An Introduction to
ETHICS

An Introduction to
ETHICS

EDITED BY

Robert E. Dewey
University of Nebraska—Lincoln

Robert H. Hurlbutt III
University of Nebraska—Lincoln

Macmillan Publishing Co., Inc.

NEW YORK

To Betsey and Laurie

Macmillan Publishing Co., Inc.
866 Third Avenue, New York, New York 10022

Collier Macmillan Canada, Ltd.

Library of Congress Cataloging in Publication Data
Main entry under title:

An Introduction to ethics.

  Includes bibliographies.
  1. Ethics—Addresses, essays, lectures.
I. Dewey, Robert E. II. Hurlbutt, Robert H.
BJ71.I57   170   75–43648
ISBN 0–02–329480–9

Printing: 1 2 3 4 5 6 7 8   Year: 7 8 9 0 1 2 3

Preface

Among those decisions that are a vital part of man's practical life, there is a class of choices that are characterized as moral or ethical. These choices are, and always have been, distinguished from the choices related to other practical activities, such as table manners and other rules of etiquette. In comparison to these activities, ethical decisions have an importance, a profound significance, that has led modern thinkers to use the term "overriding" for them. They involve responsibility and negligence, blame and reward, happiness and degradation, respect and disgrace. In a sense, morality is man's most significant enterprise, for its rules relate to, and sometimes take precedence over, those of physical sustenance. In a number of powerful ways, ethical or moral considerations are linked into other institutional structures. Political, economic, religious, educational, and aesthetic policies, and other related decisions, are ineluctably tied to moral standards. Men of all ages and types of character have considered some kinds of conduct as preferable to others, and, within such preferred conduct, have marked off certain kinds as moral or ethical.

The subject matter of ethics is perhaps most simply exhibited by sentences that are used in a number of related ways, and whose constituents commonly include a cluster of related words. These sentences, ordinarily called "ethical" or "moral" judgments, include such words as "right," "wrong," "good," "evil," "ought," "ought not," "justice," "injustice," "responsibility," and so on. The sentences or judgments relate to actions in which men do such things as assess character, levy praise and blame, make recommendations, give commands, commend and advise. They also involve assessing the character, consequences, and implications of institutions and laws, including accepted moral practices. Viewed systematically, related ethical principles and judgments, combined in coherent, consistent, and, presumably, true sets, make up the great classical ethical theories or *normative* ethical theories, as we will call them. Ethics or morality concerns what men ought to do and what is good for them, as distinct from what men are and what they want, although the relationships between these at least verbally distinct aspects of human activity are the source of much of the controversy that surrounds contemporary and classical ethical theory.

In addition to normative ethics, writers in ethics have been concerned with another important field of inquiry. There is the characteristically modern analysis of the meaning or meanings of constituent normative words. These analyses, together with discussions about the nature of the evidence and proof necessary for the justification of ethical judgments, provide the topics of meta-ethics.

There are many ways in which the materials of an anthology of philosophical readings may be organized. It can be done historically, in a chronological survey of claims about right and wrong, good and evil, beginning with Plato, perhaps, and running through Aristotle, the Stoics, and on into modern times. It can be organized topically, into the great classical types of ethical theory: teleological and deontological, utilitarian and formalistic, naturalistic and supernaturalistic, pragmatic and existentialist. It could be comparative and explore the conflicting claims which make up the major issues of ethics. It could be a systematic attempt to formulate and defend a coherent ethical theory, as in the work of Aristotle or Kant. There is the "problems" approach, which seeks to set out the materials of ethics in terms of the most basic or significant problems in classical and contemporary ethical theories. Ethics courses do not always exemplify consistent purposes, and competing ends often impose demands which are not always compatible with one another. The relationships among the need for information, teaching effectiveness, interest for students, and exposition of new philosophic methods or techniques to students are not easily combined.

Ours is a text that seeks to satisfy a number of these purposes and interests. We deal with the main problems of classical and contemporary ethical theories. We present these problems in a dialectical format which has important thinkers presenting the main arguments pro and con regarding the problems and theories. We attempt to cover the main topical elements of classical and contemporary ethical thought. In addition, we seek, in our introductions, to provide some of the relevant technical and methodological considerations needed by the student for a view of contemporary philosophic direction. Finally, a basic bibliographical guide for further reading is provided.

The book, therefore, is organized along lines that serve a number of functions. It allows the student to become conversant with, first, the main classical theories of good and evil, right and wrong—normative ethics; second, the basic critical concepts of contemporary philosophical techniques applied to ethical theories; and, third, the related critical ideas with respect to meaning and justification in ethics—meta-ethics. The organization, then, presupposes that ethics or morality involves reason, justification, rational support, and argumentation, as does any kind of disciplined rational endeavor.

More specifically, the organization of the book is as follows. There is a preliminary section which takes up the nature of ethics or morality. This section also treats three further topics which on the surface appear to stand in the path of any rational justification of normative ethical theories. There is psychological egoism, the theory that men literally cannot, in fact, act for the benefit of others. Next, there is the problem of freedom and determinism, which is taken by some thinkers to indicate that the almost universally accepted principle of causation, as (quite properly) applied to the actions of men, implies that men are not free, and therefore not reasonably subject to praise and blame or to punishment. Finally, there is the problem of cultural relativism, the claim that moral judgments and moral rules are ultimately arbitrary conventions whose only validity lies in their acceptance and approval by a majority of the members of a group or culture. This is often taken to mean that ethics is not a rationally defensible enterprise analogous to, say, the sciences.

The remainder of the book is devoted to a development of the great traditional classical and contemporary normative ethical theories and to contemporary meta-ethical theories. They are considered under traditional headings, such as deontological and teleological theories, which concern attempts to develop and to justify sets of moral rules. Here we have ethical egoism, utilitarianism, and self-realization. The issues of meta-ethics, theories concerning the meaning and justification of ethical judgments, are set out in terms of cognitivism, non-cognitivism, quasi-cognitivism. The principles behind the organization and selection of the materials are threefold: (1) to allow a range of reading materials which involve rationally stimulating and challenging sources taken from classical and contemporary theories; (2) to set them in a context for affirmation and criticism, i.e., most topics and selections are structured so as to have a thinker who supports a position, followed by a thinker who criticizes it; and (3) to help the instructor develop on the part of his students some of the skills of philosophical analysis usable in reflecting upon any subject of intellectual concern.

In the preparation of the manuscript, we are especially appreciative of the cooperation we have received from Kenneth J. Scott in his capacity as Philosophy Editor at Macmillan. We are also most grateful for the careful efficiency of Debora Palmer, Arlene Rash, and Suzie Sybouts.

R. E. D.
R. H. H.

Contents

I Preliminary Considerations: Is Ethics or Morality Possible?

The fundamental concern of ethics lies in normative issues, the development and justification of systems of moral rules which guide conduct. Nevertheless, it is not uncommon for philosophers, as well as other interested parties, to claim that some crucial problems must be resolved before normative ethics can be conceived as possible. The first of these is the problem of the nature of ethics; the second concerns the truth of psychological egoism; the third is the controversy relating to freedom and determinism; and the fourth takes up the issue of cultural relativism. Thus our first problem, the subject-matter of ethics, involves possible answers to the question, "What in general distinguishes ethics from other disciplines?" The second asks, "Do all the actions of men proceed from self-love?" The third raises the issue: "Are human choices really free?" And the final question is: "Are there any moral principles which are justifiable independently of cultural acceptance?"

The last three issues can be viewed as logical hurdles to the first. As will be seen in the readings from Plato's *Crito* and *Meno*, it has been argued from very early times that there are moral judgments about human actions that differ from the factual statements made in the sciences about human actions. It has also long been an accepted principle that these moral judgments are justifiable by standard as well as special logical and factual supports. That is, it has been held that ethics is a rational enterprise and that ethical propositions are, thus, capable of truth and falsity, coherence and incoherence, consistency and inconsistency, meaningfulness and nonsense, as are other beliefs. For such reasons, men have believed, from the time of Plato and his predecessors, that it is correct to hold persons *of any culture* responsible for their actions. To this assumption, Socrates, Meno, and Crito agreed, and therefore rejected relativism as a solution to our fourth preliminary problem.

Moreover, this claim, and others like it, such as the claims that it is correct to give moral commands, make moral recommendations, or punish people for moral offenses, all appear to presuppose that persons are capable of making free choices—"I ought" implies "I can." Those who believe that the actions of men are determined, rather than free, seem to deny the truth of this presupposition or assumption. As a result, the determinist's answer to the third preliminary problem calls in question the possibility of ethics as a rational enterprise in which men are held responsible.

Finally, traditional moralists have usually assumed that men could choose to act for the interests of others, even to their own personal harm. The psychological egoist appears to deny this claim, that is, to deny the very possibility of altruism.

It is apparent that some resolution of these problems is necessary if normative ethics is to be conceived as logically and conceptually respectable. The first articles, then, present debates over some of the basic hurdles to be surmounted in order that traditional normative ethical theories can be considered as possible.

A THE SUBJECT MATTER OF ETHICS: *WHAT DISTINGUISHES ETHICS FROM OTHER DISCIPLINES?*

The distinct but related issues and theories, for which we use the terms "normative ethics" and "meta-ethics," are set out and developed in a relatively clear and sophisticated manner as early as Plato. It is true that he did not consider this distinction to be as important as contemporary ethical thinkers do. Nevertheless, we find that in his works such key issues as the nature and criteria of virtue, good and evil, and justice, together with the systematic analysis and development of related normative theories, are treated as in many respects contingent upon meta-ethical issues such as the meaning of ethical terms and judgments, their susceptibility to standards of truth and falsity, and the standards of knowing their truth.

Thus, in the *Crito*, we find Socrates and Crito engaged in a debate over the relevant principles and facts relating to the recommendation of Crito and others that Socrates attempt to escape from his Athenian prison and his sentence of death—a sentence based upon what his friends see as a spurious charge. It is clear that in the *Crito* the protagonists (1) appeal to rational considerations about ethical issues, and hence are committed to the use of reason in ethical matters and to the belief that men can know what is right and good; (2) invoke reasons which state or imply most of the basic normative considerations which have formed the understructure of the classical normative ethical theories: *viz.*, they invoke utilitarian, deontological, theological, and conventional criteria; (3) maintain that some rules or considerations or reasons are more basic than others; (4) argue that facts are relevant to ethical decisions; and (5) assume that men can choose to do what they decide to do; they are free.

In the second selection, from the *Meno*, Socrates and Meno are concerned with a number of issues, among them the subject of moral or ethical knowledge. They argue about what virtue and the good are, and whether or not they are knowable, or teachable. In the process, they discover, and we discover along with them, that it is first necessary to know if ethical judgments are or can be true. Through their consideration of this and related issues, they find themselves forced back to a consideration of the nature of the meaning of such terms as "virtue" and "good." They argue that to find the meaning of such terms involves discovering, and having clearly in mind, what properties these terms designate or denote. One must know the meaning of such terms before one can consider the truth of the moral judgments in which these key terms are constituents. In this, and in other dialogues of Plato, we have the initiation of the field of meta-ethics.

1

Crito

PLATO

PERSONS OF THE DIALOGUE: *Socrates, Crito*
SCENE: The Prison of Socrates

Socrates Why have you come at this hour, Crito? it must be quite early?
Crito Yes, certainly.

FROM *Crito* by Plato. Translated by Benjamin Jowett (1892).

Soc. What is the exact time?

Cr. The dawn is breaking.

Soc. I wonder that the keeper of the prison would let you in.

Cr. He knows me, because I often come, Socrates; moreover, I have done him a kindness.

Soc. And are you only just arrived?

Cr. No, I came some time ago.

Soc. Then why did you sit and say nothing, instead of at once awakening me?

Cr. I should not have liked myself, Socrates, to be in such great trouble and unrest as you are—indeed I should not: I have been watching with amazement your peaceful slumbers; and for that reason I did not awake you, because I wished to minimize the pain. I have always thought you to be of a happy disposition; but never did I see anything like the easy, tranquil manner in which you bear this calamity.

Soc. Why, Crito, when a man has reached my age he ought not be repining at the approach of death.

Cr. And yet other old men find themselves in similar misfortunes, and age does not prevent them from repining.

Soc. That is true. But you have not told me why you come at this early hour.

Cr. I come to bring you a message which is sad and painful; not, as I believe, to yourself, but to all of us who are your friends, and saddest of all to me.

Soc. What? Has the ship come from Delos, on the arrival of which I am to die?

Cr. No, the ship has not actually arrived, but she will probably be here to-day, as persons who have come from Sunium tell me that they left her there; and therefore tomorrow, Socrates, will be the last day of your life.

Soc. Very well, Crito; if such is the will of God, I am willing; but my belief is that there will be a delay of a day.

Cr. Why do you think so?

Soc. I will tell you. I am to die on the day after the arrival of the ship.

Cr. Yes; that is what the authorities say.

Soc. But I do not think that the ship will be here until to-morrow; this I infer from a vision which I had last night, or rather only just now, when you fortunately allowed me to sleep.

Cr. And what was the nature of the vision?

Soc. There appeared to me the likeness of a woman, fair and comely, clothed in bright raiment, who called to me and said: O Socrates,

"The third day hence to fertile Phthia shalt thou go." [1]

Cr. What a singular dream, Socrates!

Soc. There can be no doubt about the meaning, Crito, I think.

Cr. Yes; the meaning is only too clear. But, oh! my beloved Socrates, let me entreat you once more to take my advice and escape. For if you die I shall not only lose a friend who can never be replaced, but there is another evil: people

[1] Homer, Il. ix. 363

who do not know you and me will believe that I might have saved you if I had been willing to give money, but that I did not care. Now, can there be a worse disgrace than this—that I should be thought to value money more than the life of a friend? For the many will not be persuaded that I wanted you to escape, and that you refused.

Soc. But why, my dear Crito, should we care about the opinion of the many? Good men, and they are the only persons who are worth considering, will think of these things truly as they occurred.

Cr. But you see, Socrates, that the opinion of the many must be regarded, for what is now happening shows that they can do the greatest evil to any one who has lost their good opinion.

Soc. I only wish it were so, Crito; and that the many could do the greatest evil; for then they would also be able to do the greatest good—and what a fine thing this would be! But in reality they can do neither; for they cannot make a man either wise or foolish; and whatever they do is the result of chance.

Cr. Well, I will not dispute with you; but please to tell me, Socrates, whether you are not acting out of regard to me and your other friends: are you not afraid that if you escape from prison we may get into trouble with the informers for having stolen you away, and lose either the whole or a great part of our property; or that even a worse evil may happen to us? Now, if you fear on our account, be at ease; for in order to save you, we ought surely to run this, or even a greater risk; be persuaded, then, and do as I say.

Soc. Yes, Crito, that is one fear which you mention, but by no means the only one.

Cr. Fear not—there are persons who are willing to get you out of prison at no great cost; and as for the informers, they are far from being exorbitant in their demands—a little money will satisfy them. My means, which are certainly ample, are at your service, and if you have a scruple about spending all mine, here are strangers who will give you the use of theirs; and one of them, Simmias the Theban, has brought a large sum of money for this very purpose; and Cebes and many others are prepared to spend their money in helping you to escape. I say, therefore, do not hesitate on our account, and do not say, as you did in the court, that you will have a difficulty in knowing what to do with yourself anywhere else. For men will love you in other places to which you may go, and not in Athens only; there are friends of mine in Thessaly, if you like to go to them, who will value and protect you, and no Thessalian will give you any trouble. Nor can I think that you are at all justified, Socrates, in betraying your own life when you might be saved; in acting thus you are playing into the hands of your enemies, who are hurrying on your destruction. And further I should say that you are deserting your own children; for you might bring them up and educate them; instead of which you go away and leave them, and they will have to take their chance; and if they do not meet with the usual fate of orphans, there will be small thanks to you. No man should bring children into the world who is unwilling to persevere to the end in their nurture and education. But you appear to be choosing the easier part, not the better and manlier, which would have been more becoming in one who professes to care for virtue in all his actions, like yourself. And, indeed, I am ashamed not only of you, but of us who are your friends, when I reflect that the whole business will be attributed entirely to our want of courage. The trial need never have come on, or might have been managed differently; and this last act, of crowning folly, will seem to have occurred through our negligence and cowardice, who might have saved you, if we had been good for anything; and you might have saved yourself, for there was no difficulty at all. See now, Socrates, how sad and discreditable are the consequences, both to us and you. Make up your mind, then, or rather have your mind already made up, for the time of deliberation is over, and there is only one thing to be done, which must be done this very night, and if we delay at all will be no longer practicable or possible; I beseech you therefore, Socrates, be persuaded by me, and do as I say.

Soc. Dear Crito, your zeal is invaluable, if a right one; but if wrong, the greater the zeal the greater the danger; and therefore we ought to consider whether I shall or shall not do as you say. For I am and always have been one of those natures who must be guided by reason, whatever the reason may be which upon reflection appears to me to be the best; and now that this chance has befallen me, I cannot repudiate my own words: the principles which I have hitherto honoured and revered I still honour, and unless we can at once find other and better principles, I am certain not to agree with you; no, not even if the power of the multitude could inflict many more imprisonments, confiscations, deaths, frightening us like children with hobgoblin terrors. What will be the fairest way of considering the question? Shall I return to your old argument about the opinions of men?—we were saying that some of them are to be regarded, and others not. Now, were we right in maintaining this before I was condemned? And has the argument which was once good now proved to be talk for the sake of talking—mere childish nonsense? That is what I want to consider with your help, Crito:—whether, under my present circumstances, the argument appears to be in any way different or not; and is to be allowed by me or disallowed. That argument, which, as I believe, is maintained by many persons of authority, was to the effect, as I was saying, that the opinions of some men are to be regarded, and of other men not to be regarded. Now you, Crito, are not going to die to-morrow—at least, there is no human probability of this—and therefore you are disinterested and not liable to be deceived by the circumstances in which you are placed. Tell me, then, whether I am right in saying that some opinions, and the opinions of some men only, are to be valued, and that other opinions, and the opinions of other men, are not to be valued. I ask you whether I was right in maintaining this?

Cr. Certainly.

Soc. The good are to be regarded, and not the bad?

Cr. Yes.

Soc. And the opinions of the wise are good, and the opinions of the unwise are evil?

Cr. Certainly.

Soc. And what was said about another matter? Is the pupil who devotes himself to the practice of gymnastic supposed to attend to the praise and blame and opinion of every man, or of one man only—his physician or trainer, whoever he may be?

Cr. Of one man only.

Soc. And he ought to fear the censure and welcome the praise of that one only, and not of the many?

Cr. Clearly so.

Soc. And he ought to act and train, and eat and drink in the way which seems good to his single master who has understanding, rather than according to the opinion of all other men put together?

Cr. True.

Soc. And if he disobeys and disregards the opinion and approval of the one, and regards the opinion of the many who have no understanding, will he not suffer evil?

Cr. Certainly he will.

Soc. And what will the evil be, whither tending and what affecting, in the disobedient person?

Cr. Clearly, affecting the body; that is what is destroyed by the evil.

Soc. Very good; and is not this true, Crito, of other things which we need not separately enumerate? In questions of just and unjust, fair and foul, good and evil, which are the subjects of our present consultation, ought we to follow the opinion of the many and to fear them; or the opinion of the one man who has understanding? ought we not to fear and reverence him more than all the rest of the world: and if we desert him shall we not destroy and injure that principle in us which may be assumed to be improved by justice and deteriorated by injustice;—there is such a principle?

Cr. Certainly there is, Socrates.

Soc. Take a parallel instance:—if, acting under the advice of those who have no understanding, we destroy that which is improved by health and is deteriorated by disease, would life be worth having? And that which has been destroyed is—the body?

Cr. Yes.

Soc. Could we live, having an evil and corrupted body?

Cr. Certainly not.

Soc. And will life be worth having, if that higher part of man be destroyed, which is improved by justice and depraved by injustice? Do we suppose that principle, whatever it may be in man, which has to do with justice and injustice, to be inferior to the body?

Cr. Certainly not.

Soc. More honourable than the body?

Cr. Far more.

Soc. Then, my friend, we must not regard what the many say of us: but what he, the one man who has understanding of just and unjust, will say, and what the truth will say. And therefore you begin in error when you advise that we should regard the opinion of the many about just and unjust, good and evil, honourable and dishonourable.—"Well," some one will say, "But the many can kill us."

Cr. Yes, Socrates; that will clearly be the answer.

Soc. And it is true: but still I find with surprise that the old argument is unshaken as ever. And I should like to know whether I may say the same of another proposition—that not life, but a good life, is to be chiefly valued?

Cr. Yes, that also remains unshaken.

Soc. And a good life is equivalent to a just and honourable one—that holds also?

Cr. Yes, it does.

Soc. From these premises I proceed to argue the question whether I ought or ought not to try to escape without the consent of the Athenians: and if I am clearly right in escaping, then I will make the attempt; but if not, I will abstain. The other considerations which you mention, of money and loss of character and the duty of educating one's children, are, I fear, only the doctrines of the multitude, who would be as ready to restore people to life, if they were able, as they are to put them to death—and with as little reason. But now, since the argument has thus far prevailed, the only question which remains to be considered is, whether we shall do rightly either in escaping or in suffering others to aid in our escape and paying them in money and thanks, or whether in reality we shall not do rightly; and if the latter, then death or any other calamity which may ensue on my remaining here must not be allowed to enter into the calculation.

Cr. I think that you are right, Socrates; how then shall we proceed?

Soc. Let us consider the matter together, and do you either refute me if you can, and I will be convinced; or else cease, my dear friend, from repeating to me that I ought to escape against the wishes of the Athenians: for I highly value your attempts to persuade me to do so, but I may not be persuaded against my own better judgment. And now please to consider my first position, and try how you can best answer me.

Cr. I will.

Soc. Are we to say that we are never intentionally to do wrong, or that in one way we ought and in another way we ought not to do wrong, or is doing wrong always evil and dishonourable, as I was just now saying, and as has been already acknowledged by us? Are all our former admissions which were made within a few days to be thrown away? And have we, at our age, been earnestly discoursing with one another all our life long only to discover that we are no better than children? Or, in spite of the opinion of the many, and in spite of consequences whether better or worse, shall we insist on the truth of what was then said, that injustice is always an evil and dishonour to him who acts unjustly? Shall we say so or not?

Cr. Yes.

Soc. Then we must do no wrong?

Cr. Certainly not.

Soc. Nor when injured injure in return, as the many imagine; for we must injure no one at all?

Cr. Clearly not.

Soc. Again, Crito, may we do evil?

Cr. Surely not, Socrates.

Soc. And what of doing evil in return for evil, which is the morality of the many—is that just or not?

Cr. Not just.

Soc. For doing evil to another is the same as injuring him?

Cr. Very true.

Soc. Then we ought not to retaliate or render evil for evil to any one, whatever evil we may have suffered from him. But I would have you consider, Crito, whether you really mean what you are saying. For this opinion has never been held, and never will be held, by any considerable number of persons; and those who are agreed and those who are not agreed upon this point have no common ground, and can only despise one another when they see how widely they differ. Tell me, then, whether you agree with and assent to my first principle, that neither injury nor retaliation nor warding off evil by evil is ever right. And shall that be the premise of our argument? Or do you decline and dissent from this? For so I have ever thought, and continue to think; but, if you are of another opinion, let me hear what you have to say. If, however, you remain of the same mind as formerly, I will proceed to the next step.

Cr. You may proceed, for I have not changed my mind.

Soc. Then I will go on to the next point, which may be put in the form of a question:—Ought a man to do what he admits to be right, or ought he to betray the right?

Cr. He ought to do what he thinks right.

Soc. But if this is true, what is the application? In leaving the prison against the will of the Athenians, do I wrong any? or rather do I not wrong those whom I ought least to wrong? Do I not desert the principles which were acknowledged by us to be just—what do you say?

Cr. I cannot tell, Socrates; for I do not know.

Soc. Then consider the matter in this way:—Imagine that I am about to play truant (you may call the proceeding by any name which you like), and the laws and the government come and interrogate me: "Tell us, Socrates," they say; "what are you about? are you not going by an act of yours to overturn us—the laws, and the whole state, as far as in you lies? Do you imagine that a state can subsist and not be overthrown, in which the decisions of law have no power, but are set aside and trampled upon by individuals?" What will be our answer, Crito, to these and the like words? Any one, and especially a rhetorician, will have a good deal to say on behalf of the law which requires a sentence to be carried out. He will argue that this law should not be set aside; and shall we reply, "Yes; but the state has injured us and given an unjust sentence." Suppose I say that?

Cr. Very good, Socrates.

Soc. "And was that our agreement with you?" the law would answer; "or were you to abide by the sentence of the state?" And if I were to express my astonishment at their words, the law would probably add: "Answer, Socrates, instead of opening your eyes—you are in the habit of asking and answering questions. Tell us,—What complaint have you to make against us which justifies you in attempting to destroy us and the state? In the first place did we not bring you into existence? Your father married your mother by our aid and begat you. Say whether you have any objection to urge against those of us who regulate marriage?" None, I should reply. "Or against those of us who after birth regulate the nurture and education of children, in which you also were trained? Were not the laws, which have the charge of education, right in commanding your father to train you in music and gymnastic?" Right, I should reply. "Well, then, since you were brought into the world and nurtured and educated by us, can you deny in the first place that you are our child and slave, as your fathers were before you? And if this is true, you are not on equal terms with us; nor can you think that you have a right to do to us what we are doing to you. Would you have any right to strike or revile or do any other evil to your father or your master, if you had one, because you have been struck or reviled by him, or received some other evil at his hands?—you would not say this? And because we think right to destroy you, do you think that you have any right to destroy us in return, and your country as far as in you lies? Will you, O professor of true virtue, pretend that you are justified in this? Has a philosopher like you failed to discover that our country is more to be valued and higher and holier far than mother or father or any ancestor, and more to be regarded in the eyes of the gods and of men of understanding? also to be soothed, and gently and reverently entreated when angry, even more than a father, and either to be persuaded, or if not persuaded, to be obeyed? And when we are punished by her, whether with imprisonment or stripes, the punishment is to be endured in silence; and if she lead us to wounds or death in battle, thither we follow as is right; neither may any one yield or retreat or leave his rank, but whether in battle or in a court of law, or in any other place, he must do what his city and his country order him; or he must change their view of what is just: and if he may do no violence to his father or mother, much less may he do violence to his country." What answer shall we make to this, Crito? Do the laws speak truly, or do they not?

Cr. I think that they do.

Soc. Then the laws will say: "Consider, Socrates, if we are speaking truly that in your present attempt you are going to do us an injury. For, having brought you into the world, and nurtured and educated you, and given you and every other citizen a share in every good which we had to give, we further proclaim to any Athenian by the liberty which we allow him, that if he does not like us when he has become of age and has seen the ways of the city, and made our acquaintance, he may go where he pleases and take his goods with him. None of us laws will forbid him or interfere with him. Any one who does not like us and the city, and who wants to emigrate to a colony or to any other city, may go where he likes, retaining his property. But he who has experience of the manner in which we order justice and administer the State, and still remains, has entered into an implied contract that he will do as we command him. And he who disobeys us is, as we maintain, thrice wrong; first, because in disobeying us he is disobeying his parents; secondly, because we are the authors of his education; thirdly, because he has made an agreement with us that he will duly obey our commands; and he neither obeys them nor convinces us that our commands are unjust; and we do not rudely impose them, but give him the alternative of obeying or convincing us;—that is what we offer, and he does neither.

"These are the sort of accusations to which, as we were saying, you, Socrates, will be exposed if you accomplish your intentions; you, above all other Athenians." Suppose now I ask, why I rather than anybody else? they will justly retort upon me that I above all other men have acknowledged the agreement. "There is clear proof," they will say, "Socrates, that we and the city were not displeasing to you. Of all Athenians you have been the most constant resident in the city, which, as you never leave, you may be supposed to love. For you never went out of the city either to see the games, except once when you went to the Isthmus, or to any other place unless when you were on military service; nor did you travel as other men do. Nor had you any curiosity to know other States or their laws: your affections did not go beyond us and our State; we were your special favourites, and you acquiesced in our government of you; and here in this city you begat your children, which is a proof of your satisfaction. Moreover, you might in the course of the trial, if you had liked, have fixed the penalty at banishment; the State which refuses to let you go now would have let you go then. But you pretended that you preferred death to exile, and that you were not unwilling to die. And now you have forgotten these fine sentiments, and pay no respect to us, the laws, of whom you are the destroyer; and are doing what only a miserable slave would do, running away and turning your back upon the compacts and agreements which you made as a citizen. And, first of all, answer this very question: Are we right in saying that you agreed to be governed according to us in deed, and not in word only? Is that true or not?" How shall we answer, Crito? Must we not assent?

Cr. We cannot help it, Socrates.

Soc. Then will they not say: "You, Socrates, are breaking the covenants and agreements which you made with us at your leisure, not in any haste or under any compulsion or deception, but after you have had seventy years to think of them, during which time you were at liberty to leave the city, if we were not to your mind, or if our covenants appeared to you to be unfair. You had your choice, and might have gone either to Lacedaemon or Crete, both which

States are often praised by you for their good government, or to some other Hellenic or foreign State. Whereas you, above all other Athenians, seemed to be so fond of the State, or, in other words, of us, her laws (and who would care about a State which has no laws?), that you never stirred out of her; the halt, the blind, the maimed were not more stationary in her than you were. And now you run away and forsake your agreements. Not so, Socrates, if you will take our advice; do not make yourself ridiculous by escaping out of the city.

"For just consider, if you transgress and err in this sort of way, what good will you do either to yourself or to your friends? That your friends will be driven into exile and deprived of citizenship, or will lose their property, is tolerably certain; and you yourself, if you fly to one of the neighbouring cities, as, for example, Thebes or Megara, both of which are well governed, will come to them as an enemy, Socrates, and their government will be against you, and all patriotic citizens will cast an evil eye upon you as a subverter of the laws, and you will confirm in the minds of the judges the justice of their own condemnation of you. For he who is a corrupter of the laws is more than likely to be a corrupter of the young and foolish portion of mankind. Will you then flee from well-ordered cities and virtuous men? and is existence worth having on these terms? Or will you go to them without shame, and talk to them, Socrates? And what will you say to them? What you say here about virtue and justice and institutions and laws being the best things among men? Would that be decent of you? Surely not. But if you go away from well-governed States to Crito's friends in Thessaly, where there is great disorder and licence, they will be charmed to hear the tale of your escape from prison, set off with ludicrous particulars of the manner in which you were wrapped in a goatskin or some other disguise, and metamorphosed as the manner is of runaways; but will there be no one to remind you that in your old age you were not ashamed to violate the most sacred laws from a miserable desire of a little more life? Perhaps not, if you keep them in a good temper; but if they are out of temper you will hear many degrading things; you will live, but how?— as the flatterer of all men, and the servant of all men; and doing what?— eating and drinking in Thessaly, having gone abroad in order that you may get a dinner. And where will be your fine sentiments about justice and virtue? Say that you wish to live for the sake of your children—you want to bring them up and educate them—will you take them into Thessaly and deprive them of Athenian citizenship? Is this the benefit which you will confer upon them? Or are you under the impression that they will be better cared for and educated here if you are still alive, although absent from them; for your friends will take care of them? Do you fancy that if you are an inhabitant of Thessaly they will take care of them, and if you are an inhabitant of the other world that they will not take care of them? Nay; but if they who call themselves friends are good for anything, they will—to be sure they will.

"Listen, then, Socrates, to us who have brought you up. Think not of life and children first, and of justice afterwards, but of justice first, that you may be justified before the princes of the world below. For neither will you nor any that belong to you be happier or holier or juster in this life, or happier in another, if you do as Crito bids. Now you depart in innocence, a sufferer and not a doer of evil; a victim, not of the laws but of men. But if you go forth, returning evil for evil; and injury for injury, breaking the covenants and agreements which you have made with us, and wronging those whom you ought least of all to wrong, that is to say, yourself, your friends, your country, and us, we shall be angry with you while you live, and our brethren, the laws in the world below, will receive you as an enemy; for they will know that you have done your best to destroy us. Listen, then, to us and not to Crito."

This, dear Crito, is the voice which I seem to hear murmuring in my ears, like the sound of the flute in the ears of the mystic; that voice, I say, is humming in my ears, and prevents me from hearing any other. And I know that anything more which you may say will be vain. Yet speak, if you have anything to say.

Cr. I have nothing to say, Socrates.

Soc. Leave me then, Crito, to fulfil the will of God, and to follow whither he leads.

2

Meno

PLATO

PERSONS OF THE DIALOGUE: *Meno, Socrates, a slave of Meno, Anytus*

Meno Can you tell me, Socrates, whether virtue is acquired by teaching or by practice; or if neither by teaching nor practice, then whether it comes to man by nature, or in what other way?

Socrates O Meno, there was a time when the Thessalians were famous among the other Hellenes only for their riches and their riding; but now, if I am not mistaken, they are equally famous for their wisdom, especially at Larissa, which is the native city of your friend Aristippus. And this is Gorgias' doing; for when he came there, the flower of the Aleuadae, among them your admirer Aristippus, and the other chiefs of the Thessalians, fell in love with his wisdom. And he has taught you the habit of answering questions in a grand and bold style, which becomes those who know, and is the style in which he himself answers all comers; and any Hellene who likes may ask him anything. How different is our lot! my dear Meno. Here at Athens, there is a dearth of the commodity, and all wisdom seems to have emigrated from us to you. I am certain that if you were to ask any Athenian whether virtue was natural or

FROM *Meno* by Plato. Translated by Benjamin Jowett (1892).

acquired, he would laugh in your face and say: "Stranger, you have far too good an opinion of me if you think that I can answer your question. For I literally do not know what virtue is, and much less whether it is acquired by teaching or not." And I myself, Meno, living as I do in this region of poverty, am as poor as the rest of the world, and I confess with shame that I know literally nothing about virtue; and when I do not know the "*quid*" of anything, how can I know the "*quale*"? How, if I knew nothing at all of Meno, could I tell if he was fair or the opposite of fair; rich and noble, or the reverse of rich and noble? Do you think that I could?

Men. No, indeed. But are you in earnest, Socrates, in saying that you do not know what virtue is? And am I to carry back this report of you to Thessaly?

Soc. Not only that, my dear boy, but you may say further that I have never known of any one else who did, in my judgment.

Men. Then you have never met Gorgias when he was at Athens?

Soc. Yes, I have.

Men. And did you not think that he knew?

Soc. I have not a good memory, Meno, and therefore I cannot now tell what I thought of him at the time. And I dare say that he did know, and that you know what he said: please, therefore, do remind me of what he said; or, if you would rather, tell me your own view; for I suspect that you and he think much alike.

Men. Very true.

Soc. Then as he is not here, never mind him, and do you tell me: By the gods, Meno, be generous and tell me what you say that virtue is; for I shall be truly delighted to find that I have been mistaken, and that you and Gorgias do really have this knowledge, although I have been just saying that I have never found anybody who had.

Men. There will be no difficulty, Socrates, in answering your question. Let us take first the virtue of a man—he should know how to administer the state, and in the administration of it to benefit his friends and harm his enemies; and he must also be careful not to suffer harm himself. A woman's virtue, if you wish to know about that, may also be easily described: her duty is to order her house and keep what is indoors, and obey her husband. Every age, every condition of life, young or old, male or female, bond or free, has a different virtue: there are virtues numberless, and no lack of definitions of them; for virtue is relative to the actions and ages of each of us in all that we do. And the same may be said of vice, Socrates.

Soc. How fortunate I am, Meno! When I ask you for one virtue, you present me with a swarm of them, which are in your keeping. Suppose that I carry on the figure of the swarm, and ask of you, What is the nature of the bee? and you answer that there are many kinds of bees, and I reply: But do bees differ as bees because there are many and different kinds of them; or are they not rather to be distinguished by some other quality, as, for example, beauty, size, or shape? How would you answer me?

Men. I should answer that bees do not differ from one another, as bees.

Soc. And if I went on to say: That is what I desire to know, Meno; tell me what is the quality in which they do not differ, but are all alike—would you be able to answer?

Men. I should.

Soc. And so of the virtues, however many and different they may be, they have all a common nature which makes them virtues; and on this he who would answer the question, "What is virtue?" would do well to have his eye fixed; do you understand?

Men. I am beginning to understand; but I do not as yet take hold of the question as I could wish.

Soc. When you say, Meno, that there is one virtue of a man, another of a woman, another of a child, and so on, does this apply only to virtue, or would you say the same of health, and size, and strength? Or is the nature of health always the same, whether in man or woman?

Men. I should say that health is the same, both in man and woman.

Soc. And is not this true of size and strength? If a woman is strong, she will be strong by reason of the same form and of the same strength subsisting in her which there is in the man—I mean to say that strength, as strength, whether of man or woman, is the same. Is there any difference?

Men. I think not.

Soc. And will not virtue, as virtue, be the same, whether in a child or in a grown-up person, in a woman or in a man?

Men. I cannot help feeling, Socrates, that this case is different from the others.

Soc. But why? Were you not saying that the virtue of a man was to order a state, and the virtue of a woman was to order a house?

Men. I did say so.

Soc. And can either house or state or anything be well ordered without temperance and without justice?

Men. Certainly not.

Soc. Then they who order a state or a house temperately or justly order them with temperance and justice?

Men. Certainly.

Soc. Then both men and women, if they are to be good men and women, must have the same virtues of temperance and justice?

Men. True.

Soc. And can either a young man or an elder one be good if they are intemperate and unjust?

Men. They cannot.

Soc. They must be temperate and just?

Men. Yes.

Soc. Then all men are good in the same way, and by participation in the same virtues?

Men. Such is the inference.

Soc. And they surely would not have been good in the same way unless their virtue had been the same?

Men. They would not.

Soc. Then now that the sameness of all virtue has been proven, try and remember what you and Gorgias say that virtue is.

Men. Will you have one definition of them all?

Soc. That is what I am seeking.

Men. If you want to have one definition of them all, I know not what to say but that virtue is the power of governing mankind.

Soc. And does this definition of virtue include all virtue? Is virtue the same in a child and in a slave, Meno? Can the child govern his father, or the slave his master; and would he who governed be any longer a slave?

Men. I think not, Socrates.

Soc. No, indeed; there would be small reason in that. Yet once more, fair friend; according to you, virtue is "the power of governing"; but do you not add "justly and not unjustly"?

Men. Yes, Socrates; I agree there; for justice is virtue.

Soc. Would you say "virtue," Meno, or "a virtue"?

Men. What do you mean?

Soc. I mean as I might say about anything; that a round, for example, is "a figure" and not simply "figure", and I should adopt this mode of speaking, because there are other figures.

Men. Quite right; and that is just what I am saying about virtue—that there are other virtues as well as justice.

Soc. What are they? Tell me the names of them, as I would tell you the names of the other figures if you asked me.

Men. Courage and temperance and wisdom and magnanimity are virtues; and there are many others.

Soc. Yes, Meno; and again we are in the same case: in searching after one virtue we have found many, though not in the same way as before; but we have been unable to find the common virtue which runs through them all. . . .

Soc. . . . tell me what virtue is in the universal; and do not make a singular into a plural, as the facetious say of those who break a thing, but deliver virtue to me whole and sound, and not broken into a number of pieces; . . .

Men. Well then, Socrates, virtue, as I take it, is when he, who desires the honorable, is able to provide it for himself; so the poet says, and I say, too—

Virtue is the desire of things honorable and the power of attaining them.

Soc. And does he who desires the honorable also desire the good?

Men. Certainly.

Soc. Then are there some who desire the evil and others who desire the good? Do not all men, my dear sir, desire good?

Men. I think not.

Soc. There are some who desire evil?

Men. Yes.

Soc. Do you mean that they think the evils which they desire to be good; or do they know that they are evil and yet desire them?

Men. Both, I think.

Soc. And do you really imagine, Meno, that a man knows evils to be evils and desires them notwithstanding?

Men. Certainly I do.

Soc. And desire is of possession?

Men. Yes, of possession.

Soc. And does he think that the evils will do good to him who possesses them, or does he know that they will do him harm?

Men. There are some who think that the evils will do them good, and others who know that they will do them harm.

Soc. And, in your opinion, do those who think that they will do them good know that they are evils?

Men. Certainly not.

Soc. Is it not obvious that those who are ignorant of their nature do not desire them; but they desire what they suppose to be goods although they are really evils; and if they are mistaken and suppose the evils to be goods, they really desire goods?

Men. Yes, in that case.

Soc. Well, and do those who, as you say, desire evils, and think that evils are hurtful to the possessor of them, know that they will be hurt by them?

Men. They must know it.

Soc. And must they not suppose that those who are hurt are miserable in proportion to the hurt which is inflicted upon them?

Men. How can it be otherwise?

Soc. But are not the miserable ill fated?

Men. Yes, indeed.

Soc. And does anyone desire to be miserable and ill fated?

Men. I should say not, Socrates.

Soc. But if there is no one who desires to be miserable, there is no one, Meno, who desires evil; for what is misery but the desire and possession of evil?

Men. That appears to be the truth, Socrates, and I admit that nobody desires evil.

Soc. And yet, were you not saying just now that virtue is the desire and power of attaining good?

Men. Yes, I did say so.

Soc. But if this be affirmed, then the desire of good is common to all, and one man is no better than another in that respect?

Men. True.

Soc. And if one man is not better than another in desiring good, he must be better in the power of attaining it?

Men. Exactly.

Soc. Then, according to your definition, virtue would appear to be the power of attaining good?

Men. I entirely approve, Socrates, of the manner in which you now view this matter.

Soc. Then let us see whether what you say is true from another point of view; for very likely you may be right—you affirm virtue to be the power of attaining goods?

Men. Yes.

Soc. And the goods which you mean are such as health and wealth and the possession of gold and silver, and having office and honor in the state—those are what you would call goods?

Men. Yes, I should include all those.

Soc. Then, according to Meno, who is the hereditary friend of the great king, virtue is the power of getting silver and gold; and would you add that they must be gained piously, justly, or do you deem this to be of no consequence? And is any mode of acquisition, even if unjust and dishonest, equally to be deemed virtue.

Men. Not virtue, Socrates, but vice.

Soc. Then justice or temperance or holiness, or some other part of virtue, as would appear, must accompany the acquisition, and without them the mere acquisition of good will not be virtue.

Men. Why, how can there be virtue without these?

Soc. And the non-acquisition of gold and silver in a dishonest manner for oneself or another; or, in other words, the want of them may be equally virtue?

Men. True.

Soc. Then the acquisition of such goods is no more virtue than the non-acquisition and want of them, but whatever is accompanied by justice or honesty is virtue, and whatever is devoid of justice is vice.

Men. It cannot be otherwise, in my judgment.

Soc. And were we not saying just now that justice, temperance, and the like, were each of them a part of virtue?

Men. Yes.

Soc. And so, Meno, this is the way in which you mock me.

Men. Why do you say that, Socrates?

Soc. Why, because I asked you to deliver virtue into my hands whole and unbroken, and I gave you a pattern according to which you were to frame your answer; and you have forgotten already and tell me that virtue is the power of attaining good justly, or with justice; and justice you acknowledge to be a part of virtue.

Men. Yes.

Soc. Then it follows from your own admissions that virtue is doing what you do with a part of virtue; for justice and the like are said by you to be parts of virtue.

Men. What of that?

Soc. What of that! Why, did not I ask you to tell me the nature of virtue as a whole? And you are very far from telling me this, but declare every action to be virtue which is done with a part of virtue, as though you had told me and I must already know the whole of virtue, and this, too, when frittered away into little pieces. And, therefore, my dear Meno, I fear that I must begin again and repeat the same question: What is virtue? for otherwise I can only say that every action done with a part of virtue is virtue; what else is the meaning of saying that every action done with justice is virtue? Ought I not to ask the question over again; for can anyone who does not know virtue know a part of virtue?

Men. No; I do not say that he can.

Soc. Do you remember how, in the example of figure, we rejected any answer given in terms which were as yet unexplained or unadmitted?

Men. Yes, Socrates; and we were quite right in doing so.

Soc. But then, my friend, do not suppose that we can explain to anyone the nature of virtue as a whole through some unexplained portion of virtue, or anything at all in that fashion; we should only have to ask over again the old question, What is virtue? Am I not right?

Men. I believe that you are.

Soc. Then begin again, and answer me. What, according to you and your friend Gorgias, is the definition of virtue?

Men. O Socrates, I used to be told, before I knew you, that you were always doubting yourself and making others doubt; and now you are casting your spells over me, and I am simply getting bewitched and enchanted, and am at my wits' end. And if I may venture to make a jest upon you, you seem to me both in your appearance and in your power over others to be very like the flat torpedo fish, who torpifies those who come near him and touch him, as you have now torpified me, I think. For my soul and my tongue are really torpid, and I do not know how to answer you; and though I have been delivered of an infinite variety of speeches about virtue before now, and to many persons— and very good ones they were, as I thought—at this moment I cannot even say what virtue is. And I think that you are very wise in not voyaging and going away from home, for if you did in other places as you do in Athens, you would be cast into prison as a magician.

Soc. You are a rogue, Meno, and had all but caught me.

Men. What do you mean, Socrates?

Soc. I can tell why you made a simile about me.

Men. Why?

Soc. In order that I might make another simile about you. For I know that all pretty young gentlemen like to have pretty similes made about them—as well they may—but I shall not return the compliment. As to my being a torpedo, if the torpedo is torpid as well as the cause of torpidity in others, then indeed I am a torpedo, but not otherwise; for I perplex others, not because I am clear, but because I am utterly perplexed myself. And now I know not what virtue is, and you seem to be in the same case, . . .

Men. . . . yet I would much rather return to my original question, Whether in seeking to acquire virtue we should regard it as a thing to be taught, or as a gift of nature, or as coming to men in some other way?

Soc. Had I the command of you as well as of myself, Meno, I would not have inquired whether virtue is given by instruction or not, until we had first ascertained "what it is." But as you think only of controlling me who am your slave, and never of controlling yourself—such being your notion of freedom—I must yield to you, for you are irresistible. And therefore I have now to inquire into the qualities of a thing of which I do not as yet know the nature. At any rate, will you condescend a little and allow the question "Whether virtue is given by instruction, or in any other way," to be argued upon hypothesis? As the geometrician, when he is asked whether a certain triangle is capable of being inscribed in a certain circle, will reply: "I cannot tell you as yet, but I will offer a hypothesis which may assist us in forming a conclusion. If the figure be such that when you have produced a given side of it, the given area of the triangle falls short by an area corresponding to the part produced, then one consequence follows, and if this is impossible, then some other; and therefore I wish to assume a hypothesis before I tell you whether this triangle is capable of being inscribed in the circle"—that is a geometrical hypothesis. And we too, as we know not the nature and qualities of virtue, must ask whether virtue is or is not taught, under a hypothesis: as thus, if virtue is of such a class of mental goods, will it be taught or not? Let the first hypothesis be that virtue is or is not knowledge—in that case will it be taught or not, or, as we were just now saying, "remembered"? For there is no use in disputing about the name. But is virtue taught or not, or rather, does not everyone see that knowledge alone is taught?

Men. I agree.

Soc. Then if virtue is knowledge, virtue will be taught?

Men. Certainly.

Soc. Then now we have made a quick end of this question: if virtue is of such a nature, it will be taught; and if not, not?

Men. Certainly.

Soc. The next question is whether virtue is knowledge or of another species?

Men. Yes, that appears to be the question which comes next in order.

Soc. Do we not say that virtue is a good?—This is a hypothesis which is not set aside.

Men. Certainly.

Soc. Now, if there be any sort of good which is distinct from knowledge, virtue may be that good; but if knowledge embraces all good, then we shall be right in thinking that virtue is knowledge?

Men. True.

Soc. And virtue makes us good?

Men. Yes.

Soc. And if we are good, then we are profitable; for all good things are profitable?

Men. Yes.

Soc. Then virtue is profitable?

Men. That is the only inference.

Soc. Then now let us see what are the things which severally profit us. Health and strength, and beauty and wealth—these, and the like of these, we call profitable?

Men. True.

Soc. And yet these things may also sometimes do us harm, would you not think so?

Men. Yes.

Soc. And what is the guiding principle which makes them profitable or the reverse? Are they not profitable when they are rightly used, and harmful when they are not rightly used?

Men. Certainly.

Soc. Next, let us consider the goods of the soul: they are temperance, justice, courage, quickness of apprehension, memory, magnanimity, and the like?

Men. Surely.

Soc. And such of these as are not knowledge, but of another sort, are sometimes profitable and sometimes hurtful; as, for example, courage wanting prudence, which is only a sort of confidence? When a man has no sense he is harmed by courage, but when he has sense he is profited?

Men. True.

Soc. And the same may be said of temperance and quickness of apprehension; whatever things are learned or done with sense are profitable, but when done without sense they are hurtful?

Men. Very true.

Soc. And in general, all that the soul attempts or endures, when under the guidance of wisdom, ends in happiness; but when she is under the guidance of folly, in the opposite?

Men. That appears to be true.

Soc. If then virtue is a quality of the soul, and is admitted to be profitable, it must be wisdom or prudence, since none of the things of the soul are either profitable or hurtful in themselves, but they are all made profitable or hurtful by the addition of wisdom or of folly; and therefore, if virtue is profitable, virtue must be a sort of wisdom or prudence?

Men. I quite agree.

Soc. And the other goods, such as wealth and the like, of which we were just now saying that they are sometimes good and sometimes evil, do not they also become profitable or hurtful, accordingly as the soul guides and uses them rightly or wrongly; just as the things of the soul herself are benefited when under the guidance of wisdom, and harmed by folly?

Men. True.

Soc. And the wise soul guides them rightly, and the foolish soul wrongly?

Men. Yes.

Soc. And is not this universally true of human nature? All other things hang upon the soul, and the things of the soul herself hang upon wisdom, if they are to be good; and so wisdom is inferred to be that which profits—and virtue, as we say, is profitable?

Men. Certainly.

Soc. And thus we arrive at the conclusion that virtue is either wholly or partly wisdom?

Men. I think that what you are saying, Socrates, is very true.

Soc. But if this is true, then the good are not by nature good?

Men. I think not.

Soc. If they had been, there would assuredly have been discerners of characters among us who would have known our future great men; and on their showing we should have adopted them, and when we had got them, we should have kept them in the citadel out of the way of harm, and set a stamp upon them far rather than upon a piece of gold, in order that no one might tamper with them; and when they grew up they would have been useful to the state?

Men. Yes, Socrates, that would have been the right way.

Soc. But if the good are not by nature good, are they made good by instruction?

Men. There appears to be no other alternative, Socrates. On the supposition that virtue is knowledge, there can be no doubt that virtue is taught.

Soc. Yes, indeed; but what if the supposition is erroneous?

Men. I certainly thought just now that we were right.

Soc. Yes, Meno; but a principle which has any soundness should stand firm not only just now, but always.

Men. Well; and why are you so slow of heart to believe that knowledge is virtue?

Soc. I will try and tell you why, Meno. I do not retract the assertion that if virtue is knowledge it may be taught; but I fear that I have some reason in doubting whether virtue is knowledge; for consider now and say whether virtue, and not only virtue but anything that is taught, must not have teachers and disciples?

Men. Surely.

Soc. And conversely, may not the art of which neither teachers nor disciples exist be assumed to be incapable of being taught?

Men. True; but do you think that there are no teachers of virtue?

Soc. I have certainly often inquired whether there were any, and taken great pains to find them, and have never succeeded; and many have assisted me in the search, and they were the persons whom I thought the most likely to know. Here at the moment when he is wanted we fortunately have sitting by us Anytus, the very person of whom we should make inquiry; to him then let us repair. In the first place, he is the son of a wealthy and wise father, Anthemion, who acquired his wealth, not by accident or gift, like Ismenias the Theban (who has recently made himself as rich as Polycrates), but by his own skill and industry, and who is a well-conditioned, modest man, not insolent, or overbearing, or annoying; moreover, this son of his has received a good education, as the Athenian people certainly appear to think, for they choose him to fill the highest offices. And these are the sort of men from whom you are likely to learn whether there are any teachers of virtue, and who they are. Please, Anytus, to help me and your friend Meno in answering our question, Who are the teachers? Consider the matter thus: If we wanted Meno to be a good physician, to whom should we send him? Should we not send him to the physicians?

Anytus. Certainly.

Soc. Or if we wanted him to be a good cobbler, should we not send him to the cobblers?

Any. Yes.

Soc. And so forth?

Any. Yes.

Soc. Let me trouble you with one more question. When we say that we should be right in sending him to the physicians if we wanted him to be a physician, do we mean that we should be right in sending him to those who profess the art rather than to those who do not, and to those who demand payment for teaching the art and profess to teach it to anyone who will come and learn? And if these were our reasons, should we not be right in sending him?

Any. Yes.

Soc. And might not the same be said of flute-playing and of the other arts? Would a man who wanted to make another a flute-player refuse to send him to those who profess to teach the art for money, and be plaguing other persons to give him instruction, who are not professed teachers and who never had a single disciple in that branch of knowledge which he wishes him to acquire— would not such conduct be the height of folly?

Any. Yes, by Zeus, and of ignorance, too.

Soc. Very good. And now you are in a position to advise with me about my friend Meno. He has been telling me, Anytus, that he desires to attain that kind of wisdom and virtue by which men order the state or the house, and honor their parents, and know when to receive and when to send away citizens and strangers, as a good man should. Now, to whom should he go in order that he may learn this virtue? Does not the previous argument imply clearly that we should send him to those who profess and avouch that they are the common teachers of all Hellas, and are ready to impart instruction to anyone who likes, at a fixed price?

Any. Whom do you mean, Socrates?

Soc. You surely know, do you not, Anytus, that these are the people whom mankind call Sophists?

Any. By Heracles, Socrates, forebear! I only hope that no friend or kinsman or acquaintance of mine, whether citizen or stranger, will ever be so mad as to allow himself to be corrupted by them; for they are a manifest pest and corrupting influence to those who have to do with them.

Soc. What, Anytus? Of all the people who profess that they know how to do men good, do you mean to say that these are the only ones who not only do them no good, but positively corrupt those who are entrusted to them, and in return for this disservice have the face to demand money? Indeed, I cannot believe you; for I know of a single man, Protagoras, who made more out of his craft than the illustrious Phidias, who created such noble works, or any ten other statuaries. How could that be? A mender of old shoes, or patcher-up of clothes, who made the shoes or clothes worse than he received them, could not have remained thirty days undetected, and would very soon have starved; whereas, during more than forty years, Protagoras was corrupting all Hellas and sending his disciples from him worse than he received them, and he was never found out. For, if I am not mistaken, he was about seventy years old at his death, forty of which were spent in the practice of his profession; and during all that time he had a good reputation, which to this day he retains: and not only Protagoras, but many others are well spoken of some who lived before him, and others who are still living. Now, when you say that they deceived and corrupted the youth, are they to be supposed to have corrupted them consciously or unconsciously? Can those who were deemed by many to be the wisest men of Hellas have been out of their minds?

Any. Out of their minds! No, Socrates, the young men who gave their money to them were out of their minds; and their relations and guardians who entrusted their youth to the care of these men were still more out of their minds, and most of all, the cities who allowed them to come in, and did not drive them out, citizen and stranger alike.

Soc. Has any of the Sophists wronged you, Anytus? What makes you so angry with them?

Any. No, indeed, neither I nor any of my belongings has ever had, nor would I suffer them to have, anything to do with them.

Soc. Then you are entirely unacquainted with them?

Any. And I have no wish to be acquainted.

Soc. Then, my dear friend, how can you know whether a thing is good or bad of which you are wholly ignorant?

Any. Quite well; I am sure that I know what manner of men these are, whether I am acquainted with them or not.

Soc. You must be a diviner, Anytus, for I really cannot make out, judging from your own words, how, if you are not acquainted with them, you know about them. But I am not inquiring of you who are the teachers who will corrupt Meno (let them be, if you please, the Sophists); I only ask you to tell him who there is in this great city who will teach him how to become eminent in the virtues which I was just now describing. He is the friend of your family, and you will oblige him.

Any. Why do you not tell him yourself?

Soc. I have told him whom I supposed to be the teachers of these things; but I learn from you that I am utterly at fault, and I dare say that you are right. And now I wish that you, on your part, would tell me to whom among the Athenians he should go. Whom would you name?

Any. Why single out individuals? Any Athenian gentleman, taken at random, if he will mind him, will do far more good to him than the Sophists.

Soc. And did those gentlemen grow of themselves; and without having been taught by anyone, were they nevertheless able to teach others that which they had never learned themselves?

Any. I imagine that they learned of the previous generation of gentlemen. Have there not been many good men in this city?

Soc. Yes, certainly, Anytus; and many good statesmen also there always have been, and there are still, in the city of Athens. But the question is whether they were also good teachers of their own virtue—not whether there are, or have been, good men in this part of the world, but whether virtue can be taught, is the question which we have been discussing. Now, do we mean to say that the good men of our own and of other times knew how to impart to others that virtue which they had themselves; or is virtue a thing incapable of being communicated or imparted by one man to another? That is the question which I and Meno have been arguing. Look at the matter in your own way: Would you not admit that Themistocles was a good man?

Any. Certainly; no man better.

Soc. And must not he then have been a good teacher, if any man ever was a good teacher, of his own virtue?

Any. Yes, certainly—if he wanted to be so.

Soc. But would he not have wanted? He would, at any rate, have desired to make his own son a good man and a gentleman; he could not have been jealous of him, or have intentionally abstained from imparting to him his own virtue. Did you never hear that he made his son Cleophantus a famous horseman; and had him taught to stand upright on horseback and hurl a javelin, and to do many other marvelous things; and in anything which could be learned from a master he was well trained? Have you not heard from our elders of him?

Any. I have.

Soc. Then no one could say that his son showed any want of capacity?

Any. Very likely not.

Soc. But did anyone, old or young, ever say in your hearing that Cleophantus, son of Themistocles, was a wise or good man, as his father was?

Any. I have certainly never heard anyone say so.

Soc. And if virtue could have been taught, would his father Themistocles have sought to train him in these minor accomplishments, and allowed him who, as you must remember, was his own son, to be no better than his neighbours in those qualities in which he himself excelled?

Any. Indeed, indeed, I think not.

Soc. Here was a teacher of virtue whom you admit to be among the best men of the past. Let us take another—Aristides, the son of Lysimachus; would you not acknowledge that he was a good man?

Any. To be sure I should.

Soc. And did not he train his son Lysimachus better than any other Athenian in all that could be done for him by the help of masters? But what has been the result? Is he a bit better than any other mortal? He is an acquaintance of yours, and you see what he is like. There is Pericles, again, magnificent in his wisdom; and he, as you are aware, had two sons, Paralus and Xanthippus.

Any. I know.

Soc. And you know, also, that he taught them to be unrivaled horsemen, and had them trained in music and gymnastics and all sorts of arts—in these respects they were on a level with the best—and had he no wish to make good men of them? Nay, he must have wished it. But virtue, as I suspect, could not be taught. And that you may not suppose the incompetent teachers to be only the meaner sort of Athenians and few in number, remember again that Thucydides had two sons, Melesias and Stephanus, whom, besides giving them a good education in other things, he trained in wrestling, and they were the best wrestlers in Athens: one of them he committed to the care of Xanthias, and the other to Eudorus, who had the reputation of being the most celebrated wrestlers of that day. Do you remember them?

Any. I have heard of them.

Soc. Now, can there be a doubt that Thucydides, whose children were taught things for which he had to spend money, would have taught them to be good men, which would have cost him nothing, if virtue could have been taught? Will you reply that he was a mean man, and had not many friends amg theon Athenians and allies? Nay, but he was of a great family, and a man of influence at Athens and in all Hellas, and, if virtue could have been taught, he would have found out some Athenian or foreigner who would have made good men of his sons if he could not himself spare the time from cares of state. Once more, I suspect, friend Anytus, that virtue is not a thing which can be taught.

Any. Socrates, I think that you are too ready to speak evil of men: and, if you will take my advice, I would recommend you to be careful. Perhaps there is no city in which it is not easier to do men harm than to do them good, and this is certainly the case at Athens, as I believe that you know.

Soc. O Meno, I think that Anytus is in a rage. And he may well be in a rage, for he thinks, in the first place, that I am defaming these gentlemen; and in the second place, he is of opinion that he is one of them himself. But some day he will know what is the meaning of defamation, and if he ever does, he will forgive me. Meanwhile I will return to you, Meno; for I suppose that there are gentlemen in your region, too?

Men. Certainly there are.

Soc. And are they willing to teach the young, and do they profess to be teachers, and do they agree that virtue is taught?

Men. No, indeed, Socrates, they are anything but agreed; you may hear them saying at one time that virtue can be taught, and then again the reverse.

Soc. Can we call those "teachers" who do not acknowledge the possibility of their own vocation?

Men. I think not, Socrates.

Soc. And what do you think of these Sophists, who are the only professors? Do they seem to you to be teachers of virtue?

Men. I often wonder, Socrates, that Gorgias is never heard promising to teach virtue; and when he hears others promising he only laughs at them, but he thinks that men should be taught to speak.

Soc. Then do you not think that the Sophists are teachers?

Men. I cannot tell you, Socrates; like the rest of the world, I am in doubt, and sometimes I think that they are teachers, and sometimes not.

Soc. And are you aware that not you only and other politicians have doubts whether virtue can be taught or not, but that Theognis the poet says the very same thing?

Men. Where does he say so?

Soc. In these elegiac verses:

Eat and drink and sit with the mighty, and make yourself agreeable to them; for from the good you will learn what is good, but if you mix with the bad, you will lose the intelligence which you already have.

Do you observe that here he seems to imply that virtue can be taught?

Men. Clearly.

Soc. But in some other verses he shifts about and says:

If understanding could be created and put into a man, then they (who were able to perform this feat) would have obtained great rewards.

And again:

Never would a bad son have sprung from a good sire, for he would have heard the voice of instruction; but not by teaching will you ever make a bad man into a good one.

And this, as you may remark, is a contradiction of the other.

Men. Clearly.

Soc. And is there anything else of which the professors are affirmed not only not to be teachers of others, but to be ignorant themselves, and bad at the knowledge of that which they are professing to teach; or is there anything about which even the acknowledged "gentlemen" are sometimes saying that "this thing can be taught," and sometimes the opposite? Can you say that they are teachers in any true sense whose ideas are in such confusion?

Men. I should say, certainly not.

Soc. But if neither the Sophists nor the gentlemen are teachers, clearly there can be no other teachers?

Men. No.

Soc. And if there are no teachers, neither are there disciples?

Men. Agreed.

Soc. And we have admitted that a thing cannot be taught of which there are neither teachers nor disciples?

Men. We have.

Soc. And there are no teachers of virtue to be found anywhere?

Men. There are not.

Soc. And if there are no teachers, neither are there scholars?

Men. That, I think, is true.

Soc. Then virtue cannot be taught?

Men. Not if we are right in our view. But I cannot believe, Socrates, that there are no good men; and if there are, how did they come into existence?

Soc. I am afraid, Meno, that you and I are not good for much, and that Gorgias has been as poor an educator of you as Prodicus has been of me. Certainly we shall have to look to ourselves, and try to find someone who will help in some way or other to improve us. This I say, because I observe that in the previous discussion none of us remarked that right and good action is possible to man under other guidance than that of knowledge—and indeed if this be denied, there is no seeing how there can be any good men at all.

Men. How do you mean, Socrates?

Soc. I mean that good men are necessarily useful or profitable. Were we not right in admitting this? It must be so.

Men. Yes.

Soc. And in supposing that they will be useful only if they are true guides to us of action—there we were also right?

Men. Yes.

Soc. But when we said that a man cannot be a good guide unless he has knowledge, in this we were wrong.

Men. What do you mean by the word "right"?

Soc. I will explain. If a man knew the way to Larisa, or anywhere else, and went to the place and led others thither, would he not be a right and good guide?

Men. Certainly.

Soc. And a person who had a right opinion about the way, but had never been and did not know, might be a good guide also, might he not?

Men. Certainly.

Soc. And while he has true opinion about that which the other knows, he will be just as good a guide if he thinks the truth, as he who knows the truth?

Men. Exactly.

Soc. Then true opinion is as good a guide to correct action as knowledge; and that was the point which we omitted in our speculation about the nature of virtue, when we said that knowledge only is the guide of right action; whereas there is also right opinion.

Men. True.

Soc. Then right opinion is not less useful than knowledge?

Men. The difference, Socrates, is only that he who has knowledge will always be right; but he who has right opinion will sometimes be right, and sometimes not.

Soc. What do you mean? Can he be wrong who has right opinion, so long as he has right opinion?

Men. I admit the cogency of your argument, and therefore, Socrates, I wonder that knowledge should be preferred to right opinion—or why they should ever differ.

Soc. And shall I explain this wonder to you?

Men. Do tell me.

Soc. You would not wonder if you had ever observed the images of Daedalus, but perhaps you have not got them in your country?

Men. What have they to do with the question?

Soc. Because they require to be fastened in order to keep them, and if they are not fastened, they will play truant and run away.

Men. Well, what of that?

Soc. I mean to say that they are not very valuable possessions if they are at liberty, for they will walk off like runaway slaves; but when fastened, they are of great value, for they are really beautiful works of art. Now this is an illustration of the nature of true opinions: while they abide with us they are beautiful and fruitful, but they run away out of the human soul, and do not remain long, and therefore they are not of much value until they are fastened by the tie of the cause; and this fastening of them, friend Meno, is recollection, as you and I have agreed to call it. But when they are bound, in the first place, they have the nature of knowledge; and, in the second place, they are abiding. And this is why knowledge is more honorable and excellent than true opinion, because fastened by a chain.

Men. What you are saying, Socrates, seems to be very like the truth.

Soc. I too, speak rather in ignorance; I only conjecture. And yet that knowledge differs from true opinion is no matter of conjecture with me. There are not many things which I profess to know, but this is most certainly one of them.

Men. Yes, Socrates; and you are quite right in saying so.

Soc. And am I not also right in saying that true opinion leading the way perfects action quite as well as knowledge?

Men. There again, Socrates, I think you are right.

Soc. Then right opinion is not a whit inferior to knowledge, or less useful in action; nor is the man who has right opinion inferior to him who has knowledge?

Men. True.

Soc. And surely the good man has been acknowledged by us to be useful?

Men. Yes.

Soc. Seeing then that men become good and useful to states, not only because they have knowledge, but because they have right opinion, and that neither knowledge nor right opinion is given to man by nature or acquired by him— (do you imagine either of them to be given by nature?

Men. Not I.)

Soc. Then if they are not given by nature, neither are the good by nature good?

Men. Certainly not.

Soc. And nature being excluded, then came the question whether virtue is acquired by teaching?

Men. Yes.

Soc. If virtue was wisdom (or knowledge), then, as we thought, it was taught?

Men. Yes.

Soc. And if it was taught, it was wisdom?

Men. Certainly.

Soc. And if there were teachers, it might be taught; and if there were no teachers, not?

Men. True.

Soc. But surely we acknowledged that there were no teachers of virtue?

Men. Yes.

Soc. Then we acknowledged that it was not taught, and was not wisdom.

Men. Certainly.

Soc. And yet we admitted that it was a good?

Men. Yes.

Soc. And the right guide is useful and good?

Men. Certainly.

Soc. And the only right guides are knowledge and true opinion—these are the guides of man; for things which happen by chance are not under the guidance of man; but the guides of man are true opinion and knowledge.

Men. I think so, too.

Soc. But if virtue is not taught, neither is virtue knowledge.

Men. Clearly not.

Soc. Then of two good and useful things, one, which is knowledge, has been set aside and cannot be supposed to be our guide in political life.

Men. I think not.

Soc. And therefore not by any wisdom, and not because they were wise, did Themistocles and those others of whom Anytus spoke govern states. This was the reason why they were unable to make others like themselves—because their virtue was not grounded on knowledge.

Men. That is probably true, Socrates.

Soc. But if not by knowledge, the only alternative which remains is that statesmen must have guided states by right opinion, which is in politics what divination is in religion; for diviners and also prophets say many things truly, but they know not what they say.

Men. So I believe.

Soc. And may we not, Meno, truly call those men "divine" who, having no understanding, yet succeed in many a grand deed and word?

Men. Certainly.

Soc. Then we shall also be right in calling divine those whom we were just now speaking of as diviners and prophets, including the whole tribe of poets. Yes, and statesmen above all may be said to be divine and illumined, being inspired and possessed of the god, in which condition they say many grand things, not knowing what they say.

Men. Yes.

Soc. And the women, too, Meno, call good men divine—do they not? And the Spartans, when they praise a good man, say "that he is a divine man."

Men. And I think, Socrates, that they are right, although very likely our friend Anytus may take offense at the word.

Soc. I do not care; as for Anytus, there will be another opportunity of talking with him. To sum up our inquiry—the result seems to be, if we are at all right in our view, that virtue is neither natural nor acquired, but an instinct given by God to the virtuous. Nor is the instinct accompanied by reason, unless there may be supposed to be among statesmen someone who is capable of educating statesmen. And if there be such a one, he may be said to be among the living what Homer says that Tiresias was among the dead, "he alone has understanding; but the rest are flitting shades"; and he and his virtue in like manner will be a reality among shadows.

Men. That is excellent, Socrates.

Soc. Then, Meno, the conclusion is that virtue comes to the virtuous by divine dispensation. But we shall never know the certain truth until, before asking how virtue is given, we inquire into the actual nature of virtue. I fear that I must go away, but do you, now that you are persuaded yourself, persuade our friend Anytus. And do not let him be so exasperated; if you can conciliate him, you will have done good service to the Athenian people.

The Subject Matter of Ethics—Further Readings

Abelson, Raziel, and Kai Nielsen, "Ethics, History of," in Paul Edwards (ed.), *The Encyclopedia of Philosophy*, Vol. 3 (New York: Macmillan, 1967), pp. 81–117. General survey covering most of the theories presented in this book.

Ayer, A. J., *Language, Truth and Logic* (London: Victor Gollancz, 1936; 2d ed., 1946), Chap. 6. Argues that ethics should be concerned only with defining ethical concepts.

Bourke, Vernon J., *Ethics* (New York: Macmillan, 1951; 2d ed., 1966), Chap. 1. Expounds a Thomistic view of the nature of ethics.

Dewey, John, and James H. Tufts, *Ethics* (rev. ed., New York: Henry Holt, 1932), Chap. 10. Gives a conception of the nature of moral theory.

Frankena, William K., *Ethics* (Englewood Cliffs, N.J.: Prentice-Hall, 1963; 2d ed., 1973), Chaps. 1 and 6. Treats both the nature of morality and meta-ethics.

Hudson, W. D., *Modern Moral Philosophy* (Garden City, N.Y.: Doubleday, 1970), Chap. 1. Treats the nature of moral discourse and moral philosophy.

Moore, G. E., *Principia Ethica* (Cambridge: Cambridge U.P., 1903), Chap. 1. Argues that the peculiarity of ethics is that it investigates assertions about those properties of things which are denoted by the terms "good" and "bad."

Nielsen, Kai, "Ethics, Problems of," in Paul Edwards (ed.), *The Encyclopedia of Philosophy*, Vol. 3 (New York: Macmillan, 1967), pp. 117–134. Helpful survey of problems and of the relation between normative ethics and meta-ethics.

Nowell-Smith, P. H., *Ethics* (Baltimore: Penguin Books, 1954), Part I. Discusses ethics in theory and practice.

Schlick, Moritz, *Problems of Ethics*, trans. by David Rynin (New York: Prentice-Hall, 1939), Chap. 1. Offers a view about the aim of ethics and argues that the method of ethics is psychological.

Sidgwick, Henry, *The Methods of Ethics* (7th ed., London: Macmillan, 1907), Bk. I, Chap. 1. Treats the nature and methods of ethics.

Taylor, Paul W., *Principles of Ethics: An Introduction* (Encino, Calif.: Dickenson, 1975), Chap. 1. Describes descriptive, normative, and analytic ethics.

Toulmin, Stephen E., *An Examination of the Place of Reason in Ethics* (Cambridge: Cambridge U.P., 1950), Chaps. 9 and 10. Discusses whether ethics is a science. Also, presents a view of the function and development of ethics.

Warnock, G. J., *The Object of Morality* (London: Methuen, 1971), Chap. 1. Discusses three different ways of looking at the subject matter of ethics.

B PSYCHOLOGICAL EGOISM:
DO ALL THE ACTIONS OF MEN PROCEED FROM THE SOLE MOTIVE OF SELF-LOVE?

This section sets out two classical philosophical positions concerning the doctrine of psychological egoism: the factual claim that all human actions are done for reasons of self-interest. The first is that of Thomas Hobbes, who supports the claim. The second is that of Bishop Joseph Butler, who attempts its refutation. Butler's arguments are quite contemporary in tone.

There are several aspects of psychological egoism which make it of interest to ethical theory. If it is true, then it appears to follow that a decision to help others, an altruistic act, is impossible, and that it is therefore illogical to blame a person for not seeing to the welfare of others. Traditionally ethical theorists have presupposed that men have the ability to act altruistically and that it makes sense to tell them they ought to promote the general welfare, even if such action requires self-sacrifice. But, if psychological egoism is correct, then the only possible normative ethical theory seems to be that of ethical egoism: the claim that an individual *ought* to act only for his own benefit.

It is true that one can be an ethical egoist without being a psychological egoist. For this reason, we have devoted a separate section in this text to ethical egoism. Nevertheless, it is often maintained that there is a connection between the two doctrines. Accepting the view that they are connected, Hobbes argues that one ought to serve his own interests because he can do nothing else. This leads to a common criticism, that such thinking seeks illicitly to deduce what people ought to do from what people in fact do.

Whatever the merits of this criticism, it is a law of nature, for Hobbes, that men seek only to serve themselves. Society, in so far as it serves the interests and welfare of others, is artificial. Of course, many actions appear at first sight to be for the benefit of others or to serve ideals concerning the welfare of others. But Hobbes argues that below the surface they are found to be means chosen by the agent in order to satisfy his own interests. In other words, they arise from the sole motive of self-love. Butler points out that such defenses often have an air of paradox—to help another person in distress is then to worry about one's own welfare, a form of cowardice or timidity.

In what is considered by many philosophers to be one of the great classical philosophical refutations, Butler seeks to show that the arguments of Hobbes rest upon psychological, as well as logical and semantic confusions. As noted above, his arguments have an amazingly contemporary tone and character. He accuses Hobbes of what is called an *analytical dilemma*. He shows, among other things, that if one takes the claim of psychological egoism seriously as a factual claim about human behavior, then it is false because, in the ordinary sense of "help," people do help other people. But if the claim is taken in the sense in which it *must* be true, i.e., the claim that identifies self-interest with motivation in general, the term "self-interest" picks out or distinguishes nothing in the range of human behavior. The term is therefore vacuous, circular in the vicious sense, and has no linguistic function.

3

Egoism and Human Nature

THOMAS HOBBES

CHAPTER 1
OF THE STATE OF MEN WITHOUT CIVIL SOCIETY

1. The faculties of human nature may be reduced unto four kinds; bodily strength, experience, reason, passion. Taking the beginning of this following doctrine from these, we will declare, in the first place, what manner of inclinations men who are endued with these faculties bear towards each other, and whether, and by what faculty they are born apt for society, and to preserve themselves against mutual violence; then proceeding, we will shew what advice was necessary to be taken for this business, and what are the conditions of society, or of human peace; that is to say, (changing the words only), what are the fundamental *laws of nature*.

2. The greatest part of those men who have written aught concerning commonwealths, either suppose, or require us or beg of us to believe, that man is a

FROM *Philosophical Rudiments Concerning Government and Society* by Thomas Hobbes, Chapter 1 (1651).

creature born fit[1] for society. The Greeks call him ζῶονπολιτικον; and on this foundation they so build up the doctrine of civil society, as if for the preservation of peace, and the government of mankind, there were nothing else necessary than that men should agree to make certain covenants and conditions together, which themselves should then call laws. Which axiom, though received by most, is yet certainly false; and an error proceeding from our too slight contemplation of human nature. For they who shall more narrowly look into the causes for which men come together, and delight in each other's company, shall easily find that this happens not because naturally it could happen no otherwise, but by accident. For if by nature one man should love another, that is, as man, there could no reason be returned why every man should not equally love every man, as being equally man; or why he should rather frequent those, whose society affords him honour or profit. We do not therefore by nature seek society for its own sake, but that we may receive some honour or profit from it; these we desire primarily, that secondarily. How, by what advice, men do meet, will be best known by observing those things which they do when they are met. For if they meet for traffic, it is plain every man regards not his fellow, but his business; if to discharge some office, a certain market-friendship is begotten, which hath more of jealousy in it than true love, and whence factions sometimes may arise, but good will never; if for pleasure and recreation of mind, every man is wont to please himself most with those things which stir up laughter, whence he may, according to the nature of that which is ridiculous, by comparison of another man's defects and infirmities, pass the more current in his own opinion. And although this be sometimes innocent and without offence, yet it is manifest they are not so much delighted with the society, as their own vain glory. But for the most part, in these kinds of meeting we wound the absent; their whole life, sayings, actions are examined, judged, condemned. Nay, it is very rare but some present receive a fling as soon as they part; so as his reason was not ill, who was wont always at parting to go out last. And these are indeed the true

[1] Since we now see actually a constituted society among men, and none living out of it, since we discern all desirous of congress and mutual correspondence, it may seem a wonderful kind of stupidity, to lay in the very threshold of this doctrine such a stumbling block before the reader, as to deny *man to be born fit for society*. Therefore I must more plainly say, that it is true indeed, that to man by nature, or as man, that is, as soon as he is born, solitude is an enemy; for infants have need of others to help them to live, and those of riper years to help them to live well. Wherefore I deny not that men (even nature compelling) desire to come together. But civil societies are not mere meetings, but bonds, to the making whereof faith and compacts are necessary; the virtue whereof to children and fools, and the profit whereof to those who have not yet tasted the miseries which accompany its defects, is altogether unknown; whence it happens, that those, because they know not what society is, cannot enter into it; these, because ignorant of the benefit it brings, care not for it. Manifest therefore it is, that all men, because they are born in infancy, are born unapt for society. Many also, perhaps most men, either through defect of mind or want of education, remain unfit during the whole course of their lives; yet have they, infants as well as those of riper years, a human nature. Wherefore man is made fit for society not by nature, but by education. Furthermore, although man were born in such a condition as to desire it, it follows not, that he therefore were born fit to enter into it. For it is one thing to desire, another to be in capacity fit for what we desire; for even they, who through their pride, will not stoop to equal conditions, without which there can be no society, do yet desire it.

delights of society, unto which we are carried by nature, that is, by those passions which are incident to all creatures, until either by sad experience or good precepts it so fall out, which in many it never happens, that the appetite of present matters be dulled with the memory of things past: without which the discourse of most quick and nimble men on this subject, is but cold and hungry.

But if it so happen, that being met they pass their time in relating some stories, and one of them begins to tell one which concerns himself; instantly every one of the rest most greedily desires to speak of himself too; if one relate some wonder, the rest will tell you miracles, if they have them; if not, they will feign them. Lastly, that I may say somewhat of them who pretend to be wiser than others: if they meet to talk of philosophy, look, how many men, so many would be esteemed masters, or else they not only love not their fellows, but even persecute them with hatred. So clear is it by experience to all men who a little more narrowly consider human affairs, that all free congress ariseth either from mutual poverty, or from vain glory, whence the parties met endeavour to carry with them either some benefit, or to leave behind them that same ἐυδοκιμεῖν, some esteem and honour with those, with whom they have been conversant. The same is also collected by reason out of the definitions themselves of *will, good, honour, profitable*. For when we voluntarily contract society, in all manner of society we look after the object of the will, that is, that which every one of those who gather together, propounds to himself for good. Now whatsoever seems good, is pleasant, and relates either to the senses, or the mind. But all the mind's pleasure is either glory, (or to have a good opinion of one's self), or refers to glory in the end; the rest are sensual, or conducing to sensuality, which may be all comprehended under the word *conveniences*. All society therefore is either for gain, or for glory; that is, not so much for love of our fellows, as for the love of ourselves. But no society can be great or lasting, which begins from vain glory. Because that glory is like honour; if all men have it no man hath it, for they consist in comparison and precellence. Neither doth the society of others advance any whit the cause of my glorying in myself; for every man must account himself, such as he can make himself without the help of others. But though the benefits of this life may be much furthered by mutual help; since yet those may be better attained to by dominion than by the society of others, I hope no body will doubt, but that men would much more greedily be carried by nature, if all fear were removed, to obtain dominion, than to gain society. We must therefore resolve, that the original of all great and lasting societies consisted not in the mutual good will men had towards each other, but in the mutual fear[2] they had of each other.

[2] It is objected: it is so improbable that men should grow into civil societies out of fear, that if they had been afraid, they would not have endured each other's looks. They presume, I believe, that to fear is nothing else than to be affrighted. I comprehend in this word *fear*, a certain foresight of future evil; neither do I conceive flight the sole property of fear, but to distrust, suspect, take heed, provide so that they may not fear, is also incident to the fearful. They who go to sleep, shut their doors; they who travel, carry their swords with them, because they fear thieves. Kingdoms guard their coasts and frontiers with forts and castles; cities are compact with walls; and all for fear of neighbouring kingdoms and towns. Even the strongest

3. The cause of mutual fear consists partly in the natural equality of men, partly in their mutual will of hurting; whence it comes to pass, that we can neither expect from others, nor promise to ourselves the least security. For if we look on men full-grown, and consider how brittle the frame of our human body is, which perishing, all its strength, vigour, and wisdom itself perisheth with it; and how easy a matter it is, even for the weakest man to kill the strongest: there is no reason why any man, trusting to his own strength, should conceive himself made by nature above others. They are equals, who can do equal things one against the other; but they who can do the greatest things, namely, kill, can do equal things. All men therefore among themselves are by nature equal; the inequality we now discern, hath its spring from the civil law.

4. All men in the state of nature have a desire and will to hurt, but not proceeding from the same cause, neither equally to be condemned. For one man, according to that natural equality which is among us, permits as much to others as he assumes to himself; which is an argument of a temperate man, and one that rightly values his power. Another, supposing himself above others, will have a license to do what he lists, and challenges respect and honour, as due to him before others; which is an argument of a fiery spirit. This man's will to hurt ariseth from vain glory, and the false esteem he hath of his own strength; the other's from the necessity of defending himself, his liberty, and his goods, against this man's violence.

5. Furthermore, since the combat of wits is the fiercest, the greatest discords which are, must necessarily arise from this contention. For in this case it is not only odious to contend against, but also not to consent. For not to approve of what a man saith, is no less than tacitly to accuse him of an error in that thing which he speaketh: as in very many things to dissent, is as much as if you accounted him a fool whom you dissent from. Which may appear hence, that there are no wars so sharply waged as between sects of the same religion, and factions of the same commonweal, where the contestation is either concerning doctrines or politic prudence. And since all the pleasure and jollity of the mind consists in this, even to get some, with whom comparing, it may find somewhat wherein to triumph and vaunt itself; it is impossible but men must declare sometimes some mutual scorn and contempt, either by laughter, or by words, or by gesture, or some sign or other; than which there is no greater vexation of mind, and than from which there cannot possibly arise a greater desire to do hurt.

6. But the most frequent reason why men desire to hurt each other, ariseth hence, that many men at the same time have an appetite to the same thing; which yet very often they can neither enjoy in common, nor yet divide it; whence

---

armies, and most accomplished for fight, yet sometimes parley for peace, as fearing each other's power, and lest they might be overcome. It is through fear that men secure themselves by flight indeed, and in corners, if they think they cannot escape otherwise; but for the most part, by arms and defensive weapons; whence it happens, that daring to come forth they know each other's spirits. But then if they fight, civil society ariseth from the victory; if the agree, from their agreement.

it follows that the strongest must have it, and who is strongest must be decided by the sword.

7. Among so many dangers therefore, as the natural lusts of men do daily threaten each other withal, to have a care of one's self is so far from being a matter scornfully to be looked upon, that one has neither the power nor wish to have done otherwise. For every man is desirous of what is good for him, and shuns what is evil, but chiefly the chiefest of natural evils, which is death; and this he doth by a certain impulsion of nature, no less than that whereby a stone moves downward. It is therefore neither absurd nor reprehensible, neither against the dictates of true reason, for a man to use all his endeavours to preserve and defend his body and the members thereof from death and sorrows. But that which is not contrary to right reason, that all men account to be done justly, and with right. Neither by the word *right* is anything else signified, than that liberty which every man hath to make use of his natural faculties according to right reason. Therefore the first foundation of natural right is this, that *every man as much as in him lies endeavour to protect his life and members.*

8. But because it is in vain for a man to have a right to the end, if the right to the necessary means be denied him, it follows, that since every man hath a right to preserve himself, he must also be allowed a right *to use all the means, and do all the actions, without which he cannot preserve himself.*

9. Now whether the means which he is about to use, and the action he is performing, be necessary to the preservation of his life and members or not, he himself, by the right of nature, must be judge. For if it be contrary to right reason that I should judge of mine own peril, say, that another man is judge. Why now, because he judgeth of what concerns me, by the same reason, because we are equal by nature, will I judge also of things which do belong to him. Therefore it agrees with right reason, that is, it is the right of nature that I judge of his opinion, that is, whether it conduce to my preservation or not.

10. Nature hath given to *every one a right to all;* that is, it was lawful for every man, in the bare state of nature,[3] or before such time as men had engaged

[3] This is thus to be understood: what any man does in the bare state of nature, is injurious to no man; not that in such a state he cannot offend God, or break the laws of nature; for injustice against men presupposeth human laws, such as in the state of nature there are none. Now the truth of this proposition thus conceived, is sufficiently demonstrated to the mindful reader in the articles immediately foregoing; but because in certain cases the difficulty of the conclusion makes us forget the premises, I will contract this argument, and make it most evident to a single view. Every man hath right to protect himself, as appears by the seventh article. The same man therefore hath a right to use all the means which necessarily conduce to this end, by the eighth article. But those are the necessary means which he shall judge to be such, by the ninth article. He therefore hath a right to make use of, and to do all whatsoever he shall judge requisite for his preservation; wherefore by the judgment of him that doth it, the thing done is either right or wrong, and therefore right. True it is therefore in the bare state of nature, &c. But if any man pretend somewhat to tend necessarily to his preservation, which yet he himself doth not confidently believe so, he may offend against the laws of nature, as in the third chapter of this book is more at large declared. It hath been objected by some: if a son kill his father, doth he him no injury? I have answered, that a son cannot be understood to be at any time in the state of nature, as being under the power and command of them to whom he owes his protection as soon as ever he is born, namely, either his father's or his mother's, or him that nourished him; as is demonstrated in the ninth chapter.

themselves by any covenants or bonds, to do what he would, and against whom he thought fit, and to possess, use, and enjoy all what he would, or could get. Now because whatsoever a man would, it therefore seems good to him because he wills it, and either it really doth, or at least seems to him to contribute towards his preservation, (but we have already allowed him to be judge, in the foregoing article, whether it doth or not, insomuch as we are to hold all for necessary whatsoever he shall esteem so), and by the 7th article it appears that by the right of nature those things may be done, and must be had, which necessarily conduce to the protection of life and members, it follows, that in the state of nature, to have all, and do all, is lawful for all. And this is that which is meant by that common saying, *nature hath given all to all.* From whence we understand likewise, that in the state of nature profit is the measure of right.

11. But it was the least benefit for men thus to have a common right to all things. For the effects of this right are the same, almost, as if there had been no right at all. For although any man might say of every thing, *this is mine*, yet could he not enjoy it, by reason of his neighbour, who having equal right and equal power, would pretend the same thing to be his.

12. If now to this natural proclivity of men, to hurt each other, which they derive from their passions, but chiefly from a vain esteem of themselves, you add, the right of all to all, wherewith one by right invades, the other by right resists, and whence arise perpetual jealousies and suspicions on all hands, and how hard a thing it is to provide against an enemy invading us with an intention to oppress and ruin, though he come with a small number, and no great provision; it cannot be denied but that the natural state of men, before they entered into society, was a mere war, and that not simply, but a war of all men against all men. For what is WAR, but that same time in which the will of contesting by force is fully declared, either by words or deeds? The time remaining is termed PEACE.

13. But it is easily judged how disagreeable a thing to the preservation either of mankind, or of each single man, a perpetual war is. But it is perpetual in its own nature; because in regard of the equality of those that strive, it cannot be ended by victory. For in this state the conqueror is subject to so much danger, as it were to be accounted a miracle, if any, even the most strong, should close up his life with many years and old age. They of America are examples hereof, even in this present age: other nations have been in former ages; which now indeed are become civil and flourishing, but were then few, fierce, short-lived, poor, nasty, and deprived of all that pleasure and beauty of life, which peace and society are wont to bring with them. Whosoever therefore holds, that it had been best to have continued in that state in which all things were lawful for all men, he contradicts himself. For every man by natural necessity desires that which is good for him: nor is there any that esteems a war of all against all, which necessarily adheres to such a state, to be good for him. And so it happens, that through fear of each other we think it fit to rid ourselves of this condition, and to get some fellows; that if there needs must be war, it may not yet be against all men, nor without some helps.

14. Fellows are gotten either by constraint, or by consent; by constraint, when after fight the conqueror makes the conquered serve him, either through fear of death, or by laying fetters on him: by consent, when men enter into society to help each other, both parties consenting without any constraint. But the conqueror may by right compel the conquered, or the strongest the weaker, (as a man in health may one that is sick, or he that is of riper years a child), unless he will choose to die, to give caution of his future obedience. For since the right of protecting ourselves according to our own wills, proceeded from our danger, and our danger from our equality, it is more consonant to reason, and more certain for our conservation, using the present advantage to secure ourselves by taking caution, than when they shall be full grown and strong, and got out of our power, to endeavour to recover that power again by doubtful fight. And on the other side, nothing can be thought more absurd, than by discharging whom you already have weak in your power, to make him at once both an enemy and a strong one. From whence we may understand likewise as a corollary in the natural state of men, that *a sure and irresistible power confers the right of dominion and ruling over those who cannot resist;* insomuch, as the right of all things that can be done, adheres essentially and immediately unto this omnipotence hence arising.

15. Yet cannot men expect any lasting preservation, continuing thus in the state of nature, that is, of war, by reason of that equality of power, and other human faculties they are endued withal. Wherefore to seek peace, where there is any hopes of obtaining it, and where there is none, to enquire out for auxiliaries of war, is the dictate of right reason, that is, the law of nature; as shall be showed in the next chapter.

4

The Refutation of Egoism

JOSEPH BUTLER

SERMON XI   UPON THE LOVE OF OUR NEIGHBOUR (PREACHED ON ADVENT SUNDAY)

And if there be any other commandment, it is briefly comprehended in this saying, namely, Thou shalt love thy neighbour as thyself.—ROM. 13:9

It is commonly observed that there is a disposition in men to complain of the viciousness and corruption of the age in which they live, as greater than that of former ones; which is usually followed with this further observation that mankind has been in that respect much the same in all times. Now, not to determine

FROM *Fifteen Sermons Upon Human Nature* by Joseph Butler; Sermon XI (1726).

whether this last be not contradicted by the accounts of history, thus much can scarce be doubted—that vice and folly take different turns, and some particular kinds of it are more open and avowed in some ages than in others; and I suppose it may be spoken of as very much the distinction of the present to profess a contracted spirit and greater regards to self-interest than appears to have been done formerly. Upon this account it seems worth while to inquire whether private interest is likely to be promoted in proportion to the degree in which self-love engrosses us, and prevails over all other principles, or whether the contracted affection may not possibly be so prevalent as to disappoint itself, and even contradict its own end, private good.

And since, further, there is generally thought to be some peculiar kind of contrariety between self-love and the love of our neighbour, between the pursuit of public and of private good, insomuch that when you are recommending one of these, you are supposed to be speaking against the other; and from hence arises a secret prejudice against and frequently open scorn of all talk of public spirit and real goodwill to our fellow creatures; it will be necessary to inquire what respect benevolence hath to self-love, and the pursuit of private interest to the pursuit of public; or whether there be anything of that peculiar inconsistency and contrariety between them, over and above what there is between self-love and other passions and particular affections, and their respective pursuits.

These inquiries, it is hoped, may be favorably attended to; for there shall be all possible concessions made to the favorite passion, which hath so much allowed to it, and whose cause is so universally pleaded: it shall be treated with the utmost tenderness and concern for its interests.

In order to this, as well as to determine the forementioned questions, it will be necessary to consider the nature, the object, and end of that self-love, as distinguished from other principles or affections in the mind and their respective objects.

Every man hath a general desire of his own happiness; and likewise a variety of particular affections, passions, and appetites, to particular external objects. The former proceeds from, or is, self-love, and seems inseparable from all sensible creatures, who can reflect upon themselves and their own interest or happiness, so as to have that interest an object to their minds: what is to be said of the latter is, that they proceed from, or together make up, that particular nature, according to which man is made. The object the former pursues is somewhat internal, our own happiness, enjoyment, satisfaction; whether we have or have not a distinct particular perception what it is, or wherein it consists: the objects of the latter are this or that particular external thing, which the affections tend towards, and of which it hath always a particular idea or perception. The principle we call self-love never seeks anything external for the sake of the thing, but only as a means of happiness or good: particular affections rest in the external things themselves. One belongs to man as a reasonable creature reflecting upon his own interest or happiness: the other, though quite distinct from reason, are as much a part of human nature.

That all particular appetites and passions are towards *external things them-*

selves, distinct from the *pleasure arising from them*, is manifested from hence, that there could not be this pleasure, were it not for that prior suitableness between the object and the passion: there could be no enjoyment or delight for one thing more than another, from eating food more than from swallowing a stone, if there were not an affection or appetite to one thing more than another.

Every particular affection, even the love of our neighbour, is as really our own affection, as self-love; and the pleasure arising from its gratification is as much my own pleasure, as the pleasure self-love would have from knowing I myself should be happy some time hence, would be my own pleasure. And if, because every particular affection is a man's own, and the pleasure arising from its gratification his own pleasure, or pleasure to himself, such particular affection must be called self-love. According to this way of speaking, no creature whatever can possibly act but merely from self-love; and every action and every affection whatever is to be resolved up into this one principle. But then this is not the language of mankind: or, if it were, we should want words to express the difference between the principle of an action, proceeding from cool consideration that it will be to my own advantage; and an action, suppose of revenge, or of friendship by which a man runs upon certain ruin, to do evil or good to another. It is manifest the principles of these actions are totally different, and so want different words to be distinguished by: all that they agree in is, that they both proceed from, and are done to gratify an inclination in a man's self. But the principle or inclination in one case is self-love; in the other, hatred, or love of another. There is then a distinction between the cool principle of self-love, or general desire of our own happiness, as one part of our nature, and one principle of action; and the particular affections towards particular external objects, as another principle of action. How much soever, therefore, is to be allowed to self-love, yet it cannot be allowed to be the whole of our inward constitution; because, you see, there are other parts or principles which come into it.

Further, private happiness or good is all which self-love can make us desire or be concerned about. In having this consists its gratification; it is an affection to ourselves—a regard to our own interest, happiness, and private good: and in the proportion a man hath this, he is interested, or a lover of himself. Let this be kept in mind, because there is commonly, as I shall presently have occasion to observe, another sense put upon these words. On the other hand, particular affections tend towards particular external things; these are their objects; having these is their end; in this consists their gratification: no matter whether it be, or be not, upon the whole, our interest or happiness. An action, done from the former of these principles, is called an interested action. An action, proceeding from any of the latter, has its denomination of passionate, ambitious, friendly, revengeful, or any other, from the particular appetite or affection from which it proceeds. Thus self-love, as one part of human nature, and the several particular principles as the other part, are themselves, their objects, and ends, stated and shown.

From hence it will be easy to see how far, and in what ways, each of these can contribute and be subservient to the private good of the individual. Happiness does not consist in self-love. The desire of happiness is no more the thing itself, than the desire of riches is the possession or enjoyment of them. People may love themselves with the most entire and unbounded affection, and yet be extremely miserable. Neither can self-love any way help them out, but by setting them on work to get rid of the causes of their misery, to gain or make use of those objects which are by nature adapted to afford satisfaction. Happiness or satisfaction consists only in the enjoyment of those objects which are by nature suited to our several particular appetites, passions, and affections. So that if self-love wholly engrosses us and leaves no room for any other principle, there can be absolutely no such thing at all as happiness or enjoyment of any kind whatever; since happiness consists in the gratification of particular passions, which supposes the having of them. Self-love then does not constitute *this* or *that* to be our interest or good; but our interest or good being constituted by nature and supposed self-love, only puts us upon obtaining and securing it. Therefore, if it be possible that self-love may prevail and exert itself in a degree or manner which is not subservient to this end, then it will not follow that our interest will be promoted in proportion to the degree in which that principle engrosses us, and prevails over others. Nay, further, the private and contracted affection, when it is not subservient to this end, private good, may, for anything that appears, have a direct contrary tendency and effect. And if we will consider the matter, we shall see that it often really has. Disengagement is absolutely necessary to enjoyment; and a person may have so steady and fixed an eye upon his own interest, whatever he places it in, as may hinder him from attending to many gratifications within his reach, which others have their minds free and open to. Overfondness for a child is not generally thought to be for its advantage; and, if there be any guess to be from appearances, surely that character we call *selfish* is not the most promising for happiness. Such a temper may plainly be, and exert itself in a degree and manner which may give unnecessary and useless solicitude and anxiety, in a degree and manner which may prevent obtaining the means and materials of enjoyment, as well as the making use of them. Immoderate self-love does very ill consult its own interest; and how much soever a paradox it may appear, it is certainly true, that, even from self-love, we should endeavour to get over all inordinate regard to, and consideration of, ourselves. Every one of our passions and affections hath its natural stint and bound, which may easily be exceeded; whereas our enjoyments can possibly be but in a determinate measure and degree. Therefore such excess of the affection, since it cannot procure any enjoyment, must in all cases be useless, but is generally attended with inconveniences, and often is down-right pain and misery. This holds as much with regard to self-love as to all other affections. The natural degree of it, so far as it sets us on work to gain and make use of the materials of satisfaction, may be to our real advantage; but beyond or beside this, it is in several respects an inconvenience and disadvantage. Thus it appears that private interest is so far from being likely to be promoted in proportion to the degree in which self-love engrosses us, and prevails over all other principles, that *the contracted affection may be so prevalent as to disappoint itself and even contradict its own end, private good.*

"But who, except the most sordidly covetous, ever thought there was any rivalship between the love of greatness, honour, power, or between sensual appetites, and self-love? No; there is a perfect harmony between them. It is by means of these particular appetites and affections that self-love is gratified in enjoyment, happiness, and satisfaction. The competition and rivalship is between self-love and the love of our neighbour. That affection which leads us out of ourselves, makes us regardless of our own interest, and substitute that of another in its stead." Whether then there be any peculiar competition and contrariety in this case, shall now be considered.

Self-love and interestedness was stated to consist in or be an affection to ourselves, a regard to our own private good: it is, therefore, distinct from benevolence, which is an affection to the good of our fellow creatures. But that benevolence is distinct from, that is, not the same thing with self-love, is no reason for its being looked upon with any peculiar suspicion, because every principle whatever, by means of which self-love is gratified, is distinct from it. And all things, which are distinct from each other, are equally so. A man has an affection or aversion to another: that one of these tends to, and is gratified by doing good, that the other tends to, and is gratified by doing harm, does not in the least alter the respect which either one or the other of these inward feelings has to self-love. We use the word *property* so as to exclude any other persons having an interest in that, of which we say a particular man has the property: and we often use the word *selfish* so as to exclude in the same manner all regards to the good of others. But the cases are not parallel: for though that exclusion is really part of the idea of property, yet such positive exclusion, or bringing this peculiar disregard to the good of others into the idea of self-love, is in reality adding to the idea, or changing it from what it was before stated to consist in, namely, in an affection to ourselves. This being the whole idea of self-love, it can no otherwise exclude good-will or love of others, than merely by not including it, no otherwise than it excludes love of arts, or reputation, or of anything else. Neither, on the other hand, does benevolence, any more than love of art or of reputation, exclude self-love. Love of our neighbour, then has just the same respect to, is no more distant from self-love, than hatred of our neighbour, or than love and hatred of anything else. Thus the principles, from which men rush upon certain ruin for the destruction of an enemy, and for the preservation of a friend, have the same respect to the private affection, are equally interested, or equally disinterested: and it is of no avail, whether they are said to be one or the other. Therefore, to whose who are shocked to hear virtue spoken of as disinterested, it may be allowed, that it is indeed absurd to speak thus of it; unless hatred, several particular instances of vice, and all the common affections and aversions in mankind are acknowledged to be disinterested too. Is there any less inconsistence between the love of inanimate things, or of creatures merely sensitive, and self-love, than between self-love, and the love of our neighbour? Is desire of, and delight in the happiness of another any more a diminution of self-love, than desire of and delight in the esteem of another? They are both equally desire of and delight in somewhat external to ourselves: either both or neither are so. The object of self-love is expressed in the term self: and every appetite of sense, and every particular affection of the heart, are equally interested or disinterested, because the objects of them all are equally self or somewhat else. Whatever ridicule, therefore, the mention of a disinterested principle or action may be supposed to lie open to, must, upon the matter being thus stated, relate to ambition, and every appetite and particular affection, as much as to benevolence. And indeed all the ridicule, and all the grave perplexity, of which this subject hath had its full share, is merely from words. The most intelligible way of speaking of it seems to be this: that self-love, and the actions done in consequence of it, (for these will presently appear to be the same as to this question) are interested; that particular affections towards external objects, and the actions done in consequence of those affections, are not so. But every one is at liberty to use words as he pleases. All that is here insisted upon is, that ambition, revenge, benevolence, all particular passions whatever, and the actions they produce, are equally interested or disinterested.

Thus it appears, that there is no peculiar contrariety between self-love and benevolence; no greater competition between these, than between any other particular affections and self-love. This relates to the affections themselves. Let us now see whether there be any peculiar contrariety between the respective courses of life which these affections lead to; whether there be any greater competition between the pursuit of private and of public good, than between any other particular pursuits and that of private good.

There seems no other reason to suspect that there is any such peculiar contrariety, but only that the course of action which benevolence leads to, has a more direct tendency to promote the good of others, than that course of action, which love of reputation, suppose, or any other particular affection, leads to. But that any affection tends to the happiness of another, does not hinder its tending to one's own happiness too. That others enjoy the benefit of the air and the light of the sun, does not hinder but that these are as much one's own private advantage now, as they would be if we had the property of them exclusive of all others. So a pursuit which tends to promote the good of another, yet may have as great tendency to promote private interest, as a pursuit which does not tend to the good of another at all, or which is mischievous to him. All particular affections whatever, resentment, benevolence, love of the arts, equally lead to a course of action for their own gratification, *i.e.*, the gratification of ourselves: and the gratification of each gives delight: so far, then, it is manifest they have all the same respect to private interest. Now, take into consideration further, concerning these three pursuits, that the end of the first is the harm; of the second, the good of another; of the last, somewhat indifferent: and is there any necessity, that these additional considerations should alter the respect which we before saw these three pursuits had to private interest; or render any one of them less conducive to it than any other? Thus, one man's affection is to honour, as his end; in order to obtain which, he thinks no pains too great. Suppose another, with such a singularity of mind, as to have the same affection to public good, as his end, which he endeavours with the same labour to obtain. In case of success, surely the man of benevolence hath as great enjoyment as the man of ambition; they both equally having the end, their affections, in the same degree, tended to; but in case of disappointment, the benevolent man has clearly the advantage; since endeavouring to do good, considered as a virtuous pursuit, is gratified by its own consciousness, *i. e.*, is in a degree its own reward.

And as to these two, or benevolence and any other particular passions whatever, considered in a further view, is forming a general temper, which more or less disposes us for enjoyment of all the common blessings of life, distinct from their own gratification: is benevolence less the temper of tranquility and freedom, than ambition or covetousness? Does the benevolent man appear less easy with himself, from his love to his neighbour? Does he less relish his being? Is there any peculiar gloom seated on his face? Is his mind less open to entertainment, or to any particular gratification? Nothing is more manifest, than that being in good humour, which is benevolence whilst it last, is itself the temper of satisfaction and enjoyment.

Suppose, then, a man sitting down to consider how he might become most easy to himself, and attain the greatest pleasure he could; all that which is his real natural happiness; this can only consist in the enjoyment of those objects which are by nature adapted to our several faculties. These particular enjoyments make up the sum total of our happiness; and they are supposed to arise from riches, honours, and the gratification of sensual appetites. Be it so: yet none profess themselves so completely happy in these enjoyments, but that there is room left in the mind for others, if they were presented to them. Nay, these, as much as they engage us, are not thought so high, but that human nature is capable even of greater. Now there have been persons in all ages, who have professed that they found satisfaction in the exercise of charity, in the love of their neighbour, in endeavouring to promote the happiness of all they had to do with, and in the pursuit of what is just, and right, and good, as the general bent of their mind and end of their life; and that doing an action of baseness or cruelty, would be as great violence to *their* self, as much breaking in upon their nature, as any external force. Persons of this character would add, if they might be heard, that they consider themselves as acting in the view of an infinite Being, who is in a much higher sense the object of reverence and of love, than all the world besides; and, therefore, they could have no more enjoyment from a wicked action done under his eye, than the persons to whom they are making their apology could, if all mankind were the spectators of it; and that the satisfaction of approving themselves to his unerring judgment, to whom they thus refer all their actions, is a more continued settled satisfaction than any this world can afford; as also that they have, no less than others, a mind free and open to all the common innocent gratifications of it such as they are. And, if we go no further, does there appear any absurdity in this? Will any one take upon him to say, that a man cannot find his account in this general course of life, as much as in the most unbounded ambition, or the excesses of pleasure?

Or that such a person has not consulted so well for himself, for the satisfaction and peace of his own mind, as the ambitious or dissolute man? And though the consideration, that God himself will in the end justify their taste, and support their cause, is not formally to be insisted upon here; yet thus much comes in, that all enjoyments whatever are much more clear and unmixed, from the assurance that they will end well. Is it certain, then, that there is nothing in these pretensions to happiness, especially when there are not wanting persons, who have supported themselves with satisfactions of this kind in sickness, poverty, disgrace, and in the very pangs of death? whereas, it is manifest all other enjoyments fail in these circumstances. This surely looks suspicious of having somewhat in it. Self-love, methinks, should be alarmed. May she not possibly pass over greater pleasures, than those she is so wholly taken up with?

The short of the matter is no more than this. Happiness consists in the gratification of certain affections, appetites, passions, with objects which are by nature adapted to them. Self-love may indeed set us on work to gratify these: but happiness or enjoyment has no immediate connexion with self-love, but arises from such gratification alone. Love of our neighbour is one of those affections. This, considered as a virtuous principle, is gratified by a consciousness of endeavouring to promote the good of others: but considered as a natural affection, its gratification consists in the actual accomplishment of this endeavour. Now, indulgence or gratification of this affection, whether in that consciousness, or this accomplishment, has the same respect to interest, as indulgence of any other affection; they equally proceed from, or do not proceed from, self-love; they equally include or equally exclude, this principle. Thus it appears, that "benevolence and the pursuit of public good have at least as great respect to self-love and the pursuit of private good, as any other particular passions, and their respective pursuits."

Neither is covetousness, whether as a temper or pursuit, any exception to this. For if by covetousness is meant the desire and pursuit of riches for their own sake, without any regard to or consideration of the uses of them; this hath as little to do with self-love, as benevolence hath. But by this word is usually meant, not such madness and total distraction of mind, but immoderate affection to and pursuit of riches as possessions, in order to some further end; namely, satisfaction, interest, or good. This, therefore, is not a particular affection, or particular pursuit, but it is the general principle of self-love, and the general pursuit of our own interest; for which reason, the word *selfish* is by every one appropriated to this temper and pursuit. Now, as it is ridiculous to assert that self-love and the love of our neighbour are the same; so neither is it asserted that following these different affections hath the same tendency and respect to our own interest. The comparison is not between self-love and the love of our neighbour; between pursuit of our own interest, and the interest of others; but between the several particular affections in human nature towards external objects, as one part of the comparison; and the one particular affection to the good of our neighbour, as the one part of it: and it has been shown, that all these have the same respect to self-love and private interest.

There is indeed frequently an inconsistence, or interfering between self-love or private interest, and the several particular appetites, passions, affections, or the pursuits they lead to. But this competition or interfering is merely accidental, and happens much oftener between pride, revenge, sensual gratifications, and private interest, than between private interest and benevolence. For nothing is more common than to see men give themselves up to a passion or an affection to their known prejudice and ruin, and in direct contradiction to manifest and real interest, and the loudest calls of self-love: whereas the seeming competitions and interfering between benevolence and private interest, relate much more to the materials or means of enjoyment, than to enjoyment itself. There is often an interfering in the former, where there is none in the latter. Thus, as to riches: so much money as a man gives away, so much less will remain in his possession. Here is a real interfering. But though a man cannot possibly give without lessening his fortune, yet there are multitudes might give without lessening their own enjoyment; because they may have more than they can turn to any real use or advantage to themselves. Thus, the more thought and time any one employs about the interests and good of others, he must necessarily have less to attend his own; but he may have so ready and large a supply of his own wants, that such thought might be really useless to himself, though of great service and assistance to others.

The general mistake, that there is some greater inconsistence between endeavouring to promote the good of another and self-interest, than between self-interest and pursuing anything else, seems, as hath already been hinted to arise from our notions of property; and to be carried on by this property's being supposed to be itself our happiness or good. People are so very much taken up with this one subject, that they seem from it to have formed a general way of thinking, which they apply to other things that they have nothing to do with. Hence, in a confused and slight way, it might well be taken for granted, that another's having no interest in an affection (*i. e.*, his good not being the object of it,) renders, as one may speak, the proprietor's interest in it greater; and that if another had an interest in it, this would render his less, or occasion that such affection could not be so friendly to self-love, or conducive to private good, as an affection or pursuit which has not a regard to the good of another. This, I say, might be taken for granted, whilst it was not attended to, that the object of every particular affection is equally somewhat external to ourselves: and whether it be the good of another person, or whether it be any other external thing, makes no alteration with regard to its being one's own affection, and the gratification of it one's own private enjoyment. And so far as it is taken for granted, that barely having the means and materials of enjoyment is what constitutes interest and happiness; that our interest and good consists in possessions themselves, in having the property of riches, houses, lands, gardens, not in the enjoyment of them; so far it will even more strongly be taken for granted, in the way already explained, that an affection's conducing to the good of another, must even necessarily occasion it to conduce less to private good, if not to be positively detrimental to it. For, if property and happiness are one and the same thing, as by increasing the property of another, you lessen your own property, so by promoting the happiness of another, you must lessen your own happiness. But whatever occasioned the mistake, I hope it has been fully proved to be one; as it has been proved, that there is no peculiar rivalship or competition between self-love and benevolence; that as there may be a competition between these two, so there may also between any particular affection whatever and self-love; that every particular affection, benevolence among the rest, is subservient to self-love, by being the instrument of private enjoyment; and that in one respect benevolence contributes more to private interest, *i. e.*, enjoyment or satisfaction, than any other of the particular common affections, as it is in a degree its own gratification.

And to all these things may be added, that religion, from whence arises our strongest obligation to benevolence, is so far from disowning the principle of self-love, that it often addresses itself to that very principle, and always to the mind in that state when reason presides; and there can no access be had to the understanding, but by convincing men, that the course of life we would persuade them to is not contrary to their interest. It may be allowed, without any prejudice to the cause of virtue and religion, that our ideas of happiness and misery are, of all our ideas, the nearest and most important to us; that they will, nay, if you please, that they ought to prevail over those of order, and beauty, and harmony, and proportion, if there should ever be, as it is impossible there ever should be, any inconsistency between them; though these last, too, as expressing the fitness of action, are real as truth itself. Let it be allowed, though virtue or moral rectitude does indeed consist in affection to and pursuit of what is right and good, as such; yet that, when we sit down in a cool hour, we can neither justify to ourselves this or any other pursuit, till we are convinced that it will be for our happiness, or at least not contrary to it.

Psychological Egoism—Further Readings

Baylis, Charles A., *Ethics* (New York: Henry Holt, 1958), Chap. 7, pp. 144–164. Critic.

Broad, C. D., "Egoism as a Theory of Human Motives," *Hibbert Journal*, XLVIII (1949–50), pp. 105–114. Critic.

Clemens, Samuel (Mark Twain), *What is Man?* (1906), Papers 1–4. Proponent.

Gauthier, David P. (ed.), *Morality and Rational Self-Interest* (Englewood Cliffs, N.J.: Prentice-Hall, 1970). Ten selections debating the merits of psychological and ethical egoism.

Helvétius, Claude-Adrien, *A Treatise on Man* (1772), Vol. I, Sec. II, Chaps. 6–7 and Vol. I, Sec. IV. Proponent.

Hobbes, Thomas, *Leviathan* (1651), especially Chaps. 6, 11, and 13–15. Proponent.

Hospers, John, *Human Conduct* (New York: Harcourt, Brace and World, 1961), Chap. 4, pp. 141–157. Critic.

Hume, David, *An Enquiry Concerning the Principles of Morals* (1751), Appendix II. Critic.

Mandeville, Bernard, *The Fable of the Bees: or, Private Vices, Public Benefits* (Oxford: Clarendon, 1924), Vols. I and II. Proponent.

Milo, Ronald D. (ed.), *Egoism and Altruism* (Belmont, Calif.: Wadsworth, 1973). Nine classical and contemporary authors debating the merits of psychological and ethical egoism.

Nielsen, Kai, "Egoism in Ethics," *Philosophy and Phenomenological Research*, XIX (1959), pp. 502–510. Critic of both psychological and ethical egoism.

C FREEDOM AND DETERMINISM:
 ARE HUMAN CHOICES REALLY FREE?

The idea of freedom is related to a vast range of social, political, aesthetic, as well as moral issues. Political, social, economic, and personal freedoms assume a general sense of freedom which is commonly thought to form a presupposition for all assessments of moral responsibility. To claim that a person is morally responsible for an action, and therefore subject to praise or to blame and punishment, is taken to imply that the person was *able* to do or not to do the act that he in fact did.

This presupposition has traditionally been linked to another—that the moral agent causes, or determines, his actions. At this point, a difficulty arises. First, the traditional concept of causation, the principle of determinism, states that all events and objects and processes are in some sense produced by, or conjoined with, necessary and sufficient prior conditions. If this principle is applied to human actions (decisions, choices), then it appears to follow that such actions are determined by prior conditions constituted by hereditary, environmental, educational, and other situational conditions over which the agent had, and has, no control. Thus, it is argued, all actions, being caused, are *compelled* or *constrained*. The agent therefore does not in fact choose; and he therefore is neither free nor responsible.

From these considerations, it can be seen that the classical problem of freedom of the will results from the application of the conceptual apparatus of scientific explanation, with its links to the concepts of regular laws of nature, causal laws, and predictability, to human actions. Doubt is thereby cast upon a group of traditional moral assumptions.

At the same time, it is not obvious that the denial of determinism is helpful for morality. The conceptual framework, in terms of which we explain and understand objects and events, is one in which we discover their position with respect to prior causal conditions. That is, we show events and objects to be instances of laws of nature. To claim that human choices and decisions are *not* instances of such laws (physical or psychological) appears to imply that they are in some basic sense irrational and unknowable—outside the confines of scientific and rational understanding.

Accordingly, we seem caught in a dilemma. On the one hand, to claim the truth of the view that human actions are determined, and in principle predictable, seems to imply that they are compelled or constrained. Hence, the actions are unfree in principle, with the consequence that the predication of moral responsibility is illicit. On the other hand, a denial of the claim that human actions are determined, a rejection of the causal nexus between the agent and his act, drives a logical wedge between the agent and his action. This implies the no less distasteful conclusion that the action is unrelated to the agent or to his interests, and therefore that the action is unknowable and nonsensical. Again, the predication of moral praise and blame seems to be illicit. How could a moral agent be responsible for an action which he did not "bring about" or "cause?"

The classical positions with respect to the controversy are as follows. First, the vigorously deterministic position, represented by a great Enlightenment thinker, Baron D'Holbach, concludes, on grounds of standard arguments, that man is not free, and hence moral praise and blame are not warranted. This position is called "hard determinism," or "non–compatibilism," in contemporary philosophical literature. There are two ways of attempting to avoid this view, which is unacceptable to many because it runs counter to their basic belief that responsibility is a key to morality. One position denies the first premise of the argument; that is, it denies that all actions are caused. This position is called "libertarianism" in the literature, and is developed in our text by a contemporary thinker, C. A. Campbell, who seeks to refute the main claims of hard determinism. The second position, called "soft determinism," or "compatibilism," is argued by Walter T. Stace, who contends that freedom of choice is compatible with our choices being caused.

5

In Defence of Free Will

C. Arthur Campbell

In casting about for a suitable topic upon which to address you to-day, I have naturally borne in mind that an inaugural lecture of this sort should be devoted to some theme of much more than merely esoteric import: to some theme, for preference, sufficiently central in character to have challenged the attention of all who possess a speculative interest in the nature of the universe and man's place within it. That is a principal reason why I have chosen to-day to speak on free will. Mighty issues turn, and turn directly, on the solution of the free will problem. It is in no way surprising that for centuries past it has exercised a fascination for thinkers both within and without the ranks of the professional philosophers that is probably not paralleled in the case of any of the other great problems of metaphysics.

There are, however, other considerations also which have governed my choice of subject. More particularly, I have been influenced by a conviction that the present state of philosophical opinion on free will is, for certain definitely assignable reasons, profoundly unsatisfactory. In my judgment, a thoroughly perverse attitude to the whole problem has been created by the almost universal acquiescence in the view that free will in what is often called the "vulgar" sense is too obviously nonsensical a notion to deserve serious discussion. Free will in a more "refined" sense—which is apt to mean free will purged of all elements that may cause embarrassment to a Deterministic psychology or a Deterministic metaphysics—is, it is understood, a conception which may be defended by the philosopher without loss of caste. But in its "vulgar" sense, as maintained, for example, by the plain man, who clings to a belief in genuinely open possibilities, it is (we are told) a wild and even obnoxious delusion, long ago discredited for sober thinkers.

Now, as it happens, I myself firmly believe that free will, in something extremely like the "vulgar" sense, is a fact. And I am anxious to-day to do what I can, within the limits of a single lecture, to justify that belief. I propose therefore to develop a statement of the Libertarian's position which will try to make clear why he finds himself obliged to hold what he does hold, and to follow this up with a critical examination of the grounds most in vogue among philosophers for impugning this position. Considerations of time will, I fear, compel a somewhat close economy in my treatment of objections. But I shall hope to say enough to instigate a doubt in some minds concerning the validity of certain very fashionable objections whose authority is often taken to be virtually final.

FROM C. A. Campbell, "In Defense of Free Will," Inaugural Lecture on assuming the Glasgow University Chair of Logic and Rhetoric, 1938.

And if no other good purpose is served, it will at least be of advantage if I can offer, in my positive statement, a target for the missiles of the critics more truly representative of Libertarianism than the targets at which they sometimes direct their fire—targets, I may add, upon which even the clumsiest of marksmen could hardly fail to register bull's-eyes.

Let us begin by noting that the problem of free will gets its urgency for the ordinary educated man by reason of its close connection with the conception of moral responsibility. When we regard a man as morally responsible for an act, we regard him as a legitimate object of moral praise or blame in respect of it. But it seems plain that a man cannot be a legitimate object of moral praise or blame for an act unless in willing the act he is in some important sense a "free" agent. Evidently free will in some sense, therefore, is a pre-condition of moral responsibility. Without doubt it is the realization that any threat to freedom is thus a threat to moral responsibility—with all that that implies—combined with the knowledge that there are a variety of considerations, philosophic, scientific, and theological, tending to place freedom in jeopardy, that gives to the problem of free will its perennial and universal appeal. And it is therefore in close connection with the question of the conditions of moral responsibility that any discussion of the problem must proceed, if it is not to be academic in the worst sense of the term.

We raise the question at once, therefore, what are the conditions, in respect of freedom, which must attach to an act in order to make it a morally responsible act? It seems to me that the fundamental conditions are two. I shall state them with all possible brevity, for we have a long road to travel.

The first condition is the universally recognised one that the act must be *self*-caused, *self*-determined. But it is important to accept this condition in its full rigour. The agent must be not merely *a* cause but the *sole* cause of that for which he is deemed morally responsible. If entities other than the self have also a causal influence upon an act, then that act is not one for which we can say without qualification that the *self* is morally responsible. If in respect of it we hold the self responsible at all, it can only be for some feature of the act—assuming the possibility of disengaging such a feature—of which the self *is* the sole cause. I do not see how this conclusion can be evaded. But it has awkward implications which have led not a few people to abandon the notion of individual moral responsibility altogether.

This first condition, however, is quite clearly not sufficient. It is possible to conceive an act of which the agent is the sole cause, but which is at the same time an act *necessitated* by the agent's nature. Some philosophers have contended, for example, that the act of Divine creation is an act which issues necessarily from the Divine nature. In the case of such an act, where the agent could not do otherwise than he did, we must all agree, I think, that it would be inept to say that he *ought* to have done otherwise and is thus morally blameworthy, or *ought not* to have done otherwise and is thus morally praiseworthy. It is perfectly true that we do sometimes hold a person morally responsible for an act, even when we believe that he, being what he now is, virtually could not do otherwise. But underlying that judgment is always the assumption that the person has *come* to be what he now is in virtue of past acts of will in which he *was* confronted by real alternatives, by genuinely open possibilities: and, strictly speaking, it is in respect of these *past* acts of his that we praise or blame the agent *now*. For ultimate analysis, the agent's power of alternative action would seem to be an inexpugnable condition of his liability to moral praise or blame, i.e. of his moral responsibility.

We may lay down, therefore, that an act is a "free" act in the sense required for moral responsibility only if the agent (*a*) is the sole cause of the act; and (*b*) could exert his causality in alternative ways. And it may be pointed out in passing that the acceptance of condition (*b*) implies the recognition of the inadequacy for moral freedom of mere "self-determination". The doctrine called "Self-determinism" is often contrasted by its advocates with mere Determinism on the one hand and Indeterminism on the other, and pronounced to be the one true gospel. I must insist, however, that if "Self-determinism" rejects condition (*b*), it cannot claim to be a doctrine of free will in the sense required to vindicate moral responsibility. The doctrine which demands, and asserts, the fulfilment of both conditions is the doctrine we call "Libertarianism". And it would in my opinion minister greatly to clarity if it were more widely recognized that for any doctrine which is not a species of Libertarianism to pose as a doctrine of "free will" is mere masquerade.

And now, the conditions of free will being defined in these general terms, we have to ask whether human beings are in fact capable of performing free acts; and if so, where precisely such acts are to be found. . . .

Let us ask, why do human beings so obstinately persist in believing that there is an indissoluble core of purely *self*-originated activity which even heredity and environment are powerless to affect? There can be little doubt, I think, of the answer in general terms. They do so, at bottom, because they feel certain of the existence of such activity from their immediate practical experience of themselves. Nor can there be in the end much doubt, I think, in what function of the self that activity is to be located. There seems to me to be one, and only one, function of the self with respect to which the agent can even pretend to have an assurance of that absolute self-origination which is here at issue. But to render precise the nature of that function is obviously of quite paramount importance: and we can do so, I think, only by way of a somewhat thorough analysis—which I now propose to attempt—of the experiential situation in which it occurs, viz., the situation of "moral temptation".

It is characteristic of that situation that in it I am aware of an end A which I believe to be morally right, and also of an end B, incompatible with A, towards which, in virtue of that system of conative dispositions which constitutes my "character" as so far formed, I entertain a strong desire. There may be, and perhaps must be, desiring elements in my nature which are directed to A also. But what gives to the situation its specific character as one of moral temptation is that the urge of our desiring nature towards the right end, A, is felt to be *relatively* weak. We are sure that if our desiring nature is permitted to issue directly in action, it is end B that we shall choose. That is what is meant by saying, as William James does, that end B is "in the line of least resistance" relatively to our conative dispositions. The expression is, of course, a meta- phorical one, but it serves to describe, graphically enough, a situation of which we all have frequent experience, viz., where we recognize a specific end as that towards which the "set" of our desiring nature most strongly inclines us, and which we shall indubitably choose if no inhibiting factor intervenes.

But inhibiting factors, we should most of us say, *may* intervene: and that in two totally different ways which it is vital to distinguish clearly. The inhibiting factor may be of the nature of another desire (or aversion), which operates by changing the balance of the desiring situation. Though at one stage I desire B, which I believe to be wrong, more strongly than I desire A, which I believe to be right, it may happen that before action is taken I become aware of certain hitherto undiscerned consequences of A which I strongly desire, and the result may be that now not *B* but *A* presents itself to me as the end in the line of least resistance. Moral temptation is here overcome by the simple process of ceasing to be a moral temptation.

That is one way, and probably by far the commoner way, in which an inhibit- ing factor intervenes. But it is certainly not regarded by the self who is confronted by moral temptation as the *only* way. In such situations we all believe, rightly or wrongly, that even although B *continues* to be in the line of least resistance, even although, in other words, the situation remains one with the characteristic marks of moral temptation, we *can* nevertheless align ourselves with A. We can do so, we believe, because we have the power to introduce a new energy, to make what we call an "effort of will", whereby we are able to act contrary to the felt balance of mere desire, and to achieve the higher end despite the fact that it continues to be in the line of greater resistance relatively to our desiring nature. The self in practice believes that it has this power; and believes, moreover, that the decision rests solely with its self, here and now, whether this power be exerted or not.

Now the objective validity or otherwise of this belief is not at the moment in question. I am here merely pointing to its existence as a psychological fact. No amount of introspective analysis, so far as I can see, even tends to disprove that we do as a matter of fact believe, in situations of moral temptation, that it rests with our self absolutely to decide whether we exert the effort of will which will enable us to rise to duty, or whether we shall allow our desiring nature to take its course.

I have now to point out, further, how this act of moral decision, at least in the significance which it has for the agent himself, fulfils in full the two conditions which we found it necessary to lay down at the beginning for the kind of "free" act which moral responsibility presupposes.

For obviously it is, in the first place, an act which the agent believes he could perform in alternative ways. He believes that it is genuinely open to him to put forth effort—in varying degrees, if the situations admits of that—or withhold it altogether. And when he *has* decided—in whatever way—he remains convinced that these alternative courses were really open to him.

It is perhaps a little less obvious, but, I think, equally certain, that the agent believes the second condition to be fulfilled likewise, i.e. that the act of decision is determined *solely* by his self. It appears less obvious, because we all realize that formed character has a great deal to do with the choices that we make; and formed character is, without a doubt, partly dependent on the external factors of heredity and environment. But it is crucial here that we should not misunderstand the precise nature of the influence which formed character brings to bear upon the choices that constitute conduct. No one denies that it determines, at least largely, what things we desire, and again how greatly we desire them. It may thus fairly be said to determine the felt balance of desires in the situation of moral temptation. But all that that amounts to is that formed character prescribes the nature of the situation *within* which the act of moral decision takes place. It does not in the least follow that it has any influence whatsoever in determining the act of decision itself—the decision as to whether we shall exert effort or take the easy course of following the bent of our desiring nature: take, that is to say, the course which, in virtue of the determining influence of our character as so far formed, we feel to be in the line of least resistance.

When one appreciates this, one is perhaps better prepared to recognize the fact that the agent himself in the situation of moral temptation does not, and indeed could not, regard his formed character as having any influence whatever upon his act of decision as such. For the very nature of that decision, as it presents itself to him, is as to whether he will or will not permit his formed character to dictate his action. In other words, the agent distinguishes sharply between the self which makes the decision, and the self which, as formed character, determines not the decision but the situation within which the decision takes place. Rightly or wrongly, the agent believes that through his act of decision he can oppose and transcend his own formed character in the interest of duty. We are therefore obliged to say, I think, that the agent *cannot* regard his formed character as in any sense a determinant of the act of decision as such. The act is felt to be a genuinely creative act, originated by the self *ad hoc*, and by the self alone.

Here then, if my analysis is correct, in the function of moral decision in situations of moral temptation, we have an act of the self which at least *appears to the agent* to satisfy both of the conditions of freedom which we laid down at the beginning. The vital question now is, is this "appearance" true or false? Is the act of decision really what it appears to the agent to be, determined solely by the self, and capable of alternative forms of expression? If it is, then we have here a free act which serves as an adequate basis for moral responsibility. We shall be entitled to regard the agent as morally praiseworthy or morally blameworthy according as he decides to put forth effort or to let his desiring nature have its way. We shall be entitled, in short, to judge the agent as he most certainly judges himself in the situation of moral temptation. If, on the other hand, there is good reason to believe that the agent is the victim of illusion in supposing his act of decision to bear this character, then in my opinion the whole conception of moral responsibility must be jettisoned altogether. For it seems to me certain that there is no other function of the self that even looks as though it satisfied the required conditions of the free act.

Now in considering the claim to truth of this belief of our practical consciousness, we should begin by noting that the onus of proof rests upon the critic who rejects this belief. Until cogent evidence to the contrary is adduced, we are entitled to put our trust in a belief which is so deeply embedded in our experience as practical beings as to be, I venture to say, ineradicable from it. Anyone who doubts whether it is ineradicable may be invited to think himself imaginatively into a situation of moral temptation as we have above described it, and then to ask himself whether in that situation he finds it possible to *disbelieve* that his act of decision has the characteristics in question. I have no misgivings about the answer. It is possible to disbelieve only when we are thinking abstractly about the situation; not when we are living through it, either actually or in imagination. This fact certainly establishes a strong prima facie presumption in favour of the Libertarian position. Nevertheless I agree that we shall have to weigh carefully several criticisms of high authority before we can feel justified in asserting free will as an ultimate and unqualified truth. . . .

I may turn at once, therefore, to lines of argument which do still enjoy a wide currency among anti-Libertarians. And I shall begin with one which, though it is a simple matter to show its irrelevance to the Libertarian doctrine as I have stated it, is so extremely popular that it cannot safely be ignored.

The charge made is that the Libertarian view is incompatible with the *predictability* of human conduct. For we do make rough predictions of people's conduct, on the basis of what we know of their character, every day of our lives, and there can be no doubt that the practice, within certain limits, is amply justified by results. Indeed if it were not so, social life would be reduced to sheer chaos. The close relationship between character and conduct which prediction postulates really seems to be about as certain as anything can be. But the Libertarian view, it is urged, by ascribing to the self a mysterious power of decision uncontrolled by character, and capable of issuing in acts inconsistent with character, denies that continuity between character and conduct upon which prediction depends. If Libertarianism is true, prediction is impossible. But prediction *is* possible, therefore Libertarianism is untrue.

My answer is that the Libertarian view is perfectly compatible with prediction within certain limits, and that there is no empirical evidence at all that prediction is in fact possible beyond these limits. The following considerations will, I think, make the point abundantly clear.

(1) There is no question, on our view, of a free will that can will just anything at all. The range of possible choices is limited by the agent's character in every case; for nothing can be an object of possible choice which is not suggested by either the agent's desires or his moral ideals, and these depend on "character" for us just as much as for our opponents. We have, indeed explicitly recognized at an earlier stage that character determines the situation within which the act of moral decision takes place, although not the act of moral decision itself. This

consideration obviously furnishes a broad basis for at least approximate predictions.

(2) There is *one* experiential situation, and *one only*, on our view, in which there is any possibility of the act of will not being in accordance with character; viz. the situation in which the course which formed character prescribes is a course in conflict with the agent's moral ideal: in other words, the situation of moral temptation. Now this is a situation of comparative rarity. Yet with respect to all other situations in life we are in full agreement with those who hold that conduct is the response of the agent's formed character to the given situation. Why should it not be so? There could be no reason, on our view any more than on another, for the agent even to consider deviating from the course which his formed character prescribes and he most strongly desires, *unless* that course is believed by him to be incompatible with what is right.

(3) Even within that one situation which is relevant to free will, our view can still recognize a certain basis for prediction. In that situation our character as so far formed prescribes a course opposed to duty, and an effort of will is required if we are to deviate from that course. But of course we are all aware that a greater effort of will is required in proportion to the degree in which we have to transcend our formed character in order to will the right. Such action is, as we say, "harder". But if action is "harder" in proportion as it involves deviation from formed character, it seems reasonable to suppose that, on the whole, action will be of rarer occurrence in that same proportion: though perhaps we may not say that at any level of deviation it becomes flatly impossible. It follows that even with respect to situations of moral temptation we may usefully employ our knowledge of the agent's character as a clue to prediction. It will be a clue of limited, but of by no means negligible, value. It will warrant us in predicting, e.g., of a person who has become enslaved to alcohol, that he is unlikely, even if fully aware of the moral evil of such slavery, to be successful immediately and completely in throwing off its shackles. Predictions of this kind we all make often enough in practice. And there seems no reason at all why a Libertarian doctrine should wish to question their validity.

Now when these three considerations are borne in mind, it becomes quite clear that the doctrine we are defending is compatible with a very substantial measure of predictability indeed. And I submit that there is not a jot of empirical evidence that any larger measure than this obtains in fact.

Let us pass on then to consider a much more interesting and, I think, more plausible criticism. It is constantly objected against the Libertarian doctrine that it is fundamentally *unintelligible*. Libertarianism holds that the act of moral decision is the *self's* act, and yet insists at the same time that it is not influenced by any of those determinate features in the self's nature which go to constitute its "character". But, it is asked, do not these two propositions contradict one another? Surely a *self*-determination which is determination by something other than the self's *character* is a contradiction in terms? What meaning is there in the conception of a "self" in abstraction from its "character"? If you really wish to maintain, it is urged, that the act of decision is not determined by the self's character, you ought to admit frankly that it is not determined by the *self* at all. But in that case, of course, you will not be advocating a freedom which lends any kind of support to moral responsibility; indeed very much the reverse.

Now this criticism, and all of its kind, seem to me to be the product of a simple, but extraordinarily pervasive, error: the error of confining one's self to the categories of the external observer in dealing with the actions of human agents. Let me explain.

It is perfectly true that the standpoint of the external observer, which we are obliged to adopt in dealing with physical processes, does not furnish us with even a glimmering of a notion of what can be meant by an entity which acts causally and yet not through any of the determinate features of its character. So far as we confine ourselves to external observation, I agree that this notion must seem to us pure nonsense. But then we are *not* obliged to confine ourselves to external observation in dealing with the human agent. Here, though here alone, we have the inestimable advantage of being able to apprehend operations from the *inside*, from the standpoint of *living experience*. But if we do adopt this internal standpoint—surely a proper standpoint, and one which we should be only too glad to adopt if we could in the case of other entities—the situation is entirely changed. We find that we not merely can, but constantly do, attach meaning to a causation which is the self's causation but is yet not exercised by the self's character. We have seen as much already in our analysis of the situation of moral temptation. When confronted by such a situation, we saw, we are certain that it lies with our *self* to decide whether we shall let our character as so far formed dictate our action or whether we shall by effort oppose its dictates and rise to duty. We are certain, in other words, that the act is *not* determined by our *character*, while we remain equally certain that the act *is* determined by our *self*.

Or look, for a further illustration (since the point we have to make here is of the very first importance for the whole free will controversy), to the experience of effortful willing itself, where the act of decision has found expression in the will to rise to duty. In such an experience we are certain that it is our self which makes the effort. But we are equally certain that the effort does not flow from that system of conative dispositions which we call our formed character; for the very function that the effort has for us is to enable us to act against the "line of least resistance", i.e. to act in a way *contrary* to that to which our formed character inclines us.

I conclude, therefore, that those who find the Libertarian doctrine of the self's causality in moral decision inherently unintelligible find it so simply because they restrict themselves, quite arbitrarily, to an inadequate standpoint: a standpoint from which, indeed, a genuinely creative activity, if it existed, never *could* be apprehended.

It will be understood, of course, that it is no part of my purpose to deny that the act of moral decision is in *one* sense "unintelligible". If by the "intelligibility" of an act we mean that it is capable, at least in principle, of being inferred as a consequence of a given ground, then naturally my view is that the act in question is "*un*intelligible." But that, presumably, is not the meaning of "intelligibility" in the critic's mind when he says that the Libertarian holds an "unintelligible" doctrine. If it were all he meant, he would merely be pointing out that Libertarianism is not compatible with Determinism! And that tautologous pronouncement would hardly deserve the title of "criticism". Yet, strangely enough, not all of the critics seem to be quite clear on this matter. The Libertarian often has the experience of being challenged by the critic to tell him *why*, on his view, the agent now decides to put forth moral effort and now decides not to, with the obviously intended implication that if the Libertarian cannot say "why" he should give up his theory. Such critics apparently fail to see that if the Libertarian *could* say why he would already have given up his theory! Obviously to demand "intelligibility" in this sense is simply to prejudge the whole issue in favour of Determinism. The sense in which the critic is entitled to demand intelligibility of our doctrine is simply this; he may demand that the kind of action which our doctrine imputes to human selves should not be, for ultimate analysis, meaningless. And in that sense, as I have already argued, our doctrine is perfectly intelligible.

6

Determinism

BARON HOLBACH

MOTIVES AND THE DETERMINATION OF THE WILL. In whatever manner man is considered, he is connected to universal nature, and submitted to the necessary and immutable laws that she imposes on all the beings she contains, according to their peculiar essences or to the respective properties with which, without consulting them, she endows each particular species. Man's life is a line that nature commands him to describe upon the surface of the earth, without his ever being able to swerve from it, even for an instant. He is born without his own consent; his organization does in nowise depend upon himself; his ideas come to him involuntarily; his habits are in the power of those who cause him to contract them; he is unceasingly modified by causes, whether visible or concealed, over which he has no control, which necessarily regulate his mode of existence, give the hue to his way of thinking, and determine his manner of acting. He is good or bad, happy or miserable, wise or foolish, reasonable or irrational, without his will being for anything in these various states. Nevertheless, in spite of the shackles by which he is bound, it is pretended he is a free agent, or that independent of the causes by which he is moved, he determines his own will, and regulates his own condition.

FROM *The System of Nature* by Baron Holbach, Vol. I, Chapters 11 and 12. Translated by H. D. Robinson (1853).

However slender the foundation of this opinion, of which everything ought to point out to him the error, it is current at this day and passes for an incontestable truth with a great number of people, otherwise extremely enlightened; it is the basis of religion, which, supposing relations between man and the unknown being she has placed above nature, has been incapable of imagining how man could merit reward or deserve punishment from this being, if he was not a free agent. Society has been believed interested in this system; because an idea has gone abroad, that if all the actions of man were to be contemplated as necessary, the right of punishing those who injure their associates would no longer exist. At length human vanity accommodated itself to a hypothesis which, unquestionably, appears to distinguish man from all other physical beings, by assigning to him the special privilege of a total independence of all other causes, but of which a very little reflection would have shown him the impossibility. . . .

The will, as we have elsewhere said, is a modification of the brain, by which it is disposed to action, or prepared to give play to the organs. This will is necessarily determined by the qualities, good or bad, agreeable or painful, of the object or the motive that acts upon his senses, or of which the idea remains with him, and is resuscitated by his memory. In consequence, he acts necessarily, his action is the result of the impulse he receives either from the motive, from the object, or from the idea which has modified his brain, or disposed his will. When he does not act according to this impulse, it is because there comes some new cause, some new motive, some new idea, which modifies his brain in a different manner, gives him a new impulse, determines his will in another way, by which the action of the former impulse is suspended: thus, the sight of an agreeable object, or its idea, determines his will to set him in action to procure it; but if a new object or a new idea more powerfully attracts him, it gives a new direction to his will, annihilates the effect of the former, and prevents the action by which it was to be procured. This is the mode in which reflection, experience, reason, necessarily arrests or suspends the action of man's will: without this he would of necessity have followed the anterior impulse which carried him towards a then desirable object. In all this he always acts according to necessary laws from which he has no means of emancipating himself.

If when tormented with violent thirst, he figures to himself in idea, or really perceives a fountain, whose limpid streams might cool his feverish want, is he sufficient master of himself to desire or not to desire the object competent to satisfy so lively a want? It will no doubt be conceded, that it is impossible he should not be desirous to satisfy it; but it will be said—if at this moment it is announced to him that the water he so ardently desires is poisoned, he will, notwithstanding his vehement thirst, abstain from drinking it: and it has, therefore, been falsely concluded that he is a free agent. The fact, however, is, that the motive in either case is exactly the same: his own conservation. The same necessity that determined him to drink before he knew the water was deleterious upon this new discovery equally determined him not to drink; the desire of conserving himself either annihilates or suspends the former impulse; the second motive becomes stronger than the preceding, that is, the fear of death, or the desire of preserving himself, necessarily prevails over the painful sensation caused by his eagerness to drink: but, it will be said, if the thirst is very parching, an inconsiderate man without regarding the danger will risk swallowing the water. Nothing is gained by this remark: in this case, the anterior impulse only regains the ascendency; he is persuaded that life may possibly be longer preserved, or that he shall derive a greater good by drinking the poisoned water than by enduring the torment, which, to his mind, threatens instant dissolution; thus the first becomes the strongest and necessarily urges him on to action. Nevertheless, in either case, whether he partakes of the water, or whether he does not, the two actions will be equally necessary; they will be the effect of that motive which finds itself most puissant; which consequently acts in the most coercive manner upon his will.

This example will serve to explain the whole phenomena of the human will. This will, or rather the brain, finds itself in the same situation as a bowl, which, although it has received an impulse that drives it forward in a straight line, is deranged in its course whenever a force superior to the first obliges it to change its direction. The man who drinks the poisoned water appears a madman; but the actions of fools are as necessary as those of the most prudent individuals. The motives that determine the voluptuary and the debauchee to risk their health, are as powerful, and their actions are as necessary, as those which decide the wise man to manage his. But, it will be insisted, the debauchee may be prevailed on to change his conduct: this does not imply that he is a free agent; but that motives may be found sufficiently powerful to annihilate the effect of those that previously acted upon him; then these new motives determine his will to the new mode of conduct he may adopt as necessarily as the former did to the old mode. . . .

The errors of philosophers on the free agency of man, have arisen from their regarding his will as the *primum mobile*, the original motive of his actions; for want of recurring back, they have not perceived the multiplied, the complicated causes which, independently of him, give motion to the will itself; or which dispose and modify his brain, whilst he himself is purely passive in the motion he receives. Is he the master of desiring or not desiring an object that appears desirable to him? Without doubt it will be answered, no: but he is the master of resisting his desire, if he reflects on the consequences. But, I ask, is he capable of reflecting on these consequences, when his soul is hurried along by a very lively passion, which entirely depends upon his natural organization, and the causes by which he is modified? Is it in his power to add to these consequences all the weight necessary to counterbalance his desire? Is he the master of preventing the qualities which render an object desirable from residing in it? I shall be told: he ought to have learned to resist his passions; to contract a habit of putting a curb on his desires. I agree to it without any difficulty. But in reply, I again ask, is his nature susceptible of this modification? Does his boiling blood, his unruly imagination, the igneous fluid that circulates in his veins, permit him to make, enable him to apply true experience in the moment when it is wanted? And even when his temperament has capacitated him, has his education, the examples set before him, the ideas with which he has been inspired in early life, been suitable to make him contract this habit of repressing his desires? Have not all these things rather contributed to induce him to seek with avidity, to make him actually desire those objects which you say he ought to resist?

The *ambitious man* cries out: you will have me resist my passion; but have they not unceasingly repeated to me that rank, honours, power, are the most desirable advantages in life? Have I not seen my fellow citizens envy them, the nobles of my country sacrifice every thing to obtain them? In the society in which I live, am I not obliged to feel, that if I am deprived of these advantages, I must expect to languish in contempt; to cringe under the rod of oppression?

The *miser* says: you forbid me to love money, to seek after the means of acquiring it: alas! does not every thing tell me that, in this world, money is the greatest blessing; that it is amply sufficient to render me happy? In the country I inhabit, do I not see all my fellow citizens covetous of riches? but do I not also witness that they are little scrupulous in the means of obtaining wealth? As soon as they are enriched by the means which you censure, are they not cherished, considered and respected? By what authority, then, do you defend me from amassing treasure? What right have you to prevent my using means, which, although you call them sordid and criminal, I see approved by the sovereign? Will you have me renounce my happiness?

The *voluptuary* argues: you pretend that I should resist my desires; but was I the maker of my own temperament, which unceasingly invites me to pleasure? You call my pleasures disgraceful; but in the country in which I live, do I not witness the most dissipated men enjoying the most distinguished rank? Do I not behold that no one is ashamed of adultery but the husband it has outraged? Do not I see men making trophies of their debaucheries, boasting of their libertinism, rewarded with applause?

The *choleric man* vociferates: you advise me to put a curb on my passions, and to resist the desire of avenging myself: but can I conquer my nature? Can I alter the received opinions of the world? Shall I not be forever disgraced, infallibly dishonoured in society, if I do not wash out in the blood of my fellow creatures the injuries I have received?

The *zealous enthusiast* exclaims: you recommend me mildness; you advise me to be tolerant; to be indulgent to the opinions of my fellow men; but is not my temperament violent? Do I not ardently love my God? Do they not assure me, that zeal is pleasing to him; that sanguinary inhuman persecutors have been his friends? As I wish to render myself acceptable in his sight, I therefore adopt the same means.

In short, the actions of man are never free; they are always the necessary consequence of his temperament, of the received ideas, and of the notions, either true or false, which he has formed to himself of happiness; of his opinions, strengthened by example, by education, and by daily experience. So many crimes are witnessed on the earth only because every thing conspires to render man vicious and criminal; the religion he has adopted, his government, his education, the examples set before him, irresistibly drive him on to evil: under these circumstances, morality preaches virtue to him in vain. In those societies where vice is esteemed, where crime is crowned, where venality is constantly recompensed, where the most dreadful disorders are punished only in those who are too weak to enjoy the privilege of committing them with impunity, the practice of virtue is considered nothing more than a painful sacrifice of happiness. Such societies chastise, in the lower orders, those excesses which they respect in the higher ranks; and frequently have the injustice to condemn those in the penalty of death, whom public prejudices, maintained by constant example, have rendered criminal.

Man, then, is not a free agent in any one instant of his life; he is necessarily guided in each step by those advantages, whether real or fictitious, that he attaches to the objects by which his passions are roused: these passions themselves are necessary in a being who unceasingly tends towards his own happiness; their energy is necessary, since that depends on his temperament; his temperament is necessary, because it depends on the physical elements which enter into his composition; the modification of this temperament is necessary, as it is the infallible and inevitable consequence of the impulse he receives from the incessant action of moral and physical beings.

CHOICE DOES NOT PROVE FREEDOM. In spite of these proofs of the want of free agency in man, so clear to unprejudiced minds, it will, perhaps be insisted upon with no small feeling of triumph, that if it be proposed to any one, to move or not to move his hand, an action in the number of those called indifferent, he evidently appears to be the master of choosing; from which it is concluded that evidence has been offered of free agency. The reply is, this example is perfectly simple; man in performing some action which he is resolved on doing, does not by any means prove his free agency; the very desire of displaying this quality, excited by the dispute, becomes a necessary motive, which decides his will either for the one or the other of these actions: What deludes him in this instance, or that which persuades him he is a free agent at this moment, is, that he does not discern the true motive which sets him in action, namely, the desire of convincing his opponent: if in the heat of the dispute he insists and asks, "Am I not the master of throwing myself out of the window?" I shall answer him, no; that whilst he preserves his reason there is no probability that the desire of proving his free agency, will become a motive sufficiently powerful to make him sacrifice his life to the attempt: if, notwithstanding this, to prove he is a free agent, he should actually precipitate himself from the window, it would not be a sufficient warranty to conclude he acted freely, but rather that it was the violence of his temperament which spurred him on to this folly. Madness is a state, that depends upon the heat of the blood, not upon the will. A fanatic or a hero, braves death as necessarily as a more phlegmatic man or coward flies from it.

There is, in point of fact, no difference between the man that is cast out of the window by another, and the man who throws himself out of it, except that the impulse in the first instance comes immediately from without whilst that which determines the fall in the second case, springs from within his own peculiar machine, having its more remote cause also exterior. When Mutius Scaevola held his hand in the fire, he was as much acting under the influence of necessity (caused by interior motives) that urged him to this strange action, as if his arm had been held by strong men: pride, despair, the desire of braving his enemy, a wish to astonish him, and anxiety to intimidate him, etc., were the invisible chains that held his hand bound to the fire. The love of glory, enthusiasm for their country, in like manner caused Codrus and Decius to devote themselves for their fellow-citizens. The Indian Colanus and the philosopher Peregrinus were equally obliged to burn themselves, by desire of exciting the astonishment of the Grecian assembly.

It is said that free agency is the absence of those obstacles competent to oppose themselves to the actions of man, or to the exercise of his faculties: it is pretended that he is a free agent whenever, making use of these faculties, he produces the effect he has proposed to himself. In reply to this reasoning, it is sufficient to consider that it in nowise depends upon himself to place or remove the obstacles that either determine or resist him; the motive that causes his action is no more in his own power than the obstacle that impedes him, whether this obstacle or motive be within his own machine or exterior of his person: he is not master of the thought presented to his mind, which determines his will; this thought is excited by some cause independent of himself.

To be undeceived on the system of his free agency, man has simply to recur to the motive by which his will is determined; he will always find this motive is out of his own control. It is said: that in consequence of an idea to which the mind gives birth, man acts freely if he encounters no obstacle. But the question is, what gives birth to this idea in his brain? was he the master either to prevent it from presenting itself, or from renewing itself in his brain? Does not this idea depend either upon objects that strike him exteriorly and in despite of himself, or upon causes, that without his knowledge, act within himself and modify his brain? Can he prevent his eyes, cast without design upon any object whatever, from giving him an idea of this object, and from moving his brain? He is not more master of the obstacles; they are the necessary effects of either interior or exterior causes, which always act according to their given properties. A man insults a coward; this necessarily irritates him against his insulter; but his will cannot vanquish the obstacle that cowardice places to the object of his desire, because his natural conformation, which does not depend upon himself, prevents his having courage. In this case, the coward is insulted in spite of himself; and against his will is obliged patiently to brook the insult he has received.

ABSENCE OF RESTRAINT IS NOT ABSENCE OF NECESSITY. The partisans of the system of free agency appear ever to have confounded constraint with necessity. Man believes he acts as a free agent, every time he does not see any thing that places obstacles to his actions; he does not perceive that the motive which causes him to will, is always necessary and independent of himself. A prisoner loaded with chains is compelled to remain in prison; but he is not a free agent in the desire to emancipate himself; his chains prevent him from acting, but they do not prevent him from willing; he would save himself if they would loose his fetters; but he would not save himself as a free agent; fear or the idea of punishment would be sufficient motives for his action.

Man may, therefore, cease to be restrained, without, for that reason, becoming a free agent: in whatever manner he acts, he will act necessarily, according to motives by which he shall be determined. He may be compared to a heavy body that finds itself arrested in its descent by any obstacle whatever: take away this obstacle, it will gravitate or continue to fall; but who shall say this dense body is free to fall or not? Is not its descent the necessary effect of its own specific gravity? The virtuous Socrates submitted to the laws of his country, although they were unjust; and though the doors of his jail were left open to him, he would not save himself; but in this he did not act as a free agent: the invisible chains of opinion, the secret love of decorum, the inward respect for the laws, even when they were iniquitous, the fear of tarnishing his glory, kept him in his prison; they were motives sufficiently powerful with this enthusiast for virtue, to induce him to wait death with tranquility; it was not in his power to save himself, because he could find no potential motive to bring him to depart, even for an instant, from those principles to which his mind was accustomed.

Man, it is said, frequently acts against his inclination, from whence it is falsely concluded he is a free agent; but when he appears to act contrary to his inclination, he is always determined to it by some motive sufficiently efficacious to vanquish this inclination. A sick man, with a view to his cure, arrives at conquering his repugnance to the most disgusting remedies: the fear of pain, or the dread of death, then become necessary motives; consequently this sick man cannot be said to act freely.

When it is said, that man is not a free agent, it is not pretended to compare him to a body moved by a simple impulsive cause: he contains within himself causes inherent to his existence; he is moved by an interior organ, which has its own peculiar laws, and is itself necessarily determined in consequence of ideas formed from perception resulting from sensation which it receives from exterior objects. As the mechanism of these sensations, of these perceptions, and the manner they engrave ideas on the brain of man, are not known to him; because he is unable to unravel all these motions; because he cannot perceive the chain of operations in his soul, or the motive principle that acts within him, he supposes himself a free agent; which literally translated, signifies, that he moves himself by himself; that he determines himself without cause: when he rather ought to say, that he is ignorant how or why he acts in the manner he does. It is true the soul enjoys an activity peculiar to itself: but it is equally certain that this activity would never be displayed, if some motive or some cause did not put it in a condition to exercise itself: at least it will not be pretended that the soul is able either to love or to hate without being moved, without knowing the objects, without having some idea of their qualities. Gunpowder has unquestionably a particular activity, but this activity will never display itself, unless fire be applied to it; this, however, immediately sets it in motion.

THE COMPLEXITY OF HUMAN CONDUCT AND THE ILLUSION OF FREE AGENCY. It is the great complication of motion in man, it is the variety of his action, it is the multiplicity of causes that move him, whether simultaneously or in continual succession, that persuades him he is a free agent: if all his motions were simple, if the causes that move him did not confound themselves with each other, if they were distinct, if his machine were less complicated, he would perceive that all his actions were necessary, because he would be enabled to recur instantly to the cause that made him act. A man who should be always obliged to go towards the west, would always go on that side; but he would feel that, in so going, he was not a free agent: if he had another sense, as his actions or his motion, augmented by a sixth, would be still more varied and much more complicated, he would believe himself still more a free agent than he does with his five senses.

It is, then, for want of recurring to the causes that move him; for want of being able to analyze, from not being competent to decompose the complicated motion of his machine, that man believes himself a free agent: it is only upon his own ignorance that he founds the profound yet deceitful notion he has of his free agency; that he builds those opinions which he brings forward as a striking proof of his pretended freedom of action. If, for a short time, each man was willing to examine his own peculiar actions, search out their true motives to discover their concatenation, he would remain convinced that the sentiment he has of his natural free agency, is a chimera that must speedily be destroyed by experience.

Nevertheless it must be acknowledged that the multiplicity and diversity of the causes which continually act upon man, frequently without even his knowledge, render it impossible, or at least extremely difficult for him to recur to the true principles of his own peculiar actions, much less the actions of others: they frequently depend upon causes so fugitive, so remote from their effects, and which, superficially examined, appear to have so little analogy, so slender a relation with them, that it requires singular sagacity to bring them into light. This is what renders the study of the moral man a task of such difficulty; this is the reason why his heart is an abyss, of which it is frequently impossible for him to fathom the depth. . . .

If he understood the play of his organs, if he were able to recall to himself all the impulsions they have received, all the modifications they have undergone, all the effects they have produced, he would perceive that all his actions are submitted to the fatality, which regulates his own particular system, as it does the entire system of the universe: no one effect in him, any more than in nature, produces itself by chance; this, as has been before proved, is word void of sense. All that passes in him; all that is done by him; as well as all that happens in nature, or that is attributed to her, is derived from necessary causes, which act according to necessary laws, and which produce necessary effects from whence necessarily flow others.

Fatality, is the eternal, the immutable, the necessary order, established in nature; or the indispensable connexion of causes that act, with the effects they operate. Conforming to this order, heavy bodies fall: light bodies rise; that which is analogous in matter reciprocally attracts; that which is heterogeneous mutually repels; man congregates himself in society, modifies each his fellow; becomes either virtuous or wicked; either contributes to his mutual happiness, or reciprocates his misery; either loves his neighbour, or hates his companion necessarily, according to the manner in which the one acts upon the other. From whence it may be seen, that the same necessity which regulates the physical, also regulates the moral world, in which every thing is in consequence submitted to fatality. Man, in running over, frequently without his own knowledge, often in spite of himself, the route which nature has marked out for him, resembles a swimmer who is obliged to follow the current that carries him along: he believes himself a free agent, because he sometimes consents, sometimes does not consent, to glide with the stream, which notwithstanding, always hurries him forward; he believes himself the master of his condition, because he is obliged to use his arms under the fear of sinking. . . .

7

Determinism and Freedom

WALTER T. STACE

It is certain that if there is no free will there can be no morality. Morality is concerned with what men ought and ought not to do. But if a man has no freedom to choose what he will do, if whatever he does is done under compulsion, then it does not make sense to tell him that he ought not to have done what he did and that he ought to do something different. All moral precepts would in such case be meaningless. Also if he acts always under compulsion, how can he be held morally responsible for his actions? How can he, for example, be punished for what he could not help doing?

It is to be observed that those learned professors of philosophy or psychology who deny the existence of free will do so only in their professional moments and in their studies and lecture rooms. For when it comes to doing anything practical, even of the most trivial kind, they invariably behave as if they and others were free. They inquire from you at dinner whether you will choose this dish or that dish. They will ask a child why he told a lie, and will punish him for not having chosen the way of truthfulness. All of which is inconsistent with a disbelief in free will. This should cause us to suspect that the problem is not a real one; and this, I believe, is the case. The dispute is merely verbal, and is due to nothing but a confusion about the meanings of words. It is what is now fashionably called a semantic problem.

How does a verbal dispute arise? Let us consider a case which, although it is absurd in the sense that no one would ever make the mistake which is involved in it, yet illustrates the principle which we shall have to use in the solution of the

FROM *Religion and the Modern Mind* by Walter T. Stace. Copyright 1952 by W. T. Stace. Reprinted by permission of J. B. Lippincott Company.

problem. Suppose that someone believed that the word "man" means a certain sort of five-legged animal; in short that "five-legged animal" is the correct *definition* of man. He might then look around the world, and rightly observing that there are no five-legged animals in it, he might proceed to deny the existence of men. This preposterous conclusion would have been reached because he was using an incorrect definition of "man". All you would have to do to show him his mistake would be to give him the correct definition; or at least to show him that his definition was wrong. Both the problem and its solution would, of course, be entirely verbal. The problem of free will, and its solution, I shall maintain, is verbal in exactly the same way. The problem has been created by the fact that learned men, especially philosophers, have assumed an incorrect definition of free will, and then finding that there is nothing in the world which answers to their definition, have denied its existence. As far as logic is concerned, their conclusion is just as absurd as that of the man who denies the existence of men. The only difference is that the mistake in the latter case is obvious and crude, while the mistake which the deniers of free will have made is rather subtle and difficult to detect.

Throughout the modern period, until quite recently, it was assumed, both by the philosophers who denied free will and by those who defended it, that *determinism is inconsistent with free will*. If a man's actions were wholly determined by chains of causes stretching back into the remote past, so that they could be predicted beforehand by a mind which knew all the causes, it was assumed that they could not in that case be free. This implies that a certain definition of actions done from free will was assumed, namely that they are actions *not* wholly determined by causes or predictable beforehand. Let us shorten this by saying that free will was defined as meaning indeterminism. This is the incorrect definition which has led to the denial of free will. As soon as we see what the true definition is we shall find that the question whether the world is deterministic, as Newtonian science implied, or in a measure indeterministic, as current physics teaches, is wholly irrelevant to the problem.

Of course there is a sense in which one can define a word arbitrarily in any way one pleases. But a definition may nevertheless be called correct or incorrect. It is correct if it accords with a *common usage* of the word defined. It is incorrect if it does not. And if you give an incorrect definition, absurd and untrue results are likely to follow. For instance, there is nothing to prevent you from arbitrarily defining a man as a five-legged animal, but this is incorrect in the sense that it does not accord with the ordinary meaning of the word. Also it has the absurd result of leading to a denial of the existence of men. This shows that *common usage is the criterion for deciding whether a definition is correct or not*. And this is the principle which I shall apply to free will. I shall show that indeterminism is not what is meant by the phrase "free will" *as it is commonly used*. And I shall attempt to discover the correct definition by inquiring how the phrase is used in ordinary conversation.

Here are a few samples of how the phrase might be used in ordinary conversation. It will be noticed that they include cases in which the question whether a man acted with free will is asked in order to determine whether he was morally and legally responsible for his acts.

Jones I once went without food for a week.
Smith Did you do that of your own free will?
Jones No. I did it because I was lost in a desert and could find no food.

But suppose that the man who had fasted was Mahatma Gandhi. The conversation might then have gone:

Gandhi I once fasted for a week.
Smith Did you do that of your own free will?
Gandhi Yes. I did it because I wanted to compel the British Government to give India its independence.

Take another case. Suppose that I had stolen some bread, but that I was as truthful as George Washington. Then, if I were charged with the crime in court, some exchange of the following sort might take place:

Judge Did you steal the bread of your own free will?
Stace Yes. I stole it because I was hungry.

Or in different circumstances the conversation might run:

Judge Did you steal of your own free will?
Stace No. I stole because my employer threatened to beat me if I did not.

At a recent murder trial in Trenton some of the accused had signed confessions, but afterwards asserted that they had done so under police duress. The following exchange might have occurred:

Judge Did you sign this confession of your own free will?
Prisoner No. I signed it because the police beat me up.

Now suppose that a philosopher had been a member of the jury. We could imagine this conversation taking place in the jury room.

Foreman of the Jury The prisoner says he signed the confession because he was beaten, and not of his own free will.
Philosopher This is quite irrelevant to the case. There is no such thing as free will.
Foreman Do you mean to say that it makes no difference whether he signed because his conscience made him want to tell the truth or because he was beaten?
Philosopher None at all. Whether he was caused to sign by a beating or by some desire of his own—the desire to tell the truth, for example—in either case his signing was causally determined, and therefore in neither case did he act of his own free will. Since there is no such thing as free will, the question whether he signed of his own free will ought not to be discussed by us.

The foreman and the rest of the jury would rightly conclude that the philosopher must be making some mistake. What sort of a mistake could it be? There is only one possible answer. The philosopher must be using the phrase "free will" in some peculiar way of his own which is not the way in which men usually use it when they wish to determine a question of moral responsibility. That is, he must be using an incorrect definition of it as implying action not determined by causes.

Suppose a man left his office at noon, and were questioned about it. Then we might hear this:

Jones Did you go out of your own free will?
Smith Yes. I went out to get my lunch.

But we might hear:

Jones Did you leave your office of your own free will?
Smith No. I was forcibly removed by the police.

We have now collected a number of cases of actions which, in the ordinary usage of the English language, would be called cases in which people have acted of their own free will. We should also say in all these cases that they *chose* to act as they did. We should also say that they could have acted otherwise, if they had chosen. For instance, Mahatma Gandhi was not compelled to fast; he chose to do so. He could have eaten if he had wanted to. When Smith went out to get his lunch, he chose to do so. He could have stayed and done some more work, if he had wanted to. We have also collected a number of cases of the opposite kind. They are cases in which men were not able to exercise their free will. They had no choice. They were compelled to do as they did. The man in the desert did not fast of his own free will. He had no choice in the matter. He was compelled to fast because there was nothing for him to eat. And so with the other cases. It ought to be quite easy, by an inspection of these cases, to tell what we ordinarily mean when we say that a man did or did not exercise free will. We ought therefore to be able to extract from them the proper definition of the term. Let us put the cases in a table:

Free Acts	*Unfree Acts*
Gandhi fasting because he wanted to free India.	The man fasting in the desert because there was no food.
Stealing bread because one is hungry.	Stealing because one's employer threatened to beat one.
Signing a confession because one wanted to tell the truth.	Signing because the police beat one.
Leaving the office because one wanted one's lunch.	Leaving because forcibly removed.

It is obvious that to find the correct definition of free acts we must discover what characteristic is common to all the acts in the left-hand column, and is, at the same time, absent from all the acts in the right-hand column. This characteristic which all free acts have, and which no unfree acts have, will be the defining characteristic of free will.

Is being uncaused, or not being determined by causes, the characteristic of which we are in search? It cannot be, because although it is true that all the acts in the right-hand column have causes, such as the beating by the police or the absence of food in the desert, so also do the acts in the left-hand column. Mr. Gandhi's fasting was caused by his desire to free India, the man leaving his office by his hunger, and so on. Moreover there is no reason to doubt that these causes of the free acts were in turn caused by prior conditions, and that these were again the results of causes, and so on back indefinitely into the past. Any physiologist can tell us the causes of hunger. What caused Mr. Gandhi's tremendously powerful desire to free India is no doubt more difficult to discover. But it must have had causes. Some of them may have lain in peculiarities of his glands or brain, others in his past experiences, others in his heredity, others in his education. Defenders of free will have usually tended to deny such facts. But to do so is plainly a case of special pleading, which is unsupported by any scrap of evidence. The only reasonable view is that all human actions, both those which are freely done and those which are not, are either wholly determined by causes, or at least as much determined as other events in nature. It may be true, as the physicists tell us, that nature is not as deterministic as was once thought. But whatever degree of determinism prevails in the world, human actions appear to be as much determined as anything else. And if this is so, it cannot be the case that what distinguishes actions freely chosen from those which are not free is that the latter are determined by causes while the former are not. Therefore, being uncaused or being undetermined by causes, must be an incorrect definition of free will.

What, then, is the difference between acts which are freely done and those which are not? What is the characteristic which is present to all the acts in the left-hand column and absent from all those in the right-hand column? Is it not obvious that, although both sets of actions have causes, the causes of those in the left-hand column are *of a different kind* from the causes of those in the right-hand column? The free acts are all caused by desires, or motives, or by some sort of internal psychological states of the agent's mind. The unfree acts, on the other hand, are all caused by physical forces or physical conditions, outside the agent. Police arrest means physical force exerted from the outside; the absence of food in the desert is a physical condition of the outside world. We may therefore frame the following rough definitions. *Acts freely done are those whose immediate causes are psychological states in the agent. Acts not freely done are those whose immediate causes are states of affairs external to the agent.*

It is plain that if we define free will in this way, then free will certainly exists, and the philosopher's denial of its existence is seen to be what it is—nonsense. For it is obvious that all those actions of men which we should ordinarily attribute to the exercise of their free will, or of which we should say that they freely chose to do them, are in fact actions which have been caused by their own desires, wishes, thoughts, emotions, impulses, or other psychological states.

In applying our definition we shall find that it usually works well, but that there are some puzzling cases which it does not seem exactly to fit. These puzzles can always be solved by paying careful attention to the ways in which words are used, and remembering that they are not always used consistently. I have space for only one example. Suppose that a thug threatens to shoot you unless you give him your wallet, and suppose that you do so. Do you, in giving him your wallet, do so of your own free will or not? If we apply our definition, we find that you acted freely, since the immediate cause of the action was not an actual outside force but fear of death, which is a psychological cause. Most people, however, would say that you did not act of your own free will but under compulsion. Does this show that our definition is wrong? I do not think so. Aristotle, who gave a solution of the problem of free will substantially the same as ours (though he did not use the term "free will") admitted that there are what he called "mixed" or borderline cases in which it is difficult to know whether we ought to call the acts free or compelled. In the case under discussion, though no actual force was used, the gun at your forehead so nearly approximated to actual force that we tend to say the case was one of compulsion. It is a borderline case.

Here is what may seem like another kind of puzzle. According to our view an action may be free though it could have been predicted beforehand with certainty. But suppose you told a lie, and it was certain beforehand that you would tell it. How could one then say, "You could have told the truth"? The answer is that it is perfectly true that you could have told the truth *if* you had wanted to. In fact you would have done so, for in that case the causes producing your action, namely, your desires, would have been different, and would therefore have produced different effects. It is a delusion that predictability and free will are incompatible. This agrees with common sense. For if, knowing your character, I predict that you will act honorably, no one would say when you do act honorably, that this shows you did not do so of your own free will.

Since free will is a condition of moral responsibility, we must be sure that our theory of free will gives a sufficient basis for it. To be held morally responsible for one's actions means that one may be justly punished or rewarded, blamed or praised, for them. But it is not just to punish a man for what he cannot help doing. How can it be just to punish him for an action which it was certain beforehand that he would do? We have not attempted to decide whether, as a matter of fact, all events, including human actions, are completely determined. For that question is irrelevant to the problem of free will. But if we assume for the purposes of argument that complete determinism is true, but that we are nevertheless free, it may then be asked whether such a deterministic free will is compatible with moral responsibility. For it may seem unjust to punish a man for an action which it could have been predicted with certainty beforehand that he would do.

But that determinism is incompatible with moral responsibility is as much a delusion as that it is incompatible with free will. You do not excuse a man for doing a wrong act because, knowing his character, you felt certain beforehand that he would do it. Nor do you deprive a man of a reward or prize because, knowing his goodness or his capabilities, you felt certain beforehand that he would win it.

Volumes have been written on the justification of punishment. But so far as it affects the question of free will, the essential principles involved are quite simple. The punishment of a man for doing a wrong act is justified, either on the ground that it will correct his own character, or that it will deter other people from doing similar acts. The instrument of punishment has been in the past, and no doubt still is, often unwisely used; so that it may often have done more harm than good. But that is not relevant to our present problem. Punishment, if and when it is justified, is justified only on one or both of the grounds just mentioned. The question then is how, if we assume determinism, punishment can correct character or deter people from evil actions.

Suppose that your child develops a habit of telling lies. You give him a mild beating. Why? Because you believe that his personality is such that the usual motives for telling the truth do not cause him to do so. You therefore supply the missing cause, or motive, in the shape of pain and the fear of future pain if he repeats his untruthful behavior. And you hope that a few treatments of this kind will condition him to the habit of truth-telling, so that he will come to tell the truth without the infliction of pain. You assume that his actions are determined by causes, but that the usual causes of truth-telling do not in him produce their usual effects. You therefore supply him with an artificially injected motive, pain and fear, which you think will in the future cause him to speak truthfully.

The principle is exactly the same where you hope, by punishing one man, to deter others from wrong actions. You believe that the fear of punishment will cause those who might otherwise do evil to do well.

We act on the same principle with non-human, and even with inanimate, things, if they do not behave in the way we think they ought to behave. The rose bushes in the garden produce only small and poor blooms, whereas we want large and rich ones. We supply a cause which will produce large blooms, namely fertilizer. Our automobile does not go properly. We supply a cause which will make it go better, namely oil in the works. The punishment for the man, the fertilizer for the plant, and the oil for the car, are all justified by the same principle and in the same way. The only difference is that different kinds of things require different kinds of causes to make them do what they should. Pain may be the appropriate remedy to apply, in certain cases, to human beings, and oil to the machine. It is, of course, of no use to inject motor oil into the boy or to beat the machine.

Thus we see that moral responsibility is not only consistent with determinism, but requires it. The assumption on which punishment is based is that human behavior is causally determined. If pain could not be a cause of truth-telling there would be no justification at all for punishing lies. If human actions and volitions were uncaused, it would be useless either to punish or reward, or indeed to do anything else to correct people's bad behavior. For nothing that you could do would in any way influence them. Thus moral responsibility would entirely disappear. If there were no determinism of human beings at all, their actions would be completely unpredictable and capricious, and therefore irresponsible. And this is in itself a strong argument against the common view of philosophers that free will means being undetermined by causes.

The Problem of Freedom and Determinism—Further Readings

Berofsky, Bernard (ed.), *Free Will and Determinism* (New York: Harper, 1966). Twenty essays, mostly by contemporary authors, arranged in such a way that proponents and opponents debate various issues about free will and determinism.

Dworkin, Gerald (ed.), *Determinism, Free Will, and Moral Responsibility* (Englewood Cliffs, N.J.: Prentice-Hall, 1970). Twelve selections from classical and contemporary authors expressing different views.

Enteman, Willard F. (ed.), *The Problem of Free Will: Selected Readings* (New York: Scribner, 1967). Seventeen articles by classical and contemporary authors organized to bring out different points of view on issues involved in the problem of free will.

Hook, Sidney (ed.), *Determinism and Freedom in the Age of Modern Science* (New York: New York U.P., 1958). Twenty-seven contemporaries contribute papers concerning freedom and determinism.

Lehrer, Keith (ed.), *Freedom and Determinism* (New York: Random House, 1966). Seven essays by contemporary American philosophers on problems involved in the debate between free-willists and determinists.

Morgenbesser, Sidney, and James Walsh (eds.), *Free Will* (Englewood Cliffs, N.J.: Prentice-Hall, 1962). Twelve selections from classical and contemporary sources arranged to present different views on some of the key issues concerning free will.

Morris, Herbert (ed.), *Freedom and Responsibility* (Stanford, Calif.: Stanford U.P., 1961). A book of readings in philosophy and law, with sections on responsibility, free will, and punishment.

Pears, D. F. (ed.), *Freedom and the Will* (New York: St. Martin's, 1963). Seven essays by contemporary British philosophers on the nature of the will and its freedom. Most of the essays originated as talks in the Third Programme of the B.B.C., in which there was a direct exchange of views between the participants.

D CULTURAL RELATIVISM:
IS ETHICS MERE CONFORMITY?

The issues surrounding relativism are quite confusing. In the general logical sense, all relativisms involve the claim that right and wrong, good and evil, are relative to something or another. Thus "good" and "right" designate relational properties, like, for example the words, *father of* in the sentence "John is the *father of* Jane." There can be many forms of relativism, depending upon the ways in which the ethical thinker defines or characterizes the relationships he takes to be basic to ethical judgments. Logical positivists, like Ayer and Carnap, make good and evil relative to the approvals and disapprovals of the individual moral agent. Existentialists appear to agree. Pragmatists like James and Dewey make good and right relative to the solution of problems. The most common kind of relativism encountered today is probably cultural relativism, and our selections, from William Graham Sumner and Paul Taylor, reflect this view, although Taylor considers other types. Cultural relativists maintain that good and evil, right and wrong, are relative to the interests of the members of a society or culture. What is good, and what is right, are the actions and things approved by a majority of the members of a society or culture.

All forms of relativism contrast with absolutism, that is, with views which maintain that there are independent and unchanging ethical objects or properties named by normative terms like "right" and "good." This, as will be clear later, would not concern many modern ethical thinkers; but relativism also appears to deny one of those characteristic presuppositions of any ethical theory to which we keep returning. It looks, in other words, as if cultural and other forms of relativism may reject the very possibility of normative ethics, since they deny that there exist meaningful and coherent systems of rationally justifiable moral principles.

William Graham Sumner echoes the opinions characteristic of anthropologists and sociologists, who have been influenced by the wide variety of moral views discovered by contemporary social scientists in their studies of the conventions of primitive cultures. Folkways are habitually followed, learned or conditioned rules. Mores, or moral rules, are folkways with the added characteristic of concern for one's fellows. Neither kind of rule is rationally founded or based. They are habit patterns, together with associated emotional and social expressions. Even the principles and criteria ethical philosophers themselves use in the analysis and criticism of ethical concepts are products of folkways, and are "secondary" or "derived." What is true, what is right, what ought to be, reflect, not rationally justified principles, but learned, uncritically accepted, and often downright stupid, habit-patterns.

Paul Taylor distinguishes three varieties of culturally based ethical relativism. They are, in order, "descriptive," "normative," and "meta-ethical" relativism. It is clear that the term "relativism" is ambiguous, and thus cuts across the lines of organization in our text.

The descriptive relativist maintains, as an empirical claim, the position that moral rules are culture-bound, and that moral behavior is merely a matter of conformity. These "facts," he believes, are shown to be true by observation of the variation in norms among different cultures concerning the same kinds of actions. Taylor argues that this view, in the main, founders on a failure to distinguish between *ultimate* and *subsidiary* (or specific) moral rules. It is not obvious that ultimate principles, such as injunctions against lying and stealing, are variant from culture to culture, although their specific formulations may so vary.

Normative relativism, however, maintains that what is actually right in one society is wrong in another, and thus that cross-cultural comparisons are illegitimate. It is incorrect, therefore, for a person in one culture to morally condemn the actions of a person who lives in another, so long as the latter person is following the rules of his own culture. Conflicts between members of different cultures do not even represent true contradictories (a position which is also held by those theorists who make value and obligation relative to the individual). The proposition "*x* is right for Joe in culture A," does not contradict the proposition, "*x* is wrong for Manolo in culture B." As Taylor points out, the normative relativist faces the peculiar problem of being unable to propose, recommend, or justify his own position without incoherence. He is in a situation not unlike that of the absolute skeptic when he asserts that he knows that nothing can be known. The cultural relativist wishes to assert that it is right to believe (independent of his culture) that nothing is right.

Meta-ethical relativism can be formulated, according to Taylor, in two ways. The first, called "conceptual relativism," takes the views of one culture as meaningless or unintelligible to members of other cultures because each view is based upon an unique conceptual scheme. "Methodological relativism," Taylor's name for the second variety of meta-ethical relativism, claims that since variant techniques of justification are used in each culture, no cross-cultural rational grounds are available for comparative judgment. This stance, perhaps all of them, appears to be similar to what is called "the sociology of knowledge," as developed in the thought of Karl Mannheim and his followers. It is claimed that even the criteria of truth are culture-bound.

Two critical points may be (briefly) made. With respect to the latter view, it is difficult to see how their protagonists can escape having their claims turned upon them, i.e., these claims are *merely* expressions of their own cultural or personal preferences. Further, the normative variety of relativism, resting as it does on the notion of the uniqueness of each culture, seems to imply the false proposition that sentences in different languages, including of course moral sentences, cannot be translated into one another.

8

Mores as Folkways

William Graham Sumner

1. Definition and Mode of Origin of the Folkways. If we put together all that we have learned from anthropology and ethnography about primitive men and primitive society, we perceive that the first task of life is to live. Men begin with acts, not with thoughts. Every moment brings necessities which must be satisfied at once. Need was the first experience, and it was followed at once by a blundering effort to satisfy it. It is generally taken for granted that men inherited some guiding instincts from their beast ancestry, and it may be true, although it has never been proved. If there were such inheritances, they controlled and aided the first efforts to satisfy needs. Analogy makes it easy to assume that the ways of beasts had produced channels of habit and predisposition along which dexterities and other psychophysical activities would run easily. Experiments with newborn animals show that in the absence of any experience of the relation of means to ends, efforts to satisfy needs are clumsy and blundering. The method is that of trial and failure, which produces repeated pain, loss, and disappointments. Nevertheless, it is a method of rude experiment and selection. The earliest efforts of men were of this kind. Need was the impelling force. Pleaure and pain, on the one side and the other, were the rude constraints which defined the line on which efforts must proceed. The ability to distinguish between pleasure and pain is the only psychical power which is to be assumed. Thus ways of doing things were selected, which were expedient. They answered the purpose better than other ways, or with less toil and pain. Along the course on which efforts

were compelled to go, habit, routine, and skill were developed. The struggle to maintain existence was carried on, not individually, but in groups. Each profited by the other's experience; hence there was concurrence towards that which proved to be most expedient. All at last adopted the same way for the same purpose; hence the ways turned into customs and became mass phenomena. Instincts were developed in connection with them. In this way folkways arise. The young learn them by tradition, imitation, and authority. The folkways, at a time, provide for all the needs of life then and there. They are uniform, universal in the group, imperative, and invariable. As time goes on, the folkways become more and more arbitrary, positive, and imperative. If asked why they act in a certain way in certain cases, primitive people always answer that it is because they and their ancestors always have done so. A sanction also arises from ghost fear. The ghosts of ancestors would be angry if the living should change the ancient folkways.

3. FOLKWAYS ARE MADE UNCONSCIOUSLY. It is of the first importance to notice that, from the first acts by which men try to satisfy needs, each act stands by itself, and looks no further than the immediate satisfaction. From recurrent needs arise habits for the individual and customs for the group, but these results are consequences which were never conscious, and never foreseen or intended. They are not noticed until they have long existed, and it is still longer before they are appreciated. Another long time must pass, and a higher stage of mental development must be reached, before they can be used as a basis from which to deduce rules for meeting, in the future, problems whose pressure can be foreseen. The folkways, therefore, are not creations of human purpose and wit. They are like products of natural forces which men unconsciously set in operation, or they are like the instinctive ways of animals, which are developed out of experience, which reach a final form of maximum adaptation to an interest, which are handed down by tradition and admit of no exception or variation, yet change to meet new conditions, still within the same limited methods, and without rational reflection or purpose. From this it results that all the life of human beings, in all ages and stages of culture, is primarily controlled by a vast mass of folkways handed down from the earliest existence of the race, having the nature of the ways of other animals, only the topmost layers of which are subject to change and control, and have been somewhat modified by human philosophy, ethics, and religion, or by other acts of intelligent reflection. We are told of savages that "It is difficult to exhaust the customs and small ceremonial usages of a savage people. Custom regulates the whole of a man's actions—his bathing, washing, cutting his hair, eating, drinking, and fasting. From his cradle to his grave he is the slave of ancient usage. In his life there is nothing free, nothing original, nothing spontaneous, no progress towards a higher and better life, and no attempt to improve his condition, mentally, morally, or spiritually." All men act in this way with only a little wider margin of voluntary variation.

28. FOLKWAYS DUE TO FALSE INFERENCE. Furthermore, folkways have been formed by accident, that is, by irrational and incongruous action, based on

pseudo-knowledge. In Molembo a pestilence broke out soon after a Portuguese had died there. After that the natives took all possible measures not to allow any white man to die in their country. On the Nicobar islands some natives who had just begun to make pottery died. The art was given up and never again attempted. White men gave to one Bushman in a kraal a stick ornamented with buttons as a symbol of authority. The recipient died leaving the stick to his son. The son soon died. Then the Bushmen brought back the stick lest all should die. Until recently no building of incombustible materials could be built in any big town of the central province of Madagascar, on account of some ancient prejudice. A party of Eskimos met with no game. One of them returned to their sledges and got the ham of a dog to eat. As he returned with the ham bone in his hand he met and killed a seal. Ever afterwards he carried a ham bone in his hand when hunting. The Belenda women (peninsula of Malacca) stay as near to the house as possible during the period. Many keep the door closed. They know no reason for this custom. "It must be due to some now forgotten superstition." Soon after the Yakuts saw a camel for the first time smallpox broke out amongst them. They thought the camel to be the agent of the disease. A woman amongst the same people contracted an endogamous marriage. She soon afterwards became blind. This was thought to be on account of the violation of ancient customs. A very great number of such cases could be collected. In fact they represent the current mode of reasoning of nature people. It is their custom to reason that, if one thing follows another, it is due to it. A great number of customs are traceable to the notion of the evil eye, many more to ritual notions of uncleanness. No scientific investigation could discover the origin of the folkways mentioned, if the origin had not chanced to become known to civilized men. We must believe that the known cases illustrate the irrational and incongruous origin of many folkways. In civilized history also we know that customs have owed their origin to "historical accident"—the vanity of a princess, the deformity of a king, the whim of a democracy, the love intrigue of a statesman or prelate. By the institutions of another age it may be provided that no one of these things can affect decisions, acts, or interests, but then the power to decide the ways may have passed to clubs, trades unions, trust, commercial rivals, wire-pullers, politicians, and political fanatics. In these cases also the causes and origins may escape investigation.

29. HARMFUL FOLKWAYS. There are folkways which are positively harmful. Very often these are just the ones for which a definite reason can be given. The destruction of a man's goods at his death is a direct deduction from other-worldliness; the dead man is supposed to want in the other world just what he wanted here. The destruction of a man's goods at his death was a great waste of capital, and it must have had a disastrous effect on the interests of the living, and must have very seriously hindered the development of civilization. With this custom we must class all the expenditure of labor and capital on graves, temples, pyramids, rites, sacrifices, and support of priests, so far as these were supposed to benefit the dead. The faith in goblinism produced other-worldly interests

which overruled ordinary worldly interests. Foods have often been forbidden which were plentiful, the prohibition of which injuriously lessened the food supply. There is a tribe of Bushmen who will eat no goat's flesh, although goats are the most numerous domestic animals in the district. Where totemism exists it is regularly accompanied by a taboo on eating the totem animal. Whatever may be the real principle in totemism, it overrules the interest in an abundant food supply. "The origin of the sacred regard paid to the cow must be sought in the primitive nomadic life of the Indo-European race," because it is common to Iranians and Indians of Hindostan. The Libyans ate oxen but not cows. The same was true of the Phœnicians and Egyptians. In some cases the sense of a food taboo is not to be learned. It may have been entirely capricious. Mohammed would not eat lizards, because he thought them the offspring of a metamorphosed clan of Israelites. On the other hand, the protective taboo which forbade killing crocodiles, pythons, cobras, and other animals enemies of man was harmful to his interests, whatever the motive. "It seems to be a fixed article of belief throughout southern India, that all who have willfully or accidentally killed a snake, especially a cobra, will certainly be punished, either in this life or the next, in one of three ways: either by childlessness, or by leprosy, or by ophthalmia." Where this faith exists man has a greater interest to spare a cobra than to kill it. India furnishes a great number of cases of harmful mores. "In India every tendency of humanity seems intensified and exaggerated. No country in the world is so conservative in its traditions, yet no country has undergone so many religious changes and vicissitudes." "Every year thousands perish of disease that might recover if they would take proper nourishment, and drink the medicine that science prescribes, but which they imagine that their religion forbids them to touch." "Men who can scarcely count beyond twenty, and know not the letters of the alphabet, would rather die than eat food which had been prepared by men of lower caste, unless it had been sanctified by being offered to an idol; and would kill their daughters rather than endure the disgrace of having unmarried girls at home beyond twelve or thirteen years of age." In the last case the rule of obligation and duty is set by the mores. The interest comes under vanity. The sanction of the caste rules is in a boycott by all members of the caste. The rules are often very harmful. "The authority of caste rests partly on written laws, partly on legendary fables or narratives, partly on the injunctions of instructors and priests, partly on custom and usage, and partly on the caprice and convenience of its votaries." The harm of caste rules is so great that of late they have been broken in some cases, especially in regard to travel over sea, which is a great advantage to Hindoos. The Hindoo folkways in regard to widows and child marriages must also be recognized as socially harmful.

30. How "True" and "Right" are Found. If a savage puts his hand too near the fire, he suffers pain and draws it back. He knows nothing of the laws of the radiation of heat, but his instinctive action conforms to that law as if he did know it. If he wants to catch an animal for food, he must study its habits and prepare a device adjusted to those habits. If it fails, he must try again, until his observation is "true" and his device is "right." All the practical and direct

element in the folkways seems to be due to common sense, natural reason, intuition, or some other original mental endowment. It seems rational (or rationalistic) and utilitarian. Often in the mythologies this ultimate rational element was ascribed to the teaching of a god or a culture hero. In modern mythology it is accounted for as "natural."

Although the ways adopted must always be really "true" and "right" in relation to facts, for otherwise they could not answer their purpose, such is not the primitive notion of true and right.

31. The Folkways are "Right." Rights. Morals. The folkways are the "right" ways to satisfy all interests, because they are traditional, and exist in fact. They extend over the whole of life. There is a right way to catch game, to win a wife, to make one's self appear, to cure disease, to honor ghosts, to treat comrades or strangers, to behave when a child is born, on the warpath, in council, and so on in all cases which can arise. The ways are defined on the negative side, that is, by taboos. The "right" way is the way which the ancestors used and which has been handed down. The tradition is its own warrant. It is not held subject to verification by experience. The notion of right is in the folkways. It is not outside of them, of independent origin, and brought to them to test them. In the folkways, whatever is, is right. This is because they are traditional, and therefore contain in themselves the authority of the ancestral ghosts. When we come to the folkways we are at the end of our analysis. The notion of right and ought is the same in regard to all the folkways, but the degree of it varies with the importance of the interest at stake. The obligation of conformable and cooperative action is far greater under ghost fear and war than in other matters, and the social sanctions are severer, because group interests are supposed to be at stake. Some usages contain only a slight element of right and ought. It may well be believed that notions of right and duty, and of social welfare, were first developed in connection with ghost fear and other-worldliness, and therefore that, in that field also, folkways were first raised to mores. "Rights" are the rules of mutual give and take in the competition of life which are imposed on comrades in the in-group, in order that the peace may prevail there which is essential to the group strength. Therefore rights can never be "natural" or "God-given," or absolute in any sense. The morality of a group at a time is the sum of the taboos and prescriptions in the folkways by which right conduct is defined. Therefore morals can never be intuitive. They are historical, institutional, and empirical.

World philosophy, life policy, right, rights, and morality are all products of the folkways. They are reflections on, and generalizations from, the experience of pleasure and pain which is won in efforts to carry on the struggle for existence under actual life conditions. The generalizations are very crude and vague in their germinal forms. They are all embodied in folklore, and all our philosophy and science have been developed out of them.

15. Ethnocentrism is the technical name for this view of things in which one's own group is the center of everything, and all others are scaled and rated with reference to it. Folkways correspond to it to cover both the inner and

the outer relation. Each group nourishes its own pride and vanity, boasts itself superior, exalts its own divinities, and looks with contempt on outsiders. Each group thinks its own folkways the only right ones, and if it observes that other groups have other folkways, these excite its scorn. Opprobrious epithets are derived from these differences. "Pig-eater," "cow-eater," "uncircumcised," "jabberers," are epithets of contempt and abomination. The Tupis called the Portuguese by a derisive epithet descriptive of birds which have feathers around their feet, on account of trousers. For our present purpose the most important fact is that ethnocentrism leads a people to exaggerate and intensify everything in their own folkways which is peculiar and which differentiates them from others. It therefore strengthens the folkways.

16. ILLUSTRATIONS OF ETHNOCENTRISM. The Papuans on New Guinea are broken up into village units which are kept separate by hostility, cannibalism, head hunting, and divergences of language and religion. Each village is integrated by its own language, religion, and interests. A group of villages is sometimes united into a limited unity by connubium. A wife taken inside of this group unit has full status; one taken outside of it has not. The petty group units are peace groups within and are hostile to all outsiders. The Mbayas of South America believed that their deity had bidden them live by making war on others, taking their wives and property, and killing their men.

17. When Caribs were asked whence they came, they answered, "We alone are people." The meaning of the name Kiowa is "real or principal people." The Lapps call themselves "men," or "human beings." The Greenland Eskimo think that Europeans have been sent to Greenland to learn virtue and good manners from the Greenlanders. Their highest form of praise for a European is that he is, or soon will be, as good as a Greenlander. The Tunguses call themselves "men." As a rule it is found that nature peoples call the themselves "men." Others are something else—perhaps not defined—but not real men. In myths the origin of their own tribe is that of the real human race. They do not account for the others. The Ainos derive their name from that of the first man, whom they worship as a god. Evidently the name of the god is derived from the tribe name. When the tribal name has another sense, it is always boastful or proud. The Ovambo name is a corruption of the name of the tribe for themselves, which means "the wealthy." Amongst the most remarkable people in the world for ethnocentrism are the Seri of Lower California. They observe an attitude of suspicion and hostility to all outsiders, and strictly forbid marriage with outsiders.

18. The Jews divided all mankind into themselves and Gentiles. They were the "chosen people." The Greeks and Romans called all outsiders "barbarians." In Euripides' tragedy of *Iphigenia in Aulis* Iphigenia says that it is fitting that Greeks should rule over barbarians, but not contrariwise, because Greeks are free, and barbarians are slaves. The Arabs regarded themselves as the noblest nation and all others as more or less barbarous. In 1896, the Chinese minister of education and his counselors edited a manual in which this statement occurs: 'How grand and glorious is the Empire of China, the middle kingdom! She is

the largest and richest in the world. The grandest men in the world have all come from the middle empire." In all the literature of all the states equivalent statements occur, although they are not so naively expressed. In Russian books and newspapers the civilizing mission of Russia is talked about, just as, in the books and journals of France, Germany, and the United States, the civilizing mission of those countries is assumed and referred to as well understood. Each state now regards itself as the leader of civilization, the best, the freest, and the wisest, and all others as inferior. Within a few years our own man-on-the-curbstone has learned to class all foreigners of the Latin peoples as "dagos," and "dago" has become an epithet of contempt. These are all cases of ethnocentrism.

34. DEFINITION OF THE MORES. When the elements of truth and right are developed into doctrines of welfare, the folkways are raised to another plane. They then become capable of producing inferences, developing into new forms, and extending their constructive influence over men and society. Then we call them the mores. The mores are the folkways, including the philosophical and ethical generalizations as to societal welfare which are suggested by them, and inherent in them, as they grow.

42. PURPOSE OF THE PRESENT WORK. "Ethology" would be a convenient term for the study of manners, customs, usages, and mores, including the study of the way in which they are formed, how they grow or decay, and how they affect the interests which it is their purpose to serve. The Greeks applied the term "ethos" to the sum of the characteristic usages, ideas, standards, and codes by which a group was differentiated and individualized in character from other groups. "Ethics" were things which pertained to the ethos and therefore the things which were the standard of right. The Romans used "mores" for customs in the broadest and richest sense of the word, including the notion that customs served welfare, and had traditional and mystic sanction, so that they were properly authoritative and sacred. It is a very surprising fact that modern nations should have lost these words and the significant suggestions which inhere in them. The English language has no derivative noun from "mores," and no equivalent for it. The French *mœurs* is trivial compared with "mores." The German *Sitte* renders "mores" but very imperfectly. The modern peoples have made morals and morality a separate domain, by the side of religion, philosophy, and politics. In that sense, morals is an impossible and unreal category. It has no existence, and can have none. The word "moral" means what belongs or appertains to the mores. Therefore the category of morals can never be defined without reference to something outside of itself. Ethics, having lost connection with the ethos of a people, is an attempt to systematize the current notions of right and wrong upon some basic principle, generally with the purpose of establishing morals on an absolute doctrine, so that it shall be universal, absolute, and everlasting. In a general way also, whenever a thing can be called moral, or connected with some ethical generality, it is thought to be "raised," and disputants whose method is to employ ethical generalities assume especial authority for themselves and their views. These methods of discussion

are most employed in treating of social topics, and they are disastrous to sound study of facts. They help to hold the social sciences under the dominion of metaphysics. The abuse has been most developed in connection with political economy, which has been almost robbed of the character of a serious discipline by converting its discussions into ethical disquisitions.

43. WHY USE THE WORD MORES. "Ethica," in the Greek sense, or "ethology," as above defined, would be good names for our present work. We aim to study the ethos of groups, in order to see how it arises, its power and influence, the modes of its operation on members of the group, and the various attributes of it (ethica). "Ethology" is a very unfamiliar word. It has been used for the mode of setting forth manners, customs, and mores in satirical comedy. The Latin word "mores" seems to be, on the whole, more practically convenient and available than any other for our purpose, as a name for the folkways with the connotations of right and truth in respect to welfare, embodied in them. The analysis and definition above given show that in the mores we must recognize a dominating force in history, constituting a condition as to what can be done, and as to the methods which can be employed.

44. MORES ARE A DIRECTIVE FORCE. Of course the view which has been stated is antagonistic to the view that philosophy and ethics furnish creative and determining forces in society and history. That view comes down to us from the Greek philosophy and it has now prevailed so long that all current discussion conforms to it. Philosophy and ethics are pursued as independent disciplines, and the results are brought to the science of society and to statesmanship and legislation as authoritative dicta. We also have *Völkerpsychologie*, *Sozialpolitik*, and other intermediate forms which show the struggle of metaphysics to retain control of the science of society. The "historic sense," the *Zeitgeist*, and other terms of similar import are partial recognitions of the mores and their importance in the science of society. It can be seen also that philosophy and ethics are products of the folkways. They are taken out of the mores, but are never original and creative; they are secondary and derived. They often interfere in the second stage of the sequence—act, thought, act. Then they produce harm, but some ground is furnished for the claim that they are creative or at least regulative. In fact, the real process in great bodies of men is not one of deduction from any great principle of philosophy or ethics. It is one of minute efforts to live well under existing conditions, which efforts are repeated indefinitely by great numbers, getting strength from habit and from the fellowship of united action. The resultant folkways become coercive. All are forced to conform, and the folkways dominate the societal life. Then they seem true and right, and arise into mores as the norm of welfare. Thence are produced faiths, ideas, doctrines, religions, and philosophies, according to the stage of civilization and the fashions of reflection and generalization.

61. THE MORES AND INSTITUTIONS. Institutions and laws are produced out of mores. An institution consists of a concept (idea, notion, doctrine, interest) and a structure. The structure is a framework, or apparatus, or perhaps only a number of functionaries set to cooperate in prescribed ways at a certain con-

juncture. The structure holds the concept and furnishes instrumentalities for bringing it into the world of facts and action in a way to serve the interests of men in society. Institutions are either crescive or enacted. They are crescive when they take shape in the mores, growing by the instinctive efforts by which the mores are produced. Then the efforts, through long use, become definite and specific. Property, marriage, and religion are the most primary institutions. They began in folkways. They became customs. They developed into mores by the addition of some philosophy of welfare, however crude. Then they were made more definite and specific as regards the rules, the prescribed acts, and the apparatus to be employed. This produced a structure and the institution was complete. Enacted institutions are products of rational invention and intention. They belong to high civilization. Banks are institutions of credit founded on usages which can be traced back to barbarism. There came a time when, guided by rational reflection on experience, men systematized and regulated the usages which had become current, and thus created positive institutions of credit, defined by law and sanctioned by the force of the state. Pure enacted institutions which are strong and prosperous are hard to find. It is too difficult to invent and create an institution, for a purpose, out of nothing. The electoral college in the constitution of the United States is an example. In that case the democratic mores of the people have seized upon the device and made of it something quite different from what the inventors planned. All institutions have come out of mores, although the rational element in them is sometimes so large that their origin in the mores is not to be ascertained except by an historical investigation (legislatures, courts, juries, joint stock companies, the stock exchange). Property, marriage, and religion are still almost entirely in the mores. Amongst nature men any man might capture and hold a woman at any time, if he could. He did it by superior force which was its own supreme justification. But his act brought his group and her group into war, and produced harm to his comrades. They forbade capture, or set conditions for it. Beyond the limits, the individual might still use force, but his comrades were no longer responsible. The glory to him, if he succeeded, might be all the greater. His control over his captive was absolute. Within the prescribed conditions, "capture" became technical and institutional, and rights grew out of it. The woman had a status which was defined by custom, and was very different from the status of a real captive. Marriage was the institutional relation, in the society and under its sanction, of a woman to a man, where the woman had been obtained in the prescribed way. She was then a "wife." What her rights and duties were was defined by the mores, as they are to-day in all civilized society.

62. LAWS. Acts of legislation come out of the mores. In low civilization all societal regulations are customs and taboos, the origin of which is unknown. Positive laws are impossible until the stage of verification, reflection, and criticism is reached. Until that point is reached there is only customary law, or common law. The customary law may be codified and systematized with respect to some philosophical principles, and yet remain customary. The codes of Manu and Justinian are examples. Enactment is not possible until reverence for

ancestors has been so much weakened that it is no longer thought wrong to interfere with traditional customs by positive enactment. Even then there is reluctance to make enactments, and there is a stage of transition during which traditional customs are extended by interpretation to cover new cases and to prevent evils. Legislation, however, has to seek standing ground on the existing mores, and it soon becomes apparent that legislation, to be strong, must be consistent with the mores. Things which have been in the mores are put under police regulation and later under positive law. It is sometimes said that "public opinion" must ratify and approve police regulations, but this statement rests on an imperfect analysis. The regulations must conform to the mores, so that the public will not think them too lax or too strict. The mores of our urban and rural populations are not the same; consequently legislation about intoxicants which is made by one of these sections of the population does not succeed when applied to the other. The regulation of drinking places, gambling places, and disorderly houses has passed through the above-mentioned stages. It is always a question of expediency whether to leave a subject under the mores, or to make a police regulation for it, or to put it into the criminal law. Betting, horse racing, dangerous sports, electric cars, and vehicles are cases now of things which seem to be passing under positive enactment and out of the unformulated control of the mores. When an enactment is made there is a sacrifice of the elasticity and automatic self-adaptation of custom, but an enactment is specific and is provided with sanctions. Enactments come into use when conscious purposes are formed, and it is believed that specific devices can be framed by which to realize such purposes in the society. Then also prohibitions take the place of taboos, and punishments are planned to be deterrent rather than revengeful. The mores of different societies, or of different ages, are characterized by greater or less readiness and confidence in regard to the use of positive enactments for the realization of societal purposes.

63. HOW LAWS AND INSTITUTIONS DIFFER FROM MORES. When folkways have become institutions or laws they have changed their character and are to be distinguished from the mores. The element of sentiment and faith inheres in the mores. Laws and institutions have a rational and practical character, and are more mechanical and utilitarian. The great difference is that institutions and laws have a positive character, while mores are unformulated and undefined. There is a philosophy implicit in the folkways; when it is made explicit it becomes technical philosophy. Objectively regarded, the mores are the customs which actually conduce to welfare under existing life conditions. Acts under the laws and institutions are conscious and voluntary; under the folkways they are always unconscious and involuntary, so that they have the character of natural necessity. Educated reflection and skepticism can disturb this spontaneous relation. The laws, being positive prescriptions, supersede the mores so far as they are adopted. It follows that the mores come into operation where laws and tribunals fail. The mores cover the great field of common life where there are no laws or police regulations. They cover an immense and undefined domain,

and they break the way in new domains, not yet controlled at all. The mores, therefore, build up new laws and police regulations in time.

83. Inertia and Rigidity of the Mores. We see that we must conceive of the mores as a vast system of usages, covering the whole of life, and serving all its interests; also containing in themselves their own justification by tradition and use and wont, and approved by mystic sanctions until, by rational reflection, they develop their own philosophical and ethical generalizations, which are elevated into "principles" of truth and right. They coerce and restrict the new-born generation. They do not stimulate to thought, but the contrary. The thinking is already done and is embodied in the mores. They never contain any provision for their own amendment. They are not questions, but answers, to the problem of life. They present themselves as final and unchangeable, because they present answers which are offered as "the truth." No world philosophy, until the modern scientific world philosophy, and that only within a generation or two, has ever presented itself as perhaps transitory, certainly incomplete, and liable to be set aside to-morrow by more knowledge. No popular world philosophy or life policy ever can present itself in that light. It would cost too great a mental strain. All the groups whose mores we consider far inferior to our own are quite as well satisfied with theirs as we are with ours. The goodness or badness of mores consists entirely in their adjustment to the life conditions and the interests of the time and place. . . . Therefore it is a sign of ease and welfare when no thought is given to the mores, but all cooperate in them instinctively. The nations of southeastern Asia show us the persistency of the mores, when the element of stability and rigidity in them becomes predominant. Ghost fear and ancestor worship tend to establish the persistency of the mores by dogmatic authority, strict taboo, and weighty sanctions. The mores then lose their naturalness and vitality. They are stereotyped. They lose all relation to expediency. They become an end in themselves. They are imposed by imperative authority without regard to interests or conditions (caste, child marriage, widows). When any society falls under the dominion of this disease in the mores it must disintegrate before it can live again. In that diseased state of the mores all learning consists in committing to memory the words of the sages of the past who established the formulæ of the mores. Such words are "sacred writings," a sentence of which is a rule of conduct to be obeyed quite independently of present interests, or of any rational considerations.

232. Mores and Morals; Social Code. For every one the mores give the notion of what ought to be. This includes the notion of what ought to be done, for all should cooperate to bring to pass, in the order of life, what ought to be. All notions of propriety, decency, chastity, politeness, order, duty, right, rights, discipline, respect, reverence, cooperation, and fellowship, especially all things in regard to which good and ill depend entirely on the point at which the line is drawn, are in the mores. The mores can make things seem right and good to one group or one age which to another seem antagonistic to every instinct of human nature. The thirteenth century bred in every heart such a sentiment in

regard to heretics that inquisitors had no more misgivings in their proceedings than men would have now if they should attempt to exterminate rattlesnakes. The sixteenth century gave to all such notions about witches that witch persecutors thought they were waging war on enemies of God and man. Of course the inquisitors and witch persecutors constantly developed the notions of heretics and witches. They exaggerated the notions and then gave them back again to the mores, in their expanded form, to inflame the hearts of men with terror and hate and to become, in the next stage, so much more fantastic and ferocious motives. Such is the reaction between the mores and the acts of the living generation. The world philosophy of the age is never anything but the reflection on the mental horizon, which is formed out of the mores, of the ruling ideas which are in the mores themselves. It is from a failure to recognize the to and fro in this reaction that the current notion arises that mores are produced by doctrines. The "morals" of an age are never anything but the consonance between what is done and what the mores of the age require. The whole revolves on itself, in the relation of the specific to the general, within the horizon formed by the mores. Every attempt to win an outside standpoint from which to reduce the whole to an absolute philosophy of truth and right, based on an unalterable ɪrinciple, is a delusion. New elements are brought in only by new conquests of nature through science and art. The new conquests change the conditions of life and the interests of the members of the society. Then the mores change by adaptation to new conditions and interests. The philosophy and ethics then follow to account for and justify the changes in the mores; often, also, to claim that they have caused the changes. They never do anything but draw new lines of bearing between the parts of the mores and the horizon of thought within which they are inclosed, and which is a deduction from the mores. The horizon is widened by more knowledge, but for one age it is just as much a generalization from the mores as for another. It is always unreal. It is only a product of thought. The ethical philosophers select points on this horizon from which to take their bearings, and they think that they have won some authority for their systems when they travel back again from the generalization to the specific custom out of which it was deduced. The cases of the inquisitors and witch persecutors who toiled arduously and continually for their chosen ends, for little or no reward, show us the relation between mores on the one side and philosophy, ethics, and religion on the other.

494. HONOR, SEEMLINESS, COMMON SENSE, CONSCIENCE. Honor, common sense, seemliness, and conscience seem to belong to the individual domain. They are reactions produced in the individual by the societal environment. Honor is the sentiment of what one owes to one's self. It is an individual prerogative, and an ultimate individual standard. Seemliness is conduct which befits one's character and standards. Common sense, in the current view, is a natural gift and universal outfit. As to honor and seemliness, the popular view seems to be that each one has a fountain of inspiration in himself to furnish him with guidance. Conscience might be added as another natural or supernatural "voice," intuition, and part of the original outfit of all human beings

as such. If these notions could be verified, and if they proved true, no discussion of them would be in place here, but as to honor it is a well-known and undisputed fact that societies have set codes of honor and standards of it which were arbitrary, irrational, and both individually and socially inexpedient, as ample experiment has proved. These codes have been and are imperative, and they have been accepted and obeyed by great groups of men who, in their own judgment, did not believe them sound. Those codes came out of the folkways of the time and place. Then comes the question whether it is not always so. Is honor, in any case, anything but the code of one's duty to himself which he has accepted from the group in which he was educated? Family, class, religious sect, school, occupation, enter into the social environment. In every environment there is a standard of honor. When a man thinks that he is acting most independently, on his personal prerogative, he is at best only balancing against each other the different codes in which he has been educated, e.g., that of the trades union against that of the Sunday school, or of the school against that of the family. What we think "natural" and universal, and to which we attribute an objective reality, is the sum of traits whose origin is so remote, and which we share with so many, that we do not know when or how we took them up, and we can remember no rational selection by which we adopted them. The same is true of common sense. It is the stock of ways of looking at things which we acquired unconsciously by suggestion from the environment in which we grew up. Some have more common sense than others, because they are more docile to suggestion, or have been taught to make judgments by people who were strong and wise. Conscience also seems best explained as a sum of principles of action which have in one's character the most original, remote, undisputed, and authoritative position, and to which questions of doubt are habitually referred. If these views are accepted, we have in honor, common sense, and conscience other phenomena of the folkways, and the notions of eternal truths of philosophy or ethics, derived from somewhere outside of men and their struggles to live well under the conditions of earth, must be abandoned as myths.

438. SPECIFICATION OF THE SUBJECT. The ethnographers write of a tribe that the "morality" in it, especially of the women, is low or high, etc. This is the technical use of morality—as a thing pertaining to the sex relation only or especially, and the ethnographers make their propositions by applying our standards of sex behavior, and our form of the sex taboo, to judge the folkways of all people. All that they can properly say is that they find a great range and variety of usages, ideas, standards, and ideals, which differ greatly from ours. Some of them are far stricter than ours. Those we do not consider nobler than ours. We do not feel that we ought to adopt any ways because they are more strict than our traditional ones. We consider many to be excessive, silly, and harmful. A Roman senator was censured for impropriety because he kissed his wife in the presence of his daughter.

439. MEANING OF "IMMORAL." When, therefore, the ethnographers apply condemnatory or depreciatory adjectives to the people whom they study, they beg the most important question which we want to investigate; that is, What are

standards, codes, and ideas of chastity, decency, propriety, modesty, etc., and whence do they arise? The ethnographical facts contain the answer to this question. . . . "Immoral" never means anything but contrary to the mores of the time and place. Therefore the mores and the morality may move together, and there is no permanent or universal standard by which right and truth in regard to these matters can be established and different folkways compared and criticised.

9

Ethical Relativism

PAUL W. TAYLOR

One of the most commonly held opinions in ethics is that all moral norms are *relative* to particular cultures. The rules of conduct that are applicable in one society, it is claimed, do not apply to the actions of people in another society. Each community has its own norms, and morality is entirely a matter of conforming to the standards and rules accepted in one's own culture. To put it simply: What is right is what my society approves of; what is wrong is what my society disapproves of.

This view raises serious doubts about the whole enterprise of normative ethics. For if right and wrong are completely determined by the given moral code of a particular time and place, and if moral codes vary from time to time and place to place, it would seem that there are no unchanging cross-cultural principles that could constitute an ideal ethical system applicable to everyone. Since the purpose of normative ethics is to construct and defend just such a universal system of principles, belief in the relativity of moral norms denies the possibility of normative ethics. It is therefore important at the outset to examine the theory of ethical relativism.

The question raised by the ethical relativist may be expressed thus: Are moral values absolute, or are they relative? We may understand this question as asking, Are there any moral standards and rules of conduct that are universal (applicable to all mankind) or are they all culture-bound (applicable only to the members of a particular society or group)? Even when the question is interpreted in this way, however, it still remains unclear. For those who answer the question by claiming that all moral values are relative or culture-bound may be expressing any one of three different ideas. They may, first, be making an empirical or

FROM *Principles of Ethics: An Introduction* by Paul W. Taylor, pp. 13–29. Copyright 1975 by Dickenson Publishing Company, Inc., 16250 Ventura Boulevard, Encino, California. Reprinted by permission of the publisher.

factual assertion. Or secondly, they may be making a normative claim. And thirdly, they may be understood to be uttering a metaethical principle. The term "ethical relativism" has been used to refer to any or all of these three positions. In order to keep clear the differences among them, the following terminology will be used. We shall call the first position "descriptive relativism," the second "normative ethical relativism," and the third "metaethical relativism." Let us consider each in turn.

DESCRIPTIVE RELATIVISM

Certain facts about the moral values of different societies and about the way an individual's values are dependent on those of his society have been taken as empirical evidence in support of the claim that all moral values are relative to the particular culture in which they are accepted. These facts are cited by the relativist as reasons for holding a general theory about moral norms, namely, that no such norms are universal. This theory is what we shall designate "descriptive relativism." It is a factual or empirical theory because it holds that, as a matter of historical and sociological fact, no moral standard or rule of conduct has been universally recognized to be the basis of moral obligation. According to the descriptive relativist there are no moral norms common to all cultures. Each society has its own view of what is morally right and wrong and these views vary from society to society because of the differences in their moral codes. Thus it is a mistake to think there are common norms that bind all mankind in one moral community.

Those who accept the position of descriptive relativism point to certain facts as supporting evidence for their theory. These facts may be conveniently summed up under the following headings:

(1) The facts of cultural variability.
(2) Facts about the origin of moral beliefs and moral codes.
(3) The fact of ethnocentrism.

(1) The facts of cultural variability are now so familiar to everyone that they need hardly be enumerated in detail. We all know from reading anthropologists' studies of primitive cultures how extreme is the variation in the customs and taboos, the religions and moralities, the daily habits and the general outlook on life to be found in the cultures of different peoples. But we need not go beyond our own culture to recognize the facts of variability. Historians of Western civilization have long pointed out the great differences in the beliefs and values of people living in different periods. Great differences have also been discovered among the various socioeconomic classes existing within the social structure at any one time. Finally, our own contemporary world reveals a tremendous

variety of ways of living. No one who dwells in a modern city can escape the impact of this spectrum of different views on work and play, on family life and education, on what constitutes personal happiness, and on what is right and wrong.

(2) When we add to these facts of cultural and historical variability the recent psychological findings about how the individual's values reflect those of his own social group and his own time, we may begin to question the universal validity of our own values. For it is now a well-established fact that no moral values or beliefs are inborn. All our moral attitudes and judgments are learned from the social environment. Even our deepest convictions about justice and the rights of man are originally nothing but the "introjected" or "internalized" views of our culture, transmitted to us through our parents and teachers. Our very conscience itself is formed by the internalizing of the sanctions used by our society to support its moral norms. When we were told in childhood what we ought and ought not to do, and when our parents expressed their approval and disapproval of us for what we did, we were being taught the standards and rules of conduct accepted in our society. The result of this learning process (sometimes called "acculturation") was to ingrain in us a set of attitudes about our own conduct, so that even when our parents were no longer around to guide us or to blame us, we would guide or blame ourselves by thinking, "This is what I ought to do"; "That would be wrong to do"; and so on. If we then did something we believed was wrong we would feel guilty about it, whether or not anyone caught us at it or punished us for it.

It is this unconscious process of internalizing the norms of one's society through early childhood training that explains the origin of an individual's moral values. If we go beyond this and ask about the origin of society's values, we find a long and gradual development of traditions and customs which have given stability to the society's way of life and whose obscure beginnings lie in ritual magic, taboos, tribal ceremonies, and practices of religious worship. Whether we are dealing with the formation of an individual's conscience or the development of a society's moral code, then, the origin of a set of values seems to have little or nothing to do with rational, controlled thought. Neither individuals nor societies originally acquire their moral beliefs by means of logical reasoning or through the use of an objective method for gaining knowledge.

(3) Finally, the descriptive relativist points out another fact about people and their moralities that must be acknowledged. This is the fact that most people are ethnocentric (group centered). They think not only that there is but one true morality for all mankind, but that the one true morality is their own. They are convinced that the moral code under which they grew up and which formed their deepest feelings about right and wrong—namely, the moral code of their own society—is the only code for anyone to live by. Indeed, they often refuse even to entertain the possiblity that their own values might be false or that another society's code might be more correct, more enlightened, or more advanced than their own. Thus ethnocentrism often leads to intolerance and dogmatism. It causes people to be extremely narrow-minded in their ethical

outlook, afraid to admit any doubt about a moral issue, and unable to take a detached, objective stance regarding their own moral beliefs. Being absolutely certain that their beliefs are true, they can think only that those who disagree with them are in total error and ignorance on moral matters. Their attitude is: We are advanced, they are backward. We are civilized, they are savages.

It is but a short step from dogmatism to intolerance. Intolerance is simply dogmatism in action. Because the moral values of people directly affect their conduct, those who have divergent moral convictions will often come into active conflict with one another in the area of practical life. Each will believe he alone has the true morality and the other is living in the darkness of sin. Each will see the other as practicing moral abominations. Each will then try to force the other to accept the truth, or at least will not allow the other to live by his own values. The self-righteous person will not tolerate the presence of "shocking" acts which he views with outraged indignation. Thus it comes about that no differences of opinion on moral matters will be permitted within a society. The ethnocentric society will tend to be a closed society, as far as moral belief and practice are concerned.

The argument for descriptive relativism, then, may be summarized as follows. Since every culture varies with respect to its moral rules and standards, and since each individual's moral beliefs—including his inner conviction of their absolute truth—have been learned within the framework of his own culture's moral code, it follows that there are no universal moral norms. If a person believes there are such norms, this is to be explained by his ethnocentrism, which leads him to project his own culture's norms upon everyone else and to consider those who disagree with him either as innocent but "morally blind" people or as sinners who do not want to face the truth about their own evil ways.

In order to assess the soundness of this argument it is necessary to make a distinction between (a) specific moral standards and rules, and (b) ultimate moral principles. Both (a) and (b) can be called "norms," and it is because the descriptive relativist often overlooks this distinction that his argument is open to doubt. A specific moral standard (such as personal courage or trustworthiness) functions as a criterion for judging whether and to what degree a person's character is morally good or bad. A specific rule of conduct (such as "Help others in time of need" or "Do not tell lies for one's own advantage") is a prescription of how people ought or ought not to act. It functions as a criterion for judging whether an action is right or wrong. In contrast with specific standards and rules, an ultimate moral principle is a universal proposition or statement about the conditions that must hold if a standard or rule is to be used as a criterion for judging *any* person or action. Such a principle will be of the form: Standard S or rule R applies to a person or action if and only if condition C is fulfilled. An example of an ultimate moral principle is that of utility, which we shall be examining in detail in Chapter 4. The principle of utility may be expressed thus: A standard or rule applies to a person or action if, and only if, the use of the standard or rule in the actual guidance of people's conduct will result in an increase in everyone's happiness or a decrease in everyone's unhappiness.

Now it is perfectly possible for an ultimate moral principle to be consistent with a variety of specific standards and rules as found in the moral codes of different societies. For if we take into account the traditions of a culture, the beliefs about reality and the attitudes toward life that are part of each culture's world-outlook, and if we also take into account the physical or geographical setting of each culture, we will find that a standard or rule which increases people's happiness in one culture will not increase, but rather decrease, people's happiness in another. In one society, for example, letting elderly people die when they can no longer contribute to economic production will be necessary for the survival of everyone else. But another society may have an abundant economy that can easily support people in their old age. Thus the principle of utility would require that in the first society the rule "Do not keep a person alive when he can no longer produce" be part of its moral code, and in the second society it would require a contrary rule. In this case the very same kind of action that is wrong in one society will be right in another. Yet there is a single principle that makes an action of that kind wrong (in one set of circumstances) and another action of that kind right (in a different set of circumstances). In other words, the reason why one action is wrong and the other right is based on one and the same principle, namely utility.

Having in mind this distinction between specific standards and rules on the one hand and ultimate moral principles on the other, what can we say about the argument for descriptive relativism given above? It will immediately be seen that the facts pointed out by the relativist as evidence in support of his theory do not show that ultimate moral principles are relative or culture-bound. They show only that specific standards and rules are relative or culture-bound. The fact that different societies accept different norms of good and bad, right and wrong, is a fact about the standards and rules that make up the various moral codes of those societies. Such a fact does not provide evidence that there is no single ultimate principle which, explicitly or implicitly, every society appeals to as the final justifying ground for its moral code. For if there were such a common ultimate principle, the actual variation in moral codes could be explained in terms of the different world-outlooks, traditions, and physical circumstances of the different societies.

Similarly, facts about ethnocentrism and the causal dependence of an individual's moral beliefs upon his society's moral code do not count as evidence against the view that there is a universal ultimate principle which everyone would refer to in giving a final justification for his society's standards and rules, if he were challenged to do so. Whether there is such a principle and if there is, what sort of conditions it specifies for the validity of specific standards and rules, are questions still to be explored. (In later chapters of this book we shall be considering some of the answers that philosophers have given to these questions.) But the facts cited by the descriptive relativist leave these questions open. We may accept those facts and still be consistent in affirming a single universal ultimate moral principle.

NORMATIVE ETHICAL RELATIVISM

The statement, "What is right in one society may be wrong in another," is a popular way of explaining what is meant by the "relativity of morals." It is usually contrasted with "ethical universalism," taken as the view that "right and wrong do not vary from society to society." These statements are ambiguous, however, and it is important for us to be mindful of their ambiguity. For they may be understood either as factual claims or as normative claims, and it makes a great deal of difference which way they are understood. (They may also be taken as metaethical claims, but we shall postpone this way of considering them until later.)

When it is said that what is right in one society may be wrong in another, this may be understood to mean that what is *believed* to be right in one society is *believed* to be wrong in another. And when it is said that moral right and wrong vary from society to society, this may be understood to mean that different moral norms are adopted by different societies, so that an act which fulfills the norms of one society may violate the norms of another. If this is what is meant, then we are here being told merely of the cultural variability of specific standards and rules, which we have already considered in connection with descriptive relativism.

But the statement, "What is right in one society may be wrong in another," may be interpreted in quite a different way. It may be taken as a normative claim rather than as a factual assertion. Instead of asserting the unsurprising fact that what is believed to be right in one society is believed to be wrong in another, it expresses the far more radical and seemingly paradoxical claim that what *actually is* right in one society may *actually be* wrong in another. According to this view, moral norms are to be considered valid only within the society which has adopted them as part of its way of life. Such norms are not to be considered valid outside that society. The conclusion is then drawn that is is not legitimate to judge people in other societies by applying the norms of one's own society to their conduct. This is the view we shall designate "normative ethical relativism." In order to be perfectly clear about what it claims, we shall examine two ways in which it can be stated, one focusing our attention upon moral judgments, the other on moral norms.

With regard to moral judgments, normative ethical relativism holds that two *apparently* contradictory statements can both be true. The argument runs as follows. Consider the two statements:

(1) It is wrong for unmarried women to have their faces unveiled in front of strangers.

(2) It is not wrong for . . . (as above).

Here it seems as if there is a flat contradiction between two moral judgments, so that if one is true the other must be false. But the normative ethical relativist holds that they are both true, because the statements as given in (1) and (2) are incomplete. They should read as follows:

(3) It is wrong for unmarried women *who are members of society S* to have their faces unveiled in front of strangers.

(4) It is not wrong for unmarried women *outside of society S* to have their faces unveiled in front of strangers.

Statements (3) and (4) are not contradictories. To assert one is not to deny the other. The normative ethical relativist simply translates all moral judgments of the form "Doing act X is right" into statements of the form "Doing X is right when the agent is a member of society S." The latter statement can then be seen to be consistent with statements of the form "Doing X is wrong when the agent is not a member of society S."

The normative ethical relativist's view of moral norms accounts for the foregoing theory of moral judgments. A moral norm, we have seen, is either a standard used in a judgment of good and bad character or a rule used in a judgment of right and wrong conduct. Thus a person is judged to be good insofar as he fulfills the standard, and an action is judged to be right or wrong according to whether it conforms to or violates the rule. Now when a normative ethical relativist says that moral norms vary from society to society, he does not intend merely to assert the fact that different societies have adopted different norms. He is going beyond descriptive relativism and is making a normative claim. He is denying any universal validity to moral norms. He is saying that a moral standard or rule is correctly applicable only to the members of the particular society which has adopted the standard or rule as part of its actual moral code. He therefore thinks it is illegitimate to judge the character or conduct of those outside the society by such a standard or rule. Anyone who uses the norms of one society as the basis for judging the character or conduct of persons in another society is consequently in error.

It is not that a normative ethical relativist necessarily believes in *tolerance* of other people's norms. Nor does his position imply that he grants others the *right* to live by their own norms, for he would hold a relativist view even about tolerance itself. A society whose code included a rule of tolerance would be right in tolerating others, while one that denied tolerance would be right (relative to its own norm of intolerance) in prohibiting others from living by different norms. The normative ethical relativist would simply say that *we* should not judge the tolerant society to be any better than the intolerant one, for this would be applying our own norm of tolerance to other societies. Tolerance, like any other norm, is culture-bound. Anyone who claims that every society has a *right* to live by its own norms, provided that it respects a similar right in other societies, is an ethical universalist, since he holds at least one norm valid for all societies, namely, the right to practice a way of life without interference from others. And he deems this universal norm a valid one, whether or not every society does in fact accept it.

If the normative ethical relativist is challenged to prove his position, he may do either of two things. On the one hand, he may try to argue that his position follows from, or is based on the very same facts that are cited by the descriptive relativist as evidence for *his* position. Or, on the other hand, he may turn for support to metaethical considerations. Putting aside the second move for the moment, let us look more closely at the first.

The most frequent argument given in defense of normative ethical relativism is that, if the facts pointed out by the descriptive relativist are indeed true, then we must accept normative ethical relativism as the only position consistent with those facts. For it seems that if each person's moral judgments are formed within the framework of the norms of his own culture and historical epoch, and if such norms vary among cultures and epochs, it would follow necessarily that it is unwarranted for anyone to apply his own norms to conduct in other societies and times. To do so would be ethnocentrism, which is, as the descriptive relativist shows, a kind of blind, narrow-minded dogmatism. To escape the irrationality of being ethnocentric, we need but realize that the only norms one may legitimately apply to any given group are the ones accepted by that group. Since different peoples accept different norms, there are no universal norms applicable to everyone throughout the world. Now, to say that there are no universal norms applicable worldwide is to commit oneself to normative ethical relativism. Thus, the argument concludes, normative ethical relativism follows from the facts of descriptive relativism.

Is this a valid argument? Suppose one accepts the facts pointed out by the descriptive relativist. Must he then also accept normative ethical relativism? Let us examine some of the objections that have been raised to this argument. In the first place, it is claimed that the facts of cultural variability do not, *by themselves*, entail normative ethical relativism. The reason is that it is perfectly possible for someone to accept those facts and deny normative ethical relativism without contradicting himself. No matter how great may be the differences in the moral beliefs of different cultures and in the moral norms they accept, it is still possible to hold that some of these beliefs are true and others false, or that some of the norms are more correct, justified, or enlightened than others. The fact that societies differ about what is right and wrong does not mean that one society may not have better reasons for holding its views than does another. After all, just because two people (or two groups of people) disagree about whether a disease is caused by bacteria or by evil spirits does not lead to the conclusion that there is no correct or enlightened view about the cause of the disease. So it does not follow from the fact that two societies differ about whether genocide is right that there is no correct or enlightened view about this moral matter.

A similar argument can be used with regard to the second set of facts asserted by the descriptive relativist. No contradiction is involved in affirming that all moral beliefs come from the social environment and denying normative ethical relativism. The fact that a belief is learned from one's society does not mean that it is neither true nor false, or that if it is true, its truth is "relative" to the society in which it was learned. All of our beliefs, empirical ones no less than moral ones, are learned from our society. We are not born with any innate beliefs about chemistry or physics; we learn these only in our schools. Yet this does not make us skeptical about the universal validity of these sciences. So the fact that our moral beliefs come from our society and are learned in our homes and schools has no bearing on their universal validity. The origin or cause of a person's *acquiring* a belief does not determine whether the *content* of the belief is true or false, or even whether there are good grounds for his accepting that content to be true or false.

If it is claimed that our moral beliefs are based on attitudes or feelings culturally conditioned in us from childhood, the same point can still be made. Suppose, for example, that a person who believes slavery is wrong feels disapproval, dislike, or even abhorrence towards the institution of slavery. His negative attitude, which has undoubtedly been influenced by the value system of his culture, may be contrasted with a positive stance (approval, liking, admiring) of someone brought up in an environment where slave owning was accepted. Here are positive and negative attitudes toward slavery, each being causally conditioned by the given cultural environment. It does not follow from this that the two are equally justified, or that neither can be justified. The question of whether a certain attitude toward slavery is justified or unjustified depends on whether good reasons can be given *for* anyone taking the one attitude and *against* anyone taking the other. This question requires the exercise of our reasoning powers. Exactly how we can justify attitudes, or show them to be unjustified, is a complex problem that will be dealt with in later chapters of this book. But the mere fact that the attitudes which underlie moral beliefs are all learned from the social environment leaves open the question of what attitudes an intelligent, rational, and well-informed person would take toward a given action or social practice.

The same kind of argument also holds with respect to the third fact of descriptive relativism: ethnocentrism. People who are ethnocentric *believe* that the one true moral code is that of their own society. But this leaves open the question, Is their belief true or false? Two people of different cultures, both ethnocentric but with opposite moral beliefs, may each think his particular moral norms are valid for everyone; however, this has no bearing on whether either one—or neither one—is correct. We must inquire independently into the possibility of establishing the universal validity of a set of moral norms, regardless of who might or might not believe them to be universally true.

It should be noted that these various objections to the first argument for normative ethical relativism, even if sound, are not sufficient to show that normative ethical relativism is false. They only provide reasons for rejecting one argument in support of that position. To show that the position is false, it would be necessary to give a sound argument in defense of ethical universalism. The sorts of arguments set forth by philosophers to establish universalism will be disclosed in later chapters. It is only if one or more of these arguments proves acceptable that normative ethical relativism is refuted.

A second argument by which the normative ethical relativist defends his position was mentioned earlier. This argument is based on metaethical considerations, so it is appropriate now to examine the bearing of metaethics on the relativism-universalism controversy.

METAETHICAL RELATIVISM

It will be convenient to distinguish between two forms of metaethical relativism, called "conceptual relativism" and "methodological relativism." Conceptual relativism is the view that moral concepts vary from culture to culture and therefore the moral judgments of one society are meaningless or unintelligible to the members of another. For example, the idea in our own society of individual freedom as a basic human right may not be understandable to a society lacking the concept of human rights or with a view of individual freedom different from ours. The conceptual relativist holds that the meaning of a moral idea can be understood only within the context of a given culture's ethical system as a whole. The conclusion drawn from this is that intercultural comparisons of moral judgments cannot be made. There is no standpoint outside of all cultures from which to decide whether the moral judgments of one society are more enlightened or correct than those of another. Such a comparison would require that both sets of judgments be intelligible to the same individual and this, the conceptual relativist claims, is impossible.

One logical consequence of this view is the following. Suppose a person from culture X utters the judgment "Polygamy is wrong," and a person from culture Y replies, "No, polygamy is not wrong." It would appear that the person from Y is contradicting the person from X. But according to the conceptual relativist this appearance is false; there is actually no contradiction at all between them. For the word "wrong" stands for a different idea—that is, has a different meaning—in each statement. The two persons are not talking about the same thing when they use the word "wrong" (even if they are talking about the same thing when they say "polygamy"—a point also open to doubt in the conceptual relativist's view). Thus in culture X "wrong" might mean "what is detrimental to the common good" while in culture Y it might mean "prohibited by the gods." It may be that polygamy is detrimental to the common good in culture X and is permitted by the gods of culture Y. In these circumstances both statements are true, and thus there can be no contradiction between them.

A further point is now made by the conceptual relativist. Not only do the *meanings* of words like "right" and "wrong," "good" and "bad" vary from culture to culture, but there is also great variation in what the words *refer to*. In one culture, for instance, the term "a good man" will refer to anyone who is meek and forgiving. In another culture the same term will refer to one who is quick to avenge himself on others and is ruthless with his enemies. Similarly, in one society the statement "That act is right" will be applied to every case in which it is believed that the given act is necessary to uphold the honor of one's family. In another society the same statement will apply to all situations where the given act involves treating everyone concerned—friends and strangers alike—fairly and impartially.

On the basis of considerations like these, the conceptual relativist argues that what a particular word means and what it refers to in moral discourse depend on the specific system of moral norms accepted by the society in which the discourse takes place. He concludes that it makes no sense to talk, as the ethical universalist does, about a *true view* of right action or a *correct* conception of the good man. Such talk assumes that intercultural comparisons of moral concepts are possible. But, he asserts, this assumption is false, since the meaning and application of every moral concept must be relativized to a particular culture.

Is the conceptual relativist right? Can his theory stand up to critical scrutiny when it is examined with care? The answer depends on what analysis is made of the meaning and reference of words and statements used in moral discourse, a matter which will be of concern throughout the rest of this book. So the question must be left open at this juncture.

The second form of metaethical relativism, methodological relativism, maintains that different cultures use different methods of reasoning to justify moral judgments. The conclusion drawn is that the same judgment may be justified in one culture but not in another. Each method provides its own criteria for determining whether a reason given in a moral argument is a good or valid one. If such criteria vary from culture to culture, it may be possible to establish the truth of a moral belief in one social environment and to show it to be false in another. Moral knowledge, being based on different verification procedures, would then be culturally relative. Unless there were some uniform, cross-cultural method for gaining moral knowledge or a uniform, cross-cultural set of rules of reasoning that could tell us whether a person in *any* culture is thinking correctly, no claim could be made for the universal validity of moral norms. And the methodological relativist argues that there is no such method or set of rules of reasoning. Whether his argument is to be accepted is a question that must be considered in the light of those ways that have been proposed by moral philosophers for obtaining genuine moral knowledge. A number of such ways will be found in later chapters of this book.

It has been claimed that one serious implication of methodological relativism is ethical skepticism, or the complete denial of moral knowledge. The reasoning behind this claim is as follows. When the methodological relativist asserts that all moral knowledge is "relative" to a given culture, he is ruling out the very conditions that make it possible for such a thing as genuine moral knowledge to exist at all. In effect he is saying that, if we investigate the assumptions under-lying the alleged universal methods adopted by different cultures, we find that in every case one procedure will define "valid" or "good" reasons in one way and another will define them differently. It follows that the question of which, if any, of these given procedures really does lead to moral knowledge is *logically undecidable*. For to choose between any two methods, a neutral third method must be used—one that would enable us to give reasons for accepting one method and rejecting the other. But any such third way will itself merely postulate its own criteria of "valid" reasons, and we would then have to justify our choice of *these* criteria. This however, would in turn also require our giving reasons for our choice, presupposing still another procedure. Since we cannot go to infinity in seeking methods for justifying other methods, we are left at some point with an arbitrary decision. But no claim to genuine moral knowledge can to a movie with him on Saturday night, we must do so even if our parents are injured in an automobile accident Saturday afternoon and desperately need our help. Extreme cases like these show that, at least in our ordinary unreflective moral judgments, the rule "Do not break promises" has exceptions and that, consequently, ethical absolutism in the second sense of the term is not true of that particular moral rule.

Are there *any* rules of conduct that are "absolute" in the second sense? The reader should try to work out his own answer to this question for himself. What is important for present purposes is to notice the *logical independence* of the two meanings of "ethical absolutism."

According to the first meaning, an ethical absolutist holds that there are moral norms that apply to everyone, no matter what norms are actually accepted in a given society. According to the second meaning, an ethical absolutist is one who claims that at least some moral norms allow for no legitimate or justifiable exceptions. It is clear that the first meaning of ethical absolutism does not necessarily entail the second. In other words, it is possible to be an ethical absolutist in the first sense but not in the second. For it may be that all moral norms valid for everyone in any society are norms that allow for legitimate exceptions in special circumstances, *whenever* those circumstances occur. Let us consider an example.

Suppose we think that in almost all situations of life it is wrong for one person to take the life of another. Suppose, further, that we hold the rule "Thou shalt not kill" to be a universal moral norm, believing that it applies to all persons in all societies (even if a certain group of people in a given society do not accept the rule). Thus, with respect to this rule we are ethical universalists. Now suppose that we also think that there are very unusual conditions which, when they occur, make it permissible for one person to kill another. For instance, we might think that if a person's only means of defending his life or the lives of his children against the attack of a madman is to kill him, then it is not wrong to kill him. Or we might think that killing is permissible when such an act is necessary to overthrow a totalitarian government carrying out a policy of systematic genocide. If we hold these cases to be legitimate exceptions to the rule "Thou shalt not kill," are we contradicting our position of ethical universalism with regard to that rule? The answer is no, since we may be willing to consider these exceptions universally legitimate whenever they occur, no matter whether a given society accepts them as legitimate exceptions or not. In this case the *full* statement of our rule against killing would be expressed thus: It is wrong for anyone, in any society, to take the life of another, except when such an act is necessary for self-defense or the prevention of systematic genocide.

When a moral rule is stated in this manner, it encompasses its own exceptions. In other words, the complete rule stipulates all the kinds of situations in which an action of the sort *generally* forbidden by the rule is right. If we then accept the rule in its complete form, *including the list of exceptions*, as validly applicable to all human beings, we are ethical universalists (and hence ethical absolutists in the first sense of the term) with respect to this rule. However, we are not

rest on an arbitrary decision, since a different decision—as unjustifie(
first—might lead to opposite conclusions regarding a moral issue. Thi
cisely the kind of situation that the word "knowledge" precludes, if tha(
to be understood in its ordinary sense. Therefore genuine moral knov
impossible.

Moral philosophers reply to this argument simply by constructing
and systematically, a method of moral reasoning whose logical principl(
shown to be in fact presupposed by anyone, in any culture, who intends
rationally about moral matters. By considering how any reasonable beii
carry on his thinking when he understands clearly the meaning of m(
cepts, the uses of moral language, and the function of moral norms in
ance of conduct, the philosopher attempts to show that there *is* a vali
determining whether any moral judgment is true or false and, hence, t
is a warranted method for obtaining genuine moral knowledge. In this
shall become acquainted with some of the most important of these att

ETHICAL ABSOLUTISM

When someone asks, "Are moral norms relative or absolute?" ther
an ambiguity in his question, not only with respect to the word "rela
also with respect to the word "absolute." We have seen that "rela
mean, among other things, "causally dependent on variable factors ir
cultures" (descriptive relativism); *or* "validly applicable only within tl
which accepts the norm" (normative ethical relativism); *or* "impossible
on cross-cultural grounds" (methodological relativism). Let us now e?
important ambiguity in the term "absolute" as it is applied to moral n(
unless this ambiguity is cleared up, we cannot give a straightforward
the question of whether moral norms are relative or absolute.

That moral norms (that is, specific moral rules and standards) are "
can mean either of two things. It can mean that at least some moral ị
justifiable on grounds that can be established by a cross-cultural r
reasoning and that, consequently, these norms correctly apply to th
of all human beings. This, we have seen, is ethical universalism. It (
denial of normative ethical relativism and also the denial of metaetl
tivism. Hence, in this first sense of the term "absolute," ethical absol(
simply be equated with ethical universalism.

The second meaning of the term "absolute" is entirely different fror
According to the second meaning, to say that moral norms are "at
to say that they *have no exceptions*. Thus, if the rule "It is wrong t
promise" is an absolute moral norm in this second sense, then one r
break a promise no matter what the circumstances. It follows that it i
to keep a promise, even if doing so brings suffering to innocent people
for example, that a hired gunman who promises his boss to murde]
should commit the murder. It signifies that, if we have promised a fr

ethical absolutists in the second sense of the term, since we hold that the simple rule "Thou shalt not kill" does have legitimate exceptions.

It is true that in this case we may not be willing to allow for exceptions to the whole rule in its *complete* form, since we may think our statement of the rule includes all the possible exceptions it could have. With regard to the rule in its complete form, we would then be ethical absolutists in both senses of the term. On the other hand, if we are not sure we have included all the exceptions that could possibly be legitimate, then with regard to such an *incomplete* rule we would not be ethical absolutists in the second sense. The rule as we have formulated it may still have legitimate exceptions which we have overlooked, but we can nevertheless be ethical universalists about such an incomplete rule. For we might believe that, even in its incomplete form, it correctly applies to all mankind.

The main point of this discussion may now be indicated. When an ethical universalist says that there are moral norms applicable to everyone everywhere, he does not mean that the application of these norms to particular circumstances must determine that one kind of action is always right (or that it is always wrong). He means only that, whenever the norms do apply, they apply regardless of whether a given society may have accepted them in its actual moral code and another society may have excluded them from *its* moral code. The (normative) ethical relativist, on the other hand, claims that what makes an act right is precisely its conformity to the accepted norms of the society in which it occurs, while its violation of such accepted norms makes it wrong. Consider, then, two acts of the very same kind done in the very same sort of circumstances, but each occurring in a different society. One can be right and the other wrong, according to the relativist, since the moral norms of the two societies may disagree concerning the behavior in question. The ethical universalist (or "absolutist" in the first sense), however, would say that if one act is right the other is too and if one is wrong so is the other. For both are acts of an identical kind performed in identical circumstances. Therefore a rule which required or prohibited the one would also require or prohibit the other, and only one rule validly applies to such actions performed in circumstances of that sort. Thus the universalist holds that the rightness and wrongness of actions do not change according to variations in the norms accepted by different societies, even though (contrary to what the "absolutist" in the second sense says) the rightness and wrongness of actions do vary with differences in the sorts of circumstances in which they are performed.

If we keep this distinction between the two meanings of ethical absolutism clearly in mind, we can then see that it is possible to be an absolutist in one sense and not in the other. Whether either sense of absolutism is a correct view is a matter that cannot be settled without further study of normative and analytic ethics. Perhaps the reader will be able to decide these questions for himself as he pursues his own ethical inquiry.

Cultural Relativism—Further Readings

Benedict, Ruth, "Anthropology and the Abnormal," *Journal of General Psychology*, X (1934), pp. 59–82. Proponent.

——, *Patterns of Culture* (Boston: Houghton Mifflin, 1934), especially Chaps. 2, 3, 7. Proponent.

Brandt, Richard B., *Ethical Theory* (Englewood Cliffs, N.J.: Prentice-Hall, 1959), Chaps. 5, 6, and 11. Critical but also sympathetic to a qualified view of relativism.

Herskovits, Melville J., *Man and His Works* (New York: Alfred A. Knopf, 1948), Chap. 5. Proponent.

Ladd, John (ed.), *Ethical Relativism* (Belmont, Calif.: Wadsworth, 1973). Ten classical and contemporary authors debate the merits of relativism.

Norman, Richard, *Reasons for Actions: A Critique of Utilitarian Rationality* (Basil Blackwell: Oxford, 1971), especially Chaps. 3–6. Defence of a qualified cultural relativism.

Phillips, D. Z., and H. O. Mounce, *Moral Practices* (London: Routledge and Kegan Paul, 1969), especially Chaps. 6, 7, and 9. Defence of a qualified form of relativism.

Stace, Walter, T., *The Concept of Morals* (New York: Macmillan, 1937), Chaps. 1 and 2. Critic.

Taylor, Paul W., "Four Types of Ethical Relativism," *Philosophical Review*, LXIII (1954), pp. 500–516. Critic.

Wellman, Carl, "The Ethical Implications of Cultural Relativity," *Journal of Philosophy*, LX (1963), pp. 169–184. Critic.

Westermarck, Edward, *Ethical Relativity* (New York: Harcourt, Brace, 1932). Proponent.

II Normative Ethics: What Is Right and What Is Good?

If the conclusions of our first section are taken optimistically, the following *tentative* presuppositions seem to characterize ethics. (1) It is possible to have knowledge of moral rules or standards that are used as reasons in judging whether human actions and objects are right or wrong, good or evil, and whether persons are obligated or responsible with respect to these actions and objects. In other words, ethics is a rational enterprise, both in the development and justification of its rules and principles, and in the justification or assessment of particular actions and objects. Thus, ethical judgments, general and specific, are meaningful, and true or false, in more or less standard ways. (2) Therefore, moral behavior is not simply a matter of habitual conformity with conventional cultural rules. (3) Men are free, in their choices, to act or not to act in accordance with moral rules. (4) Among the reasons which are presupposed by the rules used by individuals to justify actions or to assess the actions of others persons are moral rules or principles. (5) The maxim of an action is universalizable, i.e., if an act is morally right for the agent in certain conditions, it is right for any other person in the same conditions. (6) Moral rules or conventions are social, i.e., they involve common acceptance and commitment, and the related concern for the interests of others. (7) Moral rules or principles are overriding with respect to other conventions; and some moral rules are considered as taking precedence over others, e.g., saving the life of an innocent is more important than keeping a promise to attend a tea-party. (8) Moral actions typically involve certain characteristic emotions, or attitudes, or feelings. (9) Moral rules and actions are often related to human interests, needs, and desires. It will be recalled that Socrates and Crito disagreed over many of these matters.

From the standpoint of the agent, a person can be held responsible if he knows what he is doing, if he is free to do it, if he considers the interests of others in doing it, and if his doing it can be justified by reasons which include moral standards.

Postulating or presupposing some or all of these general traits of ethics, and assuming therefore that normative ethics is possible, we can begin the consideration of normative ethical theories and their attendant problems.

Generally speaking, we make two types of normative judgment, and these types are reflected in two major kinds of ethical theory. There are, first, judgments which predicate or ascribe rightness or wrongness to actions or to rules. These may be called judgments of moral obligation. There are, second, judgments which predicate or ascribe value to objects, processes, and personal character. These may be called judgments of value. Although intimately related, these kinds of judgment are distinguishable, and the great classical and contemporary ethical theories tend to take their conceptual point of departure from one or the other of them.

There are thus two main kinds of normative ethical theory. In the first place, there are those theories which tend to take the rightness or wrongness of actions or rules as basic. For them, judgments of moral obligation are logically and conceptually prior to judgments of value. They are called *deontological theories*. All affirm, in ways which will be more carefully specified below, that there are properties of actions or rules, and ways of knowing these properties, which make the actions or rules right or wrong, without necessarily considering the value to be produced. Brunner, who connects the rightness of an action to God's approval; Aquinas, who relates it to the natural law of God; Butler, who relates it to conscience; and Ewing, who connects it with intuitions, develop theories of this sort.

A profound contrast is found in the ethical ideas of the second group of thinkers who make judgments of value basic. Their theories are called *teleological*. They maintain that men can know how they ought to act, only if they know whether their actions are likely to produce good results. For these theorists, then, judgments of obligation depend upon judgments of value. The ethical egoism of Hospers, the utilitarianism of Bentham and Mill, the self-realization of Aristotle, Bradley, and Dewey, are of this variety. In contrast to both deontological and teleological theories, some writers are inclined to be suspicious of any kind of traditional normative ethics. Nietzsche and Sartre are philosophers of this type, and we have concluded the section with selections from their work.

In this section of our text, then, we have the main body of classical and contemporary ethics, the great theories which formulate, propose, and defend comprehensive views of the nature and standards of right and wrong, good and evil, duty and obligation, virtue and vice. We have also included critics of the particular theories proposed, as well as concluding with critics who question the entire enterprise of normative ethics. We will first consider deontological theories.

A DEONTOLOGICAL THEORIES: *ARE ACTIONS RIGHT OR WRONG REGARDLESS OF CONSEQUENCES?*

1 Act Deontological Theories

Deontological theories are usually grouped under two main headings: "act deontological" and "rule deontological." Thinkers who hold to the first type maintain that rightness and wrongness are properties of the *particular actions* of individuals or of groups. Thinkers who hold to the second type maintain that these properties belong rather to *rules* or to *classes* of rules.

As representatives of the first group, we have chosen Brunner, who maintains that God communicates the rightness of a particular action to believers, and Butler, who believes that we have a faculty, conscience, by means of which men directly know the rightness of an action. With respect to the authors who are to criticize these views, Ewing attempts to refute Brunner and others of his persuasion, and Russell seeks to refute conscience theories.

a   *The Authority of God*

The theory to be considered in this section holds that the rightness and wrongness of particular actions are established by God's will. According to this kind of doctrine, men may justify an action, or a judgment about what is right or wrong, by the claim that it was approved or commanded by God. Moreover, the rightness of the action is independent of its consequences.

Our first author, Brunner, maintains that God's approval or disapproval of a particular act at a particular place and time can be directly known by the moral agent. He therefore rejects in principle any type of theory which appeals to moral rules. He does admit that Scriptural descriptions of the events and actions in Christ's life provide some indication of what it means to act according to Christian love. Nevertheless, he believes that the existence of set and unchanging moral rules would constitute a limitation on God's freedom. The moral agent learns the rightness or wrongness of an act by means of a direct, unique, and particular command of God. God's relationship to the moral agent in some respects is like that between persons, one of whom directs the other to act in this or that way, and whose directions cannot be anticipated for all occasions, or codified into sets of rules. Indeed, one of the most obvious corruptions of Christianity, according to Brunner, lies in the "legalistic" spirit of those who seek to capture God's will in abstract principles. Right and wrong, then, are revealed in the "word" of God, and the possible reception of such divine communications is contingent upon faith. Given this position, the moral rightness of an action is found through absolute obedience to the commands of God. This position involves a radical excision of many of the traditional presuppositions of ethics summarized above. There is, thus, a rejection of the principle that ethical codes are important; a refusal to accept the idea that there are systems of rules founded on rational grounds with anything like universal validity, or anything like either inductive or deductive proof. There is no commitment to, or attempt to institute, the criteria of evidence and proof, of consistency and soundness, that make up the constituents of rational justification from Plato onwards.

A. C. Ewing sets out a classical response to Brunner's antirationalism and particularism. He argues that Brunner's concept of good is vacuous. It is defined as "whatever God wills," a definition which supplies no general criteria to identify or differentiate what acts, or kinds of acts,

God would approve or will. For Ewing, this position leads to several clear and "fatal" objections. Ewing observes that if "what God wills" is the only criterion of what acts are right, then if God were to will that a person murder his neighbor, then the murder would be right—which is absurd. Brunner might attempt to defend himself against this charge by claiming that God would not command one to murder a neighbor. Or Brunner might argue that the term, "murder," being by definition related to evil, could not be related to an act willed and commanded by God, because He is by definition good. If Brunner were to defend his views in this way, then Ewing would accuse him of a vicious circle, a question-begging attempt to define God in terms of good and right, and right and good in terms of God.

10

The Divine Imperative

EMIL BRUNNER

CHAPTER IX. THE DEFINITION OF THE CHRISTIAN ETHIC

1. There is no general conception of ethics which would also include the Christian ethic. Such a general definition of ethics does not even exist for rational thought. . . .

It is of course true that even the Christian ethic is concerned with the definition of conduct, which as "right" conduct has to be distinguished from conduct which is accidental or wrong; but this distinction or definition does not take place by means of an ultimate principle, which, as such, would be intelligible and valid. . . . The Christian conception of the Good differs from every other conception of the Good at this very point: that it cannot be defined in terms of principle at all.

Whatever can be defined in accordance with a principle—whether it be the principle of pleasure or the principle of duty—is legalistic. This means that it is possible—by the use of this principle—to pre-determine "the right" down to the smallest detail of conduct. . . . This legalistic spirit corrupts the true conception of the Good from its very roots. The Christian moralist and the extreme individualist are at·one in their emphatic rejection of legalistic conduct; they join hands, as it were, in face of the whole host of legalistic moralists; they are convinced that conduct which is regulated by abstract principles can never be

FROM *The Divine Imperative* by Emil Brunner. Copyright © MCMXLVII by W. L. Jenkins. Used by permission of The Westminster Press.

good. But equally sternly the Christian moralist rejects the individualistic doctrine of freedom, according to which there is no longer any difference between "right" and "wrong." Rather, in the Christian view, that alone is "good" which is free from all caprice, which takes place in unconditional obedience. There is no Good save obedient behaviour, save the obedient will. But this obedience is rendered not to a law or a principle which can be known beforehand, but only to the free, sovereign will of God. The Good consists in always doing what God wills at any particular moment.

This statement makes it clear that for us the will of God cannot be summed up under any principle, that it is not at our disposal, but that so far as we are concerned the will of God is absolutely free. The Christian is therefore "a free lord over all things," because he stands directly under the personal orders of the free Sovereign God. This is why genuine "Christian conduct"—if we may use this idea as an illustration—is so unaccountable, so unwelcome to the moral rigorist and to the hedonist alike. The moral rigorist regards the Christian as a hedonist, and the hedonist regards him as a rigorist. In reality, the Christian is neither, yet he is also something of both, since he is indeed absolutely *bound* and obedient, but, since he is bound to the *free* loving will of God, he is himself free from all transparent bondage to principles or to legalism. Above all it is important to recognize that even love is not a principle of this kind, neither the love which God Himself *has*, nor the love which He *requires*. Only God Himself defines love in His action. We, for our part, do not know what God is, nor do we know what *love* is, unless we learn to know God in His action, in faith. To be in this His Love, is the commandment. Every attempt to conceive love as a principle leads to this result: it becomes distorted, either in the rigoristic, legalistic sense, or in the hedonistic sense. Man only knows what the love of God is when he sees the way in which God acts, and he only knows how he himself ought to love by allowing himself to be drawn by faith into this activity of God.

2. "To know God in His action" is only possible in faith. The action of God, in which He manifests Himself—and this means His love—is His revelation. God reveals Himself in His Word—which is at the same time a deed—in an actual event—in Jesus Christ; and He reveals Himself operatively in His living Word, which is now taking place—in the Holy Spirit. Because only conduct which takes place on the basis of this faith (and indeed in this faith in God's Word) can be "good conduct," in the sense of the Christian ethic, therefore, the science of good conduct, of ethics, is only possible within that other science which speaks of the Divine act of revelation, that is, within dogmatics. Reflection on the good conduct of man is only one part of more comprehensive reflection on the action of God in general. For human conduct can only be considered "good" when, and in so far as, God Himself acts in it, through the Holy Spirit. Hence just as this action is connected with the Divine action, so the Christian ethic is connected with dogmatics.

The attempt to make a clear-cut distinction between dogmatics and ethics from the point of view that the one is concerned with Divine and the other with human action spoils both dogmatics and ethics. The New Testament proclamation of the Word of God is characterized by the fact that it makes no distinction between the "dogmatic" and the "ethical" elements. The great Christological passages occur in the midst of practical exhortations, and moral instructions are always most closely connected with "dogmatic" ideas. As the indicative and the imperative suddenly alternate, as speech about the redeeming love of God flows directly into the claim for human love, so the whole New Testament is an indissoluble blend of "ethics" and "dogmatics." This is true also, more or less, of the great confessional works of the Reformation; this is also true of the greatest—and, indeed, the only genuinely reformatory—dogmatic work of the Reformation: Calvin's *Institutes*. Every theme of dogmatics is also inevitably a theme of ethics. Dogmatics does not exist independently, nor does ethics, but dogmatic knowledge as such always aims at existential, that is, ethical, thought, and ethical knowledge is rooted in knowledge of dogmatics.

We can only rightly represent the whole of ethics as a part of dogmatics, because it is concerned with God's action in and through man. Not only the commandments of God, not only the New Birth and conversion, but also man's sanctification—if it really *is* what it is called—is wholly the work of God, certainly with this distinction: it is that one of His works which is expressed in our own external conduct.

On the other hand, once we have recognized legalism as *the* evil, once we have seen that the Good, in the moral sense, is that which God does in us and through us, how could we possibly seriously consider severing ethics from dogmatics? The specific element in the Christian ethic . . . is precisely this: that the Good in human conduct only arises out of the fact that it is set within the action of God. All other forms of conduct are legalistic. This is what the authors of the Heidelberg Catechism meant when they summed up all ethics under the heading—which is certainly easy to misunderstand—of "gratitude." Good can only take place in grateful acknowledgment of the action of God. The separation of dogmatics from ethics would lay dogmatics open to the danger of speculative aberrations and ethics to the danger of moralistic distortions.

Really good Christian conduct—speaking from the point of view of principle—ought to have the whole of the Christian knowledge of God "behind" it. Luther, in his Shorter Catechism, has expressed this very well, since he begins the explanation of every commandment with the words: "we ought thus to fear and love God, in order that we . . ."

The God who is thus to be feared and loved, however, is the One who is manifested in His revelation, "the whole God." Every ethical consideration is thus connecetd with the whole Idea of God. . . .

4. . . . The scientific presentation of the Christian ethic can certainly never represent the Good as a general truth, easy to be perceived, and based on a universal principle. Were it to do this, it would be an act of treason towards the Christian Faith. The meaning of the Christian ethic is the exact opposite; its task is to work out scientifically the characteristic element in the Christian

knowledge of the Good, namely, that the Good, as faith knows it, can never be legalistic, or a matter of abstract principle; thus that the Christian ethic can never count on general recognition in the sense of a truth of reason, but, explicitly, only on the recognition of those who believe. For one who does not believe cannot understand the Christian conception of the Good.

But this does not mean that the Christian ethic makes no claim to universal validity. Whatever God demands *can* only be universal, that is, valid for all men, even if those who do not hear this demand do not admit this validity and indeed do not even understand the claim to universal validity. The believer alone clearly perceives that the Good, as it is recognized in faith, is the sole Good, and that all that is otherwise called good cannot lay claim to this title, at least not in the ultimate sense of the word. It is precisely faith and faith alone which knows this: that alone is good which God does; and, indeed, faith really consists in the fact that man knows this—and that he knows it in such a way as it alone can be known, namely in the recognition of faith. But once man does know this he also knows the unlimited unconditional validity of this conception and of the divine demand. . . .

5. But what is the function of a system of ethics in regard to the central ethical question: What ought we to do? Can ethics tell us what we are to do? If it could, it would mean that the Christian ethic also is an ethical system based on law and on abstract principles. For where ethics is regarded purely as a science, there general, and to some extent timeless, propositions are stated. If these were to define what we ought to do, then the Good would be defined in legalistic terms. Therefore no such claim can be made either by or for ethics. The service it renders cannot be that of relieving us of the necessity for making moral decisions, but that it prepares the way for such decisions. How this takes place can only be made clear in the explication of the part which is played by law within a morality which is not legalistic. The significance of the law is the same as the significance of ethics, namely: that it prepares the way for a voluntary decision, or for the hearing of the divine command.

In this explicit rejection of the legalistic definition of the Good the truly Christian ethic is also distinguished from the Roman Catholic ethic. In accordance with its juridically defined conception of faith and of the Church its conception of the Good is also rigidly legalistic, and therefore its ethical system is fundamentally a system of casuistry. The lesser stipulations are logically derived from the universal law, and by means of a closely woven network of further minor regulations the whole realm of human life is legally defined, so that for every case, in actual practice, it is possible to look up the ethical code and find out what is commanded and what is forbidden. The relation of knowledge in general and application to the particular case is determined by the purely logical relation of subsumption of the particular under the universal. . . . This conception cannot be combined with the knowledge of justification by faith alone. Ethical" orthodoxy"—the legalistic view of the Good—is just as bad as dogmatic orthodoxy, that is, as a legalistic view of faith and of the Word of God. . . .

CHAPTER XI. THE DIVINE COMMAND AS GIFT AND DEMAND

2. . . . *The Good consists simply and solely in the fact* that man receives and deliberately accepts his life as a gift from God, as life dependent on "grace," as the state of "being justified" because it has been granted as a gift, as "justification by faith." Only thus can we know the Will of God, that is, in this revelation of Himself in which He manifests Himself as disinterested, generous Love.

3. But this Divine giving is not accomplished in any magical way; it simply takes place in the fact that *God "apprehends" man;* God *claims* us for His love, for His generous giving. But this means that He claims our whole existence for Himself, for this love of His; He gives us His love. He gives us His love in such a way that He captures us completely by the power of His love. *To belong* to Him, to this love, and through His love, means that we are the *bondslaves* of this will. To believe means to become a captive, to become His property, or rather, to know that we are His property. The revelation which makes it plain that the will of God is lavish in giving *to* man, makes it equally clear that His will makes a demand *on* man. His will *for* us also means that He wants something *from* us. He claims us for His love. This is His Command. It is the "*new* commandment," because only now can man perceive that it is the command of One who gives before He demands, and who only demands something from us in the act of giving Himself to us. . . .

4. He claims us for *His* love, not for an *idea* of love—and not for a conception of the divine love which can be gained from merely reading the Bible. He claims us for His present, living activity of love, which can only be, and must always remain, His work. Therefore we can never know beforehand what God will require. God's command can only be perceived at the actual moment of hearing it. It would denote a breaking away from obedience if we were to think of the Divine Command as one which had been enacted once for all, to be interpreted by us in particular instances. To take this line would mean reverting to the legalistic distortion of His love. Love would then have become a "principle." The *free* love of God requires us to remain *free*, that we may be freely at His disposal. *You* cannot say what it means to love here and now; *He* alone can tell you what this means for you at this moment.

The Good is simply what *God* wills that we should do, not that which we would do on the basis of a principle of love. God wills to do something quite definite and particular through us, here and now, something which no other person could do at any other time. Just as the commandment of love is absolutely universal so also it is absolutely individual. But just as it is absolutely individual so also it is absolutely devoid of all caprice. "I will guide thee with Mine eye." No one can experience this "moment" save I myself. The Divine Command is made known to us "in the secret place." Therefore it is impossible for us to know it beforehand; to wish to know it beforehand—legalism—is an infringement of the divine honour. The fact that the holiness of God must be remembered when we dwell on His love means that we cannot have His love at our disposal, that it cannot ever be perceived as a universal principle, but only in the act in which He speaks to us Himself; even in His love He remains our *Master* and Lord. But He is our "Lord" in the sense that He tells us Himself what it means to "love," here and now. . . .

7. It is *His* will that God wills to accomplish in the world; He is not the servant of some purpose outside Himself. God Himself is His own End. In His love, however, He sets up an End outside Himself—without ceasing to be His own End; this "end" is the communion of the creature with Himself, the Creator. This Divine will for "community" is God's Sovereign Will. Therefore salvation, beatitude, the fulfilment of the purpose of life, both for humanity as a whole, and for the individual, is included in God's royal purpose. The tables of prohibition in the Bible may be compared with the notices on power circuits: Do Not Touch! Because God wills to control our life, He commands and He forbids. This is the "eudaemonism" of the Gospel, and at the same time its absolutely serious view of duty. God wills our true happiness; but *He* wills it, and He wills it in such a way that no one else knows what His will is. It remains outside our disposal, and indeed we do not know it. We never know what is right for us, nor what is best for the other person. We go astray when we think that we can deduce this from some principle or another, or from some experience, and we distort the thought of the divine love if we think that we know what He ought to do for us in accordance with His love. But of one thing we may be quite sure: His will is love, even when we do not understand it—when He commands as well as when He gives.

Therefore in His revelation God's will is expressed by His sanctions, by rewards and punishments. God alone gives life; to be with Him is life, to resist Him is ruin. It is impossible to exist apart from God; it is impossible to be neutral towards Him. He who is not for Him is against Him. God's Command means eternal life and God means nothing else than this. He is Love. But His will is utterly serious; it is the will of the Lord of Life and Death. Anyone who—finally—resists Him, will only dash himself to pieces against the rock of His Being. This is the holiness of the love of God. As the divine love cannot be separated from His gift of life, so the Holiness of God cannot be separated from His judicial wrath, the denial and destruction of life. To have a share in the will of God, in the sense of union with His will, means salvation; to resist Him spells utter disaster.

The abstract legalistic system of ethics, because ideas have no connexion with life, can only judge this connexion of the moral element with reward and punishment as heteronomy, as the perversion of the moral endeavour. "We ought to do the Good for the sake of the Good." It does not perceive that behind this phrase, "for the sake of the Good," there lies concealed, "for My sake." And it does not understand that the Good is done for the sake of the Good when it is done for the sake of God, in obedience to the Divine Command. We ought to obey God because He commands it, not because obedience means happiness and disobedience means unhappiness. Faith would not be faith, obedience would not be obedience, if things were otherwise. But obedience would not be obedience towards *God*, did we not know that His Command means life and His prohibition death. The primary concern is not that which refers to my Ego, to my life; no, the primary concern is this: that it is God's will, the will of Him to whom my life belongs. But that which refers to *me*, that which refers to *my* life, is the necessary second element for it concerns the will of Him who Himself is life—even *my* life. Obedience would be impure if this second element were made the first. But it would be unreal, and indeed impossible, if this second element, as the second, were not combined with the first. We cannot do anything good which has no significance for life, and we cannot avoid anything evil, unless at the same time we know it to be harmful. It is not the question whether all morality is not mingled with self-interest—without self-interest nothing would concern us at all—but the question is this: is this self-interest regarded as founded in God or in myself? To do the Good for the sake of the Good is only a pale reflection of the genuine Good; to do the Good for the sake of God means to do the Good not because my moral dignity requires it, but because it is that which is commanded by God.

11

Morality and the Commands of God

A. C. EWING

Now the simplest and most radical way of making all ethical principles dependent on God would be to say that their validity just depended on their being decrees fixed by the will of God. In that case it would naturally follow that "I ought to do *A*" was to be defined as "it is God's will that I should do *A*". . . . This view is one to which there are very serious objections. In the first place, if "obligatory" just means "commanded by God", the question arises why God should command any one thing rather than any other. We cannot say that he commands it because it ought to be done, for that would have to be translated into "God commands it because it is commanded by God". If it were said in reply that God's commands determined what we ought to do but that these commands were only issued because it was good that they should be or because obedience to them did good, this would still make judgments about the good, at least, independent of the will of God, and we should not have given a definition of all fundamental ethical concepts in terms of God or made ethics dependent on God. If what was good or bad as well as what ought to be done were fixed by God's will, then there could be no reason whatever for God willing in any particular way. His commands would become purely arbitrary, and while the idea of God as issuing arbitrary commands has sometimes been welcomed

FROM *Prospect for Metaphysics* by A. C. Ewing, pp. 39–41. Copyright 1961 by George Allen & Unwin, Ltd., London.

as a tribute to his omnipotence, omnipotence without goodness is surely an idea of no religious value whatever, and the idea of God would be deprived of all ethical content. For to say that God was good would be just to say he was God: he would be good by definition whatever he should do. Since there was no ethical reason for his commands, God might in that case just as well command us to cheat, torture and murder, and then it would really be our duty to act like this.

Secondly, why obey God's commands? Because I ought to do so. Since "I ought to do *A*" is held to mean "God commands me to do *A*", this can only mean that I am commanded by God to obey God's commands, which supplies no further reason whatever. Because God is good? This could only mean on the definition given that God carries out his own commands. Because I love God? This presupposes two propositions as to what I ought to do which could not without a vicious circle be validated by referring again to God's commands, i.e. that I ought to obey the commands of God if I love him and that I ought to love God. Because God will punish me if I do not obey? This might be a very good reason from the prudential point of view, but these considerations of self-interest cannot be an adequate basis for ethics. Even if there is some affinity between command and obligation, a mere command, however powerful the being who issues it, cannot of itself create obligation. Without a prior conception of God as good or his commands as right God would have no more claim on our obedience than Hitler or Stalin except that he would have more power than even they ever had to make things uncomfortable for those who disobey him. It is only because the notion of God (for Christians at least) already includes the notion of perfect goodness that we are inclined to think it self-evident that we ought to obey God.

It should be noted that this theological definition fails for the same kind of reason as do the naturalistic definitions of the fundamental concepts of ethics. It is not subject, indeed, to the same specific objections. We cannot, for instance, argue against it on the ground that God is sometimes wrong, as we argued against the naturalistic definitions on the ground that men are so. But it shares with the naturalistic definitions the error of either reducing ethical statements to merely factual ones, here about the acts of God, or producing a circular definition by presupposing specifically ethical concepts in the terms intended to define them. If God is not conceived as good in a specifically ethical sense but "good" functions just as an adjective to mean "what God wants," ethics is reduced to a mere prudent subservience to superior power; if on the other hand in the definition of good or right as willed by God goodness in a properly ethical sense is already presupposed, the definition is a circular one and leaves undefined some fundamental ethical term. As we can find no necessary relation between goodness and obligation on the one hand and the alleged naturalist definitions on the other, so we can find no necessary relation between being commanded or willed by God and being obligatory or good, unless we already assume the goodness of God, thus exposing ourselves to the charge of being guilty of a vicious circle, since we should in that case have defined both God in terms of goodness and goodness in terms of God. Just as it is a fatal objection to the naturalist definitions of good that they do not provide ground for obligation or any ethical reason why we ought to do any one thing rather than any other, so the theological definition is open to the objection that a command cannot in itself be a moral reason for action. Like naturalist definitions the theological definition would destroy what Kant calls the autonomy of ethics by refusing to recognize the uniqueness of its fundamental concepts and trying to make it a mere branch of another study, in this case not a natural science but theology. Both types of view overlook the gulf between the "ought" and the "is" so far as to maintain that you can reduce propositions about the former to propositions about what actually is the case. The theological view is more ethical than the naturalist only in so far as it covertly reintroduces ethical concepts which it had verbally tried to explain away by analysing them in terms of commands. Except in so far as it smuggles such concepts in again, it makes the fulfilment of duty consist just in obeying the stronger, for if you once exclude the specifically ethical element from the concept of the deity God has no claim on us except of mere power, and if you include it ethics is needed to define the fundamental concepts of theology and not theology to define the fundamental concepts of ethics.

The Authority of God—Further Readings

Barth, Karl, *The Word of God and the Word of Man* (Boston: Pilgrim, 1928), especially Chap. 5. Proponent.

Brandt, Richard B., *Ethical Theory* (Englewood Cliffs, N.J.: Prentice-Hall, 1959), Chap. 4. Critic.

Martin, C. B., *Religious Belief* (Ithaca, N.Y.: Cornell U.P., 1959), Chap. 3. Critic.

Nielsen, Kai, *Ethics Without God* (London: Pemberton Books, 1973), especially Chap. 1. Critic.

Nowell-Smith, Patrick H., "Religion and Morality," in Paul Edwards (ed.), *The Encyclopedia of Philosophy*, Vol. 7 (New York: Macmillan, 1967), pp. 150–158. Critic.

Paley, William, *The Principles of Moral and Political Philosophy* (1785), Bk. II. Proponent.

Plato, *Euthyphro*. Critic.

Ramsey, Ian T. (ed.), *Christian Ethics and Contemporary Philosophy* (New York: Macmillan, 1966), Part III. Seven selections from contemporary authors who take different views about morality and its relation to God's will.

Tolstoy, Leo, "Religion and Morality," in *On Life and Essays on Religion* (London: Oxford U.P., 1934). Preponent.

Trethowan, Illtyd, *Absolute Value: A Study in Christian Theism* (London: George Allen and Unwin, 1970), Chap. 4. Proponent.

Yandell, Keith E. (ed.), *God, Man, and Religion* (New York: McGraw-Hill, 1973), Chap. 10. Contains selections from contemporary proponents and critics.

b   Conscience

A second variety of act deontological theory contends that the rightness or wrongness of an action is known by some faculty or capacity called "conscience." Generally, those who hold this theory assert that there is some faculty analogous to vision and heaing which detects, by a kind of immediate awareness, the property of rightness or wrongness in particular actions. Conscience theorists thus agree with the intuitionists that normal human beings possess immediate, noninferential moral knowledge.

Historically, Joseph Butler has been one of the most widely influential proponents of a conscience theory. He argues from the analogy of a machine—a watch—a thing with a design whose parts are related into a systematic whole. Both the whole and the parts have purposes. The watch has the (main) purpose of telling time to interested humans. The parts have various subordinate purposes; for instance, the mainspring provides power for the whole works, the numbers and hands indicate the hours, the jewels provide bearings, etc. Let us suppose that one of these parts, the mainspring, is the most important part and that it is supreme over the others, so to speak. In this analogy, one has Butler's concept of human nature. Man, an organism, is also a systematic whole having a purpose. And his eyes, ears, arms, etc. are organs having subordinate purposes "geared" to the larger purpose. Among man's faculties are some basic psychological "propensities": the particular impulses, self-love, benevolence, and conscience, which is supreme over the others. It is a matter of fact for Butler that there is a conscience, whose dictates are properly supreme over the other propensities, and that its approvals and disapprovals of *particular actions* as moral or immoral have good consequences for man (a claim Russell denies). Thus, a bad man is, like an inaccurate watch, "out of order." His natural inclinations are out of balance or out of proper relationship.

Furthermore, Butler maintains that we directly know the rightness or wrongness of action through the natural faculty of conscience. This faculty operates much like vision and hearing. He calls the latter "outer senses," and conscience an "inner sense." Since Butler holds that we should "follow nature" by acting in accord with the dictates of conscience, he feels obligated to refute the claims that his theory reduces moral judgment to a "natural" passion or emotion, and that he makes man a "law unto himself," so that he may do anything he pleases. Butler rejects such claims, because conscience expresses our "real proper nature." Thus, to "follow nature" is to behave morally and not to act as one pleases. It is important to understand that Butler does not claim that conscience is authoritative in a *causal* sense. Men can, and do, act contrary to conscience. When Butler argues for the supremacy of conscience, he means only that conscience is the proper governor of our actions.

Although Butler expressed his views in the early eighteenth century, conscience theories are by no means out of date or irrelevant. In addition to their continuing connection with religious faith, they have been in vogue recently as providing justification for acts of civil disobedience. A particular instance would be the refusal of many young men to participate in military actions on grounds of "conscientious objection."

Russell attacks the concept of conscience squarely in terms of its rational pretensions. In his opinion, the "voices of conscience" are not, in fact, moral intuitions from God or any other faculty or rational source. Indeed, the pangs of conscience are feelings of discomfort whose sources lie in infantile training and experience. These feelings, when attached to moral rules, function as a substitute for rational support for moral beliefs, and, in Russell's view, through the identification of such emotions with irrationality, they increase and sustain unhappiness. The sense of sin—conscience—is therefore not the product of a moral faculty; rather, it is a product of infantile conditioning (introjection, hostility, guilt, repression, sublimation, etc., to use Freudian terminology). Russell's argument, thus, is essentially an application of Occam's Razor to the faculty psychology which characterizes conscience theories. Modern psychology explains the feelings of conscience according to laws of nature; and there is no need to appeal to a special faculty. In addition, Russell disagrees with Butler concerning the consequences of feelings of conscience. He believes them to be the source not, as did Butler, of good consequences, but rather of bad ones. Both, it appears, fished for examples in biased waters.

While Russell states some common objections, he does not develop the most obvious criticism of conscience theories; namely, that they are vacuous as to moral content and in consequence imply absurdities. The same act, say burning heretics at the stake, is right and wrong, depending on whose conscience is consulted.

12

The Authority of Conscience

JOSEPH BUTLER

PREFACE

Mankind has various instincts and principles of action, as brute creatures have; some leading most directly and immediately to the good of the community, and some more directly to private good.

Man has several which brutes have not; particularly reflection or conscience, an approbation of some principles or actions, and disapprobation of others.

Brutes obey their instincts or principles of action, according to certain rules; suppose the constitution of their body, and the objects around them.

The generality of mankind also obey their instincts and principles, all of them; those propensions we call good, as well as the bad, according to the same rules; namely, the constitution of their body, and the external circumstances which they are in. (Therefore it is not a true representation of mankind to affirm, that they are wholly governed by self-love, the love of power and sensual appetites: since, as on the one hand they are often actuated by these, without any regard to right or wrong; so on the other it is manifest fact, that the same persons, the generality, are frequently influenced by friendship, compassion, gratitude; and even a general abhorrence of what is base, and liking of what is fair and just, takes its turn amongst the other motives of action. This is the partial inadequate notion of human nature treated of in the first Discourse: and it is by this nature, if one may speak so, that the world is in fact influenced, and kept in that tolerable order, in which it is.)

Brutes in acting according to the rules before mentioned, their bodily constitution and circumstances, act suitably to their whole nature. (It is however to be distinctly noted, that the reason why we affirm this is not merely that brutes in fact act so; for this alone, however universal, does not at all determine, whether such course of action be correspondent to their whole nature: but the reason of the assertion is, that as in acting thus they plainly act conformably to somewhat in their nature, so, from all observations we are able to make upon them, there does not appear the least ground to imagine them to have any thing else in their nature, which requires a different rule or course of action.)

Mankind also in acting thus would act suitably to their whole nature, if no more were to be said of man's nature than what has been now said; if that, as it is a true, were also a complete, adequate account of our nature.

FROM *Fifteen Sermons Upon Human Nature* by Joseph Butler, Preface, Sermon II, III (1726).

But that is not a complete account of man's nature. Somewhat further must be brought in to give us an adequate notion of it; namely, that one of those principles of action, conscience or reflection, compared with the rest as they all stand together in the nature of man, plainly bears upon it marks of authority over all the rest, and claims the absolute direction of them all, to allow or forbid their gratification: a disapprobation of reflection being in itself a principle manifestly superior to a mere propension. And the conclusion is, that to allow no more to this superior principle or part of our nature, than to other parts; to let it govern and guide only occasionally in common with the rest, as its turn happens to come, from the temper and circumstances one happens to be in; this is not to act conformably to the constitution of man: neither can any human creature be said to act conformably to his constitution of nature, unless he allows to that superior principle the absolute authority which is due to it. And this conclusion is abundantly confirmed from hence, that one may determine what course of action the economy of man's nature requires without so much as knowing in what degrees of *strength* the several principles prevail, or which of them have actually the greatest influence.

The practical reason of insisting so much upon this natural authority of the principle of reflection or conscience is, that it seems in great measure overlooked by many, who are by no means the worse sort of men. It is thought sufficient to abstain from gross wickedness, and to be humane and kind to such as happen to come in their way. Whereas in reality the very constitution of our nature requires, that we bring our whole conduct before this superior faculty; wait its determination; enforce upon ourselves its authority, and make it the business of our lives, as it is absolutely the whole business of a moral agent, to conform ourselves to it. This is the true meaning of that ancient precept, *Reverence thyself.* . . .

There is a principle of reflection in men, by which they distinguish between, approve, and disapprove their own actions. We are plainly constituted such sort of creatures as to reflect upon our own nature. The mind can take a view of what passes within itself, its propensions, aversions, passions, affections, as respecting such objects, and in such degrees; and of the several actions consequent thereupon. In this survey it approves of one, disapproves of another, and towards a third is affected in neither of these ways, but is quite indifferent. This principle in man, by which he approves or disapproves his heart, temper, and actions, is conscience; for this is the strict sense of the word, though sometimes it is used so as to take in more. And that this faculty tends to restrain men from doing mischief to each other, and leads them to do good, is too manifest to need being insisted upon. Thus a parent has the affection of love to his children: this leads him to take care of, to educate, to make due provision for them: the natural affection leads to this; but the reflection that it is his proper business, what belongs to him, that it is right and commendable so to do, this added to the affection becomes a much more settled principle, and carries him on through more labour and difficulties for the sake of his children, than he would undergo from that affection alone, if he thought it, and the course of action it led to, either indifferent or criminal. This indeed is impossible, to do that which is good and not to approve of it; for which reason they are frequently not considered as distinct, though they really are; for men often approve of the actions of others, which they will not imitate, and likewise do that which they approve not. It cannot possibly be denied that there is this principle of reflection or conscience in human nature. Suppose a man to relieve an innocent person in great distress; suppose the same man afterwards, in the fury of anger, to do the greatest mischief to a person who had given no just cause of offence; to aggravate the injury, add the circumstances of former friendship, and obligation from the injured person; let the man who is supposed to have done these two different actions, coolly reflect upon them afterwards, without regard to their consequences to himself: to assert that any common man would be affected in the same way towards these different actions, that he would make no distinction between them, but approve or disapprove them equally, is too glaring a falsity to need being confuted. There is therefore this principle of reflection or conscience in mankind. It is needless to compare the respect it has to private good, with the respect it has to public; since it plainly tends as much to the latter as to the former, and is commonly thought to tend chiefly to the latter. This faculty is now mentioned merely as another part in the inward frame of man, pointing out to us in some degree what we are intended for, and as what will naturally and of course have some influence. The particular place assigned to it by nature, what authority it has, and how great influence it ought to have, shall be hereafter considered. . . .

SERMONS II AND III. UPON THE NATURAL SUPREMACY OF CONSCIENCE

For when the Gentiles, which have not the law, do by nature the things contained in the law, these, having not the law, are a law unto themselves.—ROM. 2: 14

As speculative truth admits of different kinds of proof, so likewise moral obligations may be shown by different methods. If the real nature of any creature leads him and is adapted to such and such purposes only, or more than to any other; this is a reason to believe the author of that nature intended it for those purposes. Thus there is no doubt the eye was intended for us to see with. And the more complex any constitution is, and the greater variety of parts there are which thus tend to some one end, the stronger is the proof that such end was designed. However, when the inward frame of man is considered as any guide in morals, the utmost caution must be used that none make peculiarities in their own temper, or any thing which is the effect of particular customs, though observable in several, the standard of what is common to the species, and above all, that the highest principle be not forgot or excluded, that to which belongs the adjustment and correction of all other inward movements and affections: which principle will of course have some influence, but which being in nature supreme, as shall now be shown, ought to preside over and govern all the rest.

The difficulty of rightly observing the two former cautions; the appearance there is of some small diversity amongst mankind with respect to this faculty, with respect to their natural sense of moral good and evil; and the attention necessary to survey with any exactness what passes within, have occasioned that it is not so much agreed what is the standard of the internal nature of man, as of his external form. Neither is this last exactly settled. Yet we understand one another when we speak of the shape of a human body; so likewise we do when we speak of the heart and inward principles, how far soever the standard is from being exact or precisely fixed. There is therefore ground for an attempt of showing men to themselves, of showing them what course of life and behaviour their real nature points out and would lead them to. Now obligations of virtue shown, and motives to the practice of it enforced, from a review of the nature of man, are to be considered as an appeal to each particular person's heart and natural conscience; as the external senses are appealed to for the proof of things cognizable by them. Since then our inward feelings, and the perceptions we receive from our external senses, are equally real; to argue from the former to life and conduct is as little liable to exception, as to argue from the latter to absolutely speculative truth. A man can as little doubt whether his eyes were given him to see with, as he can doubt of the truth of the science of *optics*, deduced from ocular experiments. And allowing the inward feeling, shame; a man can as little doubt whether it was given him to prevent his doing shameful actions, as he can doubt whether his eyes were given him to guide his steps. And as to these inward feelings themselves; that they are real, that man has in his nature passions and affections, can no more be questioned, than that he has external senses. Neither can the former be wholly mistaken; though to a certain degree liable to greater mistakes than the latter.

There can be no doubt but that several propensions or instincts, several principles in the heart of man, carry him to society, and to contribute to the happiness of it, in a sense and a manner in which no inward principle leads him to evil. These principles, propensions, or instincts which lead him to do good, are approved of by a certain faculty within, quite distinct from these propensions themselves. All this hath been fully made out in the foregoing discourse.

But it may be said, "What is all this, though true, to the purpose of virtue and religion? these require, not only that we do good to others when we are led this way, by benevolence or reflection, happening to be stronger than other principles, passions, or appetites; but likewise that the *whole* character be formed upon thought and reflection; that *every* action be directed by some determinate rule, some other rule than the strength and prevalency of any principle or passion. What sign is there in our nature (for the inquiry is only about what is to be collected from thence) that this was intended by its Author? Or how does so various and fickle a temper as that of man appear adapted thereto? It may indeed be absurd and unnatural for men to act without any reflection; nay, without regard to that particular kind of reflection which you call conscience; because this does belong to our nature. For as there never was a man but who approved one place, prospect, building, before another, so it does not appear that there ever was a man who would not have approved an action of humanity rather than of cruelty; interest and passion being quite out of the case. But interest and passion do come in, and are often too strong for and prevail over reflection and conscience. Now as brutes have various instincts, by which they are carried on to the end the Author of their nature intended them for: is not man in the same condition; with this difference only, that to his instincts (*i.e.* appetites and passions) is added the principle of reflection or conscience? And as brutes act agreeably to their nature, in following that principle or particular instinct which for the present is strongest in them; does not man likewise act agreeably to his nature, or obey the law of his creation, by following that principle, be it passion or conscience, which for the present happens to be strongest in him? Thus different men are by their particular nature hurried on to pursue honour or riches or pleasure: there are also persons whose temper leads them in an uncommon degree to kindness, compassion, doing good to their fellow-creatures: as there are others who are given to suspend their judgment, to weigh and consider things, and to act upon thought and reflection. Let every one then quietly follow his nature; as passion, reflection, appetite, the several parts of it, happen to be strongest: but let not the man of virtue taken upon him to blame the ambitious, the covetous, the dissolute; since these equally with him obey and follow their nature. Thus, as in some cases we follow our nature in doing the works *contained in the law*, so in other cases we follow nature in doing contrary."

Now all this licentious talk entirely goes upon a supposition, that men follow their nature in the same sense, in violating the known rules of justice and honesty for the sake of a present gratification, as they do in following those rules when they have no temptation to the contrary. And if this were true, that could not be so which St. Paul asserts, that men are *by nature a law to themselves.* If by following nature were meant only acting as we please, it would indeed be ridiculous to speak of nature as any guide in morals: nay the very mention of deviating from nature would be absurd; and the mention of following it, when spoken by way of distinction, would absolutely have no meaning. For did ever any one act otherwise than as he pleased? And yet the ancients speak of deviating from nature as vice; and of following nature so much as a distinction, that according to them the perfection of virtue consists therein. So that language itself should teach people another sense to the words *following nature*, than barely acting as we please. Let it however be observed, that though the words *human nature* are to be explained, yet the real question of this discourse is not concerning the meaning of words, any other than as the explanation of them may be needful to make out and explain the assertion, that *every man is naturally a law to himself*, that *every one may find within himself the rule of right, and obligations to follow it.* This St. Paul affirms in the words of the text, and this the foregoing objection really denies by seeming to allow it. And the objection will be fully answered, and the text before us explained, by observing that *nature* is considered in different views, and the word used in different senses; and by showing in what view it is considered, and in what sense the word is used, when intended to express and signify that which is the guide of life, that by which men are a law to themselves. I say, the explanation of the term will be sufficient, because from thence it will appear, that in some senses of the word *nature* cannot be, but that in another sense it manifestly is, a law to us.

I. By nature is often meant no more than some principle in man, without regard either to the kind or degree of it. Thus the passion of anger, and the affection of parents to their children, would be called equally *natural*. And as the same person hath often contrary principles, which at the same time draw contrary ways, he may by the same action both follow and contradict his nature in this sense of the word; he may follow one passion and contradict another.

II. *Nature* is frequently spoken of as consisting in those passions which are strongest, and most influence the actions; which being vicious ones mankind is in this sense naturally vicious, or vicious by nature. Thus St. Paul says of the Gentiles, *who were dead in trespasses and sins, and walked according to the spirit of disobedience, that they were by nature the children of wrath.* They could be no otherwise *children of wrath* by nature, than they were vicious by nature.

Here then are two different senses of the word *nature*, in neither of which men can at all be said to be a law unto themselves. They are mentioned only to be excluded; to prevent their being confounded, as the latter is in the objection, with another sense of it, which is now to be inquired after and explained.

III. The apostle asserts, that the Gentiles *do by* NATURE *the things contained in the law.* Nature is indeed here put by way of distinction from revelation, but yet it is not a mere negative. He intends to express more than that by which they *did not*, that by which they *did* the works of the law; namely, by *nature*. It is plain the meaning of the word is not the same in this passage as in the former, where it is spoken of as evil; for in this latter it is spoken of as good; as that by which they acted, or might have acted virtuously. What that is in man by which he is *naturally a law to himself*, is explained in the following words: *Which show the work of the law written in their hearts, their consciences also bearing witness, and their thoughts the mean while accusing or else excusing one another.* If there be a distinction to be made between the *works written in their hearts*, and the *witness of conscience;* by the former must be meant the natural disposition to kindness and compassion, to do what is of good report, to which this apostle often refers, that part of the nature of man, treated of in the foregoing discourse, which with very little reflection and of course leads him to society, and by means of which he naturally acts a just and good part in it, unless other passions or interest lead him astray. Yet since other passions, and regards to private interest, which lead us (though indirectly, yet they lead us) astray, are themselves in a degree equally natural, and often most prevalent; and since we have no method of seeing the particular degrees in which one or the other is placed in us by nature; it is plain the former, considered merely as natural, good and right as they are, can no more be a law to us than the latter. But there is a superior principle of reflection or conscience in every man, which distinguishes between the internal principles of his heart, as well as his external actions; which passes judgment upon himself and them; pronounces determinately some actions to be in themselves just, right, good; others to be in themselves evil, wrong, unjust; which, without being consulted, without being advised with, magisterially exerts itself, and approves or condemns him the doer of them accordingly; and which, if not forcibly stopped, naturally and always of course goes on to anticipate a higher and more effectual sentence, which shall hereafter second and affirm its own. But this part of the office of conscience is beyond my present design explicitly to consider. It is by this faculty, natural to man, that he is a moral agent, that he is a law to himself; but this faculty, I say, is not to be considered merely as a principle in his heart, which is to have some influence as well as others; but considered as a faculty in kind and in nature supreme over all others, and which bears its own authority of being so.

This *prerogative*, this *natural supremacy*, of the faculty which surveys, approves or disapproves the several affections of our mind and actions of our lives, being that by which men *are a law to themselves*, their conformity or disobedience to which law of our nature renders their actions, in the highest and most proper sense, natural or unnatural; it is fit it be further explained to you: and I hope it will be so, if you will attend to the following reflections.

Man may act according to that principle or inclination which for the present happens to be strongest, and yet act in a way disproportionate to, and violate his real proper nature. Suppose a brute creature by any bait to be allured into a snare, by which he is destroyed. He plainly followed the bent of his nature, leading him to gratify his appetite; there is an entire correspondence between his whole nature and such an action: such action therefore is natural. But suppose a man, foreseeing the same danger of certain ruin, should rush into it for the sake of a present gratification; he in this instance would follow his strongest desire, as did the brute creature: but there would be as manifest a disproportion, between the nature of a man and such an action, as between the meanest work of art and the skill of the greatest master in that art: which disproportion arises, not from considering the action singly in *itself*, or in its *consequences;* but from *comparison* of it with the nature of the agent. And since such an action is utterly disproportionate to the nature of man, it is in the strictest and most proper sense unnatural; this word expressing that disproportion. Therefore instead of the words *disproportionate to his nature*, the word *unnatural* may now be put; this being more familiar to us: but let it be observed, that it stands for the same thing precisely.

Now what is it which renders such a rash action unnatural? Is it that he went against the principle of reasonable and cool self-love, considered *merely* as a part of his nature? No: for if he had acted the contrary way, he would equally have gone against a principle, or part of his nature, namely, passion or appetite. But to deny a present appetite, from foresight that the gratification of it would end in immediate ruin or extreme misery, is by no means an unnatural action; whereas to contradict or go against cool self-love for the sake of such gratification, is so in the instance before us. Such an action then being unnatural; and its being so not arising from a man's going against a principle or desire barely, nor in going against that principle or desire which happens for the present to be strongest; it necessarily follows, that there must be some other difference or distinction to be made between these two principles, passion and cool self-love, than what I have yet taken notice of. And this difference, not being a difference in strength or degree, I call a difference in *nature* and in *kind*. And since, in the instance still before us, if passion prevails over self-love, the consequent action is unnatural; but if self-love prevails over passion, the action is natural: it is manifest that self-love is in human nature a superior principle to passion. This may be contradicted without violating that nature; but the former cannot. So that, if we will act conformably to the economy of man's nature, reasonable self-love must govern. Thus, without particular consideration of conscience, we may have a clear conception of the *superior nature* of one inward principle to another; and see that there really is this natural superiority, quite distinct from degrees of strength and prevalency.

Let us now take a view of the nature of man, as consisting partly of various appetites, passions, affections, and partly of the principle of reflection or conscience; leaving quite out all consideration of the different degrees of strength, in which either of them prevail, and it will further appear that there is this natural superiority of one inward principle to another, and that it is even part of the idea of reflection or conscience.

Passion or appetite implies a direct simple tendency towards such and such objects, without distinction of the means by which they are to be obtained. Consequently it will often happen there will be a desire of particular objects, in cases where they cannot be obtained without manifest injury to others. Reflection or conscience comes in, and disapproves the pursuit of them in these circumstances; but the desire remains. Which is to be obeyed, appetite or reflection? Cannot this question be answered, from the economy and constitution of human nature merely, without saying which is strongest? Or need this at all come into consideration? Would not the question be *intelligibly* and fully answered by saying, that the principle of reflection or conscience being compared with the various appetites, passions, and affections in men, the former is manifestly superior and chief, without regard to strength? And how often soever the latter happens to prevail, it is mere *usurpation:* the former remains in nature and in kind its superior; and every instance of such prevalence of the latter is an instance of breaking in upon and violation of the constitution of man.

All this is no more than the distinction, which everybody is acquainted with, between *mere power* and *authority:* only instead of being intended to express the difference between what is possible, and what is lawful in civil government; here it has been shown applicable to the several principles in the mind of man. Thus that principle, by which we survey, and either approve or disapprove our own heart, temper, and actions, is not only to be considered as what is in its turn to have some influence; which may be said of every passion, of the lowest appetites; but likewise as being superior; as from its very nature manifestly claiming superiority over all others: insomuch that you cannot form a notion of this faculty, conscience, without taking in judgment, direction, superintendency. This is a constituent part of the idea, that is, of the faculty itself:

and, to preside and govern, from the very economy and constitution of man, belongs to it. Had it strength, as it had right; had it power, as it had manifest authority, it would absolutely govern the world.

This gives us a further view of the nature of man; shows us what course of life we were made for: not only that our real nature leads us to be influenced in some degree by reflection and conscience; but likewise in what degree we are to be influenced by it, if we will fall in with, and act agreeably to the constitution of our nature: that this faculty was placed within to be our proper governor; to direct and regulate all under principles, passions, and motives of action. This is its right and office: thus sacred is its authority. And how often soever men violate and rebelliously refuse to submit to it, for supposed interest which they cannot otherwise obtain, or for the sake of passion which they cannot otherwise gratify; this makes no alteration as to the *natural right* and *office* of conscience.

13

The Sense of Sin

BERTRAND RUSSELL

Concerning the sense of sin we have already in Chapter I had occasion to say something, but we must now go into it more fully, since it is one of the most important of the underlying psychological causes of unhappiness in adult life.

There is a traditional religious psychology of sin which no modern psychologist can accept. It was supposed, especially by Protestants, that conscience reveals to every man when an act to which he is tempted is sinful, and that after committing such an act he may experience either of two painful feelings: one called remorse, in which there is no merit, and the other called repentance, which is capable of wiping out his guilt. In Protestant countries even many of those who lost their faith continued for a time to accept with greater or smaller modifications the orthodox view of sin. In our own day, partly owing to psychoanalysis, we have the opposite state of affairs: not only do the unorthodox reject the old doctrine of sin, but many of those who still consider themselves orthodox do so likewise. Conscience has ceased to be something mysterious which, because it was mysterious, could be regarded as the voice of God. We know that conscience enjoins different acts in different parts of the world, and that broadly speaking it is everywhere in agreement with tribal custom. What then is really happening when a man's conscience pricks him?

REPRINTED FROM *The Conquest of Happiness* by Bertrand Russell with the permission of Liveright Publishing Corporation, New York. Copyright 1930 by Horace Liveright, Inc. Copyright renewed 1958 by Bertrand Russell.

The word "conscience" covers as a matter of fact several different feelings; the simplest of these is the fear of being found out. You, reader, have, I am sure, lived a completely blameless life, but if you will ask some one who has at some time acted in a manner for which he would be punished if it became known, you will find that when discovery seemed imminent, the person in question repented of his crime. I do not say that this would apply to the professional thief who expects a certain amount of prison as a trade risk, but it applies to what may be called the respectable offender, such as the bank manager who has embezzled in a moment of stress, or the clergyman who has been tempted by passion into some sexual irregularity. Such men can forget their crime when there seems little chance of detection, but when they are found out or in grave danger of being so, they wish they had been more virtuous, and this wish may give them a lively sense of the enormity of their sin. Closely allied with this feeling is the fear of becoming an outcast from the herd. A man who cheats at cards or fails to pay his debts of honor has nothing within himself by which to stand up against the disapproval of the herd when he is found out. In this he is unlike the religious innovator, the anarchist, and the revolutionary, who all feel that, whatever may be their fate in the present, the future is with them and will honor them as much as they are execrated in the present. These men, in spite of the hostility of the herd, do not feel sinful, but the man who entirely accepts the morality of the herd while acting against it suffers great unhappiness when he loses caste, and the fear of this disaster or the pain of it when it has happened may easily cause him to regard his acts themselves as sinful.

But the sense of sin in its most important forms is something which goes deeper. It is something which has its roots in the unconscious, and does not appear in consciousness as fear of other people's disapproval. In consciousness certain kinds of acts are labeled Sin for no reason visible to introspection. When a man commits these acts he feels uncomfortable without quite knowing why. He wishes he were the kind of man who could abstain from what he believes to be sin. He gives moral admiration only to those whom he believes to be pure in heart. He recognizes with a greater or less degree of regret that it is not for him to be a saint; indeed his conception of saintship is probably one which it is nearly impossible to carry out in an ordinary everyday life. Consequently he goes through life with a sense of guilt, feeling that the best is not for him and that his highest moments are those of maudlin penitence.

The source of all this in practically every case is the moral teaching which the man received before he was six years old at the hands of his mother or his nurse. He learned before that age that it is wicked to swear and not quite nice to use any but the most ladylike language, that only bad men drink, and that tobacco is incompatible with the highest virtue. He learned that one should never tell a lie. And above all he learned that any interest in the sexual parts is an abomination. He knew these to be the views of his mother, and believed them to be those of his Creator. To be affectionately treated by his mother, or, if she was neglectful, by his nurse, was the greatest pleasure of his life, and was only obtainable when he had not been known to sin against the moral code. He therefore came to associate something vaguely awful with any conduct of which his mother or nurse would disapprove. Gradually as he grew older he forgot where his moral code had come from and what had originally been the penalty for disobeying it, but he did not throw off the moral code or cease to feel that something dreadful was liable to happen to him if he infringed it.

Now very large parts of this infantile moral teaching are devoid of all rational foundation and such as cannot be applied to the ordinary behavior of ordinary men. A man who uses what is called "bad language," for example, is not from a rational point of view any worse than a man who does not. Nevertheless practically everybody in trying to imagine a saint would consider abstinence from swearing as essential. Considered in the light of reason this is simply silly. The same applies to alcohol and tobacco. With regard to alcohol the feeling does not exist in Southern countries, and indeed there is an element of impiety about it, since it is known that Our Lord and the Apostles drank wine. With regard to tobacco it is easier to maintain a negative position, since all the greatest saints lived before its use was known. But here also no rational argument is possible. The view that no saint would smoke is based in the last analysis upon the view that no saint would do anything solely because it gave him pleasure. This ascetic element in ordinary morality has become almost unconscious, but it operates in all kinds of ways that make our moral code irrational. In a rational ethic it will be held laudable to give pleasure to any one, even to oneself, provided there is no counterbalancing pain to oneself or to others. The ideally virtuous man, if we had got rid of asceticism, would be the man who permits the enjoyment of all good things whenever there is no evil consequence to outweigh the enjoyment. Take again the question of lying. I do not deny that there is a great deal too much lying in the world and that we should all be the better for an increase of truthfulness; but I do deny, as I think every rational person must, that lying is in no circumstances justified. I once in the course of a country walk saw a tired fox at the last stages of exhaustion still forcing himself to run. A few minutes afterwards I saw the hunt. They asked me if I had seen the fox and I said I had. They asked me which way he had gone and I lied to them. I do not think I should have been a better man if I had told the truth.

But it is above all in the realm of sex that early moral teaching does harm. If a child has been conventionally educated by somewhat stern parents or nurses, the association between sin and the sex organs is so firmly established by the time he is six years old that it is unlikely ever to be completely undone throughout the rest of his life. This feeling is of course reënforced by the Œdipus complex, since the woman most loved in childhood is one with whom all sexual freedoms are impossible. The result is that adult men feel women to be degraded by sex, and cannot respect their wives unless their wives hate sexual intercourse. But the man whose wife is cold will be driven by instinct to seek instinctive satisfaction elsewhere. His instinctive satisfaction, however, even if he momentarily finds it, will be poisoned by the sense of guilt, so that he cannot be happy in any relation with a woman, whether in marriage or outside it. On the woman's side the same sort of thing happens if she has been very emphatically taught to

be what is called "pure." She instinctively holds herself back in her sexual relations with her husband, and is afraid of deriving any pleasure from them. In the present day, however, there is very much less of this on the part of women than there was fifty years ago. I should say that at present among educated people the sex life of men is more contorted and more poisoned by the sense of sin than that of women.

There is beginning to be widespread awareness, though not of course on the part of public authorities, of the evils of traditional sex education in regard to the very young. The right rule is simple: until a child is nearing the age of puberty teach him or her no sexual morality whatever, and avoid carefully instilling the idea that there is anything disgusting in the natural bodily functions. As the time approaches when it becomes necessary to give moral instruction, be sure that it is rational and that at every point you can give good grounds for what you say. But it is not on education that I wish to speak in this book. In this book I am concerned rather with what the adult can do to minimize the evil effects of unwise education in causing an irrational sense of sin.

The problem here is the same as has confronted us in earlier chapters, namely that of compelling the unconscious to take note of the rational beliefs that govern our conscious thought. Men must not allow themselves to be swayed by their moods, believing one thing at one moment and another at another. The sense of sin is especially prominent at moments when the concious will is weakened by fatigue, by illness, by drink, or by any other cause. What a man feels at these moments (unless caused by drink) is supposed to be a revelation from his higher self. "The devil was sick, the devil a saint would be." But it is absurd to suppose that moments of weakness give more insight than moments of strength. In moments of weakness it is difficult to resist infantile suggestions, but there is no reason whatsoever for regarding such suggestions as preferable to the beliefs of the adult man when in full possession of his faculties. On the contrary, what a man deliberately believes with his whole reason when he is vigorous ought to be to him the norm as to what he had better believe at all times. It is quite possible to overcome infantile suggestions of the unconscious, and even to change the contents of the unconscious, by employing the right kind of technique. Whenever you begin to feel remorse for an act which your reason tells you is not wicked, examine the causes of your feeling of remorse, and convince yourself in detail of their absurdity. Let your conscious beliefs be so vivid and emphatic that they make an impression upon your unconscious strong enough to cope with the impressions made by your nurse or your mother when you were an infant. Do not be content with an alternation between moments of rationality and moments of irrationality. Look into the irrationality closely with a determination not to respect it and not to let it dominate you. Whenever it thrusts foolish thoughts or feelings into your consciousness, pull them up by the roots, examine them, and reject them. Do not allow yourself to remain a vacillating creature, swayed half by reason and half by infantile folly. Do not be afraid of irreverence towards the memory of those who controlled your childhood. They seemed to you then strong and wise because you were weak and foolish; now that you are neither, it is your business to examine their apparent strength and wisdom, to consider whether they deserve that reverence that from force of habit you still bestow upon them. Ask yourself seriously whether the world is the better for the moral teaching traditionally given to the young. Consider how much of unadulterated superstition goes into the make-up of the conventionally virtuous man, and reflect that while all kinds of imaginary moral dangers were guarded against by incredibly foolish prohibitions, the real moral dangers to which an adult is exposed were practically unmentioned. What are the really harmful acts to which the average man is tempted? Sharp practice in business of the sort not punished by law, harshness towards employees, cruelty towards wife and children, malevolence towards competitors, ferocity in political conflicts— these are the really harmful sins that are common among respectable and respected citizens. By means of these sins a man spreads misery in his immediate circle and does his bit towards destroying civilization. Yet these are not the things that make him, when he is ill, regard himself as an outcast who has forfeited all claim to divine favor. These are not the things that cause him in nightmares to see visions of his mother bending reproachful glances upon him. Why is his subconscious morality thus divorced from reason? Because the ethic believed in by those who had charge of his infancy was silly; because it was not derived from any study of the individual's duty to the community; because it was made up of old scraps of irrational taboos; and because it contained within itself elements of morbidness derived from the spiritual sickness that troubled the dying Roman Empire. Our nominal morality has been formulated by priests and mentally enslaved women. It is time that men who have to take a normal part in the normal life of the world learned to rebel against this sickly nonsense.

But if the rebellion is to be successful in bringing individual happiness and in enabling a man to live consistently by one standard, not to vacillate between two, it is necessary that he should think and feel deeply about what his reason tells him. Most men, when they have thrown off superficially the superstitions of their childhood, think that there is no more to be done. They do not realize that these superstitions are still lurking underground. When a rational conviction has been arrived at, it is necessary to dwell upon it, to follow out its consequences, to search out in oneself whatever beliefs inconsistent with the new conviction might otherwise survive, and when the sense of sin grows strong, as from time to time it will, to treat it not as a revelation and a call to higher things, but as a disease and a weakness, unless of course it is caused by some act which a rational ethic would condemn. I am not suggesting that a man should be destitute of morality, I am only suggesting that he should be destitute of superstitious morality, which is a very different thing.

But even when a man has offended against his own rational code, I doubt whether a sense of sin is the best method of arriving at a better way of life. There is in the sense of sin something abject, something lacking in self-respect. No good was ever done to any one by the loss of self-respect. The rational man will regard his own undesirable acts, as he regards those of others, as acts produced by certain circumstances, and to be avoided either by a fuller realization that they are undesirable, or, where this is possible, by avoidance of the circumstances that caused them.

As a matter of fact the sense of sin, so far from being a cause of a good life, is quite the reverse. It makes a man unhappy and it makes him feel inferior. Being unhappy, he is likely to make claims upon other people which are excessive and which prevent him from enjoying happiness in personal relations. Feeling inferior, he will have a grudge against those who seem superior. He will find admiration difficult and envy easy. He will become a generally disagreeable person and will find himself more and more solitary. An expansive and generous attitude towards other people not only gives happiness to others, but is an immense source of happiness to its possessor, since it causes him to be generally liked. But such an attitude is scarcely possible to the man haunted by a sense of sin. It is an outcome of poise and self-reliance, it demands what may be called mental integration, by which I mean that the various layers of a man's nature, conscious, subconscious, and unconscious, work together harmoniously and are not engaged in perpetual battle. To produce such harmony is possible in most cases by wise education, but where education has been unwise it is a more difficult process. It is the process which the psychoanalysts attempt, but I believe that in a very great many cases the patient can himself perform the work which in more extreme cases requires the help of the expert. Do not say, "I have no time for such psychological labors, my life is a busy one filled with affairs, and I must leave my unconscious to its tricks." Nothing so much diminishes not only happiness but efficiency as a personality divided against itself. The time spent in producing harmony between the different parts of one's personality is time usefully employed. I do not suggest that a man should set apart, say, an hour a day for self-examination. This is to my mind by no means the best method, since it increases self-absorption, which is part of the disease to be cured, for a harmonious personality is directed outward. What I suggest is that a man should make up his mind with emphasis as to what he rationally believes, and should never allow contrary irrational beliefs to pass unchallenged or obtain a hold over him, however brief. This is a question of reasoning with himself in those moments in which he is tempted to become infantile, but the reasoning if it is sufficiently emphatic may be very brief. The time involved therefore should be negligible.

There is in many people a dislike of rationality, and where this exists the kind of thing that I have been saying will seem irrelevant and unimportant. There is an idea that rationality, if allowed free play, will kill all the deeper emotions. This belief appears to me to be due to an entirely erroneous conception of the function of reason in human life. It is not the business of reason to generate emotions, though it may be part of its function to discover ways of preventing such emotions as are an obstacle to well-being. To find ways of minimizing hatred and envy is no doubt part of the function of a rational psychology. But it is a mistake to suppose that in minimizing these passions we shall at the same time diminish the strength of those passions which reason does not condemn. In passionate love, in parental affection, in friendship, in benevolence, in devotion to science or art, there is nothing that reason should wish to diminish. The rational man, when he feels any or all of these emotions, will be glad that he feels them and will do nothing to lessen their strength, for all these emotions are parts of the good life, the life, that is, that makes for happiness both in oneself and in others. There is nothing irrational in the passions as such, and many irrational people feel only the most trivial passions. No man need fear that by making himself rational he will make his life dull. On the contrary, since rationality consists in the main of internal harmony, the man who achieves it is freer in his contemplation of the world and in the use of his energies to achieve external purposes than is the man who is perpetually hampered by inward conflicts. Nothing is so dull as to be encased in self, nothing so exhilarating as to have attention and energy directed outwards.

Our traditional morality has been unduly self-centered, and the conception of sin is part of this unwise focusing of attention upon self. To those who have never passed through the subjective moods induced by this faulty morality, reason may be unnecessary. But to those who have once acquired the sickness, reason is necessary in effecting a cure. And perhaps the sickness is a necessary stage in mental development. I am inclined to think that the man who has passed beyond it by the help of reason has reached a higher level than the man who has never experienced either the sickness or the cure. The hatred of reason which is common in our time is very largely due to the fact that the operations of reason are not conceived in a sufficiently fundamental way. The man divided against himself looks for excitement and distraction; he loves strong passions, not for sound reasons, but because for the moment they take him outside himself and prevent the painful necessity of thought. Any passion is to him a form of intoxication, and since he cannot conceive of fundamental happiness, all relief from pain appears to him solely possible in the form of intoxication. This, however, is the symptom of a deep-seated malady. Where there is no such malady, the greatest happiness comes with the most complete possession of one's faculties. It is in the moments when the mind is most active and the fewest things are forgotten that the most intense joys are experienced. This indeed is one of the best touchstones of happiness. The happiness that requires intoxication of no matter what sort is a spurious and unsatisfying kind. The happiness that is genuinely satisfying is accompanied by the fullest exercise of our faculties and, the fullest realization of the world in which we live.

Conscience—Further Readings

Aronfreed, Justin, *Conduct and Conscience* (New York: Academic, 1968). Summarizes work by psychologists on conscience.

Bain, Alexander, *Moral Science* (1869), Part I, Chap. 3. Critic.

Baylis, Charles A., *Ethics* (New York: Holt, 1958), Chap. 4, pp. 80–94. Critic.

Fromm, Erich, *Man for Himself* (New York: Rinehart, 1947), pp. 141–172. Distinguishes the "authoritarian" from the "humanistic conscience" and urges cultivating the latter.

Martineau, James, *Types of Ethical Theory* (3d ed., Oxford: Clarendon, 1898), Part II, Bk. I, Chaps. 1, 5, and 6. Proponent.

Nowell-Smith, P. H., *Ethics* (Baltimore: Penguin Books, 1954), Chap. 18. Critic.

Raphael, D. Daiches, *The Moral Sense* (London: Oxford U.P., 1947). A scholarly and sympathetic treatment of major philosophers who have held a moral sense theory.

Stephenson, Geoffrey M., *The Development of Conscience* (London: Routledge and Kegan Paul, 1966). A psychological study of the development of conscience in normal persons and psychopaths.

Wayland, Francis, *The Elements of Moral Science* (1835), Chap. 2. Proponent.

2 Rule Deontological Theories

In the last two sections, we have been concerned with act deontological theories, which assert that men can know the rightness or wrongness of particular actions without necessarily considering the value produced as a result of the actions. We now turn to rule deontological theories, which also hold that it is not necessary to consider value produced. In contrast to act deontological theories, however, rule deontological theories assert that men can know the rightness or wrongness of moral rules, or classes of action. Aquinas, Ewing, and Kant, in quite different formulations of the theory, maintain that the properties of rightness and wrongness are predicated of rules, or maxims, or of classes of "prima-facie" rules, which in turn provide standards for judging the rightness or wrongness of particular actions. O'Connor, Hudson, and Field argue that these proponents of rule deontology are mistaken.

a God and Natural Law

Aquinas links reason, moral rules, commands of God, and human and divine purposes and ends in a complex and subtle doctrine that seeks to unify faith and morality. The fundamental elements of his theory combine Aristotelian and Christian sources to form the view that God, the first cause of the universe, is the perfectly good, perfectly reasonable, divine law-giver. His laws constitute moral rules which are rational in character. Men know them both from religious sources and by reason. According to Aquinas, revelation and reason are two ways of comprehending God's rules for human conduct. He believes that, in following God's natural laws, men will realize the highest and happiest kind of life.

We have selected for study sections of three Questions—90, 91, and 94—from the *Summa Theologica*. In his answers to these questions, Aquinas is concerned to show that there is an important connection between moral laws and happiness. After a consideration of the competency of man to make laws and the requirement that they be promulgated, he turns to the matter of eternal law and natural law. He concludes that human natural law is man's participation in the eternal law of God. In the last of our sections, Aquinas argues that the more specific rules and laws flow from one natural and eternal law, and relates virtue and virtuous actions to these laws.

D. J. O'Connor attacks the attempt to derive moral rules from nature. He shows how the arguments that David Hume and (later) G. E. Moore leveled against naturalist moralists also tell against Thomistic theory. One can neither reduce moral properties to natural properties, or derive or deduce what is right and good from what is the case. O'Connor also attacks the attempt to connect the natural ends and purposes of things in the world to moral criteria or standards.

He notes that Aquinas is an intuitionist in the sense that he "likens" the primary principles of ethics to the principles of logic. Thus Aquinas believes the basic precepts of the natural law to be self-evident. In support of this belief, Aquinas held that some ultimate principles must be self-evident because the attempt to prove every principle would lead either to an infinite regress or to a vicious circle. For O'Connor, such an argument in behalf of self-evident principles confuses what is logically basic with what is psychologically obvious. Further, Aquinas' inclusion of statements such as "cruelty to animals is wrong" and "$2 + 2 = 4$" within the same category, is a blunder—a type or category mistake—in that "true" does not have the same meaning or have the same criteria of application in the two examples.

Aquinas holds that propositions about man's specific obligations can in some manner be derived from the primary principles of natural law. O'Connor points out that it is unclear how such derivations are made. Unless the manner of derivation is known, then the relations of "natural law" to the right action are also unclear.

Finally, O'Connor argues that there is a problem for Aquinas with respect to the extent that natural laws and subordinate moral principles are regarded as unchanging. On the one hand, if the unchanging character of morality is emphasized, specific moral precepts will cease to be applicable to changing social conditions. On the other hand, if changes in specific moral principles are admitted, Aquinas' position will move toward a relativism inconsistent with his stress upon the objectivity and rationality of natural law.

14

Reason and Divine Law

St. Thomas Aquinas

QUESTION XC. ON THE ESSENCE OF LAW

First Article. Whether Law is Something Pertaining to Reason?

We proceed thus to the First Article:—Objection 1. It would seem that law is not something pertaining to reason. For the Apostle says (*Rom.* vii. 23): *I see another law in my members*, etc. But nothing pertaining to reason is in the members, since the reason does not make use of a bodily organ. Therefore law is not something pertaining to reason. . . .

On the contrary, It belongs to the law to command and to forbid. But it belongs to reason to command, as was stated above. Therefore law is something pertaining to reason.

I answer that, Law is a rule and measure of acts, whereby man is induced to act or is restrained from acting; for *lex* [*law*] is derived from *ligare* [*to bind*], because it binds one to act. Now the rule and measure of human acts is the reason, which is the first principle of human acts, as is evident from what has been stated above. For it belongs to the reason to direct to the end, which is the first principle in all matters of action, according to the Philosopher. Now that which is the principle in any genus is the rule and measure of that genus: for instance, unity in the genus of numbers, and the first movement in the genus of movements. Consequently, it follows that law is something pertaining to reason. . . .

Second Article. Whether Law is Always Directed to the Common Good?

We proceed thus to the Second Article:—Objection 1. It would seem that law is not always directed to the common good as to its end. For it belongs to law to command and to forbid. But commands are directed to certain individual goods. Therefore the end of law is not always the common good.

From *Introduction to St. Thomas Aquinas*, edited by Anton C. Pegis. Copyright 1948 by Random House, Inc. New York.

OBJ. 2. Further, law directs man in his actions. But human actions are concerned with particular matters. Therefore law is directed to some particular good.

OBJ. 3. Further, Isidore says: *If law is based on reason, whatever is based on reason will be a law.* But reason is the foundation not only of what is ordained to the common good, but also of that which is directed to private good. Therefore law is not directed only to the good of all, but also to the private good of an individual.

On the contrary, Isidore says that *laws are enacted for no private profit, but for the common benefit of the citizens.*

I answer that, As we have stated above, law belongs to that which is a principle of human acts, because it is their rule and measure. Now as reason is a principle of human acts, so in reason itself there is something which is the principle in respect of all the rest. Hence to this principle chiefly and mainly law must needs be referred. Now the first principle in practical matters, which are the object of the practical reason, is the last end: and the last end of human life is happiness or beatitude, as we have stated above. Consequently, law must needs concern itself mainly with the order that is in beatitude. Moreover, since every part is ordained to the whole as the imperfect to the perfect, and since one man is a part of the perfect community, law must needs concern itself properly with the order directed to universal happiness. Therefore the Philosopher, in the above definition of legal matters, mentions both happiness and the body politic, since he says that we call those legal matters *just which are adapted to produce and preserve happiness and its parts for the body politic.* For the state is a perfect community, as he says in *Politics* i.

Now, in every genus, that which belongs to it chiefly is the principle of the others, and the others belong to that genus according to some order towards that thing. Thus fire, which is chief among hot things, is the cause of heat in mixed bodies, and these are said to be hot in so far as they have a share of fire. Consequently, since law is chiefly ordained to the common good, any other precept in regard to some individual work must needs be devoid of the nature of a law, save in so far as it regards the common good. Therefore every law is ordained to the common good.

REPLY OBJ. 1. A command denotes the application of a law to matters regulated by law. Now the order to the common good, at which law aims, is applicable to particular ends. And in this way commands are given even concerning particular matters.

REPLY OBJ. 2. Actions are indeed concerned with particular matters, but those particular matters are referable to the common good, not as to a common genus or species, but as to a common final cause, according as the common good is said to be the common end.

REPLY OBJ. 3. Just as nothing stands firm with regard to the speculative reason except that which is traced back to the first indemonstrable principles, so nothing stands firm with regard to the practical reason, unless it be directed to the last end which is the common good. Now whatever stands to reason in this sense has the nature of a law.

Third Article. Whether the Reason of Any Man Is Competent to Make Laws?

WE PROCEED THUS TO THE THIRD ARTICLE:—OBJECTION 1. It would seem that the reason of any man is competent to make laws. For the Apostle says (*Rom.* ii. 14) that *when the Gentiles, who have not the law, do by nature those things that are of the law, . . . they are a law to themselves.* Now he says this of all in general. Therefore anyone can make a law for himself. . . .

On the contrary, Isidore says, and the *Decretals* repeat: *A law is an ordinance of the people, whereby something is sanctioned by the Elders together with the Commonalty.* Therefore not everyone can make laws.

I answer that, A law, properly speaking, regards first and foremost the order to the common good. Now to order anything to the common good belongs either to the whole people, or to someone who is the viceregent of the whole people. Hence the making of a law belongs either to the whole people or to a public personage who has care of the whole people; for in all other matters the directing of anything to the end concerns him to whom the end belongs. . . .

Fourth Article. Whether Promulgation is Essential to Law?

WE PROCEED THUS TO THE FOURTH ARTICLE:—OBJECTION 1. It would seem that promulgation is not essential to law. For the natural law, above all, has the character of law. But the natural law needs no promulgation. Therefore it is not essential to law that it be promulgated. . . .

I answer that, As was stated above, a law is imposed on others as a rule and measure. Now a rule or measure is imposed by being applied to those who are to be ruled and measured by it. Therefore, in order that a law obtain the binding force which is proper to a law, it must needs be applied to the men who have to be ruled by it. But such application is made by its being made known to them by promulgation. Therefore promulgation is necessary for law to obtain its force.

Thus, from the four preceding articles, the definition of law may be gathered. Law is nothing else than an ordinance of reason for the common good, promulgated by him who has the care of the community.

REPLY OBJ. 1. The natural law is promulgated by the very fact that God instilled it into man's mind so as to be known by him naturally. . . .

QUESTION XCI. ON THE VARIOUS KINDS OF LAW

First Article. Whether There Is an Eternal Law?

WE PROCEED THUS TO THE FIRST ARTICLE:—OBJECTION 1. It would seem that there is no eternal law. For every law is imposed on someone. But there was not someone from eternity on whom a law could be imposed, since God alone was from eternity. Therefore no law is eternal. . . .

I answer that, As we have stated above, law is nothing else but a dictate of practical reason emanating from the ruler who governs a perfect community. Now it is evident, granted that the world is ruled by divine providence, as was stated in the First Part, that the whole community of the universe is governed by the divine reason. Therefore the very notion of the government of things in God, the ruler of the universe, has the nature of a law. And since the divine reason's conception of things is not subject to time, but is eternal, according to *Prov.* viii. 23, therefore it is that this kind of law must be called eternal. . . .

Second Article. Whether There Is in Us a Natural Law?

WE PROCEED THUS TO THE SECOND ARTICLE:—OBJECTION 1. It would seem that there is no natural law in us. For man is governed sufficiently by the eternal law, since Augustine says that *the eternal law is that by which it is right that all things should be most orderly.* But nature does not abound in superfluities as neither does she fail in necessaries. Therefore man has no natural law.

OBJ. 2. Further, by the law man is directed, in his acts, to the end, as was stated above. But the directing of human acts to their end is not a function of nature, as is the case in irrational creatures, which act for an end solely by their natural appetite; whereas man acts for an end by his reason and will. Therefore man has no natural law.

OBJ. 3. Further, the more a man is free, the less is he under the law. But man is freer than all the animals because of his free choice, with which he is endowed in distinction from all other animals. Since, therefore, other animals are not subject to a natural law, neither is man subject to a natural law.

On the contrary, The *Gloss* on *Rom.* ii. 14 (*When the Gentiles, who have not the law, do by nature those things that are of the law*) comments as follows: *Although they have no written law, yet they have the natural law, whereby each one knows, and is conscious of, what is good and what is evil.*

I answer that, As we have stated above, law, being a rule and measure, can be in a person in two ways: in one way, as in him that rules and measures; in another way, as in that which is ruled and measured, since a thing is ruled and measured in so far as it partakes of the rule or measure. Therefore, since all things subject to divine providence are ruled and measured by the eternal law, as was stated above, it is evident that all things partake in some way in the eternal law, in so far as, namely, from its being imprinted on them, they derive their respective inclinations to their proper acts and ends. Now among all others, the rational creature is subject to divine providence in a more excellent way, in so far as it itself partakes of a share of providence, by being provident both for itself and for others. Therefore it has a share of the eternal reason, whereby it has a natural inclination to its proper act and end; and this participation of the eternal law in the rational creature is called the natural law. Hence the Psalmist, after saying (*Ps.* iv. 6): *Offer up the sacrifice of justice,* as though someone asked what the works of justice are, adds: *Many say, Who showeth us good things?* in answer to which question he says: *The light of Thy countenance, O Lord, is signed upon us.* He thus implies that the light of natural reason, whereby we discern what is good and what is evil, which is the function of the natural law, is nothing else than an imprint on us of the divine light. It is therefore evident that the natural law is nothing else than the rational creature's participation of the eternal law.

REPLY OBJ. 1. This argument would hold if the natural law were something different from the eternal law; whereas it is nothing but a participation thereof, as we have stated above.

REPLY OBJ. 2. Every act of reason and will in us is based on that which is according to nature, as was stated above. For every act of reasoning is based on principles that are known naturally, and every act of appetite in respect of the means is derived from the natural appetite in respect of the last end. Accordingly, the first direction of our acts to their end must needs be through the natural law.

REPLY OBJ. 3. Even irrational animals partake in their own way of the eternal reason, just as the rational creature does. But because the rational creature partakes thereof in an intellectual and rational manner, therefore the participation of the eternal law in the rational creature is properly called a law, since a law is something pertaining to reason, as was stated above. Irrational creatures, however, do not partake thereof in a rational manner, and therefore there is no participation of the eternal law in them, except by way of likeness.

Third Article. Whether There Is a Human Law?

WE PROCEED THUS TO THE THIRD ARTICLE:—OBJECTION 1. It would seem that there is not a human law. For the natural law is a participation of the eternal law, as was stated above. Now through the eternal law *all things are most orderly*, as Augustine states. Therefore the natural law suffices for the ordering of all human affairs. Consequently there is no need for a human law. . . .

On the contrary, Augustine distinguishes two kinds of law, the one eternal, the other temporal, which he calls human.

I answer that, As we have stated above, a law is a dictate of the practical reason. Now it is to be observed that the same procedure takes place in the practical and in the speculative reason, for each proceeds from principles to conclusions, as was stated above. Accordingly, we conclude that, just as in the speculative reason, from naturally known indemonstrable principles we draw the conclusions of the various sciences, the knowledge of which is not imparted to us by nature, but acquired by the efforts of reason, so too it is that from the precepts of the natural law, as from common and indemonstrable principles, the human reason needs to proceed to the more particular determination of certain matters. These particular determinations, devised by human reason, are called human laws, provided that the other essential conditions of law be observed, as was stated above. Therefore Tully says in his *Rhetoric* that *justice has its source in nature; thence certain things came into custom by reason of their utility; afterwards these things which emanated from nature, and were approved by custom, were sanctioned by fear and reverence for the law.*

REPLY OBJ. 1. The human reason cannot have a full participation of the dictate of the divine reason, but according to its own mode, and imperfectly. Consequently, just as on the part of the speculative reason, by a natural participation of divine wisdom, there is in us the knowledge of certain common principles, but not a proper knowledge of each single truth, such as that contained in the divine wisdom, so, too, on the part of the practical reason, man has a natural participation of the eternal law, according to certain common principles, but not as regards the particular determinations of individual cases, which are, however, contained in the eternal law. Hence the need for human reason to proceed further to sanction them by law. . . .

Fourth Article. Whether There Was Any Need for a Divine Law?

WE PROCEED THUS TO THE FOURTH ARTICLE:—OBJECTION 1. It would seem that there was no need for a divine law. For, as was stated above, the natural law is a participation in us of the eternal law. But the eternal law is the divine law, as was stated above. Therefore there is no need for a divine law in addition to the natural law and to human laws derived therefrom. . . .

I answer that, Besides the natural and the human law it was necessary for the directing of human conduct to have a divine law. And this for four reasons. First, because it is by law that man is directed how to perform his proper acts in view of his last end. Now if man were ordained to no other end than that which is proportionate to his natural ability, there would be no need for man to have any further direction, on the part of his reason, in addition to the natural law and humanly devised law which is derived from it. But since man is ordained to an end of eternal happiness which exceeds man's natural ability, as we have stated above, therefore it was necessary that, in addition to the natural and the human law, man should be directed to his end by a law given by God.

Secondly, because, by reason of the uncertainty of human judgment, especially on contingent and particular matters, different people form different judgments on human acts; whence also different and contrary laws result. In order, therefore, that many may know without any doubt what he ought to do and what he ought to avoid, it was necessary for man to be directed in his proper acts by a law given by God, for it is certain that such a law cannot err.

Thirdly, because man can make laws in those matters of which he is competent to judge. But man is not competent to judge of interior movements, that are hidden, but only of exterior acts which are observable; and yet for the perfection of virtue it is necessary for man to conduct himself rightly in both kinds of acts. Consequently, human law could not sufficiently curb and direct interior acts, and it was necessary for this purpose that a divine law should supervene.

Fourthly, because, as Augustine says, human law cannot punish or forbid all evil deeds, since, while aiming at doing away with all evils, it would do away with many good things, and would hinder the advance of the common good, which is necessary for human living. In order, therefore, that no evil might remain unforbidden and unpunished, it was necessary for the divine law to supervene, whereby all sins are forbidden. . . .

Fifth Article. Whether There Is But One Divine Law?

WE PROCEED THUS TO THE FIFTH ARTICLE:—OBJECTION 1. It would seem that there is but one divine law. For, where there is one king in one kingdom, there is but one law. Now the whole of mankind is compared to God as to one king, according to *Ps.* xlvi. 8: *God is the King of all the earth.* Therefore there is but one divine law. . . .

I answer that, As we have stated in the First Part, distinction is the cause of number. Now things may be distinguished in two ways. First, as those things that are altogether specifically different, *e.g.,* a horse and an ox. Secondly, as perfect and imperfect in the same species, *e.g.,* a boy and a man; and in this way the divine law is distinguished into Old and New. Hence the Apostle (*Gal.* iii. 24, 25) compares the state of man under the Old Law to that of a child *under a pedagogue*; but the state under the New Law, to that of a full grown man, who is *no longer under a pedagogue.*

Now the perfection and imperfection of these two laws is to be taken in connection with the three conditions pertaining to law, as was stated above. For, in the first place, it belongs to law to be directed to the common good as to its end, as was stated above. This good may be twofold. It may be a sensible and earthly good, and to this man was directly ordained by the Old Law. Hence it is that, at the very outset of the Law, the people were invited to the earthly kingdom of the Chananæans (*Exod.* iii. 8, 17). Again it may be an intelligible and heavenly good, and to this, man is ordained by the New Law. Therefore, at the very beginning of His preaching, Christ invited men to the kingdom of heaven, saying (*Matt.* iv. 17): *Do penance, for the kingdom of heaven is at hand.* Hence Augustine says that *promises of temporal goods are contained in the Old Testament, for which reason it is called old; but the promise of eternal life belongs to the New Testament.*

Secondly, it belongs to law to direct human acts according to the order of justice; wherein also the New Law surpasses the Old Law, since it directs our internal acts, according to *Matt.* v. 20: *Unless your justice abound more than that of the Scribes and Pharisees, you shall not enter into the kingdom of heaven.* Hence the saying that *the Old Law restrains the hand, but the New Law controls the soul.*

Thirdly, it belongs to law to induce men to observe its commandments. This the Old Law did by fear of punishment, but the New Law, by love, which is poured into our hearts by the grace of Christ, bestowed in the New Law, but foreshadowed in the Old. Hence Augustine says that *there is little difference between the Law and the Gospel—fear* [timor] *and love* [amor]. . . .

QUESTION XCIV. THE NATURAL LAW

Second Article. Whether the Natural Law Contains Several Precepts, or Only One?

We proceed thus to the Second Article:—Objection 1. It would seem that the natural law contains not several precepts, but only one. For law is a kind of precept, as was stated above. If therefore there were many precepts of the natural law, it would follow that there are also many natural laws.

Obj. 2. Further, the natural law is consequent upon human nature. But

human nature, as a whole, is one, though, as to its parts, it is manifold. Therefore, either there is but one precept of the law of nature because of the unity of
nature as a whole, or there are many by reason of the number of parts of human
nature. The result would be that even things relating to the inclination of the
concupiscible power would belong to the natural law.

OBJ. 3. Further, law is something pertaining to reason, as was stated above.
Now reason is but one in man. Therefore there is only one precept of the natural
law.

On the contrary, The precepts of the natural law in man stand in relation to
operable matters as first principles do to matters of demonstration. But there are
several first indemonstrable principles. Therefore there are also several precepts of the natural law.

I answer that, As was stated above, the precepts of the natural law are to the
practical reason what the first principles of demonstrations are to the speculative
reason, because both are self-evident principles. Now a thing is said to be self-
evident in two ways: first, in itself; secondly, in relation to us. Any proposition
is said to be self-evident in itself, if its predicate is contained in the notion of the
subject; even though it may happen that to one who does not know the definition
of the subject, such a proposition is not self-evident. For instance, this proposition, *Man is a rational being,* is, in its very nature, self-evident, since he who
says *man,* says *a rational being*; and yet to one who does not know what a man
is, this proposition is not self-evident. Hence it is that, as Boethius says, certain
axioms or propositions are universally self-evident to all; and such are the
propositions whose terms are known to all, as, *Every whole is greater than its
part,* and, *Things equal to one and the same are equal to one another.* But some
propositions are self-evident only to the wise, who understand the meaning of
the terms of such propositions. Thus to one who understands that an angel is
not a body, it is self-evident that an angel is not circumscriptively in a place.
But this is not evident to the unlearned, for they cannot grasp it.

Now a certain order is to be found in those things that are apprehended by
men. For that which first falls under apprehension is *being,* the understanding
of which is included in all things whatsoever a man apprehends. Therefore the
first indemonstrable principle is that *the same thing cannot be affirmed and denied
at the same time,* which is based on the notion of *being* and *not-being*: and on this
principle all others are based, as is stated in *Metaph.* iv. Now as *being* is the
first thing that falls under the apprehension absolutely, so *good* is the first thing
that falls under the apprehension of the practical reason, which is directed to
action (since every agent acts for an end, which has the nature of good). Consequently, the first principle in the practical reason is one founded on the nature
of good, viz., that *good is that which all things seek after.* Hence this is the first
precept of law, that *good is to be done and promoted, and evil is to be avoided.*
All other precepts of the natural law are based upon this; so that all the things
which the practical reason naturally apprehends as man's good belong to the
precepts of the natural law under the form of things to be done or avoided.

Since, however, good has the nature of an end, and evil, the nature of the contrary, hence it is that all those things to which man has a natural inclination are naturally apprehended by reason as being good, and consequently as objects of pursuit, and their contraries as evil, and objects of avoidance. Therefore, the order of the precepts of the natural law is according to the order of natural inclinations. For there is in man, first of all, an inclination to good in accordance with the nature which he has in common with all substances, inasmuch, namely, as every substance seeks the preservation of its own being, according to its nature; and by reason of this inclination, whatever is a means of preserving human life, and of warding off its obstacles, belongs to the natural law. Secondly, there is in man an inclination to things that pertain to him more specially, according to that nature which he has in common with other animals; and in virtue of this inclination, those things are said to belong to the natural law *which nature has taught to all animals*, such as sexual intercourse, the education of offspring and so forth. Thirdly, there is in man an inclination to good according to the nature of his reason, which nature is proper to him. Thus man has a natural inclination to know the truth about God, and to live in society; and in this respect, whatever pertains to this inclination belongs to the natural law: *e.g.*, to shun ignorance, to avoid offending those among whom one has to live, and other such things regarding the above inclination.

Reply Obj. 1. All these precepts of the law of nature have the character of one natural law, inasmuch as they flow from one first precept.

Reply Obj. 2. All the inclinations of any parts whatsoever of human nature, *e.g.*, of the concupiscible and irascible parts, in so far as they are ruled by reason, belong to the natural law, and are reduced to one first precept, as was stated above. And thus the precepts of the natural law are many in themselves, but they are based on one common foundation.

Reply Obj. 3. Although reason is one in itself, yet it directs all things regarding man; so that whatever can be ruled by reason is contained under the law of reason.

Third Article. Whether All the Acts of the Virtues are Prescribed by the Natural Law?

We proceed thus to the Third Article:—Objection 1. It would seem that not all the acts of the virtues are prescribed by the natural law. For, as was stated above, it is of the nature of law that it be ordained to the common good. But some acts of the virtues are ordained to the private good of the individual, as is evident especially in regard to acts of temperance. Therefore, not all the acts of the virtues are the subject of natural law. . . .

I answer that, We may speak of virtuous acts in two ways: first, in so far as they are virtuous; secondly, as such and such acts considered in their proper species. If, then, we are speaking of the acts of the virtues in so far as they are virtuous, thus all virtuous acts belong to the natural law. For it has been stated that to the natural law belongs everything to which a man is inclined according to his nature. Now each thing is inclined naturally to an operation that is suitable to it according to its form: *e.g.*, fire is inclined to give heat. Therefore, since the rational soul is the proper form of man, there is in every man a natural inclination to act according to reason; and this is to act according to virtue. Consequently, considered thus, all the acts of the virtues are prescribed by the natural law, since each one's reason naturally dictates to him to act virtuously. But if we speak of virtuous acts, considered in themselves, *i.e.*, in their proper species, thus not all virtuous acts are prescribed by the natural law. For many things are done virtuously, to which nature does not primarily incline, but which, through the inquiry of reason, have been found by men to be conducive to well-living.

REPLY OBJ. 1. Temperance is about the natural concupiscences of food, drink and sexual matters, which are indeed ordained to the common good of nature, just as other matters of law are ordained to the moral common good.

REPLY OBJ. 2. By human nature we may mean either that which is proper to man, and in this sense all sins, as being against reason, are also against nature, as Damascene states; or we may mean that nature which is common to man and other animals, and in this sense, certain special sins are said to be against nature: *e.g.*, contrary to sexual intercourse, which is natural to all animals, is unisexual lust, which has received the special name of the unnatural crime. . . .

Fourth Article. Whether the Natural Law Is the Same in All Men?

WE PROCEED THUS TO THE FOURTH ARTICLE:—OBJECTION 1. It would seem that the natural law is not the same in all. For it is stated in the *Decretals* that *the natural law is that which is contained in the Law and the Gospel.* But this is not common to all men, because, as it is written (*Rom.* x. 16), *all do not obey the gospel.* Therefore the natural law is not the same in all men. . . .

On the contrary, Isidore says: *The natural law is common to all nations.*

I answer that, As we have stated above, to the natural law belong those things to which a man is inclined naturally; and among these it is proper to man to be inclined to act according to reason. Now it belongs to the reason to proceed from what is common to what is proper, as is stated in *Physics* i. The speculative reason, however, is differently situated, in this matter, from the practical reason. For, since the speculative reason is concerned chiefly with necessary things, which cannot be otherwise than they are, its proper conclusions, like the universal principles, contain the truth without fail. The practical reason, on the other hand, is concerned with contingent matters, which is the domain of human actions; and, consequently, although there is necessity in the common principles, the more we descend towards the particular, the more frequently we encounter defects. Accordingly, then, in speculative matters truth is the same in all men, both as to principles and as to conclusions; although the truth is not known to all as regards the conclusions, but only as regards the principles which are called *common notions.* But in matters of action, truth or practical rectitude is not the same for all as to what is particular, but only as to the common principles; and where there is the same rectitude in relation to particulars, it is not equally known to all.

It is therefore evident that, as regards the common principles whether of speculative or of practical reason, truth or rectitude is the same for all, and is equally known by all. But as to the proper conclusions of the speculative reason, the truth is the same for all, but it is not equally known to all. Thus, it is true for all that the three angles of a triangle are together equal to two right angles, although it is not known to all. But as to the proper conclusions of the practical reason, neither is the truth or rectitude the same for all, nor, where it is the same, is it equally known by all. Thus, it is right and true for all to act according to reason, and from this principle it follows, as a proper conclusion, that goods entrusted to another should be restored to their owner. Now this is true for the majority of cases. But it may happen in a particular case that it would be injurious, and therefore unreasonable, to restore goods held in trust; for instance, if they are claimed for the purpose of fighting against one's country. And this principle will be found to fail the more, according as we descend further towards the particular, *e.g.*, if one were to say that goods held in trust should be restored with such and such a guarantee, or in such and such a way; because the greater the number of conditions added, the greater the number of ways in which the principle may fail, so that it be not right to restore or not to restore.

Consequently, we must say that the natural law, as to the first common principles, is the same for all, both as to rectitude and as to knowledge. But as to certain more particular aspects, which are conclusions, as it were, of those common principles, it is the same for all in the majority of cases, both as to rectitude and as to knowledge; and yet in some few cases it may fail, both as to rectitude, by reason of certain obstacles (just as natures subject to generation and corruption fail in some few cases because of some obstacle), and as to knowledge, since in some the reason is perverted by passion, or evil habit, or an evil disposition of nature. Thus at one time theft, although it is expressly contrary to the natural law, was not considered wrong among the Germans, as Julius Cæsar relates.

REPLY OBJ. 1. The meaning of the sentence quoted is not that whatever is contained in the Law and the Gospel belongs to the natural law, since they contain many things that are above nature; but that whatever belongs to the natural law is fully contained in them. Therefore Gratian, after saying that *the natural law is what is contained in the Law and the Gospel*, adds at once, by way of example, *by which everyone is commanded to do to others as he would be done by.*

15

Aquinas and Natural Law

D. J. O'CONNOR

Of the important philosophical questions raised by St. Thomas, I shall consider the following:

(1) Is St. Thomas an intuitionist in ethics? And if so, does his version of intuitionism escape the standard objections to theories of this type?
(2) How can we argue from what is 'natural'—in whatever sense of that very ambiguous word—to what is morally obligatory?
(3) What are the primary precepts of the natural law and how are they related to the secondary precepts?
(4) To what extent do St. Thomas' concessions about the variability of the natural law destroy the basic character of his theory?

(1) St. Thomas certainly affirms that the precepts of the natural law are self-evident, like the first principles of logic. (He uses the phrase *per se notum*, 'known through itself', to describe such propositions.)

There have been two main types of intuitionism in the history of moral thinking. The first, exemplified by St. Thomas, likens the basic principles of ethics to principles of logic. The second, more familiar in modern times, dates from the eighteenth century, and is well-known to contemporary philosophers through the work of G. E. Moore. This theory draws an analogy between sensory awareness and moral awareness, and likens the moral qualities that we descry in actions and situations to sensory qualities like 'red' or 'sweet' which are presented to us in sense experience. In the phrase of G. E. Moore, good, like yellow, is 'a simple and indefinable quality'.

Of these two accounts, the second is the simpler but also the easier to refute. Indeed, it fails on the simple issue that although it claims that moral qualities are objective and directly knowable features of experience, there is no acceptable and public test for resolving disagreements about them. If A claims that action X is good and B that it is bad and both claim to know this by intuition, there can be no way of deciding the issue. There are independent ways of deciding whether a thing is yellow, and we can distinguish between 'this is yellow' and 'this looks yellow'. But no such tests and distinctions are available, for the intuitionist, in the case of moral disagreements. And so the analogy with sense experience breaks down. But the earlier form of the intuitionist thesis is more difficult to deal with.

F R O M *Aquinas and Natural Law* by D. J. O'Connor. Copyright 1967 by Macmillan, London and Basingstoke, England.

St. Thomas certainly affirms that the precepts of the natural law, like the first principles of logic, are self-evident. The phrase that he uses most often to describe such principles, whether logical or practical, is *per se notum*, 'known through itself'. He distinguishes two grades or levels of self-evidence. A proposition may be self-evident in itself (*secundum se*) if its predicate is 'contained in the notion of the subject'. His examples are not well chosen, but convenient examples might be 'All bachelors are unmarried' or 'All criminals have broken the law'. Further, a proposition may be self-evident to us (*quoad nos*) when we understand the meanings of the terms involved. Many propositions, in consequence, are obvious 'only to the wise' who are familiar with the meanings in question. The example he cites is that angels are not located in space. A less controversial one might be, say, that every tetrahedron has six edges. The basic practical principle is 'good should be done and pursued and evil avoided'. This corresponds to the basic theoretical principle, the principle of non-contradiction.

Before we consider the implications of what he says here, it will be useful to recall that it is basic to his theory of knowledge, as it was to Aristotle's, that some propositions must be known by intuition (*intellectus, intuitus*). The reason for this is that we cannot prove every statement unless we commit ourselves either to an infinite regress or to a vicious circle. So there must be certain basic propositions which are known without inference and for certain. Intuitive knowledge is non-inferential knowledge giving us certainty.

This argument mixes up two quite disparate concepts, that of being logically primitive and that of being psychologically obvious. One is a logical concept and one is psychological. Let us consider them in turn.

(*a*) It is not true that if we trace every deductive argument back to the basic premisses on which the conclusion rests we must arrive in all cases at the *same* starting-points. This has been made amply clear by the development of geometry since St. Thomas' day and, in particular, by the development of logic in modern times. We must have *some* set of axioms as our starting-point. Further, we need rules to develop consequences from the axioms (a point that Aristotle and St. Thomas did not fully appreciate). But as long as these axioms and rules satisfy certain conditions, principally that of consistency, we may use now one set and now another. What propositions we take as primitive will be relative to the system of logic or geometry in which we are operating. It is not even true, in the extreme case, that we must respect St. Thomas' basic speculative principle: 'the same thing cannot be affirmed and denied at the same time'. If we do defy this principle and base our reasonings on inconsistent premisses, we shall find that *anything at all* can be proved. Our inferences become useless and uninteresting not because reasoning is no longer possible under these conditions but because no restrictions are placed upon its outcome.

(*b*) When a proposition P is self-evident, it must always be self-evident *to somebody*. St. Thomas' distinction between propositions self-evident *in themselves* and *to us* tends to hide this important truth. And P is said to be self-evident to those people to whom its truth *seems* obvious without inference.

There are three important facts which render self-evidence useless as a criterion of truth. (i) False propositions may seem (and often have seemed) self-evident. (ii) Whether P seems self-evident to a person depends upon factors other than the logical character of P itself. It will depend on the intelligence and training of the person concerned. Propositions will seem self-evident to the skilled mathematician which to the schoolboy are difficult or unintelligible. (This is the basis of Aquinas' category of statements obvious 'only to the wise'.) (iii) There is no way of testing whether or not P, which seems self-evident to A (but not to B), is really true without adducing other tests than its putative self-evidence. To say that P is self-evident to A is to tell us a good deal about A but not very much about P. And this is just a way of saying that psychological obviousness, by itself, is no test of truth.

But how can we guarantee the truth of a conclusion if the truth is not manifest in the preceding premisses? It is certainly a condition for the truth of any conclusion to which we argue by a valid deductive inference that the premisses should be true. That is to say, we cannot know that the conclusion is true unless we are assured that our premisses are so. There are complexities here into which we need not go; it is sufficient to say that 'truth' is a word that cannot be applied unambiguously to propositions of different types. Most people would be prepared to assert that the following four propositions are all true:

(*a*) $2 + 3 = 5$.
(*b*) All men are mortal.
(*c*) Cruelty to animals is wrong.
(*d*) The sun will rise tomorrow.

But it is not difficult to show that the sense of the word 'true' is different in each of these cases. And other examples could be given which require still other senses of the word. St. Thomas' parallel between the principle of non-contradiction and the basic practical principle 'good should be done and pursued and evil avoided' ignores the important logical differences between propositions of different types—in particular between type (*a*) and type (*c*) above.

We have considered some of the disadvantages of the theory that the truth of certain propositions can be known by intuition. But this kind of intuitionism, as I said above, is not so naïve and easily refuted as the type that asserts that we intuit moral *qualities*. This is because it is a fundamental characteristic of propositions that they can have logical relations to other propositions. And this will, at least in theory, give us the possibility of testing the value of moral principles by observing their logical consequences. For if we can trace the logical relations between moral principles, we might be able to argue as follows:

(i)   Q follows from P; but Q is obviously false.
      So P must be false too.
(ii) Q follows from P; and Q seems to be true.
      So this is some evidence (though not conclusive evidence) in favour of P.

Now St. Thomas does have a theory about logical relations between the primary and secondary precepts of the natural law. But before we look at this to see what support, if any, it provides for his intuitionism, we must look at the more fundamental question of the relation between facts and values in his moral theory.

(2) Any form of a natural-law theory of morals entails the belief that propositions about man's duties and obligations can be inferred from propositions about his nature. Because man has the nature that he has, it follows that he has certain specific duties. This claim can be met by two different challenges: (*a*) to someone who claims that Q follows from P or that P entails Q, one can always say: 'Show me the proof'. If anything is provable, then it can be proved—a tautology that is often conveniently ignored. We shall look in the next section at some of the difficulties of meeting this challenge for a defender of Aquinas' version of natural law. (*b*) It is often held by contemporary philosophers that there is a general logical objection to any doctrine of this kind, an objection first clearly formulated by David Hume. A very distinguished philosopher puts the matter as follows: 'Perhaps the simplest and the most important point about ethics is purely logical. I mean the impossibility to derive non-tautological ethical rules—imperatives; principles of policy; aims; or however we may describe them—from statements of facts. Only if this fundamental logical position is realised can we begin to formulate the real problems of moral philosophy, and to appreciate their difficulty'. There is an extensive literature on this question and in recent years there has been some reaction from philosophers who wish to refute Hume. I shall consider the matter only in the rather restricted context of St. Thomas' theory of natural law.

It is worth noting that there are at least two distinct points at issue here. (i) It is said that it is a logical fallacy to argue to a conclusion which contains terms not present in the premisses. (ii) Descriptive words and value words are meaningful in entirely different ways; and it is claimed that these differences make it impossible for any statements of fact to have a statement of value as a logical consequence.

(i) In virtue of the first point, arguments of the following kind are invalid:

All cats are carnivores.
All carnivores have sharp teeth.
Therefore: All cats have sharp teeth and claws.

The conclusion, though true, does not follow from the premisses, since the term 'claws' does not occur there. However, this is a case of syllogistic reasoning. We could use examples of this type to make a point against anyone who thought *both* that all valid reasoning was syllogistic *and* that statements of value can be validly deduced from statements of fact. (It may be that St. Thomas did believe this.) But it is easy to devise examples where a term (and indeed a term standing for a value concept) appears in the conclusion without appearing in the premisses and without invalidating the argument. For example:

(*a*) Cruelty to animals is illegal.
   Therefore: Cruelty to animals is either illegal or immoral.
(*b*) All actions involve expenditure of energy.
   Therefore: All right actions involve expenditure of energy.

However, these instances can do no more than show that conclusions may validly *contain* value terms even though such terms do not occur in the premises. But so far no one has constructed an example where the argument is clearly valid and where the value term appears *effectively* in the conclusion. By 'appears effectively', I mean that the value word is the predicate purporting to give information about a certain type of action. For example: 'X is right', 'Y is obligatory', or 'Z is wrong' would be such effective uses of value terms where the X, Y, and Z stood for human actions or types of action. Examples of the kind shown at (*a*) and (*b*) above would be dismissed by Hume's followers as trivial and irrelevant to the important question raised at (ii): Are there any facts about human nature from which we can deduce information about our moral obligations?

(ii) We can, of course, approach the question from the other side and argue in the following way: any acts which are morally obligatory for me must lie within what I am capable of doing; and what I am capable of doing is determined by my nature. This seems to be a conclusion validly drawn from true premises and so must itself be true. Unfortunately, it is a perfectly general conclusion and gives us no guide to what our duties may be. Even if we had a clear notion of 'human nature' we would still know only that our duties lay somewhere within the range of actions that this nature made possible for us. And, of course, we all know this already. What we want to know is which of those many actions are right and which are wrong. Our hope of doing that depends, among other things, on having an agreed, unambiguous and factually well-founded concept of 'human nature'. And as we have seen, there are difficulties in the way of this that St. Thomas did not recognise. Moreover, this is only a necessary and not a sufficient condition for what we need. The theory of natural law must further contain as a basic principle not just the useless (because over-general) statement:

(*a*) Human nature determines human duties
   but something much more specific to the following effect:

(*b*) Human nature having properties $P_1, P_2 \ldots, P_n$ determines obligations $O_1, O_2 \ldots, O_n$ where the variables P and O can be made quite specific.

(*b*) is much stronger than (*a*) not only because it contains specific information about human nature and moral duties, but also because the word 'determines' means 'entails' in (*b*) and not just 'sets the boundaries of' as in (*a*).

How far can St. Thomas' theory be stretched to meet this requirement? He has a specific concept of human nature—that man is a rational animal and so has all those capacities and tendencies bound up in the concept of being rational. (It is worth remembering that he lists among *self-evident* propositions the statement that man is rational.) We have seen that his concept of rationality can be challenged. So let us make the difficulty clearer by sketching a more acceptable version of rationality and asking whether it can be seen to commit us in any way to specific moral obligations. Let us say that a man is rational if, among other things, he is consistent, open-minded, and unprejudiced, if he usually draws correct conclusions from the evidence available to him and proportions the degree of his belief in any proposition to the amount of good evidence that he has for it. It is true that one can, on these criteria, be rational in varying degrees and true also that not all human beings are rational in this sense. This contrasts with St. Thomas' notion of rationality which is an 'all or nothing' concept not susceptible of variation in degree and one which applies to every human being. However, to the extent that someone does meet these standards, he would nowadays be accounted a rational animal. Can we say anything about how a man ought to behave from the mere fact that he has this kind of disposition? We might say, for example, that a man ought to act consistently and guide his conduct by rules of some kind. But apart from the fact that this is not so much a consequence of being rational as part of the concept itself, it is still quite unspecific. It does not tell us *exactly what* rules we should respect in our behaviour. It is indeed difficult to see how any process of argument could be used to demonstrate from the fact that man is rational in this sense, or indeed in any other, that he has specific and definable duties.

But St. Thomas does make an attempt to draw specific recommendations about human conduct from the fact that man is rational in his sense of the term. This fact about man is a special kind of natural inclination. We have natural inclinations which we share with the rest of creation, such as the tendency to keep ourselves in existence; we have some which we share with other animals, such as sexual and parental instincts; and we have some arising specifically from our role as rational beings. 'Thus man has a natural inclination to know the truth about God, and to live in society: and in this respect, whatever pertains to this inclination belongs to the natural law; for instance, to shun ignorance, to avoid offending those among whom one has to live, and other such things regarding the above inclination.'

Granted that these are 'natural inclinations', why *ought* we to strive after them? How does the obligation follow from these facts, if facts they are? St. Thomas answers that it is because those things to which we have a natural inclination are 'apprehended by reason as being good and consequently as objects of pursuit'. But why are those things which are good in the sense of being sought after necessarily also good in the sense of being the right kind of things for us to choose? For clearly, not every action done by man in accordance with his natural inclinations leads to his last end. For wrong acts are not, in one sense of the phrase, contrary to nature and yet they do not so lead us. Thomas seems to speak with two voices in answering this question. On the one hand, since we are rational creatures, we know both what our end is and what is its relation (*proportio*) with those things which lead to it. On the other hand, he confesses, as we have seen, that reason may go astray in the complex contingencies of everyday actions so that we make the wrong choice without being aware of our mistake. But virtue is not the same as rational clear-sightedness. And if wrong actions are simply the outcome of intellectual error, how are we to be blamed for them? An over-intellectualised approach to ethics tends to raise the question with which Socrates struggled unsuccessfully: if virtue is knowledge, how can we ever willingly do evil? St. Thomas was, of course, aware of Socrates' mistake. But his own theory, in its attempt to show a rational connection between man's nature and his duties, moves towards the same paradox.

Nor can we say, indeed, that he has *demonstrated* the connection. Let us remember the useful truism cited above: What is demonstrable can be demonstrated.

(3) We can now consider St. Thomas' views on the relation between the primary and the secondary precepts of the natural law. As we have seen, his general position is as follows: there is a close analogy between theoretical reasoning and practical reasoning. Just as there are self-evident and necessary propositions on which all our genuinely scientific knowledge is grounded, so too *synderesis* gives us the first principles of practical reason. And just as we can derive further necessarily true propositions from the basic truths of logic, so too we can derive more detailed moral rules from the general precepts of *synderesis*. We have seen that he does not, at least in some passages, try to press this rather bold simile too closely, presumably on the ground that it is not obvious how the derivations are to be performed. However, this is certainly a point that his expositors and critics must examine in some detail. We want to know just how the specific moral rules which we need to guide our conduct can be shown to be connected with allegedly self-evident principles. We must know therefore:

(*a*) what are the primary principles of natural law;
(*b*) what are the secondary precepts derivable from (*a*);
(*c*) how the secondary precepts are derived from the primary.

Unless a clear and satisfactory account can be given of (*a*), (*b*), and (*c*), the doctrine of natural law will be no guide to right action. And if this is so, it will have failed as an ethical theory. For unlike many modern moral philosophers, St. Thomas does not seek merely to analyse moral language. He tries also to give a rational justification for specific moral precepts.

The chief difficulty in the way of getting adequate information on (*a*), (*b*), and (*c*) above is that Aquinas gives few examples and those that he does give are not always helpful. He says, for example, that 'this is the first precept of law that good is to be done and pursued and evil is to be avoided. All other precepts of the natural law are based upon this.' He also cites as a general precept 'that one should do evil to no man', adding unhelpfully 'and similar principles'. Both of these principles can be regarded as tautologies whose truth depends on the meaning of the terms used in expressing them. Indeed, in view of St. Thomas' account of the nature of self-evident propositions, he would probably have agreed to this. And his most recent commentators seem to agree in so regarding them. But if so, it is hard to see how any informative and specific ethical propositions can be said to follow from them. He also says, in illustration of his statement that whatever belongs to the natural law is contained in the teaching of the Old and New Testaments, that the following proposition belongs to the natural law: 'Everyone is commanded to do to others as he would be done by.' But it is not clear from the context if this is a primary or a secondary precept. It is certainly not self-evident, and the enormous variations in human tastes and temperaments make it a very uncertain principle to act on unless it is carefully qualified. And he even suggests that to act in accordance with reason belongs to the natural law. But again, it is not obvious if this precept, if it is a precept, is primary or secondary.

Thus Aquinas sometimes suggests that there is only one primary precept and sometimes that there are more than one, though without ever listing them. It is clear, however, that there are very many secondary precepts. Indeed, any of the moral rules of medieval Christianity falls into this class with the exception of those for which we are dependent on divine revelation. (Keeping the Sabbath would be such an instance.) St. Thomas lists as examples injunctions against stealing, against breaking agreements, against sexual activities outside marriage, and so on.

But the most important question here is: How does St. Thomas understand the secondary principles to be related to the primary ones? His treatment of this key question is very sketchy, and it is impossible to know how he would have answered the objections to what appears to have been his position and which seem such obvious difficulties to critics writing in the middle of the twentieth century. How are we to understand the statement that moral rules are derived (*derivantur*) from the general precepts of the natural law? He is quite specific about this: 'Something may be derived from natural law in two ways: first, as a conclusion from premises, secondly, by way of determination of certain generalities. The first way is like to that by which, in sciences, demonstrated conclusions are drawn from the principles: while the second mode is likened to that whereby, in the arts, general forms are particularised as to details: thus the craftsman needs to determine the general form of a house to some particular shape. Some things are therefore derived from the general principles of the natural law by way of conclusions; e.g. that *one must not kill* may be derived as a conclusion from the principle that *one should do harm to no man*: while some are derived therefrom by way of determination; e.g. the law of nature has it that the evil-doer should be punished; but that he should be punished in this or that way, is a determination of the law of nature.' And he goes on to say that it is derivation and not determination that preserves the force of the natural law. (His reason for saying this is not obvious.)

The answer to this is simply that the proposition:

(*a*) One should do harm to no man.

does not, by itself, imply the proposition:

(*b*) One must not kill.

The argument requires another premiss to the effect that all killing is doing harm. And this is at least disputable. For example, a defender of euthanasia or suicide might well deny it to be a general principle applicable in all circumstances. And, in general, no conclusions can be obtained, by derivation, from the master principle, 'Good is to be done and evil avoided', without the help of other more disputable propositions.

Indeed, in other passages, St. Thomas seems to want to soften the analogy between strict logical derivation and the logical relationships between the primary and secondary precepts of morals. We have seen that he admits that 'in matters of action, truth or practical rectitude is not the same for all, as to matters of detail, but only as to general principles'. But it is a rule of logic that if P is true and Q is validly derived from P, then Q must be true. Thus the analogy between reasoning in logic and mathematics and reasoning in morals is not a strict one. But if there are differences between these two kinds of reasoning, we need to know exactly what they are.

St. Thomas does not enlighten us on this. He makes several references to the derivation of conclusions from moral principles 'known naturally'; and he distinguishes between such conclusions according to whether they follow more or less immediately from intuitively-known first principles. Some such conclusions, he says, are known after only a little reflection (*modica consideratio*), while others require a great deal of thought (*multa consideratio*). The former are obvious to most of us while the latter are known only to experts (*sapientes*), 'just as it is not possible for all to consider the particular conclusions of sciences, but only for those who are versed in philosophy'. Here again he is pursuing his misleading analogy with formal reasoning; and this analogy is pointless unless the derivations to which he refers can actually be performed. He is faced with a dilemma which he sometimes seems to be uneasily aware of but which he never meets squarely. Either moral rules are derivable from the general precepts given in *synderesis* or they are not. If they are, we require to see the derivations, since what is provable can be proved. If they are not, how are they to be justified?

In one of his early writings, the *Commentary on the Sentences*, St. Thomas sketched another approach to the distinction between the primary and secondary precepts of natural law. If an action is unfitting or unsuitable (*inconveniens*) to the ends which nature 'intends to obtain' by the act in question, then it is against the natural law. And if the act is *inconveniens* to the chief end of the act, it violates the primary precepts; if it is unfitting for the secondary ends, it violates only secondary precepts. He discusses this in connection with the question: Is polygamy wrong? And in this context he distinguishes the primary end of marriage, the production and rearing of children, from the secondary end, the mutual affection and companionship of husband and wife. However, apart from the fact that talk of nature's intentions is under suspicion of being a simple confusion between the distinct concepts of *purpose* and *function*, there is no effective way of deciding what are the primary and secondary ends of any human activity, or even of knowing if such a distinction is meaningful. Much use has been made of this kind of argument in discussions about the morality of contraception. But it is worth noting that in his mature writings St. Thomas makes little appeal to arguments of this sort. It is a pity that his modern disciples have not followed his example in this respect.

(4) St. Thomas has said that natural law is unchangeable in its first principles but that its secondary precepts may be modified in rare and special cases. The examples that he has chiefly in mind here are of little interest to moral philosophy. (They are alleged cases, reported in the Old Testament, of wrong acts done by divine command.) We have seen that he makes the cryptic remark that truth is not the same for all in matters of action, but it is not clear what this implies. We should therefore look briefly at the question: Is it possible on St. Thomas' theory of natural law for specific act A to be wrong at time t_1 and right or even obligatory at t_2? At least it is beyond argument that some acts are *believed* to be permitted at one time and wrong at another. The conspicuous moral defects of the twentieth century should not blind us to the fact that our moral *standards* may reasonably be claimed to show progress on those of earlier times. Slavery, torture of suspects and witnesses, child labour, cruelty to animals, the killing of prisoners of war—these are instances, among many others, of conduct now widely regarded as immoral and indeed proscribed by law. The charter of human rights promulgated by the United Nations Organisation is evidence at least of our lip service to virtue and so of an improvement of moral standards overtly endorsed if not always set to work.

If we assume for the sake of the argument that Aquinas' account of natural law may be accepted, are we to say that moral progress consists in bringing to light the consequences of the first principles of morals in the way that advances in mathematics bring to light the consequences of principles long accepted? Or are we to say that human nature changes and so our obligations change with it? Or that the great social and technological transformation of the modern world presents us with new duties by altering the environment in which we have to live and act? These questions have been much discussed in modern times by St. Thomas' commentators, and the complexities and variety of their opinions are some indication of the difficulty of getting an answer from the text of St. Thomas himself.

There are a few passages where he states that human nature is changeable (*mutabilis*), though it is not clear what he means by this. There are, in any case, many more passages in his writings where he asserts the opposite. So we can hardly credit St. Thomas with the view that morality can change with changes in human nature, though on some versions of a theory of natural law this might be maintained. But he does admit that human law (based upon natural law) changes both on account of alterations in human circumstances and in human reason (which is 'changeable and imperfect').

Again it is unclear what he meant by this. Perhaps his own teaching about usury would be an illustration. He condemned lending money for interest as a sin against justice and so against the law of nature. But a belief in the immorality of taking interest for money lent could be reasonably maintained only in a society in which commerce and industry played a small part. When European society came to depend more and more on economic development and therefore upon investment, for its prosperity and welfare, this interdiction of usury was quietly dropped by Christian moralists. In the same way, the traditional doctrine of the 'just war' has become increasingly hard to defend since the development of nuclear weapons. So too, the proscription of contraception has been made unplausible by changing moral attitudes to sexual relations and by the growing menace of overpopulation. It is now possible to find reputable Roman Catholic theologians who deny, even in public, that contraception is always against the natural law.

We are not concerned here with the truth or falsity of such claims. There is a more interesting and important question: If the detailed precepts of the natural law can be supposed to change in this way or even, less radically, if *our knowledge* of these detailed precepts changes, what becomes of the theory of natural law as an objectively based and rationally defensible basis for morality? This objectivity and rationality is, after all, its great apparent advantage. Yet it seems inevitable either that its detailed prescriptions become irrelevant and inapplicable to a society changed by education and technology or that they are accommodated to these changes. In that case, the theory is, in its application, as relativist as any other.

God and Natural Law—Further Readings

Armstrong, R. A., *Primary and Secondary Precepts in Thomistic Natural Law Teaching* (The Hague: Martinus Nijhoff, 1966). Sympathetic exposition and defence of natural law.

Copleston, F. C., *Aquinas* (Baltimore: Penguin Books, 1955), Chap. 5. Sympathetic exposition.

d'Entrèves, A. P., *Natural Law: An Introduction to Legal Philosophy* (London: Hutchinson, 1951; rev. ed., 1970). Defence of natural law.

Evans, Illtud, O.P., *Light on the Natural Law* (Baltimore: Helicon, 1965). Five contemporary authors debate issues about natural law.

Fried, Charles, "Natural Law and the Concept of Justice," *Ethics*, LXXIV (1964), pp. 237–254. Defence of natural law.

Gilson, Etienne, *The Christian Philosophy of St. Thomas Aquinas* (New York: Random House, 1956), Part III. Sympathetic exposition.

Hart, H. L. A., *The Concept of Law* (Oxford: Clarendon, 1961), especially Chap. 9. Argues for a modified version of natural law.

Kelsen, Hans, *General Theory of Law and State*, trans. by Anders Wedberg (Cambridge, Mass.: Harvard U.P., 1945) with Appendix, "Natural Law Doctrine and Legal Positivism," trans. by Wolfgang Herbert Kraus. The Appendix is a critical discussion of natural and positive law.

Mill, John Stuart, "Nature," in *Three Essays on Religion* (1874). Critic of natural law.

Muelder, Walter G., *Moral Law in Christian Social Ethics* (Richmond, Va.: John Knox, 1966), pp. 139–142. Critic of natural law.

Outka, Gene H., and Paul Ramsey, *Norm and Context in Christian Ethics* (New York: Charles Scribner's Sons, 1968), Part II. Five selections from contemporary authors reassessing the natural law tradition.

Simon, Yves R., *The Tradition of Natural Law*, ed. by Vukan Kuic (New York: Fordham U.P., 1965). Defence of the natural law tradition.

Weldon, T. D., *The Vocabulary of Politics* (Baltimore: Penguin Books, 1953), Chap. 3, Sec. 5. Analyzes different senses of "law," concluding that the natural law tradition in ethics and politics is based upon linguistic confusion.

Wollheim, Richard, "Natural Law," in Paul Edwards (ed.), *The Encyclopedia of Philosophy*, Vol. 5 (New York: Macmillan, 1967), pp. 450–454. A brief survey of the natural law tradition and its critics.

b *Ethical Intuitionism*

In our second rule deontological theory, A. C. Ewing formulates a version of ethical intuitionism. Ewing, along with W. D. Ross (whose work is most important in its critical capacity as the main refutation of act utilitarianism, and therefore is included in the section on utilitarianism), is probably the best known of contemporary intuitionists. Like their colleagues among the conscience theorists, Ewing and Ross maintain that we know rightness and wrongness directly and noninferentially. Thus, they hold to the cognitivist line in maintaining that ethical judgments are rational, true or false, objective and defensible—views which have characterized in some manner all of the normative theories so far considered with the exception of Brunner. Ewing, then, is following a time-honored tradition when he argues that we do know what is right or wrong, and that we know these moral truths by intuition in a way similar to knowing the interconnections among the steps in deductive sequences of formal or mathematical arguments. We also meet again the claim made by Aquinas that some principles must be known as true without proof if we are to avoid an infinite regress.

It follows from the intuitionist position that a person who holds incorrect moral beliefs is in some sense either blind or stupid. The "blindness" allegation, although not considered by Russell in our selection critical of Butler's conscience theory, is common to both intuitionism and to conscience theories. The views of Ewing and Ross are more sophisticated in this respect. Nevertheless, they appear to conceive the knowledge of right and wrong as a product of a kind of faculty which "sees" the moral properties these terms denote.

W. H. Hudson aims the first shots of his attack on intuitionism at this target. He argues, first, that intuitionism confuses belief with knowledge. His procedure is to set forth the most common criteria of knowledge and then to ask whether intuitionist claims about moral knowledge conform to them. These criteria are: a proposition is known if it is true, if it is believed, and if it has satisfactory evidence with which to answer the question, "How do you know?" Intuitionism fails the test on several counts, Hudson argues. First, it confuses the second and third criteria—it assimilates "feeling sure" (belief) with evidence. Second, it cannot show why and how cases of mistaken intuitive claims are false—it cannot distinguish them on independent grounds from those which are true. Third, we do not, in fact, accept our feelings of certainty as final. We revise our most firmly held beliefs in the light of new evidence. Further, there are no common, independent tests such as tests of vision, or of correctness in mathematics. Intuitionists offer nothing that corresponds to color-blindness tests, or to the definitions and proofs found in mathematics. Moral knowledge is not like "seeing" a red thing, or "seeing" the relationships among definitions, axioms, theorems, and rules of inference. Mathematical and empirical models, or put another way, concepts of self-evidence and of perception—the two great paradigms of immediate knowledge—are incorrectly exploited by intuitionism.

Some writers, William Frankena for instance,* appear to believe that the continued acceptance of basic and unprovable principles such as benevolence and justice, and the necessity for us to appeal to them in justifications, supports the rule deontologist. This position appears either to beg an important question concerning the cognitive character of these ultimate principles or to modify the cognitive claims commonly made by deontological theorists. Such continued acceptance could be explained on grounds held by nonintuitionists, whom we shall consider in later sections. For example, the acceptance might be explained by Hare or Sartre as reflecting widely-shared decisions or commitments. Stevenson could view the principles as manifesting commonly expressed emotions of approval. Some of the new naturalists might regard the principles as rules for meeting human interests. As Hudson makes the case, such basic principles may not be correctly considered as instances of knowledge at all, since they do not fulfill the criteria of knowledge claims. More will be said on this issue in the meta-ethical section.

*William Frankena, *Ethics* (Englewood Cliffs, New Jersey: Prentice-Hall, Inc., 1963), pp. 33–62.

Rule deontologists appear to resolve an important problem in connection with act deontologist theories—the fact that it is extremely difficult to behave morally and think over each particular action; i.e., we need to cite rules in practical life, at least rules "of thumb." Moreover, normal patterns of justification involve the use of such rules which, on pain of inconsistency, must be extended generally to other similar persons and situations. If a thinker denies that a general rule is a necessary part of the justification of the moral rightness of an action—as the act deontologist does—he has no satisfactory pattern with which to replace it.

16

Ethical Intuitionism

A. C. Ewing

The present seems to me a suitable occasion for saying something more about "intuition" and its place in ethics. It is a well-known fact that propositions, particularly in ethics, but also in other fields of thought, sometimes present themselves to a person in such a way that without having even in his own opinion established them by empirical observation or by argument he seems to himself to see them directly and clearly to be true. This is often expressed by saying that he has or at least seems to himself to have an *intuition* of their truth. It might be expressed without using the term *intuition* by saying simply that he knows or rationally believes them to be true without having any reasons or at least seems to himself to do so. Some such intuitions or apparent intuitions are no doubt explicable as due to quick and half-conscious, or even in some sense unconscious, inference, deductive or inductive, but I do not see how we can explain all or even most ethical "intuitions" in this way. For in the absence of a conclusive proof of ethical propositions from non-ethical, which it would take a bold man at the present stage of the development of thought to regard as possible, some ethical propositions must be known immediately if any are to be known at all. Ethical facts are not the sort of thing that can be discovered by sense-perception, and we can know no ethical truths by argument unless we know the ethical premises to be true. This in the eyes of some people casts suspicion and doubt on the objective truth of ethics, but these doubts will be lessened when it is realized that the need for admitting intuition is by no means confined to ethics. This we can show by a simple logical argument to the effect that some intuition is necessarily presupposed in all reasoning. Suppose I argue A, ∴ B, ∴ C. Now the argument is invalid unless B does really follow from A, but how can I know that it does so? I may be able to interpolate an

FROM *Ethics* by A. C. Ewing. Copyright 1953 by Hodder & Stoughton, London.

intermediate proposition D which itself follows from A and from which B follows, but this only puts the problem further back. I must know that D follows from A, and though I might perhaps be able to interpolate a further intermediate stage, I obviously cannot go on in this way *ad infinitum*. Sooner or later, and probably very soon indeed, I must come to some link between A and the next term in the inference which I can see immediately to hold without being able to prove this by further argument. We may take it then that, if we are to have any knowledge by inference, intuitive knowledge must occur, and the same is true if we substitute for "knowledge" in both places "justified (rational) belief." The argument shows that all apparent intuitions cannot possibly be reduced to suppressed inferences, since inference itself presupposes intuition of the connections between the different stages in the inference. Even if we made explicit all the intermediate steps of a suppressed inference, they would never justify our conclusion in the absence of this. Ethical intuitions are not indeed intuitions of logical connections, but at least the present argument shows that, if we are to have inference in any sphere, the possibility of intuition cannot be rejected on principle. The mere fact that intuitions have to be admitted in ethics cannot be made an objection against ethics, since it has been shown that we have also to admit intuition with all knowledge outside ethics that involves inference. The term intuition is apt to be suspect, but to say somebody knows something intuitively is only to say that he knows it otherwise than by simple observation or reasoning.

Now when we examine the nature of our ethical thought on its own merits, we do find that it presupposes certain ethical truths which we must know intuitively or not at all. For instance, we object to a man doing something because, we say, it is unkind, meaning that it will cause unnecessary pain to others. But why should he not cause unnecessary pain to others if he so desires? Our objection that he ought not to do so presupposes that pain is evil, and that we ought not unnecessarily to inflict evil on other men. I do not see how these truths can be proved: they are known intuitively, if at all. And in general it is very hard to see how we can know anything to be intrinsically good or bad except by intuition. What argument could prove it? Yet nothing can be really good or bad in the instrumental sense unless it can produce what is intrinsically good or bad, so that ethics is at a complete standstill without knowledge of the latter. I think, however, that both in the development of the individual and of the race particular intuitions come first and general ones later: we saw the evil of a particular pain before we generalized and said that pain was evil, but once we have made the generalization we can without having to prove it see it to be true.

Intuitions also seem to be necessarily present in ethical judgement when we consider the final stage in which we after estimating the factual consequences see or judge an act to be right or wrong. For we have to balance the good and evil in the consequences against each other, and there are no rules of logic or calculations of mathematics by which we can do that. We just see that one set of consequences or one act is preferable to a suggested alternative after having viewed them as a whole, paying attention to their relevant factual aspects. The

points we adduce on either side do not prove (except in simple cases) that an act is right or wrong, but rather put us in a position in which we have more chance of seeing whether it is right or wrong.

Most philosophical defenders of intuition have preferred not to use the word except in cases where they claimed certain knowledge. But at any rate we must admit that people sometimes seem to themselves to know something intuitively when they do not really have the knowledge, and it does not seem to me to matter very much whether we express this by saying that they seemed to have intuitions but did not really, or by saying that they had intuitions but the intuitions were wrong. I have a preference, however, for the latter mode of expression because the former suggests that there is some specific recognizable psychological state, that of having intuitions, which has the proud privilege of infallibility, and this does not seem to be the case. If we say that all intuitions are true or certain, this can only be justified because we refuse to call anything an intuition if we think it false or uncertain. It is thus only verbal. We do not conclude that memory is an infallible faculty because it is bad English to say we remembered something which did not happen.

The fallibility of intuition, or if we prefer to say this, apparent intuition, enhances greatly the importance of the various testing processes to which I have referred. It seems only reasonable to regard intuition as a developing capacity and therefore capable of error, and, as we have seen, a genuine intuition may well be mixed up with false beliefs accepted on authority or derived from mistaken inference. It is not therefore a necessary condition of the validity of an intuition that everybody should agree with it. We ought to have the courage of our opinions even if everybody does not agree, and even the *certainty* of an ethical proposition is not upset by every rogue who shuts his eyes to the truth because he does not want to believe in it or every fool who cannot see it. We need not doubt that it was wrong to put Jews in concentration camps because some Nazis persuaded themselves into thinking it right. On the other hand it is even more important to insist that we must not think that what strikes us as good or right is necessarily always really so, though it is our duty to act on it as long as it really after careful consideration strikes us as so. It is not error but error which could never be corrected that would constitute a serious difficulty for the intuitionist, and there is no reason to think that ethical beliefs cannot be progressively and indefinitely improved with the help of the testing methods of which I have spoken. The uncertainty which these admissions allow must be accepted as an inevitable element in human life like all the other risks and disadvantages inherent in our limitations, but this need not prevent some ethical judgements being completely and others practically certain. Most logicians will tell you (I think quite rightly) that all the general laws which physical science establishes are, strictly speaking, uncertain, but this is not incompatible with a great many of them being practically certain, i.e. so near certainty that we need not bother about the difference, nor necessarily with some particular judgements about physical objects being absolutely certain. It is a disputed question among philosophers indeed whether any judgements at all can be absolutely certain in the strictest sense, but at least most people will be satisfied if some ethical judgements can be maintained to be at any rate as certain as the judgement, e.g. that they have bodies or that the earth existed before they were born.

An intuition must be regarded as a rational judgement, though one not based on argument, even if capable of confirmation by it, and not as a mere feeling. It is of great practical importance to realize this, for it is easy, and I should imagine common enough, to think one knows something to be true or some action right just because one has a certain kind of emotional feeling about it or even because it is the only idea which on first thoughts comes into a man's head. The best and most reliable intuition comes after reasoning and not before. There is such a thing as intuition in science, but those who excel in it are men who have already studied science carefully and systematically and practised its inferences. Intuition may even spring from reasoning in the first instance, though it goes beyond it, and it certainly must be subject to the test of reasoning. Only, since we have seen that everything we know cannot possibly be established by reasoning, we are not entitled to reject a view merely because we cannot prove it. If, though it cannot be proved, it is in accord with the rest of our well-established beliefs, and if it continues to strike us as clear and certain whenever we consider it we are entitled even in the absence of strict proof securely to hold to it.

I think, however, that intuition and inference are more closely connected than I have yet suggested. Intuition should not be regarded as a quasi-miraculous flash of insight standing by itself and not essentially linked with any other thought process at all. It presupposes at least a rational selection between different aspects of the situation, whether this is done instantaneously or gradually, and it is certainly affected deeply by our previous experience, thought and action. What I seem to see immediately when I make a particular ethical decision may be the fruit of long experience and thought about similar situations, without being itself a logical deduction or induction from definite features in the situations in question. In that case the more reasoned and reasonable my thought, the more likely is my intuition to be reliable. What presents itself as an intuition, even though it cannot be regarded as a definite inference from premises, may be determined by our whole previous slowly developed view of ethical conduct and ethical ideals. We may think of the ethical process of balancing the good and evil, the advantages and disadvantages, of one action against another as analogous to the process which occurs when we have to balance probabilities against each other in order to decide what to regard as most likely to happen or which of two theories to accept. We have to consider the points on each side, but we cannot usually thereby *prove* which act is right or which event or theory is more probable. Yet though not a matter of proof, it is a rational matter, whether we attribute the decision to "intuition" or to "good judgement," and it is certainly not one in which infallibility is general.

My insistence on intuition must not be in any way regarded as a protest against the use of reasoning in ethics. What we need is more reasoning and not less. People often talk as if modern psychology had shown that we ought not to reason: what it has shown is merely that reason does not influence us as much as we thought and that there is a lot of bad reasoning. But that reason influences us little is no ground for denying that it ought to influence us more, and that there is much bad reasoning is no ground for not trying to make it good. The deplorable effects on individual life of the neglect to use our reason properly the psychologists themselves have shown; and as regards public affairs what has happened in this generation is surely a vivid enough demonstration of the evils of irrationalism. The ideologies which have devastated the world in recent years would never have gained a grip if people had not been prepared to satisfy their emotions by accepting what was thoroughly unreasonable. The better we reason the better our intuitions: the two are not enemies but indispensable allies.

17

Critique of Intuitionism

W. D. Hudson

The fundamental belief of all the authors with whom we are concerned in this study was that there are moral truths which, when known, are known by intuition; and, if men do not know them, their defect of intuition is comparable either to a defect of physical sight or of intellectual discernment. We will deal with the elements of this belief in turn.

First, does it make sense to speak of knowing by intuition? The word "know" usually differs in meaning from "believe." To know X is not simply to believe, i.e. to be convinced, or *feel* sure, of X. Admittedly, "know" is sometimes used with some such meaning. People say that they know when they mean that they feel very sure. But this feeling often turns out to have been mistaken. It is intelligible, then, in any context to insist on a distinction between knowing and feeling sure. "You say that you know. But do you really *know* or do you only feel sure?"

When "know" is used in accordance with this distinction between knowing and merely believing firmly, there are three conditions which must be fulfilled. I am entitled to say "I know X" if: (i) X is true. I cannot know that London is the capital of Scotland. (ii) I believe X. It does not make sense to say "I know London is the capital of England but I do not believe it." (iii) I have a satisfactory answer to the question, "How do you know X?", giving me what Professor A. J. Ayer calls "the right to be sure."

Is "By intuition" such an answer? Three objections can be brought against it. (i) It assimilates the third condition of knowledge to the second; it simply

FROM *Ethical Intuitionism* by W. D. Hudson. Copyright 1967 by Macmillan, London and Basingstoke, England.

reaffirms that one feels sure. (ii) Intuition is indistinguishable in cases where it is ultimately shown to have been mistaken from those in which it is not. For instance, so-called "men of destiny," such as Hitler, claim to know intuitively what to do to ensure victory in battle or success in some other enterprise. Sometimes their intuitions, when acted upon, meet with success, sometimes with failure. But, so far as one can tell, there is no discernible difference in the two cases, so far as the feeling of certainty is concerned. (iii) We do not, in fact, accept this answer. If we did, we should persist in our claim to know by intuition, whatever contrary evidence came to light. But only mad men do that. If sufficient weight of evidence comes to light, we are always prepared to concede that what we claimed to know by intuition we did not know.

Now, can failure to intuit such moral "truths" as that promise-breaking is wrong, be attributed, as intuitionists have often attributed it, to a sort of blindness or stupidity? Take first the analogy with physical blindness. If a group of people, looking at a lawn, all saw a tree on it, except one, Smith, then, given obvious conditions (that no one was obstructing Smith's line of vision, etc.), we should conclude that Smith's sight was in some way defective. Similarly, intuitionists argue, if Smith does not "see" the wrongness of promise-breaking, we are entitled to say that he is morally "blind."

The first and most obvious objection to this view is that there are no *agreed* tests for deciding whether or not a man is morally "blind," as there are for deciding whether or not his eyesight is defective. It is conceivable that Smith does not see the tree on the lawn because he is deceived by some trick of the light; and it is even possible that there is no tree there and everyone, except Smith, is suffering from an hallucination. If such possibilities worry us, how can we eliminate them? We can take Smith to a specialist who will test his eyes. The tests will be *independent* of Smith's not seeing the tree; and they will be such as other specialists—and plain men in so far as they understand them—consider appropriate for testing eyesight. But there do not seem to be any such independent, agreed tests which all moralists—much less all plain men—accept as tests for moral "blindness."

This contention may conceivably be questioned. Suppose Smith does not "see" that promise-breaking is wrong. We could investigate his other moral beliefs and his conduct. If we found that he rejected other moral principles (besides that concerning promise-breaking), which most other men accept, and that his behaviour was frequently such as most other men would call licentious or dissolute, would not these discoveries constitute agreed, independent, corroborative evidence of his moral "blindness"? Yes. But the point is that such evidence may *not* exist. Yet, even if Smith is at one with most other men in his moral beliefs and conduct on everything except promise-breaking, the intuitionist, *qua* intuitionist, is committed to explaining his failure to "see" the wrongness of promise-breaking as due to a defect of intuition. He does not "see" it because he is morally "blind." Presumably the intuitionist means more by this than the vacuous tautology, he does not "see" it because he does not "see" it. Yet what more does this tell us than that? Recall the tree on the lawn. To say that Smith does not see it because his eyesight is defective explains why he does not see it because there is more to having defective eyesight than simply not seeing this tree on the lawn. If Smith failed every test for defective eyesight known to specialists, yet still did not see the tree on the lawn, it would tell us nothing to say that he did not see it because his eyesight was defective, which we did not already know when we were told simply that he did not see it. Nor does it tell us anything, when the intuitionist says that Smith does not "see" the wrongness of promise-breaking because something is wrong with his capacity for moral intuition, where there is no further evidence of moral "blindness." All the intuitionist is saying, in such a case, is that Smith does not "see" it because he does not "see" it.

Is the comparison with intellectual stupidity any more plausible? If Smith's moral judgment on an act in a particular situation differs from that of other men, then this could be because he lacks the intelligence to see how a certain moral principle, or principles, apply in such situations. His "stupidity," then, would be comparable to that of a man who could not see how certain axioms, rules of inference, etc., can be used to solve a mathematical problem. But suppose Smith simply says that he cannot "see" the wrongness of promise-breaking. This is not a matter of unravelling the moral aspects of a complicated situation, but of "seeing" a single principle which rational intuitionists say that all men who are not morally stupid do "see." Can Smith's failure to "see" it be plausibly called a kind of stupidity? If Smith is a moron, then, of course, he may not understand the sentence, "Promise-breaking is wrong," but *ex hypothesi* any comparison with such stupidity is excluded. The intuitionist does not say that Smith cannot understand the meaning of this sentence, but that he cannot "see" the moral truth which it expresses. On the rational intuitionist's own presuppositions, however, does this make sense? He compares principles such as "Promise-breaking is wrong" with mathematical axioms. Well, would it make sense if someone, who was being instructed in Euclidean geometry, said that he did not see the truth of "Things equal to the same thing are equal to one another"? This is not a proposition which he is required to judge true or false. It is a definition which, if he is going to do Euclidean geometry at all, he must accept. He may, of course, refuse to accept it. But if this refusal is called stupidity, then to say that anyone refused to accept the axiom because he was stupid would be to utter the tautology that he refused to accept it because he refused to accept it. Similarly, if moral principles are comparable to mathematical axioms, to say that Smith does not think that promise-breaking is wrong because he is stupid is vacuous. All it means is that he does not accept this principle because he does not accept it.

CONCLUSION

The writers whom we have considered in this study were men of their time. They worked out their moral philosophy in the light of contemporary empirical facts and the alternative philosophical viewpoints which then prevailed. But times have changed. New approaches have emerged in philosophy and influenced the account which thinkers give of morals; and it would seem that even the empirical facts of morality are not what they were.

The rationalists and the "moral sense" philosophers claimed that all men intuit certain moral truths to be self-evident; and that any plain man has only to look into his own breast to become aware of the overriding authority of conscience. Now, unless these empirical claims had, in the past, answered to something in the experience of their readers, the ethical intuitionists would have been quickly forgotten. They, and many of their readers in the past so far as one can tell, did indeed "hear" the magisterial "voice" of conscience within; and there was, in point of fact, a high degree of unanimity in its deliverances as between one man and another. The reasons for this state of things are perhaps not far to seek. In times when authority—parental, pedagogic, and priestly— is austere and unquestioned, it is hardly surprising if men develop imperious super-egos. And where the prevailing moral code is clear and stable, it is not surprising to find them at one on where their duty lies. Past ages have, of course, all had their moral rebels. But, by contrast with our own day, the times in which our authors wrote were marked by uncritical respect for authority and general agreement on moral issues. Today consciences appear to be less imperious; and they are certainly less assured and agreed in their pronouncements upon any issue. This contrast, between the empirical facts of man's moral life then and now, explains, in part at least, why ethical intuitionism, which has seemed to many past generations plausible and convincing, strikes a modern reader like Mr. J. O. Urmson as "obscurantist," and, if we are to believe Professor P. Edwards, seems "incredible" to most contemporary students of philosophy nowadays, when they first encounter it.

Because so many moral judgments appeared to eighteenth-century intuition- ists clear-cut and indisputable, they concluded that the moral properties of actions or states of affairs are objective. They are, that is to say, not matters of variable human opinion, but part of the unchanging structure of reality. What account, then, was to be given of the faculty which discerns them? Turning to philosophical empiricism for the answer, Shaftesbury and Hutcheson said that, since our most reliable guides to the nature of objective reality are the elemental data of our senses, the moral faculty must be a sense. The rationalists contended that the deliverances of the moral faculty are more certain than that view would allow. It is conceivable that our senses should have been other than they are and that the reality which we experience through them should be other than it seems to us to be. So, if moral intuitions are attributed to a sense, it becomes conceivable that they also could have been other than they are, or could mislead us. This the rationalists would not have. They saw that it would have meant conceding, not only that promise-breaking, for instance, might have *seemed to us* to be right, but that it could conceivably have *been* right. This latter, they said, is as inconceivable as that two and two should not make four, or the whole not be greater than one of its parts. To what, then, must we attribute moral intuitions, if not to a sense? Cartesian intuitionism gave them their answer. According to this philosophy, the ultimate logical constituents of reasoning are clear and distinct ideas which cannot conceivably be other than they are. These are apprehended by reason, or understanding, in its intuitive function. Euclidean axioms provide one example of clear and distinct ideas. The rationalists believed that certain fundamental moral intuitions (such as that promise-breaking is wrong) provide another. The givenness, or objectivity, of morals, they held, can only be accounted for adequately, if the moral faculty is taken to be reason.

Both these philosophical viewpoints reify moral judgment in two ways. They conceive of some "thing," or entity, the moral faculty, existing "within" the minds of men; and of another kind of "thing," the moral properties of actions or states of affairs, existing "out there" in objective reality. Moral judgment occurs when the "thing" in man "comes into touch with" the "thing" in objective reality. Of course, these are "things" in a qualified, non-spatio-temporal sense. The "thing" in man is said to be spiritual, not material; and the "things" in reality to be, not natural, but "non-natural," properties. But the reification remains. Behind moral words are the entities to which they refer and the entity which uses them so to refer. Moral experience is the activity, or interrelationship, of these entities. Moral philosophy is the study of how they work. Moral language is the medium within which they work, or the tool which they use.

But need we postulate such entities? It has seemed to many modern philosophers that here is a clear case for *Occam's Razor*: Entities must not be multiplied without necessity. If we dispense with these entities, we are left only with the language which men use. But could not an intelligible and satisfactory account of moral judgment be given in terms of this alone?

Suppose we accept the contention of rational intuitionists that moral thinking, like mathematical, can be broken down ultimately into appeals to what is axiomatic or self-evident. Then, in making a moral judgment, one is applying a principle, or principles, to which one is committed, just as in geometry one is applying axioms. The principles referred to are "self-evident," at least in the sense that one cannot justify them in terms of anything beyond themselves, and perhaps also in the sense that one cannot conceive of any circumstances in which one would be prepared to abandon them. What is going on in moral judgment would now amount to this: words like "right" and "good" are being used to commend actions or states of affairs; and one is committed to axiomatic or self-evident principles, such as "Happiness is good" or "Promise-keeping is right," in accordance with which one uses these moral words. The "intuitions" into which moral thinking breaks down are, on this view, rules for the use of the words "good," "right," etc., not discernments of the nature of objective reality. It is conceivable that the rules should be other than they are. They vary from age to age, culture to culture. And sometimes an individual person changes his moral principles and uses moral words in accordance with a new set of rules. But all that is involved here is words, and men using them in accordance with rules.

The rationalists were perfectly correct to find an analogy between morals and mathematics. But their Cartesian mentors had taken it for granted that the axioms of the mathematical systems which they used were not simply rules for the use of words, or signs, but ultimate truths about the nature of reality. This was a mistake. Reality may require axioms to be abandoned or altered. Modern mathematicians use other geometries than that of Euclid, constituted by different axioms and, for some purposes, more useful in describing the world or coming to terms with it. The mistake which the rationalists made about the intuitions of morality was simply a "carry over" from the mistake which the Cartesians had made about mathematics.

If we reject the intuitionist account of the objectivity of moral judgment, it is important to clarify what goes with it and what does not. The contention that we can show men to have knowledge of a metaphysical moral order, comparable to their knowledge of the physical order of nature, must, presumably, go, or find some other ground. But some people appear to think that, if this contention has to be abandoned, morality is evacuated of its significance and seriousness. Moral judgment then becomes no more than the expression of subjective taste or distaste; and it really means nothing any longer to say that man is a moral being. But these conclusions do not necessarily follow.

Moral discourse—whether we regard it as referring to non-natural facts or as registering options—remains *sui generis*. That is to say—if we may conceive of it as a "language-game"—that the rules of this game are distinctively its own. One need only compare the way in which men talk about what they regard as matters of taste with the way in which they talk about what they regard as moral issues. If a man, having tasted a wine, exlaimed, "Ugh!", and we said to him, "Why don't you like?", he might reply, "I just don't"; or he might give a reason, such as, "It's too sweet." Now, in either case, it would be eccentric on our part, if we tried to argue with him. We should not be likely to pester him for a reason why he did not like the wine, if he said, "I just don't." And, if he told us that he did not like it because it was too sweet, it would be rather silly of us to rebuke him for inconsistency because we happened to know that he liked sugar in his tea. But now suppose that this man said, "Capital punishment is wrong." It would not be at all eccentric of us to argue with him, if we held another opinion. We should not be behaving oddly if we pressed him for a reason why he thought capital punishment wrong. What would be eccentric is if he were to reply, "I just do." Or—if that is putting it rather strongly—we should at least feel that it was not quite playing the game to go around voicing moral judgments and then refusing to give reasons for them. Suppose that he replies to our request for a reason why he thinks capital punishment wrong with some such remark as: "Because it requires one man to take another man's life and society has no right to ask that of anybody." It will not now be at all silly to ask him whether he thinks that war is wrong; and if he says that he does not, to accuse him of inconsistency. Faced with such an accusation, he will, no doubt, try to think of some morally relevant respect in which the killing involved in war differs from that which society requires in the case of capital punishment. Enough has been said to show that, in moral discourse, one is expected to give reasons for one's judgments, and to accept the implications of universalising these reasons, as one is not expected to do when merely expressing taste or distaste. There are, no doubt, other defining characteristics of moral discourse besides those noted here. What makes a judgment moral is a question about which a lively discussion is going on at the present time among linguistic philosophers. All it is necessary to bring out for our purpose, however, is that moral discourse does have its own distinctive defining characteristics and cannot logically be reduced to anything other than itself.

Moreover, it is characteristic of man to play this moral language 'game." Morality is a distinctively human concern. In this sense, man is indeed a moral being. Any account of human life, which ignored the fact that men ask questions, and debate answers, in terms of moral words, such as "ought," "right," "good," would be seriously inadequate.

Some recent Christian authors have suggested—to quote one—that "Christian morality is indissolubly bound up with the principle of 'the objectivity of moral judgments'"; and have even gone so far as to say—to quote another—that, unless moral language has "objective reference," it is "impossible . . . to believe in God at all." If these quotations mean that the Christian faith or ethic stand or fall with philosophical intuitionism, they are surely absurd! The so-called moral argument for the existence of God may do so, but that is another matter. Religious moralists—just like other kinds of moralist, e.g. evolutionists, hedonists etc.—hold two sorts of view. On the one hand, they believe that something is in fact the case: that X will fulfil the will of God (cf. will conduce to evolution, will produce the greatest happiness of the greatest number, etc.). This belief may, of course, be either true or false. On the other hand, religious moralists, like other kinds of moralist, are committed to a principle of action: We ought to do what conforms to the will of God! (cf. what conduces to evolution, produces the greatest happiness of the greatest number, etc.). Both these sorts of view are logically quite distinct from the philosophical contention that men can be shown to know moral truths by intuition. The relationship between the two sorts of view is, indeed, a matter about which there is animated discussion among modern moral philosophers. It may well be that the logical gap between "is" and "ought"—between factual description and moral evaluation—is not so deep and wide as some analytical philosophers have supposed. And it may be that some "is" statements in religious terms logically imply "ought" statements. But, whatever opinions ultimately prevail on such matters, they will be concerned with the language men use and the relationship between saying one kind of thing and saying another. The discrediting of intuitionism—if it has been discredited—will have no bearing upon them.

Intuitionism—Further Readings

Edwards, Paul, *The Logic of Moral Discourse* (Glencoe, Ill.: Free Press, 1955), especially Chap. 4. Critic.

Hudson, W. D., *Modern Moral Philosophy* (Garden City, N.Y.: Doubleday, 1970), Chap. 3. Exposition and criticism.

Moore, G. E., *Ethics* (London: Oxford U.P., 1912). Proponent.

——, *Principia Ethica* (Cambridge: Cambridge U.P., 1903). Proponent.

Nowell-Smith, P. H., *Ethics* (Baltimore: Penguin Books, 1954), Chaps. 2–4. Critic.

Prichard, H. A., "Does Moral Philosophy Rest on a Mistake?" *Mind*, XXI (1912), pp. 21–37. Proponent.

Ross, W. D., *Foundations of Ethics* (Oxford: Clarendon, 1939). Proponent.

——, *The Right and the Good* (Oxford: Clarendon, 1930). Proponent.

Strawson, P. F., "Ethical Intuitionism," *Philosophy*, XXIV (1949), pp. 23–33. Critic.

Warnock, G. J., *Contemporary Moral Philosophy* (London: Macmillan, 1967), Chap. 2. Critic.

Wellman, Carl, *The Language of Ethics* (Cambridge, Mass.: Harvard U.P., 1961), Chap. 3. Critic.

C The Categorical Imperative

The significance of Kant's ethical thought is indicated in a number of ways. It is seen, for example, in the continuing attention to Kant's requirement that the maxim or rule of any action, if morally correct, be universalizable. This requirement remains a major source of controversy in contemporary ethical thought. Kantian concepts are an important constituent in *prescriptivism*, the ethical theory of R. M. Hare, whose work will be considered below.

Moreover, since Kant's ethical writings appeared, almost all writers in the field have felt obliged to develop their position, at least partially, in response to his views. Kant's ethical "formalism," as it is sometimes called, differs from act deontological theories as well as other rule deontological theories in that he has an abstract criterion—the various formulations of the categorical imperative—which he believes applicable to any possible moral decision. He thinks that the moral character of a particular action can be determined only when the action has been related to the maxim or moral rule behind the action. In turn, the maxim of an action must conform to his abstract criterion, the categorical imperative. His views differ from those of Aquinas in a number of ways. In particular, he rejects the doctrine that specific content rules can be found in nature, and linked to God in the Thomist manner. His theory differs from those of intuitionists, such as Ross and Ewing, who believe that men intuitively know the rightness or wrongness of certain classes or types of acts; in contrast, Kant thinks that such judgments must be tested in the light of his supreme principle of morality, the categorical imperative. Our selection centers on Kant's concept of moral duty and its articulation in different formulations of the *categorical imperative*. The two most famous formulations are: "Act as if the maxim of your action were to become by your will a universal law of nature," and "So act as to treat humanity, whether in your own person or in that of any other, in every case as an end, never as means only."

G. C. Field's attack on Kant is classical in form. He sets out counter-instances which enable him to deduce contradictions from Kant's position. He points out, for instance, that certain rules, such as "thou shalt not lie," if taken absolutely, lead to the absurd conclusion that one could with moral rectitude contribute to a murder by refusing to lie to a murderer concerning the whereabouts of his intended victim. On the other hand, if one attempts to qualify the maxim to something such as "thou shalt not lie except in cases where, etc., etc.," one faces the difficulty of specifying the criteria which distinguish the exceptions without bringing in nonformal criteria, i.e., utilitarianism. Field proceeds in this fashion, often offering a possible defense of Kant. He concludes that Kantian doctrine cannot serve as a practical set of normative ethical principles.

Most contemporary ethical thinkers, among them Richard Brandt,* feel that while Kant's principle of universalizing maxims hits (confusedly) upon a key presupposition of ethics, it nevertheless suffers from grave difficulties: (1) it permits highly immoral actions to be approved; (2) it permits a maxim to be universalizable for one person, but not another; and (3) it allows an agent to so qualify a maxim with exceptions that it cannot fail to be universalizable because it ranges over only one person and one situation. Despite these difficulties, it appears likely that Kant must be credited with a clear understanding that certain elements must characterize, or be presupposed by, any human ethic. First, if an action is right for one person in a certain set of circumstances, it is right for any other person in the same set of circumstances. Second, ethics involves as an essential element concern for other humans as being worthwhile in themselves. Finally, ethics is social, i.e., a shared activity (cf., Kant's kingdom of ends) involving mutually accepted rules and goals. Where Kant seems to go awry is in his belief that formal considerations can confer content on ethical rules.

* Richard Brandt, *Ethical Theory* (Englewood Cliffs, New Jersey: Prentice-Hall, Inc., 1959), pp. 27–35.

18

Fundamental Principles of the Metaphysic of Morals

IMMANUEL KANT

FIRST SECTION. TRANSITION FROM THE COMMON RATIONAL KNOWLEDGE OF MORALITY TO THE PHILOSOPHICAL

Nothing can possibly be conceived in the world, or even out of it, which can be called good without qualification, except a *good will*. Intelligence, wit, judgment, and other *talents* of the mind, however they may be named, or courage, resolution, perseverance, as qualities of temperament, are undoubtedly good and desirable in many respects; but these gifts of nature may also become extremely bad and mischievous if the will which is to make use of them, and which, therefore, constitutes what is called *character*, is not good. It is the same with the *gifts of fortune*. Power, riches, honor, even health, and the general well-being and contentment with one's condition which is called *happiness*, inspire pride, and often presumption, if there is not a good will to correct the influence of these on the mind, and with this also to rectify the whole principle of acting, and adapt it to its end. The sight of a being who is not adorned with a single feature of a pure and good will, enjoying unbroken prosperity, can never give pleasure to an impartial rational spectator. Thus a good will appears to constitute the indispensable condition even of being worthy of happiness.

There are even some qualities which are of service to this good will itself, and may facilitate its action, yet which have no intrinsic unconditional value, but always presuppose a good will, and this qualifies the esteem that we justly have for them, and does not permit us to regard them as absolutely good. Moderation in the affections and passions, self-control, and calm deliberation are not only good in many respects, but even seem to constitute part of the intrinsic worth of the person; but they are far from deserving to be called good without qualification, although they have been so unconditionally praised by the ancients. For without the principles of a good will, they may become extremely bad; and the coolness of a villain not only makes him far more dangerous, but also directly makes him more abominable in our eyes than he would have been without it.

A good will is good not because of what it performs or effects, not by its aptness for the attainment of some proposed end, but simply by virtue of the

FROM *Fundamental Principles of the Metaphysic of Morals* by Immanuel Kant, Sections 1 and 2. Translated by T. K. Abbott (1898).

volition—that is, it is good in itself, and considered by itself is to be esteemed much higher than all that can be brought about by it in favor of any inclination, nay, even of the sum-total of all inclinations. Even if it should happen that, owing to special disfavor of fortune, or the niggardly provision of a step-motherly nature, this will should wholly lack power to accomplish its purpose, if with its greatest efforts it should yet achieve nothing, and there should remain only the good will (not, to be sure, a mere wish, but the summoning of all means in our power), then, like a jewel, it would still shine by its own light, as a thing which has its whole value in itself. Its usefulness or fruitlessness can neither add to nor take away anything from this value. It would be, as it were, only the setting to enable us to handle it the more conveniently in common commerce, or to attract to it the attention of those who are not yet connoisseurs, but not to recommend it to true connoisseurs, or to determine its value.

There is, however, something so strange in this idea of the absolute value of the mere will, in which no account is taken of its utility, that notwithstanding the thorough assent of even common reason to the idea, yet a suspicion must arise that it may perhaps really be the product of mere high-flown fancy, and that we may have misunderstood the purpose of nature in assigning reason as the governor of our will. Therefore we will examine this idea from this point of view.

In the physical constitution of an organized being, that is, a being adapted suitably to the purposes of life, we assume it as a fundamental principle that no organ for any purpose will be found but what is also the fittest and best adapted for that purpose. Now in a being which has reason and a will, if the proper object of nature were its *conservation*, its *welfare*, in a word, its *happiness*, then nature would have hit upon a very bad arrangement in selecting the reason of the creature to carry out this purpose. For all the actions which the creature has to perform with a view to this purpose, and the whole rule of its conduct, would be far more surely prescribed to it by instinct, and that end would have been attained thereby much more certainly than it ever can be by reason. Should reason have been communicated to this favored creature over and above, it must only have served it to contemplate the happy constitution of its nature, to admire it, to congratulate itself thereon, and to feel thankful for it to the beneficent cause, but not that it should subject its desires to that weak and delusive guidance, and meddle bunglingly with the purpose of nature. In a word, nature would have taken care that reason should not break forth into *practical exercise*, nor have the presumption, with its weak insight, to think out for itself the plan of happiness and of the means of attaining it. Nature would not only have taken on herself the choice of the ends but also of the means, and with wise foresight would have entrusted both to instinct.

And, in fact, we find that the more a cultivated reason applies itself with deliberate purpose to the enjoyment of life and happiness, so much the more does the man fail of true satisfaction. And from this circumstance there arises in many, if they are candid enough to confess it, a certain degree of *misology*, that is, hatred of reason, especially in the case of those who are most experienced in the use of it, because after calculating all the advantages they derive—I do not say from the invention of all the arts of common luxury, but even from the sciences (which seem to them to be after all only a luxury of the understanding)—they find that they have, in fact, only brought more trouble on their shoulders rather than gained in happiness; and they end by envying rather than despising the more common stamp of men who keep closer to the guidance of mere instinct, and do not allow their reason much influence on their conduct. And this we must admit, that the judgment of those who would very much lower the lofty eulogies of the advantages which reason gives us in regard to the happiness and satisfaction of life, or who would even reduce them below zero, is by no means morose or ungrateful to the goodness with which the world is governed, but that there lies at the root of these judgments the idea that our existence has a different and far nobler end, for which, and not for happiness, reason is properly intended, and which must, therefore, be regarded as the supreme condition to which the private ends of man must, for the most part, be postponed.

For as reason is not competent to guide the will with certainty in regard to its objects and the satisfaction of all our wants (which it to some extent even multiplies), this being an end to which an implanted instinct would have led with much greater certainty; and since, nevertheless, reason is imparted to us as a practical faculty, that is, as one which is to have influence on the *will*, therefore, admitting that nature generally in the distribution of her capacities has adapted the means to the end, its true destination must be to produce a *will*, not merely good as a *means* to something else, but *good in itself*, for which reason was absolutely necessary. This will then, though not indeed the sole and complete good, must be the supreme good and the condition of every other, even of the desire of happiness. Under these circumstances, there is nothing inconsistent with the wisdom of nature in the fact that the cultivation of the reason, which is requisite for the first and unconditional purpose, does in many ways interfere, at least in this life, with the attainment of the second, which is always conditional—namely, happiness. Nay, it may even reduce it to nothing, without nature thereby failing of her purpose. For reason recognizes the establishment of a good will as its highest practical destination, and in attaining this purpose is capable only of a satisfaction of its own proper kind, namely, that from the attainment of an end, which end again is determined by reason only, notwithstanding that this may involve many a disappointment to the ends of inclination.

We have then to develop the notion of a will which deserves to be highly esteemed for itself, and is good without a view to anything further, a notion which exists already in the sound natural understanding, requiring rather to be cleared up than to be taught, and which in estimating the value of our actions always takes the first place and constitutes the condition of all the rest. In order to do this, we will take the notion of duty, which includes that of a good will, although implying certain subjective restrictions and hindrances. These, however, far from concealing it or rendering it unrecognizable, rather bring it out by contrast and make it shine forth so much the brighter.

I omit here all actions which are already recognized as inconsistent with duty, although they may be useful for this or that purpose, for with these the question whether they are done *from duty* cannot arise at all, since they even conflict with it. I also set aside those actions which really conform to duty, but to which men have *no* direct *inclination*, performing them because they are impelled thereto by some other inclination. For in this case we can readily distinguish whether the action which agrees with duty is done *from duty* or from a selfish view. It is much harder to make this distinction when the action accords with duty, and the subject has besides a *direct* inclination to it. For example, it is always a matter of duty that a dealer should not overcharge an inexperienced purchaser; and wherever there is much commerce the prudent tradesman does not overcharge, but keeps a fixed price for everyone, so that a child buys of him as well as any other. Men are thus *honestly* served; but this is not enough to make us believe that the tradesman has so acted from duty and from principles of honesty; his own advantage required it; it is out of the question in this case to suppose that he might besides have a direct inclination in favor of the buyers, so that, as it were, from love he should give no advantage to one over another. Accordingly the action was done neither from duty nor from direct inclination, but merely with a selfish view.

On the other hand, it is a duty to maintain one's life; and, in addition, everyone has also a direct inclination to do so. But on this account the often anxious care which most men take for it has no intrinsic worth, and their maxim has no moral import. They preserve their life a*s duty requires*, no doubt, but not *because duty requires*. On the other hand, if adversity and hopeless sorrow have completely taken away the relish for life, if the unfortunate one, strong in mind, indignant at his fate rather than desponding or dejected, wishes for death, and yet preserves his life without loving it—not from inclination or fear, but from duty—then his maxim has a moral worth.

To be beneficent when we can is a duty; and besides this, there are many minds so sympathetically constituted that, without any other motive of vanity or self-interest, they find a pleasure in spreading joy around them, and can take delight in the satisfaction of others so far as it is their own work. But I maintain that in such a case an action of this kind, however proper, however amiable it may be, has nevertheless no true moral worth, but is on a level with other inclinations, for example, the inclination to honor, which, if it is happily directed to that which is in fact of public utility and accordant with duty, and consequently honorable, deserves praise and encouragement, but not esteem. For the maxim lacks the moral import, namely, that such actions be done *from duty*, not from inclination. Put the case that the mind of that philanthropist was clouded by sorrow of his own, extinguishing all sympathy with the lot of others, and that while he still has the power to benefit others in distress, he is not touched by their trouble because he is absorbed with his own; and now suppose that he tears himself out of his dead insensibility and performs the action without any inclination to it, but simply from duty, then first has his action its genuine moral worth. Further still, if nature has put little sympathy in the heart of this or that man, if he, supposed to be an upright man, is by temperament cold and indifferent to the sufferings of others, perhaps because in respect of his own he is provided with the special gift of patience and fortitude, and supposes, or even requires, that others should have the same—and such a man would certainly not be the meanest product of nature—but if nature had not specially framed him for a philanthropist, would he not still find in himself a source from whence to give himself a far higher worth than that of a good-natured temperament could be? Unquestionably. It is just in this that the moral worth of the character is brought out which is incomparably the highest of all, namely, that he is beneficent, not from inclination, but from duty.

To secure one's own happiness is a duty, at least indirectly; for discontent with one's condition, under a pressure of many anxieties and amidst unsatisfied wants, might easily become a great *temptation to transgression of duty*. But here again, without looking to duty, all men have already the strongest and most intimate inclination to happiness, because it is just in this idea that all inclinations are combined in one total. But the precept of happiness is often of such a sort that it greatly interferes with some inclinations, and yet a man cannot form any definite and certain conception of the sum of satisfaction of all of them which is called happiness. It is not then to be wondered at that a single inclination, definite both as to what it promises and as to the time within which it can be gratified, is often able to overcome such a fluctuating idea, and that a gouty patient, for instance, can choose to enjoy what he likes, and to suffer what he may, since, according to his calculation, on this occasion at least, he has [only] not sacrificed the enjoyment of the present moment to a possibly mistaken expectation of a happiness which is supposed to be found in health. But even in this case, if the general desire for happiness did not influence his will, and supposing that in his particular case health was not a necessary element in this calculation, there yet remains in this, as in all other cases, this law—namely, that he should promote his happiness not from inclination but from duty, and by this would his conduct first acquire true moral worth.

It is in this manner, undoubtedly, that we are to understand those passages of Scripture also in which we are commanded to love our neighbor, even our enemy. For love, as an affection, cannot be commanded, but beneficence for duty's sake may, even though we are not impelled to it by any inclination— nay, are even repelled by a natural and unconquerable aversion. This is *practical* love, and not *pathological*—a love which is seated in the will, and not in the propensions of sense—in principles of action and not of tender sympathy; and it is this love alone which can be commanded.

The second* proposition is: That an action done from duty derives its moral

---

* The first proposition was that to have moral worth an action must be done from duty. Translator's footnote.

worth, *not from the purpose* which is to be attained by it, but from the maxim by which it is determined, and therefore does not depend on the realization of the object of the action, but merely on the *principle of volition* by which the action has taken place, without regard to any object of desire. It is clear from what precedes that the purposes which we may have in view in our actions, or their effects regarded as ends and springs of the will, cannot give to actions any unconditional or moral worth. In what, then, can their worth lie if it is not to consist in the will and in reference to its expected effect? It cannot lie anywhere but in the *principle of the will* without regard to the ends which can be attained by the action. For the will stands between its *a priori* principle, which is formal, and its *a posteriori* spring, which is material, as between two roads, and as it must be determined by something, it follows that it must be determined by the formal principle of volition when an action is done from duty, in which case every material principle has been withdrawn from it.

The third proposition, which is a consequence of the two preceding, I would express thus: *Duty is the necessity of acting from respect for the law.* I may have *inclination* for an object as the effect of my proposed action, but I cannot have *respect* for it just for this reason that it is an effect and not an energy of will. Similarly, I cannot have respect for inclination, whether my own or another's; I can at most, if my own, approve it; if another's, sometimes even love it, that is, look on it as favorable to my own interest. It is only what is connected with my will as a principle, by no means as an effect—what does not subserve my inclination, but overpowers it, or at least in case of choice excludes it from its calculation—in other words, simply the law of itself, which can be an object of respect, and hence a command. Now an action done from duty must wholly exclude the influence of inclination, and with it every object of the will, so that nothing remains which can determine the will except objectively the *law*, and subjectively *pure respect* for this practical law, and consequently the maxim that I should follow this law even to the thwarting of all my inclinations.

Thus the moral worth of an action does not lie in the effect expected from it, nor in any principle of action which requires to borrow its motive from this expected effect. For all these effects—agreeableness of one's condition, and even the promotion of the happiness of others—could have been also brought about by other causes, so that for this there would have been no need of the will of a rational being; whereas it is in this alone that the supreme and unconditional good can be found. The pre-eminent good which we call moral can therefore consist in nothing else than *the conception of law* in itself, *which certainly is only possible in a rational being*, in so far as this conception, and not the expected effect, determines the will. This is a good which is already present in the person who acts accordingly, and we have not to wait for it to appear first in the result.

But what sort of law can that be the conception of which must determine the will, even without paying any regard to the effect expected from it, in order that this will may be called good absolutely and without qualification? As I have deprived the will of every impulse which could arise to it from obedience to any law, there remains nothing but the universal conformity of its actions to law in general, which alone is to serve the will as a principle, that is, I am never to act otherwise than so *that I could also will that my maxim should become a universal law*. Here, now, it is the simple conformity to law in general, without assuming any particular law applicable to certain actions, that serves the will as its principle, and must so serve it if duty is not to be a vain delusion and a chimerical notion. The common reason of men in its practical judgments perfectly coincides with this, and always has in view the principle here suggested. Let the question be, for example: May I when in distress make a promise with the intention not to keep it? I readily distinguish here between the two significations which the question may have: whether it is prudent or whether it is right to make a false promise? The former may undoubtedly often be the case. I see clearly indeed that it is not enough to extricate myself from a present difficulty by means of this subterfuge, but it must be well considered whether there may not hereafter spring from this lie much greater inconvenience than that from which I now free myself, and as, with all my supposed *cunning*, the consequences cannot be so easily foreseen but that credit once lost may be much more injurious to me than any mischief which I seek to avoid at present, it should be considered whether it would not be more *prudent* to act herein according to a universal maxim, and to make it a habit to promise nothing except with the intention of keeping it. But it is soon clear to me that such a maxim will still only be based on the fear of consequences. Now it is a wholly different thing to be truthful from duty, and to be so from apprehension of injurious consequences. In the first case, the very notion of the action already implies a law for me; in the second case, I must first look about elsewhere to see what results may be combined with it which would affect myself. For to deviate from the principle of duty is beyond all doubt wicked; but to be unfaithful to my maxim of prudence may often be very advantageous to me, although to abide by it is certainly safer. The shortest way, however, and an unerring one, to discover the answer to this question whether a lying promise is consistent with duty, is to ask myself, Should I be content that my maxim (to extricate myself from difficulty by a false promise) should hold good as a universal law, for myself as well as for others; and should I be able to say to myself, "Every one may make a deceitful promise when he finds himself in a difficulty from which he cannot otherwise extricate himself"? Then I presently become aware that, while I can will the lie, I can by no means will that lying should be a universal law. For with such a law there would be no promises at all, since it would be in vain to allege my intention in regard to my future actions to those who would not believe this allegation, or if they over-hastily did so, would pay me back in my own coin. Hence my maxim, as soon as it should be made a universal law, would necessarily destroy itself.

I do not, therefore, need any far-reaching penetration to discern what I have to do in order that my will may be morally good. Inexperienced in the course of the world, incapable of being prepared for all its contingencies, I only ask myself: Canst thou also will that thy maxim should be a universal law? If not, then it must be rejected, and that not because of a disadvantage accruing from it to myself or even to others, but because it cannot enter as a principle into a possible universal legislation, and reason extorts from me immediate respect for such legislation. I do not indeed as yet *discern* on what this respect is based (this the philosopher may inquire), but at least I understand this—that it is an estimation of the worth which far outweighs all worth of what is recommended by inclination, and that the necessity of acting from *pure* respect for the practical law is what constitutes duty, to which every other motive must give place because it is the condition of a will being good *in itself*, and the worth of such a will is above everything. . . .

SECOND SECTION. TRANSITION FROM POPULAR MORAL PHILOSOPHY TO THE METAPHYSIC OF MORALS

. . . Everything in nature works according to laws. Rational beings alone have the faculty of acting according *to the conception* of laws—that is, according to principles, that is, have a *will*. Since the deduction of actions from principles requires *reason*, the will is nothing but practical reason. If reason infallibly determines the will, then the actions of such a being which are recognized as objectively necessary are subjectively necessary also, that is, the will is a faculty to choose *that only* which reason independent on inclination recognizes as practically necessary, that is, as good. But if reason of itself does not sufficiently determine the will, if the latter is subject also to subjective conditions (particular impulses) which do not always coincide with the objective conditions, in a word, if the will does not *in itself* completely accord with reason (which is actually the case with men), then the actions which objectively are recognized as necessary are subjectively contingent, and the determination of such a will according to objective laws is *obligation*, that is to say, the relation of the objective laws to a will that is not thoroughly good is conceived as the determination of the will of a rational being by principles of reason, but which the will from its nature does not of necessity follow.

The conception of an objective principle, in so far as it is obligatory for a will, is called a command (of reason), and the formula of the command is called an Imperative.

All imperatives are expressed by the word *ought* [*or shall*], and thereby indicate the relation of an objective law of reason to a will which from its subjective constitution is not necessarily determined by it (an obligation). They say that something would be good to do or to forbear, but they say it to a will which does not always do a thing because it is conceived to be good to do it. That is practically *good*, however, which determines the will by means of the conceptions of reason, and consequently not from subjective causes, but objectively, that is, on principles which are valid for every rational being as such. It is distinguished from the *pleasant* as that which influences the will only by means of sensation from merely subjective causes, valid only for the sense of this or that one, and not as a principle of reason which holds for every one.

A perfectly good will would therefore be equally subject to objective laws (viz., laws of good), but could not be conceived as *obliged* thereby to act lawfully, because of itself from its subjective constitution it can only be determined by the conception of good. Therefore no imperatives hold for the Divine will, or in general for a *holy* will; *ought* is here out of place because the volition is already of itself necessarily in unison with the law. Therefore imperatives are only formulae to express the relation of objective laws of all volition to the subjective imperfection of the will of this or that rational being, for example, the human will.

Now all *imperatives* command either *hypothetically* or *categorically*. The former represent the practical necessity of a possible action as means to something else that is willed (or at least which one might possibly will). The categorical imperative would be that which represented an action as necessary of itself without reference to another end, that is, as objectively necessary.

Since every practical law represents a possible action as good, and on this account, for a subject who is practically determinable by reason as necessary, all imperatives are formulae determining an action which is necessary according to the principle of a will good in some respects. If now the action is good only as a means *to something else*, then the imperative is *hypothetical*; if it is conceived as good *in itself* and consequently as being necessarily the principle of a will which of itself conforms to reason, then it is *categorical*.

Thus the imperative declares what action possible by me would be good, and presents the practical rule in relation to a will which does not forthwith perform an action simply because it is good, whether because the subject does not always know that it is good, or because, even if it know this, yet its maxims might be opposed to the objective principles of practical reason.

Accordingly the hypothetical imperative only says that the action is good for some purpose, *possible* or *actual*. In the first case it is a *problematical*, in the second an *assertorial* practical principle. The categorical imperative which declares an action to be objectively necessary in itself without reference to any purpose, that is, without any other end, is valid as an *apodictic* (practical) principle.

Whatever is possible only by the power of some rational being may also be conceived as a possible purpose of some will; and therefore the principles of action as regards the means necessary to attain some possible purpose are in fact infinitely numerous. All sciences have a practical part consisting of problems expressing that some end is possible for us, and of imperatives directing how it may be attained. These may, therefore, be called in general imperatives of *skill*. Here there is no question whether the end is rational and good, but only what one must do in order to attain it. The precepts for the physician to make his patient thoroughly healthy, and for a poisoner to ensure certain death, are of equal value in this respect, that each serves to effect its purpose perfectly. Since in early youth it cannot be known what ends are likely to occur to us in the course of life, parents seek to have their children taught a *great many things*, and provide for their *skill* in the use of means for all sorts of arbitrary ends, of none of which can they determine whether it may not perhaps hereafter be an object to their pupil, but which it is at all events *possible* that he might aim at; and this anxiety is so great that they commonly neglect to form and correct their judgment on the value of the things which may be chosen as ends.

There is *one* end, however, which may be assumed to be actually such to all rational beings (so far as imperatives apply to them, viz., as dependent beings), and, therefore, one purpose which they not merely *may* have, but which we may with certainty assume that they all actually *have* by a natural necessity, and this is *happiness*. The hypothetical imperative which expresses the practical necessity of an action as means to the advancement of happiness is *assertorial*. We are not to present it as necessary for an uncertain and merely possible purpose, but for a purpose which we may presuppose with certainty and *a priori* in every man, because it belongs to his being. Now skill in the choice of means to his own greatest well-being may be called *prudence*, in the narrowest sense. And thus the imperative which refers to the choice of means to one's own happiness, that is, the precept of prudence, is still always *hypothetical;* the action is not commanded absolutely, but only as means to another purpose.

Finally, there is an imperative which commands a certain conduct immediately, without having as its condition any other purpose to be attained by it, This imperative is *categorical*. It concerns not the matter of the action, or its intended result, but its form and the principle of which it is itself a result; and what is essentially good in it consists in the mental disposition, let the consequence be what it may. This imperative may be called that of *morality*. . . .

When I conceive a hypothetical imperative, in general I do not know beforehand what it will contain until I am given the condition. But when I conceive a categorical imperative, I know at once what it contains. For as the imperative contains besides the law only the necessity that the maxims[1] shall conform to this law, while the law contains no conditions restricting it, there remains nothing but the general statement that the maxim of the action should conform to a universal law, and it is this conformity alone that the imperative properly represents as necessary.

There is therefore but one categorical imperative, namely, this: *Act only on that maxim whereby thou canst at the same time will that it should become a universal law*.

Now if all imperatives of duty can be deduced from this one imperative as from their principle, then, although it should remain undecided whether what is called duty is not merely a vain notion, yet at least we shall be able to show what we understand by it and what this notion means.

Since the universality of the law according to which effects are produced constitutes what is properly called *nature* in the most general sense (as to form)—

---

[1] A "maxim" is a subjective principle of action, and must be distinguished from the *objective principle*, namely, practical law. The former contains the practical rule set by reason according to the conditions of the subject (often its ignorance or its inclinations), so that it is the principle on which the subject *acts;* but the law is the objective principle valid for every rational being, and is the principle on which it *ought to act*—that is an imperative.

that is, the existence of things so far as it is determined by general laws—the imperative of duty may be expressed thus: *Act as if the maxim of thy action were to become by thy will a universal law of nature.*

We will now enumerate a few duties, adopting the usual division of them into duties to ourselves and to others, and into perfect and imperfect duties.

1. A man reduced to despair by a series of misfortunes feels wearied of life, but is still so far in possession of his reason that he can ask himself whether it would not be contrary to his duty to himself to take his own life. Now he inquires whether the maxim of his action could become a universal law of nature. His maxim is: From self-love I adopt it as a principle to shorten my life when its longer duration is likely to bring more evil than satisfaction. It is asked then simply whether this principle founded on self-love can become a universal law of nature. Now we see at once that a system of nature of which it should be a law to destroy life by means of the very feeling whose special nature it is to impel to the improvement of life would contradict itself, and therefore could not exist as a system of nature; hence that maxim cannot possibly exist as a universal law of nature, and consequently would be wholly inconsistent with the supreme principle of all duty.

2. Another finds himself forced by necessity to borrow money. He knows that he will not be able to repay it, but sees also that nothing will be lent to him unless he promises stoutly to repay it in a definite time. He desires to make this promise, but he has still so much conscience as to ask himself: Is it not unlawful and inconsistent with duty to get out of a difficulty in this way? Suppose, however, that he resolves to do so, then the maxim of his action would be expressed thus: When I think myself in want of money, I will borrow money and promise to repay it, although I know that I never can do so. Now this principle of self-love or of one's own advantage may perhaps be consistent with my whole future welfare; but the question now is, Is it right? I change then the suggestion of self-love into a universal law, and state the question thus: How would it be if my maxim were a universal law? Then I see at once that it could never hold as a universal law of nature, but would necessarily contradict itself. For supposing it to be a universal law that everyone when he thinks himself in a difficulty should be able to promise whatever he pleases, with the purpose of not keeping his promise, the promise itself would become impossible, as well as the end that one might have in view in it, since no one would consider that anything was promised to him, but would ridicule all such statements as vain pretenses.

3. A third finds in himself a talent which with the help of some culture might make him a useful man in many respects. But he finds himself in comfortable circumstances and prefers to indulge in pleasure rather than to take pains in enlarging and improving his happy natural capacities. He asks, however, whether his maxim of neglect of his natural gifts, besides agreeing with his inclination to indulgence, agrees also with what is called duty. He sees then that a system of nature could indeed subsist with such a universal law, although men (like the South Sea islanders) should let their talents rest and resolve to

devote their lives merely to idleness, amusement, and propagation of their species—in a word, to enjoyment; but he cannot possibly *will* that this should be a universal law of nature, or be implanted in us as such by a natural instinct. For, as a rational being, he necessarily wills that his faculties be developed, since they serve him, and have been given him, for all sorts of possible purposes.

4. A fourth, who is in prosperity, while he sees that others have to contend with great wretchedness and that he could help them, thinks: What concern is it of mine? Let everyone be as happy as Heaven pleases, or as he can make himself; I will take nothing from him nor even envy him, only I do not wish to contribute anything to his welfare or to his assistance in distress! Now no doubt, if such a mode of thinking were a universal law, the human race might very well subsist, and doubtless even better than in a state in which everyone talks of sympathy and good-will, or even takes care occasionally to put it into practice, but, on the other side, also cheats when he can, betrays the rights of men, or otherwise violates them. But although it is possible that a universal law of nature might exist in accordance with that maxim, it is impossible to *will* that such a principle should have the universal validity of a law of nature. For a will which resolved this would contradict itself, inasmuch as many cases might occur in which one would have need of the love and sympathy of others, and in which, by such a law of nature, sprung from his own will, he would deprive himself of all hope of the aid he desires.

These are a few of the many actual duties, or at least what we regard as such, which obviously fall into two classes on the one principle that we have laid down. We must be *able to will* that a maxim of our action should be a universal law. This is the canon of the moral appreciation of the action generally. Some actions are of such a character that their maxim cannot without contradiction be even *conceived* as a universal law of nature, far from it being possible that we should *will* that it *should* be so. In others, this intrinsic impossibility is not found, but still it is impossible to *will* that their maxim should be raised to the universality of a law of nature, since such a will would contradict itself. It is easily seen that the former violate strict or rigorous (inflexible) duty; the latter only laxer (meritorious) duty. Thus it has been completely shown by these examples how all duties depend as regards the nature of the obligation (not the object of the action) on the same principle.

If now we attend to ourselves on occasion of any transgression of duty, we shall find that we in fact do not will that our maxim should be a universal law, for that is impossible for us; on the contrary, we will that the opposite should remain a universal law, only we assume the liberty of making an *exception* in our own favor or (just for this time only) in favor of our inclination. Consequently, if we considered all cases from one and the same point of view, namely, that of reason, we should find a contradiction in our own will, namely, that a certain principle should be objectively necessary as a universal law, and yet subjectively should not be universal, but admit of exceptions. As, however, we at one moment regard our action from the point of view of a will wholly conformed to reason, and then again look at the same action from the point of view of a will affected by inclination, there is not really any contradiction, but an antagonism of inclination to the precept of reason, whereby the universality of the principle is changed into a mere generality, so that the practical principle of reason shall meet the maxim half way. Now, although this cannot be justified in our own impartial judgment, yet it proves that we do really recognize the validity of the categorical imperative and (with all respect for it) only allow ourselves a few exceptions which we think unimportant and forced from us.

We have thus established at least this much—that if duty is a conception which is to have any import and real legislative authority for our actions, it can only be expressed in categorical, and not at all in hypothetical, imperatives. We have also, which is of great importance, exhibited clearly and definitely for every practical application the content of the categorical imperative, which must contain the principle of all duty if there is such a thing at all. We have not yet, however, advanced so far as to prove *a priori* that there actually is such an imperative, that there is a practical law which commands absolutely of itself and without any other impulse, and that the following of this law is duty.

With the view of attaining to this it is of extreme importance to remember that we must not allow ourselves to think of deducing the reality of this principle from the *particular attributes of human nature*. For duty is to be a practical, unconditional necessity of action; it must therefore hold for all rational beings (to whom an imperative can apply at all), and *for this reason only* be also a law for all human wills. On the contrary, whatever is deduced from the particular natural characteristics of humanity, from certain feelings and propensions, nay, even, if possible, from any particular tendency proper to human reason, and which need not necessarily hold for the will of every rational being—this may indeed supply us with a maxim but not with a law; with a subjective principle on which we may have a propension and inclination to act, but not with an objective principle on which we should be *enjoined* to act, even though all our propensions, inclinations, and natural dispositions were opposed to it. In fact, the sublimity and intrinsic dignity of the command in duty are so much the more evident, the less the subjective impulses favor it and the more they oppose it, without being able in the slightest degree to weaken the obligation of the law or to diminish its validity.

Here then we see philosophy brought to a critical position, since it has to be firmly fixed, notwithstanding that it has nothing to support it in heaven or earth. Here it must show its purity as absolute director of its own laws, not the herald of those which are whispered to it by an implanted sense or who knows what tutelary nature. Although these may be better than nothing, yet they can never afford principles dictated by reason, which must have their source wholly *a priori* and thence their commanding authority, expecting everything from the supremacy of the law and the due respect for it, nothing from inclination, or else condemning the man to self-contempt and inward abhorrence.

Thus every empirical element is not only quite incapable of being an aid to the principle of morality, but is even highly prejudicial to the purity of morals; for the proper and inestimable worth of an absolutely good will consists just in this that the principle of action is free from all influence of contingent grounds, which alone experience can furnish. We cannot too much or too often repeat our warning against this lax and even mean habit of thought which seeks for its principle among empirical motives and laws; for human reason in its weariness is glad to rest on this pillow, and in a dream of sweet illusions (in which, instead of Juno, it embraces a cloud) it substitutes for morality a bastard patched up from limbs of various derivation, which looks like anything one chooses to see in it; only not like virtue to one who has once beheld her in her true form.[2]

The question then is this: Is it a necessary law *for all rational beings* that they should always judge of their actions by maxims of which they can themselves will that they should serve as universal laws? If it is so, then it must be connected (altogether *a priori*) with the very conception of the will of a rational being generally. . . .

The will is conceived as a faculty of determining oneself to action *in accordance with the conception of certain laws*. And such a faculty can be found only in rational beings. Now that which serves the will as the objective ground of its self-determination is the *end*, and if this is assigned by reason alone, it must hold for all rational beings. On the other hand, that which merely contains the ground of possibility of the action of which the effect is the end, this is called the *means*. The subjective ground of the desire is the *spring*, the objective ground of the volition is the *motive;* hence the distinction between subjective ends which rest on springs, and objective ends which depend on motives valid for every rational being. Practical principles are *formal* when they abstract from all subjective ends; they are *material* when they assume these, and therefore particular, springs of action. The ends which a rational being proposes to himself at pleasure as *effects* of his actions (material ends) are all only relative, for it is only their relation to the particular desires of the subject that gives them their worth, which therefore cannot furnish principles universal and necessary for all rational beings and for every volition, that is to say, practical laws. Hence all these relative ends can give rise only to hypothetical imperatives.

Supposing, however, that there were something *whose existence* has *in itself* an absolute worth, something which, being *an end in itself*, could be a source of definite laws, then in this and this alone would lie the source of a possible categorical imperative, that is, a practical law.

Now I say: man and generally any rational being *exists* as an end in himself, *not merely as a means* to be arbitrarily used by this or that will, but in all his actions, whether they concern himself or other rational beings, must be always regarded at the same time as an end. All objects of the inclinations have only a conditional worth; for if the inclinations and the wants founded on them did not exist, then their object would be without value. But the inclinations them-

---

[2] To behold virtue in her proper form is nothing else but to contemplate morality stripped of all admixture of sensible things and of every spurious ornament of reward or self-love. How much she then eclipses everything else that appears charming to the affections, every one may readily perceive with the least exertion of his reason, if it be not wholly spoiled for abstraction.

selves, being sources of want, are so far from having an absolute worth for which they should be desired that, on the contrary, it must be the universal wish of every rational being to be wholly free from them. Thus the worth of any object which is *to be acquired* by our action is always conditional. Beings whose existence depends not on our will but on nature's, have nevertheless, if they are irrational beings, only a relative value as means, and are therefore called *things;* rational beings, on the contrary, are called *persons*, because their very nature points them out as ends in themselves, that is, as something which must not be used merely as means, and so far therefore restricts freedom of action (and is an object of respect). These, therefore, are not merely subjective ends whose existence has a worth *for us* as an effect of our action, but *objective ends*, that is, things whose existence is an end in itself—an end, moreover, for which no other can be substituted, which they should subserve *merely* as means, for otherwise nothing whatever would possess *absolute worth;* but if all worth were conditioned and therefore contingent, then there would be no supreme practical principle of reason whatever.

If then there is a supreme practical principle or, in respect of the human will, a categorical imperative, it must be one which, being drawn from the conception of that which is necessarily an end for everyone because it is *an end in itself*, constitutes an *objective* principle of will, and can therefore serve as a universal practical law. The foundation of this principle is: *rational nature exists as an end in itself.* Man necessarily conceives his own existence as being so; so far then this is a *subjective* principle of human actions. But every other rational being regards its existence similarly, just on the same rational principle that holds for me; so that it is at the same time an objective principle from which as a supreme practical law all laws of the will must be capable of being deduced. Accordingly the practical imperative will be as follows: *So act as to treat humanity, whether in thine own person or in that of any other, in every case as an end withal, never as means only.* We will now inquire whether this can be practically carried out.

To abide by the previous examples:

First, under the head of necessary duty to oneself: He who contemplates suicide should ask himself whether his action can be consistent with the idea of humanity *as an end in itself*. If he destroys himself in order to escape from painful circumstances, he uses a person merely as *a mean* to maintain a tolerable condition up to the end of life. But a man is not a thing, that is to say, something which can be used merely as means, but must in all his actions be always considered as an end in himself. I cannot, therefore, dispose in any way of a man in my own person so as to mutilate him, to damage or kill him. (It belongs to ethics proper to define this principle more precisely, so as to avoid all misunderstanding, for example, as to the amputation of the limbs in order to preserve myself; as to exposing my life to danger with a view to preserve it, etc. This question is therefore omitted here.)

Secondly, as regards necessary duties, or those of strict obligation, towards others: He who is thinking of making a lying promise to others will see at once that he would be using another man *merely as a mean*, without the latter containing at the same time the end in himself. For he whom I propose by such a promise to use for my own purposes cannot possibly assent to my mode of acting towards him, and therefore cannot himself contain the end of this action. This violation of the principle of humanity in other men is more obvious if we take in examples of attacks on the freedom and property of others. For then it is clear that he who transgresses the rights of men intends to use the person of others merely as means, without considering that as rational beings they ought always to be esteemed also as ends, that is, as beings who must be capable of containing in themselves the end of the very same action.

Thirdly, as regards contingent (meritorious) duties to oneself: It is not enough that the action does not violate humanity in our own person as an end in itself, it must also *harmonize with it*. Now there are in humanity capacities of greater perfection which belong to the end that nature has in view in regard to humanity in ourselves as the subject; to neglect these might perhaps be consistent with the *maintenance* of humanity as an end in itself, but not with the *advancement* of this end.

Fourthly, as regards meritorious duties towards others: The natural end which all men have is their own happiness. Now humanity might indeed subsist although no one should contribute anything to the happiness of others, provided he did not intentionally withdraw anything from it; but after all, this would only harmonize negatively, not positively, with *humanity as an end in itself*, if everyone does not also endeavor, as far as in him lies, to forward the ends of others. For the ends of any subject which is an end in himself ought as far as possible to be *my* ends also, if that conception is to have its *full* effect with me.

This principle that humanity and generally every rational nature is *an end in itself* (which is the supreme limiting condition of every man's freedom of action), is not borrowed from experience, *first*, because it is universal, applying as it does to all rational beings whatever, and experience is not capable of determining anything about them; *secondly*, because it does not present humanity as an end to men (subjectively), that is, as an object which men do of themselves actually adopt as an end; but as an objective end which must as a law constitute the supreme limiting condition of all our subjective ends, let them be what we will; it must therefore spring from pure reason. In fact the objective principle of all practical legislation lies (according to the first principle) in *the rule* and its form of universality which makes it capable of being a law (say, for example, a law of nature); but the *subjective* principle is in the *end*; now by the second principle, the subject of all ends is each rational being inasmuch as it is an end in itself. Hence follows the third practical principle of the will, which is the ultimate condition of its harmony with the universal practical reason, viz., the idea of *the will of every rational being as a universally legislative will*.

On this principle all maxims are rejected which are inconsistent with the will being itself universal legislator. Thus the will is not subject to the law, but so subject that it must be regarded *as itself giving the law*, and on this ground only subject to the law (of which it can regard itself as the author).

In the previous imperatives, namely, that based on the conception of the conformity of actions to general laws, as in a *physical system of nature*, and that based on the universal *prerogative* of rational beings as *ends* in themselves— these imperatives just because they were conceived as categorical excluded from any share in their authority all admixture of any interest as a spring of action; they were, however, only *assumed* to be categorical, because such an assumption was necessary to explain the conception of duty. But we could not prove independently that there are practical propositions which command categorically, nor can it be proved in this section; one thing, however, could be done, namely, to indicate in the imperative itself, by some determinate expression, that in the case of volition from duty all interest is renounced, which is the specific criterion of categorical as distinguished from hypothetical imperatives. This is done in the present (third) formula of the principle, namely, in the idea of the will of every rational being as a *universally legislating will*.

For although a will *which is subject to laws* may be attached to this law by means of an interest, yet a will which is itself a supreme lawgiver, so far as it is such, cannot possibly depend on any interest, since a will so dependent would itself still need another law restricting the interest of its self-love by the condition that it should be valid as universal law.

Thus the *principle* that every human will is *a will which in all its maxims gives universal laws*,[3] provided it be otherwise justified, would be very *well adapted* to be the categorical imperative, in this respect, namely, that just because of the idea of universal legislation it is *not based on any interest*, and therefore it alone among all possible imperatives can be *unconditional*. Or still better, converting the proposition, if there is a categorical imperative (that is, a law for the will of every rational being), it can only command that everything be done from maxims of one's will regarded as a will which could at the same time will that it should itself give universal laws, for in that case only the practical principle and the imperative which it obeys are unconditional, since they cannot be based on any interest.

Looking back now on all previous attempts to discover the principle of morality, we need not wonder why they all failed. It was seen that man was bound to laws by duty, but it was not observed that the laws to which he is subject are *only those of his own giving*, though at the same time they are *universal*, and that he is only bound to act in conformity with his own will—a will, however, which is designed by nature to give universal laws. For when one has conceived man only as subject to a law (no matter what), then this law required some interest, either by way of attraction or constraint, since it did not originate as a law from *his own will*, but this will was according to a law obliged by *something else* to act in a certain manner. Now by this necessary consequence all the labor spent in finding a supreme principle of *duty* was

---

[3] I may be excused from adducing examples to elucidate this principle, as those which have already been used to elucidate the categorical imperative and its formula would all serve for the like purpose here.

irrevocably lost. For men never elicited duty, but only a necessity of acting from a certain interest. Whether this interest was private or otherwise, in any case the imperative must be conditional, and could not by any means be capable of being a moral command. I will therefore call this the principle of *Autonomy* of the will, in contrast with every other which I accordingly reckon as *Heteronomy*.

The conception of every rational being as one which must consider itself as giving in all the maxims of its will universal laws, so as to judge itself and its actions from this point of view—this conception leads to another which depends on it and is very fruitful, namely, that of a *kingdom of ends*.

By a "kingdom" I understand the union of different rational beings in a system by common laws. Now since it is by laws that ends are determined as regards their universal validity, hence, if we abstract from the personal differences of rational beings, and likewise from all the content of their private ends, we shall be able to conceive all ends combined in a systematic whole (including both rational beings as ends in themselves, and also the special ends which each may propose to himself), that is to say, we can conceive a kingdom of ends, which on the preceding principles is possible.

For all rational beings come under the *law* that each of them must treat itself and all others *never merely as means*, but in every case *at the same time as ends in themselves*. Hence results a systematic union of rational beings by common objective laws, that is, a kingdom which may be called a kingdom of ends, since what these laws have in view is just the relation of these beings to one another as ends and means. It is certainly only an ideal.

A rational being belongs as a *member* to the kingdom of ends when, although giving universal laws in it, he is also himself subject to these laws. He belongs to it *as sovereign* when, while giving laws, he is not subject to the will of any other.

A rational being must always regard himself as giving laws either as member or as sovereign in a kingdom of ends which is rendered possible by the freedom of will. He cannot, however, maintain the latter position merely by the maxims of his will, but only in case he is a completely independent being without wants and with unrestricted power adequate to his will.

Morality consists then in the reference of all action to the legislation which alone can render a kingdom of ends possible. This legislation must be capable of existing in every rational being, and of emanating from his will, so that the principle of this will is never to act on any maxim which could not without contradiction be also a universal law, and accordingly always so to act *that the will could at the same time regard itself as giving in its maxims universal laws.* If now the maxims of rational beings are not by their own nature coincident with this objective principle, then the necessity of acting on it is called practical necessitation that is, *duty*. Duty does not apply to the sovereign in the kingdom of ends, but it does to every member of it and to all in the same degree.

The practical necessity of acting on this principle, that is, duty, does not rest at all on feelings, impulses, or inclinations, but solely on the relation of rational beings to one another, a relation in which the will of a rational being must always be regarded as *legislative*, since otherwise it could not be conceived as *an end in itself*. Reason then refers every maxim of the will, regarding it as legislating universally, to every other will and also to every action towards oneself; and this not on account of any other practical motive or any future advantage, but from the idea of the *dignity* of a rational being, obeying no law but that which he himself also gives.

In the kingdom of ends everything has either *value* or *dignity*. Whatever has a value can be replaced by something else which is *equivalent;* whatever, on the other hand, is above all value, and therefore admits of no equivalent, has a dignity.

Whatever has reference to the general inclinations and wants of mankind has a *market value;* whatever, without presupposing a want, corresponds to a certain taste, that is, to a satisfaction in the mere purposeless play of our faculties, has a *fancy value;* but that which constitutes the condition under which alone anything can be an end in itself, this has not merely a relative worth, that is, value, but an intrinsic worth, that is, *dignity*.

Now morality is the condition under which alone a rational being can be an end in himself, since by this alone it is possible that he should be a legislating member in the kingdom of ends. Thus morality, and humanity as capable of it, is that which alone has dignity. Skill and diligence in labor have a market value; wit, lively imagination, and humor have fancy value; on the other hand, fidelity to promises, benevolence from principle (not from instinct), have an intrinsic worth. Neither nature nor art contains anything which in default of these it could put in their place, for their worth consists not in the effects which spring from them, not in the use and advantage which they secure, but in the disposition of mind, that is, the maxims of the will which are ready to manifest themselves in such actions, even though they should not have the desired effect. These actions also need no recommendation from any subjective taste or sentiment, that they may be looked on with immediate favor and satisfaction; they need no immediate propension or feeling for them; they exhibit the will that performs them as an object of an immediate respect, and nothing but reason is required to *impose* them on the will; not to *flatter* it into them, which, in the case of duties, would be a contradiction. This estimation therefore shows that the worth of such a disposition is dignity, and places it infinitely above all value, with which it cannot for a moment be brought into comparison or competition without as it were violating its sanctity.

What then is it which justifies virtue or the morally good disposition, in making such lofty claims? It is nothing less than the privilege it secures to the rational being of participating in the giving of universal laws, by which it qualifies him to be a member of a possible kingdom of ends, a privilege to which he was already destined by his own nature as being an end in himself, and on that account legislating in the kingdom of ends; free as regards all laws of physical nature, and obeying those only which he himself gives, and by which his maxims can belong to a system of universal law to which at the same time he submits himself. For nothing has any worth except what the law assigns it. Now the legislation itself which assigns the worth of everything must for that very reason possess dignity, that is, an unconditional incomparable worth; and the word *respect* alone supplies a becoming expression for the esteem which a rational being must have for it. *Autonomy* then is the basis of the dignity of human and of every rational nature. . . .

The Autonomy of the Will as the Supreme Principle of Morality

Autonomy of the will is that property of it by which it is a law to itself (independently of any property of the objects of volition). The principle of autonomy then is: Always so to choose that the same volition shall comprehend the maxims of our choice as a universal law. . . . That the principle of autonomy in question is the sole principle of morals can be readily shown by mere analysis of the conceptions of morality. For by this analysis we find that its principle must be a categorical imperative, and that what this commands is neither more nor less than this very autonomy.

Heteronomy of the Will as the Source of All Spurious Principles of Morality

If the will seeks the law which is to determine it *anywhere else* than in the fitness of its maxims to be universal laws of its own dictation, consequently if it goes out of itself and seeks this law in the character of any of its objects, there always results *heteronomy*. The will in that case does not give itself the law, but it is given by the object through its relation to the will. This relation, whether it rests on inclination or on conceptions of reason, only admits of hypothetical imperatives: I ought to do something *because I wish for something else*. On the contrary, the moral, and therefore categorical, imperative says: I ought to do so and so, even though I should not wish for anything else. For example, the former says: I ought not to lie if I would retain my reputation; the latter says: I ought not to lie although it should not bring me the least discredit. The latter therefore must so far abstract from all objects that they shall have no *influence* on the will, in order that practical reason (will) may not be restricted to administering an interest not belonging to it, but may simply show its own commanding authority as the supreme legislation. Thus, for example, I ought to endeavour to promote the happiness of others, not as if its realization involved any concern of mine (whether by immediate inclination or by any satisfaction indirectly gained through reason), but simply because a maxim which excludes it cannot be comprehended as a universal law in one and the same volition.

Classification Of All Principles of Morality Which Can Be Founded on the Conception of Heteronomy

Here as elsewhere human reason in its pure use, so long as it was not critically examined, has first tried all possible wrong ways before it succeeded in finding the one true way.

All principles which can be taken from this point of view are either *empirical* or *rational*. The *former*, drawn from the principle of *happiness*, are built on physical or moral feelings; the *latter*, drawn from the principle of *perfection*, are built either on the rational conception of perfection as a possible effect, or on that of an independent perfection (the will of God) as the determining cause of our will.

Empirical principles are wholly incapable of serving as a foundation for moral laws. For the universality with which these should hold for all rational beings without distinction, the unconditional practical necessity which is thereby imposed on them is lost when their foundation is taken from the *particular constitution of human nature* or the accidental circumstances in which it is placed. The principle of *private happiness*, however, is the most objectionable, not merely because it is false, and experience contradicts the supposition that prosperity is always proportioned to good conduct, nor yet merely because it contributes nothing to the establishment of morality—since it is quite a different thing to make a prosperous man and a good man, or to make one prudent and sharp-sighted for his own interests, and to make him virtuous—but because the springs it provides for morality are such as rather undermine it and destroy its sublimity, since they put the motives to virtue and to vice in the same class, and only teach us to make a better calculation, the specific difference between virtue and vice being entirely extinguished. On the other hand, as to moral feeling, this supposed special sense, the appeal to it is indeed superficial when those who cannot *think* believe that *feeling* will help them out, even in what concerns general laws; and besides, feelings which naturally differ infinitely in degree cannot furnish a uniform standard of good and evil, nor has anyone a right to form judgments for others by his own feelings; nevertheless this moral feeling is nearer to morality and its dignity in this respect that it pays virtue the honor of ascribing to her *immediately* the satisfaction and esteem we have for her, and does not, as it were, tell her to her face that we are not attached to her by her beauty but by profit.

Among the *rational* principles of morality, the ontological conception of *perfection*, notwithstanding its defects, is better than the theological conception which derives morality from a Divine absolutely perfect will. The former is, no doubt, empty and indefinite, and consequently useless for finding in the boundless field of possible reality the greatest amount suitable for us; moreover, in attempting to distinguish specifically the reality of which we are now speaking from every other, it inevitably tends to turn in a circle and cannot avoid tacitly presupposing the morality which it is to explain; it is nevertheless preferable to the theological view, first, because we have no intuition of the Divine perfection, and can only deduce it from our own conceptions the most important of which is that of morality, and our explanation would thus be involved in a gross circle; and, in the next place, if we avoid this, the only notion of the Divine will remaining to us is a conception made up of the attributes of desire of glory and dominion, combined with the awful conceptions of might and vengeance, and any system of morals erected on this foundation would be directly opposed to morality.

However, if I had to choose between the notion of the moral sense and that of perfection in general (two systems which at least do not weaken morality, although they are totally incapable of serving as its foundation), then I should decide for the latter, because it at least withdraws the decision of the question from the sensibility and brings it to the court of pure reason; and although even here it decides nothing, it at all events preserves the indefinite idea (of a will good in itself) free from corruption, until it shall be more precisely defined.

For the rest I think I may be excused here from a detailed refutation of all these doctrines; that would only be superfluous labor, since it is so easy, and is probably so well seen even by those whose office requires them to decide for one of those theories (because their hearers would not tolerate suspension of judgment). But what interests us more here is to know that the prime foundation of morality laid down by all these principles is nothing but heteronomy of the will, and for this reason they must necessarily miss their aim.

In every case where an object of the will has to be supposed, in order that the rule may be prescribed which is to determine the will, there the rule is simply heteronomy; the imperative is conditional, namely, *if* or *because* one wishes for this object, one should act so and so; hence it can never command morally, that is, categorically. Whether the object determines the will by means of inclination, as in the principle of private happiness, or by means of reason directed to objects of our possible volition generally, as in the principle of perfection, in either case the will never determines itself *immediately* by the conception of the action, but only by the influence which the foreseen effect of the action has on the will; *I ought to do something, on this account, because I wish for something else;* and here there must be yet another law assumed in me as its subject, by which I necessarily will this other thing, and this law again requires an imperative to restrict this maxim. For the influence which the conception of an object within the reach of our faculties can exercise on the will of the subject in consequence of its natural properties, depends on the nature of the subject, either the sensibility (inclination and taste) or the understanding and reason, the employment of which is by the peculiar constitution of their nature attended with satisfaction. It follows that the law would be, properly speaking, given by nature, and as such it must be known and proved by experience, and would consequently be contingent, and therefore incapable of being an apodictic practical rule, such as the moral rule must be. Not only so, but it is *inevitably only heteronomy;* the will does not give itself the law, but it is given by a foreign impulse by means of a particular natural constitution of the subject adapted to receive it. An absolutely good will, then, the principle of which must be a categorical imperative, will be indeterminate as regards all objects, and will contain merely the *form of volition* generally, and that as autonomy, that is to say, the capability of the maxims of every good will to make themselves a universal law, is itself the only law which the will of every rational being imposes on itself, without needing to assume any spring or interest as a foundation.

19

Critique of Kant

G. C. FIELD

In criticisms of Kant's ethical theory in text-books of Philosophy and else-where, we often find the chief emphasis laid on the supposed practical con-sequences of Kant's view, which are represented as being obviously at variance with our ordinary moral ideas, and in some cases amounting almost to a *reductio ad absurdum* of his whole theory.

It is argued, for instance, that none of these so-called moral rules can really be universalized in practice. The rule, Thou shalt not lie, for instance, leads to the conclusion that if a man pursued by murderers could be saved by a timely lie, it would nevertheless be wrong for us to tell this lie, and that it would be our duty to help the murderers to commit the crime by telling them which way their victim had gone. Kant, indeed, seems ready to accept this conclusion. But almost everyone would feel that a conclusion like this violates our strongest moral feelings, and that a view which really led to this conclusion would have to be abandoned. Or again, "Thou shalt not kill," if universalized, would forbid war, capital punishment, and even legitimate self-defence or defence of other people. And, though there are people who have gone to these lengths, it is certain that the moral sense of the majority of mankind is against them. We should say that "Thou shalt not kill," is a sound rule, in general, but that there are cir-cumstances in which we may or must break it. If we modify the rule and say, "Thou shalt not kill, except under certain circumstances," to make it a universal and at the same time a practical rule we should have to mention all the circum-stances in the formula. And if we try we shall find this absolutely impossible. Thus if we say that one may kill in defence of the life of another, we find that this would not apply if the other was a murderer we were defending from justice. If we say that one may kill in defence of the life of another who ought not to be killed, then of course we have said nothing. We have only raised the question again when or under what circumstances ought or ought not a man to be killed, which is just the question we are asking.

We can strengthen this line of argument by finding cases of actions which would be universally recognized as good and yet which could not possibly be universalized, where the attempt to universalize them would lead to as great logical absurdities as universal lying. Take the question of self-sacrifice, for instance. The universal moral sentiment of mankind recognizes self-sacrifice

FROM *Moral Theory* by G. C. Field. Copyright 1932 by Methuen & Co., Ltd., London. First published 1921.

as a great good. Yet the attempt to universalize it would be absolutely self-contradictory. For self-sacrifice, giving up what we want ourselves to other people, involves for it to be possible the existence of other people who accept the sacrifice. But if every-one is sacrificing himself, there will be no one to accept the sacrifice, and self-sacrifice itself becomes impossible.

The same question, really, comes up from a different point of view when we find two principles of action, both apparently right, clashing with each other. We have the rule forbidding the telling of lies. And we have another rule bidding us preserve innocent human life by every means in our power. Both these would be recognized as wholly laudable principles of action. But, as we have seen, in the case of the man escaping from murderers they come into conflict. If we ask how we are to decide between them, all we can say is that it depends on the circumstances of the particular case. But with that we have already abandoned Kant's principle. We recognize that it is impossible to have any general rule, absolutely universal and admitting of no exceptions. We cannot lay down beforehand a general formula which can be applied ready-made to each particular case. We have to examine each particular case on its merits, because we never can be sure beforehand that its special circumstances will not be of importance.

We shall probably be ready to accept all that is said in criticism of this kind as quite true. And, if it is true, as against Kant's exposition of his system it is perfectly conclusive, so far as it goes. There can be no doubt that he really thought that he had got hold of a principle of supreme importance for practice, which would really enable us to decide in actual cases what we ought or ought not to do. And equally without doubt is it, if there is anything in the above criticisms, that he had not in fact found such a principle. We cannot apply his test, as he thought we could, to all practical cases. But, in spite of all this, it still remains open to question whether these objections are fatal to the Kantian system as a whole. They are fatal to the practical conclusions that Kant draws from the central and fundamental points of his system. But it remains to be seen whether it was really necessary to draw these conclusions. It is still possible that we may be able to abandon these conclusions, against which we have found such decisive objections, and yet still retain these central and fundamental points.

If we wished to essay this kind of salvage work, we should probably argue something in these terms:—Let us admit, we should say, that we cannot get a definition or account of the good which we can use as an absolute criterion to decide in each particular case what is right or not. But that is not to admit that Kant's general account of what constitutes good or right is false: it merely shows that we cannot use his definition in the way he thought that we could. Still less is it to say that no general account of the nature of goodness or rightness is possible. But it does say that any general account of the good that we get will have to be *ex post facto*. That is to say, after we have decided that a particular action or kind of action is good or right, we can look for and discover in it what it was that made it good or right.

This procedure may be illustrated from other subjects of philosophical investigation. Thus the general account of the nature of causation, which Philosophy tries to arrive at, would not help us to decide in any particular case what was the cause of what. It would only enable us to say what the general nature of the connexion was, which we had already discovered to exist between certain things. Or again, we might arrive at a definition of truth, we might come to the conclusion that it was the agreement of two ideas or the agreement of an idea with reality or any other of the definitions which different schools of philosophers have mentioned. But whatever definition we adopt, it will be derived from an examination of instances of propositions which are true. And it will not enable us to tell whether any proposition is true or false. At the most, it tells us the exact meaning of the question we are asking when we ask whether any particular proposition is true or false.

Now this distinction was perfectly familiar to Kant, who was probably, indeed, the first person who really grasped it. But he does not seem to have applied it, as we might have expected him to do, to his moral theory. But if we apply it, as he ought to have done, we shall no longer ask or expect that our account of the nature of good should give us a practical criterion which would decide at once whether any particular action was right or wrong. The most we can expect of it is that it should help us to get clear in our own minds about the real nature of the question we ought to ask in particular moral cases.

This it does do when it tells us that the essence of the rightness of an action is its universality. But here we come up against the objection already given that this is impossible, because there is really no such thing as universality in moral precepts. As we saw, all so-called rules of right conduct have exceptions in certain cases, and each case has to be considered on its merits. For the possibility of a universal rule applying to more actions than one, depends upon these different actions being of the same kind. And, of course, as a matter of fact no action is exactly the same as any other in all its circumstances, and we can never say beforehand that its special circumstances are irrelevant to its moral worth. So that really we should need a special rule for each action.

"Well," the reply to this objection would be, "and why not?" For, it would be urged, this argument really rests on a confusion about the meaning of universality. It would apply equally, for instance, against the Law of the Uniformity of Nature. We express this law by saying that the same causes always produce the same effects. But of course we know all the time really that there never is exactly the same cause or the same effect repeated: exactly the same event or series of events never does and never can occur twice over. But that does not invalidate the law, if we understand it rightly. For universality does not necessarily involve there being actually more than one case of a particular law. Perhaps there would be less danger of confusion if, for the misleading word "universality," we substituted a word such as "necessity," which is really a better expression of the same idea. We should then say that the Law of the Uniformity of Nature means that the cause is necessarily connected with the effect. And in a moral question we should say that this action is necessarily right, that it necessarily follows from all these circumstances that the action should be done; We may say, if we like, that if *per impossibile* we could get exactly the same circumstances over again, exactly the same action would have to be done. The fact that exactly the same circumstances cannot really be repeated does not make this an empty phrase. We can surely attach some meaning to the question, Supposing that anyone else were in exactly the same circumstances, should we will him to act in this way? even though, as a matter of fact, no one else is or ever could be in exactly the same circumstances. In fact, this is really the right question to ask, the right attitude in which to approach particular moral problems. And so universality or necessity can be maintained to be the essence of rightness or goodness, even though it does not give us the infallible practical guidance that Kant expected from it.

Besides this we have a contribution of more practical value in the second maxim which bids us always treat humanity, whether in oneself or in others, as an end not as a means. The wrongness of treating any human being as a means is deduced, of course, from the first maxim. It is wrong, because we do not will that anyone else should treat all other people, including ourselves, merely as a means. But this rule is really of more practical value than the first maxim and in some cases can be applied as a practical test. Not that it is always a sufficient guide by itself, because there might be cases where there was an honest difference of opinion whether a particular course of action did involve treating any human beings merely as a means or not. And we may allow, in general, that Kant does not help much to resolve honest doubts and difference of opinion. But he shows us the right questions to ask, and he prevents us, if we follow him, from allowing our own wishes to blind us to what is right.

We may sum up, then, by saying that although we cannot apply his tests in practice with the certainty that he claimed for them, yet there is no reason why we should not accept them as really a correct account of what right action consists in.

So far the case for the defence. And as against the criticisms previously advanced, it seems sound enough. It preserves the essence of the doctrine, while recognizing that we must drop certain applications of it which were originally made. But we must not think that with this the whole case against Kant's ethical theory falls to the ground. There are far more serious and fundamental objections to his view, which we must now consider.

We shall find that the previous objection, even though we do not think it holds good by itself, will suggest to us the lines on which a much more serious attack may be launched. For it is, after all, by a consideration of its practical consequences that we begin to find the view unsatisfactory.

Probably we should all feel that no one would be really satisfied by being told that good or right merely meant necessary or capable of universal application or any other term of this kind. Of course, a vague feeling like that would not by itself be decisive against the view, though it might raise a doubt whether the view was really derived so directly from our universally received notions of morality as was claimed. But, apart from what has been already discussed, we shall find on further consideration some practical consequences of the view which will certainly give us pause before accepting it. We must remember that, according to Kant, this is the essential nature of the good, and not merely one of its qualities. It is what goodness means. And, if that is so, we may invert the proposition, All good or right actions can be universalized, into, Anything that can be universalized is good or right. And the consequences of that are much more serious than those mentioned in the previous objections. In fact, they are such as we could hardly accept. Truth-telling, for instance, certainly can be universalized as a practical law. And yet we have seen extreme cases where, according to our ordinary moral ideas, it is not right to tell the truth.

The point will become even clearer if we consider the very significant passage in which Kant discusses the practical application of his own maxims. "A third finds in himself a talent which with the help of some culture might make him a useful man in many respects. But he finds himself in comfortable circumstances, and prefers to indulge in pleasure rather than to take pains in enlarging and improving his happy natural capacities. He asks, however, whether his maxim of neglect of his natural gifts, besides agreeing with his inclination to indulgence, agrees also with what is called duty. He sees then that a system of nature could indeed subsist with such a universal law although men (like the South Sea islanders) should let their talents rust, and resolve to devote their lives merely to idleness, amusement, and propagation of their species—in a word to enjoyment; but he cannot possibly *will* that this should be a universal law of nature, or be implanted in us as such by a natural instinct. For, as a rational being, he necessarily wills that his faculties be developed, since they serve him, and have been given him, for all sorts of possible purposes."

Even more striking, perhaps, is his next imaginary case, of the man who declares that he will not help others who are in misfortune, even when it is in his power. Of course, as Kant sees, it would be a quite possible universal law that none should help others in misfortune. "But," he asserts, "although it is possible that a universal law of nature might exist in accordance with that maxim, it is impossible to *will* that such a principle should have the universal validity of a law of nature. For a will which resolved this would contradict itself, inasmuch as many cases might occur in which one would have need of the love and sympathy of others, and in which, by such a law of nature, sprung from his own will, he would deprive himself of all hope of the aid he desires." But supposing that the man replied to this, "I accept these consequences, and I am perfectly willing, in fact I should prefer that none should help me when I am in misfortune, so long as it is understood that I need not help them when they are." There is no impossibility, no self-contradiction in this position. What is Kant going to reply?

The fact of the matter is that these passages really give away the whole case. We have here a maxim or principle of action which could be perfectly well made into a universal law, but which as a matter of fact we do not will to be universally observed. If we ask why we do not so will it, the only possible answer is that we do not will it, because it is not right. And as we have seen that such a law could quite easily be universally applied, the inevitable conclusion is that being right means something other and more than being capable of universal application. In the last instance, indeed, Kant by a woeful departure from his principles expressly gives as the reason the fact that the results would be unpleasant to us, thus, in spite of all he has said, putting the reason for our not willing the action in our feelings, in this particular case, in our desire for a certain state of society. But even without this, the case is clear enough. We find that on his own showing, we may think an action not to be right even though it could be universally applied. So that the essence of rightness does not lie in universality, but in something else, whatever it may be. It may be true that we should will to make any right maxim universal. But we should universalize it because it was right, not think it right because it could be universalized.

The point may be emphasized further. Kant says that as rational beings we *could* not will such a course of action to be universal. But why not? As rational beings, we are only concerned with the bare form of universality. Our only reason for not making any rule universal would be that it could not be done, that it would contradict itself. And in these cases the rule would not contradict itself at all. Or we may meet Kant on his own ground and ask how he knows that a rational being could not will such an action to be universal. It certainly does not follow from the conception of a rational being. A rational being simply *qua* rational can will anything so long as it is possible to do so consistently, so long as it does not contradict itself. In this case there is no contradiction. And if in spite of this we do not will it or think it right, the reason must lie in something else not in the nature of reason as such nor in the bare form of universality. Defenders of Kant, such as the translator of the work under discussion, Dr. T. K. Abbott, who argues that he only meant to give a negative test,[1] really concede the whole point at issue. For if we have only got a negative test, we cannot have discovered the essential nature and the real meaning of goodness. At best we have only discovered one of its symptoms, some fact about it which follows from its essential nature. But what we set out to look for has not been discovered, and the whole search has to begin over again.

Kant, then, has not succeeded in the task he set himself. He thought that the nature of goodness or rightness could be derived from the conception of a rational being. If, as we have seen to be the case, his attempt thus to derive it was unsuccessful, the reason must be sought in one or both of two possible directions. On the one hand, it may be that he had not really understood what was involved in the nature of a rational being. On the other, he may have been mistaken in thinking that it was connected in this way with the conception of goodness or rightness. It would be well, perhaps, if we want to see which alternative to accept, to examine the conception of rational being a little more closely.

A rational being, of course, is a being endowed with reason. But what is reason? Whatever else it is, it is in the first place a cognitive faculty of the conscious being, it is something in us which enables us to know something

---

[1] As a matter of fact, of course, we have seen that his principle gives us no practical test at all, not even a negative one.

We shall probably best distinguish it from other cognitive faculties by the kind of object that we know by it. Kant would say, for instance, that reason was that which enabled us to know universal and necessary truths. But however we distinguish it, the important point is that it is a form of knowing. As applied to actions, it tells us facts about the actions, it tells us the kind of action each one is. And we are here face to face with the crucial question, "Can reason be practical?" Or, in other words, "Can a knowledge of the nature of an action by itself move us to take that action?" Kant thought that it could: it is essential to his whole position. And if he is wrong in this, we have discovered the fundamental fallacy of his theory.

Let us try to realize the point of view of those who would hold that on this fundamental point Kant was wrong. We may, to begin with, set against Kant's view the dictum of Aristotle, The intellect by itself moves nothing, has no motive force. Or, in other words the mere knowing that an action, or anything else, is of such-and-such a kind cannot possibly move us to act.

The point is of such vital importance that we must elaborate this point of view a little further. In the elementary stages of reflection, it might seem to us that this was obviously at variance with certain observable facts. We say that the would-be criminal knows that if he commits a murder, he will be hanged. This knowledge is enough to make him refrain from doing so, however much he may want to. I know, when I am ill, that a certain medicine will make me well, and therefore I take it, however unpleasant it may be. Here we have cases of knowledge moving us to action. The argument is really a very superficial one, and only worth mentioning because it helps to illustrate and emphasize the view against which it is directed. For the point is, of course, that it is not the mere knowledge that moves us to action at all. If the criminal did not mind being hanged, if I am absolutely indifferent whether I get well or not, then the knowledge would have no effect on our action one way or another. The reason why the knowledge moves us to action is that it is the knowledge that that particular kind of action will have an effect that we want or desire. But the bare knowledge that a particular action is of a certain kind or will have a certain effect has no influence on us unless we have an interest in that effect or that kind of action, unless, that is, we have some feeling towards it. In short, action of any kind will not take place without the presence of a desire or some element of feeling or emotion. So that if we were pure reason without any desire or feelings, we should not, as Kant thought, act in a particular way, but we should simply not act at all.[2]

If this is true, Kant's fallacy lies in thinking that just the bare knowledge that an action is of a certain kind is sufficient to move us to do that action. Why that may sound plausible, at first hearing, is that when we speak of the kind of

---

[2] We might express this in Kantian terms by saying that the reason cannot be free in his sense. If our reason acts, it acts according to certain laws of its own nature, no doubt. But to start it acting it needs an efficient cause, just as much as natural objects do, in this case, some form of desire or feeling. So far therefore, is reason from supplying a possible motive for action, that it cannot itself act without a previous desire or feeling to set it in motion.

action we are apt to include in the meaning of that phrase the effect the action has on us: thus, for instance, we may speak of pleasant and unpleasant actions as being different kinds of actions, though the difference lies not necessarily at all in the actions themselves but simply in the effect they have on us. But Kant, of course, is careful to avoid this confusion. When he speaks of the kind of action, he means simply what the action is in itself, apart from its effects on us or any relation to our feelings.

In the light of this, we can get a clearer view of the place of reason in action and the real meaning of reasonable action. Practical reason will mean for us what it meant for Aristotle, who first used the phrase: that is, the ability to discover what will be the best means to an end which we want to attain. The essence of unreasonable action will lie in doing something which will defeat our own ends: for instance, in doing something in obedience to an immediate desire which will hinder the attainment of something else which we really want more. Practical reason will really be the capacity of finding means to ends.

We can apply the same consideration to the meaning of the term "ends." In that connexion we may recall the passage where Kant argues that all rational beings must be ends in themselves, because each one regards himself as an end. And as they are all rational beings, what holds of one must hold of the others. So that they must all be ends in themselves. However ready we may be to accept the valuable practical consequences that Kant draws from the principle we should probably all feel that the argument as it stands is singularly unconvincing. And, in the light of the above consideration, we begin to see the reason for that. For it becomes clearer that the argument really rests on a confusion about the sort of fact that being an end really is. Being an end is not, in our ordinary use of the term, a fact about things like being a human being or being green or being a triangle, a fact about the thing itself, a fact which belongs to the thing in its own right. Being an end is not really a fact about the thing at all. My end in ordinary speech means my object or purpose, what I am aiming at or trying to get at or want or desire. It is made an end by being wanted, and if I cease to want it it ceases to be my end. If no one wants it any longer, it ceases to be an end at all. That is, there is strictly no such thing as an end in itself unless we are going to attach an entirely new meaning to the word. Being an end implies some relation to the desires or purposes of some conscious being: and a thing is made an end by this relation. It follows, then, that nothing can be just an end: it could only be an end for someone, the purpose or desire of some conscious being. And there would, of course, be nothing self-contradictory in the view that each conscious being might have a different end, or that the same thing might be an end for one being and not for another.

The same consideration, would apply, surely, to a conception like that of value. We should ask whether value must not be value for someone, whether we do not find that, if we are to think of value at all, we must think of it as essentially related to our feelings or the feelings of some conscious being or beings. This, at any rate, is our ordinary use of it. And ultimately we shall begin to ask ourselves whether we may not be finally forced to say the same of a wider conception like that of good. If we are, we shall have to say that our conception of good necessarily contains in itself a reference to some conscious being. We shall not be able to allow any such ideas as that of good, which was just good and not good for some being. Good would be found to be essentially related to and in some way dependent on the wishes or desires or feelings of some conscious being.

The Kantian would, of course, object here that Kant had already considered the claims of the desires and feelings and given reasons for rejecting them. In the first place, he had argued that to make goodness depend on desires or feelings, would make it something uncertain and fluctuating, because some people might desire a thing and others not, or the same person might desire it at one time and not at another. This is certainly a weighty objection, and will have to be considered at length later. Here it will suffice to suggest a possible line on which it might be met: that is, if we developed the idea of some end which every conscious being, by its very nature, must and would desire, if it only realized what it was. We shall meet with this conception later. In the second place he had argued that such a view would make what we desired not good in itself but only as a means to an end. Here we can only say that Kant, doubtless largely under the influence of a faulty psychology, seems to fail to realize the possibility or the true meaning of anything being desired purely for its own sake. Finally it would be argued that such a view would not give us a thing good in itself, because its goodness would depend upon something else outside of it, namely, our desire of or feeling towards it. This we should readily admit. And we should reply that we do not and cannot recognize the existence or possibility of any such thing as good in itself in that sense, out of all relation to anything else. It simply has no meaning for us. And if it had, it would make goodness something of no interest or importance to us, and of no possible influence upon our actions.

With this, we really return to the point from which Kant started. We shall remember that one of the assumptions on which he seemed to base his theory was that which was expressed by saying that if a thing is really good, it must be good in itself. If that appealed to us at first as a reasonable statement of our own ordinary ideas, it was only because we had not yet realized what it really meant. When we did realize this, instead of accepting it as a correct starting-point, we should be more inclined to describe it as the fundamental fallacy of Kant, as indeed of many other writers. Goodness, we should say now, is not a quality which belongs to things in themselves, quite apart from their effect on or their relation to us[3] or some conscious being. If it were, it could only be related to us as an object of cognition. And if it were simply an object of cognition, something that we merely knew without having any feeling towards it, it could not move us to action, or indeed be of any practical interest or importance to us at all.

[3] Of course, in a sense, as we have seen, Kant does make goodness related to us, because it is an essential quality of rational beings. But that merely means that we, in so far as we are rational, are the things which have this quality. It is obviously a very different thing from asserting that goodness itself consists in a relation to us or to any conscious being. And nothing short of this will satisfy the above criticism.

There are many other objections to Kant's view. But if the argument has been correct, we have found his fundamental fallacy in the false assumptions from which he starts. They are really two in number. He starts from the assumption that what is good must be good in itself, apart from all relations to anything else. And in consequence of this he is forced to assume that the mere intellectual apprehension of the fact is sufficient to move us to action. The other assumptions which we have ascribed to him follow from these two or are different forms which they take. But, if our argument has been at all correct, we must maintain against this that the simple intellectual apprehension, the bare knowledge of anything can never move us to action. And consequently his idea of a good in itself is incompatible with one of the most deeply recognized characteristics of the moral fact, namely, that it is somehow a reason for action.

The Categorical Imperative—Further Readings

Acton, H. B., *Kant's Moral Philosophy* (London: Macmillan, 1970). Primarily exposition, with some criticism.

Broad, C. D., *Five Types of Ethical Theory* (New York: Harcourt, Brace, 1930), Chap. 5. Exposition and criticism.

Carritt, E. F., *The Theory of Morals* (London: Humphrey Milford, 1928), Chap. 9. Critic.

Duncan, A. R. C., *Practical Reason and Morality: A Study of Immanuel Kant's FOUNDATIONS FOR THE METAPHYSIC OF MORALS* (London: Thomas Nelson, 1957). Primarily exposition, with some criticism.

Kant, Immanuel, *Critique of Practical Reason* (1788).

Körner, S., *Kant* (Baltimore: Penguin Books, 1955), Chap. 6. Exposition and criticism.

Liddell, Brendan E. A., *Kant on the Foundation of Morality: A Modern Version of the GRUNDLEGUNG*, Translated with commentary (Bloomington: Indiana U.P., 1970). Seeks primarily to make Kant's thought clear to readers who have no philosophical background.

Paton, H. J., *The Categorical Imperative* (4th ed., London: Hutchinson, 1963). Sympathetic exposition.

Rashdall, Hastings, *The Theory of Good and Evil* (Oxford: Clarendon, 1907; 2d ed., 1924), Vol. 1, Chap. 5. Critic.

Ross, W. D., *Kant's Ethical Theory* (Oxford: Clarendon, 1954). Exposition and criticism.

Teale, A. E., *Kantian Ethics* (London: Oxford U.P.: 1951). Exposition and constructive criticism.

Williams, T. C., *The Concept of the Categorical Imperative* (Oxford: Clarendon, 1968). A sympathetic study of Kant's categorical imperative and its place in his ethics.

Wolff, Robert Paul, *The Autonomy of Reason: A Commentary on Kant's GROUNDWORK OF THE METAPHYSIC OF MORALS* (New York: Harper and Row, 1973). Exposition, criticism, and critical reconstruction.

—— (ed.), *Immanuel Kant: FOUNDATIONS OF THE METAPHYSICS OF MORALS with Critical Essays* (New York: Bobbs-Merrill, 1969). Contains nine critical essays by contemporary authors on Kant's ethics.

B TELEOLOGICAL THEORIES:
DOES THE AMOUNT OF GOOD PRODUCED MAKE AN ACTION RIGHT?

In the light of the foregoing, it would be difficult to argue that deontological theories are altogether successful in their attempts to found normative ethics without considering the consequences of actions for good and evil. It is of theoretical, as well as pedagogical importance, therefore, that we consider the large and often quite disparate group of theories which in both classical and contemporary times have opposed deontological views, namely, teleological theories.

As was pointed out in the introduction to this section, teleological theories propose the general thesis that obligation and rightness depend upon the value of the consequences of the actions performed by a moral agent at a given time and place. We know how we ought to act if and when we know what is good. The theories vary mainly in terms of (1) their understanding of the properties which make the consequences good (e.g., pleasure or self-realization); (2) their answer to the question of whether it is the consequences of particular actions, or the consequences of acting in conformity with rules which must be considered in judging the rightness of an action; and (3) whether they hold that the value to be considered is that of the agent alone (egoism), or of the greatest number of persons (altruism or utilitarianism). Teleological theories, then, divide into a number of types according to the ways in which these elements can be combined. There are egoisms, hedonisms, egoistic hedonisms, ethical egoisms, hedonistic utilitarianisms, "ideal" utilitarianisms, act and rule utilitarianisms, self-realization theories, interest theories, etc.; and, unfortunately, the terminology is not uniform.* The articles which follow include a selection broad enough to introduce the reader to the major teleological theories and to the criticisms most frequently lodged against them.

*See Brandt, *op. cit.*, Chapters 14 and 15.

1 Ethical Egoism

We have already encountered the psychological form of egoism in the selections from Thomas Hobbes and Bishop Butler. Some of the issues related to ethical egoism surfaced in that section. We are now prepared to consider some contemporary positions with respect to the continuing controversy over egoism, here understood as the doctrine that a person ought to act in his own interest, even to the exclusion of, and potential harm to, the interests of others.

Brian Medlin, in a widely read article, exploints a modern technique relating to different modes of meaning in his treatment of this ancient controversy. He agrees that ultimate ethical principles are beyond inductive or deductive proof; and this allows the ethical egoist to defend his position as rationally equal to any other ethical view. But he argues that the egoist can be refuted by means of another rational criterion, the principle of consistency. He first rejects "individual" egoism on the ground that it implies the attempt to persuade other persons that no possible morality can pay. This, he believes, rejects morality in principle and withdraws individual egoism from the class of moral theories. Medlin next argues that if egoism is to qualify as an ethical theory, it must be both universal and categorical. To be universal, the theory must maintain that everyone ought to look after his own interests, disregarding all others except as they further his interests. To be categorical, the theory must claim that to act in our own interests is right in itself, as distinct from the hypothetical form, which claims that if each of us acts in his own interest, some other end such as happiness will result—which, according to Medlin, is a "perverse" utilitarian theory. Having thus clarified what ethical egoism asserts, Medlin then argues that the doctrine is inconsistent.

Hospers seeks to support ethical egoism. Pursuant to this end, he first takes up an argument, which he quotes for us, from Kurt Baier. Baier has argued* that ethical egoism leads to a *reductio ad absurdum* in that an action which fulfills the interests of one of two persons to the exclusion of the interests of the other, is by egoistic criteria both right and not right, which leads egoism into inconsistency. Hospers maintains that this argument confuses two different things: (1) the thesis that

*Kurt Baier, *The Moral Point of View* (New York: Random House, 1966).

adequate ethical theories should resolve conflicts, and (2) the claim that egoist theory is self-contradictory. He distinguishes between personal and impersonal egoism, and concludes that neither is refuted on grounds of inadequacy with respect to the resolution of conflicts. Hospers then argues that the inconsistency results only if one states the ethical egoist's position in certain (unnecessary) ways. His way, according to what might be called the "disinterested spectator at a game" model, is "I hope each of you tries to come out on top"; and this is surely not, he claims, contradictory.

Our third philosopher, Baumer, argues against Hospers that his game analogy fails. Baumer also contends that impersonal egoism leads to absurdities.

20

Ultimate Principles and Ethical Egoism

BRIAN MEDLIN

I believe that it is now pretty generally accepted by professional philosophers that ultimate ethical principles must be arbitrary. One cannot derive conclusions about what should be merely from accounts of what is the case; one cannot decide how people ought to behave merely from one's knowledge of how they do behave. To arrive at a conclusion in ethics one must have at least one ethical premiss. This premiss, if it be in turn a conclusion, must be the conclusion of an argument containing at least one ethical premiss. And so we can go back, indefinitely but not for ever. Sooner or later, we must come to at least one ethical premiss which is not deduced but baldly asserted. Here we must be arational; neither rational nor irrational, for here there is no room for reason even to go wrong.

But the triumph of Hume in ethics has been a limited one. What appears quite natural to a handful of specialists appears quite monstrous to the majority of decent intelligent men. At any rate, it has been my experience that people who are normally rational resist the above account of the logic of moral language, not by argument—for that can't be done—but by tooth and nail. And they resist from the best motives. They see the philosopher wantonly unravelling the whole fabric of morality. If our ultimate principles are arbitrary, they say, if those principles came out of thin air, then anyone can hold any principle he pleases. Unless moral assertions are statements of fact about the world and either true or false, we can't claim that any man is wrong, whatever his prin-

FROM "Ultimate Principles and Ethical Egoism" by Brian Medlin (*Australasian Journal of Philosophy*, Vol. XXXV, No. 2, 1957).

ciples may be, whatever his behaviour. We have to surrender the luxury of calling one another scoundrels. That this anxiety flourishes because its roots are in confusion is evident when we consider that we don't call people scoundrels, anyhow, for being mistaken about their facts. Fools, perhaps, but that's another matter. Nevertheless, it doesn't become us to be high-up. The layman's uneasiness, however irrational it may be, is very natural and he must be reassured.

People cling to objectivist theories of morality from moral motives. It's a very queer thing that by doing so they often thwart their own purposes. There are evil opinions abroad, as anyone who walks abroad knows. The one we meet with most often, whether in pub or parlour, is the doctrine that everyone should look after himself. However refreshing he may find it after the high-minded pomposities of this morning's editorial, the good fellow knows this doctrine is wrong and he wants to knock it down. But while he believes that moral language is used to make statements either true or false, the best he can do is to claim that what the egoist says is false. Unfortunately, the egoist can claim that it's true. And since the supposed fact in question between them is not a publicly ascertainable one, their disagreement can never be resolved. And it is here that even good fellows waver, when they find they have no refutation available. The egoist's word seems as reliable as their own. Some begin half to believe that perhaps it is possible to supply an egoistic basis for conventional morality, some that it may be impossible to supply any other basis. I'm not going to try to prop up our conventional morality, which I fear to be a task beyond my strength, but in what follows I do want to refute the doctrine of ethical egoism. I want to resolve this disagreement by showing that what the egoist says is inconsistent. It is true that there are moral disagreements which can never be resolved, but this isn't one of them. The proper objection to the man who says "Everyone should look after his own interests regardless of the interests of others" is not that he isn't speaking the truth, but simply that he isn't speaking.

We should first make two distinctions. This done, ethical egoism will lose much of its plausibility.

1. UNIVERSAL AND INDIVIDUAL EGOISM

Universal egoism maintains that everyone (including the speaker) ought to look after his own interests and to disregard those of other people except in so far as their interests contribute towards his own.

Individual egoism is the attitude that the egoist is going to look after himself and no one else. The egoist cannot promulgate that he is going to look after himself. He can't even preach that he *should* look after himself and preach this alone. When he tries to convince me that he should look after himself, he is attempting so to dispose me that I shall approve when he drinks my beer and steals Tom's wife. I cannot approve of his looking after himself and himself alone without so far approving of his achieving his happiness, regardless of the happiness of myself and others. So that when he sets out to persuade me that he should look after himself regardless of others, he must also set out to persuade me that I should look after him regardless of myself and others. Very small chance he has! And if the individual egoist cannot promulgate his doctrine without enlarging it, what he has is no doctrine at all.

A person enjoying such an attitude may believe that other people are fools not to look after themselves. Yet he himself would be a fool to tell them so. If he did tell them, though, he wouldn't consider that he was giving them *moral* advice. Persuasion to the effect that one should ignore the claims of morality because morality doesn't pay, to the effect that one has insufficient selfish motive and, therefore, insufficient motive for moral behaviour is not moral persuasion. For this reason I doubt that we should call the individual egoist's attitude an ethical one. And I don't doubt this in the way someone may doubt whether to call the ethical standards of Satan "ethical" standards. A malign morality is none the less a morality for being malign. But the attitude we're considering is one of mere contempt for all moral considerations whatsoever. An indifference to morals may be wicked, but it is not a perverse morality. So far as I am aware, most egoists imagine that they are putting forward a doctrine in ethics, though there may be a few who are prepared to proclaim themselves individual egoists. If the good fellow wants to know how he should justify conventional morality to an individual egoist, the answer is that he shouldn't and can't. Buy your car elsewhere, blackguard him whenever you meet, and let it go at that.

2. CATEGORICAL AND HYPOTHETICAL EGOISM

Categorical egoism is the doctrine that we all ought to observe our own interests, *because that is what we ought to do*. For the categorical egoist the egoistic dogma is the ultimate principle in ethics.

The hypothetical egoist, on the other hand, maintains that we all ought to observe our own interests, because . . . If we want such and such an end, we must do so and so (look after ourselves). The hypothetical egoist is not a real egoist at all. He is very likely an unwitting utilitarian who believes mistakenly that the general happiness will be increased if each man looks wisely to his own. Of course, a man may believe that egoism is enjoined on us by God and he may therefore promulgate the doctrine and observe it in his conduct, not in the hope of achieving thereby a remote end, but simply in order to obey God. But neither is *he* a real egoist. He believes, ultimately, that we should obey God, even should God command us to altruism.

An ethical egoist will have to maintain the doctrine in both its universal and categorical forms. Should he retreat to hypothetical egoism he is no longer an egoist. Should he retreat to individual egoism his doctrine, while logically impregnable, is no longer ethical, no longer even a doctrine. He may wish to quarrel with this and if so, I submit peacefully. Let him call himself what he will, it makes no difference. I'm a philosopher, not a rat-catcher, and I don't see it as my job to dig vermin out of such burrows as individual egoism.

Obviously something strange goes on as soon as the ethical egoist tries to promulgate his doctrine. What is he doing when he urges upon his audience that they should each observe his own interests and those interests alone? Is he not acting contrary to the egoistic principle? It cannot be to his advantage to convince them, for seizing always their own advantage they will impair his. Surely if he does believe what he says, he should try to persuade them otherwise. Not perhaps that they should devote themselves to his interests, for they'd hardly swallow that; but that everyone should devote himself to the service of others. But is not to believe that someone should act in a certain way to try to persuade him to do so? Of course, we don't always try to persuade people to act as we think they should act. We may be lazy, for instance. But in so far as we believe that Tom should do so and so, we have a tendency to induce him to do so and so. Does it makes sense to say: "Of course you should do this, but for goodness' sake don't"? Only where we mean: "You should do this for certain reasons, but here are even more persuasive reasons for not doing it." If the egoist believes ultimately that others should mind themselves alone, then, he must persuade them accordingly. If he doesn't persuade them, he is no universal egoist. It certainly makes sense to say: "I know very well that Tom should act in such and such a way. But I know also that it's not to my advantage that he should so act. So I'd better dissuade him from it." And this is just what the egoist must say, if he is to consider his own advantage and disregard everyone else's. That is, he must behave as an individual egoist, if he is to be an egoist at all.

He may want to make two kinds of objection here:

1. That it will not be to his disadvantage to promulgate the doctrine, provided that his audience fully understand what is to their ultimate advantage. This objection can be developed in a number of ways, but I think that it will always be possible to push the egoist into either individual or hypothetical egoism.

2. That it is to the egoist's advantage to preach the doctrine if the pleasure he gets out of doing this more than pays for the injuries he must endure at the hands of his converts. It is hard to believe that many people would be satisfied with a doctrine which they could only consistently promulgate in very special circumstances. Besides, this looks suspiciously like individual egoism in disguise.

I shall say no more on these two points because I want to advance a further criticism which seems to me at once fatal and irrefutable.

Now it is time to show the anxious layman that we have means of dealing with ethical egoism which are denied him; and denied him by just that objectivism which he thinks essential to morality. For the very fact that our ultimate principles must be arbitrary means they can't be anything we please. Just because they come out of thin air they can't come out of hot air. Because these principles are not propositions about matters of fact and cannot be deduced from propositions about matters of fact, they must be the fruit of our own attitudes. We assert them largely to modify the attitudes of our fellows but by asserting them we express our own desires and purposes. This means that we cannot use moral language cavalierly. Evidently we cannot say something like "All human desires and purposes are bad." This would be to express our own desires and purposes, thereby committing a kind of absurdity. Nor, I shall argue, can we say "Everyone should observe his own interests regardless of the interests of others."

Remembering that the principle is meant to be both universal and categorical, let us ask what kind of attitude the egoist is expressing. Wouldn't that attitude be equally well expressed by the conjunction of an infinite number of avowals thus?—

I want myself to come out on top	and	I don't care about Tom, Dick, Harry . . .
and		and
I want Tom to come out on top	and	I don't care about myself, Dick, Harry . . .
and		and
I want Dick to come out on top	and	I don't care about myself, Tom, Harry . . .
and		and
I want Harry to come out on top	and	I don't care about myself, Dick, Tom . . .
etc.		etc.

From this analysis it is obvious that the principle expressing such an attitude must be inconsistent.

But now the egoist may claim that he hasn't been properly understood. When he says "Everyone should look after himself and himself alone," he means "Let each man do what he wants regardless of what anyone else wants." The egoist may claim that what he values is merely that he and Tom and Dick and Harry should each do what he wants and not care about what anyone else may want and that this doesn't involve his principle in any inconsistency. Nor need it. But even if it doesn't, he's no better off. Just what does he value? Is it the well-being of himself, Tom, Dick and Harry or merely their going on in a certain way regardless of whether or not this is going to promote their well-being? When he urges Tom, say, to do what he wants, is he appealing to Tom's self-interest? If so, his attitude can be expressed thus:

I want myself to be happy		I want myself not to care about Tom,
and	and	Dick, Harry . . .
I want Tom to be happy		

We need go no further to see that the principle expressing such an attitude must be inconsistent. I have made this kind of move already. What concerns me now is the alternative position the egoist must take up to be safe from it. If the egoist values merely that people should go on in a certain way, regardless of whether or not this is going to promote their well-being, then he is not appealing to the self-interest of his audience when he urges them to regard their own interests. If Tom has any regard for himself at all, the egoist's blandishments will leave him cold. Further, the egoist doesn't even have his own interest in mind when he says that, like everyone else, he should look after himself. A funny kind of egoism this turns out to be.

Perhaps now, claiming that he is indeed appealing to the self-interest of his audience, the egoist may attempt to counter the objection of the previous paragraph. He may move into "Let each man do what he wants and let each man disregard what others want when their desires clash with his own." Now his attitude may be expressed thus:

I want everyone to be happy   and   I want everyone to disregard the happiness of others when their happiness clashes with his own.

The egoist may claim justly that a man can have such an attitude and also that in a certain kind of world such a man could get what he wanted. Our objection to the egoist has been that his desires are incompatible. And this is still so. If he and Tom and Dick and Harry did go on as he recommends by saying "Let each man disregard the happiness of others, when their happiness conflicts with his own," then assuredly they'd all be completely miserable. Yet he wants them to be happy. He is attempting to counter this by saying that it is merely a fact about the world that they'd make one another miserable by going on as he recommends. The world could conceivably have been different. For this reason, he says, this principle is not inconsistent. This argument may not seem very compelling, but I advance it on the egoist's behalf because I'm interested in the reply to it. For now we don't even need to tell him that the world isn't in fact like that. (What it's like makes no difference.) Now we can point out to him that he is arguing not as an egoist but as a utilitarian. He has slipped into hypothetical egoism to save his principle from inconsistency. If the world were such that we always made ourselves and others happy by doing one another down, then we could find good utilitarian reasons for urging that we should do one another down.

If, then, he is to save his principle, the egoist must do one of two things. He must give up the claim that he is appealing to the self-interest of his audience, that he has even his own interest in mind. Or he must admit that, in the conjunction above, although "I want everyone to be happy" refers to ends, nevertheless "I want everyone to disregard the happiness of others when their happiness conflicts with his own" can refer only to means. That is, his so-called ultimate principle is really compounded of a principle and a moral rule subordinate to that principle. That is, he is really a utilitarian who is urging everyone to go on in a certain way so that everyone may be happy. A utilitarian, what's more, who is ludicrously mistaken about the nature of the world. Things being as they are, his moral rule is a very bad one. Things being as they are, it can only be deduced from his principle by means of an empirical premiss which is manifestly false. Good fellows don't need to fear him. They may rest easy that the world is and must be on their side and the best thing they can do is be good.

It may be worth pointing out that objections similar to those I have brought against the egoist can be made to the altruist. The man who holds that the principle "Let everyone observe the interests of others" is both universal and categorical can be compelled to choose between two alternatives, equally repugnant. He must give up the claim that he is concerned for the well-being of himself and others. Or he must admit that, though "I want everyone to be happy" refers to ends, nevertheless "I want everyone to disregard his own happiness when it conflicts with the happiness of others' can refer only to means.

I have said from time to time that the egositic principle is inconsistent. I have not said it is contradictory. This for the reason that we can, without contradiction, express inconsistent desires and purposes. To do so is not to say anything like "Goliath was ten feet tall and not ten feet tall." Don't we all want to eat our cake and have it too? And when we say we do we aren't asserting a contradiction. We are not asserting a contradiction whether we be making an avowal of our attitudes or stating a fact about them. We all have conflicting motives. As a utilitarian exuding benevolence I want the man who mows my landlord's grass to be happy, but as a slug-a-bed I should like to see him scourged. None of this, however, can do the egoist any good. For we assert our ultimate principles not only to express our own attitudes but also to induce similar attitudes in others, to dispose them to conduct themselves as we wish. In so far as their desires conflict, people don't know what to do. And, therefore, no expression of incompatible desires can ever serve for an ultimate principle of human conduct.

21

Baier and Medlin on Ethical Egoism

JOHN HOSPERS

In his excellent book *The Moral Point of View*, Professor Kurt Baier attempts to refute ethical egoism—the doctrine that my sole duty is to promote my own interests exclusively—in the following way:

Let B and K be candidates for the presidency of a certain country and let it be granted that it is in the interest of either to be elected, but that only one can succeed. It would then be in the interest of B but against the interest of K if B were elected, and vice versa, and therefore in the interest of B but against the interest of K if K were liquidated, and vice versa. But from this it would follow that B ought to liquidate K, that it is wrong for B not to do so, that B has not "done his duty" until he has liquidated K; and vice versa. Similarly K, knowing that his own liquidation is in the interest of B and therefore anticipating B's attempts to secure it, ought to take steps to foil B's endeavors. It would be wrong for him not to do so. He would "not have done his duty" until he had made sure of stopping B. It follows that if K prevents B from liquidating him, his act must be said to be both wrong and not wrong—wrong

FROM "Baier and Medlin on Ethical Egoism" (*Philosophical Studies*, Vol. XII, Nos. 1 and 2). Copyright 1961 by D. Reidel Publishing Company, Dordrecht, Holland.

because it is the prevention of what B ought to do, his duty, and wrong for B not to do it; not wrong because it is what K ought to do, his duty, and wrong for K not to do it. But one and the same act (logically) cannot be both morally wrong and not morally wrong. . . .

This is obviously absurd. For morality is designed to apply in just such cases, namely, those where interests conflict. But if the point of view of morality were that of self-interest, then there could *never* be moral solutions of conflicts of interest.[1]

We are to assume at the outset that killing K not only seems to be, but really *is* to B's interest and that killing B really is to K's interest. (If it were to the interest of each to work out a compromise, then no problem would arise.) Operating on this assumption, what can be said of Professor Baier's one-shot refutation of egoism? His argument can be schematized in the following way:

1. Every adequate ethical theory must be able to provide solutions for conflicts of interest.
2. Ethical egoism is unable to provide solutions for conflicts of interest.
3. Therefore, ethical egoism is not an adequate ethical theory.

So much for the argument for the inadequacy of ethical egoism. But his criticism goes even further:

4. Any view which is guilty of self-contradiction is thereby refuted.
5. Ethical egoism is guilty of self-contradiction.
6. Therefore, ethical egoism is refuted.

We may examine the second argument first, since if a theory is guilty of self-contradiction no further refutation of it is necessary.

Let it be admitted that to say that one and the same act is both right and wrong is to be guilty of a self-contradiction, since the proposition that it is wrong entails that it is not right, and an act cannot be both right and not right. (I shall waive any discussion of a point whose truth is presupposed in Baier's argument, namely that rightness and wrongness are properties. I shall also waive discussion of the possibility that even if they are properties they are to-you and to-me properties, e.g., something can be interesting to you and not interesting to me, and rightness might be like interestingness.)

We may admit, then, at least for purposes of the argument, that to say that Brutus killing Caesar was both right and wrong involves a contradiction. But the case presented by Professor Baier is not that of one and the same act being both right and wrong. It is a case of *two* acts, one by B and the other by K. They are two acts of the same *kind*, namely attempted murder (or the attempt to foil the murder-attempt of the other), but there is no contradiction in two such acts being attempted or in both being right. It might well be B's duty to try to dispose of K, and K's duty to try to dispose of B. Since there are two acts here, one by B and one by K, the situation of one and the same act being both right and wrong does not arise, and no contradiction arises either.

[1] *The Moral Point of View.* (Ithaca, N.Y.: Cornell University Press, 1958), pp. 189–90.

So much for the argument concerning contradiction. But the inadequacy argument remains, and it seems much more plausible. It is true that we usually expect an ethical theory to be able to settle conflicts of interest; for example, if husband and wife both want custody of the children, we expect the ethical theory to tell us (in conjunction, of course, with empirical premises) which one's wish should be granted; every judge in a courtroom must make such decisions. The judge in arbitrating such a case could not use ethical egoism as a way of settling it, for if it is the interest of both husband and wife to have the same thing and they can't both have it, he will *have* to decide against the interest of one of them; and egoism, which tells each person to follow his own interest exclusively, can provide no basis for settling the dispute. This does seem to be a very serious criticism.

What would the egoist reply to such a charge? I must first distinguish the *personal* egoist from the *impersonal* egoist. The personal egoist is one who says that *his* sole duty is to promote his own interest exclusively, but makes no pronouncement about what other people should do. (Some would not consider this an ethical theory at all, since it does not fulfill the criterion of generality. And if the theory is restated so as not to talk about duties at all—not "It is my duty to promote my own interest exclusively" but "*I'm going* to promote my own interest exclusively," which is the kind of thing that most practicing egoists say—then of course there is no ethical theory at all, but only a prediction or expression of determination with regard to one's future behavior). The impersonal egoist is one who says that the duty of *each and every person* (including himself) is to pursue his own interest exclusively.

How will the egoist react to Baier's inadequacy argument? The *personal* egoist will not be disturbed at all. According to him, his one duty is to pursue exclusively his own interest; so if he happens to be B he will try to kill K and if he is K he will try to kill B (and foil K's attempts to kill him); and if he is neither B nor K he will not concern himself with the conflict of interest one way or the other. Of course if there is something in it for him, he will: if he stands to gain a fortune if K wins, then he will do what he can to assist K's victory in order to gain the fortune. But otherwise he will ignore the matter. "But doesn't an ethical theory have to have a means of deciding what to do or say in cases of conflict of interest? If you had to advise B or K, what would you say?" The answer is, of course, that if there is nothing in it for him the personal egoist will not bother to advise either party or to aid either cause. If asked for advice on the matter, he would probably say, "Get lost, you bother me." (Nor would the personal egoist be likely to engage in philosophical discussion. It would hardly be to his interest to allow other people to plant in his mind the seeds of skepticism concerning his egoistic doctrine.)

So far, then, egoism has not been refuted. It has been shown to be inadequate *only if* you expect an ethical theory to arbitrate conflicts of interest. Thus, it *would* be insufficient for the judge in a divorce court. The judge has nothing to gain either way, but he has to decide on a matter of conflict of interest between husband and wife. If the judge were a personal egoist, his principle would simply be to follow *his own* interest; but this principle wouldn't help him at all in dealing with the case at hand. Here he needs instructions, not for promoting his own interest, but for settling cases of conflict of interest between *other* people.

And this, of course, the theory cannot provide; but the personal egoist doesn't mind this at all. He has no wish to arbitrate other people's conflicts of interest. He will gladly leave such activities to the "suckers."

What of the *impersonal* egoist? His view is that he should pursue his own interest exclusively, that B should pursue B's, that K should pursue K's, and so on for everyone else. What will he say in the case of B and K? He will advise K to try to win out over B by whatever means he can, and will advise B to try to win out over K by whatever means he can: in other words, to settle the thing by force or craft, and may the strongest or cleverest man win. Does his advice to B contradict his advice to K? Not at all; he is urging each one to try to gain victory over the other; this is not very different from telling each of the two competing teams to try and win the game. His view does not, of course, provide a *rational* means of settling the conflict of interest, but it does provide a means: it tells each party to try to emerge victorious, though of course only one of them *can* emerge victorious.

So far, there seems to be no difficulty for the impersonal egoist. But, as an impersonal egoist, he does have a stake in the general acceptance of his doctrine; for he does say of other people, not just himself, that each should pursue his own interest exclusively. If he sees B, he will urge B to try to win over K (even if he has nothing to gain personally by B's victory), and if he sees K, he will urge K to try to win over B. But there is, while no outright contradiction, a curious *tactical incongruity* in his view. For if the impersonal egoist advises others to pursue their own interest, might not this interfere with the promotion of *his own* interest and yet is he not committed by his own doctrine to pursuing his own interest exclusively? If he advises B and K, but neither B nor K is a threat to him, there is no problem; but if I advise my business competitor to pursue his own interest with a vengeance, may he not follow my advice and pursue his interest so wholeheartedly that he forces me out of business? For the sake of *my own* interest, then, I may be well advised to keep my egoistic doctrine to myself, lest others use it against me.

An impersonal egoist, therefore, may simply prefer to keep his own counsel and not advise others at all. In this case, he escapes the difficulty just as the personal egoist did. He will pursue his own interest regardless of who else opposes it; and while he does, as an impersonal egoist, advise others to pursue *their* own interests, he will do this only when doing it does not imperil *his* interest.

Thus, *if* you are an impersonal egoist, and *if* as an impersonal egoist you have a stake in advising others—and only then—you will feel a conflict between the promotion of your egoistic doctrine and the promotion of your own interests, which will be damaged if others pursue their interests at the expense of yours. But this hardly *refutes* the impersonal egoist's doctrine; it concerns only a tactical matter of when to publicize it.

But now another objection to ethical egoism presents itself. Suppose you are an impersonal egoist, and are suggesting courses of action to your acquaintances. Acquaintance A asks you what to do, and you say to him, "Pursue your own interest exclusively, and if B tries to get the better of you, cut him down. Even if you could save B's life by lifting a finger, there is no reason for you to do so as long as it doesn't promote your interest." Later on, B asks you what you think *he* should do. So you say to him, "Pursue your own interest exclusively, and if A tries to get the better of you, cut him down. Even if you could save A's life by lifting a finger, there is no reason for you to do so as long as it doesn't promote your interest." And you say similar things to your other acquaintances.

Suppose, now, that an onlooker heard you say all these things. He might wonder (with good reason) exactly what you were advising—what the general drift of your advice was. You tell A to do what is to his interest and ignore B, so our onlooker thinks you are a friend of A's and an enemy of B's. But then you tell B to do what is to his interest and ignore A, and our onlooker now concludes that you are a friend of B and an enemy of A. And in fact what are you anyway? It sounds to the onlooker as if you are pathologically addicted to changing your mind. Perhaps, like some people, you are so impressed by whoever you are with at the moment that you forget all about the interests of those who aren't right there before you. This might explain the sudden shift in attitude.

But the curious thing is that the egoist doesn't consider this a shift in attitude at all, but a consistent expression of *one* attitude, the "impersonal egoistic" attitude. But that is just the point of the objection. *Is* it a single consistent attitude? When you are in the presence of A, it is only A's interest that counts; but a moment later, when you are in the presence of B, it is only B's interest that counts. Isn't this very strange? Can the question of whose interests count really depend on whom you happen to be addressing or confronting at the moment?

The charge, in short, is that the impersonal egoist is guilty of issuing *inconsistent directives*. This charge is made, for example, by Dr. Brian Medlin.[2] According to Medlin, when the (impersonal) egoist is talking to himself he says "I want myself to come out on top, and I don't care about Tom, Dick, Harry . . ."; when he is talking to Tom he says (in effect), "I want Tom to come out on top and I don't care about myself, Dick, Harry . . ."; when he is talking to Dick he says, "I want Dick to come out on top, and I don't care about myself, Tom, Harry . . ."; and so on in a conjunction of an infinite number of avowals. "From this analysis," he concludes, "it is obvious that the principle expressing such an attitude must be inconsistent." (The same conclusion follows if the egoist says to Tom, "You alone count," and to Dick, "You alone count," and so on.)

Now, if this is what the impersonal egoist really means to say, then of course what he says *is* inconsistent. But perhaps that is not what he means to say; at any rate, it is not what he *needs* to say. What else might he mean?

---

[2] "Ultimate Principles and Ethical Egoism," *Australasian Journal of Philosophy*, 35 (No. 2): 111–18 (August 1957).

It might be suggested, first, that all that the egoist wants to say is that if you tend to your interests (happiness, or welfare, or whatever) and I to my interests and Tom to Tom's interests, and so on, everyone will be happier (or have more welfare, etc.) than they would if they did not adopt such a completely laissez-faire policy with regard to one another's interests. But two things should be noted about this: (1) If the egoist says this, he is making an *empirical* claim—a claim that human beings will be happier pursuing a policy of splendid isolation with regard to each other than by behaving cooperatively, helping one another in time of need, and so on—and this empirical claim is very dubious indeed; it seems rather to be the case that the welfare of human beings is not independent but *inter*dependent, and that "no man is an island." If each person pursued his own interest to the exclusion of others, there would be less happiness in the world, not more. But whatever may be said of this empirical claim, (2) when the egoist makes this claim he is no longer can egoist but a utilitarian; he is arguing that the general welfare (or the maximum total fulfillment of human interests) is what should be striven for, and that the best means of achieving it is by a policy of isolation. But in admitting that the general welfare is the end to be aimed at he is already forsaking his egoism.

Is there anything else, then, that the impersonal egoist can be alleged to mean? The charge against him is that his directives to different people are inconsistent with one another. He, Tom, Dick, and Harry cannot each be the *only* person who counts, or the only person he hopes will come out on top. Is not the egoist, if he abandons the utilitarian argument (above) and retreats back to his egoism, caught in this web of inconsistency? Is he not saying to Tom that he hopes Tom will come out on top (and by implication that Dick won't), and then the next moment saying to Dick that he hopes Dick will come out on top (and by implication that Tom won't), and so on, thereby patting each one on the back before his face and poking him in the nose behind his back?

The egoist *need* not, I think, be guilty of such duplicity. What if he assembled Tom, Dick, Harry, and everyone else into his presence at the same moment? What would he say to them all together? He might say, "I *hope* that each of you comes out on top." But in that case, he *is* saying something self-contradictory, since of course each of them cannot come out on top—only one of them can. But he need not say this; suppose that instead he says, "I hope each of you *tries* to come out on top," or "Each of you should *try* to come out the victor." There is surely no inconsistency here. The hope he is expressing here is the kind of hope that the interested but impartial spectator expresses at a game. Perhaps the egoist likes to live life in a dangerous cutthroat manner, unwilling to help others in need but not desiring others to help him either. He wants life to be spicy and dangerous; to him the whole world is one vast egoistic game, and living life accordingly is the way to make it interesting and exciting. It may be that, if our egoist says this, his egoism is somewhat diluted from the stronger and earlier form of "I hope that you all win" or "Each of you alone counts"—but at least, in this latest formulation, he is not caught in an inconsistency.

Whether or not the egoist, then, is caught in an inconsistency depends on what, exactly, we take him to be saying. It should not be assumed that because the egoist in some formulations of his doctrine is guilty of inconsistency, he is therefore inconsistent in all of them.

22

Indefensible Impersonal Egoism

WILLIAM H. BAUMER

It has recently been argued by Peter Hare, following the lead of John Hospers, that impersonal egoism is at least a not impossible ethical view, and not accompanied by such odd self-referring characteristics as would make it tantamount to impossible.[1] The purpose of this discussion is to show that this view is mistaken. The discussion includes three parts. First is a formulation of the basic principle of impersonal egoism. Second is an argument to show that Hare's and Hospers' analogy with trying to win a game both fails and is unnecessary. Third is an argument to show that, pace Hare, Hospers, and Brian Medlin, impersonal ethical egoism is absurd even given a non-emotive analysis of ethical language.[2]

Impersonal egoism is supposed to be a view which involves the determination of all questions of right and wrong, if not also good and bad, in terms of the satisfactions of the interests of each particular agent. No appeal to any sort of general happiness principle is admissible. The satisfactions, however, may well be long-term ones; it is not to be supposed that impersonal egoism is non-prudential. Its principle is formulable as follows:

> Each person ought to do those acts, and only those acts, which lead to the most efficient satisfaction of the most interests he himself has.

Hare might object that this principle introduces a teleological element, whereas it was his intent to evade Daniel Kading and Martin Kramer's position by arguing for a "deontological" impersonal egoism.[3] But this principle is, using Medlin's term, categorical; it does not depend upon any obviously teleological principle such as a utilitarian one or a Deweyan endorsement of more growth

FROM "Indefensible Impersonal Egoism" by William H. Baumer (*Philosophical Studies*, Vol. XVIII, No. 5). Copyright 1967 by D. Reidel Publishing Company, Dordrecht, Holland.

[1] Peter Hare, "In Defense of Impersonal Egoism," *Philosophical Studies*, 17: 94–95 (1966). John Hospers, "Baier and Medlin on Ethical Egoism," *Philosophical Studies*, 12: 10–16 (1961); cf. his *Human Conduct* (New York: Harcourt, Brace, and World, 1961), pp. 157–72.

[2] Brian Medlin, "Ultimate Principles and Ethical Egoism," *Australasian Journal of Philosophy*, 35: 111–18 (1957).

[3] Cf. Daniel Kading and Martin Kramer, "Mr. Hospers' Defense of Impersonal Egoism," *Philosophical Studies*, 15: 44–46 (1964).

for more people more of the time. Unlike Medlin's, this formulation is not offered with an emotive analysis of ethical language in the background. Indeed, it is not possible to press for a more deontological or categorical principle here without seeking one which even the traditional deontologists never supposed was necessary: a principle governing one's pursuit of his interests which makes no mention of any interests to be pursued. Finally, it is not possible to do without such a principle here, to follow the more traditional deontologist pattern of simply having a set of rules. Such an approach would not involve the general prohibition of anything not in one's own interests which is the defining characteristic of impersonal egoism.

Hare and Hospers attempt to make impersonal egoism plausible by presenting it as a view which urges that everyone should try to win, claiming that this is analogous to the spectator at a sports contest impartially cheering on both sides. This is supposed to remove the embarrassment of a view which cannot be preached if it is to be practiced, since it is hardly apparent that the promotion of the doctrine of impersonal egoism is in the interests of any particular agent. Unfortunately, one element overlooked by Hare and Hospers is that everyone is both spectator and player in this "game," and thus must be urging on everyone, including himself. A far more serious difficulty, and one which invalidates the analogy, is this: We think of sports contests as going on according to certain rules and conventions. One does not, for example, turn a pea shooter on one's opponent in a golf match at the moment he is attempting to blast out of a sand trap. But impersonal egoism does not apply within such a larger context, and is not to be applied within the customary limitations of a non-egoistic moral scheme. If an analogy with a contest is to be introduced, the appropriate one is warfare conducted with no consideration of any humanitarian concerns. After all, the obligation one has on the basis of impersonal egoism is not to try to fulfill one's interests in a competitively balanced or fair situation, as a game analogy might suggest. Rather, this obligation is to fulfill, or try to fulfill, one's interests *simpliciter*. On the view of impersonal egoism it is not merely odd but downright "immoral" for someone not to take *every* possible advantage which promotes his own interests most efficiently. In only this sense is anything "against the rules" of the "game." The proposed analogy, in short, assimilates a peripheral aspect of impersonal egoism to a peripheral aspect of a sports contest while neglecting the dissimilarities between the central aspects of these. Thus it fails.

The impersonal egoist, though, need not be disturbed by the collapse of this analogy, for he did not need it in the first place. It is only on the assumption of an emotive analysis of ethical language that the egoist must preach his view to others. If this is rejected, as it certainly can be, all the impersonal egoist has to be able to do is to express his view consistently should this be required. Hare and Hospers suppose he can, and thus suppose that this is a possible ethical position. But he cannot, and it is not. Consider the following sort of situation where Mr. Alpha and Mr. Bravo have conflicting interests. These are not merely conflicting interests prima facie but on balance; they are also precisely the interests each ought to fulfill on the basis of the impersonal egoism principle. To say these interests conflict is to say that Alpha's fulfillment of his interests will prevent Bravo's fulfilling his and conversely. Such a situation, it might be remarked, is hardly unlikely; it arises whenever each of two (or more) agents can best fulfill his own interests by gaining one goal which only one of all those involved can gain, e.g., a particular socio-economic position. In such a situation it follows from impersonal egoism that Alpha ought to do those acts which will bring about the fulfillment of his interests while Bravo ought to do certain acts which will prevent Alpha's fulfilling his interests, and conversely. Unfortunately for impersonal egoism, this is absurd. The following makes this clear.

If someone ought, on balance, to do a certain act, it cannot on pain of contradiction be, on balance, wrong for him to do that. But to say it is not wrong for him to do that act is to say that he has the right to do it, i.e., that the act is permissively right for him. It follows that if an act is one which someone ought to do, then it is an act which it is permissively right for him to do. Furthermore, if it is permissively right for someone to do a given act, then no one has the right to prevent him from doing that. This is so since to say that someone has such a right of prevention is to say that the act to be prevented is in some sense wrong, and the same act cannot be both in some sense wrong and also permissively right, at least on balance. It is, in this connection, important to differentiate preventing an act from urging its non-performance or some such. At least so far as acts which are only permissively right are concerned, it is perfectly appropriate to suggest that the agent do something else, etc. To prevent an act, though, is not merely to urge it not be done, advise against it, etc.; it is to *stop* its being done. But note what this yields: if someone ought, on balance, to do a certain act, then it is wrong for anyone to prevent his doing that act.

The foregoing development of the interrelations of the meanings of the terms involved applies to the conflicting interests of Alpha and Bravo with interesting results. Alpha, while he ought to prevent Bravo's fulfilling his own interests, is at the same time wrong in doing so, for Bravo ought to fulfill his own interests. Bravo, while he ought to prevent Alpha's fulfilling his own interests, is wrong in doing so since Alpha ought to fulfill his own interests. In short, given impersonal egoism and the interrelations of the meanings of "ought to do," "wrong," and "prevent," it follows that each one, Alpha and Bravo, is doing what he ought and ought not do. Further absurdities involved in impersonal egoism could be generated, but two are twice enough.[4] It cannot, incidentally, be supposed that these can successfully be removed by insisting upon an emotive analysis of the terms here. Though such an appeal might be supposed to destroy the above introduction of interrelations of meanings of ethical terms, it does not prevent inconsistency. Medlin has shown that.

Impersonal egoism, then, can be formulated as something other than unintentional utilitarianism, and can be formulated on the basis of some alternative

---

[4] For a somewhat similar argument, see Kurt Baier, *The Moral Point of View* (Ithaca, N.Y.: Cornell University Press, 1958), pp. 189–90.

to an emotive analysis of ethical language. It cannot, however, be helpfully assimilated to cheering on participants in a sporting contest. It also cannot be taken as a possible ethical position, for absurd positions are not possible ones, ethical or otherwise.

Ethical Egoism—Further Readings

Baier, Kurt, *The Moral Point of View* (Ithaca, N.Y.: Cornell U.P., 1958), Chap. 8. Critic.

Brunton, J. A., "Egoism and Morality," *The Philosophical Quarterly*, VI (1956), pp. 289–303. Argues that ethical egoism can be regarded properly as a moral theory.

Ewing, A. C., *Ethics* (London: English Universities, 1953), Chap. 2. Critic.

Gauthier, David P. (ed.), *Morality and Rational Self-Interest* (Englewood Cliffs, N.J.: Prentice-Hall, 1970). Ten selections debating the merits of psychological and ethical egoism.

Hobbes, Thomas, *Leviathan* (1651), especially Chaps. 6, 11, 13–15. Proponent, using psychological egoism to support his position.

Hospers, John, *Human Conduct* (New York: Harcourt, Brace and World, 1961), Chap. 4, pp. 157–174. Critic.

Milo, Ronald D. (ed.), *Egoism and Altruism* (Belmont, Calif.: Wadsworth, 1973). Nine classical and contemporary authors debating the merits of psychological and ethical egoism.

Moore, G. E., *Principia Ethica* (Cambridge: Cambridge U.P., 1903), pp. 96–105. Critic.

Nielsen, Kai, "Egoism in Ethics," *Philosophy and Phenomenological Research*, XIX (1959), pp. 502–510. Critic of both psychological and ethical egoism.

Olson, Robert G., *The Morality of Self-Interest* (New York: Harcourt, Brace and World, 1965). Proponent.

Rand, Ayn, *The Virtue of Selfishness* (New York: New American Library, 1961). Proponent.

2 Act Utilitarianism

The material in this section introduces one of the most sustained controversies in the history of philosophy—the development of the intuitionist attack upon, and the contemporary defense of, naturalistic utilitarianism. Although normative and meta-ethical issues, as usual, overlap, our treatment will separate them. As a result, part of the controversy is covered in this section, and part of it in the meta-ethical section.

The articles set out the classic formulations of hedonistic utilitarianism in the works of Jeremy Bentham and John Stuart Mill. Taken as act utilitarians, although this perhaps too narrowly restricts their thought, Bentham and Mill argue that particular actions are right or wrong in so far as they produce the greatest balance of good over evil for the greatest number of persons. The good is further characterized as happiness, and happiness is defined in terms of pleasure. Bentham and Mill are, therefore, hedonistic in their value theory. While Bentham and Mill state classic versions of utilitarianism, it is important to remember that it is possible to be utilitarian in theory of obligation and yet not be hedonistic in theory of value—G. E. Moore, for instance, is a utilitarian who claims that good is not definable at all.

Bentham, in contrast with Mill, holds to a *quantitative* conception of pleasure. He believes (*a*) that we know pleasure empirically, and (*b*) that units of pleasure may be added up in the fashion of a calculus. We can, therefore, justify moral decisions, justify actions, settle disagreements, in an essentially scientific and rational manner. Mill, while agreeing in substance with this position, insists that there are *qualitative* differences in pleasures, and that some kinds of pleasure are more valuable than others. Intellectual pleasures are, for instance, often more important, higher on the scale of values, than physical pleasures. To Bentham's "pushpin is as good as poetry," Mill responds, "better to be Socrates dissatisfied than a fool satisfied." The basic contrast between utilitarianism and egoistic hedonism relates to the *universalistic* principle to which Bentham and Mill subscribe—the principle that the good to be promoted must be for the greatest number of persons. They subscribe, in other words, to the view that morality involves concern for the interests of others.

Both Bentham and Mill maintain that ethical hedonism has some sort of logical footing in *psychological hedonism*—the tendency for humans to in fact pursue pleasure and avoid pain. This position has elicited two main avenues of criticism. First is the argument that they have committed some kind of fallacy which involves the attempt to define the normative in terms of the non-normative, *viz.*: "good" in terms of pleasure (see G. E. Moore's criticism in the selection taken from his writings). Second is the supposedly logically fallacious blooper which attempts to deduce "ought" from an "is." On the latter point, a considerable amount of attention is paid to Mill's argument that the only ground for asserting that something is desirable is that it is desired. A third line of criticism attempts to show that the application of the utilitarian standard to moral decisions leads to absurdities, and this is the territory of Ross.*

The debate over utilitarianism, with respect both to meta-ethical and normative ethical issues, is still very much alive in moral philosophy. We will begin its consideration with the work of W. D. Ross.

It is generally agreed that W. D. Ross set out the most biting contemporary criticism of the view that has come to be called "act utilitarianism." Utilitarian criteria of right and wrong cannot, he claims, be applied to particular actions without the production of a number of absurdities. In the first place, there are a number of personal and other ties to duty which are, at least in any clear sense, ignored by the utilitarian theory. Thus, if two possible actions have the same amount of good consequences, and one of them involves a *prima-facie* duty (i.e., comes under a moral rule or principle), such as helping one who is distressed, or telling the truth, or keeping a promise, or punishing an innocent person, utilitarian theory would seem to imply that the two actions are morally equivalent. But, according to Ross, this is so counter-intuitive as to be absurd. It seems obvious that given two actions equally productive of good consequences, and given that one in addition comes under a relevant moral rule, say, keeping a promise, then the latter is the right one and the other wrong. Of course, the act utilitarians will claim that the argument begs an important question in its assumption that a person can lie, for instance, without producing an increment of bad consequences, such as loss of self-respect, etc., which would make the action wrong on their account also. Ross argues, in the second place, that act utilitarianism would seem to allow certain other absurd consequences. The punishment of innocents, the killing of ill and useless citizens, failure to keep a promise or to tell the truth would all seem to be morally acceptable actions, if it could be shown that they would be productive of good consequences.

The upshot of these arguments is that most modern moral philosophers have found it necessary to reject or to modify act utilitarianism, although, as we will see in future selections below, the dispute is by no means settled.

---

*For a consideration of these arguments against Mill, see W. H. Hudson, *Modern Moral Philosophy* (New York: Doubleday and Company, Inc., 1970), pp. 74 *et seq.*; also Mary Warnock, *Ethics Since 1900* (London: Oxford University Press, 1966), pp. 19–27.

23

An Introduction to the Principles of Morals and Legislation

JEREMY BENTHAM

CHAPTER 1. OF THE PRINCIPLE OF UTILITY

I. Nature has placed mankind under the governance of two sovereign masters, *pain* and *pleasure*. It is for them alone to point out what we ought to do, as well as to determine what we shall do. On the one hand the standard of right and wrong, on the other the chain of causes and effects, are fastened to their throne. They govern us in all we do, in all we say, in all we think; every effort we can make to throw off our subjection, will serve but to demonstrate and confirm it. In words a man may pretend to abjure their empire: but in reality he will remain subject to it all the while. The *principle of utility*[1] recognizes the subjection, and assumes it for the foundation of that system, the object of which is to rear the fabric of felicity by the hands of reason and of law. Systems which attempt to question it, deal in sounds instead of sense, in caprice instead of reason, in darkness instead of light.

But enough of metaphor and declamation: it is not by such means that moral science is to be improved.

II. The principle of utility is the foundation of the present work; it will be proper therefore at the outset to give an explicit and determinate account of what is meant by it. By the principle of utility is meant that principle which approves or disapproves of every action whatsoever, according to the tendency which it appears to have to augment or diminish the happiness of the party

FROM *An Introduction to the Principles of Morals and Legislation* by Jeremy Bentham, Chapters 1, 4, 10 (1789).

[1] To this denomination has of late been added, or substituted, the *greatest happiness or greatest felicity* principle: this for shortness, instead of saying at length *that principle* which states the greatest happiness of all those whose interest is in question, as being the right and proper, and only right and proper and universally desirable, end of human action: of human action in every situation, and in particular in that of a functionary or set of functionaries exercising the powers of government. The word *utility* does not so clearly point to the ideas of *pleasure* and *pain as* the words *happiness* and *felicity* do: nor does it lead us to the consideration of the *number*, of the interests affected; to the *number*, as being the circumstance, which contributes, in the largest proportion, to the formation of the standard here in question; the *standard of right and wrong*, by which alone the propriety of human conduct, in every situation, can with propriety be tried. This want of a sufficiently manifest connexion between the ideas of *happiness* and *pleasure* on the one hand, and the idea of *utility* on the other, I have every now and then found operating, and with but too much efficiency, as a bar to the acceptance, that might otherwise have been given, to this principle.

whose interest is in question; or, what is the same thing in other words, to promote or to oppose that happiness. I say of every action whatsoever; and therefore not only of every action of a private individual, but of every measure of government.

III. By utility is meant that property in any object, whereby it tends to produce benefit, advantage, pleasure, good, or happiness, (all this in the present case comes to the same thing) or (what comes again to the same thing) to prevent the happening of mischief, pain, evil, or unhappiness to the party whose interest is considered: if that party be the community in general, then the happiness of the community: if a particular individual, then the happiness of that individual.

IV. The interest of the community is one of the most general expressions that can occur in the phraseology of morals: no wonder that the meaning of it is often lost. When it has a meaning, it is this. The community is a fictitious *body*, composed of the individual persons who are considered as constituting as it were its *members*. The interest of the community then is, what?—the sum of the interests of the several members who compose it.

V. It is in vain to talk of the interest of the community, without understanding what is the interest of the individual.[2] A thing is said to promote the interest or to be *for* the interest, of an individual, when it tends to add to the sum total of his pleasures: or, what comes to the same thing, to diminish the sum total of his pains.

VI. An action then may be said to be conformable to the principle of utility, or, for shortness' sake, to utility, (meaning with respect to the community at large) when the tendency it has to augment the happiness of the community is greater than any it has to diminish it.

VII. A measure of government (which is but a particular kind of action, performed by a particular person or persons) may be said to be conformable to or dictated by the principle of utility, when in like manner the tendency which it has to augment the happiness of the community is greater than any which it has to diminish it.

VIII. When an action, or in particular a measure of government, is supposed by a man to be conformable to the principle of utility, it may be convenient, for the purposes of discourse, to imagine a kind of law or dictate, called a law or dictate of utility: and to speak of the action in question, as being conformable to such law or dictate.

IX. A man may be said to be a partizan of the principle of utility, when the approbation or disapprobation he annexes to any action, or to any measure, is determined by and proportioned to the tendency which he conceives it to have to augment or to diminish the happiness of the community: or in other words, to its conformity or unconformity to the laws or dictates of utility.

X. Of an action that is conformable to the principle of utility, one may

---

[2] Interest is one of those words, which not having any superior *genus*, cannot in the ordinary way be defined.

always say either that it is one that ought to be done, or at least that it is not
one that ought not to be done. One may say also, that it is right it should be
done; at least that it is not wrong it should be done: that it is a right action;
at least that it is not a wrong action. When thus interpreted, the words *ought*,
and *right* and *wrong*, and others of that stamp, have a meaning: when otherwise,
they have none.

XI. Has the rectitude of this principle been ever formally contested? It
should seem that it had, by those who have not known what they have been
meaning. Is it susceptible of any direct proof? It should seem not, for that
which is used to prove everything else, cannot itself be proved; a chain of proofs
must have their commencement somewhere. To give such proof is as impossible
as it is needless.

XII. Not that there is or ever has been that human creature breathing,
however stupid or perverse, who has not on many, perhaps on most occasions
of his life, deferred to it. By the natural constitution of the human frame,
on most occasions of their lives men in general embrace this principle, without
thinking of it; if not for the ordering of their own actions, yet for the trying of
their own actions, as well as of those of other men. There have been, at the
same time, not many, perhaps even of the most intelligent, who have been
disposed to embrace it purely and without reserve. There are even few who have
not taken some occasion or other to quarrel with it, either on account of their
not understanding always how to apply it, or on account of some prejudice
or other which they were afraid to examine into, or could not bear to part with.
For such is the stuff that man is made of: in principle and in practice, in a right
track and in a wrong one, the rarest of all human qualities is consistency.

XIII. When a man attempts to combat the principle of utility, it is with reason
drawn, without his being aware of it, from that very principle itself.[3] His arguments, if they prove anything, prove not that the principle is *wrong*, but that,
according to the applications he supposes to be made of it, it is *misapplied*.
Is it possible for a man to move the earth? Yes; but he must first find out another earth to stand upon.

XIV. To disapprove the propriety of it by arguments is impossible; but,
from the causes that have been mentioned, or from some confused or partial
view of it, a man may happen to be disposed not to relish it. Where this is the
case, if he thinks the settling of his opinions on such a subject worth the trouble,
let him take the following steps, and at length, perhaps, he may come to reconcile
himself to it.

1. Let him settle with himself, whether he would wish to discard this principle
altogether; if so, let him consider what it is that all his reasonings (in matters
of politics especially) can amount to?

2. If he would, let him settle with himself, whether he would judge and act
without any principle, or whether there is any other he would judge and act by?

---

[3] "The principle of utility, (I have heard it said) is a dangerous principle: it is dangerous
on certain occasions to consult it." This is as much as to say, what? that it is not consonant
to utility, to consult utility: in short, that it is *not* consulting it, to consult it.

3. If there be, let him examine and satisfy himself whether the principle he thinks he has found is really any separate intelligible principle; or whether it be not a mere principle in words, a kind of phrase, which at bottom expresses neither more nor less than the mere averment of his own unfounded sentiments; that is, what in another person he might be apt to call caprice?

4. If he is inclined to think that his own approbation or disapprobation, annexed to the idea of an act, without any regard to its consequences, is a sufficient foundation for him to judge and act upon, let him ask himself whether his sentiment is to be a standard of right and wrong, with respect to every other man, or whether every man's sentiment has the same privilege of being a standard to itself?

5. In the first case, let him ask himself whether his principle is not despotical, and hostile to all the rest of the human race?

6. In the second case, whether it is not anarchical, and whether at this rate there are not as many different standards of right and wrong as there are men? and whether even to the same man, the same thing, which is right today, may not (without the least change in its nature) be wrong tomorrow? and whether the same thing is not right and wrong in the same place at the same time? and in either case, whether all argument is not at an end? and whether, when two men have said, "I like this," and "I don't like it," they can (upon such principle) have anything more to say?

7. If he should have said to himself, No: for that the sentiment which he proposes as a standard must be grounded on reflection, let him say on what particulars the reflection is to turn? if on particulars having relation to the utility of the act, then let him say whether this is not deserting his own principle, and borrowing assistance from that every one in opposition to which he sets it up: or if not on those particulars, on what other particulars?

8. If he should be for compounding the matter, and adopting his own principle in part, and the principle of utility in part, let him say how far he will adopt it?

9. When he has settled with himself where he will stop, then let him ask himself how he justifies to himself the adopting it so far? and why he will not adopt it any farther?

10. Admitting any other principle than the principle of utility to be a right principle, a principle that it is right for a man to pursue; admitting (what is not true) that the word *right* can have a meaning without reference to utility, let him say whether there is any such thing as a *motive* that a man can have to pursue the dictates of it: if there is, let him say what that motive is, and how it is to be distinguished from those which enforce the dictates of utility: if not, then lastly let him say what it is this other principle can be good for? . . .

CHAPTER IV. VALUE OF A LOT OF PLEASURE OR PAIN, HOW TO BE MEASURED

I. Pleasures then, and the avoidance of pains, are the *ends* which the legislator has in view: it behoves him therefore to understand their *value*. Pleasures and pains are the *instruments* he has to work with: it behoves him therefore to understand their force, which is again, in other words, their value.

II. To a person considered *by himself*, the value of a pleasure or pain considered *by itself*, will be greater or less, according to the four following circumstances.[4]

1. Its *intensity*.
2. Its *duration*.

3. Its *certainty* or *uncertainty*.
4. Its *propinquity* or *remoteness*.

III. These are the circumstances which are to be considered in estimating a pleasure or a pain considered each of them by itself. But when the value of any pleasure or pain is considered for the purpose of estimating the tendency of any *act* by which it is produced, there are two other circumstances to be taken into the account; these are,

5. Its *fecundity*, or the chance it has of being followed by sensations of the *same* kind: that is, pleasures, if it be a pleasure: pains, if it be a pain.

6. Its *purity*, or the chance it has of *not* being followed by sensations of the *opposite* kind: that is, pains, if it be a pleasure: pleasures, if it be a pain.

These two last, however, are in strictness scarcely to be deemed properties of the pleasures or the pain itself; they are not, therefore, in strictness to be taken into the account of the value of that pleasure or that pain. They are in strictness to be deemed properties only of the act, or other event, by which such pleasure or pain has been produced; and accordingly are only to be taken into the account of the tendency of such act or such event.

IV. To a *number* of persons, with reference to each of whom the value of a pleasure or a pain is considered, it will be greater or less, according to seven circumstances: to wit, the six preceding ones; *viz.*

1. Its *intensity*.
2. Its *duration*.
3. Its *certainty* or *uncertainty*.

4. Its *propinquity* or *remoteness*.
5. Its *fecundity*.
6. Its *purity*.

And one other; to wit:

7. Its *extent;* that is, the number of persons to whom it *extends;* or, (in other words) who are affected by it.

V. To take an exact account then of the general tendency of any act, by which the interests of a community are affected, proceed as follows. Begin

---

[4] These circumstances have since been denominated *elements* or *dimensions* of *value* in a pleasure or a pain.

Not long after the publication of the first edition, the following memoriter verses were framed, in the view of lodging more effectually, in the memory, these points, on which the whole fabric of morals and legislation may be seen to rest:

> *Intense, long, certain, speedy, fruitful, pure—*
> Such marks in *pleasures* and in *pains* endure.
> Such pleasures seek, if *private* be thy end:
> If it be *public*, wide let them *extend*.
> Such *pains* avoid, whichever be thy view:
> If pains *must* come, let them *extend* to few.

with any one person of those whose interests seem most immediately to be affected by it: and take an account,

1. Of the value of each distinguishable *pleasure* which appears to be produced by it in the *first* instance.

2. Of the value of each *pain* which appears to be produced by it in the *first* instance.

3. Of the value of each pleasure which appears to be produced by it *after* the first. This constitutes the *fecundity* of the first *pleasure* and the *impurity* of the first *pain*.

4. Of the value of each *pain* which appears to be produced by it after the first. This constitutes the *fecundity* of the first *pain*, and the *impurity* of the first pleasure.

5. Sum up all the values of all the *pleasures* on the one side, and those of all the pains on the other. The balance, if it be on the side of pleasure, will give the *good* tendency of the act upon the whole, with respect to the interests of that *individual* person; if on the side of pain, the *bad* tendency of it upon the whole.

6. Take an account of the *number* of persons whose interests appear to be concerned; and repeat the above process with respect to each. *Sum up* the numbers expressive of the degrees of *good* tendency, which the act has, with respect to each individual, in regard to whom the tendency of it is *good* upon the whole: do this again with respect to each individual, in regard to whom the tendency of it is *bad* upon the whole. Take the *balance;* which, if on the side of *pleasure*, will give the general *good tendency* of the act, with respect to the total number of community of individuals concerned; if on the side of pain the general *evil tendency*, with respect to the same community.

VI. It is not to be expected that this process should be strictly pursued previously to every moral judgment, or to every legislative or judicial operation. It may, however, be always kept in view: and as near as the process actually pursued on these occasions approaches to it, so near will such process approach to the character of an exact one.

VII. The same process is alike applicable to pleasure and pain in whatever shape they appear: and by whatever denomination they are distinguished: to pleasure, whether it be called *good* (which is properly the cause or instrument of pleasure), or *profit* (which is distant pleasure, or the cause or instrument of distant pleasure), or *convenience*, or *advantage, benefit, emolument, happiness*, and so forth: to pain, whether it be called *evil* (which corresponds to *good*), or *mischief*, or *inconvenience*, or *disadvantage*, or *loss*, or *unhappiness*, and so forth.

VIII. Nor is this a novel and unwarranted, any more than it is a useless theory. In all this there is nothing but what the practice of mankind, wheresoever they have a clear view of their own interest, is perfectly conformable to. An article of property, an estate in land, for instance, is valuable, on what account? On account of the pleasures of all kinds which it enables a man to produce, and what comes to the same thing, the pains of all kinds which it enables him to avert. But the value of such an article of property is universally understood to rise or fall according to the length or shortness of the time which a man has in it: the certainty or uncertainty of its coming into possession: and the nearness or remoteness of the time at which, if at all, it is to come into possession. As to the *intensity* of the pleasures which a man may derive from it, this is never thought of, because it depends upon the use which each particular person may come to make of it; which cannot be estimated till the particular pleasures he may come to derive from it, or the particular pains he may come to exclude by means of it, are brought to view. For the same reason, neither does he think of the *fecundity* or *purity* of those pleasures. . . .

CHAPTER X. MOTIVES

2. *No Motives Either Constantly Good, or Constantly Bad*

IX. In all this chain of motives, the principle or original link seems to be the last internal motive in prospect; it is to this that all the other motives in prospect owe their materiality; and the immediately acting motive its existence. This motive in prospect, we see, is always some pleasure, or some pain; some pleasure, which the act in question is expected to be a means of continuing or producing: some pain which it is expected to be a means of discontinuing or preventing. A motive is substantially nothing more than pleasure or pain, operating in a certain manner.

X. Now, pleasure is in *itself* a good: nay, even setting aside immunity from pain, the only good: pain is in itself an evil; and, indeed, without exception, the only evil; or else the words good and evil have no meaning. And this is alike true of every sort of pain, and of every sort of pleasure. It follows, therefore, immediately and incontestably, that *there is no such thing as any sort of motive that is in itself a bad one.*[5]

XI. It is common, however, to speak of actions as proceeding from *good* or *bad* motives: in which case the motives meant are such as are internal. The expression is far from being an accurate one; and as it is apt to occur in the consideration of almost every kind of offence, it will be requisite to settle the precise meaning of it, and observe how far it quadrates with the truth of things.

XII. With respect to goodness and badness, as it is with everything else that is not itself either pain or pleasure, so is it with motives. If they are good or bad, it is only on account of their effects: good, on account of their tendency to produce pleasure, or avert pain: bad, on account of their tendency to produce pain, or avert pleasure. Now the case is, that from one and the same motive, and from every kind of motive, may proceed actions that are good, others that are bad, and others that are indifferent. . . .

XXIX. It appears then that there is no such thing as any sort of motive

---

[5] Let a man's motive be ill-will; call it even malice, envy, cruelty; it is still a kind of pleasure that is his motive: the pleasure he takes at the thought of the pain which he sees, or expects to see, his adversary undergo. Now even this wretched pleasure, taken by itself, is good: it may be faint; it may be short: it must at any rate be impure: yet while it lasts, and before any bad consequences arrive, it is good as any other that is not more intense.

which is a bad one in itself: nor, consequently, any such thing as a sort of motive, which in itself is exclusively a good one. And as to their effects, it appears too that these are sometimes bad, at other times either indifferent or good: and this appears to be the case with every sort of motive. *If any sort of motive then is either good or bad on the score of its effects, this is the case only on individual occasions, and with individual motives;* and this is the case with one sort of motive as well as with another. *If any sort of motive then can, in consideration of its effects, be termed with any propriety a bad one,* it can only be with reference to the balance of all the effects it may have had of both kinds within a given period, that is, of its most usual tendency.

XXX. What then? (it will be said) are not lust, cruelty, avarice, bad motives? Is there so much as any one individual occasion, in which motives like these can be otherwise than bad? No, certainly: and yet the proposition, that there is no one *sort* of motive but what will on many occasions be a good one, is nevertheless true. The fact is, that these are names which, if properly applied, are never applied but in the cases where the motives they signify happen to be bad. The names of these motives, considered apart from their effects, are sexual desire, displeasure, and pecuniary interest. To sexual desire, when the effects of it are looked upon as bad, is given the name of lust. Now lust is always a bad motive. Why? Because if the case be such, that the effects of the motive are not bad, it does not go, or at least ought not to go, by the name of lust. The case is, then, that when I say, "Lust is a bad motive," it is a proposition that merely concerns the import of the word lust; and which would be false if transferred to the other word used for the same motive, sexual desire. Hence we see the emptiness of all those rhapsodies of common-place morality, which consist in the taking of such names as lust, cruelty, and avarice, and branding them with marks of reprobation: applied to the *thing*, they are false; applied to the *name*, they are true indeed, but nugatory. Would you do a real service to mankind, show them the cases in which sexual desire *merits* the name of lust; displeasure, that of cruelty; and pecuniary interest, that of avarice.

24

Utilitarianism

JOHN STUART MILL

CHAPTER I. GENERAL REMARKS

There are few circumstances among those which make up the present condition of human knowledge more unlike what might have been expected, or more significant of the backward state in which speculation on the most

FROM *Utilitarianism* by J. S. Mill, Chapters 1, 2, 4 (1863).

important subjects still lingers, than the little progress which has been made in the decision of the controversy respecting the criterion of right and wrong. From the dawn of philosophy, the question concerning the *summum bonum*, or, what is the same thing, concerning the foundation of morality, has been accounted the main problem in speculative thought, has occupied the most gifted intellects and divided them into sects and schools, carrying on a vigorous warfare against one another. And after more than two thousand years the same discussions continue, philosophers are still ranged under the same contending banners, and neither thinkers nor mankind at large seem nearer to being unanimous on the subject than when the youth Socrates listened to the old Protagoras, and asserted (if Plato's dialogue be grounded on a real conversation) the theory of utilitarianism against the popular morality of the so-called sophist.

It is true that similar confusion and uncertainty and, in some cases, similar discordance exist respecting the first principles of all the sciences, not excepting that which is deemed the most certain of them—mathematics, without much impairing, generally indeed without impairing at all, the trustworthiness of the conclusions of those sciences. An apparent anomaly, the explanation of which is that the detailed doctrines of a science are not usually deduced from, nor depend for their evidence upon, what are called its first principles. Were it not so, there would be no science more precarious, or whose conclusions were more insufficiently made out, than algebra, which derives none of its certainty from what are commonly taught to learners as its elements, since these, as laid down by some of its most eminent teachers, are as full of fictions as English law, and of mysteries as theology. The truths which are ultimately accepted as the first principles of a science are really the last results of metaphysical analysis, practised on the elementary notions with which the science is conversant; and their relation to the science is not that of foundations to an edifice, but of roots to a tree, which may perform their office equally well though they be never dug down to and exposed to light. But though in science the particular truth precede the general theory, the contrary might be expected to be the case with a practical art, such as morals or legislation. All action is for the sake of some end, and rules of action, it seems natural to suppose, must take their whole character and color from the end to which they are subservient. When we engage in a pursuit, a clear and precise conception of what we are pursuing would seem to be the first thing we need, instead of the last we are to look forward to. A test of right and wrong must be the means, one would think, of ascertaining what is right or wrong, and not a consequence of having already ascertained it.

The difficulty is not avoided by having recourse to the popular theory of a natural faculty, a sense or instinct, informing us of right and wrong. For— besides that the existence of such a moral instinct is itself one of the matters in dispute—those believers in it who have any pretensions to philosophy have been obliged to abandon the idea that it discerns what is right or wrong in the particular case in hand, as our other senses discern the sight or sound actually present. Our moral faculty, according to all those of its interpreters who are entitled to the name of thinkers, supplies us only with the general principles of moral judgments; it is a branch of our reason, not of our sensitive faculty; and must be looked to for the abstract doctrines of morality, not for perception of it in the concrete. The intuitive, no less than what may be termed the inductive, school of ethics insists on the necessity of general laws. They both agree that the morality of an individual action is not a question of direct perception, but of the application of a law to an individual case. They recognize also, to a great extent, the same moral laws, but differ as to their evidence and the source from which they derive their authority. According to the one opinion, the principles of morals are evident *a priori*, requiring nothing to command assent except that the meaning of the terms be understood. According to the other doctrine, right and wrong, as well as truth and falsehood, are questions of observation and experience. But both hold equally that morality must be deduced from principles; and the intuitive school affirm as strongly as the inductive that there is a science of morals. Yet they seldom attempt to make out a list of the *a priori* principles which are to serve as the premises of the science; still more rarely do they make any effort to reduce those various principles to one first principle, or common ground of obligation. They either assume the ordinary precepts of morals as of *a priori* authority, or they lay down as the common groundwork of those maxims, some generality much less obviously authoritative than the maxims themselves, and which has never succeeded in gaining popular acceptance. Yet to support their pretensions there ought either to be some one fundamental principle or law at the root of all morality, or, if there be several, there should be a determinate order of precedence among them; and the one principle, or the rule for deciding between the various principles when they conflict, ought to be self-evident.

To inquire how far the bad effects of this deficiency have been mitigated in practice, or to what extent the moral beliefs of mankind have been vitiated or made uncertain by the absence of any distinct recognition of an ultimate standard, would imply a complete survey and criticism of past and present ethical doctrine. It would, however, be easy to show that whatever steadiness or consistency these moral beliefs have attained has been mainly due to the tacit influence of a standard not recognized. Although the non-existence of an acknowledged first principle has made ethics not so much a guide as a consecration of men's actual sentiments, still, as men's sentiments, both in favor and of aversion, are greatly influenced by what they suppose to be the effect of things upon their happiness, the principle of utility, or, as Bentham latterly called it, the greatest happiness principle, has had a large share in forming the moral doctrines even of those who most scornfully reject its authority. Nor is there any school of thought which refuses to admit that the influence of actions on happiness is a most material and even predominant consideration in many of the details, of morals, however unwilling to acknowledge it as the fundamental principle of morality and the source of moral obligation. I might go much further and say that to all those *a priori* moralists who deem it necessary to argue at all, utilitarian arguments are indispensable. It is not my present purpose to criticize these thinkers; but I cannot help referring, for illustration, to a systematic treatise by one of the most illustrious of them, the *Metaphysics of Ethics* by Kant. This remarkable man, whose system of thought will long remain one of the landmarks in the history of philosophical speculation, does, in the treatise in question, lay down a universal first principle as the origin and ground of moral obligation; it is this: "So act that the rule on which thou actest would admit of being adopted as a law by all rational beings." But when he begins to deduce from this precept any of the actual duties of morality, he fails, almost grotesquely, to show that there would be any contradiction, any logical (not to say physical) impossibility, in the adoption by all rational beings of the most outrageously immoral rules of conduct. All he knows is that the *consequences* of their universal adoption would be such as no one would choose to incur.

On the present occasion, I shall, without further discussion of the other theories, attempt to contribute something towards the understanding and appreciation of the "utilitarian" or "happiness" theory, and towards such proof as it is susceptible of. It is evident that this cannot be proof in the ordinary and popular meaning of the term. Questions of ultimate ends are not amenable to direct proof. Whatever can be proved to be good must be so by being shown to be a means to something admitted to be good without proof. The medical art is proved to be good by its conducing to health; but how is it possible to prove that health is good? The art of music is good, for the reason, among others, that it produces pleasure; but what proof is it possible to give that pleasure is good? If, then, it is asserted that there is a comprehensive formula, including all things which are in themselves good, and that whatever else is good is not so as an end but as a means, the formula may be accepted or rejected, but is not a subject of what is commonly understood by proof. We are not, however, to infer that its acceptance or rejection must depend on blind impulse, or arbitrary choice. There is a larger meaning of the word "proof," in which this question is as amenable to it as any other of the disputed questions of philosophy. The subject is within the cognizance of the rational faculty; and neither does that faculty deal with it solely in the way of intuition. Considerations may be presented capable of determining the intellect either to give or withhold its assent to the doctrine; and this is equivalent to proof. . . .

CHAPTER II. WHAT UTILITARIANISM IS

A passing remark is all that needs be given to the ignorant blunder of supposing that those who stand up for utility as the test of right and wrong use the term in that restricted and merely colloquial sense in which utility is opposed to pleasure. An apology is due to the philosophical opponents of utilitarianism, for even the momentary appearance of confounding them with anyone capable of so absurd a misconception; which is the more extraordinary, inasmuch as the contrary accusation, of referring everything to pleasure, and that, too, in its grossest form, is another of the common charges against utilitarianism: and, as has been pointedly remarked by an able writer, the same sort of persons, and often the very same persons, denounce the theory "as impracticably dry when the word 'utility' precedes the word 'pleasure,' and as too practically voluptuous when the word 'pleasure' precedes the word 'utility'." Those who know anything about the matter are aware that every writer, from Epicurus to Bentham, who maintained the theory of utility, meant by it, not something to be contradistinguished from pleasure, but pleasure itself, together with exemption from pain; and instead of opposing the useful to the agreeable or the ornamental, have always declared that the useful means these, among other things. Yet the common herd, including the herd of writers, not only in newspapers and periodicals, but in books of weight and pretension, are perpetually falling into this shallow mistake. Having caught up the word "utilitarian" while knowing nothing whatever about it but its sound they habitually express by it the rejection or the neglect of pleasure in some of its forms: of beauty, of ornament or of amusement. Nor is the term thus ignorantly misapplied solely in disparagement, but occasionally in compliment, as though it implied superiority to frivolity and the mere pleasures of the moment. And this perverted use is the only one in which the word is popularly known, and the one from which the new generation are acquiring their sole notion of its meaning. Those who introduced the word, but who had for many years discontinued it as a distinctive appellation, may well feel themselves called upon to resume it if by doing so they can hope to contribute anything towards rescuing it from this utter degradation.[1]

The creed which accepts as the foundation of morals "utility" or the "greatest happiness principle" holds that actions are right in proportion as they tend to promote happiness, wrong as they tend to produce the reverse of happiness. By happiness is intended pleasure, and the absence of pain; by unhappiness, pain, and the privation of pleasure. To give a clear view of the moral standard set up by the theory, much more requires to be said; in particular, what things it includes in the ideas of pain and pleasure; and to what extent this is left an open question. But these supplementary explanations do not affect the theory of life on which this theory of morality is grounded—namely, that pleasure and freedom from pain are the only things desirable as ends; and that all desirable things (which are as numerous in the utilitarian as in any other scheme) are desirable either for the pleasure inherent in themselves, or as means to the promotion of pleasure and the prevention of pain.

Now such a theory of life excites in many minds, and among them in some of the most estimable in feeling and purpose, inveterate dislike. To suppose that life has (as they express it) no higher end than pleasure—no better and

---

[1] The author of this essay has reason for believing himself to be the first person who brought the word "utilitarian" into use. He did not invent it, but adopted it from a passing expression in Mr. Galt's *Annals of the Parish*. After using it as a designation for several years, he and others abandoned it from a growing dislike to anything resembling a badge or watchword of sectarian distinction. But as a name for one single opinion, not a set of opinions—to denote the recognition of utility as a standard, not any particular way of applying it—the term supplies a want in the language, and offers, in many cases, a convenient mode of avoiding tiresome circumlocution.

nobler object of desire and pursuit—they designate as utterly mean and groveling; as a doctrine worthy only of swine, to whom the followers of Epicurus were, at a very early period, contemptuously likened; and modern holders of the doctrine are occasionally made the subject of equally polite comparisons by its German, French, and English assailants.

When thus attacked, the Epicureans have always answered that it is not they, but their accusers, who represent human nature in a degrading light, since the accusation supposes human beings to be capable of no pleasures except those of which swine are capable. If this supposition were true, the charge could not be gainsaid, but would then be no longer an imputation; for if the sources of pleasure were precisely the same to human beings and to swine, the rule of life which is good enough for the one would be good enough for the other. The comparison of the Epicurean life to that of beasts is felt as degrading, precisely because a beast's pleasures do not satisfy a human being's conceptions of happiness. Human beings have faculties more elevated than the animal appetites and, when once made conscious of them, do not regard anything as happiness which does not include their gratification. I do not, indeed, consider the Epicureans to have been by any means faultless in drawing out their scheme of consequences from the utilitarian principle. To do this in any sufficient manner, many Stoic, as well as Christian, elements require to be included. But there is no known Epicurean theory of life which does not assign to the pleasures of the intellect, of the feelings and imagination, and of the moral sentiments, a much higher value of pleasures than to those of mere sensation. It must be admitted, however, that utilitarian writers in general have placed the superiority of mental over bodily pleasures chiefly in the greater permanency, safety, uncostliness, etc., of the former—that is, in their circumstantial advantages rather than in their intrinsic nature. And on all these points utilitarians have fully proved their case; but they might have taken the other and, as it may be called, higher ground with entire consistency. It is quite compatible with the principle of utility to recognize the fact that some kinds of pleasure are more desirable and more valuable than others. It would be absurd that, while, in estimating all other things, quality is considered as well as quantity, the estimation of pleasures should be supposed to depend on quantity alone.

If I am asked what I mean by difference of quality in pleasures, or what makes one pleasure more valuable than another, merely as a pleasure, except its being greater in amount, there is but one possible answer. Of two pleasures, if there be one to which all or almost all who have experience of both give a decided preference, irrespective of a feeling of moral obligation to prefer it, that is the more desirable pleasure. If one of the two is, by those who are competently acquainted with both, placed so far above the other that they prefer it, even though knowing it to be attended with a greater amount of discontent, and would not resign it for any quantity of the other pleasure which their nature is capable of, we are justified in ascribing to the preferred enjoyment a superiority in quality so far outweighing quantity as to render it, in comparison, of small account.

Now it is an unquestionable fact that those who are equally acquainted with and equally capable of appreciating and enjoying both, do give a most marked preference to the manner of existence which employs their higher faculties. Few human creatures would consent to be changed into any of the lower animals for a promise of the fullest allowance of a beast's pleasures; no intelligent human being would consent to be a fool, no instructed person would be an ignoramus, no person of feeling and conscience would be selfish and base, even though they should be persuaded that the fool, the dunce, or the rascal is better satisfied with his lot than they are with theirs. They would not resign what they possess more than he for the most complete satisfaction of all the desires which they have in common with him. If they ever fancy they would, it is only in cases of unhappiness so extreme that to escape from it they would exchange their lot for almost any other, however undesirable in their own eyes. A being of higher faculties requires more to make him happy, is capable probably of more acute suffering, and certainly accessible to it at more points, than one of an inferior type; but in spite of these liabilities, he can never really wish to sink into what he feels to be a lower grade of existence. We may give what explanation we please of this unwillingness; we may attribute it to pride, a name which is given indiscriminately to some of the most and to some of the least estimable feelings of which mankind are capable: we may refer it to the love of liberty and personal independence, an appeal to which was with the Stoics one of the most effective means for the inculcation of it; to the love of power or to the love of excitement, both of which do really enter into and contribute to it; but its most appropriate appellation is a sense of dignity, which all human beings possess in one form or other, and in some, though by no means in exact, proportion to their higher faculties, and which is so essential a part of the happiness of those in whom it is strong that nothing which conflicts with it could be otherwise than momentarily an object of desire to them. Whoever supposes that this preference takes place at a sacrifice of happiness—that the superior being, in anything like equal circumstances, is not happier than the inferior—confounds the two very different ideas of happiness and content. It is indisputable that the being whose capacities of enjoyment are low has the greatest chance of having them fully satisfied; and a highly endowed being will always feel that any happiness which he can look for, as the world is constituted, is imperfect. But he can learn to bear its imperfections, if they are at all bearable; and they will not make him envy the being who is indeed unconscious of the imperfections, but only because he feels not at all the good which those imperfections qualify. It is better to be a human being dissatisfied than a pig satisfied; better to be Socrates dissatisfied than a fool satisfied. And if the fool, or the pig, are of a different opinion, it is because they only know their own side of the question. The other party to the comparison knows both sides.

It may be objected that many who are capable of the higher pleasures occasionally, under the influence of temptation, postpone them to the lower. But this is quite compatible with a full appreciation of the intrinsic superiority of the higher. Men often, from infirmity of character, make their election for the nearer good, though they know it to be the less valuable; and this no less when the choice is between two bodily pleasures than when it is between bodily and mental. They pursue sensual indulgences to the injury of health, though perfectly aware that health is the greater good. It may be further objected that many who begin with youthful enthusiasm for everything noble, as they advance in years, sink into indolence and selfishness. But I do not believe that those who undergo this very common change voluntarily choose the lower description of pleasures in preference to the higher. I believe that, before they devote themselves exclusively to the one, they have already become incapable of the other. Capacity for the nobler feelings is in most natures a very tender plant, easily killed, not only by hostile influences, but by mere want of sustenance; and in the majority of young persons it speedily dies away if the occupations to which their position in life has devoted them, and the society into which it has thrown them, are not favorable to keeping that higher capacity in exercise. Men lose their high aspirations as they lose their intellectual tastes, because they have not time or opportunity for indulging them; and they addict themselves to inferior pleasures, not because they deliberately prefer them, but because they are either the only ones to which they have access, or the only ones which they are any longer capable of enjoying. It may be questioned whether any one who has remained equally susceptible to both classes of pleasures, ever knowingly and calmly preferred the lower, though many, in all ages, have broken down in an ineffectual attempt to combine both.

From this verdict of the only competent judges, I apprehend there can be no appeal. On a question which is the best worth having of two pleasures, or which of two modes of existence is the most grateful to the feelings, apart from its moral attributes and from its consequences, the judgment of those who are qualified by knowledge of both, or, if they differ, that of the majority of them, must be admitted as final. And there needs be the less hesitation to accept this judgment respecting the quality of pleasures, since there is no other tribunal to be referred to even on the question of quantity. What means are there of determining which is the acutest of two pains, or the intensest of two pleasurable sensations, except the general suffrage of those who are familiar with both? Neither pains nor pleasures are homogeneous, and pain is always heterogeneous with pleasure. What is there to decide whether a particular pleasure is worth purchasing at the cost of a particular pain, except the feelings and judgment of the experienced? When, therefore, those feelings and judgment declare the pleasures derived from the higher faculties to be preferable *in kind*, apart from the question of intensity, to those of which the animal nature, disjoined from the higher faculties, is susceptible, they are entitled on this subject to the same regard.

I have dwelt on this point, as being a necessary part of a perfectly just conception of utility or happiness considered as the directive rule of human conduct. But it is by no means an indispensable condition to the acceptance of the utilitarian standard; for that standard is not the agent's own greatest happiness, but the greatest amount of happiness altogether; and if it may possibly be doubted whether a noble character is always the happier for its nobleness, there can be no doubt that it makes other people happier, and that the world in general is immensely a gainer by it. Utilitarianism, therefore, could only attain its end by the general cultivation of nobleness of character, even if each individual were only benefited by the nobleness of others, and his own, so far as happiness is concerned, were a sheer deduction from the benefit. . . .

CHAPTER IV. OF WHAT SORT OF PROOF THE PRINCIPLE OF UTILITY IS SUSCEPTIBLE

It has already been remarked that questions of ultimate ends do not admit of proof, in the ordinary acceptation of the term. To be incapable of proof by reasoning is common to all first principles, to the first premises of our knowledge, as well as to those of our conduct. But the former, being matters of fact, may be the subject of a direct appeal to the faculties which judge of fact—namely, our senses and our internal consciousness. Can an appeal be made to the same faculties on questions of practical ends? Or by what other faculty is cognizance taken of them?

Questions about ends are, in other words, questions what things are desirable. The utilitarian doctrine is that happiness is desirable, and the only thing desirable, as an end; all other things being only desirable as means to that end. What ought to be required of this doctrine, what conditions is it requisite that the doctrine should fulfill—to make good its claim to be believed?

The only proof capable of being given that an object is visible is that people actually see it. The only proof that a sound is audible is that people hear it; and so of the other sources of our experience. In like manner, I apprehend, the sole evidence it is possible to produce that anything is desirable is that people do actually desire it. If the end which the utilitarian doctrine proposes to itself were not, in theory and in practice, acknowledged to be an end, nothing could ever convince any person that it was so. No reason can be given why the general happiness is desirable, except that each person, so far as he believes it to be attainable, desires his own happiness. This, however, being a fact, we have not only all the proof which the case admits of, but all which it is possible to require, that happiness is a good; that each person's happiness is a good to that person, and the general happiness, therefore, a good to the aggregate of all persons. Happiness had made out its title as *one* of the ends of conduct, and consequently one of the criteria of morality.

But it has not, by this alone, proved itself to be the sole criterion. To do that, it would seem, by the same rule, necessary to show, not only that people desire happiness, but that they never desire anything else. Now it is palpable that they do desire things which, in common language, are decidedly distinguished from happiness. They desire, for example, virtue and the absence of vice, no less really than pleasure and the absence of pain. The desire of virtue is not as universal, but it is as authentic a fact as the desire of happiness. And hence the opponents of the utilitarian standard deem that they have a right to infer that there are other ends of human action besides happiness, and that happiness is not the standard of approbation and disapprobation.

But does the utilitarian doctrine deny that people desire virtue, or maintain that virtue is not a thing to be desired? The very reverse. It maintains not only that virtue is to be desired, but that it is to be desired disinterestedly, for itself. Whatever may be the opinion of utilitarian moralists as to the original conditions by which virtue is made virtue, however they may believe (as they do) that actions and dispositions are only virtuous because they promote another end than virtue, yet this being granted, and it having been decided, from considerations of this description, what *is* virtuous, they not only place virtue at the very head of the things which are good as means to the ultimate end, but they also recognize as a psychological fact the possibility of its being, to the individual, a good in itself, without looking to any end beyond it; and hold that the mind is not in a right state, not in a state conformable to utility, not in the state most conducive to the general happiness, unless it does love virtue in this manner—as a thing desirable in itself, even although, in the individual instance, it should not produce those other desirable consequences which it tends to produce, and on account of which it is held to be virtue. This opinion is not, in the smallest degree, a departure from the happiness principle. The ingredients of happiness are very various, and each of them is desirable in itself, and not merely when considered as swelling an aggregate. The principle of utility does not mean that any given pleasure, as music, for instance, or any given exemption from pain, as for example health, is to be looked upon as means to a collective something termed happiness, and to be desired on that account. They are desired and desirable in and for themselves; besides being means, they are a part of the end. Virtue, according to the utilitarian doctrine, is not naturally and originally part of the end, but it is capable of becoming so; and in those who love it disinterestedly it has become so, and is desired and cherished, not as a means to happiness, but as a part of their happiness.

To illustrate this further, we may remember that virtue is not the only thing originally a means, and which if it were not a means to anything else would be and remain indifferent, but which by association with what it is a means to comes to be desired for itself, and that too with the utmost intensity. What, for example, shall we say of the love of money? There is nothing originally more desirable about money than about any heap of glittering pebbles. Its worth is solely that of the things which it will buy; the desires for other things than itself, which it is a means of gratifying. Yet the love of money is not only one of the strongest moving forces of human life, but money is, in many cases, desired in and for itself; the desire to possess it is often stronger than the desire to use it, and goes on increasing when all the desires which point to ends beyond it, to be compassed by it, are falling off. It may, then, be said truly that money is desired not for the sake of an end, but as part of the end. From being a means to happiness, it has come to be itself a principal ingredient of the individual's conception of happiness. The same may be said of the majority of the great objects of human life: power, for example, or fame, except that to each of these there is a certain amount of immediate pleasure annexed, which has at least the semblance of being naturally inherent in them—a thing which cannot be said of money. Still, however, the strongest natural attraction, both of power and of fame, is the immense aid they give to the attainment of our other wishes; and it is the strong association thus generated between them and all our objects of desire which gives to the direct desire of them the intensity it often assumes, so as in some characters to surpass in strength all other desires. In these cases the means have become a part of the end, and a more important part of it than any of the things which they are means to. What was once desired as an instrument for the attainment of happiness has come to be desired for its own sake. In being desired for its own sake it is, however, desired as *part* of happiness. The person is made, or thinks he would be made, happy by its mere possession; and is made unhappy by failure to obtain it. The desire of it is not a different thing from the desire of happiness any more than the love of music or the desire of health. They are included in happiness. They are some of the elements of which the desire of happiness is made up. Happiness is not an abstract idea but a concrete whole; and these are some of its parts. And the utilitarian standard sanctions and approves their being so. Life would be a poor thing, very ill provided with sources of happiness, if there were not this provision of nature by which things originally indifferent, but conducive to, or otherwise associated with, the satisfaction of our primitive desires, become in themselves sources of pleasure more valuable than the primitive pleasures, both in permanency, in the space of human existence that they are capable of covering, and even in intensity.

Virtue, according to the utilitarian conception, is a good of this description. There was no original desire of it, or motive to it, save its conduciveness to pleasure, and especially to protection from pain. But through the association thus formed it may be felt a good in itself, and desired as such with as great intensity as any other good; and with this difference between it and the love of money, of power, or of fame, that all of these may, and often do, render the individual noxious to the other members of the society to which he belongs, whereas there is nothing which makes him so much a blessing to them as the cultivation of the disinterested love of virtue. And consequently, the utilitarian standard, while it tolerates and approves those other acquired desires, up to the point beyond which they would be more injurious to the general happiness than promotive of it, enjoins and requires the cultivation of the love of virtue up to the greatest strength possible, as being above all things important to the general happiness.

It results from the preceding considerations that there is in reality nothing desired except happiness. Whatever is desired otherwise than as a means to some end beyond itself, and ultimately to happiness, is desired as itself a part of happiness, and is not desired for itself until it has become so. Those who desire virtue for its own sake desire it either because the consciousness of it is a pleasure, or because the consciousness of being without it is a pain, or for both reasons united; as in truth the pleasure and pain seldom exist separately, but almost always together—the same person feeling pleasure in the degree of virtue attained, and pain in not having attained more. If one of these gave him no pleasure, and the other no pain, he would not love or desire virtue, or would desire it only for the other benefits which it might produce to himself or to persons whom he cared for.

We have now, then, an answer to the question, of what sort of proof the principle of utility is susceptible. If the opinion which I have now stated is psychologically true—if human nature is so constituted as to desire nothing which is not either a part of happiness or a means of happiness, we can have no other proof, and we require no other, that these are the only things desirable. If so, happiness is the sole end of human action, and the promotion of it the test by which to judge of all human conduct; from whence it necessarily follows that it must be the criterion of morality, since a part is included in the whole.

And now to decide whether this is really so, whether mankind do desire nothing for itself but that which is a pleasure to them, or of which the absence is a pain, we have evidently arrived at a question of fact and experience, dependent, like all similar questions, upon evidence. It can only be determined by practised self-conciousness and self-observation, assisted by observation of others. I believe that these sources of evidence, impartially consulted, will declare that desiring a thing and finding it pleasant, aversion to it and thinking of it as painful, are phenomena entirely inseparable or rather two parts of the same phenomenon; in strictness of language, two different modes of naming the same psychological fact; that to think of an object as desirable (unless for the sake of its consequences) and to think of it as pleasant are one and the same thing; and that to desire anything except in proportion as the idea of it is pleasant, is a physical and metaphysical impossibility.

25

The Right and the Good

W. D. ROSS

CHAPTER II. WHAT MAKES RIGHT ACTS RIGHT?

The real point at issue between hedonism and utilitarianism on the one hand and their opponents on the other is not whether "right" means "productive of so and so"; for it cannot with any plausibility be maintained that it does. The point at issue is that to which we now pass, *viz.*, whether there is any general character which makes right acts right, and if so, what it is. Among the main historical attempts to state a single characteristic of all right actions which is the foundation of their rightness are those made by egoism and utilitarianism. But I do not propose to discuss these, not because the subject is unimportant, but because it has been dealt with so often and so well already, and because there has come to be so much agreement among moral philosophers that neither of these theories is satisfactory. A much more attractive theory has been put forward by Professor Moore: that what makes actions right is that they are productive of more *good* than could have been produced by any other action open to the agent.

This theory is in fact the culmination of all the attempts to base rightness on productivity of some sort of result. The first form this attempt takes is the attempt to base rightness on conduciveness to the advantage or pleasure of the agent. This theory comes to grief over the fact, which stares us in the face, that a great part of duty consists in an observance of the rights and a furtherance of the interests of others, whatever the cost to ourselves may be. Plato and others may be right in holding that a regard for the rights of others never in the long run involves a loss of happiness for the agent, that "the just life profits a man." But this, even if true, is irrelevant to the rightness of the act. As soon as a man does an action *because* he thinks he will promote his own interests thereby, he is acting not from a sense of its rightness but from self-interest.

To the egoistic theory hedonistic utilitarianism supplies a much-needed amendment. It points out correctly that the fact that a certain pleasure will be enjoyed by the agent is no reason why he *ought* to bring it into being rather than an equal or greater pleasure to be enjoyed by another, though, human nature being what it is, it makes it not unlikely that he *will* try to bring it into being. But hedonistic utilitarianism in its turn needs a correction. On reflection it seems clear that pleasure is not the only thing in life that we think good in itself, that for instance we think the possession of a good character, or an intelligent understanding of the world, as good or better. A great advance is made by the substitution of "productive of the greatest good" for "productive of the greatest pleasure."

Not only is this theory more attractive than hedonistic utilitarianism, but its logical relation to that theory is such that the latter could not be true unless *it* were true, while it might be true though hedonistic utilitarianism were not. It is in fact one of the logical bases of hedonistic utilitarianism. For the view that what produces the maximum pleasure is right has for its bases the views (1) that what produces the maximum good is right, and (2) that pleasure is the only thing good in itself. If they were not assuming that what produces the maximum *good* is right, the utilitarians' attempt to show that pleasure is the only thing good in itself, which is in fact the point they take most pains to establish, would have been quite irrelevant to their attempt to prove that only what produces the maximum *pleasure* is right. If, therefore, it can be shown that productivity of the maximum good is not what makes all right actions right, we shall *a fortiori* have refuted hedonistic utilitarianism.

When a plain man fulfils a promise because he thinks he ought to do so, it seems clear that he does so with no thought of its total consequences, still less with any opinion that these are likely to be the best possible. He thinks in fact much more of the past than of the future. What makes him think it right to act in a certain way is the fact that he has promised to do so—that and, usually, nothing more. That his act will produce the best possible consequences is not his reason for calling it right. What lends colour to the theory we are examining, then, is not the actions (which form probably a great majority of our actions) in which some such reflection as "I have promised" is the only reason we give ourselves for thinking a certain action right, but the exceptional cases in which the consequences of fulfilling a promise (for instance) would be so disastrous to others that we judge it right not to do so. It must of course be admitted that such cases exist. If I have promised to meet a friend at a particular time for some trivial purpose, I should certainly think myself justified in breaking my engagement if by doing so I could prevent a serious accident or bring relief to the victims of one. And the supporters of the view we are examining hold that my thinking so is due to my thinking that I shall bring more good into existence by the one action than by the other. A different account may, however, be given of the matter, an account which will, I believe, show itself to be the true one. It may be said that besides the duty of fulfilling promises I have and recognize a duty of relieving distress, and that when I think it right to do the latter at the cost of not doing the former, it is not because I think I shall produce more good thereby but because I think it the duty which is in the circumstances more of a duty. This account surely corresponds much more closely with what we really think in such a situation. If, so far as I can see, I could bring equal amounts of good into being by fulfilling my promise and by helping some one to whom I had made no promise, I should not hesitate to regard the former as my duty. Yet on the view that what is right is right because it is productive of the most good I should not so regard it.

There are two theories, each in its way simple, that offer a solution of such cases of conscience. One is the view of Kant, that there are certain duties of perfect obligation, such as those of fulfilling promises, of paying debts, of telling the truth, which admit of no exception whatever in favour of duties of imperfect obligation, such as that of relieving distress. The other is the view of, for instance, Professor Moore and Dr. Rashdall, that there is only the duty of producing good, and that all "conflicts of duties" should be resolved by asking "by which action will most good be produced?" But it is more important that our theory fit the facts than that it be simple, and the account we have given above corresponds (it seems to me) better than either of the simpler theories with what we really think, *viz.*, that normally promise-keeping, for example should come before benevolence, but that when and only when the good to be produced by the benevolent act is very great and the promise comparatively trivial, the act of benevolence becomes our duty.

In fact the theory of "ideal utilitarianism," if I may for brevity refer so to the theory of Professor Moore, seems to simplify unduly our relations to our fellows. It says, in effect, that the only morally significant relation in which my neighbours stand to me is that of being possible beneficiaries by my action. They do stand in this relation to me, and this relation is morally significant. But they may also stand to me in the relation of promisee to promiser, of creditor to debtor, of wife to husband, of child to parent, of friend to friend, of fellow countryman to fellow countryman, and the like; and each of these relations is the foundation of a *prima facie* duty, which is more or less incumbent on me according to the circumstances of the case. When I am in a situation, as perhaps I always am, in which more than one of these *prima facie* duties is incumbent on me, what I have to do is to study the situation as fully as I can until I form the considered opinion (it is never more) that in the circumstances one of them is more incumbent than any other; then I am bound to think that to do this *prima facie* duty is my duty *sans phrase* in the situation.

I suggest *"prima facie* duty" or "conditional duty" as a brief way of referring to the characteristic (quite distinct from that of being a duty proper) which an act has, in virtue of being of a certain kind (e.g., the keeping of a promise), of being an act which would be a duty proper if it were not at the same time of another kind which is morally significant. Whether an act is a duty proper or actual duty depends on *all* the morally significant kinds it is an instance of. . . .

There is nothing arbitrary about these *prima facie* duties. Each rests on a definite circumstance which cannot seriously be held to be without moral significance. Of *prima facie* duties I suggest, without claiming completeness or finality for it, the following division.[1]

(1) Some duties rest on previous acts of my own. These duties seem to include two kinds, (*a*) those resting on a promise or what may fairly be called an implicit promise, such as the implicit undertaking not to tell lies which seems to be implied in the act of entering into conversation (at any rate by civilized men), or of writing books that purport to be history and not fiction. These may be called the duties of fidelity. (*b*) Those resting on a previous wrongful act. These may be called the duties of reparation. (2) Some rest on previous acts of other men, i.e., services done by them to me. These may be loosely described as the duties of gratitude. (3) Some rest on the fact or possibility of a distribution of pleasure or happiness (or of the means thereto) which is not in accordance with the merit of the persons concerned; in such cases there arises a duty to upset or prevent such a distribution. These are the duties of justice. (4) Some rest on the mere fact that there are other beings in the world whose condition

---

[1] I should make it plain at this stage that I am *assuming* the correctness of some of our main convictions as to *prima facie* duties, or, more strictly, am claiming that we *know* them to be true. To me it seems as self-evident as anything could be, that to make a promise, for instance, is to create a moral claim on us in someone else. Many readers will perhaps say that they do *not* know this to be true. If so, I certainly cannot prove it to them; I can only ask them to reflect again, in the hope that they will ultimately agree that they also know it to be true. The main moral convictions of the plain man seem to me to be, not opinions which it is for philosophy to prove or disprove, but knowledge from the start; and in my own case I seem to find little difficulty in distinguishing these essential convictions from other moral convictions which I also have, which are merely fallible opinions based on an imperfect study of the working for good or evil of certain institutions or types of action.

we can make better in respect of virtue, or of intelligence, or of pleasure. These are the duties of beneficence. (5) Some rest on the fact that we can improve our own condition in respect of virtue or of intelligence. These are the duties of self-improvement. (6) I think that we should distinguish from (4) the duties that may be summed up under the title of "not injuring others." No doubt to injure others is incidentally to fail to do them good; but it seems to me clear that non-maleficence is apprehended as a duty distinct from that of beneficence, and as a duty of a more stringent character. It will be noticed that this alone among the types of duty has been stated in a negative way. An attempt might no doubt be made to state this duty, like the others, in a positive way. It might be said that it is really the duty to prevent ourselves from acting either from an inclination to harm others or from an inclination to seek our own pleasure, in doing which we should incidentally harm them. But on reflection it seems clear that the primary duty here is the duty not to harm others, this being a duty whether or not we have an inclination that if followed would lead to our harming them; and that when we have such an inclination the primary duty not to harm others gives rise to a consequential duty to resist the inclination. The recognition of this duty of non-maleficence is the first step on the way to the recognition of the duty of beneficence; and that accounts for the prominence of the commands "thou shalt not kill," "thou shalt not commit adultery," "thou shalt not steal," "thou shalt not bear false witness," in so early a code as the Decalogue. But even when we have come to recognize the duty of beneficence, it appears to me that the duty of non-maleficence is recognized as a distinct one, and as *prima facie* more binding. We should not in general consider it justifiable to kill one person in order to keep another alive, or to steal from one in order to give alms to another.

The essential defect of the "ideal utilitarian" theory is that it ignores, or at least does not do full justice to, to the highly personal character of duty. If the only duty is to produce the maximum of good, the question who is to have the good—whether it is myself, or my benefactor, or a person to whom I have made a promise to confer that good on him, or a mere fellow man to whom I stand in no such special relation—should make no difference to my having a duty to produce that good. But we are all in fact sure that it makes a vast difference. . . .

It is necessary to say something by way of clearing up the relation between *prima facie* duties and the actual or absolute duty to do one particular act in particular circumstances. If, as almost all moralists except Kant are agreed, and as most plain men think, it is sometimes right to tell a lie or to break a promise, it must be maintained that there is a difference between *prima facie* duty and actual or absolute duty. When we think ourselves justified in breaking, and indeed morally obliged to break, a promise in order to relieve some one's distress, we do not for a moment cease to recognize a *prima facie* duty to keep our promise, and this leads us to feel, not indeed shame or repentance, but certainly compunction, for behaving as we do; we recognize, further, that it is our duty to make up somehow to the promisee for the breaking of the promise.

We have to distinguish from the characteristic of being our duty that of tending to be our duty. Any act that we do contains various elements in virtue of which it falls under various categories. In virtue of being the breaking of a promise, for instance, it tends to be wrong; in virtue of being an instance of relieving distress it tends to be right. Tendency to be one's duty may be called a parti-resultant attribute, i.e., one which belongs to an act in virtue of some one component in its nature. *Being* one's duty is a toti-resultant attribute, one which belongs to an act in virtue of its whole nature and of nothing less than this. . . .

Another instance of the same distinction may be found in the operation of natural laws. *Qua* subject to the force of gravitation towards some other body, each body tends to move in a particular direction with a particular velocity; but its actual movement depends on *all* the forces to which it is subject. It is only by recognizing this distinction that we can preserve the absoluteness of laws of nature, and only by recognizing a corresponding distinction that we can preserve the absoluteness of the general principles of morality. But an important difference between the two cases must be pointed out. When we say that in virtue of gravitation a body tends to move in a certain way, we are referring to a causal influence actually exercised on it by another body or other bodies. When we say that in virtue of being deliberately untrue a certain remark tends to be wrong, we are referring to no causal relation, to no relation that involves succession in time, but to such a relation as connects the various attributes of a mathematical figure. And if the word "tendency" is thought to suggest too much a causal relation, it is better to talk of certain types of act as being *prima facie* right or wrong (or of different persons as having different and possibly conflicting claims upon us), than of their tending to be right or wrong.

Something should be said of the relation between our apprehension of the *prima facie* rightness of certain types of act and our mental attitude towards particular acts. It is proper to use the word "apprehension" in the former case and not in the latter. That an act, *qua* fulfilling a promise, or *qua* effecting a just distribution of good, or *qua* returning services rendered, or *qua* promoting the good of others, or *qua* promoting the virtue or insight of the agent, is *prima facie* right, is self-evident; not in the sense that it is evident from the beginning of our lives, or as soon as we attend to the proposition for the first time, but in the sense that when we have reached sufficient mental maturity and have given sufficient attention to the proposition it is evident without any need of proof, or of evidence beyond itself. It is self-evident just as a mathematical axiom, or the validity of a form of inference, is evident. The moral order expressed in these propositions is just as much part of the fundamental nature of the universe (and, we may add, of any possible universe in which there were moral agents at all) as is the spatial or numerical structure expressed in the axioms of geometry or arithmetic. In our confidence that these propositions are true there is involved the same trust in our reason that is involved in our confidence in mathematics; and we should have no justification for trusting it in the latter sphere and distrusting it in the former. In both cases we are dealing with propositions that cannot be proved, but that just as certainly need no proof. . . .

Our judgments about our actual duty in concrete situations have none of the certainty that attaches to our recognition of the general principles of duty. A statement is certain, i.e., is an expression of knowledge, only in one or other of two cases: when it is either self-evident, or a valid conclusion from self-evident premises. And our judgments about our particular duties have neither of these characters. (1) They are not self-evident. Where a possible act is seen to have two characteristics, in virtue of one of which it is *prima facie* right, and in virtue of the other *prima facie* wrong, we are (I think) well aware that we are not certain whether we ought or ought not to do it; that whether we do it or not, we are taking a moral risk. We come in the long run, after consideration, to think one duty more pressing than the other, but we do not feel certain that it is so. And though we do not always recognize that a possible act has two such characteristics, and though there *may* be cases in which it has not, we are never certain that any particular possible act has not, and therefore never certain that it is right, nor certain that it is wrong. For, to go no further in the analysis, it is enough to point out that any particular act will in all probability in the course of time contribute to the bringing about of good or of evil for many human beings, and thus have a *prima facie* rightness or wrongness of which we know nothing. (2) Again, our judgments about our particular duties are not logical conclusions from self-evident premises. The only possible premises would be the general principles stating their *prima facie* rightness or wrongness *qua* having the different characteristics they do have; and even if we could (as we cannot) apprehend the extent to which an act will tend on the one hand, for example, to bring about advantages for our benefactors, and on the other hand to bring about disadvantages for fellow men who are not our benefactors, there is no principle by which we can draw the conclusion that it is on the whole right or on the whole wrong. In this respect the judgment as to the rightness of a particular act is just like the judgment as to the beauty of a particular natural object or work of art. A poem is, for instance, in respect of certain qualities beautiful and in respect of certain others not beautiful; and our judgment as to the degree of beauty it possesses on the whole is never reached by logical reasoning from the apprehension of its particular beauties or particular defects. Both in this and in the moral case we have more or less probable opinions which are not logically justified conclusions from the general principles that are recognized as self-evident. . . .

Supposing it to be agreed, as I think on reflection it must, that no one *means* by "right" just "productive of the best possible consequences," or "optimific," the attributes "right" and "optimific" might stand in either of two kinds of relation to each other. (1) They might be so related that we could apprehend *a priori*, either immediately or deductively, that any act that is optimific is right and any act that is right is optimific, as we can apprehend that any triangle that is equilateral is equiangular and *vice versa*. Professor Moore's view is, I think, that the coexistensiveness of "right" and "optimific" is apprehended immediately. He rejects the possibility of any proof of it. Or (2) the two attributes might be such that the question whether they are invariably connected had to be answered by means of an inductive inquiry. Now at first sight it might seem as if the constant connexion of the two attributes could be immediately apprehended. It might seem absurd to suggest that it could be right for any one to do an act which would produce consequences less good than those which would be produced by some other act in his power. Yet a little thought will convince us that this is not absurd. The type of case in which it is easier to see that this is so is, perhaps, that in which one has made a promise. In such a case we all think that *prima facie* it is our duty to fulfil the promise irrespective of the precise goodness of the total consequences. And though we do not think it is necessarily our actual or absolute duty to do so, we are far from thinking that any, even the slightest, gain in the value of the total consequences will necessarily justify us in doing something else instead. Suppose, to simplify the case by abstraction, that the fulfilment of a promise to A would produce 1,000 units of good for him, but that by doing some other act I could produce 1,001 units of good for B, to whom I have made no promise, the other consequences of the two acts being of equal value; should we really think it self-evident that it was our duty to do the second act and not the first? I think not. We should, I fancy, hold that only a much greater disparity of value between the total consequences would justify us in failing to discharge our *prima facie* duty to A. After all, a promise is a promise, and is not to be treated so lightly as the theory we are examining would imply. What, exactly, a promise is, is not so easy to determine, but we are surely agreed that it constitutes a serious moral limitation to our freedom of action. To produce the 1,001 units of good for B rather than fulfil our promise to A would be to take, not perhaps our duty as philanthropists too seriously, but certainly our duty as makers of promises too lightly.

Or consider another phase of the same problem. If I have promised to confer on A a particular benefit containing 1,000 units of good, is it self-evident that if by doing some different act I could produce 1,001 units of good for A himself (the other consequences of the two acts being supposed equal in value), it would be right for me to do so? Again, I think not. Apart from my general *prima facie* duty to do A what good I can, I have another *prima facie* duty to do him the particular service I have promised to do him, and this is not to be set aside in consequence of a disparity of good of the order of 1,001 to 1,000, though a much greater disparity might justify me in so doing.

Or again, suppose that A is a very good and B a very bad man, should I then, even when I have made no promise, think it self-evidently right to produce 1,001 units of good for B rather than 1,000 for A? Surely not. I should be sensible of a *prima facie* duty of justice, i.e., of producing a distribution of goods in proportion to merit, which is not outweighed by such a slight disparity in the total goods to be produced.

Such instances—and they might easily be added to—make it clear that there is no self-evident connexion between the attributes "right" and "optimific." The theory we are examining has a certain attractiveness when applied to our decision that a particular act is our duty (though I have tried to show that it does not agree with our actual moral judgements even here). But it is not even possible when applied to our recognition of *prima facie* duty. For if it were self-evident that the right coincides with the optimific, it should be self-evident that what is *prima facie* right is *prima facie* optimific. But whereas we are certain that keeping a promise is *prima facie* right, we are not certain that it is *prima facie* optimific (though we are perhaps certain that it is *prima facie* bonific). Our certainty that it is *prima facie* right depends not on its consequences but on its being the fulfilment of a promise. The theory we are examining involves too much difference between the evident ground of our conviction about *prima facie* duty and the alleged ground of our conviction about actual duty.

The coextensiveness of the right and the optimific is, then, not self-evident. And I can see no way of proving it deductively; nor, so far as I know, has any one tried to do so. There remains the question whether it can be established inductively. Such an inquiry, to be conclusive, would have to be very thorough and extensive. We should have to take a large variety of the acts which we, to the best of our ability, judge to be right. We should have to trace as far as possible their consequences, not only for the persons directly affected but also for those indirectly affected, and to these no limit can be set. To make our inquiry thoroughly conclusive, we should have to do what we cannot do, *viz.*, trace these consequences into an unending future. And even to make it reasonably conclusive, we should have to trace them far into the future. It is clear that the most we could possibly say is that a large variety of typical acts that are judged right appear, so far as we can trace their consequences, to produce more good than any other acts possible to the agents in the circumstances. And such a result falls far short of proving the constant connexion of the two attributes. But it is surely clear that no inductive inquiry justifying even this result has ever been carried through. The advocates of utilitarian systems have been so much persuaded either of the identity or of the self-evident connexion of the attributes "right" and "optimific" (or "felicific") that they have not attempted even such an inductive inquiry as is possible. And in view of the enormous complexity of the task and the inevitable inconclusiveness of the result, it is worth no one's while to make the attempt. What, after all, would be gained by it? If, as I have tried to show, for an act to be right and to be optimific are not the same thing, and an act's being optimific is not even the ground of its being right, then if we could ask ourselves (though the question is really unmeaning) which we ought to do, right acts because they are right or optimific acts because they are optimific, our answer must be "the former." If they are optimific as well as right, that is interesting but not morally important; if not, we still ought to do them (which is only another way of saying that they *are* the right acts), and the question whether they are optimific has no importance for moral theory.

There is one direction in which a fairly serious attempt has been made to show the connexion of the attributes "right" and "optimific." One of the most evident facts of our moral consciousness is the sense which we have of the sanctity of promises, a sense which does not, on the face of it, involve the thought that one will be bringing more good into existence by fulfilling the promise than by breaking it. It is plain, I think, that in our normal thought we consider that the fact that we have made a promise is in itself sufficient to create a duty of keeping it, the sense of duty resting on remembrance of the past promise and not on thoughts of the future consequences of its fulfilment. Utilitarianism tries to show that this is not so, that the sanctity of promises rests on the good consequences of the fulfilment of them and the bad consequences of their non-fulfilment. It does so in this way: it points out that when you break a promise you not only fail to confer a certain advantage on your promisee but you diminish his confidence, and indirectly the confidence of others, in the fulfilment of promises. You thus strike a blow at one of the devices that have been found most useful in the relations between man and man—the device on which, for example, the whole system of commercial credit rests—and you tend to bring about a state of things wherein each man, being entirely unable to rely on the keeping of promises by others, will have to do everything for himself, to the enormous impoverishment of human well-being.

To put the matter otherwise, utlitarians say that when a promise ought to be kept it is because the total good to be produced by keeping it is greater than the total good to be produced by breaking it, the former including as its main element the maintenance and strengthening of general mutual confidence, and the latter being greatly diminished by a weakening of this confidence. They say, in fact, that the case I put some pages back never arises—the case in which by fulfilling a promise I shall bring into being 1,000 units of good for my promisee, and by breaking it 1,001 units of good for some one else, the other effects of the two acts being of equal value. The other effects, they say, never are of equal value. By keeping my promise I am helping to strengthen the system of mutual confidence; by breaking it I am helping to weaken this; so that really the first act produces $1,000+x$ units of good, and the second $1,001-y$ units, and the difference between $+x$ and $-y$ is enough to outweigh the slight superiority in the *immediate* effects of the second act. In answer to this it may be pointed out that there must be *some* amount of good that exceeds the difference between $+x$ and $-y$ (i.e., exceeds $x+y$); say, $x+y+z$. Let us suppose the *immediate* good effects of the second act to be assessed not at 1,001 but at $1,000+x+y+z$. Then its *net* good effects are $1,000+x+z$, i.e., greater than those of the fulfilment of the promise; and the utilitarian is bound to say forthwith that the promise should be broken. Now, we may ask whether that is really the way we think about promises? Do we really think that the production of the slightest balance of good, no matter who will enjoy it, by the breach of a promise frees us from the obligation to keep our promise? We need not doubt that a system by which promises are made and kept is one that has great advantages for the general well-being. But that is not the whole truth. To make a promise is not merely to adapt an ingenious device for promoting the general well-being; it is to put oneself in a new relation to one person in particular, a relation which creates a specifically new *prima facie* duty to him, not reducible to the duty of promoting the general well-being of society. By all means let us try to foresee the net good effects of keeping one's promise and the net good effects of breaking it, but even if we assess the first at $1,000+x$ and the second at $1,000+x+z$, the question still remains whether it is not our duty to fulfil the promise. It may be suspected, too, that the effect of a single keeping or breaking of a promise in strengthening or weakening the fabric of mutual confidence is greatly exaggerated by the theory we are examining. And if we suppose two men dying together alone, do we think that the duty of one to fulfil before he dies a promise he has made to the other would be extinguished by the fact that neither act would have any effect on the general confidence? Any one who holds this may be suspected of not having reflected on what a promise is.

I conclude that the attributes "right" and "optimific" are not identical, and that we do not know either by intuition, by deduction, or by induction that they coincide in their application, still less that the latter is the foundation of the former. It must be added, however, that if we are ever under no special obligation such as that of fidelity to a promisee or of gratitude to a benefactor, we ought to do what will produce most good; and that even when we are under a special obligation the tendency of acts to promote general good is one of the main factors in determining whether they are right.

In what has preceded, a good deal of use has been made of "what we really think" about moral questions; a certain theory has been rejected because it does not agree with what we really think. It might be said that this is in principle wrong; that we should not be content to expound what our present moral consciousness tells us but should aim at a criticism of our existing moral consciousness in the light of theory. Now I do not doubt that the moral consciousness of men has in detail undergone a good deal of modification as regards the things we think right, at the hands of moral theory. But if we are told, for instance, that we should give up our view that there is a special obligatoriness attaching to the keeping of promises because it is self-evident that the only duty is to produce as much good as possible, we have to ask ourselves whether we really, when we reflect, *are* convinced that this is self-evident, and whether we really *can* get rid of our view that promise-keeping has a bindingness independent of productiveness of maximum good. In my own experience I find that I cannot, in spite of a very genuine attempt to do so; and I venture to think that most people will find the same, and that just because they cannot lose the sense of special obligation, they cannot accept as self-evident, or even as true, the theory which would require them to do so. In fact it seems, on reflection, self-evident that a promise, simply as such, is something that *prima facie* ought to be kept, and it does *not*, on reflection, seem self-evident that production of maximum good is the only thing that makes an act obligatory. And to ask us to give up at the bidding of a theory our actual apprehension of what is right and what is wrong seems like asking people to repudiate their actual experience of beauty, at the bidding of a theory which says "only that which satisfies such and such conditions can be beautiful." If what I have called our actual apprehension is (as I would maintain that it is) truly an apprehension, i.e., an instance of knowledge, the request is nothing less than absurd.

I would maintain, in fact, that what we are apt to describe as "what we think" about moral questions contains a considerable amount that we do not think but know, and that this forms the standard by reference to which the truth of any moral theory has to be tested, instead of having itself to be tested by reference to any theory. I hope that I have in what precedes indicated what in my view these elements of knowledge are that are involved in our ordinary moral consciousness.

It would be a mistake to found a natural science on "what we really think," i.e., on what reasonably thoughtful and well-educated people think about the subjects of the science before they have studied them scientifically. For such opinions are interpretations, and often misinterpretations, of sense-experience; and the man of science must appeal from these to sense-experience itself, which furnishes his real data. In ethics no such appeal is possible. We have no more direct way of access to the facts about rightness and goodness and about what things are right or good, than by thinking about them; the moral convictions of thoughtful and well-educated people are the data of ethics just as sense-perceptions are the data of a natural science. Just as some of the latter have to be rejected as illusory, so have some of the former; but as the latter are rejected only when they are in conflict with other more accurate sense-perceptions, the former are rejected only when they are in conflict with other convictions which stand better the test of reflection. The existing body of moral convictions of the best people is the cumulative product of the moral reflection of many generations, which has developed an extremely delicate power of appreciation of moral distinctions; and this the theorist cannot afford to treat with anything other than the greatest respect. The verdicts of the moral consciousness of the best people are the foundation on which he must build; though he must first compare them with one another and eliminate any contradictions they may contain.

It is worth while to try to state more definitely the nature of the acts that are right. We may try to state first what (if anything) is the universal nature of *all* acts that are right. It is obvious that any of the acts that we do has countless effects, directly or indirectly, on countless people, and the probability is that any act, however right it be, will have adverse effects (though these may be very trivial) on some innocent people. Similarly, any wrong act will probably have beneficial effects on some deserving people. Every act therefore, viewed in some aspects, will be *prima facie* right, and viewed in others, *prima facie* wrong, and right acts can be distinguished from wrong acts only as being those which, of all those possible for the agent in the circumstances, have the greatest balance of *prima facie* rightness, in those respects in which they are *prima facie* right, over their *prima facie* wrongness, in those respects in which they are *prima facie* wrong—*prima facie* rightness and wrongness being understood in the sense previously explained. For the estimation of the comparative stringency of these *prima facie* obligations no general rules can, so far as I can see, be laid down. We can only say that a great deal of stringency belongs to the duties of "perfect obligation"—the duties of keeping our promises, of repairing wrongs we have done, and of returning the equivalent of services we have received. For the rest, ἐν τῇ αἰσθήσει ἡ κρίσις. ["The decision rests with perception," *Nicomachean Ethics* 1109b, 1126b]. This sense of our particular duty in particular circumstances, preceded and informed by the fullest reflection we can bestow on the act in all its bearings, is highly fallible, but it is the only guide we have to our duty.

Act Utilitarianism—Further Readings

Note. The following readings pertain not only to act utilitarianism but also to rule utilitarianism.

Bayles, Michael D. (ed.), *Contemporary Utilitarianism* (Garden City, N.Y.: Doubleday, 1968). Ten articles by contemporary authors on act and rule utilitarianism.

Blake, Ralph Mason, "Why Not Hedonism? A Protest," *International Journal of Ethics*, XXXVII (1926–27), pp. 1–18. Proponent of hedonism.

Brandt, Richard B., *Ethical Theory* (Englewood Cliffs, N.J.: Prentice-Hall, 1959), Chaps. 15, 16, 19. Criticizes both act and rule utilitarianism, then defends a modified form of rule utilitarianism.

Carritt, E. F., *Ethical and Political Thinking* (Oxford: Clarendon, 1947), Chaps. 4 and 8. Critic of egoistic and utilitarian hedonism.

"Discussion: Rule-Utilitarianism," *Australasian Journal of Philosophy*, LXIII (1965), pp. 211–231. Four contemporary authors express different views about rule utilitarianism.

Epicurus, *Epicurus: The Extant Remains*, trans. by C. Bailey (Oxford: Clarendon 1926). A classic proponent of hedonism.

Ewing, A. C., *Ethics* (London: English Universities, 1953), Chaps. 3 and 5. Critic of both hedonistic and ideal utilitarianism.

Frankena, William K., *Ethics* (Englewood Cliffs, N.J.: Prentice-Hall, 1963; 2d ed., 1973), Chap. 3. Criticizes act and rule utilitarianism.

Gorowitz, Samuel (ed.), *John Stuart Mill: UTILITARIANISM with Critical Essays* (New York: Bobbs-Merrill, 1971). Contains twenty-eight critical essays by contemporary authors. Some treat Mill's ethics directly; others deal with act and rule utilitarianism.

Hearn, Thomas K., Jr. (ed.), *Studies in Utilitarianism* (New York: Appleton-Century-Crofts, 1971). Selections from Bentham, Mill, and Moore, together with seven contemporary essays treating various issues concerning utilitarianism. Several authors discuss act and rule utilitarianism.

Hodgson, D. H., *Consequences of Utilitarianism* (Oxford: Clarendon, 1967). A critical discussion of act and rule utilitarianism, which concludes that considerations of utility and the importance of rules might be reconcilable.

Hume, David, *An Enquiry Concerning the Principles of Morals* (1751). While not strictly utilitarian, this classic work did much to shape the utilitarian tradition.

Lyons, David, *Forms and Limits of Utilitarianism* (Oxford: Clarendon, 1965). An advanced study, critical of act and rule utilitarianism.

Mabbott, J. D., "Moral Rules," *Proceedings of the British Academy*, XXXIX (1953), pp. 97–118. Proponent of rule utilitarianism.

Moore, G. E., *Ethics* (London: Oxford U.P.: 1912), Chaps. 1, 2, 5. Proponent of ideal utilitarianism.

Narveson, Jan, *Morality and Utility* (Baltimore: The Johns Hopkins Press, 1967). Criticizes rule utilitarianism and defends act utilitarianism.

Nowell-Smith, P. H., *Ethics* (Baltimore: Penguin Books, 1954), Chaps. 15–16. Proponent of a form of rule utilitarianism.

Quinton, Anthony, *Utilitarian Ethics* (London: Macmillan, 1973). An historical and critical study of utilitarianism, with special emphasis upon Bentham and Mill.

Rescher, Nicholas, *Distributive Justice: A Constructive Critique of the Utilitarian Theory of Distribution* (New York: Bobbs-Merrill, 1966). Sympathetic to utilitarianism but acknowledges an independent principle of justice.

Schneewind, J. B., *Mill: A Collection of Critical Essays* (Garden City, N.Y.: Doubleday, 1968). Nineteen essays on different aspects of Mill's philosophy, many dealing with his ethics.

Sidgwick, Henry, *The Methods of Ethics* (7th ed., London: Macmillan, 1907), especially Bk. I, Chap. 9; Bk. II, Chap. 1; Bk. III, Chaps. 11, 13; Bk. IV. A classic statement of utilitarianism.

Singer, Marcus G., *Generalization in Ethics* (New York: Alfred A. Knopf, 1961), Chap. 7. Criticizes act and rule utilitarianism.

Smart, J. J. C., and Bernard Williams, *Utilitarianism: for and against* (Cambridge: Cambridge U.P., 1973). Smart argues for act utilitarianism; Williams provides a general critique of utilitarianism.

3 Rule Utilitarianism

A very important line of thought among contemporary ethical thinkers consists in the modification of utilitarian theory in response to criticisms, particularly those of Ross. The resulting theory is generally referred to as *rule utilitarianism*, and sometimes as "restricted" utilitarianism.

First, rule utilitarians recognize that moral rules are an essential aspect of ethical decision. There are a number of prima-facie rules which are applied by people in making moral decisions. In ordinary circumstances, these form the standards for judging the rightness or wrongness of specific actions independently of consequences. Thus, the rule utilitarian gives the deontologist his due. He can agree with the deontologist that it is right for a person to keep a secretly made promise to a dying man, and that it is right, other things being equal, to preferentially help one's own child. But—and here the utilitarian principle is applied—the test of these moral rules is the balance of intrinsic value over disvalue, good over evil, which is consequent upon their employment. In this manner, it is believed that the key criticisms which Ross leveled against utilitarianism are met. Rule utilitarianism, then, can be seen as a kind of compromise which is based upon the difference between the justification of rules, a sort of "legislative" function in morality, and the justification of particular actions, a "judicial" or "executive" function. Both, to be sure, are rational activities in the traditional sense of giving reasons in support of actions and judgments.

One powerful and influential formulation of this kind of theory is found in the article we have included by John Rawls entitled "Two Concepts of Rules." He defends utilitarianism against criticisms such as those of Ross. The main burden of the argument rests upon a distinction between rules as relating to social practices, and the particular actions which are instances of the practices. Utility provides the justification of practice as a whole, whereas particular acts are justified in terms of their conformity to the moral rules within the practice. Rawls also distinguishes between the *summary* conception of rules, or rules generated simply by generalizing from the decisions of individuals, and the *practice* conception of rules. The latter is the most significant, for it conceives rules as defining social practices. On the practice conception, it is impossible even to describe an action of a certain kind without referring to a set of rules. According to Rawls, if a person believes that he is obligated to keep his promise only if the consequences of doing so are better than the consequences of his breaking it, then that person does not understand what a promise is (i.e., he does not understand promising as a practice involving the rule that one keeps one's promises).

Recently there has been a great deal of controversy concerning act and role utilitarianism. It has been claimed, for instance, that the two theories are *extensionally equivalent* (i.e., that the two theories would approve exactly the same acts as right). On the other hand, rule utilitarians claim that there are "hard core" cases which their view handles but act utilitarianism does not.*

Our critic of rule utilitarianism, J. J. C. Smart, classifies himself as an "extreme utilitarian" and argues that moral rules are merely rules of thumb—what, as we understand it, Rawls called "summary rules." Smart believes that, ordinarily, actions that are in accord with relevant moral rules will in fact produce the greatest amount of happiness, and points out that in general there is not sufficient time for an agent to figure out all the consequences of every action. In addition, abiding by the rules usually has good consequences for the agent, and not abiding by them has bad ones. Thus, "do not lie," and "do not break promises," are ordinarily upheld by even the extreme utilitarian.

*Taylor, *op. cit.*, Chapter 4.

In one part of his argument, Smart claims that he *chooses* extreme or act utilitarianism on the ground that the common moral consciousness which is reflected in prima facie moral rules serves mainly to protect superstititions and morally bad beliefs. In another part, he argues that the defenses of rule utilitarianism, particularly with respect to the resolution of conflicts based on competing moral rules, result in the collapse of rule or restricted utilitarianism into extreme utilitarianism. Smart (and others) appear to show in some cases that it is correct and reasonable to break the law. But the rule utilitarian tries to show that either (*a*) a priority of higher and lower order principles is at issue, and the principle of utility is used in order to assign the appropriate priority; or (*b*) reference to some principle, whose test is utility, is necessary whenever an exception to a rule is indicated. Also, the principle would involve considering the utility of everyone's making such an exception as a general practice.

It should be understood that Rawls does not claim a complete justification of utilitarianism.* Rawls argues that neither form of utilitarianism completely satisfies the demands of justice. His writings, and that of other contemporary theorists, indicate that the utilitarian–deontological controversy is one of the liveliest in current ethical theory.

*See his "Justice as Fairness," *Philosophical Review*, LXVIII, 1958, pp. 164–194; and "The Sense of Justice," *Philosophical Review*, LXXII, 1963, pp. 281–305; and *A Theory of Justice* (Cambridge, Mass.: Harvard University Press, 1971).

26

Two Concepts of Rules

JOHN RAWLS

In this paper I want to show the importance of the distinction between justifying a practice[1] and justifying a particular action falling under it, and I want to explain the logical basis of this distinction and how it is possible to miss its significance. While the distinction has frequently been made, and is now becom-

FROM "Two Concepts of Rules" by John Rawls (*Philosophical Review*, Vol. LXIV, No. 1). Copyright 1955 by The Philosophical Review, Ithaca, New York. Reprinted by permission of The Philosophical Review and the author.

[1] I use the word "practice" throughout as a sort of technical term meaning any form of activity specified by a system of rules which defines offices, roles, moves, penalties, defenses, and so on, and which gives the activity its structure. As examples one may think of games and rituals, trials and parliaments.

ing commonplace, there remains the task of explaining the tendency either to overlook it altogether, or to fail to appreciate its importance.

To show the importance of the distinction I am going to defend utilitarianism against those objections which have traditionally been made against it in connection with punishment and the obligation to keep promises. I hope to show that if one uses the distinction in question then one can state utilitarianism in a way which makes it a much better explication of our considered moral judgments than these traditional objections would seem to admit. Thus the importance of the distinction is shown by the way it strengthens the utilitarian view regardless of whether that view is completely defensible or not.

To explain how the significance of the distinction may be overlooked, I am going to discuss two conceptions of rules. One of these conceptions conceals the importance of distinguishing between the justification of a rule or practice and the justification of a particular action falling under it. The other conception makes it clear why this distinction must be made and what is its logical basis. . . .

I shall now consider the question of promises. The objection to utilitarianism in connection with promises seems to be this: it is believed that on the utilitarian view when a person makes a promise the only ground upon which he should keep it, if he should keep it, is that by keeping it he will realize the most good on the whole. So that if one asks the question "Why should I keep *my* promise?" the utilitarian answer is understood to be that doing so in *this* case will have the best consequences. And this answer is said, quite rightly, to conflict with the way in which the obligation to keep promises is regarded.

Now of course critics of utilitarianism are not unaware that one defense sometimes attributed to utilitarians is the consideration involving the practice of promise keeping. In this connection they are supposed to argue something like this: it must be admitted that we feel strictly about keeping promises, more strictly than it might seem our view can account for. But when we consider the matter carefully it is always necessary to take into account the effect which our action will have on the practice of making promises. The promisor must weigh, not only the effects of breaking his promise on the particular case, but also the effect which his breaking his promise will have on the practice itself. Since the practice is of great utilitarian value, and since breaking one's promise always seriously damages it, one will seldom be justified in breaking one's promise. If we view our individual promises in the wider context of the practice of promising itself we can account for the strictness of the obligation to keep promises. There is always one very strong utilitarian consideration in favor of keeping them, and this will insure that when the question arises as to whether or not to keep a promise it will usually turn out that one should, even where the facts of the particular case taken by itself would seem to justify one's breaking it. In this way the strictness with which we view the obligation to keep promises is accounted for.

Ross has criticized this defense as follows: however great the value of the practice of promising, on utilitarian grounds, there must be some value which is greater, and one can imagine it to be obtainable by breaking a promise.

Therefore there might be a case where the promisor could argue that breaking his promise was justified as leading to a better state of affairs on the whole. And the promisor could argue in this way no matter how slight the advantage won by breaking the promise. If one were to challenge the promisor his defense would be that what he did was best on the whole in view of all the utilitarian considerations, which in this case *include* the importance of the practice. Ross feels that such a defense would be unacceptable. I think he is right insofar as he is protesting against the appeal to consequences in general and without further explanation. Yet it is extremely difficult to weigh the force of Ross's argument. The kind of case imagined seems unrealistic and one feels that it needs to be described. One is inclined to think that it would either turn out that such a case came under an exception defined by the practice itself, in which case there would not be an appeal to consequences in general on the particular case, or it would happen that the circumstances were so peculiar that the conditions which the practice presupposes no longer obtained. But certainly Ross is right in thinking that it strikes us as wrong for a person to defend breaking a promise by a general appeal to consequences. For a general utilitarian defense is not open to the promisor: it is not one of the defenses allowed by the practice of making promises.

Ross gives two further counter-arguments: First, he holds that it over-estimates the damage done to the practice of promising by a failure to keep a promise. One who breaks a promise harms his own name certainly, but it isn't clear that a broken promise always damages the practice itself sufficiently to account for the strictness of the obligation. Second, and more important, I think, he raises the question of what one is to say of a promise which isn't known to have been made except to the promisor and the promisee, as in the case of a promise a son makes to his dying father concerning the handling of the estate. In this sort of case the consideration relating to the practice doesn't weigh on the promisor at all, and yet one feels that this sort of promise is as binding as other promises. The question of the effect which breaking it has on the practice seems irrelevant. The only consequence seems to be that one can break the promise without running any risk of being censured; but the obligation itself seems not the least weakened. Hence it is doubtful whether the effect on the practice ever weighs in the particular case; certainly it cannot account for the strictness of the obligation where it fails to obtain. It seems to follow that a utilitarian account of the obligation to keep promises cannot be successfully carried out. . . .

These arguments and counter-arguments fail to make the distinction between the justification of a practice and the justification of a particular action falling under it, and therefore they fall into the mistake of taking it for granted that the promisor . . . is entitled without restriction to bring utilitarian considerations to bear in deciding whether to keep *his* promise. But if one considers what the practice of promising is one will see, I think, that it is such as not to allow this sort of general discretion to the promisor. Indeed, the point of the practice is to abdicate one's title to act in accordance with utilitarian and prudential considerations in order that the future may be tied down and plans coordinated in advance. There are obvious utilitarian advantages in having a practice which denies to the promisor, as a defense, any general appeal to the utilitarian principle in accordance with which the practice itself may be justified. There is nothing contradictory, or surprising, in this: utilitarian (or aesthetic) reasons might properly be given in arguing that the game of chess, or baseball, is satisfactory just as it is, or in arguing that it should be changed in various respects, but a player in a game cannot properly appeal to such considerations as reasons for his making one move rather than another. It is a mistake to think that if the practice is justified on utilitarian grounds then the promisor must have complete liberty to use utilitarian arguments to decide whether or not to keep his promise. The practice forbids this general defense; and it is a purpose of the practice to do this. Therefore what the above arguments presuppose—the idea that if the utilitarian view is accepted then the promisor is bound if, and only if, the application of the utilitarian principle to his own case shows that keeping it is best on the whole—is false. The promisor is bound because he promised: weighing the case on its merits is not open to him.

Is this to say that in particular cases one cannot deliberate whether or not to keep one's promise? Of course not. But to do so is to deliberate whether the various excuses, exceptions and defenses, which are understood by, and which constitute an important part of, the practice, apply to one's own case. Various defenses for not keeping one's promise are allowed, but among them there isn't the one that, on general utilitarian grounds, the promisor (truly) thought his action best on the whole, even though there may be the defense that the consequences of keeping one's promise would have been *extremely* severe. While there are too many complexities here to consider all the necessary details, one can see that the general defense isn't allowed if one asks the following question: what would one say of someone who, when asked why he broke his promise, replied simply that breaking it was best on the whole? Assuming that his reply is sincere, and that his belief was reasonable (i.e., one need not consider the possibility that he was mistaken), I think that one would question whether or not he knows what it means to say "I promise" (in the appropriate circumstances). It would be said of someone who used this excuse without further explanation that he didn't understand what defenses the practice, which defines a promise, allows to him. If a child were to use this excuse one would correct him; for it is part of the way one is taught the concept of a promise to be corrected if one uses this excuse. The point of having the practice would be lost if the practice did allow this excuse.

It is no doubt part of the utilitarian view that every practice should admit the defense that the consequences of abiding by it would have been extremely severe; and utilitarians would be inclined to hold that some reliance on people's good sense and some concession to hard cases is necessary. They would hold that a practice is justified by serving the interests of those who take part in it; and as with any set of rules there is understood a background of circumstances under which it is expected to be applied and which need not—indeed which cannot—

be fully stated. Should these circumstances change, then even if there is no rule which provides for the case, it may still be in accordance with the practice that one be released from one's obligation. But this sort of defense allowed by a practice must not be confused with the general option to weigh each particular case on utilitarian grounds which critics of utilitarianism have thought it necessarily to involve. . . .

So far I have tried to show the importance of the distinction between the justification of a practice and the justification of a particular action falling under it by indicating how this distinction might be used to defend utilitarianism against two long-standing objections. One might be tempted to close the discussion at this point by saying that utilitarian considerations should be understood as applying to practices in the first instance and not to particular actions falling under them except insofar as the practices admit of it. One might say that in this modified form it is a better account of our considered moral opinions and let it go at that. But to stop here would be to neglect the interesting question as to how one can fail to appreciate the significance of this rather obvious distinction and can take it for granted that utilitarianism has the consequence that particular cases may always be decided on general utilitarian grounds. I want to argue that this mistake may be connected with misconceiving the logical status of the rules of practices; and to show this I am going to examine two conceptions of rules, two ways of placing them within the utilitarian theory.

The conception which conceals from us the significance of the distinction I am going to call the summary view. It regards rules in the following way: one supposes that each person decides what he shall do in particular cases by applying the utilitarian principle; one supposes further that different people will decide the same particular case in the same way and that there will be recurrences of cases similar to those previously decided. Thus it will happen that in cases of certain kinds the same decision will be made either by the same person at different times or by different persons at the same time. If a case occurs frequently enough one supposes that a rule is formulated to cover that sort of case. I have called this conception the summary view because rules are pictured as summaries of past decisions arrived at by the *direct* application of the utilitarian principle to particular cases. Rules are regarded as reports that cases of a certain sort have been found on *other* grounds to be properly decided in a certain way (although, of course, they do not *say* this).

There are several things to notice about this way of placing rules within the utilitarian theory.

1. The point of having rules derives from the fact that similar cases tend to recur and that one can decide cases more quickly if one records past decisions in the form of rules. If similar cases didn't recur, one would be required to apply the utilitarian principle directly, case by case, and rules reporting past decisions would be of no use.

2. The decisions made on particular cases are logically prior to rules. Since rules gain their point from the need to apply the utilitarian principle to many similar cases, it follows that a particular case (or several cases similar to it)

may exist whether or not there is a rule covering that case. We are pictured as recognizing particular cases prior to there being a rule which covers them, for it is only if we meet with a number of cases of a certain sort that we formulate a rule. Thus we are able to describe a particular case as a particular case of the requisite sort whether there is a rule regarding *that* sort of case or not. Put another way: what the A's and the B's refer to in rules of the form "Whenever A do B" may be described as A's and B's whether or not there is the rule "Whenever A do B", or whether or not there is any body of rules which make up a practice of which that rule is a part.

To illustrate this consider a rule, or maxim, which could arise in this way: suppose that a person is trying to decide whether to tell someone who is fatally ill what his illness is when he has been asked to do so. Suppose the person to reflect and then decide, on utilitarian grounds, that he should not answer truthfully; and suppose that on the basis of this and other like occasions he formulates a rule to the effect that when asked by someone fatally ill what his illness is, one should not tell him. The point to notice is that someone's being fatally ill and asking what his illness is, and someone's telling him, are things that can be described as such whether or not there is this rule. The performance of the action to which the rule refers doesn't require the stage setting of a practice of which this rule is a part. This is what is meant by saying that on the summary view particular cases are logically prior to rules.

3. Each person is in principle always entitled to reconsider the correctness of a rule and to question whether or not it is proper to follow it in a particular case. As rules are guides and aids, one may ask whether in past decisions there might not have been a mistake in applying the utilitarian principle to get the rule in question, and wonder whether or not it is best in this case. The reason for rules is that people are not able to apply the utilitarian principle effortlessly and flawlessly; there is need to save time and to post a guide. On this view a society of rational utilitarians would be a society without rules in which each person applied the utilitarian principle directly and smoothly, and without error, case by case. On the other hand, ours is a society in which rules are formulated to serve as aids in reaching these ideally rational decisions on particular cases, guides which have been built up and tested by the experience of generations. If one applies this view to rules, one is interpreting them as maxims, as "rules of thumb"; and it is doubtful that anything to which the summary conception did apply would be called a *rule*. Arguing as if one regarded rules in this way is a mistake one makes while doing philosophy.

4. The concept of a *general* rule takes the following form. One is pictured as estimating on what percentage of the cases likely to arise a given rule may be relied upon to express the correct decision, that is, the decision that would be arrived at if one were to correctly apply the utilitarian principle case by case. If one estimates that by and large the rule will give the correct decision, or if one estimates that the likelihood of making a mistake by applying the utilitarian principle directly on one's own is greater than the likelihood of making a mistake by following the rule, and if these considerations held of persons generally,

then one would be justified in urging its adoption as a general rule. In this way *general* rules might be accounted for on the summary view. It will still make sense, however, to speak of applying the utilitarian principle case by case, for it was by trying to foresee the results of doing this that one got the initial estimates upon which acceptance of the rule depends. That one is taking a rule in accordance with the summary conception will show itself in the naturalness with which one speaks of the rule as a guide, or as a maxim, or as a generalization from experience, and as something to be laid aside in extraordinary cases where there is no assurance that the generalization will hold and the case must therefore be treated on its merits. Thus there goes with this conception the notion of a particular exception which renders a rule suspect on a particular occasion.

The other conception of rules I will call the practice conception. On this view rules are pictured as defining a practice. Practices are set up for various reasons, but one of them is that in many areas of conduct each person's deciding what to do on utilitarian grounds case by case leads to confusion, and that the attempt to coordinate behavior by trying to foresee how others will act is bound to fail. As an alternative one realizes that what is required is the establishment of a practice, the specification of a new form of activity; and from this one sees that a practice necessarily involves the abdication of full liberty to act on utilitarian and prudential grounds. It is the mark of a practice that being taught how to engage in it involves being instructed in the rules which define it, and that appeal is made to those rules to correct the behavior of those engaged in it. Those engaged in a practice recognize the rules as defining it. The rules cannot be taken as simply describing how those engaged in the practice in fact behave: it is not simply that they act as if they were obeying the rules. Thus it is essential to the notion of a practice that the rules are publicly known and understood as definitive; and it is essential also that the rules of a practice can be taught and can be acted upon to yield a coherent practice. On this conception, then, rules are not generalizations from the decisions of individuals applying the utilitarian principle directly and independently to recurrent particular cases. On the contrary, rules define a practice and are themselves the subject of the utilitarian principle. . . .

If one compares the two conceptions of rules I have discussed, one can see how the summary conception misses the significance of the distinction between justifying a practice and justifying actions falling under it. On this view rules are regarded as guides whose purpose it is to indicate the ideally rational decision on the given particular case which the flawless application of the utilitarian principle would yield. One has, in principle, full option to use the guides or to discard them as the situation warrants without one's moral office being altered in any way: whether one discards the rules or not, one always holds the office of a rational person seeking case by case to realize the best on the whole. But on the practice conception, if one holds an office defined by a practice, then questions regarding one's actions in this office are settled by reference to the rules which define the practice. If one seeks to question these rules, then one's office undergoes a fundamental change: one then assumes the office of one empowered to change and criticize the rules, or the office of a reformer, and so on. The summary conception does away with the distinction of offices and the various forms of argument appropriate to each. On that conception there is one office and so no offices at all. It therefore obscures the fact that the utilitarian principle must, in the case of actions and offices defined by a practice, apply to the practice, so that general utilitarian arguments are not available to those who act in offices so defined. . . .

I have tried to show that when we fit the utilitarian view together with the practice conception of rules, where this conception is appropriate, we can formulate it in a way which saves it from several traditional objections. I have further tried to show how the logical force of the distinction between justifying a practice and justifying an action falling under it is connected with the practice conception of rules and cannot be understood as long as one regards the rules of practices in accordance with the summary view.

27

Extreme and Restricted Utilitarianism

J. J. C. Smart

Utilitarianism is the doctrine that the rightness of actions is to be judged by their consequences. What do we mean by "actions" here? Do we mean particular actions or do we mean classes of actions? According to which way we interpret the word "actions" we get two different theories, both of which merit the appellation "utilitarian".

(1) If by "actions" we mean particular individual actions we get the sort of doctrine held by Bentham, Sidgwick, and Moore. According to this doctrine we test individual actions by their consequences, and general rules, like "keep promises", are mere rules of thumb which we use only to avoid the necessity of estimating the probable consequences of our actions at every step. The rightness or wrongness of keeping a promise on a particular occasion depends only on the goodness or badness of the consequences of keeping or breaking the promise on that particular occasion. Of course part of the consequences of breaking the promise, and a part to which we will normally ascribe decisive importance, will be the weakening of faith in the institution of promising. However, if the goodness of the consequences of breaking the rule is *in toto* greater than the goodness of the consequences of keeping it, then we must break the rule, irrespective of whether the goodness of the consequences of *everybody's* obeying the rule is or is not greater than the consequences of *everybody's* breaking it. To put it shortly,

FROM "Extreme and Restricted Utilitarianism" (*The Philosophical Quarterly*, Vol. VI, No. 25). Copyright 1956 by The Philosophical Quarterly, St. Andrews, Scotland. Reprinted by permission of The Philosophical Quarterly and the author.

rules do not matter, save *per accidens* as rules of thumb and as *de facto* social institutions with which the utilitarian has to reckon when estimating consequences. I shall call this doctrine "extreme utilitarianism".

(2) A more modest form of utilitarianism has recently become fashionable. The doctrine is to be found in Toulmin's book *The Place of Reason in Ethics*, in Nowell-Smith's *Ethics* (though I think Nowell-Smith has qualms), in John Austin's *Lectures on Jurisprudence* (Lecture II), and even in J. S. Mill, if Urmson's interpretation of him is correct (*Philosophical Quarterly*, III (1953), 33–39). Part of its charm is that it appears to resolve the dispute in moral philosophy between intuitionists and utilitarians in a way which is very neat. The above philosophers hold, or seem to hold, that moral rules are more than rules of thumb. In general the rightness of an action is *not* to be tested by evaluating its consequences but only by considering whether or not it falls under a certain rule. Whether the rule is to be considered an acceptable moral rule, is, however, to be decided by considering the consequences of adopting the rule. Broadly, then, actions are to be tested by rules and rules by consequences. The only cases in which we must test an individual action directly by its consequences are (a) when the action comes under two different rules, one of which enjoins it and one of which forbids it, and (b) when there is no rule whatever that governs the given case. I shall call this doctrine "restricted utilitarianism".

It should be noticed that the distinction I am making cuts across, and is quite different from, the distinction commonly made between hedonistic and ideal utilitarianism. Bentham was an extreme hedonistic utilitarian and Moore an extreme ideal utilitarian, and Toulmin (perhaps) could be classified as a restricted ideal utilitarian. A hedonistic utilitarian holds that the goodness of the consequences of an action is a function only of their pleasurableness and an ideal utilitarian, like Moore, holds that pleasurableness is not even a necessary condition of goodness. Mill seems, if we are to take his remarks about higher and lower pleasures seriously, to be neither a pure hedonistic nor a pure ideal utilitarian. He seems to hold that pleasurableness is a necessary condition for goodness, but that goodness is a function of other qualities of mind as well. Perhaps we can call him a quasi-ideal utilitarian. When we say that a state of mind is good I take it that we are expressing some sort of *rational preference*. When we say that it is pleasurable I take it that we are saying that it is enjoyable, and when we say that something is a higher pleasure I take it that we are saying that it is more truly, or more deeply, enjoyable. I am doubtful whether "more deeply enjoyable" does not just mean "more enjoyable, even though not more enjoyable on a first look", and so I am doubtful whether quasi-ideal utilitarianism, and possibly ideal utilitarianism too, would not collapse into hedonistic utilitarianism on a closer scrutiny of the logic of words like "preference", "pleasure", "enjoy", "deeply enjoy", and so on. However, it is beside the point of the present paper to go into these questions. I am here concerned only with the issue between extreme and restricted utilitarianism and am ready to concede that both forms of utilitarianism can be either hedonistic or nonhedonistic.

The issue between extreme and restricted utilitarianism can be illustrated by considering the remark "But suppose everyone did the same". (Cf. A. K. Stout's article in *The Australasian Journal of Philosophy*, XXXII, 1–29). Stout distinguishes two forms of the universalization principle, the causal forms and the hypothetical form. To say that you ought not to do an action A because it would have bad results if everyone (or many people) did action A may be merely to point out that while the action A would otherwise be the optimific one, nevertheless when you take into account that doing A will probably cause other people to do A too, you can see that A is not, on a broad view, really optimific. If this causal influence could be avoided (as may happen in the case of a secret desert island promise) then we would disregard the universalization principle. This is the causal form of the principle. A person who accepted the universalization principle in its hypothetical form would be one who was concerned only with what would happen *if* everyone did the action A: he would be totally unconcerned with the question of whether in fact everyone would do the action A. That is, he might say that it would be wrong not to vote because it would have bad results if everyone took this attitude, and he would be totally unmoved by arguments purporting to show that my refusing to vote has no effect whatever on other people's propensity to vote. Making use of Stout's distinction, we can say that an extreme utilitarian would apply the universalization principle in the causal form, while a restricted utilitarian would apply it in the hypothetical form.

How are we to decide the issue between extreme and restricted utilitarianism? I wish to repudiate at the outset that milk and water approach which describes itself sometimes as "investigating what is implicit in the common moral consciousness" and sometimes as "investigating how people ordinarily talk about morality". We have only to read the newspaper correspondence about capital punishment or about what should be done with Formosa to realize that the common moral consciousness is in part made up of superstitious elements, of morally bad elements, and of logically confused elements. I address myself to good hearted and benevolent people and so I hope that if we rid ourselves of the logical confusion the superstitious and morally bad elements will largely fall away. For even among good hearted and benevolent people it is possible to find superstitious and morally bad reasons for moral beliefs. These superstitious and morally bad reasons hide behind the protective screen of logical confusion. With people who are not logically confused but who are openly superstitious or morally bad I can of course do nothing. That is, our ultimate pro-attitudes may be different. Nevertheless I propose to rely on *my own* moral consciousness and to appeal to *your* moral consciousness and to forget about what people ordinarily say. "The obligation to obey a rule", says Nowell-Smith (*Ethics*, p. 239), "does not, *in the opinion of ordinary men*", (my italics), "rest on the beneficial consequences of obeying it in a particular case". What does this prove? Surely it is more than likely that ordinary men are confused here. Philosophers should be able to examine the question more rationally.

For an extreme utilitarian moral rules are rules of thumb. In practice the extreme utilitarian will mostly guide his conduct by appealing to the rules ("do not lie", "do not break promises", etc.) of common sense morality. This is not because there is anything sacrosanct in the rules themselves but because he can argue that probably he will most often act in an extreme utilitarian way if he does not think as a utilitarian. For one thing, actions have frequently to be done in a hurry. Imagine a man seeing a person drowning. He jumps in and rescues him. There is no time to reason the matter out, but usually this will be the course of action which an extreme utilitarian would recommend if he did reason the matter out. If, however, the man drowning had been drowning in a river near Berchtesgaden in 1938, and if he had had the well-known black forelock and moustache of Adolf Hitler, an extreme utilitarian would, if he had time, work out the probability of the man's being the villainous dictator, and if the probability were high enough he would, on extreme utilitarian grounds, leave him to drown. The rescuer, however, has not time. He trusts to his instincts and dives in and rescues the man. And this trusting to instincts and to moral rules can be justified on extreme utilitarian grounds. Furthermore, an extreme utilitarian who knew that the drowning man was Hitler would nevertheless praise the rescuer, not condemn him. For by praising the man he is strengthening a courageous and benevolent disposition of mind, and in general this disposition has great positive utility. (Next time, perhaps, it will be Winston Churchill that the man saves!) We must never forget that an extreme utilitarian may praise actions which he knows to be wrong. Saving Hitler was wrong, but it was a member of a class of actions which are generally right, and the motive to do actions of this class is in general an optimific one. In considering questions of praise and blame it is not the expediency of the praised or blamed action that is at issue, but the expediency of the praise. It can be expedient to praise an inexpedient action and inexpedient to praise an expedient one.

Lack of time is not the only reason why an extreme utilitarian may, on extreme utilitarian principles, trust to rules of common sense morality. He knows that in particular cases where his own interests are involved his calculations are likely to be biased in his own favor. Suppose that he is unhappily married and is deciding whether to get divorced. He will in all probability greatly exaggerate his own unhappiness (and possibly his wife's) and greatly underestimate the harm done to his children by the breakup of the family. He will probably also underestimate the likely harm done by the weakening of the general faith in marriage vows. So probably he will come to the correct extreme utilitarian conclusion if he does not in this instance think as an extreme utilitarian but trusts to common sense morality.

There are many more and subtle points that could be made in connection with the relation between extreme utilitarianism and the morality of common sense. All those that I have just made and many more will be found in Book IV, Chapters 3–5, of Sidgwick's *Methods of Ethics*. I think that this book is the best book ever written on ethics, and that these chapters are the best chapters of the book. As they occur so near the end of a very long book they are unduly neglected. I refer the reader, then, to Sidgwick for the classical exposition of the relation between (extreme) utilitarianism and the morality of common sense. One further point raised by Sidgwick in this connection is whether an (extreme) utilitarian ought on (extreme) utilitarian principles to propagate (extreme) utilitarianism among the public. As most people are not very philosophical and not good at empirical calculations, it is probable that they will most often act in an extreme utilitarian way if they do not try to think as extreme utilitarians. We have seen how easy it would be to misapply the extreme utilitarian criterion in the case of divorce. Sidgwick seems to think it quite probable that an extreme utilitarian should not propagate his doctrine too widely. However, the great danger to humanity comes nowadays on the plane of public morality—not private morality. There is a greater danger to humanity from the hydrogen bomb than from an increase of the divorce rate, regrettable though that might be, and there seems no doubt that extreme utilitarianism makes for good sense in international relations. When France walked out of the United Nations because she did not wish Morocco discussed, she said that she was within her rights because Morocco and Algiers are part of her metropolitan territory and nothing to do with U.N. This was clearly a legalistic if not superstitious argument. We should not be concerned with the so-called "rights" of France or any other country but with whether the cause of humanity would be best be served by discussing Morocco in U.N. (I am not saying that the answer to this is "Yes". There are good grounds for supposing that more harm than good would come by such a discussion.) I myself have no hesitation in saying that on extreme utilitarian principles we ought to propagate extreme utilitarianism as widely as possible. But Sidgwick had respectable reasons for suspecting the opposite.

The extreme utilitarian, then, regards moral rules as rules of thumb and as sociological facts that have to be taken into account when deciding what to do, just as facts of any other sort have to be taken into account. But in themselves they do not justify any action.

The restricted utilitarian regards moral rules as more than rules of thumb for short-circuiting calculations of consequences. Generally, he argues, consequences are not relevant at all when we are deciding what to do in a particular case. In general, they are relevant only to deciding what rules are good reasons for acting in a certain way in particular cases. This doctrine is possibly a good account of how the modern unreflective twentieth-century Englishman often thinks about morality, but surely it is monstrous as an account of how it is most rational to think about morality. Suppose that there is a rule R and that in 99 per cent of cases the best possible results are obtained by acting in accordance with R. Then clearly R is a useful rule of thumb; if we have not time or are not impartial enough to assess the consequences of an action it is an extremely good bet that the thing to do is to act in accordance with R. But is it not monstrous to suppose that if we *have* worked out the consequences and if we have perfect faith in the impartiality of our calculations, and if we *know* that in this instance to break R will have better results than to keep it, we should nevertheless obey the rule? Is it not to erect R into a sort of idol if we keep it when breaking it will prevent, say, some avoidable misery? Is not this a form of superstitious rule worship (easily explicable psychologically) and not the rational thought of a philosopher?

The point may be made more clearly if we consider Mill's comparison of moral rules to the tables in the nautical almanac. (*Utilitarianism*, Everyman Edition, pp. 22–23). This comparison of Mill's is adduced by Urmson as evidence that Mill was a restricted utilitarian, but I do not think that it will bear this interpretation at all. (Though I quite agree with Urmson that many other things said by Mill are in harmony with restricted rather than extreme utilitarianism. Probably Mill had never thought very much about the distinction and was arguing for utilitarianism, restricted or extreme, against other and quite nonutilitarian forms of moral argument.) Mill says: "Nobody argues that the art of navigation is not founded on astronomy, because sailors cannot wait to calculate the Nautical Almanac. Being rational creatures, they go out upon the sea of life with their minds made up on the common questions of right and wrong, as well as on many of the far more difficult questions of wise and foolish. . . . Whatever we adopt as the fundamental principle of morality, we require subordinate principles to apply it by." Notice that this is, as it stands, only an argument for subordinate principles as rules of thumb. The example of the nautical almanac is misleading because the information given in the almanac is in all cases the same as the information one would get if one made a long and laborious calculation from the original astronomical data on which the almanac is founded. Suppose, however, that astronomy were different. Suppose that the behavior of the sun, moon, and planets was very nearly as it is now, but that on rare occasions there were peculiar irregularities and discontinuities, so that the almanac gave us rules of the form "in 99 per cent of cases where the observations are such and such you can deduce that your position is so and so." Furthermore, let us suppose that there were methods which enabled us, by direct and laborious calculation from the original astronomical data, not using the rough and ready tables of the almanac, to get our correct position in 100 per cent of cases. Seafarers might use the almanac because they never had time for the long calculations and they were content with a 99 per cent chance of success in calculating their positions. Would it not be absurd, however, if they *did* make the direct calculation, and finding that it disagreed with the almanac calculation, nevertheless they ignored it and stuck to the almanac conclusion? Of course the case would be altered if there were a high enough probability of making slips in the direct calculation: then we might stick to the almanac result, liable to error though we knew it to be, simply because the direct calculation would be open to error for a different reason, the fallibility of the computer. This would be analogous to the case of the extreme utilitarian who abides by the conventional rule against the dictates of his utilitarian calculations simply because he thinks that his calculations are probably affected by personal bias. But if the navigator were sure of his direct calculations would he not be foolish to abide by his almanac? I conclude, then, that if we change our suppositions about astronomy and the almanac (to which there are no exceptions) to bring the case into line with that of morality (to whose rules there are exceptions), Mill's example loses its appearance of supporting the restricted form of utilitarianism. Let me say once more that I am not here concerned with how ordinary men think about morality but with how they ought to think. We could quite well imagine a race of sailors who acquired a superstitious reverence for their almanac, even though it was only right in 99 per cent of cases, and who indignantly threw overboard any man who mentioned the possibility of a direct calculation. But would this behavior of the sailors be rational?

Let us consider a much discussed sort of case in which the extreme utilitarian might go against the conventional moral rule. I have promised to a friend, dying on a desert island from which I am subsequently rescued, that I will see that his fortune (over which I have control) is given to a jockey club. However, when I am rescued I decide that it would be better to give the money to a hospital, which can do more good with it. It may be argued that I am wrong to give the money to the hospital. But why? (a) The hospital can do more good with the money than the jockey club can. (b) The present case is unlike most cases of promising in that no one except me knows about the promise. In breaking the promise I am doing so with complete secrecy and am doing nothing to weaken the general faith in promises. That is, a factor, which would normally keep the extreme utilitarian from promise breaking even in otherwise unoptimific cases, does not at present operate. (c) There is no doubt a slight weakening in my own character as an habitual promise keeper, and moreover psychological tensions will be set up in me every time I am asked what the man made me promise him to do. For clearly I shall have to say that he made me promise to give the money to the hospital, and, since I am an habitual truth teller, this will go very much against the grain with me. Indeed I am pretty sure that in practice I myself would keep the promise. But we are not discussing what my moral habits would probably make me do; we are discussing what I ought to do. Moreover, we must not forget that even if it would be most rational of me to give the money to the hospital it would also be most rational of you to punish or condemn me if you did, most improbably, find out the truth (e.g. by finding a note washed ashore in a bottle). Furthermore, I would agree that though it was most rational of me to give the money to the hospital it would be most rational of you to condemn me for it. We revert again to Sidgwick's distinction between the utility of the action and the utility of the praise of it.

Many such issues are discussed by A. K. Stout in the article to which I have already referred. I do not wish to go over the same ground again, especially as I think that Stout's arguments support my own point of view. It will be useful, however, to consider one other example that he gives. Suppose that during hot weather there is an edict that no water must be used for watering gardens. I have a garden and I reason that most people are sure to obey the edict, and that as the amount of water that I use will be by itself negligible no harm will be done if I use the water secretly. So I do use the water, thus producing some lovely flowers which give happiness to various people. Still, you may say, though the action was perhaps optimific, it was unfair and wrong.

There are several matters to consider. Certainly my action should be condemned. We revert once more to Sidgwick's distinction. A right action may be rationally condemned. Furthermore, this sort of offence is normally found out. If I have a wonderful garden when everybody else's is dry and brown there is only one explanation. So if I water my garden I am weakening my respect for law and order, and as this leads to bad results an extreme utilitarian would agree that I was wrong to water the garden. Suppose now that the case is altered and that I can keep the thing secret: there is a secluded part of the garden where I grow flowers which I give away anonymously to a home for old ladies. Are you still so sure that I did the wrong thing by watering my garden? However, this is still a weaker case than that of the hospital and the jockey club. There will be tensions set up within myself: my secret knowledge that I have broken the rule will make it hard for me to exhort others to keep the rule. These psychologically ill effects in myself may be not inconsiderable: directly and indirectly they may lead to harm which is at least of the same order as the happiness that the old ladies get from the flowers. You can see that on an extreme utilitarian view there are two sides to the question. . . .

I now pass on to a type of case which may be thought to be the trump card of restricted utilitarianism. Consider the rule of the road. It may be said that since all that matters is that everyone should do the same it is indifferent which rule we have, "go on the left hand side" or "go on the right hand side". Hence the only *reason* for going on the left hand side in British countries is that this is the rule. Here the rule does seem to be a reason, in itself, for acting in a certain way. I wish to argue against this. The rule in itself is not a reason for our actions. We would be perfectly justified in going on the right hand side if (a) we knew that the rule was to go on the left hand side, and (b) we were in a country peopled by superanarchists who always on principle did the opposite of what they were told. This shows that the rule does not give us a reason for acting so much as an indication of the probable actions of others, which helps us to find out what would be our own most rational course of action. If we are in a country not peopled by anarchists, but by nonarnachist extreme utilitarians, we expect, other things being equal, that they will keep rules laid down for them. Knowledge of the rule enables us to predict their behavior and to harmonize our own actions with theirs. The rule "keep to the left hand side", then, is not a logical *reason* for action but an anthropological *datum* for planning actions.

I conclude that in every case if there is a rule R the keeping of which is in general optimific, but such that in a special sort of circumstances the optimific behavior is to break R, then in these circumstances we should break R. Of course we must consider all the less obvious effects of breaking R, such as reducing people's faith in the moral order, before coming to the conclusion that to break R is right: in fact we shall rarely come to such a conclusion. Moral rules, on the extreme utilitarian view, are rules of thumb only, but they are not bad rules of thumb. But if we *do* come to the conclusion that we should break the rule and if we have weighed in the balance our own fallibility and liability to personal bias, what good reason remains for keeping the rule? I can understand "it is optimific" as a reason for action, but why should "it is a member of a class of actions which are usually optimific" or "it is a member of a class of actions which as a class are more optimific than any alternative general class" be a good reason? You might as well say that a person ought to be picked to play for Australia just because all his brothers have been, or that the Australian team should be composed entirely of the Harvey family because this would be better than composing it entirely of any other family. The extreme utilitarian does not appeal to artificial feelings, but only to our feelings of benevolence, and what better feelings can there be to appeal to? Admittedly we can have a pro-attitude to anything, even to rules, but such artificially begotten pro-attitudes smack of superstition. Let us get down to realities, human happiness and misery, and make these the objects of our pro-attitudes and anti-attitudes.

The restricted utilitarian might say that he is talking only of *morality*, not of such things as rules of the road. I am not sure how far this objection, if valid, would affect my argument, but in any case I would reply that as a philosopher I conceive of ethics as the study of how it would be *most rational* to act. If my opponent wishes to restrict the word "morality" to a narrower use he can have the word. The fundamental question is the question of rationality of action *in general*. Similarly if the restricted utilitarian were to appeal to ordinary usage and say "it might be most rational to leave Hitler to drown but it would surely not be *wrong* to rescue him", I should again let him have the words "right" and "wrong" and should stick to "rational" and "irrational". We already saw that it would be rational to praise Hitler's rescuer, even though it would have been most rational not to have rescued Hitler. In ordinary language, no doubt, "right" and "wrong" have not only the meaning "most rational to do" and "not most rational to do" but also have the meaning "praiseworthy" and "not praiseworthy". Usually to the utility of an action corresponds utility of praise of it, but as we saw, this is not always so. Moral language could thus do with tidying up, for example by reserving "right" for "most rational" and "good" as an epithet of praise for the motive from which the action sprang. It would be more becoming in a philosopher to try to iron out illogicalities in moral language and to make suggestions for its reform than to use it as a court of appeal whereby to perpetuate confusions.

One last defence of restricted utilitarianism might be as follows. "Act optimifically" might be regarded as itself one of the rules of our system (though it would be odd to say that this rule was justified by its optimificality). According to Toulmin (*The Place of Reason in Ethics*, pp. 146–48) if "keep promises", say, conflicts with another rule we are allowed to argue the case on its merits, as if we were extreme utilitarians. If "act optimifically" is itself one of our rules then there will always be a conflict of rules whenever to keep a rule is not itself optimific. If this is so, restricted utilitarianism collapses into extreme utilitarianism. And no one could read Toulmin's book or Urmson's article on Mill without thinking that Toulmin and Urmson are of the opinion that they have thought of a doctrine which does *not* collapse into extreme utilitarianism, but which is, on the contrary, an improvement on it.

Rule Utilitarianism—Further Readings

Note. Further readings on rule utilitarianism are to be found in the bibliography which appears at the end of the section on act utilitarianism (page 256).

4 Self-Realization

The diverse theories that next occupy our attention are included under teleological theories because they share the view that right actions are those which produce the greatest amount of good. They also agree that the good produced (actualized, realized) is in some sense related to the conscious human self. The variations among the theories relate to the widely different ways in which they define the *self*, and to the different ways in which it is to be realized or actualized. For one thing, it is difficult to conceive the realization of the self as a single event or episode. Self-realization is not an "end" in the sense of a pleasant experience, or the satisfaction of a desire—as a consummatory experience. The human self may be conceived in naturalistic terms, as in Aristotle's doctrine, or in idealistic terms, as in the theories of Hegel, Green, and Bradley; it can be conceived as some sort of power, as in Nietzsche, or as the integrated realization of potentialities for experience, as in John Dewey.

Agreement on the basic teleological character of ethics, therefore, does not entail that self-realization theories will be very similar. Since the diverse concepts of the self will be reflected in widely variant concepts of the good, there is disagreement among self-realization philosophers with respect to the standards for right or wrong actions. Some theories characterize the self in terms of psychological and physical potentialities. They conceive the realization as a good, integrated, harmonious relationship among or between thse "parts" of the self. Plato, Aristotle, Aquinas, and Dewey are of this general persuasion. Some tie the realization of the self to its social roots of training and habituation, the integration and harmonization of interests, desires, roles, institutions, as reflected in personal and social relationships. Here are Hegel, Green, Bosanquet, Bradley, Royce, and, perhaps, John Dewey again. Modern psychologists, sociologists, anthropologists often construe ethics in terms of the integration and harmonization of the traits of personality as reflected in developmental levels, drives, motives, role, and status. Common to all is a conviction that goodness relates to the degree of coherence, consistency, and harmony of a variety of elements relating to and characterizing man. Since value or goodness is in part due to the relationships among these "parts," and to the degree of value, these *good* systems are often called "organic," or "organic wholes." Related to these value criteria is the theory of obligation: actions are right if they produce, and to the degree that they produce such valuable states.

The main difficulties suffered by self-realization theories relate to the vagueness and ambiguity of their respective concepts of self and human nature, and to their inability to characterize and distinguish clearly between the actual and potential properties of human beings. Therefore, a prime problem concerns the criterion or criteria which make possible a distinction between *good* potentialities and actualities and *bad* ones. That is, the problem is to distinguish those potentialities which should be realized and those which should not, since it is obvious that the realization of many capacities, for example pathological behavior or bank robbery, would be bad.

a   *Aristotle*

Our first self-realization theorist is Aristotle. Plato also falls in this category. Both conceive of right action in terms of harmonious states of the soul or of human nature. Aristotle was chosen here mainly because of the profound influence he has exercised on recent moral philosophy, with respect to both normative and meta-ethical considerations. Some of these influences should be mentioned.

First, Aristotle presaged several logical points which have come to be important in contemporary ethics. He saw that the relation between interests (and desires, pleasures, etc.), and the good is quite different from that, say, between a thing being red and its being desired. The latter is a contingent relationship, the former is not. This is a point that many recent and even present ethical philosophers, G. E. Moore, for instance, failed to recognize clearly. Mill and Bentham knew it, of course, but their critics did not.* A second factor, closely connected with the above, lies in Aristotle's concept of a practical logic, involving his notions

*See Alasdair MacIntyre, *A Short History of Ethics* (New York: Macmillan, 1966), Chapter 7.

of practical reason and the practical syllogism, which has helped inspire a revolution in contemporary logical theory as related to ethics, particularly in the work of Hare, Toulmin, Nowell-Smith, Geach, and other linguistic philosophers. Third, Aristotle's view of mental states as characterizable in terms of intentional objects has profoundly affected modern theory of action, and through it, ethics. Fourth, Aristotle rejected the "naming" theory of meaning, the commitment to the view that common properties constitute the meaning of ethical terms. This view characterized the ethics of Plato and most thinkers in the history of philosophy.

Aristotle bases his ethics on a concept of human nature which fits into his doctrines of matter and form, actuality and potentiality. The soul or self is the actuality, the form, of the potentiality of human nature. In order to determine what is the good of anything, it is necessary to discover its end or purpose; and in order to do this, it is necessary to isolate what is unique to the thing's function or purpose. Following these purposive and functional analogies, drawn from animals, organs of the body, and tools, Aristotle sees the soul as having two main divisions—the irrational and the rational. The irrational includes vegetative and appetitive elements. These elements, which are shared with animals and plants, are not unique to man, and hence cannot be the basis for his goodness or virtue. But the rational soul is the source of the good for man—his end or goal, his excellence. The highest good for man, then, is found in the exercise of his rational capacities, and, further, other goods accrue only through the active use of these capacities, for instance through the rational application of the principle of the golden mean. A harmonious and integrated realization of the rational and appetitive capacities is the good, providing man's distinctive happiness.

Following a method which involved study of the uses of moral words, in particular the word "good," Aristotle classified the uses.* The highest good, or end, must be intrinsically valuable, self-sufficient, desirable, the end of action. Happiness fulfills these criteria, but only the happiness associated with rational activity accords with them all— even the gods delight in thought, Aristotle believed. The intellectual virtues are highest, therefore; but the moral virtues, based in habit, related to appetite and to pleasure, fulfill the criteria sufficiently to be good, and lead to a secondary sort of happiness. They are, for instance, much less self-sufficient than the rational activities. Happiness, generally, is thus an activity of the soul in accordance with virtue. Following the divisions of the soul, virtues are either intellectual or moral, and each functions harmoniously when related to a principle. The rational criterion

*See Pamela Huby, *Greek Ethics* (New York: Macmillan, 1967), pp. 41–47.

or principle of moral virtue is the golden mean, right actions being those which admit of neither excess nor defect. In summary, Aristotle concludes that virtue is a state of character, concerned with choice, lying in a mean, relative to the agent, determined by a rational principle, on the part of a man of practical wisdom. Note the *per genus et differentia* approach. Aristotle concludes that man reaches fulfillment, realizes the self, in the exercise of rational faculties, directly in the intellectual order, and indirectly in the order of the moral virtues, which in turn harmonizes appetites and desires. Man can know what is good, what is right, can choose to act in accordance with such knowledge, and can justify both actions and rules.

Frederick Siegler argues that Aristotle's position founders upon the vagaries and ambiguities of the concepts of function, or end as applied to man. He grants that the ability to reason is a singular characteristic of man, but he contends that it is not clearly the case either that reason is man's function, or that the activity of reason is in itself morally praiseworthy. These claims relate to one of the difficulties with respect to self-realization theories mentioned above—the absence of a criterion with which to distinguish the good capacities, which ought to be realized, from those which are not good and ought not to be realized. Siegler maintains, further, that rational activity does not necessarily lead to happiness. Even the concept of "reason" itself is not wholly clear—is it contemplation, deduction, obedience to logical rules, application to rules, or something else? Mapping our various uses of the word "function," Siegler concludes that Aristotle either loses his hold on the relevant analogies to tools, organs, etc., or else has hold of analogies which fail to do moral duty. He suspects that in a natural or descriptive sense, man has no function at all in the way or ways that a carpenter or knife can be said to have one (or more).

Another line of attack is set out by Alasdair MacIntyre. He argues that Aristotle's doctrine of the golden mean is confused in several respects, leaving the theory without a principle with which to identify means. According to Aristotle, extremes of emotion or action are to be avoided. Yet, MacIntyre reasons that many emotions and actions do not lend themselves to the schema (envy, murder, theft), in that they are extremes already, but there is in the schema no principle or standard which indicates why they are extremes. Also, some of Aristotle's examples of extremes, for instance envy and malice, do not share the same action or emotion. In effect, therefore, Aristotle's method is basically an adducement of the mores accepted by the Greek "gentleman." His criteria for extremes, in other words, are drawn from his social biases.

28

The Nicomachean Ethics

ARISTOTLE

BOOK I

1. Every art and every inquiry, and similarly every action and pursuit, is thought to aim at some good; and for this reason the good has rightly been declared to be that at which all things aim. But a certain difference is found among ends; some are activities, others are products apart from the activities that produce them. Where there are ends apart from the actions, it is the nature of the products to be better than the activities. Now, as there are many actions, arts, and sciences, their ends also are many; the end of the medical art is health, that of shipbuilding a vessel, that of strategy victory, that of economics wealth. But where such arts fall under a single capacity—as bridle-making and the other arts concerned with the equipment of horses fall under the art of riding, and this and every military action under strategy, in the same way other arts fall under yet others—in all of these the ends of the master arts are to be preferred to all the subordinate ends; for it is for the sake of the former that the latter are pursued. It makes no difference whether the activities themselves are the ends of the actions, or something else apart from the activities, as in the case of the sciences just mentioned.

2. If, then, there is some end of the things we do, which we desire for its own sake (everything else being desired for the sake of this), and if we do not choose everything for the sake of something else (for at that rate the process would go on to infinity, so that our desire would be empty and vain), clearly this must be the good and the chief good. Will not the knowledge of it, then, have a great influence on life? Shall we not, like archers who have a mark to aim at, be more likely to hit upon what is right? If so, we must try, in outline at least to determine what it is. . . .

3. Our discussion will be adequate if it has as much clearness as the subject-matter admits of, for precision is not to be sought for alike in all discussions, any more than in all the products of the crafts. Now fine and just actions . . . admit of much variety and fluctuation of opinion, so that they may be thought to exist only by convention, and not by nature. And goods also give rise to similar fluctuation because they bring harm to many people; for before now

FROM Aristotle, *Ethica Nicomachea*, translated by W. D. Ross. (W. D. Ross, ed.: *The Oxford Translation of Aristotle*, Vol. XI, 1925.) Reprinted by permission of the Oxford University Press, Oxford.

men have been undone by reason of their wealth, and others by reason of their courage. We must be content, then, in speaking of such subjects and with such premises to indicate the truth roughly and in outline, and in speaking about things which are only for the most part true and with premises of the same kind to reach conclusions that are no better. In the same spirit, therefore, should each type of statement be *received;* for it is the mark of an educated man to look for precision in each class of things just so far as the nature of the subject admits; it is evidently equally foolish to accept probable reasoning from a mathematician and to demand from a rhetorician scientific proofs.

Now each man judges well the things he knows, and of these he is a good judge. And so the man who has been educated in a subject is a good judge of that subject, and the man who has received an all-round education is a good judge in general. Hence a young man is not a proper hearer of lectures on political science; for he is inexperienced in the actions that occur in life, but its discussions start from these and are about these; and, further, since he tends to follow his passions, his study will be vain and unprofitable, because the end aimed at is not knowledge but action. And it makes no difference whether he is young in years or youthful in character; the defect does not depend on time, but on his living, and pursuing each successive object, as passion directs. For to such persons, as to the incontinent, knowledge brings no profit; but to those who desire and act in accordance with a rational principle knowledge about such matters will be of great benefit.

These remarks about the student, the sort of treatment to be expected, and the purpose of the inquiry, may be taken as our preface.

4. Let us resume our inquiry and state, in view of the fact that all knowledge and every pursuit aims at some good, . . . what is the highest of all goods achievable by action. Verbally there is very general agreement; for both the general run of men and people of superior refinement say that it is happiness, and identifying living well and doing well with being happy; but with regard to what happiness is they differ, and the many do not give the same account as the wise. For the former think it is some plain and obvious thing, like pleasure, wealth, or honour; they differ, however, from one another—and often even the same man identifies it with different things, with health when he is ill, with wealth when he is poor; but, conscious of their ignorance, they admire those who proclaim some great ideal that is above their comprehension. Now some thought that apart from these many goods there is another which is self-subsistent and causes the goodness of all these as well. To examine all the opinions that have been held were perhaps somewhat fruitless; enough to examine those that are most prevalent or that seem to be arguable. . . .

5. . . . To judge from the lives that men lead, most men, and men of the most vulgar type, seem (not without some ground) to identify the good, or happiness, with pleasure; which is the reason why they love the life of enjoyment. For there are, we may say, three prominent types of life—that just mentioned, the political, and thirdly the contemplative life. Now the mass of mankind are evidently quite slavish in their tastes, preferring a life suitable to beasts, but they get some ground for their view from the fact that many of those in high places share the tastes of Sardanapallus. A consideration of the prominent types of life shows that people of superior refinement and of active disposition identify happiness with honour; for this is, roughly speaking, the end of the political life. But it seems too superficial to be what we are looking for, since it is thought to depend on those who bestow honour rather than on him who receives it, but the good we divine to be something proper to a man and not easily taken from him. Further, men seem to pursue honour in order that they may be assured of their goodness; at least it is by men of practical wisdom that they seek to be honoured, and among those who know them, and on the ground of their virtue; clearly, then, according to them, at any rate, virtue is better. And perhaps one might even suppose this to be, rather than honour, the end of the political life. But even this appears somewhat incomplete; for possession of virtue seems actually compatible with being asleep, or with lifelong inactivity, and, further, with the greatest sufferings and misfortunes; but a man who was living so no one would call happy, unless he were maintaining a thesis at all costs. But enough of this; for the subject has been sufficiently treated even in the current discussions. Third comes the contemplative life, which we shall consider later.

The life of money-making is one undertaken under compulsion, and wealth is evidently not the good we are seeking; for it is merely useful and for the sake of something else. And so one might rather take the aforenamed objects to be ends; for they are loved for themselves. But it is evident that not even these are ends; yet many arguments have been thrown away in support of them. Let us leave this subject, then.

6. We had perhaps better consider the universal good and discuss thoroughly what is meant by it, although such an inquiry is made an uphill one by the fact that the Forms have been introduced by friends of our own. Yet it would perhaps be thought to be better, indeed to be our duty, for the sake of maintaining the truth even to destroy what touches us closely, especially as we are philosophers or lovers of wisdom; for, while both are dear, piety requires us to honour truth above our friends.

The men who introduced this doctrine did not posit Ideas of classes within which they recognized priority and posteriority (which is the reason why they did not maintain the existence of an Idea embracing all numbers); but the term "good" is used both in the category of substance and in that of quality and in that of relation, and that which is *per se*, i.e. substance, is prior in nature to the relative (for the latter is like an offshoot and accident of being); so that there could not be a common Idea set over all these goods. Further, since "good" has as many senses as "being" (for it is predicated both in the category of substance, as of God and of reason, and in quality, i.e. of the virtues, and in quantity, i.e. of that which is moderate, and in relation, i.e. of the useful, and in time, i.e. of the right opportunity, and in place, i.e. of the right locality and the like), clearly it cannot be something universally present in all cases and single; for then it could not have been predicated in all the categories but in one only. Further, since of the things answering to one Idea there is one science. there would have been one science of all the goods; but as it is there are many sciences even of the things that fall under one category, e.g. of opportunity, for opportunity in war is studied by strategies and in disease by medicine, and the moderate in food is studied by medicine and in exercise by the science of gymnastics. And one might ask the question, what in the world they *mean* by "a thing itself", if (as is the case) in "man himself" and in a particular man the account of man is one and the same. For in so far as they are man, they will in no respect differ; and if this is so, neither will "good itself" and particular goods, in so far as they are good. But again it will not be good any the more for being eternal, since that which lasts long is no whiter than that which perishes in a day. The Pythagoreans seem to give a more plausible account of the good, when they place the one in the column of goods; and it is they that Speusippus seems to have followed.

But let us discuss these matters elsewhere; an objection to what we have said, however, may be discerned in the fact that the Platonists have not been speaking about *all* goods, and that the goods that are pursued and loved for themselves are called good by reference to a single Form, while those which tend to produce or to preserve these somehow or to prevent their contraries are called so by reference to these, and in a secondary sense. Clearly, then, goods must be spoken of in two ways, and some must be good in themselves, the others by reason of these. Let us separate, then, things good in themselves from things useful, and consider whether the former are called good by reference to a single Idea. What sort of goods would one call good in themselves? Is it those that are pursued even when isolated from others, such as intelligence, sight, and certain pleasures and honours? Certainly, if we pursue these also for the sake of something else, yet one would place them among things good in themselves. Or is nothing other than the Idea of good good in itself? In that case the Form will be empty. But if the things we have named are also things good in themselves, the account of the good will have to appear as something identical in them all, as that of whiteness is identical in snow and in white lead. But of honour, wisdom, and pleasure, just in respect of their goodness, the accounts are distinct and diverse. The good, therefore, is not some common element answering to one Idea.

But what then do we mean by the good? It is surely not like the things that only chance to have the same name. Are goods one, then, by being derived from one good or by all contributing to one good, or are they rather one by analogy? Certainly as sight is in the body, so is reason in the soul, and so on in other cases. But perhaps these subjects had better be dismissed for the present; for perfect precision about them would be more appropriate to another branch of philosophy. And similarly with regard to the Idea; even if there is some one good which is universally predicable of goods or is capable of separate and independent existence, clearly it could not be achieved or attained by man; but we are now seeking something attainable. Perhaps, however, some one might think it worth while to recognize this with a view to the goods that *are* attainable and achievable; for having this as a sort of pattern we shall know better the goods that are good for us, and if we know them shall attain them. This argument has some plausibility, but seems to clash with the procedure of the sciences; for all of these, though they aim at some good and seek to supply the deficiency of it, leave on one side the knowledge of *the* good. Yet that all the exponents of the arts should be ignorant of, and should not even seek, so great an aid is not probable. It is hard, too, to see how a weaver or a carpenter will be benefited in regard to his own craft by knowing this "good itself," or how the man who has viewed the Idea itself will be a better doctor or general thereby. For a doctor seems not even to study health in this way, but the health of man, or perhaps rather the health of a particular man; it is individuals that he is healing. But enough of these topics.

7. Let us again return to the good we are seeking, and ask what it can be. It seems different in different actions and arts; it is different in medicine, in strategy, and in the other arts likewise. What then is the good of each? Surely that for whose sake everything else is done. In medicine this is health, in strategy victory, in architecture a house, in any other sphere something else, and in every action and pursuit the end; for it is for the sake of this that all men do whatever else they do. Therefore, if there is an end for all that we do, this will be the good achievable by action, and if there are more than one, these will be the goods achievable by action.

So the argument has by a different course reached the same point; but we must try to state this even more clearly. Since there are evidently more than one end, and we choose some of these (e.g., wealth, flutes, and in general instruments) for the sake of something else, clearly not all ends are final ends; but the chief good is evidently something final. Therefore, if there is only one final end, this will be what we are seeking, and if there are more than one, the most final of these will be what we are seeking. Now we call that which is in itself worthy of pursuit more final than that which is worthy of pursuit for the sake of something else, and that which is never desirable for the sake of something else more final than the things that are desirable both in themselves and for the sake of that other thing, and therefore we call final without qualification that which is always desirable in itself and never for the sake of something else.

Now such a thing happiness, above all else, is held to be; for this we choose always for itself and never for the sake of something else, but honour, pleasure, reason, and every virtue we choose indeed for themselves (for if nothing resulted from them we should still choose each of them), but we choose them also for the sake of happiness, judging that by means of them we shall be happy. Happiness, on the other hand, no one chooses for the sake of these, nor, in general, for anything other than itself.

From the point of view of self-sufficiency the same result seems to follow; for the final good is thought to be self-sufficient. Now by self-sufficient we do not mean that which is sufficient for a man by himself, for one who lives a solitary life, but also for parents, children, wife, and in general for his friends and fellow citizens, since man is born for citizenship. But some limit must be set to this; for if we extend our requirements to ancestors and descendants and friends' friends we are in for an infinite series. . . . The self-sufficient we now define as that which when isolated makes life desirable and lacking in nothing; and such we think happiness to be; and further we think it most desirable of all things, without being counted as one good thing among others— if it were so counted it would clearly be made desirable by the addition of even the least of goods; for that which is added becomes an excess of goods, and of goods the greater is always more desirable. Happiness, then, is something final and self-sufficient, and is the end of action.

Presumably, however, to say that happiness is the chief good seems a platitude, and a clearer account of what it is is still desired. This might perhaps be given, if we could first ascertain the function of man. For just as for a flute-player, a sculptor, or any artist, and, in general, for all things that have a function or activity, the good and the "well" is thought to reside in the function, so would it seem to be for man, if he has a function. Have the carpenter, then, and the tanner certain functions or activities, and has man none? Is he born without a function? Or as eye, hand, foot, and in general each of the parts evidently has a function, may one lay it down that man similarly has a function apart from all these? What then can this be? Life seems to be common even to plants, but we are seeking what is peculiar to man. Let us exclude, therefore, the life of nutrition and growth. Next there would be a life perception, but *it* also seems to be common even to the horse, the ox, and every animal. There remains, then, an active life of the element that has a rational principle; of this, one part has such a principle in the sense of being obedient to one, the other in the sense of possessing one and exercising thought. And, as "life of the rational element" also has two meanings, we must state that life in the sense of activity is what we mean; for this seems to be the more proper sense of the term. Now if the function of man is an activity of soul which follows or implies a rational principle, and if we say "a so-and-so" and "a good so-and-so" have a function which is the same in kind, e.g., a lyre-player and a good lyre-player, and so without qualification in all cases, eminence in respect of goodness being added to the name of the function (for the function of a lyre-player is to play the lyre, and that of a good lyre-player is to do so well): if this is the case, (and we state the function of man to be a certain kind of life, and this to be an activity or actions of the soul implying a rational principle, and the function of a good man to be the good and noble performance of these, and if any action is well performed when it is performed in accordance with the appropriate excellence: if this is the case,) human good turns out to be activity of soul in accordance with virtue, and if there are more than one virtue, in accordance with the best and most complete.

But we must add "in a complete life." For one swallow does not make a summer, nor does one day; and so too one day, or a short time, does not make a man blessed and happy. . . .

13. Since happiness is an activity of soul in accordance with perfect virtue, we must consider the nature of virtue. . . .

Some things are said about it, adequately enough, even in the discussion outside our school, and we must use these; e.g., that one element in the soul is irrational and one has a rational principle. Whether these are separated as the parts of the body or of anything divisible are, or are distinct by definition but by nature inseparable, like convex and concave in the circumference of a circle, does not affect the present question.

Of the irrational element one division seems to be widely distributed, and vegetative in its nature, I mean that which causes nutrition and growth; for it is this kind of power of the soul that one must assign to all nurslings and to embryos, and this same power to full-grown creatures; this is more reasonable than to assign some different power to them. Now the excellence of this seems to be common to all species and not specifically human; for this part or faculty seems to function most in sleep, while goodness and badness are least manifest in sleep (whence comes the saying that the happy are no better off than the wretched for half their lives; and this happens naturally enough, since sleep is an inactivity of the soul in that respect in which it is called good or bad), unless perhaps to a small extent some of the movements actually penetrate to the soul, and in this respect the dreams of good men are better than those of ordinary people. Enough of this subject, however; let us leave the nutritive faculty alone, since it has by its nature no share in human excellence.

There seems to be also another irrational element in the soul—one which in a sense, however, shares in a rational principle. For we praise the rational principle of the continent man and of the incontinent, and the part of their soul that has such a principle, since it urges them aright and towards the best objects; but there is found in them also another element naturally opposed to the rational principle, which fights against and resists that principle. For exactly as paralysed limbs when we intend to move them to the right turn on the contrary to the left, so is it with the soul; the impulses of incontinent people move in contrary directions. But while in the body we see that which moves astray, in the soul we do not. No doubt, however, we must nonetheless suppose that in the soul too there is something contrary to the rational principle, resisting and opposing it. In what sense it is distinct from the other elements does not concern us. Now even this seems to have a share in a rational principle, as we said; at any rate in the continent man it obeys the rational principle—and presumably in the temperate and brave man it is still more obedient; for in him it speaks, on all matters, with the same voice as the rational principle.

Therefore the irrational element also appears to be twofold. For the vegetative element in no way shares in a rational principle, but the appetitive, and in general the desiring element in a sense shares in it, in so far as it listens to and obeys it; this is the sense in which we speak of "taking account" of one's father or one's friends, not that in which we speak of "accounting" for a mathematical property. That the irrational element is in some sense persuaded by a rational principle is indicated also by the giving of advice and by all reproof and exhortation. And if this element also must be said to have a rational principle, that which has a rational principle (as well as that which has not) will be twofold, one subdivision having it in the strict sense and in itself, and the other having a tendency to obey as one does one's father.

Virtue too is distinguished into kinds in accordance with this difference; for we say that some of the virtues are intellectual and others moral, philosophic wisdom and understanding and practical wisdom being intellectual, liberality and temperance moral. For in speaking about a man's character we do not say that he is wise or has understanding but that he is good-tempered or temperate; yet we praise the wise man also with respect to h.s state of mind; and of states of mind we call those which merit praise virtues.

BOOK II

1. Virtue, then, being of two kinds, intellectual and moral, intellectual virtue in the main owes both its birth and its growth to teaching (for which reason it requires experience and time), while moral virtue comes about as a result of habit, whence also its name *ethike* is one that is formed by a slight variation from the word *ethos* (habit). From this it is also plain that none of the moral virtues arises in us by nature; for nothing that exists by nature can form a habit contrary to its nature. For instance the stone which by nature moves downwards cannot be habituated to move upwards, not even if one tries to train it by throwing it up ten thousand times; nor can fire be habituated to move downwards, nor can anything else that by nature behaves in one way be trained to behave in another. Neither by nature, then, nor contrary to nature do the virtues arise in us; rather we are adapted by nature to receive them, and are made perfect by habit.

Again, of all the things that come to us by nature we first acquire the potentiality and later exhibit the activity (this is plain in the case of the senses; for it was not by often seeing or often hearing that we got these senses, but on the contrary we had them before we used them, and did not come to have them by using them); but the virtues we get by first exercising them, as also happens in the case of the arts as well. For the things we have to learn before we can do them, we learn by doing them, e.g., men become builders by building and lyre-players by playing the lyre; so too we become just by doing just acts, temperate by doing temperate acts, brave by doing brave acts. . . .

Again, it is from the same causes and by the same means that every virtue is both produced and destroyed, and similarly every art; for it is from playing the lyre that both good and bad lyre-players are produced. And the corresponding statement is true of builders and of all the rest; men will be good or bad builders as a result of building well or badly. For if this were not so, there would have been no need of a teacher, but all men would have been born good or bad at their craft. This, then, is the case with the virtues also; by doing the acts that we do in our transactions with other men we become just or unjust, and by doing the acts that we do in the presence of danger, and being habituated to feel fear or confidence, we become brave or cowardly. The same is true of appetites and feelings of anger; some men become temperate and good-tempered, others self-indulgent and irascible, by behaving in one way or the other in the appropriate circumstances. Thus, in one word, states of character arise out of like activities. This is why the activities we exhibit must be of a certain kind; it is because the states of character correspond to the differences between these. It makes no small difference, then, whether we form habits of one kind or of another from our very youth; it makes a very great difference, or rather *all* the difference. . . .

5. Next we must consider what virtue is. Since things that are found in the soul are of three kinds—passions, faculties, states of character—virtue must be one of these. By passions I mean appetite, anger, fear, confidence, envy, joy, friendly feeling, hatred, longing, emulation, pity, and in general the feelings that are accompanied by pleasure or pain; by faculties the things in virtue of which we are said to be capable of feeling these, e.g., of becoming angry or being pained or feeling pity; by states of character the things in virtue of which we stand well or badly with reference to the passions, e.g., with reference to anger we stand badly if we feel it violently or too weakly, and well if we feel it moderately; and similarly with reference to the other passions.

Now neither the virtues nor the vices are *passions*, because we are not called good or bad on the ground of our passions, but are so called on the ground of our virtues and our vices, and because we are neither praised nor blamed for our passions (for the man who feels fear or anger is not praised, nor is the man who simply feels anger blamed, but the man who feels it in a certain way), but for our virtues and our vices we are praised or blamed.

Again, we feel anger and fear without choice, but the virtues are modes of choice or involve choice. Further, in respect of the passions we are said to be moved, but in respect of the virtues and the vices we are said not to be moved but to be disposed in a particular way.

For these reasons also they are not *faculties;* for we are neither called good nor bad, nor praised nor blamed, for the simple capacity of feeling the passions; again, we have the faculties of nature, but we are not made good or bad by nature; we have spoken of this before.

If, then, the virtues are neither passions nor faculties, all that remains is that they should be *states of character.*

Thus we have stated what virtue is in respect of its genus.

6. We must, however, not only describe virtue as a state of character, but also say what sort of state it is. We may remark, then, that every virtue or excellence both brings into good condition the thing of which it is the excellence and makes the work of that thing be done well; e.g., the excellence of the eye makes both the eye and its work good; for it is by the excellence of the eye that we see well. Similarly the excellence of the horse makes a horse both good in itself and good at running and at carrying its rider and at awaiting the attack of the enemy. Therefore, if this is true in every case, the virtue of man also will be the state of character which makes a man good and which makes him do his own work well.

How this is to happen . . . will be made plain . . . by the following consideration of the specific nature of virtue. In everything that is continuous and divisible it is possible to take more, less, or an equal amount, and that either in terms of the thing itself or relatively to us; and the equal is an intermediate between excess and defect. By the intermediate in the object I mean that which is equidistant from each of the extremes, which is one and the same for all men; by the intermediate relatively to us that which is neither too much nor too little—and this is not one, nor the same for all. For instance, if ten is many and two is few, six is the intermediate, taken in terms of the object; for it exceeds and is exceeded by an equal amount; this is intermediate according to arithmetical proportion. But the intermediate relatively to us is not to be taken so; if ten pounds are too much for a particular person to eat and two too little, it does not follow that the trainer will order six pounds; for this also is perhaps too much for the person who is to take it, or too little—too little for Milo,* too much for the beginner in athletic exercises. The same is true of running and wrestling. Thus a master of any art avoids excess and defect, but seeks the intermediate and chooses this—the intermediate not in the object but relatively to us.

If it is thus, then, that every art does its work well—by looking to the intermediate and judging its works by this standard (so that we often say of good works of art that it is not possible either to take away or to add anything, implying that excess and defect destroy the goodness of works of art, while the mean preserves it; and good artists, as we say, look to this in their work), and if, further, virtue is more exact and better than any art, as nature also is, then virtue must have the quality of aiming at the intermediate. I mean moral virtue; for it is this that is concerned with passions and actions, and in these there is excess, defect, and the intermediate. For instance, both fear and confidence and appetite and anger and pity and in general pleasure and pain may be felt both too much and too little, and in both cases not well; but to feel them at the right times, with reference to the right objects, towards the right people, with the right motive, and in the right way, is what is both intermediate and best, and this is characteristic of virtue. Similarly with regard to actions also there is excess, defect, and the intermediate. Now virtue is concerned with passions and actions, in which excess is a form of failure, and so is defect, while the intermediate is praised and is a form of success; and being praised and being successful are both characteristics of virtue. Therefore virtue is a kind of mean, since, as we have seen, it aims at what is intermediate.

Again, it is possible to fail in many ways (for evil belongs to the class of the unlimited, as the Pythagoreans conjectured, and good to that of the limited), while to succeed is possible only in one way (for which reason also one is easy and the other difficult—to miss the mark easy, to hit it difficult); for these reasons also, then, excess and defect are characteristic of vice, and the mean of virtue;

*A famous wrestler. Translator's footnote.

For men are good in but one way, but bad in many.

Virtue, then, is a state of character concerned with choice, lying in a mean, i.e., the mean relative to us, this being determined by a rational principle, and by that principle by which the man of practical wisdom would determine it. Now it is a mean between two vices, that which depends on excess and that which depends on defect; and again it is a mean because the vices respectively fall short of or exceed what is right in both passions and actions, while virtue both finds and chooses that which is intermediate. Hence in respect of its substance and the definition which states its essence virtue is a mean, with regard to what is best and right and extreme.

But not every action nor every passion admits of a mean; for some have names that already imply badness, e.g., spite, shamelessness, envy, and in the case of actions adultery, theft, murder; for all of these and suchlike things imply by their names that they are themselves bad, and not the excesses or deficiencies of them. It is not possible, then, ever to be right with regard to them; one must always be wrong. Nor does goodness or badness with regard to such things depend on committing adultery with the right woman, at the right time, and in the right way, but simply to do any of them is to go wrong. It would be equally absurd, then, to expect that in unjust, cowardly, and voluptuous action there should be a mean, an excess, and a deficiency; for at that rate there would be a mean of excess and of deficiency, an excess of excess, and a deficiency of deficiency. But as there is no excess and deficiency of temperance and courage because what is intermediate is in a sense an extreme, so too of the actions we have mentioned there is no mean nor any excess and deficiency, but however they are done they are wrong; for in general there is neither a mean of excess and deficiency, nor excess and deficiency of a mean.

7. We must, however, not only make this general statement, but also apply it to the individual facts. For among statements about conduct those which arc general apply more widely, but those which are particular are more genuine, since conduct has to do with individual cases, and our statements must harmonize with the facts in these cases. We may take these cases from our table. With regard to feelings of fear and confidence courage is the mean; of the people who exceed, he who exceeds in fearlessness has no name (many of the states have no name), while the man who exceeds in confidence is rash, and he who exceeds in fear and falls short in confidence is a coward. With regard to pleasures and pains—not all of them, and not so much with regard to the pains— the mean is temperance, the excess self-indulgence. Persons deficient with regard to the pleasures are not often found; hence such persons also have received no name. But let us call them "insensible."

With regard to giving and taking of money the mean is liberality, the excess and the defect prodigality and meanness. In these actions people exceed and fall short in contrary ways; the prodigal exceeds in spending and falls short in taking, while the mean man exceeds in taking and falls short in spending. . . .

With regard to money there are also other dispositions—a mean, magnificence (for the magnificent man differs from the liberal man; the former deals with large sums, the latter with small ones), and excess, tastelessness and vulgarity, and a deficiency, niggardliness. . . .

With regard to honour and dishonour the mean is proper pride, the excess is known as a sort of "empty vanity," and the deficiency is undue humility; and as we said liberality was related to magnificence, differing from it by dealing with small sums, so there is a state similarly related to proper pride, being concerned with small honours while that is concerned with great. For it is possible to desire honour as one ought, and more than one ought, and less, and the man who exceeds in his desires is called ambitious, the man who falls short unambitious, while the intermediate person has no name. The dispositions also are nameless, except that that of the ambitious man is called ambition. Hence the people who are at the extremes lay claim to the middle place; and we ourselves sometimes call the intermediate person ambitious and sometimes unambitious, and sometimes praise the ambitious man and sometimes the unambitious. . . .

With regard to anger also there is an excess, a deficiency, and a mean. Although they can scarcely be said to have names, yet since we call the intermediate person good-tempered let us call the mean good temper; of the persons at the extremes let the one who exceeds be called irascible, and his vice irascibility, and the man who falls short an inirascible sort of person, and the deficiency inirascibility.

There are also three other means, which have a certain likeness to one another, but differ from one another: for they are all concerned with intercourse in words and actions, but differ in that one is concerned with truth in this sphere, the other two with pleasantness; and of this one kind is exhibited in giving amusement, the other in all the circumstances of life. We must therefore speak of these two, that we may the better see that in all things the mean is praiseworthy, and the extremes neither praiseworthy nor right, but worthy of blame. Now most of these states also have no names, but we must try, as in the other cases, to invent names ourselves so that we may be clear and easy to follow. With regard to truth, then, the intermediate is a truthful sort of person and the mean may be called truthfulness, while the pretence which exaggerates is boastfulness and the person characterized by it a boaster, and that which understates is mock modesty and the person characterized by it mock-modest. With regard to pleasantness in the giving of amusement the intermediate person is ready-witted and the disposition ready wit, the excess is buffoonery and the person characterized by it a buffoon, while the man who falls short is a sort of boor and his state is boorishness. With regard to the remaining kind of pleasantness, that which is exhibited in life in general, the man who is pleasant in the right way is friendly and the mean is friendliness, while the man who exceeds is an obsequious person if he has no end in view, a flatterer if he is aiming at his own advantage, and the man who falls short and is unpleasant in all circumstances is a quarrelsome and surly sort of person.

There are also means in the passions and concerned with the passions;

since shame is not a virtue, and yet praise is extended to the modest man. For even in these matters one man is said to be intermediate, and another to exceed, as for instance the bashful man who is ashamed of everything; while he who falls short or is not ashamed of anything at all is shameless, and the intermediate person is modest. Righteous indignation is a mean between envy and spite, and these states are concerned with the pain and pleasures that are felt at the fortunes of our neighbours; the man who is characterized by righteous indignation is pained at undeserved good fortune, the envious man, going beyond him, is pained at all good fortune, and the spiteful man falls so far short of being pained that he even rejoices. . . .

9. That moral virtue is a mean, then, and in what sense it is so, and that it is a mean between two vices, the one involving excess, the other deficiency, and that it is such because its character is to aim at what is intermediate in passions and in actions, has been sufficiently stated. Hence also it is no easy task to be good. For in everything it is no easy task to find the middle, e.g., to find the middle of a circle is not for every one but for him who knows; so, too, any one can get angry—that is easy—or give or spend money; but to do this to the right person, to the right extent, at the right time, with the right motive, and in the right way, *that* is not for every one, nor is it easy; wherefore goodness is both rare and laudable and noble. . . .

BOOK X

6. . . . What remains is to discuss in outline the nature of happiness, since his is what we state the end of human nature to be. Our discussion will be, the more concise if we first sum up what we have said already. We said, then, that it is not a disposition; for if it were it might belong to some one who was asleep throughout his life, living the life of a plant, or, again, to some one who was suffering the greatest misfortunes. If these implications are unacceptable, and we must rather class happiness as an activity, as we have said before, and if some activities are necessary, and desirable for the sake of something else, while others are so in themselves, evidently happiness must be placed among those desirable in themselves, not among those desirable for the sake of something else; for happiness does not lack anything, but is self-sufficient. Now those activities are desirable in themselves from which nothing is sought beyond the activity. And of this nature virtuous actions are thought to be; for to do noble and good deeds is a thing desirable for its own sake.

Pleasant amusements also are thought to be of this nature; we choose them not for the sake of other things; for we are injured rather than benefited by them, since we are led to neglect our bodies and our property. But most of the people who are deemed happy take refuge in such pastimes, which is the reason why those who are ready-witted at them are highly esteemed at the courts of tyrants; they make themselves pleasant companions in the tyrants' favourite pursuits, and that is the sort of man they want. Now these things are thought to be of the nature of happiness because people in despotic positions spend their leisure in them, but perhaps such people prove nothing; for virtue and reason, from which good activities flow, do not depend on despotic position; nor, if these people, who have never tasted pure and generous pleasure, take refuge in the bodily pleasures, should these for that reason be thought more desirable; for boys, too, think the things that are valued among themselves are the best. It is to be expected, then, that, as different things seem valuable to boys and to men, so they should to bad men and to good. Now . . . those things are both valuable and pleasant which are such to the good man; and to each man the activity in accordance with his own disposition is most desirable, and, therefore, to the good man that which is in accordance with virtue. Happiness, therefore, does not lie in amusement; it would, indeed, be strange if the end were amusement, and one were to take trouble and suffer hardship all one's life in order to amuse oneself. For, in a word, everything that we choose we choose for the sake of something else—except happiness, which is an end. Now to exert oneself and work for the sake of amusement seems silly and utterly childish. But to amuse oneself in order that one may exert oneself, as Anacharsis puts it, seems right; for amusement is a sort of relaxation, and we need relaxation because we cannot work continuously. Relaxation, then, is not an end; for it is taken for the sake of activity.

The happy life is thought to be virtuous; now a virtuous life requires exertion, and does not consist in amusement. And we say that serious things are better than laughable things and those connected with amusement, and that the activity of the better of any two things—whether it be two elements of our being or two men—is the more serious; but the activity of the better is *ipso facto* superior and more of the nature of happiness. And any chance person—even a slave—can enjoy the bodily pleasures no less than the best man; but no one assigns to a slave a share in happiness—unless he assigns to him also a share in human life. For happiness does not lie in such occupations, but, as we have said before, in virtuous activities.

7. If happiness is activity in accordance with virtue, it is reasonable that *it* should be in accordance with the highest virtue; and this will be that of the best thing in us. Whether it be reason or something else that is this element which is thought to be our natural ruler and guide and to take thought of things noble and divine, whether it be itself also divine or only the most divine element in us, the activity of this in accordance with its proper virtue will be perfect happiness. That this activity is contemplative we have already said.

Now this would seem to be in agreement with what we said before and with the truth. For, firstly, this activity is the best (since not only is reason the best thing in us, but the objects of reason are the best of knowable objects); and, secondly, it is the most continuous, since we can contemplate truth more continuously than we can *do* anything. And we think happiness has pleasure mingled with it, but the activity of philosophic wisdom is admittedly the pleasantest of virtuous activities; at all events the pursuit of it is thought to offer pleasures marvellous for their purity and their enduringness, and it is to be expected that those who know will pass their time more pleasantly than those who inquire. And the self-sufficiency that is spoken of must belong most to the contemplative activity. For while a philosopher, as well as a just man or one possessing any other virtue, needs the necessaries of life, when they are sufficiently equipped with things of that sort the just man needs people towards whom and with whom he shall act justly, and the temperate man, the brave man, and each of the others is in the same case, but the philosopher, even when by himself, can contemplate truth, and the better the wiser he is; he can perhaps do so better if he has fellow-workers, but still he is the most self-sufficient. And this activity alone would seem to be loved for its own sake; for nothing arises from it apart from the contemplating, while from practical activities we gain more or less apart from the action. And happiness is thought to depend on leisure; for we are busy that we may have leisure, and make war that we may live in peace. Now the activity of the practical virtues is exhibited in political or military affairs, but the actions concerned with these seem to be unleisurely. War-like actions are completely so (for no one chooses to be at war, or provokes war, for the sake of being at war; any one would seem absolutely murderous if he were to make enemies of his friends in order to bring about battle and slaughter); but the action of the statesman is also unleisurely, and—apart from the political action itself—aims at despotic power and honours, or at all events happiness, for him and his fellow citizens—a happiness different from political action, and evidently sought as being different. So if among virtuous actions, political and military actions are distinguished by nobility and greatness, and these are un-leisurely and aim at and end and are not desirable for their own sake, but the activity of reason, which is contemplative, seems both to be superior in serious worth and to aim at no end beyond itself, and to have its pleasure proper to itself (and this augments the activity), and the self-sufficiency, leisureliness, unwearied-ness (so far as this is possible for man), and all the other attributes ascribed to the supremely happy man are evidently those connected with this activity, it follows that this will be the complete happiness of man, if it be allowed a complete term of life (for none of the attributes of happiness is *in*complete).

But such a life would be too high for man; for it is not in so far as he is man that he will live so, but in so far as something divine is present in him; and by so much as this is superior to our composite nature is its activity superior to that which is the exercise of the other kind of virtue. If reason is divine, then, in comparison with man, the life according to it is divine in comparison with human life. But we must not follow those who advise us, being men, to think of human things, and, being mortal, of mortal things, but must, so far as we can, make ourselves immortal, and strain every nerve to live in accordance with the best thing in us; for even if it be small in bulk, much more does it in power and worth surpass everything. This would seem, too, to be each man himself, since it is the authoritative and better part of him. It would be strange, then, if he were to choose not the life of his self but that of something else. And what we said before will apply now; that which is proper to each thing is by nature best and most pleasant for each thing; for man, therefore, the life according to reason is best and pleasantest, since reason more than anything else *is* man. This life therefore is also the happiest.

8. But in a secondary degree the life in accordance with the other kind of virtue is happy; for the activities in accordance with this befit our human estate. Just and brave acts, and other virtuous acts, we do in relation to each other, observing our respective duties with regard to contracts and services and all manner of actions and with regard to passions; and all of these seem to be typically human. Some of them seem even to arise from the body, and virtue of character to be in many ways bound up with the passions. Practical wisdom, too, is linked to virtue of character, and this to practical wisdom, since the principles of practical wisdom are in accordance with the moral virtues and rightness in morals is in accordance with practical wisdom. Being connected with the passions also, the moral virtues must belong to our composite nature; and the virtues of our composite nature are human; so, therefore, are the life and the happiness which correspond to these. The excellence of the reason is a thing apart, we must be content to say this much about it, for to describe it precisely is a task greater than our purpose requires. It would seem, however, also to need external equipment but little, or less than moral virtue does. Grant that both need the necessaries, and do so equally, even if the statesman's work is the more concerned with the body and things of that sort; for there will be little difference there; but in what they need for the exercise of their activities there will be much difference. The liberal man will need money for the doing of his liberal deeds, and the just man too will need it for the returning of services (for wishes are hard to discern, and even people who are not just pretend to wish to act justly); and the brave man will need power if he is to accomplish any of the acts that correspond to his virtue, and the temperate man will need opportunity; for how else is either he or any of the others to be recognized? It is debated, too, whether the will or the deed is more essential to virtue, which is assumed to involve both; it is surely clear that its perfection involves both; but for deeds many things are needed, and more, the greater and nobler the deeds are. But the man who is contemplating the truth needs no such thing, at least with a view to the exercise of his activity; indeed they are, one may say, even hindrances, at all events to his contemplation; but in so far as he is a man and lives with a number of people, he chooses to do virtuous acts; he will therefore need such aids to living a human life.

But that perfect happiness is a contemplative activity will appear from the following consideration as well. We assume the gods to be above all other beings blessed and happy; but what sort of actions must we assign to them? Acts of justice? Will not the gods seem absurd if they make contracts and return deposits, and so on? Acts of a brave man, then, confronting dangers and running risks because it is noble to do so? Or liberal acts? To whom will they give? It will be strange if they are really to have money or anything of the kind. And what would their temperate acts be? Is not such praise tasteless, since they have no bad appetites? If we were to run through them all, the circumstances of action would be found trivial and unworthy of gods. Still, every one supposes that they *live* and therefore that they are active; we cannot suppose them to sleep like Endymion. Now if you take away from a living being action, and still more production, what is left but contemplation? Therefore the activity of God, which surpasses all others in blessedness, must be contemplative; and of human activities, therefore, that which is most akin to this must be most of the nature of happiness.

This is indicated, too, by the fact that the other animals have no share in happiness, being completely deprived of such activity. For while the whole life of the gods is blessed, and that of men too in so far as some likeness of such activity belongs to them, none of the other animals is happy, since they in no way share in contemplation. Happiness extends, then, just so far as contemplation does, and those to whom contemplation more fully belongs are more truly happy, not as a mere concomitant but in virtue of the contemplation; for this is in itself precious. Happiness, therefore, must be some form of contemplation.

But, being a man, one will also need external prosperity; for our nature is not self-sufficient for the purpose of contemplation, but our body also must be healthy and must have food and other attention. Still, we must not think that the man who is to be happy will need many things or great things, merely because he cannot be supremely happy without external goods; for self-sufficiency and action do not involve excess, and we can do noble acts without ruling earth and sea; for even with moderate advantages one can act virtuously (this is manifest enough; for private persons are thought to do worthy acts no less than despots—indeed even more); and it is enough that we should have so much as that; for the life of the man who is active in accordance with virtue will be happy. Solon, too, was perhaps sketching well the happy man when he described him as moderately furnished with externals but as having done (as Solon thought) the noblest acts, and lived temperately; for one can with but moderate possessions do what one ought. Anaxagoras also seems to have supposed the happy man not to be rich nor a despot, when he said that he would not be surprised if the happy man were to seem to most people a strange person; for they judge by externals, since these are all they perceive. The opinions of the wise, then, to harmonize with our arguments. But while even such things carry some conviction, the truth in practical matters is discerned from the facts of life; for these are the decisive factor. We must therefore survey what we have already said, bringing it to the test of the facts of life, and if it harmonizes with the facts we must accept it, but if it clashes with them we must suppose it to be mere theory. Now he who exercises his reason and cultivates it seems to be both in the best state of mind and most dear to the gods. For if the gods have any care for human affairs, as they are thought to have, it would be reasonable both that they should delight in that which was best and most akin to them (i.e., reason) and that they should reward those who love and honour this most, as caring for the things that are dear to them and acting both rightly and nobly.

And that all these attributes belong most of all to the philosopher is manifest. He, therefore, is the dearest to the gods. And he who is that will presumably be also the happiest; so that in this way too the philosopher will more than any other be happy.

29

Aristotle and the End of Man

FREDERICK SIEGLER

Now, what does it mean to say that acting for the sake of reasons is the function or proper function of man?

Consider the argument in the following form:

1. Man has a function.
2. The function of man is determined by what is peculiar to man.
3. What is peculiar to man is acting on reasons.
4. The function of man is acting on reasons.

Suppose for the moment that we understood what was meant by "the function of man." Then there would still be some problem as to how Aristotle establishes that man *has* one. He suggests two considerations or arguments. (1) Since the carpenter and shoemaker have their own functions and spheres of action, presumably man as man has one too (by nature). (2) Since each part of the body "has its own proper function, so man too has some function over and above the functions of his parts."

Now these arguments look inconclusive. For it is not clear what sort of implausibility or absurdity would be reached by asserting that carpenters have functions but man as man does not. Or that although the parts of man have functions man as a whole does not. If Aristotle were to assert as a general truth that every natural thing has a function then of course it would follow that man has one. But he does not assert this. And if he did there would be difficulties about e.g. the functions of the appendix. And presumably we should require some argument to support such a view. But even if, for the sake of continuing, we accept that man *has* a function, what does this *mean*?

Now we do speak of the flute player as having a function in an orchestra, but it is not clear what could be meant by the function of the flute player *qua* flute player. According to Aristotle the function of the flute player is to play the flute. Function, here, means "what constitutes being a flute player." It is

FROM "Reason, Happiness, and Goodness" by Frederick Siegler, in James J. Walsh and Henry L. Shapiro (eds.): *Aristotle's Ethics*, Copyright 1967 by Wadsworth Publishing Co., Inc., Belmont, California.

of some importance to note that if a flute player plays the flute he does not thereby discharge any moral or other kind of obligation, and he does not thereby benefit from playing the flute.

If by function of man Aristotle means what he means when he speaks of the function of a flute player, and by function of a flute player we understand "doing what constitutes being a flute player," then Aristotle means by function of man "doing what constitutes being a man." Now just as playing the flute is peculiar to being a flute player, so acting on reasons is peculiar to being a man. Consequently when Aristotle says that the function of man is acting on reasons he must or can only mean that men alone act on reasons, or that acting on reasons is what constitutes being a man. And again, by parity of reasoning, when a man acts on reasons he does not thereby discharge any moral or any other kind of obligation, nor does he thereby necessarily benefit from acting on reasons.

We have considered one sense of function which Aristotle might be said to have in mind when he says "The (proper) function of man is an activity of the soul in conjunction with the rational element." The sense we have discussed might be called a descriptive sense of "function." In this sense we speak of the function of some object as that which the object characteristically does, or is designed to do. For example the function of the blackjack is to stun temporarily. That is its function, purpose, or role in life. From this truth about the function of the blackjack it does not follow that anyone ought morally to use that tool; and if anything practical follows, it is that if you want to stun somebody then you ought (not morally) to use a blackjack.

There is another sense of function which is not so aseptic as this. Suppose somebody said "Johnson is ruining the country: after all the function of government is to leave all commercial affairs to private enterprise. He is going beyond the proper function of government." The critic is not describing how in fact the government is run or what in fact constitutes the workings of a government. Rather he is criticizing the activities of our government in terms of what he thinks ought to be the sphere of governmental activities. This notion of function might be spoken of as "the evaluative or ought sense of function."

These two notions of function can be exemplified by comparing discussion by scholars of the function of the medieval university, with discussion by contemporary educators of the function of today's university. The latter group speak in the idiom of what ought to be, recommendation, and advice. The former group speak in neutral terms. The former group are trying to say things which are true, e.g., "the medieval university functioned as a proving ground for clerics." The latter group are trying to say things which ought to be true, e.g., "the function of the university is to train young minds for the professions." Their point might be put by reference to something which may *be* true of universities, e.g., "although today's university *functions* as a mating ground for overgrown adolescents, its *real* or *proper* function is to train young minds for the professions."

We now have two notions of function. The first describes what something characteristically *does* do, and the second states what something *ought* to do. It seems possible that a third notion of function could be developed. There is general agreement that Aristotle's discussion of function is in some way derived from that in Plato's *Republic* 352dff, where examples of tools, horse, and sense organs are developed. One example of the notion of a function is Plato's analysis of the *orgon*, the work or function of an instrument or tool such as a knife. The function is determined by the producer's purpose in making it or the user's purpose in using it. Joachim comments: "the purpose is not sheerly external: i.e., the work of the tool and the tool's own nature (its material, shape, etc.) are necessarily adjusted to one another. The work of cutting demands, for example, steel (not wood), and steel of a certain shape. To that extent the tool, in serving the purpose of the craftsman, is fulfilling itself, its own destiny. A knife which will not cut is not merely a bad knife—it is not a knife at all, but for example, a mere piece of steel: steel of a certain shape (what we call a 'knife') is only itself in cutting." Joachim cites Plato's illustrations of the horse's function to make a similar point. He admits that in fulfilling its function "to bear its rider safely and quickly" the horse is fulfilling a purpose "imposed on it by man. But obviously man, in using the horse for his purposes, is taking advantage of the natural powers of the horse: i.e., the horse, in doing the work which man sets it, is also realizing its own nature or *phusis*, exercising a function in which it expresses its self. In other words the horse, in making its contribution to the well-being of man, is also achieving its own well-being." The horse thereby "fulfills its own natural tendencies and powers, as well as certain wants of man."

From this we might develop what could be called the beneficial notion of function. Man, in doing what is peculiar to him or what his natural powers enable him to do, is thereby realizing his own nature and therefore achieving his own well-being or benefitting himself.

We now have three notions of a function: (1) descriptive, what an x characteristically does, (2) evaluative, what an x ought to do, (3) beneficial, what an x does that benefits him or leads to his well-being.

We have considered the argument in terms of function in the first sense, and now we shall consider it in the third, and then the second senses. Using the third sense of function the argument would run:

1. Man has a function (doing what is beneficial to man).
2. What is beneficial to man is doing what is peculiar to him.
3. What is peculiar to man is acting on reasons.
4. What is beneficial to man is acting on reasons.

Now this conclusion 4 follows from 2 and 3, but there is some unclarity as to how to go about determining the meaning and truth of 2. In fact it is 4 that is attractive in this argument, and it does have an air of truth about it. For surely, if a man has goals or aims in life it is unlikely that he will achieve his aims if he does not act on reasons. In fact, if a man has aims then it seems that if he does not act on reasons to achieve his aims, in a clear sense he cannot be said to have *achieved* his aims. A man whose aim it is to win a chess match is less than half glad to win by forfeit. He does not thereby achieve his aim, rather it comes to him. In another way this conclusion seems plausible. We as human beings do seem to place value on rational activity, activity which involves reasoning. And if a person were to spend his life eating and sleeping we might pity him and encourage him to do something (which involves reasoning). For we think it to a man's benefit to engage in reasoning. But though in some ways the conclusion seems quite plausible, its plausibility does not derive from the premises since 2, a crucial premise, is by no means clear, or if in a way understandable, it is not clearly true.

Another difficulty in this third notion of function is that *if* it does indeed derive from Plato's discussion of the function of a knife, horse, or eye, etc. it is not clear how this aids in understanding what Aristotle might have in mind in speaking of the function of man. Now it is certainly true, in Plato's examples, that there is some notion of benefit or well-being involved in a thing's performing its function, but it is the user who is benefited when, for example, the knife performs its function, and it is difficult to attach any clear sense to the talk of the knife's "fulfilling itself, its own destiny." Let us ask this: Does the notion of the knife's fulfilling a function have any bearing on *its* happiness or moral goodness? Obviously not. There is no notion of the happiness or moral goodness of a knife, and it is difficult to see how the knife could be said to benefit in any way. But this is exactly what Aristotle has to say if an analogy between the function of a knife and the function of a man is to have any relevance to the discussion of the happiness or goodness of man.

Now consider the case of the horse. Does the notion of the horse's function have any bearing on its happiness or moral goodness? Clearly not the latter. There is some suggestion by Joachim that if a horse fulfills its function it is doing something that benefits it, but it seems that such a suggestion is gratuitous. To say that a work-horse is "realizing its own nature or *phusis*, exercising a function in which it expresses its self . . . achieving its own well being, etc." suggests that a horse is happy in doing what man wants it to do, and there seems to be no good reason to believe such a thing. There is no indication as to how one is to establish such a claim. That a horse is kept under lock and key even after it has been trained to contribute toward "achieving its own well-being" suggests, if anything, the contrary.

If what I have argued is correct, then the notion of the function of the knife, horse, or eye cannot really give us a beneficial notion of function that could be used to elucidate the happiness or moral goodness of man.

Difficulties also arise from employing sense 2 of function.

1. Man has a function (doing what man ought to do).
2. What man ought to do is what is peculiar to him.
3. What is peculiar to man is acting on reasons.
4. What man ought to do is act on reasons.

For one thing, if "ought" is taken as a moral ought, then it is not clear that

2 is true, or how we should settle the issue of its truth. And even if this were true and it were a moral ought, 4, which would follow from 2 and 3, does not seem acceptable as it stands.

For although it might well be beneficial to man to act on reasons, it does not seem right to say that if a man acts on reasons he is thereby acting as he ought. And this is because a man can act on reasons and still be morally wicked. Of course it is true that the notion of acting on reasons or for the sake of reasons is sometimes construed as acting on right reason, where this comes to "acting on reasons for morally good goals." After all when we say that a man is reasonable we mean more than that he acts on reasons; rather we mean that his reasons are good ones, and his *aims* are good ones. And in that sense of acting reasonably, the conclusion 4 seems quite plausible, though perhaps a bit circular and thereby trivial, namely, what man ought to do is to act reasonably, i.e., to act on good reasons for good aims. But if the conclusion is taken in this sense then so must the premises be taken in this sense. And then in premise 3 "acting on reasons" must mean "acting on reasons for good ends." But in that case premise 3 is *false*. For what is peculiar to human beings, we agreed, is acting on reasons, or for the sake of reasons, but not in the sense of having the right reasons, or the right ends in view. Although it does seem to be peculiarly human to help a lady because she is in need, an action for the sake of a reason, it is, unfortunately, no less peculiarly human to shoot a lady because she is a bore, an action for the sake of a reason. Acting for the sake of reasons is perhaps peculiar to human beings, but it is no more or less peculiar to human beings to act with the right reasons or for the right ends than it is to act for unjustifiable reasons or for the wrong ends.

Consequently, if we understand "acting on reasons" in premise 3 to refer to what is common to Hitler and Churchill, namely acting for the sake of reasons, then premise 2 would be false, and the conclusion 4 would not be established by the argument. On the other hand, if we construe "acting on reasons" to mean "having the right reasons for the right ends" then even if we accept premise 2, premise 3 would be false, and the conclusion, though it seems trivially true, would not be supported by the argument. It may be that Aristotle is suggesting that if a man wants to achieve his aims, and if he wants to be morally virtuous, then a *necessary* but not sufficient condition is acting for the sake of reasons, or on reasons. If one does not reason in his activities he will not be able to achieve his aims, including happiness, nor will he be able to become morally good since moral goodness involves at least reasoning with regard to one's activities.

Aristotle now offers an analogy between the function of man and the function of a harpist. Is Aristotle hoping to explicate further the concept of happiness or the concept of good? Is he hoping to show some connection between being happy and being good?

It seems unquestionable that the function of a harpist is to play the harp, if by function we mean what he *qua* harpist characteristically does. Furthermore it seems unquestionable that the function of a good harpist is to play the harp well. Now, by parity of reasoning since the function of man is acting on reasons (that is what is peculiarly characteristic of man *qua* man) a good man would be a man who reasons well or is a good reasoner.

But here again "reason well" is equivocal. It could mean (1) that he has reasons which *justify* his actions, or (2) that his reasons are well or efficiently designed for his purposes, whatever his purposes may be. Reasoning well, therefore might imply that the agent is (1) morally praiseworthy, or (2) praise-worthy in calculation or efficiency. Now I think that 1 in practice requires 2 since one can hardly do the morally right thing if he is poor in calculation. This point is discussed by Aristotle in Bk. 6 Ch. 5–13 where he finally concludes that the morally good man must have practical wisdom which is concerned with the calculation of means for reaching one's ends. But it is clear that 2 in no way requires 1, for the man who is clever in deliberation or calculation concerning his aims does not necessarily have morally praiseworthy aims. Such a man Aristotle says (1144a24ff) has cleverness, and if he has noble aims then his cleverness deserves praise, but if the goal is a bad one then the cleverness is knavery or smartness.

Now suppose that Aristotle has in mind the first sense of "reasons well." In that case there is no parallel with the harpist; for the harpist and the good harpist are related solely in terms of performing that which is his peculiar function or ability, namely playing the harp. But we agree that the peculiar function or ability of a man is acting on reasons in a neutral sense; that is, excluding the issue of the moral or beneficial nature of the ends, for it is no more or less unique for a man to make plans for a new hospital than it is for him to make plans for a bank robbery. Now if this is so, then it just does not follow that a man who performs his peculiar function well is doing something morally praiseworthy. All that follows is that if a man performs his peculiar function well his reasons reveal careful design and deliberation and efficient planning. And consequently if Aristotle has in mind sense 1 of "reasons well" then the analogy between the harpist and man is gone. Consider the argument as follows:

1. The function of a harpist is to play the harp.
2. A good harpist plays the harp well.
3. So in general if the function of an X is to f, then a good X must f well.
4. The function of man is to act on reasons or reason in his actions.
5. A good man acts well on reasons or reasons well in his actions.

Now grant for the present purposes the truth of 3 as established by or sup-ported by premises 1 and 2. Premise 4 is true if function means what it does in premise 1, namely, that which constitutes being a man, what is peculiar to being a man. But then 5, the conclusion, does not follow if by "reasons well" Aristotle means "has reasons which justify his actions," for (a) "good" in premise 3 is neither a moral nor a beneficial good, (b) "reasons" in premise 4 is morally and beneficially neutral, and (c) since "good" and "reasons well" in the conclusion, if it is to follow logically from the premises, must retain the same sense it has in the premises. Consequently, there is no room for sense 1 of "reasons well" in this argument.

Now on the other hand, suppose Aristotle has in mind the second sense of "reasons well." In that case the parallel with the harpist is maintained. For since it is the peculiar function or ability of man to act on reasons, it would follow that a man who was skilled at or had a high standard in that particular function is a man highly skilled in reasoning; he is a man who deliberates carefully, plans with precision, and organizes his activities so that he can achieve his aims, whatever they may be. But of course, from this it does not at all follow that a man who performs in accordance with the function of man (reasoning) is *eo ipso* a morally praiseworthy man. Nor does it follow that a man who performs his function (reasoning) skilfully is *eo ipso* a morally praiseworthy man. Acting on reasons or having reasons for one's actions may be a necessary condition for moral worth, and being a *skilful* reasoner may be a necessary condition for moral worth. But neither of these conditions is sufficient for moral worth, since a clever bank robber has reasons carefully designed for his aims. It is true, as Aristotle says, that "any action is well performed when it is performed in accordance with the appropriate excellence," but since the peculiar ability or function of man is acting on reasons, and the excellent functioning of man is having well designed reasons, it does not follow that an action that is well performed is a morally praiseworthy action.

Now if Aristotle thinks that a man will be happy if he performs actions in accordance with carefully designed reasons, then it follows that such a man whether he has good aims or bad aims, will be happy. And this may or may not be true. But if it is true then it by no means follows that happiness is activity of the soul in accordance with *virtue*, if by "virtue" Aristotle means having morally praiseworthy aims. Only if Aristotle means by "virtue" the exercise of the peculiar ability to deliberate and reason about aims might it be true to say that happiness is activity of the soul in accordance with virtue. But then this is only to say that a man with moral or immoral aims is happy if he reasons well about his aims. And so if this argument about the function of man is meant to elucidate the concept of happiness, then Aristotle is justified in concluding only that a man is happy if and only if he reasons well about his aims. But Aristotle wants the conclusion that happiness is virtuous activity of the soul (1099b25), and he wants virtue to mean having virtuous or praiseworthy aims, good and noble ends.

Furthermore, if Aristotle thinks that human good, or what is morally praiseworthy in human action, is activity in accordance with the efficient functioning of man, then it follows from his argument that an action is morally praiseworthy if and only if it is performed in accordance with the efficient functioning of the peculiar ability of reasoning. But that conclusion does not seem to be correct. For as we have suggested, a man might reason well about evil aims, thereby using well his peculiar ability and not be morally praiseworthy. To act on well designed reasons may be a necessary condition but it is certainly not a sufficient condition for moral praise. So the only conclusion justified by his argument is that if a man reasons carefully and successfully he is morally praise-worthy. And that conclusion is quite false. Of course Aristotle does not want to come to that conclusion. He wants to conclude that the function of a good man is the good and noble or right and proper performance of rationally based actions. And although this conclusion seems quite plausible it does not follow from his argument. And this is simply because the argument about the function of man refers to what Aristotle considers to be peculiar to human beings; yet this peculiarity does not single out morally praiseworthy aims from morally blameworthy aims. It singles out the ability to act on or for the sake of reasons. And because he referred to the ability to act on or for the sake of reasons, his claim about the peculiar ability of man seemed to be true. But if he had claimed that the peculiar ability of man was to act on reasons for morally praiseworthy aims, his claim about the peculiar ability of man would be false, since it would imply that the ability to act on reasons for morally blameworthy ends is not equally peculiar to man. And because the claim about the peculiar function of man did not separate morally praiseworthy aims from morally blameworthy aims, it is no wonder that Aristotle cannot come to any conclusions about what constitutes morally praiseworthy actions if such conclusions are based solely on the peculiar function of man.

We may have been tempted, as perhaps Aristotle was tempted, by a misleading parallel between the harpist and man. A harpist *qua* harpist is praised for performing his function well. There is nothing morally praiseworthy about that. But man *qua* man can be praised on two separate (though perhaps related) accounts. He can be praised for performing his function well. That is by no means moral praise. And he can be praised for performing his function well for morally praiseworthy ends or aims. And as I have suggested, it may be a necessary condition for moral praise that a man be able to reason well about his aims, but that is not sufficient. He must have the right aims. And having the right aims is unfortunately not any more peculiar to human beings than having the wrong aims. But to be a moral man one must be more than an efficient reasoner. There may be some sense in saying of an efficient reasoner who has aims we believe to be wrong that he is not *really* reasoning, but (1) that sounds as though one is trying to defend a thesis at any cost, and (2) surely what such a man is doing is peculiar to man.

30

Aristotle and Moral Virtue

ALASDAIR MACINTYRE

This notion of the mean is perhaps the single most difficult concept in the *Ethics*. It will be most conveniently introduced by an example. The virtue of courage is said to be the mean between two vices—a vice of excess, which is rashness, and a vice of deficiency, which is cowardice. A mean is thus a rule or principle of choice between two extremes. Extremes of what? Of emotion or of action. In the case of courage, I give way too much to the impulses which danger arouses when I am a coward, too little to them when I am foolhardy. Three obvious objections at once arise. The first is that there are many emotions and actions for which there cannot be a "too much" or a "too little." Aristotle specifically allows for this. He says that a man "can be afraid and be bold and desire and be angry and pity and feel pleasure and pain in general, too much or too little"; but he says also that malice, shamelessness, and envy are such that their names imply that they are evil. So also with actions such as adultery, theft, and murder. But Aristotle states no principle which will enable us to recognize what falls in one class, what in the other. We can, however, attempt to interpret Aristotle at this point and try to state the principle implicit in his examples.

If I merely ascribe anger or pity to a man, I thereby neither applaud nor condemn him. If I ascribe envy, I do so condemn him. Those emotions of which there can be a mean—and the actions which correspond to them—are those which I can characterize without any moral commitment. It is where I can characterize an emotion or action as a case of anger or whatever it is, prior to and independently of asking whether there is too much or too little of it, that I have a subject for the mean. But if this is what Aristotle means, then he is committed to showing that every virtue and vice are mean and extreme for some emotion or concern with pleasure and pain characterizeable and identifiable in nonmoral terms. Just this is what Aristotle sets out to show in the latter part of Book II of the *Ethics*. Envy, for example, is one extreme, and malice another, of a certain attitude to the fortunes of others. The virtue which is the mean is righteous indignation. But this very example brings out a new difficulty in the doctrine. The righteously indignant man is one who is upset by the undeserved good fortune of others (this example is perhaps the first indication that Aristotle was not a nice or a good man: the words "supercilious prig" spring to mind very often in reading the *Ethics*). The jealous man has an excess of this attitude—

he is upset even by the deserved good fortune of others; and the malicious man is alleged to have a defect here in that he falls short of being pained—he takes pleasure. But this is absurd. The malicious man rejoices in the ill-fortune of others. The Greek word for *malice*, ἐπιχειρεκακία, means this. Thus what he rejoices in is not the same as what the jealous and the righteously indignant man are pained by. His attitude cannot be placed on the same scale as theirs, and only a determination to make the schematism of mean, excess, and defect work at all costs could have led Aristotle to make this slip. Perhaps with a little ingenuity Aristotle could be emended here so as to save his doctrine. But what of the virtue of liberality? The vices here are prodigality and meanness. Prodigality is excess in giving, deficiency in getting, and meanness is excess in getting, deficiency in giving. So these are not after all excess or defect of the same emotion or action. And Aristotle himself half admits that to the virtue of temperance and the excess of profligacy there is no corresponding defect. "Men deficient in the enjoyment of pleasures scarcely occur." Thus the doctrine finally appears as at best of varying degrees of usefulness in exposition, but scarcely as picking out something logically necessary to the character of a virtue.

Moreover, there is a falsely abstract air about the doctrine. For Aristotle does not, as he might seem to, think that there is one and only one right choice of emotion or action, independent of circumstances. What is courage in one situation would in another be rashness and in a third cowardice. Virtuous action cannot be specified without reference to the judgment of a prudent man— that is, of one who knows how to take account of circumstances. Consequently, knowledge of the mean cannot just be knowledge of a formula, it must be knowledge of how to apply the rules to choices. And here the notions of excess and defect will not help us. A man who is suspicious of his own tendency to indignation will rightly consider how much envy and malice there is in it; but the connection of envy and malice with indignation is that in the one case I evince a desire to possess the goods of others, and in the other I evince a desire for the harm of others. What makes these wrong is that I desire that what is not mine should be mine, without thought for the deserts of others or myself, and that I desire harm. The viciousness of these desires is in no way due to their being excess or defect of the same desire, and therefore the doctrine of the mean is no guide here. But if this classification in terms of the mean is no practical help, what is its point? Aristotle relates it to no theoretical account of, for example, the emotions, and it therefore appears more and more as an arbitrary construction. But we can see how Aristotle may have arrived at it. For he may have examined everything commonly called a virtue, looked for a recurrent pattern, and thought that he had found one in the mean. The list of virtues in the *Ethics* is not a list resting on Aristotle's own personal choices and evaluations. It reflects what Aristotle takes to be "the code of a gentleman" in contemporary Greek society. Aristotle himself endorses this code. Just as in analyzing political constitutions he treats Greek society as normative, so in explaining the virtues he treats upper-class Greek life as normative. And what else could we have expected? To this there are two answers. The first is that it would be purely unhistorical to look in the *Ethics* for a moral virtue such as meekness, which enters only with the Christian gospels, or thrift, which enters only with the puritan ethics of work, or for an intellectual virtue such as curiosity, which enters self-consciously with systematic experimental science. (Aristotle himself, in fact, exhibited this virtue, but perhaps could not have envisaged it as a virtue.) Yet this is not good enough as an answer, for Aristotle was aware of alternative codes. There is in Aristotle's *Ethics* not merely a contempt for the morality of artisans or of barbarians, but also a systematic repudiation of the morality of Socrates. It is not just that the undeserved suffering of the good man is never attended to. But when Aristotle considers justice he so defines it that the enactments of a state are unlikely to be unjust provided that they are properly enacted, without undue haste and in due form. It cannot therefore—generally speaking— be just to break the law. Moreover, in the discussion of the virtues, the defect of the virtue of truthfulness is the vice of the self-deprecator which is named εἰρωνεία, irony. This is a word closely associated with Socrates' claim to ignorance, and its use can scarcely have been accidental. Thus at every point where a reference to Socrates occurs in Aristotle we find none of Plato's respect, although a deep respect for Plato himself is shown. It is difficult to resist the conclusion that what we see here is Aristotle's class-bound conservatism silently and partisanly rewriting the table of the virtues, and so from yet another point of view suspicion is cast upon the doctrine of the mean.

The detail of Aristotle's account of particular virtues is rendered with brilliant analysis and perceptive insight, especially in the case of courage. It is much more, as I have just suggested, the list of virtues which raises questions. The virtues discussed are courage, temperance, liberality, magnificence, greatness of soul, good temper or gentleness, being agreeable in company, wittiness, and lastly, modesty, which is treated as not a virtue, but akin to one. Of these, greatness of soul is to do in part with how to behave to one's social inferiors, and liberality and magnificence concern one's attitudes to one's wealth. Three of the other virtues have to do with what are sometimes called manners in polite society. Aristotle's social bias is thus unmistakable. This bias would not matter philosophically but for the fact that it prevents Aristotle from raising the questions, How do I decide what is in fact included in the list of the virtues? could I invent a virtue? is it logically open to me to consider a vice what others have considered a virtue? And to beg these questions is to suggest strongly that there just *are* so many virtues—in the same sense that at a given period there just are so many Greek states.

Self-Realization—Further Readings Primarily Related to Aristotle

Aristotle, *Eudemian Ethics.*
Field, G. C., *Moral Theory* (London: Methuen, 1921; 2d ed., 1932), Part II. Exposition and criticism.

Hardie, W. F. R., *Aristotle's Ethical Theory* (Oxford: Clarendon, 1968). Exposition.

Huby, Pamela M., *Greek Ethics* (London: Macmillan, 1967), Chap. 5. Exposition and criticism.

Joachim, H. H., *Aristotle: The Nicomachean Ethics* (Oxford: Clarendon, 1951). Detailed commentary.

Moravcsik, J. M. E. (ed.), *Aristotle: A Collection of Critical Essays* (Garden City, N.Y.: Doubleday, 1967), Part IV. Contains four scholarly essays on fundamental topics in Aristotle's ethics.

Ross, W. D., *Aristotle* (5th ed., London: Methuen, 1949), Chap. 7. Exposition and criticism.

Russell, Bertrand, *A History of Western Philosophy* (New York: Simon and Schuster, 1945), Chap. 20. Critical, with an occasional witty bite.

Walsh, James J., and Henry L. Shapiro (eds.), *Aristotle's Ethics: Issues and Interpretations* (Belmont, Calif.: Wadsworth, 1967). Seven critical essays on themes in Aristotle's ethics.

b *Bradley*

Bradley represents absolute idealism, a tradition originating mainly in the work of Hegel. Central to his work is a concern with the rational categories of organization, consistency, and coherence. The reason for this lies in his acceptance of Hegel's belief that reality, including moral activity, is characterized by logical connections. The realization of the self, which constitutes the end and good for men, and the criterion of right action, is not, therefore, as it was for Aristotle, placed by Bradley in man's natural faculties or in the biological model of function. In his famous article, "My Station and Its Duties," Bradley first criticizes hedonism and Kantianism, and then maintains that moral right and wrong are associated with the individual's reflective and willing obedience to the moral rules of his group or society. The good and the right incorporate, in true Hegelian synthesis, elements misconstrued by hedonism and Kantianism. For Bradley, both sensuous pleasure and duty are constituents of the good. The individual, however, is real only to the extent that he reflects his society, for therein he obtains, by training, education, and experience, all of his interests, attitudes, and habits. The self to be realized, then, is the unity of these constituents, shared by family and culture. One's selfhood is what is realized in the moral agent's character in his station and its related duties. A person can only be a person by acting and thinking and feeling; and the patterns in which these elements and their relationships emerge will be a product of his experience in his culture or society. How would an Englishman act, or be, other than an Englishman?

The self to be realized is, therefore, not the sensuous, and not the self construed as any feeling, or a series of feelings, or pleasures. Nor is it a collection of feelings, or happiness. Neither is it found in the opposite of the sensuous, that is, in the sense of duty, or of the will. The first is a mere collection of unrelated particular feelings, without form; and the second is empty form, without content. Self-realization, however, remains the end or goal of man—the good. And it is an objective end, not contingent on the opinion of any individual. The right, the "stern imperative," emerges when a man finds his station and its related duties. Try to describe an individual, demands Bradley, without using terms intrinsic to a culture. A man is a part, a member, of a social organism. His clothing styles, his language, his sentiments, his ideals are derived from a particular society or culture. The individual, apart from society, is a delusion of thinking, an abstraction. Man can, therefore, realize his physical, intellectual, emotional, moral potentialities only within the context of institutions. Social institutions provide the "outer" part of morality, the "objective" part. The "inner," "subjective" aspect involves the personal willing of the duties constituent to the station of the moral agent. The outer is, so to speak, the body, and the inner the soul, of the moral world. The duties must be willed by the soul in order to be realized. In this manner, the contradiction between the sensuous, that is, between pleasure and desire, on the one hand, and rules, duty, form, on the other, is resolved. True happiness results from willing one's duties. In this synthesis, the moral agent overcomes the contradiction by identifying his good, his pleasure and happiness, with the good will, the duties of the moral organism.

How do we know how to act? Bradley argues that we know in a particular case what is the right action by an immediate, intuitional judgment, a nondiscursive thought. In this respect he appears to have affiliations with act deontological theorists.

In his critique of Bradley, Rashdall contends that the self-realization theory is either contradictory or vacuous, ineffective, and impossible to apply. It is contradictory in that it recommends that we make real a self, but the self is already real. This argument seems a bit strained, resting upon a concept of self which takes it to be unchanging, a position which no self-realization theorist need accept. More significantly, Rashdall maintains that Bradley's position offers no criteria for distinguishing which capacities ought to be developed. It is impossible to develop all capacities. An "all round development," which Rashdall cites as the Greek ideal, cannot be achieved, since the complete development of some capacities (say, the intellectual) makes the complete development of

others (say, the physical) impossible. Even worse, the development of
"all capacities" would entail the realization of bad ones—surely a moral
absurdity. In other places, Rashdall attempts to refute Bradley's view that
men are (morally and otherwise) real only in respect to their place in a
social and institutional structure. In particular, he attacks what he conceives to be the close relationship, which Bradley holds to be of paramount importance, between the moral features of the agent's behavior
and the traditional moral rules of his society. He argues that one presupposition of moral responsibility lies in one's *deciding for himself*. Mere
habitual instantiation of social rules is not a sufficient condition of moral
praise or of good character, because it neglects the required understanding and appreciation of the moral rules involved and their relation
to moral behavior. If this were not true, a person could never be morally
justified in any action which runs counter to a conventionally accepted
moral rule. Indeed, it would be flatly inconsistent to question the validity
of a moral rule, a position which seems odd. Moral reform and innova-
tion, thus, would (paradoxically) be impossible, and the stagnation and
sterility of civilization would presumably ensue.

31

My Station and Its Duties

F. H. Bradley

We have traversed by this time, however cursorily, a considerable field, and
so far it might appear without any issue or at best with a merely negative result.
Certainly in our anticipatory remarks (Essay II), we thought we found some
answer to the question, What is the end? But that answer was too abstract to
stand by itself. And, if we may be said to know thus much, that the end is self-
realization, yet at present we do not seem to have learned anything about the
self to be realized. And the detail of Essays II and III appears at most to have
given us some knowledge of that which self-realization is not.

We have learned that the self to be realized is not the self as this or that feeling,
or as any series of the particular feelings of our own or others' streams or trains
of consciousness. It is, in short, not the self to be pleased. The greatest sum of
units of pleasure we found to be the idea of a mere collection, whereas, if we
wanted morality, it was something like a universal that we wanted. Happiness,
as the effort to construct that universal by the addition of particulars, gave us a

FROM *Ethical Studies* by F. H. Bradley, Essay 5, Second Edition (Oxford: Clarendon
Press, 1927). First published in 1876.

futile and bastard product which carried its self-destruction within it, in the continual assertion of its own universality, together with its unceasing actual particularity and finitude; so that happiness was, if we chose, nowhere not realized; or again, if we chose, not anywhere realizable. And passing then to the opposite pole, to the universal as the negative of the particulars, to the supposed pure will or duty for duty's sake, we found that too was an unreal conception. It was a mere form which, to be will, must give itself a content, and which could give itself a content only at the cost of a self-contradiction. We saw, further, that any such content was in addition arbitrarily postulated and that, even then, the form was either never realized, because real in no particular content, or always and every where realized, because equally reconcilable with any content. And so, as before with happiness, we perceived that morality could have no existence if it meant anything more than the continual asseveration of an empty formula. And, if we had chosen, we might have gone on to exhibit the falsity of asceticism, to see that the self cannot be realized as its own mere negation, since morality is practice, is will to do something, is self-affirmation; and that a will to deny one's will is not self-realization, but rather is, strictly speaking, a psychical impossibility, a self-contradictory illusion. And the possibility, again, of taking as the self to be realized the self which I happen to have, my natural being, and of making life the end of life in the sense that each should live his life as he happens to find it in his own nature, has been precluded beforehand by the result derived from the consideration of the moral consciousness, viz., that morality implies a superior, a higher self, or at all events a universal something which is above this or that self and so above mine. And, to complete the account of our negations, we saw further, with respect to duty for duty's sake, that even were it possible (as it is not) to create a content from the formula and to elaborate in this manner a system of duties, yet even then the practice required by the theory would be impossible, and so too morality, since in practice particular duties must collide and the collision of duties, if we hold to duty for duty's sake, is the destruction of all duty save the unrealized form of duty in general.

But let us view this result, which seems so unsatisfactory, from the positive side; let us see after all with what we are left. We have self-realization left as the end, the self so far being defined as neither a collection of particular feelings nor an abstract universal. The self is to be realized as something not simply one or the other; it is to be realized further as will, will not being merely the natural will, or the will as it happens to exist and finds itself here or there, but the will as the *good* will, *i.e.*, the will that realizes an end which is above this or that man, superior to them, and capable of confronting them in the shape of a law or an ought. This superior something further, which is a possible law or ought to the individual man, does not depend for its existence on his choice or opinion. Either there is no morality, so says the moral consciousness, or moral duties exist independently of their position by this or that person—my duty may be mine and no other man's, but I do not make it mine. If it is duty, it would be the duty of any person in my case and condition, whether they thought so or not—

in a word, duty is "objective," in the sense of not being contingent on the opinion or choice of this or that subject.

What we have left then (to resume it) is this—the end is the realization of the good will which is superior to ourselves; and again the end is self-realization. Bringing these together we see the end is the realization of ourselves as the will which is above ourselves. And this will (if morality exists) we saw must be "objective," because not dependent on "subjective" liking; and "universal," because not identifiable with any particular, but standing above all actual and possible particulars. Further, though universal it is not abstract since it belongs to its essence that it should be realized, and it has no real existence except in and through its particulars. The good will (for morality) is meaningless, if, whatever else it be, it be not the will of living human beings. It is a concrete universal because it not only is above but is within and throughout its details, and is so far only as they are. It is the life which can live only in and by them, as they are dead unless within it; it is the whole soul which lives so far as the body lives, which makes the body a living body and which without the body is as unreal an abstraction as the body without it. It is an organism and a moral organism; and it is conscious self-realization because only by the will of its self-conscious members can the moral organism give itself reality. It is the self-realization of the whole body because it is one and the same will which lives and acts in the life and action of each. It is the self-realization of each member because each member cannot find the function which makes him himself, apart from the whole to which he belongs; to be himself he must go beyond himself, to live his life he must live a life which is not *merely* his own, but which, none the less, but on the contrary all the more, is intensely and emphatically his own individuality. Here, and here first, are the contradictions which have beset us solved—here is a universal which can confront our wandering desires with a fixed and stern imperative, but which yet is no unreal form of the mind but a living soul that penetrates and stands fast in the detail of actual existence. It is real, and real for me. It is in its affirmation that I affirm myself, for I am but as a "heart-beat in its system." And I am real in it, for, when I give myself to it, it gives me the fruition of my own personal activity, the accomplished ideal of my life which is happiness. In the realized idea which, superior to me and yet here and now in and by me, affirms itself in a continuous process, we have found the end, we have found self-realization, duty, and happiness in one—yes, we have found ourselves when we have found our station and its duties, our function as an organ in the social organism.

"Mere rhetoric," we shall be told, "a bad metaphysical dream, a stale old story once more warmed up, which cannot hold its own against the logic of facts. That the state was prior to the individual, that the whole was sometimes more than the sum of the parts, was an illusion which preyed on the thinkers of Greece. But that illusion has been traced to its source and dispelled and is in plain words exploded. The family, society, the state, and generally every community of men consists of individuals, and there is nothing in them real except the individuals.

Individuals have made them, and make them, by placing themselves and by standing in certain relations. The individuals are real by themselves and it is because of them that the relations are real. They make them, they are real *in* them, not because of them, and they would be just as real *out* of them. The whole is the mere sum of the parts, and the parts are as real away from the whole as they are within the whole. Do you really suppose that the individual would perish if every form of community were destroyed? Do you think that anything real answers to the phrases of universal and organism? Everything is in the organism what it is out, and the universal is a name, the existing fact answering to which is particular persons in such and such relations. To put the matter shortly, the community is the sum of its parts, is made by the addition of parts, and the parts are as real before the addition as after; the relations they stand in do not make them what they are, but are accidental, not essential, to their being; and, as to the whole, if it is not a name for the individuals that compose it, it is a name of nothing actual. These are not metaphysical dreams. They are facts and verifiable facts.''

Are they facts? Facts should explain facts; and the view called "individualism" (because the one reality that it believes in is the "individual," in the sense of this, that, and the other particular) should hence be the right explanation. What are the facts here to be explained? They are human communities, the family, society, and the state. Individualism has explained them long ago. They are "collections" held together by force, illusion, or contract. It has told the story of their origin and to its own satisfaction cleared the matter up. Is the explanation satisfactory and verifiable? That would be a bold assertion when historical science has rejected and entirely discredited the individualistic origin of society, and when, if we turn to practice, we find everywhere the state asserting itself as a power which has, and, if need be, asserts the right to make use of and expend the property and person of the individual without regard to his wishes, and which, moreover, may destroy his life in punishment, and put forth other powers such as no theory of contract will explain except by the most palpable fictions, while at the same time no ordinary person calls their morality in question. Both history and practical politics refuse to verify the "facts" of the individualist; and we should find still less to confirm his theory if we examined the family.

If, then, apart from metaphysic one looks at the history and present practice of society, these would not appear to establish the "fact" that the individual is the one reality and communities mere collections. "For all that," we shall be told, "it is the truth." True that is, I suppose, not as fact but as metaphysic; and this is what one finds to soften with those who deride metaphysic and talk most of facts. Their minds, so far as such a thing may be, are not seldom mere "collective unities" of metaphysical dogmas. They decry any real metaphysic because they dimly feel that their own will not stand criticism; and they appeal to facts because while their metaphysic stands they feel they need not be afraid of them. When their view is pushed as to plain realities, such as the nature of gregarious animals, the probable origin of mankind from them, the institutions of early society, actual existing communities with the common type impressed on all their members, their organic structure and the assertion of the whole body as of paramount importance in comparison with any of the members, then they must fall back on their metaphysic. And the point we wish here to emphasize is this, that their metaphysic is mere dogmatism. It is assumed, not proved. It has a right to no refutation, for assertion can demand no more than counter-assertion; and what is affirmed on the one side we on the other side can simply deny, and we intend to do so here.

A discussion that would go to the bottom of the question, What is an individual? is certainly wanted. It would certainly be desirable, showing first what an individual is, to show then that "individualism" has not apprehended that, but taken an abstraction for reality. But, if I could do that (which I could not do), this would not be the place; nor perhaps should I have to say very much that has not been said before, and has not been attended to.

But we are not going to enter on a metaphysical question to which we are not equal; we meet the metaphysical assertion of the "individualist" with a mere denial and, turning to facts, we will try to show that they lead us in another direction. To the assertion, then, that selves are "individual" in the sense of exclusive of other selves, we oppose the (equally justified) assertion that this is a mere fancy. We say that, out of theory, no such individual men exist; and we will try to show from fact that, in fact, what we call an individual man is what he is because of and by virtue of community, and that communities are thus not mere names but something real, and can be regarded (if we mean to keep to facts) only as the one in the many.

And to confine the subject and to keep to what is familiar, we will not call to our aid the life of animals, nor early societies, nor the course of history, but we will take men as they are now; we will take ourselves and endeavour to keep wholly to the teaching of experience.

Let us take a man, an Englishman as he is now, and try to point out that apart from what he has in common with others, apart from his sameness with others, he is not an Englishman—nor a man at all; that if you take him as something by himself, he is not what he is. Of course we do not mean to say that he cannot go out of England without disappearing, nor, even if all the rest of the nation perished that he would not survive. What we mean to say is that he is what he is because he is a born and educated social being, and a member of an individual social organism; that if you make abstraction of all this, which is the same in him and in others, what you have left is not an Englishman, nor a man, but some I know not what residuum, which never has existed by itself and does not so exist. If we suppose the world of relations, in which he was born and bred, never to have been, then we suppose the very essence of him not to be; if we take that away, we have taken him away; and hence he now is not an individual, in the sense of owing nothing to the sphere of relations in which he finds himself, but does contain those relations within himself as belonging to his very being; he is what he is, in brief, so far as he is what others also are.

But we shall be cut short here with an objection. "It is impossible," we shall be told, "that two men should have the *same* thing in common. You are confusing sameness and likeness." I say in answer that I am not, and that the too probable objector I am imagining too probably knows the meaning of neither one word nor the other. But this is a matter we do not intend to stay over, because it is a metaphysical question we cannot discuss, and which, moreover, we cannot be called on to discuss. We cannot be called on to discuss it because we have to do again here with sheer assertion, which either is ignorant of or ignores the critical investigation of the subject, and which, therefore, has no right to demand an answer. We allude to it merely because it has become a sort of catchword with "advanced thinkers." All that it comes to is this: first identity and diversity are assumed to exclude one another, and therefore, since diversity is a fact, it follows that there is no identity. Hence a difficulty: because it has been seen long ago and forces itself upon everyone, that denial of all identity brings you into sharp collision with ordinary fact and leads to total skepticism[1]; so, to avoid this, while we yet maintain the previous dogma, "resemblance" is brought in—a conception which (I suppose I need not add) is not analyzed or properly defined, and so does all the better. Against these assertions I shall put some others, viz., that identity and diversity, sameness and difference, imply one another, and depend for their meaning on one another; that mere diversity is nonsense, just as mere identity is also nonsense; that resemblance or likeness, strictly speaking, falls not in the objects, but in the person contemplating (likening, *ver-gleichend*); that "is A really like B?" does not mean "does it seem like?" It may mean "would it seem like to everybody?" but it generally means "is there an 'objective identity'? Is there a point or points the same in both, whether anyone sees it or not?" We do not talk of cases of "mistaken likeness"; we do not hang one man because he is "exactly like" another, or at least we do not wish to do so. We are the same as we were, not merely more or less like. We have the same faith, hope, and purpose, and the same feelings as another man has now, as ourselves had at another time—not understanding thereby the numerical indistinguishedness of particular states and moments, but calling the feelings one and the same feeling because *what* is felt is the same, and not merely like. In short, so far is it from being true that "sameness" is really "likeness," that it is utterly false that two things are really and objectively "like," unless that means "more or less the same." So much by way of counter-assertion; and now let us turn to our facts.

The "individual" man, the man into whose essence his community with others does not enter, who does not include relation to others in his very being, is, we say, a fiction, and in the light of facts we have to examine him. Let us take him in the shape of an English child as soon as he is born; for I suppose we ought not to go further back. Let us take him as soon as he is separated from his mother and occupies a space clear and exclusive of all other human beings. At this time, education and custom will, I imagine, be allowed to have not as yet operated

---

[1] Even from Mr. Mill (in controversy) we can quote, "If every general conception, instead of being 'the One in the Many,' were considered to be as many different conceptions as there are things to which it is applicable, there would be no such thing as general language."—*Logic*, 6th ed., I, 201.

on him or lessened his "individuality." But is he now a mere "individual," in the sense of not implying in his being identity with others? We cannot say that if we hold to the teaching of modern physiology. Physiology would tell us, in one language or another, that even now the child's mind is no passive "tabula rasa"; he has an inner, a yet undeveloped nature, which must largely determine his future individuality. What is this inner nature? Is it particular to himself? Certainly not all of it, will have to be the answer. The child is not fallen from heaven. He is born of certain parents who come of certain families, and he has in him the qualities of his parents, and, as breeders would say, of the strains from both sides. Much of it we can see and more we believe to be latent and, given certain (possible or impossible) conditions, ready to come to light. On the descent of mental qualities modern investigation and popular experience, as expressed in uneducated vulgar opinion, altogether, I believe, support one another, and we need not linger here. But if the intellectual and active qualities do descend from ancestors, is it not, I would ask, quite clear that a man may have in him the same that his father and mother had, the same that his brothers and sisters have? And if anyone objects to the word "same," I would put this to him. If, concerning two dogs allied in blood, I were to ask a man, "Is that of the same strain or stock as this?" and were answered, "No, not the same, but similar," should I not think one of these things, that the man either meant to deceive me, or was a "thinker," or a fool?

But the child is not merely the member of a family; he is born into other spheres, and (passing over the subordinate wholes which nevertheless do in many cases qualify him) he is born a member of the English nation. It is, I believe, a matter of fact that at birth the child of one race is not the same as the child of another; that in the children of the one race there is a certain identity, a developed or undeveloped national type which may be hard to recognize, or which at present may even be unrecognizable, but which nevertheless in some form will appear. If that be the fact, then again we must say that one English child is in some points, though perhaps it does not as yet show itself, the same as another. His being is so far common to him with others; he is not a mere "individual."

We see the child has been born at a certain time of parents of a certain race, and that means also of a certain degree of culture. It is the opinion of those best qualified to speak on the subject that civilization is to some not inconsiderable extent hereditary; that aptitudes are developed, and are latent in the child at birth; and that it is a very different thing, even apart from education, to be born of civilized and of uncivilized ancestors. These "civilized tendencies," if we may use the phrase, are part of the essence of the child. He would only partly (if at all) be himself without them; he owes them to his ancestors, and his ancestors owe them to society. The ancestors were made what they were by the society they lived in. If in answer it be replied, "Yes, but individual ancestors were prior to their society," then that, to say the least of it, is a hazardous and unproved assertion, since man, so far as history can trace him back, is social; and if Mr. Darwin's conjecture as to the development of man from a social animal be received, we must say that man has never been anything but social, and society never was made by individual men. Nor, if the (baseless) assertion of the priority of individual men were allowed, would that destroy our case, for certainly our more immediate ancestors were social; and, whether society was manufactured previously by individuals or not, yet in their case it certainly was not so. They at all events have been so qualified by the common possessions of social mankind that, as members in the organism, they have become relative to the whole. If we suppose then that the results of the social life of the race are present in a latent and potential form in the child, can we deny that they are common property? Can we assert that they are not an element of sameness in all? Can we say that the individual is this individual because he is exclusive, when, if we deduct from him what he includes, he loses characteristics which make him himself, and when again he does include what the others include, and therefore does (how can we escape the consequence?) include in some sense the others also, just as they include him? By himself, then, what are we to call him? I confess I do not know unless we name him a theoretical attempt to isolate what cannot be isolated, and that, I suppose, has, out of our heads, no existence. But what he is really, and not in mere theory, can be described only as the specification or particularization of that which is common, which is the same amid diversity, and without which the "individual" would be so other than he is that we could not call him the same.

Thus the child is at birth; and he is born not into a desert, but into a living world, a whole which has a true individuality of its own, and into a system and order which it is difficult to look at as anything else than an organism, and which, even in England, we are now beginning to call by that name. And I fear that the "individuality" (the particularness) which the child brought into the light with him now stands but a poor chance, and that there is no help for him until he is old enough to become a "philosopher." We have seen that already he has in him inherited habits, or what will of themselves appear as such; but, in addition to this, he is not for one moment left alone, but continually tampered with; and the habituation which is applied from the outside is the more insidious that it answers to this inborn disposition. Who can resist it? Nay, who but a "thinker" could wish to have resisted it? And yet the tender care that receives and guides him is impressing on him habits, habits, alas, not particular to himself, and the "icy chains" of universal custom are hardening themselves round his cradled life. As the poet tells us, he has not yet thought of himself; his earliest notions come mixed to him of things and persons, not distinct from one another, nor divided from the feeling of his own existence. The need that he cannot understand moves him to foolish, but not futile, cries for what only another can give him; and the breast of his mother, and the soft warmth and touches and tones of his nurse, are made one with the feeling of his own pleasure and pain; nor is he yet a moralist to beware of such illusion and to see in them mere means to an end without them in his separate self. For he does not even think of his separate self; he grows with his world, his mind fills and orders itself; and when he can separate himself from that world, and know himself apart from it, then by that time his self, the object of his self-consciousness, is penetrated, infected, characterized by the existence of others. Its content implies in every fiber relations of community. He learns, or already perhaps has learned, to speak, and here he appropriates the common heritage of his race; the tongue that he makes his own is his country's language, it is (or it should be) the same that others speak, and it carries into his mind the ideas and sentiments of the race (over this I need not stay), and stamps them in indelibly. He grows up in an atmosphere of example and general custom, his life widens out from one little world to other and higher worlds, and he apprehends through successive stations the whole in which he lives, and in which he has lived. Is he now to try and develop his "individuality," his self which is not the same as other selves? Where is it? What is it? Where can he find it? The soul within him is saturated, is filled, is qualified by, it has assimilated, has got its substance, has built itself up from, it *is* one and the same life with the universal life, and if he turns against this he turns against himself; if he thrusts it from him, he tears his own vitals; if he attacks it, he sets his weapon against his own heart. He has found his life in the life of the whole, he lives that in himself, "he is a pulsebeat of the whole system, and himself the whole system."

"The child, in his character of the form of the possibility of a moral individual, is something subjective or negative; his growing to manhood is the ceasing to be of this form, and his education is the discipline or the compulsion thereof. The positive side and the essence is that he is suckled at the breast of the universal Ethos, lives in its absolute intuition, as in that of a foreign being first, then comprehends it more and more, and so passes over into the universal mind." The writer proceeds to draw the weighty conclusion that virtue "is not a troubling oneself about a peculiar and isolated morality of one's own, that the striving for a positive morality of one's own is futile, and in its very nature impossible of attainment; that in respect of morality the saying of the wisest men of antiquity is the only one which is true, that to be moral is to live in accordance with the moral tradition of one's country; and in respect of education the one true answer is that which a Pythagorean gave to him who asked what was the best education for his son, If you make him the citizen of a people with good institutions."[2]

But this is to anticipate. So far, I think, without aid from metaphysics, we have seen that the "individual" apart from the community is an abstraction. It is not anything real and hence not anything that we can realize, however much we may wish to do so. We have seen that I am myself by sharing with others, by including in my essence relations to them, the relations of the social state. If I wish to realize my true being I must therefore realize something beyond my being as a mere this or that, for my true being has in it a life which is not the life of any mere particular, and so must be called a universal life.

What is it then that I am to realize? We have said it in "my station and its duties." To know what a man is (as we have seen) you must not take him in isolation. He is one of a people, he was born in a family, he lives in a certain

---

[2] Hegel, *Philosophische Abhandlungen*, I, 389.

society, in a certain state. What he has to do depends on what his place is, what his function is, and that all comes from his station in the organism. Are there then such organisms in which he lives, and if so, what is their nature? Here we come to questions which must be answered in full by any complete system of Ethics, but which we cannot enter on. We must content ourselves by pointing out that there are such facts as the family, then in a middle position a man's own profession and society, and, over all, the larger community of the state. Leaving out of sight the question of a society wider than the state, we must say that a man's life with its moral duties is in the main filled up by his station in that system of wholes which the state is, and that this, partly by its laws and institutions and still more by its spirit, gives him the life which he does live and ought to live. That objective institutions exist is of course an obvious fact; and it is a fact which every day is becoming plainer that these institutions are organic, and further, that they are moral. The assertion that communities have been manufactured by the addition of exclusive units is, as we have seen, a mere fable; and if, within the state, we take that which seems wholly to depend on individual caprice, *e.g.*, marriage,[3] yet even here we find that a man does give up his self so far as it excludes others; he does bring himself under a unity which is superior to the particular person and the impulses that belong to his single existence, and which makes him fully as much as he makes it. In short, man is a social being; he is real only because he is social, and can realize himself only because it is as social that he realizes himself. The mere individual is a delusion of theory; and the attempt to realize it in practice is the starvation and mutilation of human nature, with total sterility or the production of monstrosities. . . .

The universal which is the end, and which we have seen is concrete and does realize itself, does also more. It gets rid of the contradiction between duty and the "empirical" self; it does not in its realization leave me forever outside and unrealized.

In "duty for duty's sake" we were always unsatisfied, no nearer our goal at the end than at the beginning. There we had the fixed antithesis of the sensuous self on one side, and a nonsensuous moral ideal on the other—a standing contradition which brought with it a perpetual self-deceit, or the depressing perpetual confession that I am not what I ought to be in my inner heart, and that I never can be so. Duty, we thus saw, was an infinite process, an unending "not-yet"; a continual "not" with an everlasting "to be," or an abiding "to be" with a ceaseless "not."

From this last peevish enemy we are again delivered by "my station and its duties." There I realize myself morally, so that not only what ought to be in the world is, but I am what I ought to be, and find so my contentment and satisfaction. If this were not the case, when we consider that the ordinary moral man is self-contented and happy, we should be forced to accuse him of immorality, and we do not do this; we say he most likely might be better, but we do not say

---

[3] Marriage is a contract, a contract to pass out of the sphere of contract; and this is possible only because the contracting parties are already beyond and above the sphere of mere contract.

that he is bad, or need consider himself so. Why is this? It is because "my station and its duties" teaches us to identify others and ourselves with the station we fill; to consider that as good, and by virtue of that to consider others and ourselves good too. It teaches us that a man who does his work in the world is good, notwithstanding his faults, if his faults do not prevent him from fulfilling his station. It tells us that the heart is an idle abstraction; we are not to think of it, nor must we look at our insides, but at our work and our life, and say to ourselves, Am I fulfilling my appointed function or not? Fulfill it we can, if we will. What we have to do is not so much better than the world that we cannot do it: the world is there waiting for it; my duties are my rights. On the one hand, I am not likely to be much better than the world asks me to be; on the other hand, if I can take my place in the world I ought not to be discontented. Here we must not be misunderstood; we do not say that the false self, the habits and desires opposed to the good will, are extinguished. Though negated, they never are all of them entirely suppressed, and cannot be. Hence we must not say that any man really does fill his station to the full height of his capacity; nor must we say of any man that he cannot perform his function better than he does, for we all can do so, and should try to do so. We do not wish to deny what are plain moral facts, nor in any way to slur them over.

How then does the contradiction disappear? It disappears by my indentifying myself with the good will that I realize in the world, by my refusing to identify myself with the bad will of my private self. So far as I am one with the good will, living as a member in the moral organism, I am to consider myself real and I am not to consider the false self real. That cannot be attributed to me in my character of member in the organism. Even in me the false existence of it has been partly suppressed by that organism; and, so far as the organism is concerned, it is wholly suppressed because contradicted in its results, and allowed no reality. Hence, not existing for the organism, it does not exist for me as a member thereof; and only as a member thereof do I hold myself to be real. And yet this is not justification by faith, for we not only trust, but see, that despite our faults the moral world stands fast, and we in and by it. It is like faith, however, in this, that not merely by thinking ourselves, but by willing ourselves as such, can we look on ourselves as organs in a good whole, and do ourselves good. And further, the knowledge that as members of the system we are real, and not otherwise, encourages us more and more to identify ourselves with that system; to make ourselves better, and so more real, since we see that the good is real, and that nothing else is.

Or, to repeat it, in education my self by habituation has been growing into one with the good self around me, and by my free acceptance of my lot hereafter I consciously make myself one with the good, so that, though bad habits cling to and even arise in me, yet I cannot but be aware of myself as the reality of the good will. That is my essential side; my imperfections are not, and practically they do not matter. The good will in the world realizes itself by and in imperfect instruments, and in spite of them. The work is done, and so long as I will my part of the work and do it (as I do), I feel that, if I perform the function, I *am* the organ, and that my faults, if they do not matter to my station, do not matter to me. My heart I am not to think of, except to tell by my work whether it is in my work, and one with the moral whole; and if that is so, I have the consciousness of absolute reality in the good because of and by myself, and in myself because of and through the good; and with that I am satisfied, and have no right to be dissatisfied.

The individual's consciousness of himself is inseparable from the knowing himself as an organ of the whole; and the residuum falls more and more into the background, so that he thinks of it, if at all, not as himself, but as an idle appendage. For his nature now is not distinct from his "artificial self." He is related to the living moral system not as to a foreign body; his relation to it is "too inward even for faith," since faith implies a certain separation. It is no other-world that he cannot see but must trust to: he feels himself in it, and it in him; in a word, the self-consciousness of himself *is* the self-consciousness of the whole in him, and his will is the will which sees in him its accomplishment by him; it is the free will which knows itself as the free will, and as this beholds its realization and is more than content. . . .

The next point we come to is the question, How do I get to know in particular what is right and wrong? and here again we find a strangely erroneous preconception. It is thought that moral philosophy has to accomplish this task for us, and the conclusion lies near at hand that any system which will not do this is worthless. Well, we first remark, and with some confidence, that there cannot be a moral philosophy which will tell us what in particular we are to do, and also that it is not the business of philosophy to do so. All philosophy has to do is "to understand what is," and moral philosophy has to understand morals which exist, not to make them or give directions for making them. Such a notion is simply ludicrous. Philosophy in general has not to anticipate the discoveries of the particular sciences nor the evolution of history; the philosophy of religion has not to make a new religion or teach an old one, but simply to understand the religious consciousness; and aesthetic has not to produce works of fine art, but to theorize the beautiful which it finds; political philosophy has not to play tricks with the state, but to understand it; and ethics has not to make the world moral, but to reduce to theory the morality current in the world. If we want it to do anything more, so much the worse for us; for it cannot possibly construct new morality, and, even if it could to any extent codify what exists (a point on which I do not enter), yet it surely is clear that in cases of collision of duties it would not help you to know what to do. Who would go to a learned theologian, as such, in a practical religious difficulty; to a system of aesthetic for suggestions on the handling of an artistic theme; to a physiologist, as such, for a diagnosis and prescription; to a political philosopher in practical politics; or to a psychologist in an intrigue of any kind? All these persons no doubt *might* be the best to go to, but that would not be because they were the best theorists, but because they were more. In short, the view which thinks moral philosophy is to supply us with particular moral prescriptions confuses science with art, and confuses, besides, reflective with intuitive judgment. That which tells us what in particular is right and wrong is not reflection but intuition.[4]

We know what is right in a particular case by what we may call an immediate judgment, or an intuitive subsumption. These phrases are perhaps not very luminous, and the matter of the "intuitive understanding" in general is doubtless difficult, and the special character of moral judgments not easy to define; and I do not say that I am in a position to explain these subjects at all, nor, I think, could anyone do so, except at considerable length. But the point that I do wish to establish here is, I think, not at all obscure. The reader has first to recognize that moral judgments are not discursive; next, that nevertheless they do start from and rest on a certain basis; and then if he puts the two together, he will see that they involve what he may call the "intuitive understanding," or any other name, so long as he keeps in sight the two elements and holds them together.

On the head that moral judgments are not discursive, no one, I think, will wish me to stay long. If the reader attends to the facts he will not want anything else; and if he does not, I confess I cannot prove my point. In practical morality, no doubt, we *may* reflect on our principles, but I think it is not too much to say that we *never* do so, except where we have come upon a difficulty of particular application. If anyone thinks that a man's *ordinary* judgment, "this is right or wrong," comes from the having a rule *before* the mind and bringing the particular case under it, he may be right, and I cannot try to show that he is wrong. I can only leave it to the reader to judge for himself. We say we "see" and we "feel" in these cases, not we "conclude." We prize the advice of persons who can give us no reasons for what they say. There is a general belief that the having a reason for all your actions is pedantic and absurd. There is a general belief that to try to have reasons for all that you do is sometimes very dangerous. Not only the woman but the man who deliberates may be lost. First thoughts are often the best,[5] and if once you begin to argue with the devil you are in a perilous state. And I think I may add (though I do it in fear) that women are remarkable for the fineness of their moral perceptions[6] and the quickness of their judgments, and yet are or (let me save myself by saying) "may be" not remarkable for corresponding discursive ability.

---

[4] I must ask the reader here not to think of "Intuitionalism," or of "Organs of the Absolute," or of anything else of the sort. "Intuitive" is used here as the opposite of "reflective" or "discursive"; "intuition" as the opposite of "reasoning" or "explicit inferring." If the reader dislike the word, he may substitute "perception" or "sense," if he will; but then he must remember that neither are to exclude the intellectual, the understanding and its implicit judgments and inferences.

[5] It is right to remark that second thoughts are often the offspring of wrong desire, but not always so. They may arise from collisions, and in these cases we see how little is to be done by theoretical deduction.

[6] Not, perhaps, on *all* matters. Nor, again, will it do to say that *everywhere* women are preeminently intuitive, and men discursive. But in *practical* matters there seems not much doubt that it is so.

Taking for granted then that our ordinary way of judging in morals is not by reflection and explicit reasoning, we have now to point to the other side of the fact, viz., that these judgments are not mere isolated impressions, but stand in an intimate and vital relation to a certain system, which is their basis. Here again we must ask the reader to pause, if in doubt, and consider the facts for himself. Different men, who have lived in different times and countries, judge a fresh case in morals differently. Why is this? There is probably no "why" before the mind of either when he judges; but *we* perhaps can say, "I know why A said so and B so," because we find some general rule or principle different in each, and in each the basis of the judgment. Different people in the same society may judge points differently, and we sometimes know why. It is because A is struck by one aspect of the case, B by another; and one principle is (not *before*, but) *in* A's mind when he judges, and another in B's. Each has subsumed, but under a different head; the one perhaps justice, the other gratitude. Every man has the morality he has made his own in his mind, and he "sees" or "feels" or "judges" accordingly, though he does not reason explicitly from data to a conclusion.

I think this will be clear to the reader; and so we must say that on their perceptive or intellectual side (and that, the reader must not forget, is the one side that we are considering) our moral judgments are intuitive subsumptions.

To the question, How am I to know what is right? the answer must be, By the αἴσθησις of the φρόνιμος; and the φρόνιμος is the man who has identified his will with the moral spirit of the community, and judges accordingly. If an immoral course be suggested to him, he "feels" or "sees" at once that the act is not in harmony with a good will, and he does not do this by saying, "this is a breach of rule A, *therefore*, etc.," but the first thing he is aware of is that he "does not like it"; and what he has done, without being aware of it, is (at least in most cases) to seize the quality of the act, that quality being a general quality. Actions of a particular kind he does not like, and he has instinctively referred the particular act to that kind. What is right is perceived in the same way; courses suggest themselves, and one is approved of, because intuitively judged to be of a certain kind, which kind represents a principle of the good will.

If a man is to know what is right, he should have imbibed by precept, and still more by example, the spirit of his community, its general and special beliefs as to right and wrong, and, with this whole embodied in his mind should particularize it in any new case, not by a reflective deduction, but by an intuitive subsumption, which does not know that it is a subsumption; by a carrying out of the self into a new case, wherein what is before the mind is the case and not the self to be carried out, and where it is indeed the whole that feels and sees, but all that is seen is seen in the form of *this* case, *this* point, *this* instance. Precept is good, but example is better; for by a series of particulars (as such forgotten) we get the general spirit, we identify ourselves both on the side of will and judgment with the basis, which basis (be it remembered) has not got to be explicit.

32

Problems of Self-Realization

HASTINGS RASHDALL

We are met by a doctrine very fashionable in philosophical circles which finds the key to all ethical problems in that comfortable word "self-realization;" . . . I shall here . . . confine myself to the purely ethical aspect of this fascinating formula—"Self-realization is the end of life."

In order to subject the doctrine to any profitable criticism, it seems necessary to attempt the by no means easy task of distinguishing the various possible senses in which this watchword seems to be used by its devotees. The formula would probably have proved less attractive, had these various senses been distinguished by those to whom it presents itself as a "short and easy way" out of all ethical perplexities.

1. Firstly, then, we may suppose that the upholder of self-realization means exactly what he says. If he does, it seems easy to show that what he is committing himself to is mere self-contradictory nonsense. To realize means to make real. You cannot make real what is real already, and the self must certainly be regarded as real before we are invited to set about realizing it. Nor is the task to which we are invited rendered easier when we are assured that the self, which is to become something that it was not, is out of time, and consequently (one might have supposed) insusceptible of change.

2. But of course it will be said that what is actually meant by self-realization is the realization of some potentiality or capacity of the self which is at present unrealized. In this sense no doubt it is true enough that Morality must consist in some kind of self-realization. But to say so is to say something "generally admitted indeed but obscure" . . . as Aristotle would have put it. In this sense the formula gives us just no information at all. For whatever you do or abstain from doing, if you only sit still or go to sleep, you must still be realizing some one of your capacities: since nobody can by any possibility do anything which he was not first capable of doing. Morality is self-realization beyond a doubt, but then so is immorality. The precious formula leaves out the whole differentia of Morality; and it is a differentia presumably which we are in search of when we ask, "What is Morality?" and are solemnly told, "It is doing or being something which you are capable of doing or being."

3. It may be maintained that Morality is the realization of *all* the capacities of human nature. But this is impossible, since one capacity can only be realized by the non-realization or sacrifice of some other capacity. There can be no self-realization without self-sacrifice. The good man and the bad alike realize one

FROM *The Theory of Good and Evil* by Hastings Rashdall, Book II, Chapter 3 (1907).

element or capacity of their nature, and sacrifice another. The whole question is which capacity is to be realized and which is to be sacrificed. And as to this our formula gives us just no information.

4. Or more vaguely self-realization may be interpreted to mean an equal, all-round development of one's whole nature—physical, intellectual, emotional. To such a view I should object that, interpreted strictly and literally, it is just as impracticable as the last. It is impossible for the most gifted person to become a first-rate Musician without much less completely realizing any capacity he has of becoming a first-rate Painter. It is impossible to become really learned in one subject without remaining ignorant of many others: impossible to develop one's athletic capacities to the full without starving and stunting the intellect, impossible (as a simple matter of Physiology) to carry to its highest point the cultivation of one's intellectual faculties without some sacrifice of physical efficiency. There is a similar collision between the demands of intellectual cultivation and those of practical work. . . . Up to a certain point it is no doubt desirable that a man should endeavour to develop different sides of his nature: but that point is soon reached. Beyond that point there must come the inevitable sacrifice—of body to mind or of mind to body, of learning or speculative insight to practical efficiency, or of practical efficiency to learning or insight.

It is the same within the intellectual sphere itself. There too the law of sacrifice prevails. Up to a certain point no doubt the man who is a mere specialist will be a bad specialist, but that point is soon reached. Charles Darwin found that the cultivation of reasoning power and observation had extinguished his once keen imagination and aesthetic sensibility. And yet who would wish—whether in the interests of the world or in the interests of what was best worthy of development in Charles Darwin's own nature—that his work should have been spoiled in order that one of the three hours which was the maximum working day his health allowed should have been absorbed by politics or philanthropy? Who would decide that the origin of species should have been undiscovered, in order that the man who might have discovered it should retain the power of enjoying Wordsworth? This notion of an equal, all-round, "harmonious" development is thus a sheer impossibility, excluded by the very constitution of human nature, and incompatible with the welfare of human society. And, in so far as some approximation to such an ideal of life is possible, it involves a very apotheosis of mediocrity, ineffectiveness, dilettantism.

And there is a more formidable objection to come. If the ideal of self-realization is to be logically carried out, it must involve the cultivation of a man's capacity for what vulgar prejudice calls immorality as well as of his capacity for Morality. It is quite arbitrary to exclude certain kinds of activity as "bad," because what we are in search of was some definition of the good in conduct, and we were told that it was the development of all his capacities. . . .

5. One possible interpretation of our formula remains. Self-realization may mean the realization of a man's highest capacities by the sacrifice of the lower. No doubt, in a sense every school of Moral Philosophy which allows of the distinction between a "higher" and a "lower" at all would admit that Morality

does mean the sacrifice of the lower to the higher—though it might be objected that this ideal, taken literally, is too ascetic: the lower capacities of human nature have a certain value; they ought to be realized to a certain extent—to be subordinated, not "sacrificed," except in so far as their realization is inconsistent with that of the higher. But then there is nothing of all this in the word "self-realization." And even with the gloss that "self-realization" means realization of the "true" or "higher" self, it tells us just nothing at all about the question what this true self-realization is. In fact the formula which is presented to us as the key to the ethical problem of the end of life, turns out on examination to mean merely "The end of life is the end of life." No doubt it has been said that every attempt to define Morality must have the appearance of moving in a circle. In a sense that may be the case. The moral cannot be defined in terms of the non-moral. But then that is just what our formula attempts to do, and that is just the source of its futility. Moreover, when the word "self-realization" is presented to us, not merely as an account of the end, but also as the immediate criterion for the individual's conduct, it is open to the objection that it says exactly nothing about the fundamental question of Ethics—the question of the relation of my end to that of others.

6. This last difficulty would be removed if, with Mr. Bradley in one of his phases (a phase difficult to reconcile with the definition given above), we contend that the self which is realized in Morality, actually includes in itself all the selves in whom I feel an interest:

'If myself which I aim at is the realization in me of a moral world which is a system of selves, an organism in which I am a member, and in whose life I live—then I cannot aim at my own well-being without aiming at that of others. The others are not mere means to me, but are involved in my essence.'

Now to the adoption of self-realization in this sense as an answer to the ethical problem I should object (*a*) that the interpretation is not the one which is naturally suggested by that term. If the end of life is (in part or in whole) to attain the ends of others besides myself, that is a most important truth which should surely be emphasized in any answer, however summary, to the question, "What is the end of life?"; and not left to be understood in a formula which takes no explicit account of it. (*b*) We are as far off as ever from knowing what the "realization" of the other selves, which is included in the realization of mine, really is. (*c*) The proposition that I cannot attain my end without promoting the end of others is at all events an intelligble proposition. Not so, I respectfully submit, the proposition that "others are involved in my essence." Such an assertion seems to me to ignore the very essence of selfhood, which excludes an absorption or inclusion in other selves, however closely related to us. Of course, Mr. Bradley will reply that we cannot distinguish a thing from its relations. And yet Mr. Bradley has himself taught us—no one more effectively—that there cannot be relations without something to relate. No doubt a *thing*, which does not exist for itself, but only in and for a mind, cannot even in thought be abstracted from its relations: the thing is made what it is by its intelligible relations, if we include in its relations the content which it has for a mind other than itself. But this is not so with a self. Unquestionably there can be no subject without an object; the very nature of a subject is constituted by its knowledge of such and such objects. The objects that it knows are part of the self; in the view of a thorough-going Idealism, indeed, the subject and its experiences make up one spiritual being. But, all the same, of such a spiritual being it is not true that it is made what it is by its relation to other spiritual beings in the same way as a mere thing, which exists for others and not for itself, is made what it is by its relations. The *thing* has no *esse* except to be felt, thought, experienced; the way it enters into the experience of minds is the only sort of being it possesses. On the other hand, the "esse" of the soul is to think, to feel, to experience. This thinking, feeling, experiencing does undoubtedly include relations to other selves; but such relations are not the whole of its being. The experiences of a soul may be *like* those of another soul: they may be caused by and dependent upon the experiences of another soul. But the experiences of one soul cannot be or become identical with the experience of another soul: the content of two consciousnesses may be the same—the universal abstracted from the particular, but not the reality: neither, therefore, can the good of one soul or self be the good of another, or be included in or be part of the good of another. Hence, if we are to avoid a mysticism which frankly takes leave of intelligibility, we cannot include any realization of the capacities of others in our conception of self-realization, however essential to such realization the good of others may be. If all that is meant is that other selves may be ends to me, not mere means, that is precisely the point which is usually disguised, if it is not denied, by those who employ the formula "self-realization." The tendency of the phrase is to represent all moral conduct as motived by a desire for my own good, into which consideration of others can only enter as means to the realization of my end. Even if there be a more ultimate metaphysical sense in which my self and others are really the same self, that is not in the sense with which we have to do with selves in Ethics: in Ethics at least we are concerned with the relations between a plurality of selves.

Further defence of this last objection would carry us more deeply into the metaphysical region than it would be in place to go at present. But I trust that what has been said will be enough to suggest that there is nothing to be gained by the use of this ambiguous, mysterious term. It tells us nothing important, nothing that could not be better expressed in some other way. It is an attempt to evade the real problems of Morality instead of answering them. . . .

Are we then to condemn the attempt to think for onself in moral matters? Are we to say that a man must simply submit himself wholly and unreservedly to the maxims, the traditions, the ideals of the society in which he finds himself? A moment's reflection is enough to negative the suggestion. A principle object of moral education is to form the habit of judging for oneself. The ancient philosopher who most emphasized the necessity of moral education by habituation insisted no less strongly that the moral education was not complete until the man had come to see and appreciate for himself the reason, the ground, the principle of the maxims which he at first accepted on authority[1]. And if the man's moral education has been a success, if he really has been taught to use his moral Reason, it cannot invariably stop in its exercise at the exact point which would prevent the deliverances of his own moral consciousness coming into collision with those of his moral instructors. The majority of men, of course, are not likely to rise on the whole far above the moral ideal of their society; but, if we do not confound Morality with the mere observance of a few traditional, and for the most part negative, maxims of conduct, it is clear that very ordinary men must have some moral originality or individuality. A man who thought and felt with the majority on every detail of life and conduct would be, as nearly as it is possible to be, a man without a character. And it is precisely to the men in whom moral education has been most successful, who have absorbed most completely all that was best in the teaching and example by which they were educated, that there are most certain to come moments at which they are impelled to question the teaching they have received; and to apply the principles which they have imbibed to the criticism of those principles themselves, or to carry them out into applications not dreamed of by those from whom they learned them. Moral innovations of this sort may of course take a great variety of forms. Sometimes there will be a violent reaction against morals that have been taught; and yet the greatest of moral revolutionaries have owed not less to their environment than the most rigid traditionalists. The environment of Athens produced Socrates as much as it produced the Sophists. . . .

To tell the man of the least gifted moral nature that he is never to think for himself about what he ought to do would be to doom him to moral stagnation or sterility. Mr. Bradley (who seems rarely to touch upon practical matters without violent and obvious exaggeration) has laid it down that for a man "to wish to be better than the world is to be already on the threshold of immorality." It would be truer to say that the man who is content to be as moral as his neighbours has already passed considerably beyond that threshold. Would not any one who really supposed that at all times "wisdom and virtue consist in living agreeably to the Ethos of one's country" inevitably have voted for the condemnation of Socrates, and have joined the crowd which shouted "Crucify him, crucify him"?

Self-Realization—Further Readings Primarily Related to Bradley

Bradley, F. H., *Appearance and Reality* (Oxford: Clarendon, 1893; 2d ed., 1897), Chap. 25.

———, *Collected Essays* (Oxford: Clarendon, 1935), Vol. I, Essays 3–8.

———, *Ethical Studies* (Oxford: Clarendon, 1876; 2d ed., 1927).

[1] Aristotle, *Ethic. Nicomach.*, VI. 12 (p. 1144 *a*).

Carritt, E. F., *The Theory of Morals* (London: Oxford U.P., 1928), Chap. 6. Critic of self-realization theories.

Green, T. H., *Prolegomena to Ethics* (Oxford: Clarendon, 1883), especially Bks. III–IV. Proponent of an allied view of self-realization.

Moore, G. E., *Principia Ethica* (Cambridge: Cambridge U.P., 1903), Chap. 4. Criticizes metaphysical ethics—a type of ethical theory which includes Bradley's.

Pratt, James Bissett, *Reason in the Art of Living* (New York: Macmillan, 1949), Chap. 9. Critic of self-realization theories.

Taylor, A. E., "Self-Realization—A Criticism," *International Journal of Ethics*, VI (1895–96), pp. 356–371. Critic.

Warnock, Mary, *Ethics Since* 1900 (London: Oxford U.P.: 1960), Chap. 1. Exposition, stating Bradley's place in twentieth-century ethics.

Wollheim, Richard, *F. H. Bradley* (Baltimore: Penguin Books, 1959; 2d ed., 1969), Chap. 6. Exposition, placing "My Station and Its Duties" in the context of Bradley's total ethics.

C *Dewey*

John Dewey generally conceives of right actions as those which resolve specific problems, and relieve the constituent tensions of problematic situations. These problems may be more or less moral in the traditional sense—Dewey does not particularly care for the distinction between the moral and the valuable. For him, moral problems are those in which judgment and choice are required prior to action. The moral situation involves, then, conflict and difficulty—tensions—and the search for satisfactory action. It therefore involves desires, potential satisfactions, natural goods like pleasure and health, which make up networks of interrelated biological, psychological, and social needs and demands. In the moral situation, these demands present the agent with a problem to be solved. A person may, for instance, have a family: a spouse, children, aged parents. This situation may occasion great friction and tension with respect to the care and training of the children. In this situation are previously established moral rules specifying different obligations to husband or wife, offspring, and parents. There may be various biological and social needs, relating to physical as well as psychological health. There also may be other relevant social and economic demands. Now, for Dewey, these moral rules do not provide fixed and final guidance. The *good* in this context will involve a resolution of the problems, a harmonious integration of the constituents of the situation which maximizes the possible satisfactions, minimizes the frictions, and, at the highest, enriches and expands the personalities and experiences of the people involved. Growth, in actively transforming situations to increase the quality of experience, is the only final end.

A person finds himself in a problematic situation, involving biological, psychological, social needs and duties, along with related moral rules and principles. Interruptions of behavior patterns produce tensions and dissatisfactions, thwarted desires, unfulfilled needs. The moral character of the situation relates not only to the moral rules involved (duties to family, etc.), but also to the necessity of making a choice, coming to a decision, among alternatives. Desires and satisfactions, "prizings," are not in themselves good, although they do provide "ends-in-view." They must be properly integrated with whatever rules, ends, or means are involved. An intelligent agent then sets up an hypothesis which proposes a solution to his problem, based upon the facts, rules, and expectations in the unique situation. The resolution should involve in balance the growth, enrichment, integration, of the related biological, psychological, social values and experiences inherent in the situation. New experiences and attitudes ensue for each person involved.

To solve problems intelligently, the agent uses a scientific method. He observes the factors involved in the problematic situation; he generates an hypothesis for a satisfactory resolution, and he then acts upon the hypothesis. If the ensuing action fails, then the process of observation, hypothesis, and test is rejected as in the more sophisticated use of the method by professional scientists. Suppose in our example that the outcome is successful. The aged parent is happy, gets better attention and medical care, makes new friends, etc. The family of the agent calms down, friction over the children is reduced, etc. The agent has then acted rightly.

Smith criticizes Dewey along typical philosophical lines. He argues that the instrumentalist theory over-states the ability of the scientific method to resolve ethical problems, or to provide a satisfactory normative theory. In particular, he believes that Dewey's theory does not provide a criterion for justifying ethical beliefs and judgments. Why, he asks, regard any ethical belief as justified at all? Arguing from several examples, Smith maintains that Dewey's pattern works only with essentially nonmoral cases, such as a situation where a roof leaks. In cases like parental obligation to children, however, moral principles are involved that do not appear to be a product of scientific proof or justification. Such principles appear to be ultimate in some sense—i.e., fixed. Finally, Smith accuses Dewey of being caught in a vicious circle. For Dewey, means and ends cannot be treated separately. The means employed affect the ends to be achieved; the ends, in turn, affect our judgment of the means to be selected. Yet, according to Smith, unless we have independent knowledge of the ends we want to achieve, we cannot proceed to consider the means for their realization.

33

Reconstruction in Moral Conceptions

JOHN DEWEY

The impact of the alteration in methods of scientific thinking upon moral ideas is, in general, obvious. Goods, ends are multiplied. Rules are softened into principles, and principles are modified into methods of understanding. Ethical theory began among the Greeks as an attempt to find a regulation for the conduct of life which should have a rational basis and purpose instead of being derived from custom. But reason as a substitute for custom was under the obligation of supplying objects and laws as fixed as those of custom had been. Ethical theory ever since has been singularly hypnotized by the notion that its business is to discover some final end or good or some ultimate and supreme law. This is the common element among the diversity of theories. Some have held that the end is loyalty or obedience to a higher power or authority; and they have variously found this higher principle in Divine Will, the will of the secular ruler, the maintenance of institutions in which the purpose of superiors is embodied, and the rational consciousness of duty. But they have differed from one another because there was one point in which they were agreed: a single and final source of law. Others have asserted that it is impossible to locate morality in conformity to law-giving power, and that it must be sought in ends that are goods. And some have sought the good in self-realization, some in holiness, some in happiness, some in the greatest possible aggregate of pleasures. And yet these schools have agreed in the assumption that there is a single, fixed and final good. They have been able to dispute with one another only because of their common premise.

The question arises whether the way out of the confusion and conflict is not to go to the root of the matter by questioning this common element. Is not the belief in the single, final and ultimate (whether conceived as good or as authoritative law) an intellectual product of that feudal organization which is disappearing historically and of that belief in a bounded, ordered cosmos, wherein rest is higher than motion, which has disappeared from natural science? It has been repeatedly suggested that the present limit of intellectual reconstruction lies in the fact that it has not as yet been seriously applied in the moral and social disciplines. Would not this further application demand precisely that we advance to a belief in a plurality of changing, moving, individualized goods and ends, and to a belief that principles, criteria, laws are intellectual instruments for analyzing individual or unique situations?

The blunt assertion that every moral situation is a unique situation having its own irreplaceable good may seem not merely blunt but preposterous. For the established tradition teaches that it is precisely the irregularity of special cases which makes necessary the guidance of conduct by universals, and that the essence of the virtuous disposition is willingness to subordinate every particular case to adjudication by a fixed principle. It would then follow that submission of a generic end and law to determination by the concrete situation entails complete confusion and unrestrained licentiousness. Let us, however, follow the pragmatic rule, and in order to discover the meaning of the idea ask for its consequences. Then it surprisingly turns out that the primary significance of the unique and morally ultimate character of the concrete situation is to transfer the weight and burden of morality to intelligence. It does not destroy responsibility; it only locates it. A moral situation is one in which judgment and choice are required antecedently to overt action. The practical meaning of the situation—that is to say the action needed to satisfy it—is not self-evident. It has to be searched for. There are conflicting desires and alternative apparent goods. What is needed is to find the right course of action, the right good. Hence, inquiry is exacted: observation of the detailed makeup of the situation; analysis into its diverse factors; clarification of what is obscure; discounting the more insistent and vivid traits; tracing the consequences of the various modes of action that suggest themselves; regarding the decision reached as hypothetical and tentative until the anticipated or supposed consequences which led to its adoption have been squared with actual consequences. This inquiry is intelligence. Our moral failures go back to some weakness of disposition, some absence of sympathy, some one-sided bias that makes us perform the judgment of the concrete case carelessly or perversely. Wide sympathy, keen sensitiveness, persistence in the face of the disagreeable, balance of interests enabling us to undertake the work of analysis and decision intelligently are the distinctively moral traits—the virtues or moral excellencies.

It is worth noting once more that the underlying issue is, after all, only the same as that which has been already thrashed out in physical inquiry. There too it long seemed as if rational assurance and demonstration could be attained only if we began with universal conceptions and subsumed particular cases under them. The men who initiated the methods of inquiry that are now everywhere adopted were denounced in their day (and sincerely) as subverters of truth and foes of science. If they have won in the end, it is because, as has already been pointed out, the method of universals confirmed prejudices and sanctioned ideas that had gained currency irrespective of evidence for them;

while placing the initial and final weight upon the individual case, stimulated painstaking inquiry into facts and examination of principles. In the end, loss of eternal truths was more than compensated for in the accession of quotidian facts. The loss of the system of superior and fixed definitions and kinds was more than made up for by the growing system of hypotheses and laws used in classifying facts. After all, then, we are only pleading for the adoption in moral reflection of the logic that has been proved to make for security, stringency and fertility in passing judgments upon physical phenomena. And the reason is the same. The old method in spite of its nominal and esthetic worship of reason discouraged reason, because it hindered the operation of scrupulous and unremitting inquiry.

More definitely, the transfer of the burden of the moral life from following rules or pursuing fixed ends over to the detection of the ills that need remedy in a special case and the formulation of plans and methods for dealing with them, eliminates the causes which have kept moral theory controversial, and which have also kept it remote from helpful contact with the exigencies of practice. The theory of fixed ends inevitably leads thought into the bog of disputes that cannot be settled. If there is one *summum bonum*, one supreme end, what is it? To consider this problem is to place ourselves in the midst of controversies that are as acute now as they were two thousand years ago. Suppose we take a seemingly more empirical view, and say that while there is not a single end, there also are not as many as there are specific situations that require amelioration; but there are a number of such natural goods as health, wealth, honor or good name, friendship, esthetic appreciation, learning and such moral goods as justice, temperance, benevolence, etc. What or who is to decide the right of way when these ends conflict with one another, as they are sure to do? Shall we resort to the method that once brought such disrepute upon the whole business of ethics: Casuistry? Or shall we have recourse to what Bentham well called the *ipse dixit* method: the arbitrary preference of this or that person for this or that end? Or shall we be forced to arrange them all in an order of degrees from the highest good down to the least precious? Again we find ourselves in the middle of unreconciled disputes with no indication of the way out.

Meantime, the special moral perplexities where the aid of intelligence is required go unenlightened. We cannot seek or attain health, wealth, learning, justice or kindness in general. Action is always specific, concrete, individualized, unique. And consequently judgments as to acts to be performed must be similarly specific. To say that a man seeks health or justice is only to say that he seeks to live healthily or justly. These things, like truth, are adverbial. They are modifiers of action in special cases. How to live healthily or justly is a matter which differs with every person. It varies with his past experience, his opportunities, his temperamental and acquired weaknesses and abilities. Not man in general but a particular man suffering from some particular disability aims to live healthily, and consequently health cannot mean for him exactly what it means for any other mortal. Healthy living is not something to be attained by itself apart from other ways of living. A man needs to be healthy *in* his life, not apart from it, and what does life mean except the aggregate of his pursuits and activities? A man who aims at health as a distinct end becomes a valetudinarian, or a fanatic, or a mechanical performer of exercises, or an athlete so one-sided that his pursuit of bodily development injures his heart. When the endeavor to realize a so-called end does not temper and color all other activities, life is portioned out into strips and fractions. Certain acts and times are devoted to getting health, others to cultivating religion, others to seeking learning, to being a good citizen, a devotee of fine art and so on. This is the only logical alternative to subordinating all aims to the accomplishment of one alone— fanaticism. This is out of fashion at present, but who can say how much of distraction and dissipation in life, and how much of its hard and narrow rigidity is the outcome of men's failure to realize that each situation has its own unique end and that the whole personality should be concerned with it? Surely, once more, what a man needs is to live healthily, and this result so affects all the activities of his life that it cannot be set up as a separate and independent good.

Nevertheless the general notions of health, disease, justice, artistic culture are of great importance: Not, however, because this or that case may be brought exhaustively under a single head and its specific traits shut out, but because generalized science provides a man as physician and artist and citizen, with questions to ask, investigations to make, and enables him to understand the meaning of what he sees. Just in the degree in which a physician is an artist in his work he uses his science, no matter how extensive and accurate, to furnish him with tools of inquiry into the individual case, and with methods of forecasting a method of dealing with it. Just in the degree in which, no matter how great his learning, he subordinates the individual case to some classification of diseases and some generic rule of treatment, he sinks to the level of the routine mechanic. His intelligence and his action become rigid, dogmatic, instead of free and flexible.

Moral goods and ends exist only when something has to be done. The fact that something has to be done proves that there are deficiencies, evils in the existent situation. This ill is just the specific ill that it is. It never is an exact duplicate of anything else. Consequently the good of the situation has to be discovered, projected and attained on the basis of the exact defect and trouble to be rectified. It cannot intelligently be injected into the situation from without. Yet it is the part of wisdom to compare different cases, to gather together the ills from which humanity suffers, and to generalize the corresponding goods into classes. Health, wealth, industry, temperance, amiability, courtesy, learning, esthetic capacity, initiative, courage, patience, enterprise, thoroughness and a multitude of other generalized ends are acknowledged as goods. But the *value* of this systematization is intellectual or analytic. Classifications *suggest* possible traits to be on the lookout for in studying a particular case; they suggest methods of action to be tried in removing the inferred causes of ill. They are tools of insight; their value is in promoting an individualized response in the individual situation.

Morals is not a catalogue of acts nor a set of rules to be applied like drugstore prescriptions or cook-book recipes. The need in morals is for specific methods of inquiry and of contrivance: Methods of inquiry to locate difficulties and evils; methods of contrivance to form plans to be used as working hypotheses in dealing with them. And the pragmatic import of the logic of individualized situations, each having its own irreplaceable good and principle, is to transfer the attention of theory from preoccupation with general conceptions to the problem of developing effective methods of inquiry.

Two ethical consequences of great moment should be remarked. The belief in fixed values has bred a division of ends into intrinsic and instrumental, of those that are really worth while in themselves and those that are of importance only as means to intrinsic goods. Indeed, it is often thought to be the very beginning of wisdom, of moral discrimination, to make this distinction. Dialectically, the distinction is interesting and seems harmless. But carried into practice it has an import that is tragic. Historically, it has been the source and justification of a hard and fast difference between ideal goods on one side and material goods on the other. At present those who would be liberal conceive intrinsic goods as esthetic in nature rather than as exclusively religious or as intellectually contemplative. But the effect is the same. So-called intrinsic goods, whether religious or esthetic, are divorced from those interests of daily life which because of their constancy and urgency form the preoccupation of the great mass. Aristotle used this distinction to declare that slaves and the working class though they are necessary *for* the state—the commonweal—are not constituents *of* it. That which is regarded as *merely* instrumental must approach drudgery; it cannot command either intellectual, artistic or moral attention and respect. Anything becomes *unworthy* whenever it is thought of as intrinsically lacking worth. So men of "ideal" interests have chosen for the most part the way of neglect and escape. The urgency and pressure of "lower" ends have been covered up by polite conventions. Or, they have been relegated to a baser class of mortals in order that the few might be free to attend to the goods that are really or intrinsically worth while. This withdrawal, in the name of higher ends, has left, for mankind at large and especially for energetic "practical" people the lower activities in complete command.

No one can possibly estimate how much of the obnoxious materialism and brutality of our economic life is due to the fact that economic ends have been regarded as *merely* instrumental. When they are recognized to be as intrinsic and final in their place as any others, then it will be seen that they are capable of idealization, and that if life is to be worth while, they must acquire ideal and intrinsic value. Esthetic, religious and other "ideal" ends are now thin and meagre or else idle and luxurious because of the separation from "instrumental" or economic ends. Only in connection with the latter can they be woven into the texture of daily life and made substantial and pervasive. The vanity and irresponsibility of values that are merely final and not also in turn means to the enrichment of other occupations of life ought to be obvious. But now the doctrine of "higher" ends gives aid, comfort and support to every socially isolated and socially irresponsible scholar, specialist, esthete and religionist. It protects the vanity and irresponsibility of his calling from observation by others and by himself. The moral deficiency of the calling is transformed into a cause of admiration and gratulation.

The other generic change lies in doing away once for all with the traditional distinction between moral goods, like the virtues, and natural goods like health, economic security, art, science and the like. The point of view under discussion is not the only one which has deplored this rigid distinction and endeavored to abolish it. Some schools have even gone so far as to regard moral excellencies, qualities of character as of value only because they promote natural goods. But the experimental logic when carried into morals makes every quality that is judged to be good according as it contributes to amelioration of existing ills. And in so doing, it enforces the moral meaning of natural science. When all is said and done in criticism of present social deficiencies, one may well wonder whether the root difficulty does not lie in the separation of natural and moral science. When physics, chemistry, biology, medicine, contribute to the detection of concrete human woes and to the development of plans for remedying them and relieving the human estate, they become moral; they become part of the apparatus of moral inquiry of science. The latter then loses its peculiar flavor of the didactic and pedantic; its ultra-moralistic and hortatory tone. It loses its thinness and shrillness as well as its vagueness. It gains agencies that are efficacious. But the gain is not confined to the side of moral science. Natural science loses its divorce from humanity; it becomes itself humanistic in quality. It is something to be pursued not in a technical and specialized way for what is called truth for its own sake, but with the sense of its social bearing, its intellectual indispensableness. It is technical only in the sense that it provides the technique of social and moral engineering.

When the consciousness of science is fully impregnated with the consciousness of human value, the greatest dualism which now weighs humanity down, the split between the material, the mechanical, the scientific and the moral and ideal will be destroyed. Human forces that now waver because of this division will be unified and reinforced. As long as ends are not thought of as individualized according to specific needs and opportunities, the mind will be content with abstractions, and the adequate stimulus to the moral or social use of natural science and historical data will be lacking. But when attention is concentrated upon the diversified concretes, recourse to all intellectual materials needed to clear up the special cases will be imperative. At the same time that morals are made to focus in intelligence, things intellectual are moralized. The vexatious and wasteful conflict between naturalism and humanism is terminated.

These general considerations may be amplified. First: Inquiry, discovery take the same place in morals that they have come to occupy in sciences of nature. Validation, demonstration become experimental, a matter of consequences. Reason, always an honorific term in ethics, becomes actualized in the methods by which the needs and conditions, the obstacles and resources, of situations are scrutinized in detail, and intelligent plans of improvement are worked out. Remote and abstract generalities promote jumping at conclusions, "anticipations of nature." Bad consequences are then deplored as due to natural perversity and untoward fate. But shifting the issue to analysis of a specific situation makes inquiry obligatory and alert observation of consequences imperative. No past decision nor old principle can ever be wholly relied upon to justify a course of action. No amount of pains taken in forming a purpose in a definite case is final; the consequences of its adoption must be carefully noted, and a purpose held only as a working hypothesis until results confirm its rightness. Mistakes are no longer either mere unavoidable accidents to be mourned or moral sins to be expiated and forgiven. They are lessons in wrong methods of using intelligence and instructions as to a better course in the future. They are indications of the need of revision, development, readjustment. Ends grow, standards of judgment are improved. Man is under just as much obligation to develop his most advanced standards and ideals as to use conscientiously those which he already possesses. Moral life is protected from falling into formalism and rigid repetition. It is rendered flexible, vital, growing.

In the second place, every case where moral action is required becomes of equal moral importance and urgency with every other. If the need and deficiencies of a specific situation indicate improvement of health as the end and good, then for that situation health is the ultimate and supreme good. It is no means to something else. It is a final and intrinsic value. The same thing is true of improvement of economic status, of making a living, of attending to business and family demands—all of the things which under the sanction of fixed ends have been rendered of secondary and merely instrumental value, and so relatively base and unimportant. Anything that in a given situation is an end and good at all is of equal worth, rank and dignity with every other good of any other situation, and deserves the same intelligent attention.

We note thirdly the effect in destroying the roots of Phariseeism. We are so accustomed to thinking of this as deliberate hypocrisy that we overlook its intellectual premises. The conception which looks for the end of action within the circumstances of the actual situation will not have the same measure of judgment for all cases. When one factor of the situation is a person of trained mind and large resources, more will be expected than with a person of backward mind and uncultured experience. The absurdity of applying the same standard of moral judgment to savage peoples that is used with civilized will be apparent. No individual or group will be judged by whether they come up to or fall short of some fixed result, but by the direction in which they are moving. The bad man is the man who no matter how good he *has* been is beginning to deteriorate, to grow less good. The good man is the man who no matter how morally unworthy he *has* been is moving to become better. Such a conception makes one severe in judging himself and humane in judging others. It excludes that arrogance which always accompanies judgment based on degree of approximation to fixed ends.

In the fourth place, the process of growth, of improvement and progress, rather than the static outcome and result, becomes the significant thing. Not health as an end fixed once and for all, but the needed improvement in health—

a continual process—is the end and good. The end is no longer a terminus or limit to be reached. It is the active process of transforming the existent situation. Not perfection as a final goal, but the ever-enduring process of perfecting, maturing, refining is the aim in living. Honesty, industry, temperance, justice, like health, wealth and learning, are not goods to be possessed as they would be if they expressed fixed ends to be attained. They are directions of change in the quality of experience. Growth itself is the only moral "end."

Although the bearing of this idea upon the problem of evil and the controversy between optimism and pessimism is too vast to be here discussed, it may be worth while to touch upon it superficially. The problem of evil ceases to be a theological and metaphysical one, and is perceived to be the practical problem of reducing, alleviating, as far as may be removing, the evils of life. Philosophy is no longer under obligation to find ingenious methods for proving that evils are only apparent, not real, or to elaborate schemes for explaining them away or, worse yet, for justifying them. It assumes another obligation:—That of contributing in however humble a way to methods that will assist us in discovering the causes of humanity's ills. Pessimism is a paralyzing doctrine. In declaring that the world is evil wholesale, it makes futile all efforts to discover the remediable causes of specific evils and thereby destroys at the root every attempt to make the world better and happier. Wholesale optimism, which has been the consequence of the attempt to explain evil away, is, however, equally an incubus.

After all, the optimism that says that the world is already the best possible of all worlds might be regarded as the most cynical of pessimisms. If this is the best possible, what would a world which was fundamentally bad be like? Meliorism is the belief that the specific conditions which exist at one moment, be they comparatively bad or comparatively good, in any event may be bettered. It encourages intelligence to study the positive means of good and the obstructions to their realization, and to put forth endeavor for the improvement of conditions. It arouses confidence and a reasonable hopefulness as optimism does not. For the latter in declaring that good is already realized in ultimate reality tends to make us gloss over the evils that concretely exist. It becomes too readily the creed of those who live at ease, in comfort, of those who have been successful in obtaining this world's rewards. Too readily optimism makes the men who hold it callous and blind to the sufferings of the less fortunate, or ready to find the cause of troubles of others in their personal viciousness. It thus co-operates with pessimism, in spite of the extreme nominal differences between the two, in benumbing sympathetic insight and intelligent effort in reform. It beckons men away from the world of relativity and change into the calm of the absolute and eternal.

The import of many of these changes in moral attitude focusses in the idea of happiness. Happiness has often been made the object of the moralists' contempt. Yet the most ascetic moralist has usually restored the idea of happiness under some other name, such as bliss. Goodness without happiness, valor and virtue without satisfaction, ends without conscious enjoyment—these things are as intolerable practically as they are self-contradictory in conception. Happiness is not, however, a bare possession; it is not a fixed attainment. Such a happiness is either the unworthy selfishness which moralists have so bitterly condemned, or it is, even if labelled bliss, an insipid tedium, a millennium of ease in relief from all struggle and labor. It could satisfy only the most delicate of molly-coddles. Happiness is found only in success; but success means succeeding, getting forward, moving in advance. It is an active process, not a passive outcome. Accordingly it includes the overcoming of obstacles, the elimination of sources of defect and ill. Esthetic sensitiveness and enjoyment are a large constituent in any worthy happiness. But the esthetic appreciation which is totally separated from renewal of spirit, from re-creation of mind and purification of emotion is a weak and sickly thing, destined to speedy death from starvation. That the renewal and re-creation come unconsciously not by set intention but makes them the more genuine.

Upon the whole, utilitarianism has marked the best in the transition from the classic theory of ends and goods to that which is now possible. It had definite merits. It insisted upon getting away from vague generalities, and down to the specific and concrete. It subordinated law to human achievement instead of subordinating humanity to external law. It taught that institutions are made for man and not man for institutions; it actively promoted all issues of reform. It made moral good natural, humane, in touch with the natural goods of life. It opposed unearthly and other worldly morality. Above all, it acclimatized in human imagination the idea of social welfare as a supreme test. But it was still profoundly affected in fundamental points by old ways of thinking. It never questioned the idea of a fixed, final and supreme end. It only questioned the current notions as to the nature of this end; and then inserted pleasure and the greatest possible aggregate of pleasures in the position of the fixed end.

Such a point of view treats concrete activities and specific interests not as worth while in themselves, or as constituents of happiness, but as mere external means to getting pleasures. The upholders of the old tradition could therefore easily accuse utilitarianism of making not only virtue but art, poetry, religion and the state into mere servile means of attaining sensuous enjoyments. Since pleasure was an outcome, a result valuable on its own account independently of the active processes that achieve it, happiness was a thing to be possessed and held onto. The acquisitive instincts of man were exaggerated at the expense of the creative. Production was of importance not because of the intrinsic worth of invention and reshaping the world, but because its external results feed pleasure. Like every theory that sets up fixed and final aims, in making the end passive and possessive, it made all active operations *mere* tools. Labor was an unavoidable evil to be minimized. Security in possession was the chief thing practically. Material comfort and ease were magnified in contrast with the pains and risk of experimental creation.

These deficiencies, under certain conceivable conditions, might have remained merely theoretical. But the disposition of the times and the interests of those who propagated the utilitarian ideas, endowed them with power for social harm. In spite of the power of the new ideas in attacking old social abuses, there were elements in the teaching which operated or protected to sanction new social abuses. The reforming zeal was shown in criticism of the evils inherited from the class system of feudalism, evils economic, legal and political. But the new economic order of capitalism that was superseding feudalism brought its own social evils with it, and some of these ills utilitarianism tended to cover up or defend. The emphasis upon acquisition and possession of enjoyments took on an untoward color in connection with the contemporary enormous desire for wealth and the enjoyments it makes possible.

If utilitarianism did not actively promote the new economic materialism, it had no means of combating it. Its general spirit of subordinating productive activity to the bare product was indirectly favorable to the cause of an unadorned commercialism. In spite of its interest in a thoroughly social aim, utilitarianism fostered a new class interest, that of the capitalistic property-owning interests, provided only property was obtained through free competition and not by governmental favor. The stress that Bentham put on security tended to consecrate the legal institution of private property provided only certain legal abuses in connection with its acquisition and transfer were abolished. *Beati possidentes*—provided possessions had been obtained in accord with the rules of the competitive game—without, that is, extraneous favors from government. Thus utilitarianism gave intellectual confirmation to all those tendencies which make "business" not a means of social service and an opportunity for personal growth in creative power but a way of accumulating the means of private enjoyments. Utilitarian ethics thus afford a remarkable example of the need of philosophic reconstruction which these lectures have been presenting. Up to a certain point, it reflected the meaning of modern thought and aspirations. But it was still tied down by fundamental ideas of that very order which it thought it had completely left behind: The idea of a fixed and single end lying beyond the diversity of human needs and acts rendered utilitarianism incapable of being an adequate representative of the modern spirit. It has to be reconstructed through emancipation from its inherited elements.

If a few words are added upon the topic of education, it is only for the sake of suggesting that the educative process is all one with the moral process, since the latter is a continuous passage of experience from worse to better. Education has been traditionally thought of as preparation: as learning, acquiring certain things because they will later be useful. The end is remote, and education is getting ready, is a preliminary to something more important to happen later on. Childhood is only a preparation for adult life, and adult life for another life. Always the future, not the present, has been the significant thing in education: Acquisition of knowledge and skill for future use and enjoyment; formation of habits required later in life in business, good citizenship and pursuit of science. Education is thought of also as something needed by some human beings merely because of their dependence upon others. We are born ignorant, unversed, unskilled, immature, and consequently in a state of social dependence. Instruction, training, moral discipline are processes by which the mature, the adult, gradually raise the helpless to the point where they can look out for themselves. The business of childhood is to grow into the independence of adulthood by means of the guidance of those who have already attained it. Thus the process of education as the main business of life ends when the young have arrived at emancipation from social dependence.

These two ideas, generally assumed but rarely explicitly reasoned out, contravene the conception that growing, or the continuous reconstruction of experience, is the only end. If at whatever period we choose to take a person, he is still in process of growth, then education is not, save as a by-product, a preparation for something coming later. Getting from the present the degree and kind of growth there is in it is education. This is a constant function, independent of age. The best thing that can be said about any special process of education, like that of the formal school period, is that it renders its subject capable of further education: more sensitive to conditions of growth and more able to take advantage of them. Acquisition of skill, possession of knowledge, attainment of culture are not ends: they are marks of growth and means to its continuing.

The contrast usually assumed between the period of education as one of social dependence and of maturity as one of social independence does harm. We repeat over and over that man is a social animal, and then confine the significance of this statement to the sphere in which sociality usually seems least evident, politics. The heart of the sociality of man is in education. The idea of education as preparation and of adulthood as a fixed limit of growth are two sides of the same obnoxious untruth. If the moral business of the adult as well as the young is a growing and developing experience, then the instruction that comes from social dependencies and interdependencies are as important for the adult as for the child. Moral independence for the adult means arrest of growth, isolation means induration. We exaggerate the intellectual dependence of childhood so that children are too much kept in leading strings, and then we exaggerate the independence of adult life from intimacy of contacts and communication with others. When the identity of the moral process with the processes of specific growth is realized, the more conscious and formal education of childhood will be seen to be the most economical and efficient means of social advance and reorganization, and it will also be evident that the test of all the institutions of adult life is their effect in furthering continued education. Government, business, art, religion, all social institutions have a meaning, a purpose. That purpose is to set free and to develop the capacities of human individuals without respect to race, sex, class or economic status. And this is all one with saying that the test of their value is the extent to which they educate every individual into the full stature of his possibility. Democracy has many meanings, but if it has a moral meaning, it is found in resolving that the supreme test of all political institutions and industrial arrangements shall be the contribution they make to the all-around growth of every member of society.

34

Critique of Dewey

JOHN E. SMITH

Value, for Dewey, is an affair of action and of conduct; the notion becomes relevant only when there arise alternative ways of behavior on the part of man or different means and pathways through which a goal is to be reached. Alternatives mean choice; allegiance to the method of intelligence demands that a choice be made on *critical* grounds. Critical choice, in short, involves us in distinguishing between the better and the worse, the good and the bad alternative. Many thinkers in the past began their reflections on the good and on how to make the right choice in this way; thus far there is nothing especially new or startling in Dewey's analysis. Normally, however, it would be thought that the only way in which scientific knowledge might help us in a problematic situation is by informing us as to the "best" (or better) way of achieving some goal previously agreed upon either as desirable or good in itself. The normal supposition would be that science can help us with regard to *means* but that it is unable to furnish us with the materials for determining what ends are valuable. Dewey dissented. Science is not confined to the determination of means alone; it has within itself resources for determining ends. The manner in which this is to be accomplished is through the regulation of our desires. By distinguishing between behavior which is direct and habitual, requiring neither evaluation nor the presence of explicit desire, and behavior which is indirect in the sense that it can take place only after reflection and judgment, Dewey tried to show that the method of intelligence is unavoidable in the framing of ends. When the course of life and events goes along "naturally" and there is no problem or struggle, there is also no need to speak of desires. Desires come into being along with difficulties. Desire for Dewey meant a specific *end in view* and one which is the *proper* end because it represents the solution to a problem. When the situation becomes discordant and a deficiency or lack is felt, habitual action will not suffice. Our sense that something is wrong leads to analysis of the situation; we want to locate the difficulty and resolve it. Genuine desire, as distinct from wish, whim, fancy, and day-dreaming, exists when there is the clear intention, expressed as an end in view, to overcome the obstacle and set the situation right again. Since ends, Dewey argued, are no more than the last stage in a series of events which serve as means, they are organically connected with the factors and conditions which lead up to them. The same is true of a desire as an end in view. It can be a genuine desire only insofar as it results from the attempt to grasp the situation and locate the difficulty in order to determine what actual means or series of events will lead to a resolution. Whims and fancies are ruled out as desires and ends in view precisely because they remain unconnected with acts and materials which would realize them. Scientific knowledge becomes relevant to the determination of ends just because it alone can inform us regarding the natures of things and the courses of action which will lead to specified results. This information, in turn, is necessary for the framing of desires or ends in view that can resolve problematic situations.

There are at least two questions to be raised. The first concerns the truth of the claim that means—the better, most-to-be-valued means—can always be best determined by following the lead of theoretical knowledge. The second asks exactly how knowledge of the conditions and relations of things can lead us to see what we *ought* to desire. Some examples will aid in the elucidation of these questions.

Suppose we discover that our roof leaks and set about to remedy the difficulty. The example is perfectly in accord with Dewey's approach; value problems arise *wherever* action is called for and it is clear that there are alternative courses of action. We are not confined to what might normally be called "moral" situations. Let us further suppose that intelligent analysis of the situation shows that we have several ways of dealing with the problem; what we want is the "best" way of fixing the defect, or at least a way which is better than other ways. There is no doubt that by taking into account such factors as cost, convenience, and the like, scientific knowledge of the materials and tools will lead us to the best way for resolving the problem. Suppose a second case, one more closely related to human concerns. A man discovers that people shun him because he rarely keeps appointments on time and then becomes angry when he is chided for his lack of punctuality. If that man should desire to change his ways he might ask, What is the best way to overcome these difficulties and to regain the favor and good graces of my friends? Here again it seems fairly obvious that finding the "best" way to proceed is simply a matter of attending to the facts of the situation. The case may be too trivial for us to use the term "scientific knowledge," but it seems fairly clear that no profound moral insight or knowledge from on high is needed in order to resolve the problem. The "best" way to achieve the end desired is dictated by the facts of human psychology. Although this second case is actually more problematic than the first, we may allow that in both examples the best way of proceeding is revealed through knowledge of the various factors in the situation.

Suppose another case involving more obviously ethical issues. A parent desires the good for her child and vows that she will be guided in all her actions by what is genuinely good for the child and not merely by her own prejudices and predilections. Now it seems clear that this vow itself as an end in view—the declared intention to seek for nothing but the good of the child—cannot be discovered merely by objective knowledge of any situation. That any course of action which follows from the initial vow represents the "best" way of acting cannot be discovered merely by appealing to the facts of human psychology, the arrangement of society, and similar sources of knowledge. The initial vow expresses an end, a goal which is good in itself; such a goal sustains itself by its own nature and does not require support from the value of any further consequences. Suppose we allow that seeking the good of the child is a good or desirable goal; the immediate question is: Is it possible to discover the best *means* of realizing that goal through the sort of knowledge which Dewey had in mind? That scientific knowledge can tell us a great deal about human life, its relation to the environment, and its social character cannot be denied. Science, however, is always dependent upon facts that are finished and done with; it draws its life from the accurate representation and explanation of what has taken place. But we do not discover ideal goods—even the general idea that we should strive for the good of the child apart from our selfish predilections— merely by investigating what has happened in the past. The child, moreover, has freedom and entertains ideas about his or her own nature and destiny; there is more than one ideal of fulfillment, and those that have been proposed in the past have not always been consistent with each other. The facts of human psychology and sociology will tell us much about human behavior, and what Dewey liked to call the results of experienced objects, but all by itself and without the intervention of *comprehensive* ideals touching on the proper vocation of man in the world, that knowledge will not suffice. And yet Dewey persistently maintained the opposite thesis; for him scientific knowledge was to be our guide not only in the discovery of means to ends previously agreed upon, but in the determination of ends themselves, which are supposed to be genuine values because they are approved on reflection and are rooted in empirical knowledge.

Dewey seems not to have seen that it is only in relatively simple situations that their problematic character is revealed on the basis of so-called factual analyses alone. The leaky roof has a way of making itself known and to know that we have a problem on our hands requires no extended diagnosis. But there is a formidable gap between a situation of that simplicity and the sort of problem which arises in connection with, for example, the divided self prevented from affirming itself by insufficient courage, or with the conflict between personal honesty and the goal of worldly success. In those cases the "problem" does not announce itself as it does when a physical system goes out of order; instead we require a standard of excellence by reference to which we can say that the situation is not as it ought to be. It is curious that the closer we come to situations which would normally be regarded as "moral" situations, the more difficult it is to see that their problematic character can be discovered merely by scientific analysis.

On Dewey's own view, the determination of means is not independent of ends, of exactly what we ought to desire and hope to achieve. But Dewey also held that the framing of ends in view taken as the proposed resolution of problematic situations depends on the tracing out of means for arriving at these ends. It is difficult to see how a vicious circle is to be avoided. We do not discover the "problematic" character of moral situations merely by analyzing the facts; to be problematic such situations must fall short of an ideal or lack a feature which would complete them. Unless we already know what ends we want to achieve, an analysis of the factual structure of a situation will not itself suffice for diagnosis. It will not do to say that only those desires or ends in view which are framed in accordance with scientific knowledge of means are genuine, because we cannot begin to consider means until we have some idea of where we want to go. Dewey did not see the relevance of goals that emerge not from the scientific appraisal of situations but out of ideal visions portraying what man and society may become. Such ideals can actually be found in his own accounts of the individual, of freedom, and of the ideal society. But it seems clear that these ends were not arrived at as a result of a scientific analysis. . . .

Self-Realization—Further Readings Primarily Related to Dewey

Bernstein, Richard J., *John Dewey* (New York: Washington Square Press, 1966), Chap. 9. Sympathetic exposition.

Blanshard, Brand, *Reason and Goodness* (London: George Allen and Unwin, 1961), Chap. 7. Critic.

Dewey, John, and James H. Tufts, *Ethics* (rev. ed., New York: Henry Holt, 1932), especially Part II.

Dewey, John, *Human Nature and Conduct* (New York: Henry Holt, 1922).

——, *Theory of Valuation*, International Encyclopedia of Unified Science, Vol. II, Foundations of the Unity of Science, No. 4 (Chicago: Univ. of Chicago Press, 1939).

Fox, Marvin, "On the Diversity of Methods in Dewey's Ethical Theory," *Philosophy and Phenomenological Research*, XII (1951), pp. 123–129. Critic.

Geiger, George R., *John Dewey in Perspective* (New York: Oxford, 1958), Chaps. 6 and 10. Sympathetic exposition.

Hook, Sidney, *John Dewey: An Intellectual Portrait* (New York: Day, 1939), Chap. 7. Sympathetic exposition.

Meenan, Daniel F. X., "John Dewey's Theory of Valuation," *Modern Schoolman*, XXX (1953), pp. 187–201. Critic.

Punzo, Vincent C., *Reflective Naturalism* (New York: Macmillan, 1969), Chap. 9. Exposition and criticism.

Romanell, Patrick, *Toward a Critical Naturalism* (New York: Macmillan, 1958), Chap. 4. Critic.

Roth, Robert J., S. J., *John Dewey and Self-Realization* (Englewood Cliffs, N.J.: Prentice-Hall, 1962). Exposition and criticism.

Vivas, Eliseo, *The Moral and the Ethical Life* (Chicago: Univ. of Chicago Press, 1950), Chaps. 6–8. Critic.

C CRITIQUE OF NORMATIVE THEORIES:
ARE ULTIMATE ETHICAL PRINCIPLES DEFENSIBLE?

Nietzsche takes the position that few, if any, ethical philosophers had bothered to ask the important question about ethics, which is: what is the basis of all morality as distinct from particular moral systems? Under the influence of Schopenhauer, Kant, heroic Greek culture, and the Darwinian theory of evolution, he responds to this question by casting doubt on all previous ethical theories. Following Schopenhauer and Darwin, he conceives nature, indeed reality as a whole, to be the product of blind, amoral, competitive, striving. From Kant and Schopenhauer, he conceives this striving in terms of the human mental process roughly indicated by the word "will." From Greek heroic culture, epitomized in vital and powerful warriors like Achilles, and contrasted with the meek and docile Christians and Jews, he conceives the superman, a charismatic leader of elite minority groups, as the characteristically good human. Nietzsche is, then, a vitalist in a most fundamental sense.

It is important to understand that he views ethics in terms of choice, of decision; of men imposing their wishes upon nature as well as upon other men. There are no ethical truths in the sense that men, by rational techniques of theoretical science—inductive or deductive—establish a correspondence between ethical beliefs and some independent and objective order of moral objects. Indeed, even scientific truth is a variety of value, and is not a matter of correspondence with nature. Ethical beliefs are not discovered; good and evil, right and wrong, are created by man.*

Nietzsche's concept of the good, then, is quite vague and obscure. It is, in a sense, whatever a man, or men, can put into effect. We may derive some ideas about the position, however, from his attack upon traditional Christian and Jewish virtue. We note that he rejects the traditional virtues of pity, charity, justice, meekness, selflessness, humility, as "slave-morality." He supports courage, psychic and physical strength, pride, egotism, cleverness, cruelty, as "master morality." Only one vague

---

*See Frederick A. Olafson, *Principles and Persons* (Baltimore: The Johns Hopkins Press, 1967), for an excellent discussion of Neitzsche and existentialistic ethics in general.

element is shared by his examples—the notion of power. The superman posits the good, makes it his, by will and action. New and comprehensive life styles, invented and enforced by men, independent of external standards, constitute virtue. The good is, then, roughly power; and right actions are those which lead to power, or are constituted by its exercise. And this gives us a relatively clear notion of a "transvaluation of values." The good, and the right, are what men are able to impose upon other men and nature. The models are animal nature and heroic warriors. Traditional morality runs counter to nature and hampers heroic spirits.

In a loose sense, Nietzsche is in the teleological camp of ethics. He might even be considered a self-realizationist. Despite the negative character of his examples, drawn mainly from his critique of traditional morality, he sees the good as involving the development of human excellences of mind and body. Indeed, he wishes the criteria of right and good kept open for this very purpose. "Right" and "good" do not name properties, qualities, universals, at all. Although his views thus have some similarities to traditional theories, they are powerfully opposed to a significant number of the presuppositions of traditional ethics, those "bases" with which, as we have seen, all ethical theories except egoism and certain kinds of relativism have more or less kept in touch. He is an egoist—he rejects the principles of altruism and universalizability which, in his view, run counter to the realization of human potential. Although he follows Kantian vitalism, he rejects the Kantian principle of universality. What is right and good for the agent, the superman, is not necessarily right and good for others—even other supermen—in the same situation. Moral decision does not involve respect for accepted rules, nor any ties to shared principles or ends. He rejects the view that ethics can be put upon a rational foundation; in fact, he considers truth and consistency as matters of choice and evaluation. Intellectualism is in his opinion a form of degeneracy. He is also a relativist. On the whole, Nietzsche almost stands outside the ethical traditions of both Western and Eastern culture, although he can perhaps be conceived as Plato's Polemarchus or Callicles (remaining recalcitrant!).

As can be seen, Nietzsche's ethics exhibits a number of decidedly modern features. Like Hare (who might be surprised at this point) he sees ethics, morality, value, as practical and not theoretical; as not, in other words, a scientific or factual enterprise. Morality is essentially a matter of choice and decision; not a matter of fact and discovery. Ethical terms do not name moral objects or properties. In modern terms, they are parasitical; they get their meaning from the situations, things, actions, to which they are attached by the moral agent. Normative terms may maintain evaluative and emotive meaning, yet change their criteria. Thus Nietzsche appears, surprisingly, to be in advance of his time on certain logical and semantic ideas as related to ethics. In addition, he reminds us, by his incisive critiques, that actions in the name of pity, charity, and other standard virtues can be counterproductive in the long run.

There are many difficulties with his theory, if it can be called a "theory." His attempts to propose and to justify his views imply that they are of worth, are valuable, and this leads to paradox in that he maintains that no such justification in ethics is possible. He tends to use terms like "cruel" in distorted ways. The model appears to be the necessary pain of, say, surgery, as the means to the cure of disease, which makes it possible for the body to prosper and develop. But no one calls this pain "cruel" in the standard use. "Cruel" is appropriately used only when certain other criteria, *viz.*, concern for the patient's interests, etc., are missing. Taking as a factual proposition his claim that actions which ignore pity, consideration for others, cooperation with others, will lead to more human excellence, the claim appears on the evidence to be false. Taking his views to embody proposals about life, they appear to be unsupportable. It appears that Nietzsche, in common with many moralists even up to the present, did not see the possibility that practical reason could be conceived in terms of the justification of decisions or proposals. Hence, he sees his and other ethical views as decisions, choices, willing, which are not open to any kind of rational appraisal. In addition, of course, there are the numerous problems relating to the kinds of choices Nietzsche makes for his model of the superman from among the limitless aspects of nature. All events are "natural" in one sense. Why does Nietzsche choose to claim that the interests and values of the powerful minority should be glorified, considered more important, than those of the weak majority? His only response is to cite reasons in justification of his choices, but this involves him in contradiction. In fact, his views, in particular his statements that the virtues, right acts, embody cruelty, pitilessness, and inhumanity, can be reduced to absurdity, i.e., cruelty is good, cruel actions are right. There is a dilemma here (or many dilemmas). From one perspective, his concepts of right and good are vacuous, yet in so far as we deduce content for them from his examples (*viz.*, cruelty), it is found that they are not actions which can be morally approved or commended. He seems to make a number of category blunders; in particular, he attempts to impose the animal model of behavior in a state of nature upon humans. It is clear, even if we ignore the "naturalistic fallacy," that simply to identify the good with the biologically evolved or with power is silly; but Nietzsche's emphasis upon choice and decision indicates that such a simple identification may not be representative of his views.

Whatever stance one takes concerning Nietzsche's moral conceptions, they had a profound if paradoxical influence upon the supporters of another kind of moral theory—existentialism—to which we turn in the next selection.

As developed by Sartre, existentialist ethics derives from an ontological characterization of man: his existence precedes his essence. Other objects and organisms in the world are profoundly different. Plants, animals, stones, artifacts like knives have a pre-existing plan, or determined character, form, behavior, independent of any self-determination. They do not choose to be what they are, or what they do, or what happens to them. Men, on the other hand, do not fulfill a plan which is imposed on them. Men choose what they are, or are to be—men are free.

Ethics and morality arise from human consciousness, particularly as it relates to desires, striving. Thus, men act for goals, ends, have intentions. Man's "being," in Sartre's terms, is created by human decision, by actions in pursuit of goals, to fill up the "nothingness"—the absence of planned behavioral and other characteristics. There is a "gap," or "void," to be filled. Animals, stones, and plants are only "objective," "beings in themselves." They have relatively fixed essences, while men are "subjective," "beings for themselves." These concepts, drawn from Sartre's *Being and Nothingness*, are Hegelian in character.

The actions, creations, and choices of men, however, are not rationally supportable. They are, so to speak, absurd in that there are no patterns or proofs which can be used as guides. Nevertheless, when they act, men act for all mankind. This assertion is an important remnant of universalizability. Further, a man, as a moral agent, conscious that his action creates the "right action," also is aware that his action thereby has consequences. Yet, there are no fixed moral rules and no moral order in which a person may ground his actions, his common sense of responsibility. Consciousness of this mixture of conditions produces a sense of anguish. He must act. He must marry or not marry, join a political party or not join it, fight for the Free French or not fight for it. The consequences are contingent, unknowable, unpredictable, disorderly and complex—to a certain extent disconnected from past and future actions and conditions. The realization by a person that he is free and must act, yet with no basis and no proof, produces anguish, feeling of abandonment, and despair. The import of the universal requirement:

"What would happen if everybody did so?" lies heavily on human consciousness, so heavily, in fact, that it produces evasions which Sartre
terms "bad faith." These attempts to avoid anguish take two general
forms. First, men deny that they did choose—deny, in other words,
that they are free—and claim they could not do otherwise than they do.
Second, they identify with group interests, whereby responsibility is
shifted to the group, and then take on roles and cite rules.

How ought we act, then? Value is created and not rationally supportable. Though men have goals and moral rules, none are universal
and provable. Some goals are worth pursuing; but only because men do
pursue them. "Good" and "evil" do not name common or objective
properties. So, how ought men to act? Obligation and the concept of
concern for the interests of others derive from a person's choice of commitment to certain shared goals. Such a choice often originates spon-
taneously in a joint action (e.g., storming the Bastille). But such a
choice restricts the agent's liberty; he is liable to violence from the
group if he breaks the implied contract. Obligations, then, like values,
are inventions. They emerge from shared ends and goals, subject to no
additional elements of proof or justification.

Sartre's existentialist ethics often appears, like that of Nietzsche,
almost anti-ethical. The conception of ethics as a rational discipline is
denied. Value and obligation are essentially individualistic. The concepts
of value and obligation are, further, essentially relativistic. On such a
view, the Kantian principle of universalizability seems strangely out of
place. Men are free, are responsible; but the responsibility seems itself
not a matter of rational support.

In several ways, Sartre's view is consistent with modern analytical
ethics. First, his view makes the meanings of ethical terms relative to
choice and invention.* They do not name properties of objects or actions.
Second, Sartre links morality to the actions and intentions of men,
making good and evil matters of creation, choice, and decision. His
examples, in particular those linked to his moral psychology, are often
extraordinarily impressive to the reader, for his sense of human frustration and trouble are profound.

Nevertheless, there are serious difficulties in his theory. It is probably correct to say that man has no purpose, like, say, a shovel or machine,
and that there are few, if any, fixed, particular moral rules. On the negative side, however, Sartre's theory is obscure. He also tends to base his

---

*See Mary Warnock, *Ethics Since 1900* (London: Oxford University Press, 1966),
Chapter 7.

theory on essentially vacuous uses of a series of terms, such as "anguish," "abandonment," "absurdity," "despair." These terms seem not to pick out traits in any clear manner. On his theory, it is impossible for men *not* to be in despair, anguish, etc. Thus, Sartre's ethical views lend themselves to dilemmas. Taken as statements about human actions and experiences, they are false. It is not the case that all choices are characterized by anguish, despair, etc. But if one persists in insisting that they are so characterized, then the terms are trivially and vacuousl true of any possible choice. A similar argument can be lodged against the existentialist claim that all actions are free. Men do not in fact choose everything they do. We do not choose all our attitudes, our bodies, our early education, etc. If it is claimed that we do so, the word "choose" has become so broad in application as to lose meaning.

Furthermore, Sartre, in his radical relativism and subjectivism, seems to have neglected the existence of common traits or ends. There are experiences of men that might make for common, even if very general, rational criteria to guide action. For instance, men have the general potential for painful and pleasant experience, and they face obvious evils like disease and discomfort. Sartre seems driven, in true Cartesian fashion, to another dilemma. He appears to think that rational proof must be straightforwardly related to assertions and propositions whose terms name common properties. Since moral rules and decisions do not fit into this context, they cannot be rational. What is needed here is the contemporary realization that other possible models are available—among them the view that acts and decisions can be viewed as proposals, pieces of advice, and thus be justifiable in different ways. The fact that an action or rule is created, invented, does not entail that it is subjective in the sense that it is beyond rational justification. Acting for no reasons is quite different from action on grounds of conscious reasons, reasons which are taken into account by the agent and may be shared with others. Sartre vacillates between the belief that the core of obligation is a logical relation (the view we are concerned with here) and the view that it is a consequence of the agent's fear of retaliation by the group, a causal relation. This same narrow concept of proof and justification is also reflected in Sartre's attitude towards anguish and despair—he connects the epistemic idea of probability to the agent's inability to be *certain* not only as to all of the consequences of an action, but also as to his own motives. Conceived in this way, anguish and despair are analytically related to actions. This neglects the wide range of meanings of the term, "certain," with respect to actions. We are often, in ordinary usage, certain of our feelings about the consequences of an action, not doubtful in mind. Normal men and women do not feel that responsibility entails anguish and despair. The bare possibility of unforeseen events, improbable eventualities, is not always taken as grounds for either the acceptance of responsibility or the attendant feelings of anguish and despair. For Sartre, the necessity of anguish and despair follow, in other words, only from his somewhat strange and limited conceptions of knowledge and probability.

35

The Will to Power

FRIEDRICH NIETZSCHE

I

WHOSE WILL TO POWER IS MORALITY? The *common factor* of all European history since the time of *Socrates* is the attempt to make the *moral values* dominate all other values, in order that they should not be only the leader and judge of life, but also of: (1) knowledge, (2) Art, (3) political and social aspirations. . . .

What is the meaning of this *will to power on the part of moral values*, which has played such a part in the world's prodigious evolutions?

Answer: Three powers lie concealed behind it: (1) the instinct of the *herd* opposed to the strong and independent; (2) the instinct of all *sufferers* and all *abortions* opposed to the happy and well-constituted; (3) the instinct of the mediocre opposed to the exceptions. . . .

II

THE TENDENCY OF MORAL EVOLUTION. Every one's desire is that there should be no other teaching and valuation of things than those by means of which he himself succeeds. Thus the *fundamental tendency* of the *weak* and *mediocre* of all times, has been to *enfeeble the strong and to reduce them to the level of the weak: their chief weapon in this process* was the *moral principle*. The attitude of the strong towards the weak is branded as evil; the higher states of the strong become bad bywords. . . .

FROM Friedrich Nietzsche, *Beyond Good and Evil* and *The Will to Power*; from *The Complete Works of Friedrich Nietzsche*, Oscar Levy, General Editor [1909–1911]. New York: Russell & Russell, 1964.

III

The instinct of the herd values the *juste milieu* and the *average* as the highest and most precious of all things: the spot where the majority is to be found, and the air that it breathes there. In this way it is the opponent of all order of rank; it regards a climb from the level to the heights in the same light as a descent from the majority to the minority. The herd regards the *exception*, whether it be above or beneath its general level, as something which is antagonistic and dangerous to itself. Their trick in dealing with the exceptions above them, the strong, the mighty, the wise, and the fruitful, is to persuade them to become guardians, herdsmen, and watchmen—in fact, to become their *headservants:* thus they convert a danger into a thing which is useful. In the middle, fear ceases: here a man is alone with nothing; here there is not much room even for misunderstandings; here there is equality; here a man's individual existence is not felt as a reproach, but as the *right* existence; here contentment reigns supreme. Mistrust is active only towards the exceptions; to be an exception is to be a sinner.

IV

The whole of the morality of Europe is based upon the values *which are useful to the herd:* the sorrow of all higher and exceptional men is explained by the fact that everything which distinguishes them from others reaches their consciousness in the form of a feeling of their own smallness and egregiousness. It is the *virtues* of modern men which are the causes of pessimistic gloominess; the mediocre, like the herd, are not troubled much with questions or with conscience—they are cheerful. (Among the gloomy strong men, Pascal and Schopenhauer are noted examples.)

The more dangerous a quality seems to the herd, the more completely it is condemned.

V

A CRITICISM OF THE VIRTUES OF THE HERD. Inertia is active: (1) In confidence, because mistrust makes suspense, reflection, and observation necessary. (2) In veneration, where the gulf that separates power is great and submission necessary: then, so that fear may cease to exist, everybody tries to love and esteem, while the difference in power is interpreted as a difference of value: and thus the relationship to the powerful *no longer has anything revolting in it.* (3) In the sense of truth. What is truth? Truth is that explanation of things which causes us the smallest amount of mental exertion (apart from this, lying is extremely fatiguing). (4) In sympathy. It is a relief to know one's self on the same level with all, to feel as all feel, and to *accept* a belief which is already current; it is something passive beside the activity which appropriates and continually carries into practice the most individual rights of valuation (the latter process allows of no repose). (5) In impartiality and coolness of judgment: people scout the strain of being moved, and prefer to be detached and "objective." (6) In uprightness: people prefer to obey a law which is to hand rather than to *create* a new one, rather than to command themselves and others; the fear of commanding—it is better to submit than to rebel. (7) In toleration; the fear of exercising a right or of enforcing a judgment.

VI

My teaching is this, that the herd seeks to maintain and preserve one type of man, and that it defends itself on two sides—that is to say, against those which are decadents from its ranks (criminals, etc.), and against those who rise superior to its dead level. The instincts of the herd tend to a stationary state of society; they merely preserve. They have no creative power. . . .

VII

THE ROOT OF ALL EVIL. That the slave morality of modesty, chastity, selflessness, and absolute obedience should have triumphed. Dominating natures were thus condemned (1) to hypocrisy, (2) to qualms of conscience—creative natures regarded themselves as rebels against God, uncertain and hemmed in by eternal values. . . .

VIII

My ultimate conclusion is, that the *real* man represents a much higher value than the "desirable" man of any ideal that has ever existed hitherto; that all "desiderata" in regard to mankind have been absurd and dangerous dissipations by means of which a particular kind of man has sought to establish *his* measures of preservation and of growth as a law for all; that every "desideratum" of this kind which has been made to dominate has *reduced* man's worth, his strength, and his trust in the future; that the indigence and mediocre intellectuality of man becomes most apparent, even today, when he reveals a *desire;* that man's ability to fix values has hitherto been developed too inadequately to do justice to the actual, not merely to the "desirable," *worth of man;* that, up to the present, ideals have really been the power which has most slandered man and the world, the poisonous fumes which have hung over reality, and which have *seduced men to yearn for nonentity.* . . .

IX

The question, and at the same time the task, is approaching with hesitation, terrible as Fate, but nevertheless inevitable: how shall the earth as a whole be ruled? And to what end shall man as a whole—no longer as a people or as a race—be reared and trained?

Legislative moralities are the principal means by which one can form mankind, according to the fancy of a creative and profound will: provided, of course, that such an artistic will of the first order gets the power into its own hands, and can make its creative will prevail over long periods in the form of legislation, religions, and morals. At present, and probably for some time to come, one will seek such colossally creative men, such really great men, as I understand them, in vain: they will be lacking, until, after many disappointments, we are forced to begin to understand why it is they are lacking, and that nothing bars with greater hostility their rise and development, at present and for some time to come, than that which is now called *the* morality in Europe. Just as if there were no other kind of morality, and could be no other kind, than the one we have already characterized as herd-morality. It is this morality which is now striving with all its power to attain to that green-meadow happiness on earth, which consists in security, absence of danger, ease, facilities for livelihood, and, last but not least, "if all goes well," even hopes to dispense with all kinds of shepherds and bellwethers. The two doctrines which it preaches most universally are "equality of rights" and "pity for all sufferers"—and it even regards suffering itself as something which must be got rid of absolutely. That such ideas may be modern leads one to think very poorly of modernity. He, however, who has reflected deeply concerning the question, how and where the plant man has hitherto grown most vigorously, is forced to believe that this has always taken place under the opposite conditions; that to this end the danger of the situation has to increase enormously, his inventive faculty and dissembling powers have to fight their way under long oppression and compulsion, and his will to life has to be increased to the unconditioned will to power, to over-power: he believes that danger, severity, violence, peril in the street and in the heart, inequality of rights, secrecy, stoicism, seductive art, and devilry of every kind—in short, the opposite of all gregarious desiderata—are necessary for the elevation of man. Such a morality with opposite designs, which would rear man upwards instead of to comfort and mediocrity; such a morality, with the intention of producing a ruling caste—the future lords of the earth—must, in order to be taught at all, introduce itself as if it were in some way correlated to the prevailing moral law, and must come forward under the cover of the latter's words and forms. But seeing that, to this end, a host of transitionary and deceptive measures must be discovered, and that the life of a single individual stands for almost nothing in view of the accomplishment of such lengthy tasks and aims, the first thing must be done is to rear a *new kind* of man in whom the duration of the necessary will and the necessary instincts is guaranteed for many generations. This must be a new kind of ruling species

and caste—this ought to be quite as clear as the somewhat lengthy and not easily expressed consequences of this thought. The aim should be to prepare a *transvaluation of values* for a particularly strong kind of man, most highly gifted in intellect and will, and, to this end, slowly and cautiously to liberate in him a whole host of slandered instincts hitherto held in check: whoever meditates about this problem belongs to us, the free spirits. . . .

X

Any doctrine would be superfluous for which everything is not already prepared in the way of accumulated forces and explosive material. A transvaluation of values can only be accomplished when there is a tension of new needs, and a new set of needy people who feel all old values as painful—although they are not conscious of what is wrong.

XI

These are the things I demand of you—however badly they may sound in your ears: that you subject moral valuations themselves to criticism. That you should put a stop to your instinctive moral impulse—which in this case demands submission and not criticism—with the question: "why precisely submission?" That this yearning for a "why?"—for a criticism of morality should not only be your present form of morality, but the sublimest of all moralities, and an honour to yourselves and to the age you live in. . . .

XII

The Lawgivers of the Future. After having tried for a long time in vain to attach a particular meaning to the word "philosopher"—for I found many antagonistic traits—I recognised that we can distinguish between two kinds of philosophers:—

(1) Those who desire to establish any large system of values (logical or moral);

(2) Those who are the *lawgivers* of such valuations.

The former try to seize upon the world of the present or the past, by embodying or abbreviating the multifarious phenomena by means of signs: their object is to make it possible for us to survey, to reflect upon, to comprehend, and to utilise everything that has happened hitherto—they serve the purpose of man by using all past things to the benefit of his future.

The second class, however, are *commanders;* they say: "Thus shall it be!" They alone determine the "whither" and the "wherefore," and that which will be useful and beneficial to man; they have command over the previous work of scientific men, and all knowledge is to them only a means to their creations. This second kind of philosopher seldom appears; and as a matter of fact their situation and their danger is appalling. How often have they not intentionally blindfolded their eyes in order to shut out the sight of the small strip of ground which separates them from the abyss and from utter destruction. Plato, for instance, when he persuaded himself that "the good," as he wanted it, was not Plato's good, but "the good in itself," the eternal treasure which a certain man of the name of Plato had chanced to find on his way! This same will to blindness prevails in a much coarser form in the case of the founders of religion; their "Thou shalt" must on no account sound to their ears like "I will"—they only dare to pursue their task as if under the command of God; their legislation of values can only be a burden they can bear if they regard it as "revelation," in this way their conscience is not crushed by the responsibility.

As soon as those two comforting expedients—that of Plato and that of Muhammed—have been overthrown, and no thinker can any longer relieve his conscience with the hypothesis "God" or "eternal values," the claim of the lawgiver to determine new values rises to an awfulness which has not yet been experienced. . . .

Beyond Good and Evil

I

I insist upon it that people finally cease confounding philosophical workers, and in general scientific men, with philosophers—that precisely here one should strictly give "each his own," and not give those far too much, these far too little. It may be necessary for the education of the real philosopher that he himself should have once stood upon all those steps upon which his servants, the scientific workers of philosophy, remain standing, and *must* remain standing: he himself must perhaps have been critic, and dogmatist, and historian, and besides, poet, and collector, and traveler, and riddle-reader, and moralist, and seer, and "free spirit," and almost everything, in order to traverse the whole range of human values and estimations, and that he may *be able* with a variety of eyes and consciences to look from a height to any distance, from a depth up to any height, from a nook into any expanse. But all these are only preliminary conditions for his task; this task itself demands something else—it requires him *to create values*. The philosophical workers, after the excellent pattern of Kant and Hegel, have to fix and formalise some great existing body of valuations—that is to say, former *determinations of value*, creations of value, which have become prevalent, and are for a time called "truths"—whether in the domain of the *logical*, the *political* (moral), or the *artistic*. It is for those investigators to make whatever has happened and been esteemed hitherto, conspicuous, conceivable, intelligible, and manageable, to shorten everything long, even "time" itself, and to *subjugate* the entire past: an immense and wonderful task, in the carrying out of which all refined pride, all tenacious will, can surely find satisfaction. *The real philosophers, however, are commanders and law-givers;* they say: "Thus *shall* it be!" They determine first the Whither and the Why of mankind, and thereby set aside the previous labor of all philosophical workers, and all subjugators of the past—they grasp at the future with a creative hand, and whatever is and was, becomes for them thereby a means, an instrument, and a hammer. Their "knowing" is *creating,* their creating is a law-giving, their will to truth is—*Will to Power.*—Are there at present such philosophers? Have there ever been such philosophers? *Must* there not be such philosophers some day? . . .

II

It is always more obvious to me that the philosopher, as a man *indispensable* for the morrow and the day after the morrow, has ever found himself, and *has been obliged* to find himself, in contradiction to the day in which he lives; his enemy has always been the ideal of his day. Hitherto all those extraordinary furtherers of humanity whom one calls philosophers—who rarely regarded themselves as lovers of wisdom, but rather as disagreeable fools and dangerous interrogators—have found their mission, their hard, involuntary, imperative mission (in the end however the greatness of their mission), in being the bad conscience of their age. In putting the vivisector's knife to the breast of the very *virtues of their age,* they have betrayed their own secret; it has been for the sake of a *new* greatness of man, a new untrodden path to his aggrandizement. They have always disclosed how much hypocrisy, indolence, self-indulgence, and self-neglect, how much falsehood was concealed under the most venerated types of contemporary morality, how much virtue was *outlived;* they have always said: "We must remove hence to where *you* are least at home." . . .

Critique of Normative Theories—Further Readings Primarily Related to Nietzsche

Copleston, Frederick, S. J., *A History of Philosophy,* Vol. VII (Westminster, Md.: Newman, 1963), Chaps. 21–22. Exposition and criticism.

Danto, Arthur C., *Nietzsche as Philosopher* (New York: Macmillan, 1965). A general and systematic treatment of Nietzsche's philosophy.

Hollingdale, R. J., *Nietzsche* (London: Routledge and Kegan Paul, 1973). A general treatment of Nietzsche's work for the nonspecialist.

——, *Nietzsche: The Man and His Philosophy* (London: Routledge and Kegan Paul, 1965). Biography of Nietzsche's life and thought.

Kaufmann, Walter, "How Nietzsche Revolutionized Ethics," in *From Shakespeare to Existentialism* (rev. ed., Garden City: N.Y.: Doubleday, 1960).

——, *Nietzsche: Philosopher, Psychologist, Antichrist* (3d ed., Princeton, N.J.: Princeton U.P., 1968). Comprehensive coverage of Nietzsche's thought with background on his life.

Jaspers, Karl, *Nietzsche: An Introduction to the Understanding of His Philosophical Activity*, trans. by Charles F. Wallraff and Frederick J. Schmitz (Tuscon: U. of Arizona Press, 1965). Treats Nietzsche's life and philosophy.

Morgan, George A., Jr., *What Nietzsche Means* (Cambridge, Mass.: Harvard U.P., 1941). General treatment of Nietzsche's philosophy.

Nietzsche, Friedrich, *Beyond Good and Evil* (1886).

——, *On the Genealogy of Morals* (1887).

——, *The Will to Power* (1909–1910).

——, *Thus Spoke Zarathustra* (1883–1885).

Solomon, Robert C., (ed.), *Nietzsche: A Collection of Critical Essays* (New York: Doubleday, 1973). Twenty-one selections treating different aspects of Nietzsche's philosophy.

36

Existentialism

JEAN-PAUL SARTRE

Atheistic existentialism, which I represent, . . . states that if God does not exist, there is at least one being in whom existence precedes essence, a being who exists before he can be defined by any concept, and that this being is man, or, . . . human reality. What is meant here by saying that existence precedes essence? It means that, first of all, man exists, turns up, appears on the scene, and, only afterwards, defines himself. If man, as the existentialist conceives him, is indefinable, it is because at first he is nothing. Only afterward will he be something, and he himself will have made that he will be. Thus, there is no human nature, since there is no God to conceive it. Not only is man what he conceives himself to be, but he is also only what he wills himself to be after this thrust toward existence.

Man is nothing else but what he makes of himself. Such is the first principle of existentialism. It is also what is called subjectivity the name we are labeled with when charges are brought against us. But what do we mean by this, if not that man has a greater dignity than a stone or table? For we mean that man first exists, that is, that man first of all is the being who hurls himself toward a future and who is conscious of imagining himself as being in the future. Man is at the start a plan which is aware of itself, rather than a patch of moss, a piece of garbage, or a cauliflower; nothing exists prior to this plan; there is nothing in

FROM *Existentialism* by Jean-Paul Sartre. Translated by Bernard Frechtman. Copyrighted 1947 by Philosophical Library, Inc., New York. Reprinted by permission of Philosophical Library, Inc.

heaven; man will be what he will have planned to be. Not what he will want to be. Because by the word "will" we generally mean a conscious decision, which is subsequent to what we have already made of ourselves. I may want to belong to a political party, write a book, get married; but all that is only a manifestation of an earlier, more spontaneous choice that is called "will." But if existence really does precede essence, man is responsible for what he is. Thus, existentialism's first move is to make every man aware of what he is and to make the full responsibility of his existence rest on him. And when we say that a man is responsible for himself, we do not only mean that he is responsible for his own individuality, but that he is responsible for all men.

The word subjectivism has two meanings, and our opponents play on the two. Subjectivism means, on the one hand, that an individual chooses and makes himself; and, on the other, that it is impossible for man to transcend human subjectivity. The second of these is the essential meaning of existentialism. When we say that man chooses his own self, we mean that every one of us does likewise; but we also mean by that that in making this choice he also chooses all men. In fact, in creating the man that we want to be, there is not a single one of our acts which does not at the same time create an image of man as we think he ought to be. To choose to be this or that is to affirm at the same time the value of what we choose, because we can never choose evil. We always choose the good, and nothing can be good for us without being good for all.

If, on the other hand, existence precedes essence, and if we grant that we exist and fashion our image at one and the same time, the image is valid for everybody and for our whole age. Thus, our responsibility is much greater than we might have supposed, because it involves all mankind. If I am a workingman and choose to join a Christian trade-union rather than be a communist, and if by being a member I want to show that the best thing for man is resignation, that the kingdom of man is not of this world, I am not only involving my own case—I want to be resigned for everyone. As a result, my action has involved all humanity. To take a more individual matter, if I want to marry, to have children; even if this marriage depends solely on my own circumstances or passion or wish, I am involving all humanity in monogamy and not merely myself. Therefore, I am responsible for myself and for everyone else. I am creating a certain image of man of my own choosing. In choosing myself, I choose man.

This helps us understand what the actual content is of such rather grandiloquent words as anguish, forlornness, despair. As you will see, it's all quite simple.

First, what is meant by anguish? The existentialists say at once that man is anguish. What that means is this: the man who involves himself and who realizes that he is not only the person he chooses to be, but also a law-maker who is, at the same time, choosing all mankind as well as himself, can not help escape the feeling of his total and deep responsibility. Of course, there are many people who are not anxious; but we claim that they are hiding their anxiety, that they are fleeing from it. Certainly, many people believe that when they do something, they themselves are the only ones involved, and when someone says to them, "What if everyone acted that way?" they shrug their shoulders and answer, "Everyone doesn't act that way." But really, one should always ask himself, "What would happen if everybody looked at things that way?" There is no escaping this disturbing thought except by a kind of double-dealing. A man who lies and makes excuses for himself by saying "not everybody does that," is someone with an uneasy conscience, because the act of lying implies that a universal value is conferred upon the lie.

Anguish is evident even when it conceals itself. This is the anguish that Kierkegaard called the anguish of Abraham. You know the story: an angel has ordered Abraham to sacrifice his son; if it really were an angel who has come and said, "You are Abraham, you shall sacrifice your son," everything would be all right. But everyone might first wonder, "Is it really an angel, and am I really Abraham? What proof do I have?"

There was a madwoman who had hallucinations; someone used to speak to her on the telephone and give her orders. Her doctor asked her, "Who is it who talks to you?" She answered, "He says it's God." What proof did she really have that it was God? If an angel comes to me, what proof is there that it's an angel? And if I hear voices, what proof is there that they come from heaven and not from hell, or from the subconscious, or a pathological condition? What proves that they are addressed to me? What proof is there that I have been appointed to impose my choice and my conception of man on humanity? I'll never find any proof or sign to convince me of that. If a voice addresses me, it is always for me to decide that this is the angel's voice; if I consider that such an act is a good one, it is I who will choose to say that it is good rather than bad.

Now, I'm not being singled out as an Abraham, and yet at every moment I'm obliged to perform exemplary acts. For every man, everything happens as if all mankind had its eyes fixed on him and were guiding itself by what he does. And every man ought to say to himself, "Am I really the kind of man who has the right to act in such a way that humanity might guide itself by my actions?" And if he does not say that to himself, he is masking his anguish.

There is no question here of the kind of anguish which would lead to quietism, to inaction. It is a matter of a simple sort of anguish that anybody who has had responsibilities is familiar with. For example, when a military officer takes the responsibility for an attack and sends a certain number of men to death, he chooses to do so, and in the main he alone makes the choice. Doubtless, orders come from above, but they are too broad; he interprets them, and on this interpretation depend the lives of ten or fourteen or twenty men. In making a decision he can not help having a certain anguish. All leaders know this anguish. That doesn't keep them from acting; on the contrary, it is the very condition of their action. For it implies that they envisage a number of possibilities, and when they choose one, they realize that it has value only because it is chosen. We shall see that this kind of anguish, which is the kind that existentialism describes, is explained, in addition, by a direct responsibility to the other men whom it involves. It is not a curtain separating us from action, but is part of action itself.

When we speak of forlornness, . . . we mean only that God does not exist and that we have to face all the consequences of this. The existentialist is strongly opposed to a certain kind of secular ethics which would like to abolish God with the least possible expense. About 1880, some French teachers tried to set up a secular ethics which went something like this: God is a useless and costly hypothesis; we are discarding it; but, meanwhile, in order for there to be an ethics, a society, a civilization, it is essential that certain values be taken seriously and that they be considered as having an *a priori* existence. It must be obligatory, *a priori*, to be honest, not to lie, not to beat your wife, to have children, etc., etc. So we're going to try a little device which will make it possible to show that values exist all the same, inscribed in a heaven of ideas, though otherwise God does not exist. In other words—and this, I believe, is the tendency of everything called reformism in France—nothing will be changed if God does not exist. We shall find ourselves with the same norms of honesty, progress, and humanism and we shall have made of God an outdated hypothesis which will peacefully die off by itself.

The existentialist, on the contrary, thinks it very distressing that God does not exist, because all possibility of finding values in a heaven of ideas disappears along with Him; there can no longer be an *a priori* Good, since there is no infinite and perfect consciousness to think it. Nowhere is it written that the Good exists, that we must be honest, that we must not lie; because the fact is we are on a plane where there are only men. Dostoievsky said, "If God didn't exist, everything would be possible." That is the very starting point of existentialism. Indeed, everything is permissible if God does not exist, and as a result man is forlorn, because neither within him nor without does he find anything to cling to He can't start making excuses for himself.

If existence really does precede essence, there is no explaining things away by reference to a fixed and given human nature. In other words, there is no determinism, man is free, man is freedom. On the other hand, if God does not exist, we find no values or commands to turn to which legitimize our conduct. So, in the bright realm of values, we have no excuse behind us, nor justification before us. We are alone, with no excuses.

That is the idea I shall try to convey when I say that man is condemned to be free. Condemned, because he did not create himself, yet, in other respects is free; because, once thrown into the world, he is responsible for everything he does. The existentialist does not believe in the power of passion. He will never agree that a sweeping passion is a ravaging torrent which fatally leads a man to certain acts and is therefore an excuse. He thinks that man is responsible for his passion.

The existentialist does not think that man is going to help himself by finding in the world some omen by which to orient himself. Because he thinks that man will interpret the omen to suit himself. Therefore, he thinks that man, with no support and no aid, is condemned every moment to invent man. . . .

To give you an example which will enable you to understand forlornness better, I shall cite the case of one of my students who came to see me under the following circumstances: his father was on bad terms with his mother, and, moreover, was inclined to be a collaborationist; his older brother had been killed in the German offensive of 1940, and the young man, with somewhat immature but generous feelings, wanted to avenge him. His mother lived alone with him, very much upset by the half-treason of her husband and the death of her older son; the boy was her only consolation.

The boy was faced with the choice of leaving for England and joining the Free French Forces—that is, leaving his mother behind—or remaining with his mother and helping her to carry on. He was fully aware that the woman lived only for him and that his going-off—and perhaps his death—would plunge her into despair. He was also aware that every act that he did for his mother's sake was a sure thing, in the sense that it was helping her to carry on, whereas every effort he made toward going off and fighting was an uncertain move which might run aground and prove completely useless; for example, on his way to England he might, while passing through Spain, be detained indefinitely in a Spanish camp; he might reach England or Algiers and be stuck in an office at a desk job. As a result, he was faced with two very different kinds of action: one, concrete, immediate, but concerning only one individual; the other concerned an incomparably vaster group, a national collectivity, but for that very reason was dubious, and might be interrupted en route. And, at the same time, he was wavering between two kinds of ethics. On the one hand, an ethics of sympathy, of personal devotion; on the other, a broader ethics, but one whose efficacy was more dubious. He had to choose between the two.

Who could help him choose? Christian doctrine? No. Christian doctrine says, "Be charitable, love your neighbor, take the more rugged path, etc., etc." But which is the more rugged path? Whom should he love as a brother? The fighting man or his mother? Which does the greater good, the vague act of fighting in a group, or the concrete one of helping a particular human being to go on living? Who can decide *a priori*? Nobody. No book of ethics can tell him. The Kantian ethics says, "Never treat any person as a means, but as an end." Very well, if I stay with my mother, I'll treat her as an end and not as a means; but by virtue of this very fact, I'm running the risk of treating the people around me who are fighting, as means; and, conversely, if I go to join those who are fighting, I'll be treating them as an end, and, by doing that, I run the risk of treating my mother as a means.

If values are vague, and if they are always too broad for the concrete and specific case that we are considering, the only thing left for us is trust our instincts. That's what this young man tried to do; and when I saw him, he said, "In the end, feeling is what counts. I ought to choose whichever pushes me in one direction. If I feel that I love my mother enough to sacrifice everything else for her—my desire for vengeance, for action, for adventure—then I'll stay with her. If, on the contrary, I feel that my love for my mother isn't enough, I'll leave."

But how is the value of a feeling determined? What gives his feeling for his mother value? Precisely the fact that he remained with her. I may say that I like so-and-so well enough to sacrifice a certain amount of money for him, but I may say so only if I've done it. I may say "I love my mother well enough to remain with her" if I have remained with her. The only way to determine the value of this affection is, precisely, to perform an act which confirms and defines it. But, since I require this affection to justify my act, I find myself caught in a vicious circle. . . .

In other words, the feeling is formed by the acts one performs; so, I can not refer to it in order to act upon it. Which means that I can neither seek within myself the true condition which will impel me to act, nor apply to a system of ethics for concepts which will permit me to act. You will say, "At least, he did go to a teacher for advice." But if you seek advice from a priest, for example, you have chosen this priest; you already knew, more or less, just about what advice he was going to give you. In other words, choosing your adviser is involving yourself. The proof of this is that if you are a Christian, you will say, "Consult a priest." But some priests are collaborating, some are just marking time, some are resisting. Which to choose? If the young man chooses a priest who is resisting or collaborating, he has already decided on the kind of advice he's going to get. Therefore, in coming to see me he knew the answer I was going to give him, and I had only one answer to give: "You're free, choose, that is, invent." No general ethics can show you what is to be done; there are no omens in the world. The Catholics will reply, "But there are." Granted—but, in any case, I myself choose the meaning they have.

When I was a prisoner, I knew a rather remarkable young man who was a Jesuit. He had entered the Jesuit order in the following way: he had had a number of very bad breaks; in childhood, his father died, leaving him in poverty, and he was a scholarship student at a religious institution where he was constantly made to feel that he was being kept out of charity; then, he failed to get any of the honors and distinctions that children like; later on, at about eighteen, he bungled a love affair; finally, at twenty-two, he failed in military training, a childish enough matter, but it was the last straw.

This young fellow might well have felt that he had botched everything. It was a sign of something, but of what? He might have taken refuge in bitterness or despair. But he very wisely looked upon all this as a sign that he was not made for secular triumphs, and that only the triumphs of religion, holiness, and faith were open to him. He saw the hand of God in all this, and so he entered the order. Who can help seeing that he alone decided what the sign meant?

Some other interpretation might have been drawn from this series of setbacks; for example, that he might have done better to turn carpenter or revolutionist. Therefore, he is fully responsible for the interpretation. Forlornness implies that we ourselves choose our being. Forlornness and anguish go together.

As for despair, the term has a very simple meaning. It means that we shall confine ourselves to reckoning only with what depends upon our will, or on the ensemble of probabilities which make our action possible. When we want something, we always have to reckon with probabilities. I may be counting on the arrival of a friend. The friend is coming by rail or street-car; this supposes that the train will arrive on schedule, or that the street-car will not jump the track. I am left in the realm of possibility; but possibilities are to be reckoned with only to the point where my action comports with the ensemble of these possibilities, and no further. The moment the possibilities I am considering are not rigorously involved by my action, I ought to disengage myself from them, because no God, no scheme, can adapt the world and its possibilities to my will. When Descartes said, "Conquer yourself rather than the world," he meant essentially the same thing. . . .

We are told, "So you're able to do anything, no matter what!" This is expressed in various ways. First we are accused of anarchy; then they say, "You're unable to pass judgment on others, because there's no reason to prefer one configuration to another"; finally they tell us, "Everything is arbitrary in this choosing of yours. You take something from one pocket and pretend you're putting it into the other."

These three objections aren't very serious. Take the first objection. "You're able to do anything, no matter what" is not to the point. In one sense choice is possible, but what is not possible is not to choose. I can always choose, but I ought to know that if I do not choose, I am still choosing. Though this may seem purely formal, it is highly important for keeping fantasy and caprice within bounds. If it is true that in facing a situation, for example, one in which, as a person capable of having sexual relations, of having children, I am obliged to choose an attitude, and if I in any way assume responsibility for a choice which, in involving myself, also involves all mankind, this has nothing to do with caprice, even if no *a priori* value determines my choice.

If anybody thinks that he recognizes here Gide's theory of the arbitrary act, he fails to see the enormous difference between this doctrine and Gide's. Gide does not know what a situation is. He acts out of pure caprice. For us, on the contrary, man is in an organized situation in which he himself is involved. Through his choice, he involves all mankind, and he can not avoid making a choice: either he will remain chaste, or he will marry and have children; anyhow, whatever he may do, it is impossible for him not to take full responsibility for the way he handles this problem. Doubtless, he chooses without refering to pre-established values, but it is unfair to accuse him of caprice. Instead, let us say that moral choice is to be compared to the making of a work of art. And before going any further, let it be said at once that we are not dealing here with an aesthetic ethics, because our opponents are so dishonest that they even accuse us of that. The example I've chosen is a comparison only.

Having said that, may I ask whether anyone has ever accused an artist who has painted a picture of not having drawn his inspiration from rules set up *a priori*? Has anyone ever asked, "What painting ought he to make?" It is clearly understood that there is no definite painting to be made, that the artist is engaged in the making of his painting, and that the painting to be made is precisely the painting he will have made. It is clearly understood that there are no *a priori* aesthetic values, but that there are values which appear subsequently in the coherence of the painting, in the correspondence between what the artist intended and the result. Nobody can tell what the painting of tomorrow will be like. Painting can be judged only after it has once been made. What connection does that have with ethics? We are in the same creative situation. We never say that a work of art is arbitrary. When we speak of a canvas of Picasso, we never say that it is arbitrary; we understand quite well that he was making himself what he is at the very time he was painting, that the ensemble of his work is embodied in his life.

The same holds on the ethical plane. What art and ethics have in common is that we have creation and invention in both cases. We can not decide *a priori* what there is to be done. I think that I pointed that out quite sufficiently when I mentioned the case of the student who came to see me, and who might have applied to all the ethical systems, Kantian or otherwise, without getting any sort of guidance. He was obliged to devise his law himself. Never let it be said by us that this man—who, taking affection, individual action, and kind-heartedness toward a specific person as his ethical first principle, chooses to remain with his mother, or who, preferring to make a sacrifice, chooses to go to England—has made an arbitrary choice. Man makes himself. He isn't ready made at the start. In choosing his ethics, he makes himself and force of circumstances is such that he can not abstain from choosing one. We define man only in relationship to involvement. It is therefore absurd to charge us with arbitrariness of choice.

In the second place, it is said that we are unable to pass judgment on others. In a way this is true, and in another way, false. It is true in this sense, that, whenever a man sanely and sincerely involves himself and chooses his configuration, it is impossible for him to prefer another configuration, regardless of what his own may be in other respects. It is true in this sense, that we do not believe in progress. Progress is betterment. Man is always the same. The situation confronting him varies. Choice always remains a choice in a situation. The problem has not changed since the time one could choose between those for and those against slavery, for example, at the time of the Civil War, and the present time, when one can side with the Maquis Resistance Party, or with the Communists.

But, nevertheless, one can still pass judgment, for, as I have said, one makes a choice in relationship to others. First, one can judge (and this is perhaps not a judgment of value, but a logical judgment) that certain choices are based on error and others on truth. If we have defined man's situation as a free choice, with no excuses and no recourse, every man who takes refuge behind the excuse of his passions, every man who sets up a determinism, is a dishonest man.

The objection may be raised, "But why mayn't he choose himself dishonestly?" I reply that I am not obliged to pass moral judgment on him, but that I do define his dishonesty as an error. One can not help considering the truth of the matter. Dishonesty is obviously a falsehood because it belies the complete freedom of involvement. On the same grounds, I maintain that there is also dishonesty if I choose to state that certain values exist prior to me; it is self-contradictory for me to want them and at the same state that they are imposed on me. Suppose someone says to me, "What if I want to be dishonest?" I'll answer, "There's no reason for you not to be, but I'm saying that that's what you are, and that the strictly coherent attitude is that of honesty."

Besides, I can bring moral judgment to bear. When I declare that freedom in every concrete circumstance can have no other aim than to want itself, if man has once become aware that in his forlornness he imposes values, he can no longer want but one thing, and that is freedom, as the basis of all values. That doesn't mean that he wants it in the abstract. It means simply that the ultimate meaning of the acts of honest men is the quest for freedom as such. A man who belongs to a communist or revolutionary union wants concrete goals; these goals imply an abstract desire for freedom; but this freedom is wanted in something concrete. We want freedom for freedom's sake and in every particular circumstance. And in wanting freedom we discover that it depends entirely on the freedom of others, and that the freedom of others depends on ours. Of course, freedom as the definition of man does not depend on others, but as soon as there is involvement, I am obliged to want others to have freedom at the same time that I want my own freedom. I can take freedom as my goal only if I take that of others as a goal as well. Consequently, when, in all honesty, I've recognized that man is a being in whom existence precedes essence, that he is a free being who, in various circumstances, can want only his freedom, I have at the same time recognized that I can want only the freedom of others.

Therefore, in the name of this will for freedom, which freedom itself implies, I may pass judgment on those who seek to hide from themselves the complete arbitrariness and the complete freedom of their existence. Those who hide their complete freedom from themselves out of a spirit of seriousness or by means of deterministic excuses, I shall call cowards; those who try to show that their existence was necessary, when it is the very contingency of man's appearance on earth, I shall call stinkers. But cowards or stinkers can be judged only from a strictly unbiased point of view.

Therefore though the content of ethics is variable, a certain form of it is universal. Kant says that freedom desires both itself and the freedom of others. Granted. But he believes that the formal and the universal are enough to constitute an ethics. We, on the other hand, think that principles which are too abstract run aground in trying to decide action. Once again, take the case of the student. In the name of what, in the name of what great moral maxim do you think he could have decided, in perfect peace of mind, to abandon his mother or to stay with her? There is no way of judging. The content is always concrete and thereby unforeseeable; there is always the element of invention. The one thing that counts is knowing whether the inventing that has been done, has been done in the name of freedom.

For example, let us look at the following two cases. You will see to what extent they correspond, yet differ. Take *The Mill on the Floss*. We find a certain young girl, Maggie Tulliver, who is an embodiment of the value of passion and who is aware of it. She is in love with a young man, Stephen, who is engaged to an insignificant young girl. This Maggie Tulliver, instead of heedlessly preferring her own happiness, chooses, in the name of human solidarity, to sacrifice herself and give up the man she loves. On the other hand, Sanseverina, in *The Charter-house of Parma*, believing that passion is man's true value, would say that a great love deserves sacrifices; that it is to be preferred to the banality of the conjugal love that would tie Stephen to the young ninny he had to marry. She would choose to sacrifice the girl and fulfil her happiness; and, as Stendhal shows, she is even ready to sacrifice herself for the sake of passion, if this life demands it. Here we are in the presence of two strictly opposed moralities. I claim that they are much the same thing; in both cases what has been set up as the goal is freedom.

You can imagine two highly similar attitudes: one girl prefers to renounce her love out of resignation; another prefers to disregard the prior attachment of the man she loves out of sexual desire. On the surface these two actions resemble those we've just described. However, they are completely different. Sanseverina's attitude is much nearer that of Maggie Tulliver, one of heedless rapacity.

Thus, you see that the second charge is true and, at the same time, false. One may choose anything if it is on the grounds of free involvement.

The third objection is the following: "You take something from one pocket and put it into the other. That is, fundamentally, values aren't serious, since you choose them." My answer to this is that I'm quite vexed that that's the way it is; but if I've discarded God the Father, there has to be someone to invent values. You've got to take things as they are. Moreover, to say that we invent values means nothing else but this: life has no meaning *a priori*. Before you come alive, life is nothing; it's up to you to give it a meaning, and value is nothing else but the meaning that you choose. In that way, you see, there is a possibility of creating a human community.

I've been reproached for asking whether existentialism is humanistic. It's been said, "But you said in *Nausea* that the humanists were all wrong. You made fun of a certain kind of humanist. Why come back to it now?" Actually, the word humanism has two very different meanings. By humanism one can mean a theory which takes man as an end and as a higher value. Humanism in this sense can be found in Cocteau's tale *Around the World in Eighty Hours* when a character, because he is flying over some mountains in an airplane, declares, "Man is simply amazing." That means that I, who did not build the airplanes, shall personally benefit from these particular inventions, and that I, as man, shall personally consider myself responsible for, and honored by, acts of a few particular men. This would imply that we ascribe a value to man on the basis of the highest deeds of certain men. This humanism is absurd, because only the dog or the horse would be able to make such an over-all judgment about man, which they are careful not to do, at least to my knowledge.

But it can not be granted that a man may make a judgment about man. Existentialism spares him from any such judgment. The existentialist will never consider man as an end because he is always in the making. Nor should we believe that there is a mankind to which we might set up a cult in the manner of Auguste Comte. The cult of mankind ends in the self-enclosed humanism of

Comte, and, let it be said, of fascism. This kind of humanism we can do without.

But there is another meaning of humanism. Fundamentally it is this: man is constantly outside of himself; in projecting himself, in losing himself outside of himself, he makes for man's existing; and, on the other hand, it is by pursuing transcendent goals that he is able to exist; man, being this state of passing-beyond, and seizing upon things only as they bear upon this passing-beyond, is at the heart, at the center of this passing-beyond. There is no universe other than a human universe, the universe of human subjectivity. This connection between transcendency, as a constituent element of man—not in the sense that God is transcendent, but in the sense of passing beyond—and subjectivity, in the sense that man is not closed in on himself but is always present in a human universe, is what we call existentialist humanism. Humanism, because we remind man that there is no law-maker other than himself, and that in his forlornness he will decide by himself; because we point out that man will fulfill himself as man, not in turning toward himself, but in seeking outside of himself a goal which is just this liberation, just this particular fulfillment.

Critique of Normative Theories—Further Readings Primarily Related to Sartre

Barnes, Hazel E., *An Existentialist Ethics* (New York: Alfred A. Knopf, 1967; New York: Vintage Books, 1971). An ethics which accepts Sartre's view of man and the world as a starting point.

——, *Sartre* (Philadelphia and New York: Lippincott, 1973). Traces the evolution of Sartre's thought.

de Beauvoir, Simone, *The Ethics of Ambiguity*, trans. by Bernard Frechtman (New York: Philosophical Library, 1948). Proponent of an allied view.

Copleston, Frederick, S. J., *Contemporary Philosophy: Studies of Logical Positivism and Existentialism* (rev. ed., New York: Newman Press, 1972), Chaps. 9–12. Exposition and criticism of both theistic and atheistic existentialism.

Danto, Arthur C., *Jean-Paul Sartre* (New York: Viking, 1975). Exposition and criticism.

Greene, Norman N., *Jean-Paul Sartre: The Existentialist Ethic* (Ann Arbor: U. of Michigan Press, 1960). Exposition.

Kaufmann, Walter, (ed.), *Existentialism from Dostoevsky to Sartre* (New York: Meridian Books, 1956). Selections from nine existentialists, including Sartre, with a helpful introduction.

Manser, Anthony, *Sartre: A Philosophic Study* (Univ. of London: Athlone Press, 1966), especially Chaps. 8–10. Exposition.

McMahon, Joseph H., *Human Beings: The World of Jean-Paul Sartre* (Chicago: U. of Chicago Press, 1971). General treatment of Sartre's philosophy and its development.

Murdoch, Iris, *Sartre: Romantic Rationalist* (New Haven: Yale U.P., 1953). Critical exposition of Sartre's thought based primarily upon his novels.

Olafson, Frederick A., *Principles and Persons: An Ethical Interpretation of Existentialism* (Baltimore: The Johns Hopkins Press, 1967). Sympathetic exposition and defence of the basic ethical views held by Heidegger, Sartre, and Merleau-Ponty.

Plantinga, Alvin, "An Existentialist's Ethics," *Review of Metaphysics*, XII (1958), pp. 235–256. Critic.

Rau, Catherine, "The Ethical Theory of J. P. Sartre," *Journal of Philosophy*, XLVI (1949), pp. 536–545. Critic, dealing with Sartre's views as expressed in *Existentialism and Humanism*.

Sartre, Jean-Paul, *Being and Nothingness*, trans. by Hazel E. Barnes (New York: Philosophical Library, 1956).

——, *No Exit and Three Other Plays*, trans. by Stuart Gilbert and Lionel Abel (New York: Vintage Books, 1955).

——, *The Roads to Freedom:* (1) *The Age of Reason*, trans. by Eric Sutton (New York: Alfred A. Knopf, 1947); (2) *The Reprieve*, trans. by Eric Sutton (New York: Alfred A. Knopf, 1947); (3) *Troubled Sleep*, trans. by Gerard Hopkins (New York: Alfred A. Knopf, 1950). Novels.

——, *The Words*, trans. by Bernard Frechtman (New York: G. Braziller, 1964). Autobiography.

Warnock, Mary, *Existentialist Ethics* (London: Macmillan, 1967). Exposition and criticism of Kierkegaard, Heidegger, and Sartre.

——, *The Philosophy of Sartre* (London: Hutchinson, 1965), especially Chaps. 5 and 6. Exposition and criticism.

III Meta-Ethics: What Do Ethical Terms Mean and Are Ethical Judgments True or False?

From time to time, we have taken note of the fact that, lurking under the great issues of normative ethics, there are criteria of meaning and justification that have, either as unassessed assumptions, or open commitments, helped in significant ways to determine theories of good and evil, right and wrong. This is true from Socrates to the present. Contemporary philosophers have been preoccupied with these issues. This is not only because of their personal interests, but because most of them see that the basic normative issues are contingent upon related conceptions of meaning and definition, justification and proof, verification and truth. Only in modern times, however, has the concern with the meaning of ethical terms and the justification of ethical statements, the topics which roughly circumscribe meta-ethics, been taken to be the whole of ethical philosophy.

Our stance in this text is that meta-ethics is a separate topic, at least in the heuristic sense, a stance which is not intended to commit us to the position that one can, among other things, hold to a meta-ethical position without at the same time being committed to a normative position of some sort. The relationships between normative and meta-ethics are both obvious and not so obvious. It is clear that issues of meaning and definition are related to issues of truth and justification, for it is impossible to know how to verify or to justify a sentence whose meaning is unclear. This is the obvious point. What is not obvious is the answer to the question: "Does commitment to a theory of meaning entail commitment to a normative theory?" And this is in itself a controversial normative issue.*

---

*See Roger Hancock, *Twentieth Century Ethics* (New York: Columbia University Press, 1974), pp. 1–18, 188–197.

Without pretending to cover all the topics which might be considered, our program is as follows. The authors whose work is presented express the ideas and issues which have dominated, and at present dominate, much of twentieth-century controversy. It is generally conceded that the major concern with meta-ethical issues began with the work of G. E. Moore. While there is no common agreement on the terms to be used in classifying Moore and other meta-ethical philosophers, some terms appear with considerable frequency in the literature. We shall use the following terms for our classification.

Those philosophers, like Moore, Ross, contemporary descriptivists, traditional and contemporary utilitarians, who believe that ethical judgments can be *known* to be true or false are, in this respect, called "*cognitivists.*" Those thinkers, such as Ayer, Stevenson, Carnap, and others, including Nietzsche, who maintain that ethical judgments cannot be known to be true or false are called "*non-cognitivists.*"

Classifying ethical theorists in yet another way, "*naturalists*" maintain either that ethical terms can be defined by reference to nonethical properties or that ethical judgments about what ought to be the case are, in some sense, factual judgments about what is the case. Here, one finds most hedonist utilitarians, Dewey, Perry, Foot, Geach, G. J. and Mary Warnock, and perhaps Brandt. "*Non-naturalists*" are those who deny either or both of the views held by naturalists. Among such philosophers are Moore, Ross, Ayer, and Stevenson.

To complicate matters, there are influential borderline cases represented by the work of Hare, Toulmin, Nowell-Smith, and Baier. These philosophers believe that rational and factual considerations provide good reasons for justifying ethical judgments; but they are not prepared to adopt a full-scale cognitivist and naturalist position. We call these thinkers "*quasi-cognitivists*" and "*quasi-naturalists.*"

Taken in historical sequence, the drama of twentieth-century, Anglo-American ethics begins with Moore, who held both a cognitivist and non-naturalist position. Reacting in large part to what were regarded as both weaknesses and strengths in Moore's ethics, a group of thinkers (here represented by Stevenson) rejected Moore's cognitivism but accepted his critique of naturalism. Subsequently, another set of philosophers, including Hare, argued that the non-cognitivism and non-naturalism of someone like Stevenson made ethical judgments untenably arbitrary. They agreed with Stevenson that ethical judgments could not be known to be true or false in the way that we can know the truth or falsity of factual judgments. Nevertheless, they believed that one could show that some ethical judgments were more justified than others by reference to rational and factual considerations. Following this quasi-cognitivist and quasi-naturalist development, we are today witnessing a revival of cognitivism and naturalism in the work of another group of philosophers, represented in the text by Foot and Searle.

A COGNITIVISM AND NON-NATURALISM: *INTUITIONISM AGAIN*

Principia Ethica by G. E. Moore, published in 1903, has preoccupied the attention of moral philosophers ever since. In particular, they tended to follow his lead in placing emphasis upon the relationships between facts and values, and upon the connection (or lack of connection) between judgments about what is and judgments about what ought to be.

Dissatisfied with the continued history of unresolved disagreement in ethics, Moore hoped to remove at least some of this dissatisfaction by carefully clarifying fundamental ethical questions and concepts. Like Socrates, Moore wants first to learn what people mean in using ethical terms before answering the more substantive questions of ethics. In short, with Moore, moral philosophy turns to meta-ethical considerations as fundamental.

From his standpoint, the central question in ethics is how to define "good." He does not want, however, a dictionary definition. For ethical purposes, what is needed is a *real* definition which sets out the property or properties named by the word, "good." But there is a hurdle, in his opinion, which dooms this approach to failure. For such a definition to be possible, the object named by the word must be complex, like, say, "man," which has many different properties. To define "man" in the desired sense is to specify the properties whose presence constitutes the necessary and sufficient conditions for the proper use of the word "man." For ethics, the hurdle, according to Moore, is that "good" does not name a complex object. Therefore, "good" is undefinable! Like yellow, goodness is a simple, unreducible, unanalyzable property. Further, like the yellowness of a visual object, we know directly, and immediately—in other words intuitively—whether an object has the property of goodness.

It is a common and major blunder of ethical philosophy, according to Moore, to attempt to define "good" in terms of some property or properties. Hedonisms, utilitarianisms, cultural relativisms, evolutionary views, all naturalisms, tend to do this, he thinks. Bentham attempted it with pleasure, Spencer with being more evolved, cultural relativism with group approval. Such attempts commit what Moore termed "the naturalistic fallacy." He supports this claim by means of what has been called the "open-question argument." He noted that if good were defined in terms of, say, pleasure, then the question, "Is pleasure good?" would mean, "Is pleasure pleasure?" But this is absurd, because the question, "Is pleasure good?" is an open and meaningful question. A similar argument can be made for whatever other nonethical property might be proposed as a definition of "good." Notice that Moore combines (a) the issue of definition in terms of properties in a general sense, and (b) the issue of defining "good" in terms of naturalistic properties. Notice also that he conceives the meaning of terms as a relation of naming, or reference, between a word and a property or set of properties.

In summary, Moore is a cognitivist in that he believes that "good" names an objective, independent (non-natural) property of things. This property can be known, and sentences predicating goodness of things are true or false. Men directly intuit this property and therefore know what things are good. He is non-naturalistic in that he believes that the property so named is not definable, but rather is simple and unanalyzable. He is a sort of an empiricist, however, in that ethical statements are always synthetic, and based upon some sort of perception-like knowledge—analogous to seeing the property yellow in yellow things.

Although it is not a central point in our selection, Moore also defends a position in normative ethics. He supports the theory that has come to be called "ideal utilitarianism." The theory maintains that right actions are those which produce, cause, bring about effects which involve the maximum amount of intrinsic value—that is, of intuited goodness and good things.

Toulmin shares the desire of most contemporary ethical thinkers: the desire to bridge in some way the logical gap between factual reasons and moral judgments without falling into the naturalistic fallacy, or into subjectivism or emotivism. He wishes, further, to show that ethics is a rational enterprise. And the way to do so, he thinks, is to attack Moore's conception of the meaning and justification of ethical beliefs. Many philosophers have felt strongly, along with Toulmin, that Moore exaggerates the separation between moral and other kinds of judgments, and that the analogy he drew between "yellow" and "good" is weak. As G. J. Warnock puts it,* Moore left moral philosophy with a puzzle, the

*G. J. Warnock, *op. cit.*, p. 16.

"idea that there is a vast corpus of moral facts about the world—known, but we cannot say how; related to other features of the world, but we cannot say why. . . ." William Frankena early pointed out that the naturalistic fallacy was not a fallacy in any traditional logical sense.* Toulmin believes that the basic problem of ethics is to overcome the difficulties in the theories of Moore (and Stevenson, see below). One of the major difficulties is that Moore's theory does not offer criteria of meaning and justification which make it possible to appraise moral argument in practice, or to settle moral disagreements. Moore's conclusions make ethical judgment irrelevant as well as untestable, given the obscurity of intuitionist epistemology. Toulmin believed that any rescue effort by thinkers must begin with a consideration of the uses of ethical language, and proceed from there to a reconsideration of the ways in which reasons support ethical judgments; not, as with Moore, with the analysis and definition of ethical terms. Thus we may discover the main use or uses of ethical judgments and moral terms. Following this line, he concludes that the rational character of ethics involves what he calls *good reasons*, and not correspondence with facts. Toulmin asserts that moral reasoning is practical, and not theoretical. He also believes that meaning is a function of use and is not tied to the model of reference or naming. From these assumptions, it follows that the logical relationship between reasons and the moral judgments they support is not one of entailment. Nevertheless, the relationship is not contingent. On this basis, he thinks that facts and norms can be brought together again. This remarriage of facts and evaluations, however, does not embrace naturalism, because he agrees with Moore that "good" cannot be defined in terms of nonethical properties. It is important to understand that this view does not preclude the use of facts as good reasons in support of moral judgments, and thus Toulmin might be called (along with Nowell-Smith, Hare, and others) a "quasi-naturalist."

We see in our article that part of Toulmin's theory which supports his rejection of Moore's meta-ethics. Toulmin directs his attention to Moore's "property" theory of the meaning of ethical terms, which he believes is one of Moore's most serious mistakes, a mistake all the more important in that it leads to others. Goodness and rightness are not, in Toulmin's opinion, directly perceived properties at all, because words like "good" and "right" are supervenient terms, that is, they depend upon, but do not name, properties. Moore, it will be recalled, was a cognitivist who held that we could intuitively know when the objective property of goodness was present. Yet, in Toulmin's opinion, he dis-

*William Frankena, "The Naturalistic Fallacy," *Mind*, XLVIII, 1939.

pensed with an essential ingredient of knowledge, the need for public verifiability. Other criticisms of Moore will emerge in later articles in this section. But, for many contemporaries, Toulmin made an important advance in the progress toward restoring the rational character of ethics, and towards linking human nature to moral standards. Moore's major confusion probably lies in his failure to separate the meaning of normative words from the criteria used to determine when normative words are correctly used. Toulmin recognized this. Toulmin also recognized another important mistake in Moore's doctrine, the "naming" theory of meaning which confuses the meaning of normative terms with their reference— the view that "good," if it has meaning, must name a property or properties. Toulmin thus was among the leaders in criticizing the assumptions that have led philosophers generally to support intuitionism and emotivism. The latter is the subject of our next section.

37

Good as Simple and Non-Natural

G. E. MOORE

PREFACE

It appears to me that in Ethics, as in all other philosophical studies, the difficulties and disagreements, of which its history is full, are mainly due to a very simple cause: namely to the attempt to answer questions, without first discovering precisely *what* question it is which you desire to answer. I do not know how far this source of error would be done away, if philosophers would *try* to discover what question they were asking, before they set about to answer it; for the work of analysis and distinction is often very difficult: we may often fail to make the necessary discovery, even though we make a definite attempt to do so. But I am inclined to think that in many cases a resolute attempt would be sufficient to ensure success; so that, if only this attempt were made, many of the most glaring difficulties and disagreements in philosophy would disappear. At all events, philosophers seem, in general, not to make the attempt; and, whether in consequence of this omission or not, they are constantly endeavouring to prove that "Yes" or "No" will answer questions, to which *neither* answer is correct, owing to the fact that what they have before their minds is not one question, but several, to some of which the true answer is "No," to others "Yes."

FROM *Principia Ethica* by G. E. Moore. Copyright 1903 by Cambridge University Press.

I have tried . . . to distinguish clearly two kinds of question, which moral philosophers have always professed to answer, but which, as I have tried to shew, they have almost always confused both with one another and with other questions. These two questions may be expressed, the first in the form: What kind of things ought to exist for their own sakes? the second in the form: What kind of actions ought we to perform? I have tried to shew exactly what it is that we ask about a thing, when we ask whether it ought to exist for its own sake, is good in itself or has intrinsic value; and exactly what it is that we ask about an action, when we ask whether we ought to do it, whether it is a right action or a duty.

But from a clear insight into the nature of these two questions, there appears to me to follow a second most important result: namely, what is the nature of the evidence, by which alone any ethical proposition can be proved or disproved, confirmed or rendered doubtful. Once we recognise the exact meaning of the two questions, I think it also becomes plain exactly what kind of reasons are relevant as arguments for or against any particular answer to them. It becomes plain that, for answers to the *first* question, no relevant evidence whatever can be adduced: from no other truth, except themselves alone, can it be inferred that they are either true or false. We can guard against error only by taking care, that, when we try to answer a question of this kind, we have before our minds that question only, and not some other or others; but that there is great danger of such errors of confusion I have tried to shew, and also what are the chief precautions by the use of which we may guard against them. As for the *second* question, it becomes equally plain, that any answer to it *is* capable of proof or disproof—that, indeed, so many different considerations are relevant to its truth or falsehood, as to make the attainment of probability very difficult, and the attainment of certainty impossible. Nevertheless the *kind* of evidence, which is both necessary and alone relevant to such proof and disproof, is capable of exact definition. Such evidence must contain propositions of two kinds and of two kinds only: it must consist, in the first place, of truths with regard to the results of the action in question—of *causal* truths—but it must *also* contain ethical truths of our first or self-evident class. Many truths of both kinds are necessary to the proof that any action ought to be done; and any other kind of evidence is wholly irrelevant. It follows that, if any ethical philosopher offers for propositions of the first kind any evidence whatever, or if, for propositions of the second kind, he either fails to adduce both causal and ethical truths, or adduces truths that are neither, his reasoning has not the least tendency to establish his conclusions. But not only are his conclusions totally devoid of weight: we have, moreover, reason to suspect him of the error of confusion; since the offering of irrelevant evidence generally indicates that the philosopher who offers it has had before his mind, not the question which he professes to answer, but some other entirely different one. Ethical discussion, hitherto, has perhaps consisted chiefly in reasoning of this totally irrelevant kind. . . .

CHAPTER I

5. . . . How "good" is to be defined, is the most fundamental question in all Ethics. That which is meant by "good" is, in fact, except its converse "bad," the *only* simple object of thought which is peculiar to Ethics. Its definition is, therefore, the most essential point in the definition of Ethics; and moreover a mistake with regard to it entails a far larger number of erroneous ethical judgments than any other. Unless this first question be fully understood, and its true answer clearly recognised, the rest of Ethics is as good as useless from the point of view of systematic knowledge. . . .

6. What, then, is good? How is good to be defined? Now, it may be thought that this is a verbal question. A definition does indeed often mean the expressing of one word's meaning in other words. But this is not the sort of definition I am asking for. Such a definition can never be of ultimate importance in any study except lexicography. If I wanted that kind of definition I should have to consider in the first place how people generally used the word "good"; but my business is not with its proper usage, as established by custom. I should, indeed, be foolish, if I tried to use it for something which it did not usually denote: if, for instance, I were to announce that, whenever I used the word "good," I must be understood to be thinking of that object which is usually denoted by the word "table." I shall, therefore, use the word in the sense in which I think it is ordinarily used; but at the same time I am not anxious to discuss whether I am right in thinking that it is so used. My business is solely with that object or idea, which I hold, rightly or wrongly, that the word is generally used to stand for. What I want to discover is the nature of that object or idea, and about this I am extremely anxious to arrive at an agreement.

But, if we understand the question in this sense, my answer to it may seem a very disappointing one. If I am asked "What is good?" my answer is that good is good, and that is the end of the matter. Or if I am asked "How is good to be defined?" my answer is that it cannot be defined, and that is all I have to say about it. But disappointing as these answers may appear, they are of the very last importance. To readers who are familiar with philosophic terminology, I can express their importance by saying that they amount to this: That propositions about the good are all of them synthetic and never analytic; and that is plainly no trivial matter. And the same thing may be expressed more popularly, by saying that, if I am right, then nobody can foist upon us such an axiom as that "Pleasure is the only good" or that "The good is the desired" on the pretence that this is "the very meaning of the word."

7. Let us, then, consider this position. My point is that "good" is a simple notion, just as "yellow" is a simple notion; that, just as you cannot, by any manner of means, explain to any one who does not already know it, what yellow is, so you cannot explain what good is. Definitions of the kind that I was asking for, definitions which describe the real nature of the object or notion denoted by a word, and which do not merely tell us what the word is used to mean, are only possible when the object or notion in question is some-

thing complex. You can give a definition of a horse, because a horse has many different properties and qualities, all of which you can enumerate. But when you have enumerated them all, when you have reduced a horse to his simplest terms, then you can no longer define those terms. They are simply something which you think of or perceive, and to any one who cannot think of or perceive them, you can never, by any definition, make their nature known. It may perhaps be objected to this that we are able to describe to others, objects which they have never seen or thought of. We can, for instance, make a man understand what a chimaera is, although he has never heard of one or seen one. You can tell him that it is an animal with a lioness's head and body, with a goat's head growing from the middle of its back, and with a snake in place of a tail. But here the object which you are describing is a complex object; it is entirely composed of parts, with which we are all perfectly familiar— a snake, a goat, a lioness; and we know, too, the manner in which those parts are to be put together, because we know what is meant by the middle of a lioness's back, and where her tail is wont to grow. And so it is with all objects, not previously known, which we are able to define: they are all complex: all composed of parts, which may themselves, in the first instance, be capable of similar definition, but which must in the end be reducible to simplest parts, which can no longer be defined. But yellow and good, we say, are not complex: they are notions of that simple kind, out of which definitions are composed and with which the power of further defining ceases.

8. When we say, as Webster says, "The definition of horse is 'A hoofed quadruped of the genus Equus,' " we may, in fact, mean three different things. (1) We may mean merely: "When I say 'horse,' you are to understand that I am talking about a hoofed quadruped of the genus Equus." This might be called the arbitrary verbal definition: and I do not mean that good is indefinable in that sense. (2) We may mean, as Webster ought to mean: "When most English people say 'horse,' they mean a hoofed quadruped of the genus Equus." This may be called the verbal definition proper, and I do not say that good is indefinable in this sense either; for it is certainly possible to discover how people use a word: otherwise, we could never have known that "good" may be translated by "gut" in German and by "bon" in French. But (3) we may, when we define horse, mean something much more important. We may mean that a certain object, which we all of us know, is composed in a certain manner: that it has four legs, a head, a heart, a liver, etc., etc., all of them arranged in definite relations to one another. It is in this sense that I deny good to be definable. I say that it is not composed of any parts, which we can substitute for it in our minds when we are thinking of it. We might think just as clearly and correctly about a horse, if we thought of all its parts and their arrangement instead of thinking of the whole: we could, I say, think how a horse differed from a donkey just as well, just as truly, in this way, as now we do, only not so easily; but there is nothing whatsoever which we could so substitute for good; and that is what I mean, when I say that good is indefinable.

9. But I am afraid I have still not removed the chief difficulty which may

prevent acceptance of the proposition that good is indefinable. I do not mean to say that *the* good, that which is good, is thus indefinable; if I did think so, I should not be writing on Ethics, for my main object is to help towards discovering that definition. It is just because I think there will be less risk of error in our search for a definition of "the good," that I am now insisting that *good* is indefinable. I must try to explain the difference between these two. I suppose it may be granted that "good" is an adjective. Well "the good," "that which is good," must therefore be the substantive to which the adjective "good" will apply: it must be the whole of that to which the adjective will apply, and the adjective must *always* truly apply to it. But if it is that to which the adjective will apply, it must be something different from that adjective itself; and the whole of that something different, whatever it is, will be our definition of *the* good. Now it may be that this some thing will have other adjectives, beside "good," that will apply to it. It may be full of pleasure, for example; it may be intelligent: and if these two adjectives are really part of its definition, then it will certainly be true, that pleasure and intelligence are good. And many people appear to think that, if we say "Pleasure and intelligence are good," or if we say "Only pleasure and intelligence are good," we are defining "good." Well, I cannot deny that propositions of this nature may sometimes be called definitions; I do not know well enough how the word is generally used to decide upon this point. I only wish it to be understood that that is not what I mean when I say there is no possible definition of good, and that I shall not mean this if I use the word again. I do most fully believe that some true proposition of the form "Intelligence is good and intelligence alone is good" can be found; if none could be found, our definition of *the* good would be impossible. As it is, I believe *the* good to be definable; and yet I still say that good itself is indefinable.

10. "Good," then, if we mean by it that quality which we assert to belong to a thing, when we say that the thing is good, is incapable of any definition, in the most important sense of that word. The most important sense of "definition" is that in which a definition states what are the parts which invariably compose a certain whole; and in this sense "good" has no definition because it is simple and has no parts. It is one of those innumerable objects of thought which are themselves incapable of definition, because they are the ultimate terms by reference to which whatever *is* capable of definition must be defined. That there must be an indefinite number of such terms is obvious, on reflection; since we cannot define anything except by an analysis, which, when carried as far as it will go, refers us to something, which is simply different from anything else, and which by that ultimate difference explains the peculiarity of the whole which we are defining: for every whole contains some parts which are common to other wholes also. There is, therefore, no intrinsic difficulty in the contention that "good" denotes a simple and indefinable quality. There are many other instances of such qualities.

Consider yellow, for example. We may try to define it, by describing its physical equivalent; we may state what kind of light-vibrations must stimulate the normal eye, in order that we may perceive it. But a moment's reflection is sufficient to shew that those light-vibrations are not themselves what we mean by yellow. *They* are not what we perceive. Indeed we should never have been able to discover their existence, unless we had first been struck by the patent difference of quality between the different colours. The most we can be entitled to say of those vibrations is that they are what corresponds in space to the yellow which we actually perceive.

Yet a mistake of this simple kind has commonly been made about "good." It may be true that all things which are good are *also* something else, just as it is true that all things which are yellow produce a certain kind of vibration in the light. And it is a fact, that Ethics aims at discovering what are those other properties belonging to all things which are good. But far too many philosophers have thought that when they named those other properties they were actually defining good; that these properties, in fact, were simply not "other," but absolutely and entirely the same with goodness. This view I propose to call the "naturalistic fallacy" and of it I shall now endeavour to dispose.

11. Let us consider what it is such philosophers say. And first it is to be noticed that they do not agree among themselves. They not only say that they are right as to what good is, but they endeavour to prove that other people who say that it is something else, are wrong. One, for instance, will affirm that good is pleasure, another, perhaps, that good is that which is desired; and each of these will argue eagerly to prove that the other is wrong. But how is that possible? One of them says that good is nothing but the object of desire, and at the same time tries to prove that it is not pleasure. But from his first assertion, that good just means the object of desire, one of two things must follow as regards his proof:

(1) He may be trying to prove that the object of desire is not pleasure. But, if this be all, where is his Ethics? The position he is maintaining is merely a psychological one. Desire is something which occurs in our minds, and pleasure is something else which so occurs; and our would-be ethical philosopher is merely holding that the latter is not the object of the former. But what has that to do with the question in dispute? His opponent held the ethical proposition that pleasure was the good, and although he should prove a million times over the psychological proposition that pleasure is not the object of desire, he is no nearer proving his opponent to be wrong. The position is like this. One man says a triangle is a circle: another replies "A triangle is a straight line, and I will prove to you that I am right: *for*" (this is the only argument) "a straight line is not a circle." "That is quite true," the other may reply; "but nevertheless a triangle is a circle, and you have said nothing whatever to prove the contrary. What is proved is that one of us is wrong, for we agree that a triangle cannot be both a straight line and a circle: but which is wrong, there can be no earthly means of proving, since you define triangle as straight line and I define it as circle."—Well, that is one alternative which any naturalistic Ethics has to face; if good is *defined* as something else, it is then impossible either to prove that any other definition is wrong or even to deny such definition.

(2) The other alternative will scarcely be more welcome. It is that the discussion is after all a verbal one. When A says "Good means pleasant" and B says "Good means desired," they may merely wish to assert that most people have used the word for what is pleasant and for what is desired respectively. And this is quite an interesting subject for discussion: only it is not a whit more an ethical discussion than the last was. Nor do I think that any exponent of naturalistic Ethics would be willing to allow that this was all he meant. They are all so anxious to persuade us that what they call the good is what we really ought to do. "Do, pray, act so, because the word 'good' is generally used to denote actions of this nature": such, on this view, would be the substance of their teaching. And in so far as they tell us how we ought to act, their teaching is truly ethical, as they mean it to be. But how perfectly absurd is the reason they would give for it! "You are to do this, because most people use a certain word to denote conduct such as this." "You are to say the thing which is not, because most people call it lying." That is an argument just as good!—My dear sirs, what we want to know from you as ethical teachers, is not how people use a word; it is not even, what kind of actions they approve, which the use of this word "good" may certainly imply: what we want to know is simply what *is* good. We may indeed agree that what most people do think good, is actually so; we shall at all events be glad to know their opinions: but when we say their opinions about what *is* good, we do mean what we say; we do not care whether they call that thing which they mean "horse" or "table" or "chair," "gut" or "bon" or "ἀγαθός"; we want to know what it is that they so call. When they say "Pleasure is good," we cannot believe that they merely mean "Pleasure is pleasure" and nothing more than that.

12. Suppose a man says "I am pleased"; and suppose that is not a lie or a mistake but the truth. Well, if it is true, what does that mean? It means that his mind, a certain definite mind, distinguished by certain definite marks from all others, has at this moment a certain definite feeling called pleasure. "Pleased" *means* nothing but having pleasure, and though we may be more pleased or less pleased, and even, we may admit for the present, have one or another kind of pleasure; yet in so far as it is pleasure we have, whether there be more or less of it, and whether it be of one kind or another, what we have is one definite thing, absolutely indefinable, some one thing that is the same in all the various degrees and in all the various kinds of it that there may be. We may be able to say how it is related to other things: that, for example, it is in the mind, that it causes desire, that we are conscious of it, etc., etc. We can, I say, describe its relations to other things, but define it we can *not*. And if anybody tried to define pleasure for us as being any other natural object; if anybody were to say, for instance, that pleasure *means* the sensation of red, and were to proceed to deduce from that that pleasure is a colour, we should be entitled to laugh at him and to distrust his future statements about pleasure. Well, that would be the same fallacy which I have called the naturalistic fallacy. That "pleased" does not mean "having the sensation of red," or anything else whatever, does not prevent us from understanding what it does mean. It is enough for us to know that "pleased" does mean "having the sensation of pleasure," and though pleasure is absolutely indefinable, though pleasure is pleasure and nothing else whatever, yet we feel no difficulty in saying that we are pleased. The reason is, of course, that when I say "I am pleased," I do *not* mean that "I" am the same thing as "having pleasure." And similarly no difficulty need be found in my saying that "pleasure is good" and yet not meaning that "pleasure" is the same thing as "good," that pleasure *means* good, and that good *means* pleasure. If I were to imagine that when I said "I am pleased," I meant that I was exactly the same thing as "pleased," I should not indeed call that a naturalistic fallacy, although it would be the same fallacy as I have called naturalistic with reference to Ethics. The reason of this is obvious enough. When a man confuses two natural objects with one another, defining the one by the other, if for instance, he confuses himself, who is one natural object, with "pleased" or with "pleasure" which are others, then there is no reason to call the fallacy naturalistic. But if he confuses "good," which is not in the same sense a natural object, with any natural object whatever, then there is a reason for calling that a naturalistic fallacy; its being made with regard to "good" marks it as something quite specific, and this specific mistake deserves a name because it is so common. As for the reasons why good is not to be considered a natural object, they may be reserved for discussion in another place. But, for the present, it is sufficient to notice this: Even if it were a natural object, that would not alter the nature of the fallacy nor diminish its importance one whit. All that I have said about it would remain quite equally true: only the name which I have called it would not be so appropriate as I think it is. And I do not care about the name: what I do care about is the fallacy. It does not matter what we call it, provided we recognise it when we meet with it. It is to be met with in almost every book on Ethics; and yet it is not recognised: and that is why it is necessary to multiply illustrations of it, and convenient to give it a name. It is a very simple fallacy indeed. When we say that an orange is yellow, we do not think our statement binds us to hold that "orange" means nothing else than "yellow," or that nothing can be yellow but an orange. Supposing the orange is also sweet! Does that bind us to say that "sweet" is exactly the same thing as "yellow," that "sweet" must be defined as "yellow"? And supposing it be recognised that "yellow" just means "yellow" and nothing else whatever, does that make it any more difficult to hold that oranges are yellow? Most certainly it does not: on the contrary, it would be absolutely meaningless to say that oranges were yellow, unless yellow did in the end mean just "yellow" and nothing else whatever— unless it was absolutely indefinable. We should not get any very clear notion about things, which are yellow—we should not get very far with our science, if we were bound to hold that everything which was yellow, *meant* exactly the same thing as yellow. We should find we had to hold that an orange was exactly the same thing as a stool, a piece of paper, a lemon, anything you like. We could prove any number of absurdities; but should we be the nearer to the truth? Why then, should it be different with "good"? Why, if good is good and indefinable, should I be held to deny that pleasure is good? Is there any difficulty in holding both to be true at once? On the contrary, there is no meaning in saying that pleasure is good, unless good is something different from pleasure. It is absolutely useless, so far as Ethics is concerned, to prove, as Mr. Spencer tries to do, that increase of pleasure coincides with increase of life, unless good *means* something different from either life or pleasure. He might just as well try to prove that an orange is yellow by shewing that it always is wrapped up in paper.

13. In fact, if it is not the case that "good" denotes something simple and indefinable, only two alternatives are possible: either it is a complex, a given whole, about the correct analysis of which there may be disagreement; or else it means nothing at all, and there is no such subject as Ethics. In general, however, ethical philosophers have attempted to define good, without recognising what such an attempt must mean. They actually use arguments which involve one or both of the absurdities considered in § 11. We are, therefore, justified in concluding that the attempt to define good is chiefly due to want of clearness as to the possible nature of definition. There are, in fact, only two serious alternatives to be considered, in order to establish the conclusion that "good" does denote a simple and indefinable notion. It might possibly denote a complex, as "horse" does; or it might have no meaning at all. Neither of these possibilities has, however, been clearly conceived and seriously maintained, as such, by those who presume to define good; and both may be dismissed by a simple appeal to facts.

(1) The hypothesis that disagreement about the meaning of good is disagreement with regard to the correct analysis of a given whole, may be most plainly seen to be incorrect by consideration of the fact that, whatever definition be offered, it may be always asked, with significance, of the complex so defined, whether it is itself good. To take, for instance, one of the more plausible, because one of the more complicated, of such proposed definitions, it may easily be thought, at first sight, that to be good may mean to be that which we desire to desire. Thus if we apply this definition to a particular instance and say "When we think that A is good, we are thinking that A is one of the things which we desire to desire," our proposition may seem quite plausible. But, if we carry the investigation further, and ask ourselves "Is it good to desire to desire A?" it is apparent, on a little reflection, that this question is itself as intelligible, as the original question "Is A good?"—that we are, in fact, now asking for exactly the same information about the desire to desire A, for which we formerly asked with regard to A itself. But it is also apparent that the meaning of this second question cannot be correctly analysed into "Is the desire to desire A one of the things which we desire to desire?": we have not before our minds anything so complicated as the question "Do we desire to desire to desire to desire A?" Moreover any one can easily convince himself by inspection that the predicate of this proposition—"good"—is positively different from the notion of "desiring to desire" which enters into its subject: "That we should desire to desire A is good" is *not* merely equivalent to "That A should be good is good." It may indeed be true that what we desire to desire is always also good; perhaps, even the converse may be true: but it is very doubtful whether this is the case, and

the mere fact that we understand very well what is meant by doubting it, shews clearly that we have two different notions before our minds.

(2) And the same consideration is sufficient to dismiss the hypothesis that "good" has no meaning whatsoever. It is very natural to make the mistake of supposing that what is universally true is of such a nature that its negation would be self-contradictory: the importance which has been assigned to analytic propositions in the history of philosophy shews how easy such a mistake is. And thus it is very easy to conclude that what seems to be a universal ethical principle is in fact an identical proposition; that, if, for example, whatever is called "good" seems to be pleasant, the proposition "Pleasure is the good" does not assert a connection between two different notions, but involves only one, that of pleasure, which is easily recognised as a distinct entity. But whoever will attentively consider with himself what is actually before his mind when he asks the question "Is pleasure (or whatever it may be) after all good?" can easily satisfy himself that he is not merely wondering whether pleasure is pleasant. And if he will try this experiment with each suggested definition in succession, he may become expert enough to recognise that in every case he has before his mind a unique object, with regard to the connection of which with any other object, a distinct question may be asked. Every one does in fact understand the question "Is this good?" When he thinks of it, his state of mind is different from what it would be, were he asked "Is this pleasant, or desired, or approved?" It has a distinct meaning for him, even though he may not recognise in what respect it is distinct. Whenever he thinks of "intrinsic value," or "intrinsic worth," or says that a thing "ought to exist," he has before his mind the unique object—the unique property of things—which I mean by "good." Everybody is constantly aware of this notion, although he may never become aware at all that it is different from other notions of which he is also aware. But, for correct ethical reasoning, it is extremely important that he should become aware of this fact; and, as soon as the nature of the problem is clearly understood, there should be little difficulty in advancing so far in analysis. . . .

38

Good as a Property

Stephen Toulmin

2.1. THREE TYPES OF PROPERTY

What is it that makes a concept a "property"? What (that is to say) makes a word a word for a "property"? Before we can answer these questions we must first ask, "What words unquestionably *are* typical words for properties?"

FROM *Reason in Ethics* by Stephen Toulmin. Copyright 1950 by Cambridge University Press.

Philosophers who treat goodness as a property often compare it to the qualities of sense (colours, etc.)—Moore goes in considerable detail into the similarities between goodness and yellowness—and some even talk about our means of perceiving "ethical properties" as "the moral sense". I shall therefore take colours as typical of one of the classes of things which we call "properties". Such properties are directly perceived by the senses, and differ in this from the third type to be mentioned below; they are also, unlike both the other two types, "unanalysable"—that is to say, they cannot be verbally defined, either in terms of simpler qualities or in terms of any set of operations, without mentioning the property itself. I can tell a red tie from a green one at sight, and I can teach any normal person to do the same; but I cannot explain how I do it either by reference to other properties of the tie or in terms of any procedure, without using the words "red" and "green" or other words for the same concepts. I shall refer to redness and other similar properties as *simple qualities*.

Another familiar class of properties consists of those which are perceived directly in the same way as the obvious qualities of sense, but which one can safely attribute to an object only after going through a certain routine. That a particular regular polygon has a fixed number of sides I may be able to tell by looking at it, but I can only be certain that it is 259-sided (rather than 257-sided or 261-sided, say) after counting its sides. For the presence of properties of this sort we require *criteria*. These are detected by means of a more or less complex routine and the properties can be defined in terms of this routine—thus "259-sided" means "having 259 sides," the operation of counting sides being familiar from other cases. Such properties are (that is to say) "analysable," and they are distinguished by this from the simple qualities. I shall refer to them as *complex qualities*.

These two types include most of the properties with which we are concerned in our day-to-day life, but there is a third which must be mentioned: this consists of properties which are detected by means of routines, in the way that complex qualities are, but which are not perceived directly—in fact we might say not perceived at all. If, for example, I say that the sun, when shining through the fog, is really yellow, although it looks as red as a blood-orange, I am not referring to any directly-perceived property of the sun at all. My remark is to be understood in the context of a scientific theory; and the property which I attribute to the sun, of being "really yellow," of radiating such-and-such types of electromagnetic wave, is defined in terms of that theory. Such properties I shall call *scientific qualities*.

Two cautions must be entered at this point. First, we need claim no deep epistemological significance for this classification. It may have some such value, but that does not concern us: all we require of it is that it shall simplify our analysis. Secondly, in saying that properties can be divided up in this way, and that such a classification exhausts the class of concepts we ordinarily refer to as properties, I do not mean that every property can be labelled once and for all as belonging to one of the types rather than another: I mean that whenever we

talk about properties we talk about them in one or another of these ways—sometimes in one, sometimes in another.

Consider some examples:

(i) Under most circumstances, when we say that anything is red or blue, hard or soft, we treat these words as words for simple qualities. But when we say that a figure is square, we sometimes treat squareness as a simple quality, telling it by eye, and sometimes, when our purposes require greater precision, demand measurements with ruler and set-square before accepting it as square—i.e. we treat "square" as a word for a complex quality, analysable into "rectangular and equilateral," these again being complex qualities analysable in terms of measurements with a set-square and a ruler respectively.

(ii) Since I have not been trained to do so, I cannot say whether or no a carpet is turkey-red unless I am given a colour-card as a "key"; I therefore treat "turkey-red" as a complex quality. A carpet-dealer, however, may get so used to telling fine shades of colour by eye that he can treat "turkey-red" as a simple quality.

(iii) We may say the sun is sodium-orange because we can see that it is (tell it by eye), *or* because we have a colour-card to compare it with, *or* because we believe a particular scientific theory: we may (that is) treat "sodium-orange" as a simple quality, *or* as a complex quality, *or* as a scientific quality.

It is one or another of these ways, however, that we treat all properties—and this is true of sense-qualities (red, green, hard, soft, loud, quiet, sweet, sour, rank and fragrant), personal characteristics (haughty and meek), shapes (square and thick), temporal distributions (rare and frequent), or what you like. In considering the objective doctrine, it will be sufficient to discuss the analogies between values and typical properties of each type.

Of course, there are cases in which our use of a concept makes it doubtful whether we should call it a property of the object or not. Judgements of taste—of what is sweet and what sour—are so erratic that we sometimes treat the concepts as though they were more like "nice" than like "red"; and by transference call the distinction between the pleasant and the unpleasant "a matter of taste." Such borderline examples draw attention to the way in which the two classes of concept shade into each other, but they do not obliterate the distinction between qualities like redness and "subjective relations"—i.e. concepts like pleasantness. In consequence they need not worry us.

Philosophers who hold that goodness is a property of those things which are good must, therefore, be taken to mean one of three things, corresponding to the three types of property which we have distinguished. They may mean that goodness is directly-perceived and unanalysable, that it is directly-perceived and analysable, or that it is to be detected only through criteria—not being perceived directly at all. In this chapter I shall concentrate on the first pair of possibilities: viz. the suggestion that goodness is a directly-perceived property, to be recognised either immediately or by means of criteria. These are the possibilities with which philosophers, especially those who talk about "the moral sense," have been most concerned. Most of the things to be said about complex qualities apply equally to scientific qualities, but I shall consider in more detail later[1] the idea that ethics is a science, and goodness a scientific quality, whose presence is to be recognised, not by direct perception, but only by indirect tests.

2.2. SIMPLE QUALITIES

What, then, is involved in asserting that an object has a particular simple quality? I have said that I can tell a red tie from a green one at sight, and can teach any normal person to do the same, but how is this? How does one, in fact, teach people to use correctly concepts of this kind? Again, in what circumstances can disagreements about simple qualities arise? And what is one to say if they do? Are we justified in correcting other people's use of simple qualities in the way in which we should correct the arithmetic of a child who said, "Seven eights are fifty-six; five and carry six; seven twos are fourteen and six makes twenty-two; so seven twenty-eights are two hundred and twenty-five"? Or can we pass over disagreements with a shrug of the shoulders, as we should the difference between one man who said, "There's nothing like an afternoon's fishing for sport and interest," and another who said, "Fishing's terribly boring"?

Imagine that I am trying to teach a foreigner (whose language I do not know and who has only a little English) to ice a cake, and suppose that I wish to explain the use of cochineal. "Cochineal?" he may inquire, not understanding me. "*Red* liquid," I shall say, "for making things *red*." If he fails to understand "red," what do I do?

The most natural thing, if I have some cochineal, will be to demonstrate to him, showing him how the icing-sugar takes up the colour of the liquid. And if that does not help him, I can try to get the idea over to him by pointing out a red rose, a book, a penny stamp or a pillar-box, and by contrasting these with $2\frac{1}{2}d.$ stamps, the lawn, sugar and shoe-polish—afterwards showing him the cochineal again. He should by then be able to understand what I mean, and pick out red objects; if he remains at a loss, all that I can do is to go through the same kind of process again and again, more slowly and with more examples, in the hope that he will get the idea. But if, whatever I do, he just fails to learn, I shall begin to think, either that he is deliberately fooling me, or that there is something wrong with him; and with reason, for the normal means of communication will have broken down.

So much for teaching people simple qualities; but what if someone else comes along and says "Cochineal is green?" Having learnt the word "red" in the ordinary way and used it successfully in everyday life, I shall wonder what is up, and I shall try to discover the cause of the contradiction. What I decide will depend on what else I find out about him. If, for instance, this is the only

---

[1] Especially in Chapter 9 below.

occasion on which I notice anything odd about his use of colour-words, I may conclude that it was a slip of the tongue. But if I try him out on pillar-boxes and penny stamps, and he calls those green, and never calls anything green except those things I call red, I shall conclude that he is talking a different language; and that, in use, his word "green" is identical with my word "red"—in fact that his "green" *means* the same as my "red". In such a case, I can learn to understand him by making appropriate substitutions (translations).

Such an example—written out at length—may seem wildly improbable, but in spoken language this kind of thing may happen quite easily. If engaged in sorting things into colours, English and Germans who understand only their own languages will get on all right as long as they only have occasion to refer to green (*grün*) things and brown (*braun*) things; but the English will be as puzzled by the Germans' talk about vice, when referring to white things, as I should be if anyone called cochineal green.

The type of disagreement manifested in these cases is one (and only one) of those arising out of *linguistic* differences. Under this heading may be included also those cases in which we should say that there was no difference in language, but only a difference of dialect, and those in which there is not even a difference of dialect, but only one of borderline usage.

This last category requires a little explanation. In everyday speech, the uses of words for properties shade into one another in ways which may lead to apparent contradictions. This fact is of great advantage to us; it would be intolerable if one might not name a colour without giving "the absolutely-exact shade"— whatever that means—or talk of "a fast car" without specifying its maximum speed in miles per hour on a level road with no wind. But there are always borderline examples which are puzzling. If two people are presented with the same object, whose colour is on the border between blue and green (i.e. such that we may not know whether to call it blue or green), one of them may be more inclined to say that it is blue, and the other that it is green. The fact that they are so inclined may reflect some difference between the sets of objects from which they learnt the words "blue" and "green": but, whether it does or not, we should expect the difference to be resolved (like so many of our disagreements) by specifying more exactly the limits being placed on the use of the words for the two properties. And if it were so resolved, we should not feel that there had been any more than a verbal difference between them.

It will, no doubt, be said that disagreements over simple qualities are not all of this kind; for what if the man is colour-blind? Colour-blindness, being exceptional and so ignored in our terminology, is a favourite source of philosophical puzzles, but it need not hold us up here. In such a case, no simple substitution or translation will be found to work: it will be found impossible to teach a colour-blind man to tell red from other colours, and indeed it is just this that leads us to call him colour-blind. There is in fact something odd in talking about a *disagreement* between a normal and a colour-blind person: the colour-blind man does not have *different* ideas about colours—he is just *without* some which most people have. In this respect his position relative to normal people is like that of normal people relative to those with absolute pitch. A man with absolute pitch can say straight off what is the position in the scale of any note which he hears: normal people do not *disagree* with him about this—they simply have no opinion.

Again, the man who says that cochineal is green may be fooling me deliberately, and he may go on doing so consistently, but this likewise leads to a situation in which we just do not know what to say—since communication breaks down—and does not lead to any relevant logical or philosophical problems. In a conceptual analysis, such as concerns us in this book, one need only examine the parts which concepts of different kinds (and words in so far as they stand for those concepts) play in our lives when language is being used literally, in the way in which we learn it—i.e. as the tool of reason (which Socrates called "the universal medium of communication").[2] The use of language for deception is not a primary use—it is in fact dependent on its unexpectedness for its success—and we need do no more than mention it.

To sum up this discussion. Simple qualities are taught "ostensively," i.e. by pointing out or instancing (which one might call "verbally-pointing-out") objects having the quality: the learner is shown how to sort out red objects from green ones, or told, "You know—like poppies and penny stamps." If two people have a disagreement about a simple quality, when the object referred to is before them (if one says that it's blue, the other that it's green; one square, the other oblong; one rare, the other frequent); then, neglecting cases of deliberate deception or organic defect, we say, "They can't mean the same by 'so-and-so'"—and we are satisfied if we discover that they are of different nationalities, or come from different parts of the country, or if one says for example, "Well, *I* should call three times a day frequent, anyway," and the other, "Good heavens, *I* shouldn't." Their disagreement, that is to say, has to be put down to a *linguistic* difference.

2.3. COMPLEX QUALITIES

The case of complex qualities may at first sight appear considerably more elaborate, but all that is involved is one further step. If I have a difference of opinion with another man as to whether a certain regular polygon is 257-sided or 259-sided, I shall not say the disagreement arises from a linguistic difference: I shall say that one of us cannot count. In the event of a disagreement over a complex quality (or a scientific quality, for that matter), one's first reaction will be to ask whether the appropriate routine (counting, measurement or comparison) has been correctly applied by both parties.

This, of course, can easily be checked: I can, for instance, make a careful joint count of the sides of the polygon with my opponent, and agree with him,

---

[2] See K. R. Popper, *The Open Society and its Enemies*, vol. 1, p. 166; and cf. *Phaedo* 89 c: "No greater evil can happen to anyone than to hate reasoning."

to begin with, that it has got 259 sides. And if after that he still calls it "257-sided," I shall have to conclude that his language or usage really is different from mine—say, that he calls a figure "n-sided" if it has $n+2$ sides. When talking to him after this I shall try making appropriate translations, using the rule, "In my usage a figure is called n-sided if it has n sides; in his if it has $n+2$." I shall ask him whether a square is "four-sided" or "two-sided" and so on. Of course, I may not succeed in finding a general translation-rule of this kind—his usage may differ from mine only in its nomenclature for figures with 259 equal sides. But, whatever the result of that attempt, the disagreement which arises in such a case will be a linguistic one—a new type of linguistic one, characteristic of complex and scientific qualities. (Two more familiar instances—numerical ones again—of words which invite similar confusions are the French term *quinzaine* for "a fortnight," and the Hebrew "on the third day" for "on the second day after.")

Taking both types of directly-perceived property together, the possible sources of disagreement can be set out as follows:

(i) deception;
(ii) organic defect;
(iii) incorrect application of the routine (in the case of complex qualities);
(iv) linguistic differences
    (*a*) in language,
    (*b*) in dialect,
    (*c*) in borderline usage,
    (*d*) in verbal definition (for complex qualities).

This list is exhaustive. If I have a disagreement with anyone about a directly-perceived property, and appear to have good evidence that none of these is the source of the difference, I can only say, "Well, one of them *must* be." And the fact that this list is exhaustive, that it is only from these sources that disagreement can arise over a concept, is part of what we mean when we say that it is "a property of the object."

2.4. IS GOODNESS A DIRECTLY-PERCEIVED PROPERTY?

This discussion of simple and complex qualities shows some of the conditions which must be met if we are to say that "X is good (or right)" attributes to X a directly-perceived property of goodness (or rightness). We must now see if any of these conditions are in fact met: this means asking about "good" and "right" the same kinds of question as we have already asked about "red" and "259-sided."

Suppose, then, that someone says to me, not "Cochineal is red," but a sentence which on the face of it is very similar, "Meekness is good." If I do not understand it, how can he make me? Will he point out to me instances of meekness, and hope to make me understand "good" in the way which would be effective if one were teaching "red"? Hardly! But this by itself is not a serious objection: he may instead try instancing—"You know, like loving your neighbour, and feeding the hungry, and honouring your parents, and paying your debts. . . ." And if I then say, "I'll take your word for it that meekness is good if paying your debts is, but how am I to know that paying your debts is?" he may reply, "Well, it just is—intrinsically."[3]

It will be tempting to conclude from this that "paying your debts" is just part of his ostensive definition of "good," just one of the examples he uses to teach people the idea (and so in a way it is); and it will be natural also to suppose that he will regard "good" as sharing *all* the logical properties of the simple qualities. But at this suggestion a supporter of the objective doctrine will begin to get worried. "It's not as arbitrary as that," he will insist. "Goodness is not a vague notion like the simple qualities—we don't mark off the 'good' from the 'indifferent' and the 'bad' in the way we mark off the 'blue' from the 'yellow' and the 'green,' or the 'tall' from the 'middling' and the 'short' "; and if we press him too hard at this point he will take refuge in vague references to "fundamental moral intuitions."

Alternatively, and especially if I say that I see no resemblance between meekness and debt-paying, he may adopt a different approach, saying, "Well, meekness makes for smoother personal relations than assertiveness or truculence: that's why I say that it's better." He may (that is) produce "criteria of goodness" ("good-making characteristics"),[4] which are at first sight to be used in the way in which "rectangularity" and "equality of sides" are used in the case of "squareness," or "having 259 sides" in the case of "259-sidedness." But again trouble arises if we ask about the standard routine for the application of the criteria. He will insist that the relation of "good-making characteristics" to "goodness" is different from the relation of the criteria for a complex quality to that quality. He will point out (quite justifiably) that the similarity between saying that a figure is "rectangular and equilateral" and saying that it is "square" is far more radical than the similarity between saying that a man beats his wife and saying that he is a "wicked" man—however good a reason his wife-beating may be for condemning him. And he will conclude that there is no standard routine, that "good" is unanalysable[5] and therefore a *simple* quality, and that the "good-making characteristics" are only *signs* of goodness, not criteria after all.

From the first, therefore, there are difficulties about the view that goodness is a directly-perceived property. If we take it that a simple (unanalysable) quality is meant, the apparent arbitrariness of an ostensive definition is puzzling: if a complex (analysable) quality is understood, no definite routine for confirming its presence is forthcoming. But these are not the greatest difficulties

[3] Cf. G. E. Moore, *Principia Ethica*, pp. 21 ff.

[4] Cf. C. D. Broad, *Proc. Aristotelian Soc.* vol. xxxiii (1933–4), on "Is 'Goodness' a Name for a Simple, Non-natural Quality?"; and also his contribution to the symposium, *The Philosophy of G. E. Moore*, pp. 43–67.

[5] Moore, op. cit. pp. 6–8.

which arise, and I shall do no more than point them out: we are in for more serious trouble when we consider the possible sources of disagreement over ethical questions.

2.5. THE SCOPE OF ETHICAL DISAGREEMENTS

What if someone else comes along and says "Meekness is bad"? What will the first man say then? Will he put the disagreement down to a linguistic difference?

No! The natural reaction will be for him to say, "Well, he's wrong," or "I may be mistaken, but I must say I like it myself," or "He may think it's bad but it's really good," or "Of course, it depends upon the circumstances." In exceptional cases he may say, "He's pulling your leg—he doesn't really mean it," or "Don't take any notice of him—he's notoriously insensitive over matters of ethics" (with implications of deliberate deception or natural defect). But the one thing I shall not expect him to say is, "He doesn't understand plain English": and this, if goodness *were* a property, is just what he should say.

If I am confident that both men are candid and in full possession of their faculties, and that they employ the same language, dialect and usage (i.e. if all the sources of disagreement over simple qualities are removed), there will be no point in my asking whether they agree or disagree about the colour of a pillar-box: there is no room for disagreement. If, in addition, I know that they have counted together the sides of a given polygon, it will be as pointless to ask whether they agree about its 259-sidedness. But, though I know all this, it will still not be silly to wonder, for example, whether they will agree that meekness is good, or that such-and-such is the right decision. Even if there is neither deception nor defect on either side, even if both parties are fully informed about the case and both mean the same by "good" and "right," it still makes sense to inquire whether their moral judgements are in fact the same.

This difference between values and properties is crucial. A few comments may help to clarify the point:

(i) There is, of course, no reason why a disagreement over values should not be based on a linguistic difference. If, for example, someone takes his moral judgements from Authority, he may mistranslate *buono* as "bad" and fall into an argument as a result. Or again, when talking about his own compositions, a musician may put on a display of uncommon self-depreciation, which leads to misunderstandings. But this kind of thing is trivial. We discover soon enough what is up—we notice that he only applies "not too awful" in *exceptional* cases, and so on—and afterwards, by substituting "all right" for "terrible," "good" for "very poor" and "excellent" for "not too awful," we come to understand him.

(ii) Apart from all linguistic matters, it is possible, that, given all the relevant facts, people's moral judgements might always agree. Hume, in his ethical theory, had to assume that there would *in fact* be no ethical disagreements between fully-informed people.

The notion of morals [he wrote] implies some sentiment common to all mankind, which recommends the same object to general approbation, and makes every man, or most men, agree in the same opinion or decision concerning it.[6]

But this apologetic assumption only accentuates the difference between "goodness" and the qualities that we have been discussing. No one thinks it necessary to make any such assumption when accounting for the general agreement about ordinary simple qualities. No one suggests that the notion of redness implies any "sentiment common to all mankind," which represents the same object to the vision of all in the same way, and so leads us to "agree in the same opinion or decision concerning it." And there need be no mystery about this, for it is a natural consequence of the function which our concept of redness serves.

This difference between values and properties, between contingent and necessary agreement, is fundamental. To contrast them, suppose that I say, "If we know all the relevant facts, there will (apart from linguistic differences) be no disagreement as to what things are and are not X." If X is a word for a property ("red," "square" or "259-sided"), the form of my statement is quite likely to be misleading: it appears to be a factual prediction, but there is actually nothing to predict—once we know all the facts there *can* be no disagreement, and it is nonsense to suggest that there might. But suppose that X is an ethical word ("good" or "right"); then my statement is a perfectly proper prediction, which may or may not be fulfilled. Ethical disagreements are not just a matter of using words differently. No set of translation-rules (like that from *weiss* to "white" or that from *rouge* to "red") would be comprehensive enough to cover all possible ethical disagreements. And, furthermore, I do not believe that anyone would ever expect there to be: our ethical concepts are not of that kind.

2.6. IS GOODNESS A "NON-NATURAL" PROPERTY?

In one unquestionably important respect, therefore, values differ from all that we should normally call directly-perceived properties. This discovery puts us in a difficult position. Is the objective doctrine quite false? Is the value of an object purely and simply *not* a property of it? Or have we missed the point? Have we been taking the doctrine too literally, supposing that more is implied by it than its supporters intend?

If the latter be the case, if the doctrine does not mean what it says but is, even in part, *figurative*, we can abandon it straight away. If all it tells us is that goodness is "as-it-were-a-property" and therefore "what-you-might-call-objective," it might, for our purposes, just as well be false. What we want is a literally-true account of our ethical concepts, an account which will show us how to distinguish between good ethical reasoning and bad. Metaphor, for us, is worse than useless.

This may be too high an aim, but we are not alone in it: some supporters of

[6] Hume, *An Enquiry Concerning the Principles of Morals* (ed. Selby-Bigge), p. 272.

the objective doctrine have the same ideal. Instead of admitting that the doctrine is metaphorical, and so a *cul-de-sac*, they insist on its literal truth. "All that you have done," they tell us, "is to show what we all know, that goodness is not just like other directly-perceived properties. Of course it isn't, but it's a directly-perceived property none the less, a special kind of property, a *non-natural* one."[7]

What happens if we try to preserve the truth of the objective doctrine in this way? As a matter of logic, the suggestion seems at first sight pretty disreputable. A townsman on his first visit to the country might be excused for thinking of rams as small, woolly bulls. (After all, they both have horns.) But if he replied to an objecting zoologist, "Ah! Don't mistake me—I know there are differences between bulls and rams. Of course there are: a ram is a very special kind of bull, a *non-tauroid* one," the zoologist might pardonably retort, "Don't be silly—it's not a bull at all. This stuff about 'non-tauroid bulls' is just verbiage conjured up *a posteriori*, in a hopeless attempt to hide the failure of your classification."

Such a retort, however justified, would fail to convince; but the zoologist could go on to bring evidence in support of his classification—for example, the mutual infertility of rams and cows. In the same way, calling or refusing to call "goodness" a "non-natural property" gets us nowhere: some kind of *grounds* must be advanced for the choice. Until we examine the case further, we have an equal reason for saying that goodness is a "non-natural" property and for saying that it is not a property at all—either suggestion is just a way of overcoming the difficulties I have pointed out, namely, the distinctions between "goodness" and "rightness," on the one hand, and all that we should normally call directly-perceived properties, on the other.

2.7. GOODNESS NOT A DIRECTLY-PERCEIVED PROPERTY

If we consider the contexts in which we normally use ethical concepts, we shall find that to treat them as properties ("non-natural" or otherwise) leads to paradoxical results.

Suppose that I am talking to a philosopher (who accepts the objective doctrine) about a mutual friend, a man noted for his high moral character, for his kindness, incorruptibility, thoughtfulness, sobriety, modesty, understanding, public spirit and wide interests; and who, when asked why he has done any particular act, always gives what we should consider good reasons, referring (for example) to the needs of others, the importance of fair dealing or the welfare of his family or community.

"Surely," I may say, "if ever a man knew what goodness was, he does!"

"I imagine that he does," the philosopher will say.

"And yet," I may reply, "I have asked him whether, when making up his mind what to do, he is conscious of observing any 'non-natural property,' any 'fittingness,'[8] in the action he decides on, and he says that he isn't. He says

---

[7] Moore, *Principia Ethica*, and *The Philosophy of G. E. Moore*, pp. 581–92.
[8] C. D. Broad, *Five Types of Ethical Theory*, p. 219.

that he does what he does because there's a good reason for doing it, and that he isn't interested in any additional, 'non-natural properties' of his actions."

To be consistent, the philosopher will have to answer, "If that is the case, he may know *what things are good*, he may know *what it is to be good*, but he cannot know *what goodness is*."

"But this is absurd," I shall retort. "Not know what goodness is? Is such a man to be classed with a kleptomaniac, a poor sneak-thief who doesn't know what goodness is? Is he to be put on the same level as a young delinquent, whose wretched home and irregular upbringing have sent him into the world with no knowledge of what goodness is? How laughable!"

How far is it fair to laugh his argument off like this? Not entirely. It is true that, in one sense, it would be ludicrous to say that a golfer who won the Open Championship did not know how to play first-class golf, even though he might not be able to explain the secrets of his success. Yet the very fact that he could not explain what was special about his strokes might lead us to say that, in another sense, he did not "know how it was done"—that he just "had the knack of doing it." But if this is all that lies behind our philosopher's objection, it has not the force he requires. Our virtuous and reasonable friend will not necessarily be able to give a *reflective account* of what is involved in reaching a moral decision, any more than the Open Golf Champion will necessarily be able to analyse his own technique—if he could, there would be no call for me to be writing this book. But there is nothing *wrong* with the way in which he reaches his own moral decisions: providing he does the right things for the right reasons, that is enough for us. A colour-blind man who overcame his initial handicap by learning from others what things were red and what green might indeed be said to be missing an essential experience, because the two colours did not look any different to him; and if goodness and rightness were "properties" our friend who is interested only in the reasons for his decisions would have to be thought of in the same way—as missing the one thing which really mattered. But this would be ridiculous.

Now this paradox shows that not even "non-naturalism" can preserve the literal truth of the objective doctrine, or justify us in adopting the objective approach to our problem. For (leaving aside the activities of moral philosophers) if I am told that someone does not know what goodness is, I shall expect him to break his promises, to lie, steal or cheat, and in so doing I shall be recognising what we do in fact mean by "goodness" and by "He does not know what goodness is." A philosopher who, out of fidelity to a theory, is driven into saying that a thoroughly virtuous and upright man does not know what goodness is, is assuredly up the garden path. He may think that, in telling us this, he is giving us factual information about the virtuous man, but he is doing nothing of the sort. If he were doing that, his remark would—philosophically—be trivial; as if he had said, "One can be upright and virtuous and yet never have read the Bible." The point of what he says is otherwise: he wants to deny something which is merely a piece of idiomatic usage—that "to be virtuous and upright and to give good reasons for one's actions" *is* "to know what goodness is"—

and to demand instead that the phrase "know-what-goodness-is" shall be reserved for "intuitive insight" (or something) into the "non-natural properties" of actions.[9]

Now this is to misrepresent our concept of "goodness," and to burke the problem with which we began. As long as we take it literally, there is something seriously at fault with the objective approach, and it is not at all likely to elucidate for us the place of reason in ethics.

Cognitivism and Non-Naturalism—Further Readings

Brandt, Richard B., *Ethical Theory* (Englewood Cliffs, N.J.: Prentice-Hall, 1959), Chap. 8. Critic.

Frankena, William K., "The Naturalistic Fallacy," *Mind*, XLVIII (1939), pp. 464–477. Critical discussion of Moore's naturalistic fallacy.

Hanock, Roger N., *Twentieth Century Ethics* (New York: Columbia U.P., 1974), Chap. 1. Exposition and criticism.

Hudson, W. D., *Modern Moral Philosophy* (Garden City, N.Y.: Doubleday, 1970), Chap. 3, Sec. 1. Exposition and criticism.

Kerner, George C., *The Revolution in Ethical Theory* (New York: Oxford U.P., 1966), Chap. 1. Exposition and criticism.

Klemke, E. D. (ed.), *Studies in the Philosophy of G. E. Moore* (Chicago: Quadrangle Books, 1969), Part I. Four critical essays by contemporary authors.

Moore, G. E., *Ethics* (London: Oxford U.P., 1912).

——, *Principia Ethica* (Cambridge: Cambridge U.P., 1903).

Nowell-Smith, P. H., *Ethics* (Baltimore: Penguin Books, 1954), Chaps. 2–5, especially Chap. 5. Critic.

Prior, Arthur N., *Logic and the Basis of Ethics* (Oxford: Clarendon, 1949), especially Chaps. 1 and 9. Historical and critical discussion of Moore's naturalistic fallacy.

Schilpp, Paul Arthur (ed.), *The Philosophy of G. E. Moore* (Evanston: Northwestern U.P., 1942). See the first six essays on Moore's ethics and Moore's reply.

Warnock, G. J., *Contemporary Moral Philosophy* (London: Macmillan, 1967), Chap. 2. Exposition and criticism.

Warnock, Mary, *Ethics Since* 1900 (London: Oxford U.P., 1960), Chap. 2. Exposition.

White, Alan R., *G. E. Moore: A Critical Exposition* (Basil Blackwell: Oxford, 1958), Chap. 7. Primarily exposition.

---

[9] For a discussion of this type of argument, see Norman Malcolm's contribution to *The Philosophy of G. E. Moore*, pp. 345–68.

B NON-COGNITIVISM AND NON-NATURALISM: *EMOTIVISM*

One of the most influential meta-ethical positions developed in the twentieth century is the emotive theory. Its proponents agree with G. E. Moore's belief that the clarification of the meaning of ethical concepts is of primary importance, and they also agree with Moore that such concepts cannot be defined in terms of nonethical properties.

Despite these areas of agreement, the emotivists rejected one of Moore's most deeply-held assumptions—the assumption that there is moral knowledge. For them, ethical judgments are not true or false. Since value terms have emotive meaning, ethical judgments function to express the speaker's emotion and to persuade others to share that emotion. For example, if a speaker says that abortion is wrong, he is expressing his emotional disapproval of abortion and seeking to influence those who hear him to adopt a similar attitude. If his listeners disagree, discussion may continue. The first speaker may mention various facts which he thinks will move others to adopt his emotional attitude toward abortion. If these and other persuasive efforts fail, the discussion will end with the speaker saying that abortion is wrong and his opponents saying that it is right. On the surface, it would appear that there is disagreement between them concerning the truth about abortion. On the emotivist view, however, the parties to the dispute are simply expressing different emotional preferences; it is what Stevenson calls a "disagreement in attitude." Having reached this point, it makes no more sense to ask which view is correct than it would to ask whether one person's preference for blondes is more correct than another person's preference for redheads.

In recent years, the most prominent defenders of the emotive theory have been A. J. Ayer and Charles Stevenson. To represent this position in our text, we have chosen Stevenson's article, "The Emotive Meaning of Emotive Terms."

Stevenson points out that the ethical, or "vital," sense of the term, "good," is ordinarily expected to meet three requirements. First, we must be able to disagree intelligently about what is "good." Second, "goodness" must be "magnetic," i.e., a person who comes to believe that a thing is "good" must thereby gain a stronger inclination to act in its favor than he would otherwise. Third, "goodness" must not be discoverable solely by use of the scientific method; otherwise, ethics would collapse into one of the sciences, such as psychology.

Stevenson then asserts that the major function of ethical judgments is to influence the interests of others. When ethical judgments are looked at in this way, Stevenson argues that our use of the term, "good," can be seen to meet all of the above requirements.

Concerning ethical disagreement in particular, Stevenson distinguishes between "disagreement in belief" and "disagreement in interest." Where there is disagreement in belief, evidence can often be brought to bear to settle the issue. Thus, if one person believes that energy conservation is unnecessary to meet the needs of Americans and another person brings in facts to change his mind, the two may reach agreement as to what conservation policies ought to be adopted. But if one person has no interest in meeting the energy needs of Americans and another does possess such an interest, they may agree on all the relevant facts and yet disagree about what ought to be done. There is then no rational method to settle their ethical disagreement.

Like Stevenson, Hare is fundamentally concerned with the function of ethical judgments. Unlike Stevenson, he does not believe that such judgments function primarily to influence the emotional attitudes of others. For him, the language of morals is prescriptive and functions to guide conduct. As such, ethical language is more closely related to imperative than to indicative sentences. That is, the language of morals is used principally by a speaker to tell someone what to do rather than to convey information. In this respect, Hare's view is similar to that of Stevenson, for Stevenson also rejects the view that ethical judgments function primarily to be informative. Nevertheless, Hare is sharply critical of Stevenson's thesis that ethical language is used to change attitudes. From Hare's standpoint, Stevenson's view cannot distinguish ethical judgments from propaganda. The main reason for Stevenson's confusion, according to Hare, lies in his mistaken ideas concerning the relationship between ethical words and actions. Stevenson makes the relationship one of causation, rather than one of logical implication. Put in another way, Stevenson confuses reasons and causes. Moreover, Stevenson's position implies that, in the final analysis, moral discourse ceases to be rational. For Hare, when we recognize that moral judgments are used prescriptively to guide conduct, we can then find a place for their rational justification. In this section, Hare is basically critical of writers like Stevenson. In the next section, we shall learn more of Hare's positive views.

39

The Emotive Meaning of Ethical Terms

C. L. STEVENSON

I

Ethical questions first arise in the form "Is so and so good?" or "Is this alternative better than that?" These questions are difficult partly because we don't quite know what we are seeking. We are asking, "Is there a needle in that haystack?" without even knowing just what a needle is. So the first thing to do is to examine the questions themselves. We must try to make them clearer, either by defining the terms in which they are expressed, or by any other method that is available.

The present paper is concerned wholly with this preliminary step of making ethical questions clear. In order to help answer the question "Is X good?" we must *substitute* for it a question which is free from ambiguity and confusion.

It is obvious that in substituting a clearer question we must not introduce some utterly different kind of question. It won't do (to take an extreme instance of a prevalent fallacy) to substitute for "Is X good?" the question "Is X pink with yellow trimmings?" and then point out how easy the question really is. This would beg the original question, not help answer it. On the other hand, we must not expect the substituted question to be strictly "identical" with the original one. The original question may embody hypostatization, anthropomorphisms, vagueness, and all the other ills to which our ordinary discourse is subject. If our substituted question is to be clearer, it must remove these ills. The questions will be identical only in the sense that a child is identical with the man he later becomes. Hence we must not demand that the substitution strike us, on immediate introspection, as making no change in meaning.

Just how, then, must the substituted question be related to the original? Let us assume (inaccurately) that it must result from replacing "good" by some set of terms which define it. The question then resolves itself to this: How must the defined meaning of "good" be related to its original meaning?

I answer that it must be *relevant*. A defined meaning will be called "relevant" to the original meaning under these circumstances: Those who have understood the definition must be able to say all that they then want to say by using the term in the defined way. They must never have occasion to use the term in the old, unclear sense. (If a person did have to go on using the word in the old sense,

FROM "The Emotive Meaning of Ethical Terms" (*Mind*, Vol. XLVI, no. 181). Copyright 1937 by Basil Blackwell, Publisher, Oxford.

then to this extent his meaning would not be clarified, and the philosophical task would not be completed.) It frequently happens that a word is used so confusedly and ambiguously that we must give it *several* defined meanings, rather than one. In this case only the whole set of defined meanings will be called "relevant," and any one of them will be called "partially relevant." This is not a rigorous treatment of *relevance*, by any means; but it will serve for the present purposes.

Let us now turn to our particular task—that of giving a relevant definition of "good." Let us first examine some of the ways in which others have attempted to do this.

The word "good" has often been defined in terms of *approval*, or similar psychological attitudes. We may take as typical examples: "good" means *desired by me* (Hobbes); and "good" means *approved by most people* (Hume, in effect). It will be convenient to refer to definitions of this sort as "interest theories," following Mr. R. B. Perry, although neither "interest" nor "theory" is used in the most usual way.

Are definitions of this sort relevant?

It is idle to deny their *partial* relevance. The most superficial inquiry will reveal that "good" is exceedingly ambiguous. To maintain that "good" is *never* used in Hobbes's sense, and never in Hume's, is only to manifest an insensitivity to the complexities of language. We must recognize, perhaps, not only these senses, but a variety of similar ones, differing both with regard to the kind of interest in question, and with regard to the people who are said to have the interest.

But this is a minor matter. The essential question is not whether interest theories are *partially* relevant, but whether they are *wholly* relevant. This is the only point of intelligent dispute. Briefly: Granted that some senses of "good" may relevantly be defined in terms of interest, is there some *other* sense which is *not* relevantly so defined? We must give this question careful attention. For it is quite possible that when philosophers (and many others) have found the question "Is X good?" so difficult, they have been grasping for this *other* sense of "good," and not any sense relevantly defined in terms of interest. If we insist on defining "good" in terms of interest, and answer the question when thus interpreted, we may be begging *their* question entirely. Of course this *other* sense of "good" may not exist, or it may be a complete confusion; but that is what we must discover.

Now many have maintained that interest theories are *far* from being completely relevant. They have argued that such theories neglect the very sense of "good" which is most vital. And certainly, their arguments are not without plausibility.

Only . . . what *is* this "vital" sense of "good"? The answers have been so vague, and so beset with difficulties, that one can scarcely determine.

There are certain requirements, however, with which this "vital" sense has been expected to comply—requirements which appeal strongly to our common sense. It will be helpful to summarize these, showing how they exclude the interest theories:

In the first place, we must be able sensibly to *disagree* about whether something is "good." This condition rules out Hobbes's definition. For consider the following argument: "This is good." "That isn't so; it's not good." As translated by Hobbes, this becomes: "I desire this." "That isn't so, for *I* don't." The speakers are not contradicting one another, and think they are, only because of an elementary confusion in the use of pronouns. The definition, "good" means *desired by my community*, is also excluded, for how could people from different communities disagree?

In the second place, "goodness" must have, so to speak, a magnetism. A person who recognizes X to be "good" must *ipso facto* acquire a stronger tendency to act in its favour than he otherwise would have had. This rules out the Humian type of definition. For according to Hume, to recognize that something is "good" is simply to recognize that the majority approve of it. Clearly, a man may see that the majority approve of X without having, himself, a stronger tendency to favour it. This requirement excludes any attempt to define "good" in terms of the interest of people *other* than the speaker.

In the third place, the "goodness" of anything must not be verifiable solely by use of the scientific method. "Ethics must not be psychology." This restriction rules out all of the traditional interest theories, without exception. It is so sweeping a restriction that we must examine its plausibility. What are the methodological implications of interest theories which are here rejected?

According to Hobbes's definition, a person can prove his ethical judgments, with finality, by showing that he is not making an introspective error about his desires. According to Hume's definition, one may prove ethical judgments (roughly speaking) by taking a vote. *This* use of the empirical method, at any rate, seems highly remote from what we usually accept as proof, and reflects on the complete relevance of the definitions which imply it.

But aren't there more complicated interest theories which are immune from such methodological implications? No, for the same factors appear; they are only put off for a while. Consider, for example, the definition: "X is good" means *most people would approve of X if they knew its nature and consequences*. How, according to this definition, could we prove that a certain X was good? We should first have to find out, empirically, just what X was like, and what its consequences would be. To this extent the empirical method, as required by the definition, seems beyond intelligent objection. But what remains? We should next have to discover whether most people would approve of the sort of thing we had discovered X to be. This couldn't be determined by popular vote— but only because it would be too difficult to explain to the voters, beforehand, what the nature and consequences of X really were. Apart from this, voting would be a pertinent method. We are again reduced to counting noses, as a *perfectly final* appeal.

Now we need not scorn voting entirely. A man who rejected interest theories as irrelevant might readily make the following statement: "If I believed that X would be approved by the majority, when they knew all about it, I should be strongly *led* to say that X was good." But he would continue: "*Need* I say that

X was good, under the circumstances? Wouldn't my acceptance of the alleged 'final proof' result simply from my being democratic? What about the more aristocratic people? They would simply say that the approval of most people, even when they knew all about the object of their approval, simply had nothing to do with the goodness of anything, and they would probably add a few remarks about the low state of people's interests." It would indeed seem, from these considerations, that the definition we have been considering has presupposed democratic ideals from the start; it has dressed up democratic propaganda in the guise of a definition.

The omnipotence of the empirical method, as implied by interest theories and others, may be shown unacceptable in a somewhat different way. Mr. G. E. Moore's familiar objection about the open question is chiefly pertinent in this regard. No matter what set of scientifically knowable properties a thing may have (says Moore, in effect), you will find, on careful introspection, that it is an open question to ask whether anything having these properties is *good*. It is difficult to believe that this recurrent question is a totally confused one, or that it seems open only because of the ambiguity of "good." Rather, we must be using some sense of "good" which is not definable, relevantly, in terms of anything scientifically knowable. That is, the scientific method is not sufficient for ethics.

These, then, are the requirements with which the "vital" sense of "good" is expected to comply: (1) goodness must be a topic for intelligent disagreement; (2) it must be "magnetic"; and (3) it must not be discoverable solely through the scientific method.

II

Let us now turn to my own analysis of ethical judgments. First let me present my position dogmatically, showing to what extent I vary from tradition.

I believe that the three requirements, given alone, are perfectly sensible; that there is some *one* sense of "good" which satisfies all three requirements; and that no traditional interest theory satisfies them all. But this does not imply that "good" must be explained in terms of a Platonic Idea, or of a Categorical Imperative, or of an unique, unanalyzable property. On the contrary, the three requirements can be met by a *kind* of interest theory. *But we must give up a presupposition which all the traditional interest theories have made.*

Traditional interest theories hold that ethical statements are *descriptive* of the existing state of interests—that they simply *give information* about interests. (More accurately, ethical judgments are said to describe what the state of interests is, was, or will be, or to indicate what the state of interests *would* be under specified circumstances.) It is this emphasis on description, on information, which leads to their incomplete relevance. Doubtless there is always *some* element of description in ethical judgments, but this is by no means all. Their major use is not to indicate facts, but to *create an influence*.

Instead of merely describing people's interests, they *change* or *intensify* them. They *recommend* an interest in an object, rather than state that the interest already exists.

For instance: When you tell a man that he oughtn't to steal, your object isn't merely to let him know that people disapprove of stealing. You are attempting, rather, to get *him* to disapprove of it. Your ethical judgment has a quasi-imperative force which, operating through suggestion, and intensified by your tone of voice, readily permits you to begin to *influence*, to *modify*, his interests. If in the end you do not succeed in getting *him* to disapprove of stealing, you will feel that you've failed to convince him that stealing is wrong. You will continue to feel this, even though he fully acknowledges that you disapprove of it, and that almost everyone else does. When you point out to him the consequences of his actions—consequences which you suspect he already disapproves of—these *reasons* which support your ethical judgment are simply a means of facilitating your influence. If you think you can change his interests by making vivid to him how others will disapprove of him, you will do so; otherwise not. So the consideration about other people's interest is just an additional means you may employ, in order to move him, and is not a part of the ethical judgment itself. Your ethical judgment doesn't merely describe interests to him, it directs his very interests. The difference between the traditional interest theories and my view is like the difference between describing a desert and irrigating it.

Another example: A munition maker declares that war is a good thing. If he merely meant that he approved of it, he would not have to insist so strongly, nor grow so excited in his argument. People would be quite easily convinced that he approved of it. If he merely meant that most people approved of war, or that most people would approve of it if they knew the consequences, he would have to yield his point if it were proved that this wasn't so. But he wouldn't do this, nor does consistency require it. He is not *describing* the state of people's approval; he is trying to *change* it by his influence. If he found that few people approved of war, he might insist all the more strongly that it was good, for there would be more changing to be done.

This example illustrates how "good" may be used for what most of us would call bad purposes. Such cases are as pertinent as any others. I am not indicating the *good* way of using "good." I am not influencing people, but am describing the way this influence sometimes goes on. If the reader wishes to say that the munition maker's influence is bad—that is, if the reader wishes to awaken people's disapproval of the man, and to make him disapprove of his own actions—I should at another time be willing to join in this undertaking. But this is not the present concern. I am not using ethical terms, but am indicating how they *are* used. The munition maker, in his use of "good," illustrates the persuasive character of the word just as well as does the unselfish man who, eager to encourage in each of us a desire for the happiness of all, contends that the supreme good is peace.

Thus ethical terms are *instruments* used in the complicated interplay and readjustment of human interests. This can be seen plainly from more general observations. People from widely separated communities have different moral attitudes. Why? To a great extent because they have been subject to different social influences. Now clearly this influence doesn't operate through sticks and stones alone; words play a great part. People praise one another, to encourage certain inclinations, and blame one another, to discourage others. Those of forceful personalities issue commands which weaker people, for complicated instinctive reasons, find it difficult to disobey, quite apart from fears of consequences. Further influence is brought to bear by writers and orators. Thus social influence is exerted, to an enormous extent, by means that have nothing to do with physical force or material reward. The ethical terms facilitate such influence. Being suited for use in *suggestion*, they are a means by which men's attitudes may be led this way or that. The reason, then, that we find a greater similarity in the moral attitudes of one community than in those of different communities is largely this: ethical judgments propagate themselves. One man says "This is good"; this may influence the approval of another person, who then makes the same ethical judgment, which in turn influences another person, and so on. In the end, by a process of mutual influence, people take up more or less the same attitudes. Between people of widely separated communities, of course, the influence is less strong; hence different communities have different attitudes.

These remarks will serve to give a general idea of my point of view. We must now go into more detail. There are several questions which must be answered: How does an ethical sentence acquire its power of influencing people—why is it suited to suggestion? Again, what has this influence to do with the *meaning* of ethical terms? And finally, do these considerations really lead us to a sense of "good" which meets the requirements mentioned in the preceding section?

Let us deal first with the question about *meaning*. This is far from an easy question, so we must enter into a preliminary inquiry about meaning in general. Although a seeming digression, this will prove indispensable.

III

Broadly speaking, there are two different *purposes* which lead us to use language. On the one hand we use words (as in science) to record, clarify, and communicate *beliefs*. On the other hand we use words to give vent to our feelings (interjections), or to create moods (poetry), or to incite people to actions or attitudes (oratory).

The first use of words I shall call "descriptive"; the second, "dynamic." Note that the distinction depends solely upon the *purpose* of the *speaker*.

When a person says "Hydrogen is the lightest known gas," his purpose *may* be simply to lead the hearer to believe this, or to believe that the speaker believes it. In that case the words are used descriptively. When a person cuts himself and says "Damn," his purpose is not ordinarily to record, clarify, or communicate any belief. The word is used dynamically. The two ways of using words, however, are by no means mutually exclusive. This is obvious from the fact that our purposes are often complex. Thus when one says "I want you to close the door," part of his purpose, ordinarily, is to lead the hearer to believe that he has this want. To that extent the words are used descriptively. But the major part of one's purpose is to lead the hearer to *satisfy* the want. To that extent the words are used dynamically.

It very frequently happens that the same sentence may have a dynamic use on one occasion, and may not have a dynamic use on another; and that it may have different dynamic uses on different occasions. For instance: A man says to a visiting neighbour, "I am loaded down with work." His purpose may be to let the neighbour know how life is going with him. This would *not* be a dynamic use of words. He may make the remark, however, in order to drop a hint. This *would* be dynamic usage (as well as descriptive). Again, he may make the remark to arouse the neighbour's sympathy. This would be a *different* dynamic usage from that of hinting.

Or again, when we say to a man, "Of course you won't make those mistakes any more," we *may* simply be making a prediction. But we are more likely to be using "suggestion," in order to encourage him and hence *keep* him from making mistakes. The first use would be descriptive; the second, mainly dynamic.

From these examples it will be clear that we can't determine whether words are used dynamically or not, merely by reading the dictionary—even assuming that everyone is faithful to dictionary meanings. Indeed, to know whether a person is using a word dynamically, we must note his tone of voice, his gestures, the general circumstances under which he is speaking, and so on.

We must now proceed to an important question: What has the dynamic use of words to do with their *meaning?* One thing is clear—we must not define "meaning" in a way that would make meaning vary with dynamic usage. If we did, we should have no use for the term. All that we could say about such "meaning" would be that it is very complicated, and subject to constant change. So we must certainly distinguish between the dynamic use of words and their meaning.

It doesn't follow, however, that we must define "meaning" in some non-psychological fashion. We must simply restrict the psychological field. Instead of identifying meaning with *all* the psychological causes and effects that attend a word's utterance, we must identify it with those that it has a *tendency* (causal property, dispositional property) to be connected with. The tendency must be a particular kind, moreover. It must exist for all who speak the language; it must be persistent; and must be realizable more or less independently of determinate circumstances attending the word's utterance. There will be further restrictions dealing with the interrelation of words in different contexts. Moreover, we must include, under the psychological responses which the words tend to produce, not only immediately introspectable experiences, but *dispositions* to react in a given way with appropriate stimuli. I hope to go into these matters in a subsequent paper. Suffice it now to say that I think "meaning" may be thus defined in a way to include "propositional" meaning as an important kind. Now a word may *tend* to have causal relations which in fact it sometimes doesn't; and it may sometimes have causal relations which it *doesn't tend* to have. And since the tendency of words which constitutes their meaning must be of a particular kind, and may include, as responses, dispositions to reactions, of which any of *several* immediate experiences may be a sign, then there is nothing surprising in the fact that words have a permanent meaning, in spite of the fact that the immediately introspectable experiences which attend their usage are so highly varied.

When "meaning" is defined in this way, meaning will not include dynamic use. For although words are sometimes accompanied by dynamic purposes, they do not *tend* to be accompanied by them in the way above mentioned. E.g., there is no tendency realizable independently of the determinate circumstances under which the words are uttered.

There will be a kind of meaning, however, in the sense above defined, which has an intimate relation to dynamic usage. I refer to "emotive" meaning (in a sense roughly like that employed by Ogden and Richards). The emotive meaning of a word is a tendency of a word, arising through the history of its usage, to produce (result from) *affective* responses in people. It is the immediate aura of feeling which hovers about a word. Such tendencies to produce affective responses cling to words very tenaciously. It would be difficult, for instance, to express merriment by using the interjection "alas." Because of the persistence of such affective tendencies (among other reasons) it becomes feasible to classify them as "meanings."

Just *what* is the relation between emotive meaning and the dynamic use of words? Let us take an example. Suppose that a man is talking with a group of people which includes Miss Jones, aged 59. He refers to her, without thinking, as an "old maid." Now even if his purposes are perfectly innocent—even if he is using the words purely descriptively—Miss Jones won't think so. She will think he is encouraging the others to have contempt for her, and will draw in her skirts, defensively. The man might have done better if instead of saying "old maid" he had said "elderly spinster." The latter words could have been put to the same descriptive use, and would not so readily have caused suspicions about the dynamic use.

"Old maid" and "elderly spinster" differ, to be sure, only in emotive meaning. From the example it will be clear that certain words, because of their emotive meaning, are suited to a certain kind of dynamic use—so well suited, in fact, that the hearer is likely to be misled when we use them in any other way. The more pronounced a word's emotive meaning is, the less likely people are to use it purely descriptively. Some words are suited to encourage people, some to discourage them, some to quiet them, and so on.

Even in these cases, of course, the dynamic purposes are not to be identified with any sort of meaning; for the emotive meaning accompanies a word much more persistently than do the dynamic purposes. But there is an important contingent relation between emotive meaning and dynamic purpose: the former assists the latter. Hence if we define emotively laden terms in a way that neglects their emotive meaning, we are likely to be confusing. *We lead people to think that the terms defined are used dynamically less often than they are.*

IV

Let us now apply these remarks in defining "good." This word may be used morally or non-morally. I shall deal with the non-moral usage almost entirely, but only because it is simpler. The main points of the analysis will apply equally well to either usage.

As a preliminary definition, let us take an inaccurate approximation. It may be more misleading than helpful, but will do to begin with. Roughly, then, the sentence "X is good" means *We like X.* ("We" includes the hearer or hearers.)

At first glance this definition sounds absurd. If used, we should expect to find the following sort of conversation: A. "This is good." B. "But I *don't* like it. What led you to believe that I did?" The unnaturalness of B's reply, judged by ordinary word-usage, would seem to cast doubt on the relevance of my definition.

B's unnaturalness, however, lies simply in this: he is assuming that "We like it" (as would occur implicitly in the use of "good") is being used descriptively. This won't do. When "We like it" is to take the place of "This is good," the former sentence must be used not purely descriptively, but dynamically. More specifically, it must be used to promote a very subtle (and for the non-moral sense in question, a very easily resisted) kind of *suggestion*. To the extent that "we" refers to the hearer, it must have the dynamic use, essential to suggestion, of leading the hearer to *make* true what is said, rather than merely to believe it. And to the extent that "we" refers to the speaker, the sentence must have not only the descriptive use of indicating belief about the speaker's interest, but the quasi-interjectory, dynamic function of giving direct expression to the interest. (This immediate expression of feelings assists in the process of suggestion. It is difficult to disapprove in the face of another's enthusiasm.)

For an example of a case where "We like this" is used in the dynamic way that "This is good" is used, consider the case of a mother who says to her several children, "One thing is certain, *we all like to be neat.*" If she really believed this, she wouldn't bother to say so. But she is not using the words descriptively. She is *encouraging* the children to like neatness. By telling them that they like neatness, she will lead them to *make* her statement true, so to speak. If, instead of saying "We all like to be neat" in this way, she had said "It's a good thing to be neat," the effect would have been approximately the same.

But these remarks are still misleading. Even when "We like it" is used for suggestion, it isn't quite like "This is good." The latter is more subtle. With such a sentence as "This is a good book" for example, it would be practically impossible to use instead "We like this book." When the latter is used, it must be accompanied by so exaggerated an intonation, to prevent its becoming confused with a descriptive statement, that the force of suggestion becomes stronger, and ludicrously more overt, than when "good" is used.

The definition is inadequate, further, in that the definiens has been restricted to dynamic usage. Having said that dynamic usage was different from meaning, I should not have to mention it in giving the *meaning* of "good."

It is in connection with this last point that we must return to emotive meaning. The word "good" has a pleasing emotive meaning which fits it especially for the dynamic use of suggesting favourable interest. But the sentence "We like it" has no such emotive meaning. Hence my definition has neglected emotive meaning entirely. Now to neglect emotive meaning is likely to lead to endless confusions, as we shall presently see; so I have sought to make up for the inadequacy of the definition by letting the restriction about dynamic usage take the place of emotive meaning. What I should do, of course, is to find a definiens whose emotive meaning, like that of "good," simply does *lead* to dynamic usage.

Why didn't I do this? I answer that it isn't possible, if the definition is to afford us increased clarity. No two words, in the first place, have quite the same emotive meaning. The most we can hope for is a rough approximation. But if we seek for such an approximation for "good," we shall find nothing more than synonyms, such as "desirable" or "valuable"; and these are profitless because they do not clear up the connection between "good" and favourable interest. If we reject such synonyms, in favour of non-ethical terms, we shall be highly misleading. For instance: "This is good" has something like the meaning of "I *do* like this; do so as well." But this is certainly not accurate. For the imperative makes an appeal to the conscious efforts of the hearer. Of course he can't like something just by trying. He must be led to like it through suggestion. Hence an ethical sentence differs from an imperative in that it enables one to make changes in a much more subtle, less fully conscious way. Note that the ethical sentence centres the hearer's attention not on his interests, but on the object of interest, and thereby facilitates suggestion. Because of its subtlety, moreover, an ethical sentence readily permits counter-suggestion, and leads to the give and take situation which is so characteristic of arguments about values.

Strictly speaking, then, it is impossible to define "good" in terms of favourable interest if emotive meaning is not to be distorted. Yet it is possible to say that "This is good" is *about* the favourable interest of the speaker and the hearer or hearers, and that it has a pleasing emotive meaning which fits the words for use in suggestion. This is a rough description of meaning, not a definition. But it serves the same clarifying function that a definition ordinarily does; and that, after all, is enough.

A word must be added about the moral use of "good." This differs from the above in that it is about a different kind of interest. Instead of being about what the hearer and speaker *like*, it is about a stronger sort of approval. When a person *likes* something, he is pleased when it prospers, and disappointed when it doesn't. When a person *morally approves* of something, he experiences a rich feeling of security when it prospers, and is indignant, or "shocked" when it doesn't. These are rough and inaccurate examples of the many factors which one would have to mention in distinguishing the two kinds of interest. In the moral usage, as well as in the non-moral, "good" has an emotive meaning which adapts it to suggestion.

And now, are these considerations of any importance? Why do I stress emotive meanings in this fashion? Does the omission of them really lead people into errors? I think, indeed, that the errors resulting from such omissions are enormous. In order to see this, however, we must return to the restrictions, mentioned in section I, with which the "vital" sense of "good" has been expected to comply.

V

The first restriction, it will be remembered, had to do with disagreement. Now there is clearly some sense in which people disagree on ethical points; but we must not rashly assume that all disagreement is modelled after the sort that occurs in the natural sciences. We must distinguish between "disagreement in belief" (typical of the sciences) and "disagreement in interest." Disagreement in belief occurs when A believes *p* and B disbelieves it. Disagreement in interest occurs when A has a favourable interest in X, when B has an unfavourable one in it, and when neither is content to let the other's interest remain unchanged.

Let me give an example of disagreement in interest. A. "Let's go to a cinema to-night." B. "I don't want to do that. Let's go to the symphony." A continues to insist on the cinema, B on the symphony. This is disagreement in a perfectly conventional sense. They can't agree on where they want to go, and each is trying to redirect the other's interest. (Note that imperatives are used in the example.)

It is disagreement in *interest* which takes places in ethics. When C says "This is good," and D says "No, it's bad," we have a case of suggestion and counter-suggestion. Each man is trying to redirect the other's interest. There obviously need be no domineering, since each may be willing to give ear to the other's influence; but each is trying to move the other none the less. It is in this sense that they disagree. Those who argue that certain interest theories make no provision for disagreement have been misled, I believe, simply because the traditional theories, in leaving out emotive meaning, give the impression that ethical judgments are used descriptively only; and of course when judgments are used purely descriptively, the only disagreement that can arise is disagreement *in belief*. Such disagreement may be disagreement in belief *about* interests; but this is not the same as disagreement *in* interest. My definition doesn't provide for disagreement in belief about interests, any more than does Hobbes's; but that is no matter, for there is no reason to believe, at least on common-sense grounds, that this kind of disagreement exists. There is only disagreement *in* interest. (We shall see in a moment that disagreement in interest does not remove ethics from sober argument—that this kind of disagreement may often be resolved through empirical means.)

The second restriction, about "magnetism," or the connection between goodness and actions, requires only a word. This rules out *only* those interest theories which do *not* include the interest of the speaker, in defining "good." My account does include the speaker's interest; hence is immune.

The third restriction, about the empirical method, may be met in a way that springs naturally from the above account of disagreement. Let us put the question in this way: When two people disagree over an ethical matter, can they completely resolve the disagreement through empirical considerations, assuming that each applies the empirical method exhaustively, consistently, and without error?

I answer that sometimes they can, and sometimes they cannot; and that at any rate, even when they can, the relation between empirical knowledge and ethical judgments is quite different from the one which traditional interest theories seem to imply.

This can best be seen from an analogy. Let's return to the example where A and B couldn't agree on a cinema or a symphony. The example differed from an ethical argument in that imperatives were used, rather than ethical judgments; but was analogous to the extent that each person was endeavouring to modify the other's interest. Now how would these people argue the case, assuming that they were too intelligent just to shout at one another?

Clearly, they would give "reasons" to support their imperatives. A might say, "But you know, Garbo is at the Bijou." His hope is that B, who admires Garbo, will acquire a desire to go to the cinema when he knows what play will be there. B may counter, "But Toscanini is guest conductor to-night, in an all-Beethoven programme." And so on. Each supports his imperative ("*Let's* do so and so") by reasons which may be empirically established.

To generalize from this: disagreement in interest may be rooted in disagreement in belief. That is to say, people who disagree in interest would often cease to do so if they knew the precise nature and consequences of the object of their interest. To this extent disagreement in interest may be resolved by securing agreement in belief, which in turn may be secured empirically.

This generalization holds for ethics. If A and B, instead of using imperatives, had said, respectively, "It would be *better* to go to the cinema," and "It would be better to go to the symphony," the reasons which they would advance would be roughly the same. They would each give a more thorough account of the object of interest, with the purpose of completing the redirection of interest which was begun by the suggestive force of the ethical sentence. On the whole, of course, the suggestive force of the ethical statement merely exerts enough pressure to start such trains of reasons, since the reasons are much more essential in resolving disagreement in interest than the persuasive effect of the ethical judgment itself.

Thus the empirical method is relevant to ethics simply because our knowledge of the world is a determining factor to our interests. But note that empirical facts are not inductive grounds from which the ethical judgment problematically follows. (This is what traditional interest theories imply.) If someone said "Close the door," and added the reason "We'll catch cold," the latter would scarcely be called an inductive ground of the former. Now imperatives are related to the reasons which support them in the same way that ethical judgments are related to reasons.

Is the empirical method *sufficient* for attaining ethical agreement? Clearly not. For empirical knowledge resolves disagreement in interest only to the extent that such disagreement is rooted in disagreement in belief. Not all disagreement in interest is of this sort. For instance: A is of a sympathetic nature, and B isn't. They are arguing about whether a public dole would be good. Suppose that they discovered all the consequences of the dole. Isn't it possible, even so, that A will say that it's good, and B that it's bad? The disagreement in interest may arise not from limited factual knowledge, but simply from A's sympathy and B's coldness. Or again, suppose, in the above argument, that A was poor and unemployed, and that B was rich. Here again the disagreement might not be due to different factual knowledge. It would be due to the different social positions of the men, together with their predominant self-interest.

When ethical disagreement is not rooted in disagreement in belief, is there *any* method by which it may be settled? If one means by "method" a *rational* method, then there is no method. But in any case there is a "way." Let's consider the above example, again, where disagreement was due to A's sympathy and B's coldness. Must they end by saying, "Well, it's just a matter of our having different temperaments"? Not necessarily. A, for instance, may try to *change* the temperament of his opponent. He may pour out his enthusiasms in such a moving way—present the sufferings of the poor with such appeal—that he will lead his opponent to see life through different eyes. He may build up, by the contagion of his feelings, an influence which will modify B's temperament, and create in him a sympathy for the poor which didn't previously exist. This is often the only way to obtain ethical agreement, if there is any way at all. It is persuasive, not empirical or rational; but that is no reason for neglecting it. There is no reason to scorn it, either, for it is only by such means that our personalities are able to grow, through our contact with others.

The point I wish to stress, however, is simply that the empirical method is instrumental to ethical agreement only to the extent that disagreement in interest is rooted in disagreement in belief. There is little reason to believe that all disagreement is of this sort. Hence the empirical method is not sufficient for ethics. In any case, ethics is not psychology, since psychology doesn't endeavour to *direct* our interests; it discovers facts about the ways in which interests are or can be directed, but that's quite another matter.

To summarize this section: my analysis of ethical judgments meets the three requirements for the "vital" sense of "good" that were mentioned in section I. The traditional interest theories fail to meet these requirements simply because they neglect emotive meaning. This neglect leads them to neglect dynamic usage, and the sort of disagreement that results from such usage, together with the method of resolving the disagreement. I may add that my analysis answers Moore's objection about the open question. Whatever scientifically knowable properties a thing may have, it *is* always open to question whether a thing having these (enumerated) qualities is good. For to ask whether it is good is to ask for *influence*. And whatever I may know about an object, I can still ask, quite pertinently, to be influenced with regard to my interest in it.

VI

And now, have I really pointed out the "vital" sense of "good"?

I suppose that many will still say "No," claiming that I have simply failed to set down *enough* requirements which this sense must meet, and that my analysis, like all others given in terms of interest, is a way of begging the issue. They will say: "When we ask 'Is X good?' we don't want mere influence, mere advice. We decidedly don't want to be influenced through persuasion, nor are we fully content when the influence is supported by a wide scientific knowledge of X. The answer to our question will, of course, modify our interests. But this is only because an unique sort of *truth* will be revealed to us—a truth which must be apprehended *a priori*. We want our interests to be guided by this truth, and by nothing else. To substitute for such a truth mere emotive meaning and suggestion is to conceal from us the very object of our search."

I can only answer that I do not understand. What is this truth to be *about*? For I recollect no Platonic Idea, nor do I know what to *try* to recollect. I find no indefinable property, nor do I know what to look for. And the "self-evident" deliverances of reason, which so many philosophers have claimed, seem, on examination, to be deliverances of their respective reasons only (if of anyone's) and not of mine.

I strongly suspect, indeed, that any sense of "good" which is expected both to unite itself in synthetic *a priori* fashion with other concepts, and to influence interests as well, is really a great confusion. I extract from this meaning the power of influence alone, which I find the only intelligible part. If the rest is confusion, however, then it certainly deserves more than the shrug of one's shoulders. What I should like to do is to *account* for the confusion—to examine the psychological needs which have given rise to it, and to show how these needs may be satisfied in another way. This is *the* problem, if confusion is to be stopped at its source. But it is an enormous problem, and my reflections on it, which are at present worked out only roughly, must be reserved until some later time.

I may add that if "X is good" is essentially a vehicle for suggestion, it is scarcely a statement which philosophers, any more than many other men, are called upon to make. To the extent that ethics predicates the ethical terms of anything, rather than explains their meaning, it ceases to be a reflective study. Ethical statements are social instruments. They are used in a co-operative enterprise in which we are mutually adjusting ourselves to the interests of others. Philosophers have a part in this, as do all men, but not the major part.

40

Critique of Emotivism

R. M. Hare

The temptation to reduce imperatives to indicatives is very strong, and has the same source as the temptation to analyse value-words in the way called "naturalistic." This is the feeling that the "proper" indicative sentence, of which there is thought to be only one kind, is somehow above suspicion in a way that other sorts of sentence are not; and that therefore, in order to put these other sorts of sentence above suspicion, it is necessary to show that they are *really* indicatives. This feeling was intensified when the so-called "verificationist" theory of meaning became popular. This theory, which is in many ways a very fruitful one in its proper sphere, holds, to put it roughly, that a sentence does not have meaning unless there is something that would be the case if it were true. Now this is a very promising account of one of the ways in which a certain class of sentences (the typical indicatives) have meaning. Obviously, if a sentence is claimed to express a statement of fact, and yet we have no idea what would be the case if it were true, then that sentence is (to us) meaningless. But if this criterion of meaningfulness, which is useful in the case of statements of fact, is applied indiscriminately to types of utterance which are not intended to express statements of fact, trouble will result. Imperative sentences do not satisfy this criterion, and it may be that sentences expressing moral judgements do not either; but this only shows that they do not express statements in the sense defined by the criterion; and this sense may be a narrower one than that of normal usage. It does not mean that they are meaningless, or even that their meaning is of such a character that no logical rules can be given for their employment.[1]

1. 5. The feeling, that only "proper indicatives" are above suspicion, can survive (surprisingly) the discovery that there are perfectly good significant

[1] See my article "Imperative Sentences," *Mind*, lviii (1949), 21, from which some material is here used.

sentences of our ordinary speech which are not reducible to indicatives. It survives in the assumption that any meaning which is discovered for these sentences must necessarily be of some logically inferior status to that of indicatives. This assumption has led philosophers such as Professor A. J. Ayer, in the course of expounding their most valuable researches into the logical nature of moral judgements, to make incidental remarks which have raised needless storms of protest.[2] The substance of Ayer's theory is that moral judgements do not ordinarily function in the same way as the class of indicative sentences marked out by his verification-criterion. But by his way of stating his view, and his assimilation of moral judgements to other (quite distinct) types of sentence which are also marked off from typical indicatives by this criterion, he stirred up dust which has not yet subsided. All this might be closely paralleled by a similar treatment of imperatives—and it seems that writers of the same general line of thought as Ayer would have said the same sort of thing about imperatives as they did about moral judgements. Suppose that we recognize the obvious fact that imperatives are not like typical indicatives. Suppose, further, that we regard only typical indicatives as above suspicion. It will be natural then to say "Imperatives do not state anything, they only express wishes." Now to say that imperatives express wishes is, like the first theory which we considered, unexceptionable on the colloquial plane; we would indeed say, if someone said "Keep my name out of this," that he had expressed a wish to have his name kept out of it. But nevertheless the extreme ambiguity of the word "express" may generate philosophical confusion. We speak of expressing statements, opinions, beliefs, mathematical relations, and so on; and if it is in one of these senses that the word is used, the theory, though it tells us little, is harmless. But unfortunately it is also used in ways which are unlike these; and Ayer's use (in speaking of moral judgements) of the word "evince" as its rough synonym was dangerous. Artists and composers and poets are said to express their own and our feelings; oaths are said to express anger; and dancing upon the table may express joy. Thus to say that imperatives express wishes may lead the unwary to suppose that what happens when we use one, is this: we have welling up inside us a kind of longing, to which, when the pressure gets too great for us to bear, we give vent by saying an imperative sentence. Such an interpretation, when applied to such sentences as "Supply and fit to door mortise dead latch and plastic knob furniture," is unplausible. And it would seem that value-judgements also may fail to satisfy the verification-criterion, and indeed be in some sense, like imperatives, prescriptive, without having this sort of thing said about them. It is perfectly unexceptionable, on the colloquial plane, to say that the sentence "A is good" is used to express approval of A (*The Shorter Oxford English Dictionary* says: "Approve: . . . to pronounce to be good"); but it is philosophically misleading if we think that the approval which is expressed is a peculiar warm feeling inside us. If the Minister of Local

---

[2] See especially *Language, Truth and Logic*, 2nd ed., pp. 108–9. For a later and more balanced statement, see "On the Analysis of Moral Judgments," *Philosophical Essays*, pp. 231 ff.

Government expresses approval of my town plan by getting his underlings to write to me saying "The Minister approves of your plan" or "The Minister thinks your plan is the best one," I shall in no circumstances confirm the letter by getting a private detective to observe the Minister for signs of emotion. In this case, to have such a letter sent *is* to approve.

1. 6. There could be no analogue, in the case of singular imperatives, of the "attitude" variety of the approval theory of value-judgements,[3] but it is possible to construct such a theory about *universal* imperative sentences. If someone said "Never hit a man when he is down," it would be natural to say that he had expressed a certain attitude towards such conduct. It is extremely hard to define exactly this attitude or give criteria for recognizing it, just as it is difficult to say exactly what *moral* approval is as opposed to other sorts of approval. The only safe way of characterizing the attitude which is expressed by a universal impera- tive is to say "The attitude that one should not (or should) do so and so"; and the only safe way of characterizing the attitude which is expressed by a moral judgement is to say "The attitude that it is wrong (or right) to do so and so." To maintain an attitude of "moral approval" towards a certain practice is to have a disposition to think, on the appropriate occasions, that it is right; or, if "think" itself is a dispositional word, it is simply to think that it is right; and our thinking that it is right may be betrayed or exhibited—behaviourists would say constituted—by our acting in certain ways (above all, doing acts of the sort in question when the occasion arises; next, saying that they are right; applauding them in other ways, and so on). But there is in all this nothing to explain just *what* one thinks when one thinks that a certain sort of act is right. And similarly, if we said that "Never hit a man when he is down" expressed an attitude that one should not hit, &c. (or an attitude of aversion from hitting, or a "contra- attitude" towards hitting), we should not have said anything that would be intelligible to someone who did not understand the sentence which we were trying to explain.

I wish to emphasize that I am not seeking to refute any of these theories. They have all of them the characteristic that, if put in everyday terms, they say nothing exceptionable so far as their main contentions go; but when we seek to understand how they explain the philosophical perplexities which generated them, we are either forced to interpret them in such a way as to render them unplausible, or else find that they merely set the same problems in a more complicated way. Sentences containing the word "approve" are so difficult of analysis that it seems perverse to use this notion to explain the meaning of moral judgements which we learn to make years before we learn the word "approve"; and similarly, it would be perverse to explain the meaning of the imperative mood in terms of wishing or any other feeling or attitude; for we learn how to respond to and use commands long before we learn the comparatively complex notions of "wish," "desire," "aversion," &c.

[3] See, for example, C. L. Stevenson, *Ethics and Language.*

1. 7. We must now consider another group of theories which have often been held concurrently with the group just considered. These hold that the function in language of either moral judgements or imperatives (which the theories often equate) is to affect causally the behaviour or emotions of the hearer. Professor R. Carnap writes:

> But actually a value-statement is nothing else than a command in a misleading grammatical form. It may have effects upon the actions of men, and these effects may either be in accordance with our wishes or not; but it is neither true nor false.[4]

and Professor Ayer writes:

> Ethical terms do not serve only to express feeling. They are calculated also to arouse feeling, and so to stimulate action. Indeed some of them are used in such a way as to give the sentences in which they occur the effect of commands.[5]

More recently this sort of view has been elaborated by Professor Stevenson.[6] Here again we have a type of theory which may be on the colloquial plane harmless, but which suggests philosophical errors by seeming to assimilate the processes of using a command or a moral judgement to other processes which are in fact markedly dissimilar.

It is indeed true of imperative sentences that if anyone, in using them, is being sincere or honest, he intends that the person referred to should *do* something (namely, what is commanded). This is indeed a test of sincerity in the case of commands, just as a statement is held to be sincere only if the speaker believes it. And there are similar criteria, as we shall later see, for sincerely assenting to commands and statements that have been given or made by someone else. But this is not quite what the theories suggest. They suggest, rather, that the function of a command is to affect the hearer causally, or get him to do something; and to say this may be misleading. In ordinary parlance there is no harm in saying that in using a command our intention is to get someone to do something; but for philosophical purposes an important distinction has to be made. The processes of *telling* someone to do something, and *getting* him to do it, are quite distinct, logically, from each other.[7] The distinction may be elucidated by considering a parallel one in the case of statements. To tell someone that something is the case is logically distinct from getting (or trying to get) him to believe it. Having told someone that something is the case we may, if he is not disposed to believe what we say, start on a quite different process of trying to get him to believe it (trying to persuade or convince him that what we have said is true). No one, in seeking to explain the function of indicative sentences, would say that they were attempts to persuade someone that something is the case.

---

[4] *Philosophy and Logical Syntax*, p. 24.

[5] *Language, Truth and Logic*, 2nd ed., p. 108.

[6] *Ethics and Language*, especially p. 21.

[7] For a fuller treatment of this question see my article, "Freedom of the Will," *Aristotelian Society*, Supplementary Vol. xxv (1951), 201, from which I have used some material here and in 10.3.

And there is no more reason for saying that commands are attempts to persuade or get someone to do something; here, too, we first tell someone what he is to do, and then, if he is not disposed to do what we say, we may start on the wholly different process of trying to get him to do it. Thus the instruction already quoted "Supply and fit to door mortise dead latch and plastic knob furniture" is not intended to *galvanize* joiners into activity; for such a purpose other means are employed.

This distinction is important for moral philosophy; for in fact the suggestion, that the function of moral judgements was to persuade, led to a difficulty in distinguishing their function from that of propaganda.[8] Since I am going to draw attention to some similarities between commands and moral judgements, and to classify them both as prescriptions, I require most emphatically to dissociate myself from the confusion of either of these things with propaganda. We have here, as often in philosophy, a mixture of two distinctions. The first is that between the language of statements and prescriptive language. The second is that between telling someone something and getting him to believe or do what one has told him. That these two distinctions are quite different, and overlap each other, should be clear after a moment's consideration. For we may tell someone, either that something is the case, or to do something; here there is no attempt at persuasion (or influencing or inducing or getting to). If the person is not disposed to assent to what we tell him, we may then resort to rhetoric, propaganda, marshalling of additional facts, psychological tricks, threats, bribes, torture, mockery, promises of protection, and a variety of other expedients. All of these are ways of inducing him or getting him to do something; the first four are also ways of getting him to believe something; none of them are ways of telling him something, though those of them which involve the employment of language may include telling him all sorts of things. Regarded as inducements or expedients for persuasion, their success is judged solely by their effects—by whether the person believes or does what we are trying to get him to believe or do. It does not matter whether the means used to persuade him are fair or foul, so long as they do persuade him. And therefore the natural reaction to the realization that someone is trying to persuade us is "He's trying to get at me; I must be on my guard; I mustn't let him bias my decision unfairly; I must be careful to make up my own mind in the matter and remain a free responsible agent." Such a reaction to moral judgements should not be encouraged by philosophers. On the other hand, these are not natural reactions either to someone's telling us that something is the case, or to his telling us to do something (for example, to fit a latch to the door). Telling someone to do something, or that something is the case, is answering the question "What shall I do?" or "What are the facts?" When we have answered these questions the hearer knows what to do or what the facts are—if what we have told him is right. He is not necessarily thereby *influenced* one way or the other, nor have we failed if he is not; for he may decide to disbelieve or disobey us, and the mere telling him

[8] Cf. Stevenson, *Ethics and Language*, ch. xi.

does nothing—and seeks to do nothing—to prevent him doing this. But persuasion is not directed to a person as a rational agent, who is asking himself (or us) "What shall I do?"; it is not an answer to this or to any other question; it is an attempt to *make* him answer it in a particular way.

It is easy to see, therefore, why the so-called "imperative theory" of moral judgements raised the protests that it did. Because based on a misconception of the function, not only of moral judgements but also of the commands to which they were being assimilated, it seemed to impugn the rationality of moral discourse. But if we realize that commands, however much they may differ from statements, are like them in this, that they consist in telling someone something, not in seeking to influence him, it does no harm to draw attention to the similarities between commands and moral judgements. For, as I shall show, commands, because they, like statements, are essentially intended for answering questions asked by rational agents, are governed by logical rules just as statements are. And this means that moral judgements may also be so governed. We remember that the greatest of all rationalists, Kant, referred to moral judgements as imperatives; though we must remember also that he was using the latter term in an extended sense, and that moral judgements, though they are like imperatives in some respects, are unlike them in others (11. 5).

Non-Cognitivism and Non-Naturalism—Further Readings

Ayer, Alfred J., *Language, Truth and Logic* (London: Victor Gollancz, 1936, 2d ed., 1946), Chap. 6. Proponent.

Blanshard, Brand, *Reason and Goodness* (London: George Allen and Unwin, 1961), Chap. 8. Critic.

Brandt, Richard B., *Ethical Theory* (Englewood Cliffs, N.J.: Prentice-Hall, 1959), Chap. 9. Exposition and criticism.

Ewing, A. C., *The Definition of Good* (New York: Macmillan, 1947), Chap. 1. Critic.

Hancock, Roger N., *Twentieth Century Ethics* (New York: Columbia U.P., 1974), Chap. 4. Exposition and criticism.

Hudson, W. D., *Modern Moral Philosophy* (Garden City, N.Y.: Doubleday, 1970), Chap. 4. Exposition and criticism.

Kerner, George C., *The Revolution in Ethical Theory* (New York: Oxford U.P., 1966), Chap. 2. Exposition and criticism.

Stevenson, Charles L., *Ethics and Language* (New Haven: Yale U.P., 1944).

——, *Facts and Values: Studies in Ethical Analysis* (New Haven: Yale U.P., 1963).

Stroll, Avrum, *The Emotive Theory of Ethics.* In *University of California Publications in Philosophy* (Berkeley: U. of California Press, 1954), Vol. XXVIII, pp. 1–92. Exposition and criticism.

Toulmin, Stephen E., *An Examination of the Place of Reason in Ethics* (Cambridge: Cambridge U.P., 1950), Chap. 3. Critic.

Urmson, J. O., *The Emotive Theory of Ethics* (New York: Oxford U.P., 1968). Exposition and criticism.

Warnock, G. J., *Contemporary Moral Philosophy* (London: Macmillan, 1967), Chap. 3. Exposition and criticism.

Warnock, Mary, *Ethics Since 1900* (London: Oxford U.P., 1960), Chap. 4. Exposition.

Wellman, Carl, "Emotivism and Ethical Objectivity," *American Philosophical Quarterly*, V (1968), pp. 90–99. Critic.

——, *The Language of Ethics* (Cambridge, Mass.: Harvard U.P., 1961), Chap. 4. Exposition and criticism.

C QUASI-COGNITIVISM AND QUASI-NATURALISM: *THE GOOD REASONS APPROACH*

The last section included Hare's rejection of emotivism, and since it is now our interest to obtain a more complete view of his work, perhaps a recapitulation would be helpful. Hare shares Stevenson's concern with the function of ethical statements; but he believes that Stevenson wrongly identifies that function as primarily one of influencing the emotional attitudes of others. For Hare, the key use of ethical language is to provide practical guidance in making choices about various courses of action. Ethical language, in other words, is prescriptive and practical; it provides answers to the question, "What shall I do?" Hare also agrees with Stevenson in his rejection of naturalism in so far as it involves defining ethical terms by reference to nonethical properties. Hare essentially agrees with Moore, then, with respect to the naturalistic fallacy. At the same time, he does not follow Moore's cognitivism. In developing his position, Hare rejects the claim that ethical judgments, either of value or obligation, are indicative statements whose function is to impart information.

Nevertheless, he does not consider ethical statements to be beyond the pale of rational justification. There are important relationships between factual statements about natural properties and the moral judgments which they support as reasons. For example, Hare devotes much attention to the term "good," and he notes that when we call something "good," we intend to commend it. This commendatory use of "good" provides what he calls the "evaluative meaning" of the term. This evaluative meaning is constant, even though we may predicate the term "good" of objects as various as motor-cars and strawberries. Furthermore, when we commend particular objects as good there are reasons which can be cited to justify our statement. There are "criteria" for calling some motor-cars "good" and others "bad." Thus, we may call them "good," because they are easy to start, handle comfortably on the road, use relatively little fuel, and do not require frequent repairs. By referring to factual traits such as these, we show our listener that our judgment is not an arbitrary one. In similar fashion, we could justify our judgment that strawberries are "good" by citing their tastiness, their food value, etc. Our "criteria" for applying the term "good" to objects of different types will vary; but the evaluative meaning of "good" will be the same.

By distinguishing the evaluative meaning of "good" from the criteria for applying the term, Hare avoids Moore's naturalistic fallacy. For Hare, "good" is not defined in terms of nonethical properties, yet, at the same time, we do need to know the relevant nonethical properties of things before we can reasonably apply the term "good" to them. As the reader will note, Hare does not object to saying that statements using the term "good" have both evaluative and descriptive meaning. Accordingly, Hare's position may be viewed as seeking a middle path between cognitivism and non-cognitivism and between naturalism and non-naturalism. For this reason, we have classified him as both a quasi-cognitivist and a quasi-naturalist.

Hare also argues both in *The Language of Morals* and, even more strongly in *Freedom and Reason* (New York: Oxford University Press, 1965), that there is another property of moral reasoning. Ethical judgments must be universalizable—a property we have seen manifested, in one form or another, by most traditional normative theories. The principle of universalizability is somewhat like the rule of consistency: if I call a pencil "yellow" under certain conditions of light, visibility, readings on a spectrometer, etc., then I must be willing to call other objects "yellow" under the same conditions. By the same token, if I call an action "right" or an object "good" under certain conditions, then I must call other actions "right" and other objects "good" under the same conditions. To tell a person that he should repay a debt in certain circumstances commits the speaker to the proposition that anybody, including the speaker himself, should repay the debt in the same circumstances. If moral judgments were not so universalizable, they could not, in Hare's opinion, perform their action-guiding (prescriptive) function.

In sum, moral judgments, or evaluations, are prescriptions which are characterized by universalizability; their common meaning or use is to commend, or to condemn, actions or objects or persons; and moral judgments can often be justified by statements which provide good reasons for the prescriptions.

Warnock's attack is directed at two main elements of Hare's doctrine: the prescriptivity of ethical language, and the principle of universalizability.

With respect to prescriptivity, Warnock wishes to claim that ethical language can be descriptive in stronger senses then Hare allows. Searle and Foot, whom we have yet to consider, also support this claim. Warnock contends that it is not at all clear that all evaluations are primarily prescriptions. But he is after bigger game. Following the pattern established by some other ethical thinkers, e.g., Nowell-Smith and J. L. Austin, he argues that it is obvious that normative and evaluative words and sentences do many things: advise, exhort, implore, command, confess, undertake. They are *multi-functional*.* Hare mistakenly restricts the evaluative context to answers to the question: "What shall I do?" It is much more plausible, Warnock thinks, to argue the more limited thesis that there is an important connection between words and deeds; and, this is, of course, one of Hare's interests. The acceptance of the correctness of a moral judgment does commit one to acting in certain ways; nevertheless, Warnock argues that the relations between moral judgments and deeds need not be construed as always prescriptive. There may be many other things going on—avowals, expressions of approval, etc. Moral discourse in general is not related to conduct in one way, any more than one who engages in moral discourse is always doing one thing.

On universalizability, Warnock believes that it does not, as Hare believes, differentiate moral from other prescriptions. Its presence, for instance, does not make a prescriptive judgment morally right. It is merely the principle of consistency set out in relation to moral judgments and their justification. As was argued in the comment on Kant's ethics in a similar context, one can merely enlarge the generalization so as to include the hard cases. One might even generalize to include what most persons would regard as immoral cases. For example, one might say: "All cases of not reporting small cash payments as income for tax purposes are permissible." There is no criterion to show that what a person is willing to universalize is wrong. Warnock believes that Hare is in this difficulty because he holds that ultimate moral rules are matters of decision, not subject to further proof. This being true, Hare really has not got far away from Stevenson's emotivism after all.

* See Brandt, *Ethical Theory*, *op. cit.*, pp. 231–239.

41

Prescriptivism

R. M. HARE

5. 2. Let me illustrate one of the most characteristic features of value-words in terms of a particular example. It is a feature sometimes described by saying that "good" and other such words are the names of "supervenient" or "consequential" properties. Suppose that a picture is hanging upon the wall and we are discussing whether it is a good picture; that is to say, we are debating whether to assent to, or dissent from, the judgement "P is a good picture." It must be understood that the context makes it clear that we mean by "good picture" not "good likeness" but "good work of art"—though both these uses would be value-expressions.

First let us notice a very important peculiarity of the word "good' as used in this sentence. Suppose that there is another picture next to P in the gallery (I will call it Q). Suppose that either P is a replica of Q or Q of P, and we do not know which, but do know that both were painted by the same artist at about the same time. Now there is one thing that we cannot say; we cannot say "P is exactly like Q in all respects save this one, that P is a good picture and Q not." If we were to say this, we should invite the comment, "But how can one be good and the other not, if they are exactly alike? There must be some *further* difference between them to make one good and the other not." Unless we at least admit the relevance of the question "What makes one good and the other not?" we are bound to puzzle our hearers; they will think that something has gone wrong with our use of the word "good." Sometimes we cannot specify just what it is that makes one good and the other not; but there always must be something. Suppose that in the attempt to explain our meaning we said: "I didn't say that there *was* any other difference between them; there is just this one difference, that one is good and the other not. Surely you would understand me if I said that one was *signed* and the other not, but that there was otherwise no difference? So why shouldn't I say that one was *good* and the other not, but that there was otherwise no difference?" The answer to this protest is that the word "good" is not like the word "signed"; there is a difference in their logic.

5. 3. The following reason might be suggested for this logical peculiarity: there is some one characteristic or group of characteristics of the two pictures on which the characteristic "good" is logically dependent, so that, of course, one cannot be good and the other not, unless these characteristics vary too. To quote a parallel case, one picture could not be *rectangular* and the other not, unless certain other characteristics also varied, for example the size of at least one of the angles. And so a natural response to the discovery that "good" behaves as it does, is to suspect that there is a set of characteristics which together *entail* a thing being good, and to set out to discover what these characteristics are. This is the genesis of that group of ethical theories which Professor Moore called "naturalist"—an unfortunate term, for as Moore says himself, substantially the same fallacy may be committed by choosing metaphysical or supra-sensible characteristics for this purpose.[1] Talking about the supernatural is no prophylactic against "naturalism." The term has, unfortunately, since Moore's introduction of it, been used very loosely. It is best to confine it to those theories against which Moore's refutation (or a recognizable version of it) is valid. In this sense most "emotive" theories are not naturalist, though they are often called so. Their error is a quite different one. I shall argue below (11.3) that what is wrong with naturalist theories is that they leave out the prescriptive or commendatory element in value-judgements, by seeking to make them derivable from statements of fact. If I am right in this opinion, my own theory, which preserves this element, is not naturalist.

We have to inquire, then, whether there is any characteristic or group of characteristics which is related to the characteristic of being good in the same way as the angle-measurements of figures are related to their rectangularity. In what way are the latter related? This involves answering the question: Why cannot it be the case that one picture is rectangular and the other not unless the angle-measurements of the two pictures also differ? The answer is clearly that "rectangular" *means* "rectilinear and having all its angles of a certain size, namely, 90 degrees"; and, therefore, that when we have said that one picture is rectangular and the other not, we have said that the measurements of their angles differ; and if we then go on to say that they do not differ, we contradict ourselves. Therefore, to say "P is exactly like Q in all respects save this one, that P is a rectangular picture and Q not," may be self-contradictory; whether it is self-contradictory depends on what we intend to include in "all respects." If we intend to include the measurements of the angles, then the sentence is self-contradictory; for it is self-contradictory to say "P is exactly like Q in all respects, *including the measurements of its angles*, save this one, that P is a rectangular picture and Q not"; this contains the assertion that the angles of P both differ and do not differ from those of Q.

Thus the impossibility that we are speaking of is a logical one, which depends upon the meaning of the word "rectangular." This is a very elementary example of a logical impossibility; there are other more complex examples. Those who in recent times have denied that there can be synthetic *a priori* truth have been asserting that all *a priori* impossibility can be shown to be of this character, i.e. dependent on the meanings assigned to the words used. Whether they are

---

[1] *Principia Ethica*, p. 39.

right is still a matter under dispute; but for the purposes of my argument I shall assume that they are. The dispute has reached the stage when it cannot be argued on abstract grounds alone, but only by the painstaking analysis of particular sentences which are claimed to be true *a priori* and yet synthetic.[2]

5. 4. Let us then ask whether "good" behaves in the way that we have noticed for the same reason that "rectangular" does; in other words, whether there are certain characteristics of pictures which are defining characteristics of a good picture, in the same way as "having all its angles 90 degrees and being a recti-linear plane figure" are defining characteristics of a rectangle. Moore thought that he could prove that there were no such defining characteristics for the word "good" as used in morals. His argument has been assailed since he propounded it; and it is certainly true that the formulation of it was at fault. But it seems to me that Moore's argument was not merely plausible; it rests, albeit insecurely, upon a secure foundation; there is indeed something about the way in which, and the purposes for which, we use the word "good" which makes it impossible to hold the sort of position which Moore was attacking, although Moore did not see clearly what this something was. Let us, therefore, try to restate Moore's argument in a way which makes it clear why "naturalism" is untenable, not only for the moral use of "good" as he thought, but also for many other uses.

Let us suppose for the sake of argument that there are some "defining characteristics" of a good picture. It does not matter of what sort they are; they can be a single characteristic, or a conjunction of characteristics, or a dis-junction of alternative characteristics. Let us call the group of these character-istics C. "P is a good picture" will then mean the same as "P is a picture and P is C." For example, let C mean "Having a tendency to arouse in people who are at that time members of the Royal Academy (or any other definitely specified group of people), a definitely recognizable feeling called 'admiration'." The words "definitely specified" and "definitely recognizable" have to be inserted, for otherwise we might find that words in the *definiens* were being used evalu-atively, and this would make the definition no longer "naturalistic." Now sup-pose that we wish to say that the members of the Royal Academy have good taste in pictures. To have good taste in pictures means to have this definitely recognizable feeling of admiration for those pictures, and only those pictures, which are good pictures. If therefore we wish to say that the members of the Royal Academy have good taste in pictures, we have, according to the definition, to say something which means the same as saying that they have this feeling of admiration for pictures which have a tendency to arouse in them this feeling.

Now this is not what we wanted to say. We wanted to say that they admired good pictures; we have succeeded only in saying that they admired pictures which they admired. Thus if we accept the definition we debar ourselves from saying something that we do sometimes want to say. What this something is will become apparent later; for the moment let us say that what we wanted to do was

---

[2] An excellent example of such analysis is to be found in an article on "The Incongruity of Counterparts," by D. F. Pears, *Mind*, lxi (1952), 78.

to *commend* the pictures which the members of the Royal Academy admired. Something about our definition prevented our doing this. We could no longer commend the pictures which they admired, we could only say that they admired those pictures which they admired. Thus our definition has prevented us, in one crucial case, from commending something which we want to commend. That is what is wrong with it.

Let us generalize. If "P is a good picture" is held to mean the same as "P is a picture and P is C," then it will become impossible to commend pictures for being C; it will be possible only to say that they are C. It is important to realize that this difficulty has nothing to do with the particular example that I have chosen. It is not because we have chosen the wrong defining characteristics; it is because, whatever defining characteristics we choose, this objection arises, that we can no longer commend an object for possessing those characteristics.

Let us illustrate this by another example. I am deliberately excluding for the moment moral examples because I want it to be clear that the logical difficulties which we are encountering have nothing to do with morals in particular, but are due to the general characteristics of value-words. Let us consider the sentence "S is a good strawberry." We might naturally suppose that this means nothing more than "S is a strawberry and S is sweet, juicy, firm, red, and large." But it then becomes impossible for us to say certain things which in our ordinary talk we do say. We sometimes want to say that a strawberry is a good strawberry because it is sweet, &c. This—as we can at once see if we think of ourselves saying it—does not mean the same as saying that a strawberry is a sweet, &c., strawberry because it is sweet, &c. But according to the proposed definition this is what it would mean. Thus here again the proposed definition would prevent our saying something that we do succeed in saying meaningfully in our ordinary talk. . . .

5.8.   Value-terms have a special function in language, that of commending; and so they plainly cannot be defined in terms of other words which themselves do not perform this function; for if this is done, we are deprived of a means of performing the function. But with words like "puppy" this does not apply; one may define "puppy" in terms of any other words which will do the same job. Whether two expressions will do the same job is decided by reference to usage. And since what we are trying to do is to give an account of the word "good" as it *is* used—not as it *might* be used if its meaning and usage were changed—this reference is final. It is therefore no answer to the above argument to claim that a "naturalist" might if he pleased define "good" in terms of some characteristics of his choice. Such an arbitrary definition is quite out of place here; the logician is, it is true, at liberty to define his own technical terms as he pleases, provided that he makes it clear how he is going to use them. But "good" in this context is not a technical term used for talking about what the logician is talking about; it itself *is* what he is talking about; it is the object of his study, not the instrument. He is studying the function of the word "good" in language; and so long as he wishes to study this, he must continue to allow the word the function which it has in language, that of commending. If by an arbitrary definition he gives the word a different function from that which it now has, then he is not studying the same thing any longer; he is studying a figment of his own devising.

Naturalism in ethics, like attempts to square the circle and to "justify induction," will constantly recur so long as there are people who have not understood the fallacy involved. It may therefore be useful to give a simple procedure for exposing any new variety of it that may be offered. Let us suppose that someone claims that he can deduce a moral or other evaluative judgement from a set of purely factual or descriptive premisses, relying on some definition to the effect that V (a value-word) means the same as C (a conjunction of descriptive predicates). We first have to ask him to be sure that C contains no expression that is covertly evaluative (for example "natural" or "normal" or "satisfying" or "fundamental human needs"). Nearly all so-called "naturalistic definitions" will break down under this test—for to be genuinely naturalistic a definition must contain no expression for whose applicability there is not a definite criterion which does not involve the making of a value-judgement. If the definition satisfies this test, we have next to ask whether its advocate ever wishes to commend anything for being C. If he says that he does, we have only to point out to him that his definition makes this impossible, for the reasons given. And clearly he cannot say that he never wishes to commend anything for being C; for to commend things for being C is the whole object of his theory. . . .

7. 1. Of all the problems raised by the preceding argument, the key problem is as follows: there are two sorts of things that we can say, for example, about strawberries; the first sort is usually called *descriptive*, the second sort *evaluative*. Examples of the first sort of remark are, "This strawberry is sweet" and "This strawberry is large, red, and juicy." Examples of the second sort of remark are "This is a good strawberry" and "This strawberry is just as strawberries ought to be." The first sort of remark is often given as a reason for making the second sort of remark; but the first sort does not by itself entail the second sort, nor vice versa. Yet there seems to be some close logical connexion between them. Our problem is: "What is this connexion?"; for no light is shed by saying that there is a connexion, unless we can say what it is.

The problem may also be put in this way: if we knew all the descriptive properties which a particular strawberry had (knew, of every descriptive sentence relating to the strawberry, whether it was true or false), and if we knew also the meaning of the word "good," then what else should we require to know, in order to be able to tell whether a strawberry was a good one? Once the question is put in this way, the answer should be apparent. We should require to know, what are the criteria in virtue of which a strawberry is to be called a good one, or what are the characteristics that make a strawberry a good one, or what is the standard of goodness in strawberries. We should require to be given the major premiss. We have already seen that we can know the meaning of "good strawberry" without knowing any of these latter things—though there is also a sense of the sentence "What does it mean to call a strawberry a good one?" in which we should not know the answer to it, unless we also knew the answer to these other questions. It is now time to elucidate and distinguish these two ways in which we can be said to know what it means to call an object a good member of its class. This will help us to see more clearly both the differences and the similarities between "good" and words like "red" and "sweet."

Since we have been dwelling for some time on the differences, it will do no harm now to mention some of the similarities. For this purpose, let us consider the two sentences "M is a red motor-car" and "M is a good motor-car." It will be noticed that "motor-car," unlike "strawberry," is a functional word, as defined in the preceding chapter. Reference to the *Shorter Oxford English Dictionary* shows that a motor-car is a carriage, and a carriage a means of conveyance. Thus, if a motor-car will not convey anything, we know from the definition of motor-car that it is not a good one. But when we know this, we know so little, compared with what is required in order to know the full criteria of a good motor-car, that I propose in what follows to ignore, for the sake of simplicity, this complicating factor. I shall treat "motor-car" as if it did not have to be defined functionally: that is to say, I shall assume that we could learn the meaning of "motor-car" (as in a sense we can) simply by being shown examples of motor-cars. It is, of course, not always easy to say whether or not a word is a functional word; it depends, like all questions of meaning, on how the word is taken by a particular speaker.

The first similarity between "M is a red motor-car" and "M is a good motor-car" is that both can be, and often are, used for conveying information of a purely factual or descriptive character. If I say to someone "M is a good motor-car," and he himself has not seen, and knows nothing of M, but does on the other hand know what sorts of motor-car we are accustomed to call "good" (knows what is the accepted standard of goodness in motor-cars), he undoubtedly receives information from my remark about what sort of motor-car it is. He will complain that I have misled him, if he subsequently discovers that M will not go over 30 m.p.h., or uses as much oil as petrol, or is covered with rust, or has large holes in the roof. His reason for complaining will be the same as it would have been if I had said that the car was red and he subsequently discovered that it was black. I should have led him to expect the motor-car to be of a certain description when in fact it was of a quite different description.

The second similarity between the two sentences is this. Sometimes we use them, not for actually conveying information, but for putting our hearer into a position subsequently to use the word "good" or "red" for giving or getting information. Suppose, for example, that he is utterly unfamiliar with motor-cars in the same sort of way as most of us are unfamiliar with horses nowadays, and knows no more about motor-cars than is necessary in order to distinguish a motor-car from a hansom cab. In that case, my saying to him "M is a good motor-car" will not give him any information about M, beyond the information that it is a motor-car. But if he is able then or subsequently to examine M, he will have learnt something. He will have learnt that some of the characteristics which M has, are characteristics which make people—or at any rate me—call it a good motor-car. This may not be to learn very much. But suppose that I make judgements of this sort about a great many motor-cars, calling some good and some not good, and he is able to examine all or most of the motor-cars about which I am speaking; he will in the end learn quite a lot, always presuming that I observe a consistent standard in calling them good or not good. He will eventually, if he pays careful attention, get into the position in which he knows, after I have said that a motor-car is a good one, what sort of a motor-car he may expect it to be—for example fast, stable on the road, and so on.

Now if we were dealing, not with "good," but with "red," we should call this process "explaining the meaning of the word"—and we might indeed, in a sense, say that what I have been doing is explaining what one means by a" good motor-car." This is a sense of "mean" about which, as we have seen, we must be on our guard. The processes, however, are very similar. I might explain the meaning of "red" by continually saying of various motor-cars "M is a red motor-car," "N is not a red motor car," and so on. If he were attentive enough, he would soon get into a position in which he was able to use the word "red" for giving or getting information, at any rate about motor-cars. And so, both with "good" and with "red," there is this process, which in the case of "red" we may call "explaining the meaning," but in the case of "good" may only call it so loosely and in a secondary sense; to be clear we must call it something like "explaining or conveying or setting forth the standard of goodness in motor-cars."

The standard of goodness, like the meaning of "red," is normally something which is public and commonly accepted. When I explain to someone the meaning of "red motor-car," he expects, unless I am known to be very eccentric, that he will find other people using it in the same way. And similarly, at any rate with objects like motor-cars where there is a commonly accepted standard, he will expect, having learnt from me what is the standard of goodness in motor-cars, to be able, by using the expression "good motor-car," to give information to other people, and get it from them, without confusion.

A third respect in which "good motor-car" resembles "rcd motor-car" is the following: both "good" and "red" can vary as regards the exactitude or vagueness of the information which they do or can convey. We normally use the expression "red motor-car" very loosely. Any motor-car that lies somewhere between the unmistakably purple and the unmistakably orange could without abuse of language be called a red motor-car. And similarly, the standard for calling motor-cars good is commonly very loose. There are certain characteristics, such as inability to exceed 30 m.p.h., which to anyone but an eccentric would be sufficient conditions for refusing to call it a good motor-car; but there is no precise set of accepted criteria such that we can say "If a motor-car satisfies these conditions, it is a good one; if not, not." And in both cases we could be precise if we wanted to. We could, for certain purposes, agree not to say that a motor-car was "really red" unless the redness of its paint reached a certain measurable degree of purity and saturation; and similarly, we might adopt a very exact standard of goodness in motor-cars. We might refuse the name "good motor-car" to any car that would not go round a certain race-track without mishap in a certain limited time, that did not conform to certain other rigid specifications as regards accommodation, &c. This sort of thing has not been done for the expression "good motor-car"; but, as Mr. Urmson has pointed out, it has been done by the Ministry of Agriculture for the expression "super apple."[3]

It is important to notice that the exactness or looseness of their criteria does absolutely nothing to distinguish words like "good" from words like "red." Words in both classes may be descriptively loose or exact, according to how rigidly the criteria have been laid down by custom or convention. It certainly is not true that value-words are distinguished from descriptive words in that the former are looser, descriptively, than the latter. There are loose and rigid examples of both sorts of word. Words like "red" can be extremely loose, without becoming to the least degree evaluative; and expressions like "good sewage effluent" can be the subject of very rigid criteria, without in the least ceasing to be evaluative. . . .

8. 1. It is now time to inquire into the reasons for the logical features of "good" that we have been describing, and to ask why it is that it has this peculiar combination of evaluative and descriptive meaning. The reason will be found in the purposes for which it, like other value-words, is used in our discourse. The examination of these purposes will reveal the relevance of the matters discussed in the first part of this book to the study of evaluative language.

I have said that the primary function of the word "good" is to commend. We have, therefore, to inquire what commending is. When we commend or condemn anything, it is always in order, at least indirectly, to guide choices, our own or other people's, now or in the future. Suppose that I say "The South Bank Exhibition is very good." In what context should I appropriately say this, and what would be my purpose in so doing? It would be natural for me to say it to someone who was wondering whether to go to London to see the Exhibition, or, if he was in London, whether to pay it a visit. It would, however, be too much to say that the reference to choices is always as direct as this. An American returning from London to New York, and speaking to some people who had no intention of going to London in the near future, might still make the same remark. In order, therefore, to show that critical value-judgements are all ultimately related to choices, and would not be made if they were not so related, we require to ask, for what purpose we have standards.

It has been pointed out by Mr. Urmson that we do not speak generally of "good" wireworms. This is because we never have any occasion for choosing between wireworms, and therefore require no guidance in so doing. We therefore need to have no standards for wireworms. But it is easy to imagine circumstances in which this situation might alter. Suppose that wireworms came into use as a special kind of bait for fishermen. Then we might speak of having dug up a very good wireworm (one, for example, that was exceptionally fat and attractive to fish), just as now, no doubt, seafishermen might talk of having dug up a very good lug-worm. We only have standards for a class of objects, we only talk

---

[3] *Mind*, lix (1950), 152 (also in *Logic and Language*, ii, ed. Flew, 166).

of the virtues of one specimen as against another, we only use value-words about them, when occasions are known to exist, or are conceivable, in which we, or someone else, would have to choose between specimens. We should not call pictures good or bad if no one ever had the choice of seeing them or not seeing them (or of studying them or not studying them in the way that art students study pictures, or of buying them or not buying them). Lest, by the way, I should seem to have introduced a certain vagueness by specifying so many alternative kinds of choices, it must be pointed out that the matter can, if desired, be made as precise as we require; for we can specify, when we have called a picture a good one, within what class we have called it good; for example, we can say "I meant a good picture to study, but not to buy."

8. 2. It should be pointed out that even judgements about past choices do not refer merely to the past. As we shall see, all value-judgements are covertly universal in character, which is the same as to say that they refer to, and express acceptance of, a standard which has an application to other similar instances. If I censure someone for having done something, I envisage the possibility of him, or someone else, or myself, having to make a similar choice again; otherwise there would be no point in censuring him. Thus, if I say to a man whom I am teaching to drive "You did that manœuvre badly" this is a very typical piece of driving-instruction; and driving-instruction consists in teaching a man to drive not in the past but in the future; to this end we censure or commend past pieces of driving, in order to impart to him the standard which is to guide him in his subsequent conduct.

When we commend an object, our judgement is not solely about that particular object, but is inescapably about objects like it. Thus, if I say that a certain motor-car is a good one, I am not merely saying something about that particular motor-car. To say something about that particular car, merely, would not be to commend. To commend, as we have seen, is to guide choices. Now for guiding a particular choice we have a linguistic instrument which is not that of commendation, namely, the singular imperative. If I wish merely to tell someone to choose a particular car, with no thought of the kind of car to which it belongs, I can say "Take that one." If instead of this I say "That is a good one," I am saying something more. I am implying that if any motor-car were just like that one, it would be a good one too; whereas by saying "Take that one," I do not imply that, if my hearer sees another car just like that one, he is to take it too. But further, the implication of the judgement "That is a good motor-car" does not extend merely to motor-cars *exactly* like that one. If this were so, the implication would be for practical purposes useless; for nothing is exactly like anything else. It extends to every motor-car that is like that one in the *relevant* particulars; and the relevant particulars are its virtues—those of its characteristics for which I was commending it, or which I was calling good about it. Whenever we commend, we have in mind something about the object commended which is the reason for our commendation. It therefore always makes sense, after someone has said "That is a good motor-car," to ask "What is good about it?" or "Why do you call it good?" or "What features of it are you commending?" It may not always be easy to answer this question precisely, but it is always a legitimate question. If we did not understand why it was always a legitimate question, we should not understand the way in which the word "good" functions.

We may illustrate this point by comparing two dialogues (similar to the one in 5.2):

(1) *X.* Jones' motor-car is a good one.
   Y. What makes you call it good?
   X. Oh, just that it's good.
   Y. But there must be some *reason* for your calling it good, I mean some property that it has in virtue of which you call it good.
   X. No; the property in virtue of which I call it good is just its goodness and nothing else.
   Y. But do you mean that its shape, speed, weight, manœuvrability, &c., are irrelevant to whether you call it good or not?
   X. Yes, quite irrelevant; the only relevant property is that of goodness, just as, if I called it yellow, the only relevant property would be that of yellowness.

(2) The same dialogue, only with "yellow" substituted for "good" and "yellowness" for "goodness" throughout, and the last clause ("just as . . . yellowness") omitted.

The reason why X's position in the first dialogue is eccentric is that since, as we have already remarked, "good" is a "supervenient" or "consequential" epithet, one may always legitimately be asked when one has called something a good something, "What is good about it?" Now to answer this question is to give the properties in virtue of which we call it good. Thus, if I have said, "That is a good motor-car" and someone asks "Why? What is good about it?" and I reply "Its high speed combined with its stability on the road," I indicate that I call it good in virtue of its having these properties or virtues. Now to do this is *eo ipso* to say something about other motor-cars which have these properties. If any motor-car whatever had these properties, I should have, if I were not to be inconsistent, to agree that it was, *pro tanto*, a good motor-car; though of course it might, although it had these properties in its favour, have other countervailing disadvantages, and so be, taken all in all, not a good motor-car.

This last difficulty can always be got over by specifying in detail why I called the first motor-car a good one. Suppose that a second motor-car were like the first one in speed and stability, but gave its passengers no protection from the rain, and proved difficult to get into and out of. I should not then call it a good motor-car, although it had those characteristics which led me to call the first one good. This shows that I should not have called the first one good either, if it too had had the bad characteristics of the second one; and so in specifying what was good about the first one, I ought to have added '. . . and the protection it gives to the passengers and the ease with which one can get into and out of it." This process could be repeated indefinitely until I had given a complete list of the characteristics of the first motor-car which were required to make me allow it to be good one. This, in itself, would not be saying all that there was to be said about my standards for judging motor-cars—for there might be other motor-cars which, although falling short to a certain extent in these characteristics, had other countervailing good characteristics; for example, soft upholstery, large accommodation, or small consumption of petrol. But it would be at any rate some help to my hearer in building up an idea of my standards in motor-cars; and in this lies the importance of such questions and answers, and the importance of recognizing their relevance, whenever a value-judgement has been made. For one of the purposes of making such judgements is to make known the standard.

When I commend a motor-car I am guiding the choices of my hearer not merely in relation to that particular motor-car but in relation to motor-cars in general. What I have said to him will be of assistance to him whenever in the future he has to choose a motor-car or advise anyone else on the choice of a motor-car or even design a motor-car (choose what sort of motor-car to have made) or write a general treatise on the design of motor-cars (which involves choosing what sort of motor-cars to advise other people to have made). The method whereby I give him this assistance is by making known to him a standard for judging motor-cars.

This process has, as we have noticed, certain features in common with the process of defining (making known the meaning or application of) a descriptive word, though there are important differences. We have now to notice a further resemblance between showing the usage of a word and showing how to choose between motor-cars. In neither case can the instruction be done successfully unless the instructor is consistent in his teaching. If I use "red" for objects of a wide variety of colours, my hearer will never learn from me a consistent usage of the word. Similarly, if I commend motor-cars with widely different or even contrary characteristics, what I say to him will not be of assistance to him in choosing motor-cars subsequently, because I am not teaching him any consistent standard—or any standard at all, for a standard is by definition consistent. He will say, "I don't see by what standards you are judging these motor-cars; please explain to me why you call them all good, although they are so different." Of course, I might be able to give a satisfactory explanation. I might say, "There are different sorts of motor-cars, each good in its way; there are sports cars, whose prime requisites are speed and manœuvrability; and family cars, which ought rather to be capacious and economical; and taxis, and so on. So when I say a car is good which is fast and manœuvrable, although it is neither capacious nor economical, you must understand that I am commending it as a sports car, not as a family car." But suppose that I did not recognize the relevance of his question; suppose that I was just doling out the predicate "good" entirely haphazard, as the whim took me. It is clear that in this case I should teach him no standard at all.

We thus have to distinguish two questions that can always be asked in elucidation of a judgement containing the word "good." Suppose that someone says "That is a good one." We can then always ask (1) "Good what—sports car or family car or taxi or example to quote in a logic-book?" Or we can ask (2) "What makes you call it good?" To ask the first question is to ask for the class within which evaluative comparisons are being made. Let us call it the class of comparison. To ask the second question is to ask for the virtues or "good-making characteristics." These two questions are, however, not independent; for what distinguishes the class of comparison "sports car" from the class "family car" is the set of virtues which are to be looked for in the respective classes. This is so in all cases where the class of comparison is defined by means of a functional word—for obviously "sports car," "family car," and "taxi" are functional to a very much higher degree than plain "motor-car." Sometimes, however, a class of comparison may be further specified without making it more functional; for example, in explaining the phrase "good wine" we might say "I mean good wine for this district, not good wine compared with all the wines that there are."

8. 3. Now since it is the purpose of the word "good" and other value-words to be used for teaching standards, their logic is in accord with this purpose. We are therefore in a position at last to explain the feature of the word "good" which I pointed out at the beginning of this investigation. The reason why I cannot apply the word "good" to one picture, if I refuse to apply it to another picture which I agree to be in all other respects exactly similar, is that by doing this I should be defeating the purpose for which the word is designed. I should be commending one object, and so purporting to teach my hearers one standard, while in the same breath refusing to commend a similar object, and so undoing the lesson just imparted. By seeking to impart two inconsistent standards, I should be imparting no standard at all. The effect of such an utterance is similar to that of a contradiction; for in a contradiction, I say two inconsistent things, and so the effect is that the hearer does not know what I am trying to say. . . .

9. 2. . . . When we use the word "good" in order to commend morally, we are always directly or indirectly commending *people*. Even when we use the expression "good act" or others like it, the reference is indirectly to human characters. This, as has often been pointed out, constitutes a difference between the words "good" and "right." In speaking, therefore, of moral goodness, I shall speak only of the expression "good man" and similar expressions. We have to consider whether in fact this expression has the same logical features as the non-moral uses of "good" which we have been discussing, remembering that clearly "man" in "good man" is not normally a functional word, and never so when moral commendation is being given.

9. 3. First, let us take that characteristic of "good" which has been called its supervenience. Suppose that we say "St. Francis was a good man." It is logi-

cally impossible to say this and to maintain at the same time that there might have been another man placed in precisely the same circumstances as St. Francis, and who behaved in them in exactly the same way, but who differed from St. Francis in this respect only, that he was not a good man. I am supposing, of course, that the judgement is made in both cases upon the whole life of the subject, "inner" and overt. This example is similar in the relevant particulars to that in 5. 2.

Next, the explanation of this logical impossibility does not lie in any form of naturalism; it is not the case that there is any conjunction C of descriptive characteristics such that to say that a man has C entails that he is morally good. For, if this were the case, we should be unable to commend any man for having those characteristics; we should only be able to say that he had them. Nevertheless, the judgement that a man is morally good is not logically independent of the judgement that he has certain other characteristics which we may call virtues or good-making characteristics; there is a relation between them although it is not one of entailment or of identity of meaning.

Our previous discussion of non-moral goodness helps us to understand what the relation is. It is that a statement of the characteristics of the man (the minor or factual premiss) *together with* a specification of a standard for judging men morally (the major premiss), entails a moral judgement upon him. And moral standards have many of the features that we have found in other value-standards. "Good," as used in morals, has a descriptive and an evaluative meaning, and the latter is primary. To know the descriptive meaning is to know by what standards the speaker is judging. Let us take a case where the standard is well known. If a parson says of a girl that she is a good girl, we can form a shrewd idea, of what description she is; we may expect her to go to church, for example. It is therefore easy to fall into the error of supposing that by calling her a good girl the parson means simply that she has these descriptive characteristics.

It is quite true that part of what the parson means is that the girl has these characteristics; but it is to be hoped that this is not all he means. He also means to commend her for having them; and this part of his meaning is primary. The reason why we know, when a parson says a girl is good, what, sort of girl she is how she normally behaves, &c., is that parsons are usually consistent in the way they award commendation. It is through being used consistently by parsons for commending certain sorts of behaviour in girls that the word comes to have a descriptive force.

42

Problems of Prescriptivism

G. J. WARNOCK

MORAL DISCOURSE AS "PRESCRIPTIVE"

Prescriptive discourse, I think we may say quite generally (expounding Hare), is that species of discourse in which practical questions are answered—much as, one might say, informative discourse is that species of discourse which answers requests for information. If you put to me the information-seeking question "Where do you live?", my answer ("I live in Oxford") is a specimen of informative discourse; if you put to me the practical question "What ought I to do?", my answer will be a specimen of prescriptive discourse.

Now the simplest of all forms of prescriptive discourse, and also in a sense the basic form, is, in Hare's view, the plain imperative. The primary case of telling someone what to do is to issue, for instance, the simple imperative "Go away"—an utterance which may or may not have the effect of *making* its addressee go away, but at any rate *tells* him to. But in Hare's view we cannot properly say, as Carnap once did, that moral judgments just *are* grammatically disguised imperatives, for, as we shall see, moral judgments have certain essential features which simple imperatives may lack. But moral judgments, he holds, do have in common with imperatives the crucial feature that they are "prescriptive"; and this in fact means, in Hare's view, that a moral judgment—or at any rate a genuine, typical, non-deviant moral judgment—*entails* an imperative. Just as, if a proposition *p* entails another proposition *q*, I cannot (consistently) assert or accept *p* and deny or reject *q*, so, in Hare's view, I cannot (consistently) assert or accept the moral judgment, say, "You ought to repay the money" and deny or reject the imperative "Repay the money." Now to "deny" or "reject" an imperative, Hare holds, is simply, having received it, *not* to act on it, not to do what it says. Thus, the thesis that moral judgments are prescriptive implies that one who accepts the moral judgment that he ought to do *X* is logically committed to doing *X*; conversely, that one who does not do *X* is logically debarred from accepting or affirming the judgment that he ought to do *X*. My moral judgment that you ought to do *X* "guides" your action, not in the sense that it necessarily *moves* you to do *X*, but in that your accepting my judgment *commits* you to doing *X*, and your not doing *X* implies your rejection of my judgment. For in saying that you ought to do it I am implicitly telling you to do it; and if you do not, you have not accepted what I said.

FROM *Contemporary Moral Philosophy* by G. J. Warnock. Copyright 1967 by Macmillan, London and Basingstoke, England.

Moral judgments, then, are supposed to resemble imperatives in being "prescriptive," and to be so, indeed, in virtue of an intimate logical relation to imperatives. But they have, Hare holds, a further most important feature which distinguishes them from at any rate many imperatives. I may, on a whim of the moment, tell you in particular to go away on this particular occasion, without thereby being logically committed to saying or doing anything in particular on any other occasion; the singular imperative "Go away," issued to you here and now, does not *bind* me to taking any particular line elsewhere or elsewhen. If on another occasion, perhaps another exactly similar occasion, I happen to want you not to go away, I may issue the imperative "Don't go" without logical impropriety. Not so, however, with moral judgments. For the moral judgment that I make in a certain situation must be founded on, made in virtue of, certain features *of* that situation; and accordingly I must, in consistency, be prepared to make the same judgment in any situation which shares those features (and does not differ in any other relevant respect). Such a judgment as "You ought to repay the money" is, in Hare's term, universalisable; that is, if I commit myself to this judgment in your particular case, I thereby commit myself to the view that anybody—including, most importantly, myself—in the circumstances in which you now are ought to act in that way. I cannot, without logical impropriety, issue a different judgment in another case, unless I can show that other case to be different in some relevant respect. Or if I judge differently some other case which I cannot show to be relevantly different, then I am bound to correct or withdraw my original judgment. Moral judgments, in effect, cannot be, as imperatives may be, purely and completely singular; in judging this case, we implicitly judge any case of this *kind*, and cannot accordingly judge differently other cases of the *same* kind.

We have before us, then, the thesis "that moral judgments are a kind of *prescriptive* judgments, and that they are distinguished from other judgments of this class by being *universalisable*." I shall now argue, first, that moral judgments are *not* essentially prescriptive, and second, that, if that is so, we need not claim for "universalisability" the importance which Hare, as I think mistakenly, claims for it.

TWO VERSIONS OF "PRESCRIPTIVISM"

I believe that there can be discerned, encapsulated in what we may call the prescriptivist thesis, at least two distinguishable doctrines which call for separate discussion. I begin with the one that seems the more obviously false.

The prescriptivist thesis is, of course, put forward as a quite general thesis about moral discourse—not only, we may note, about moral utterances in general, but even about moral words in general, which are said by Hare to have "prescriptive meaning." Now one way in which this thesis might be taken, and in which it has sometimes been put forward, would be this: it is the thesis that there is a certain class of words, which includes that class of words which occur characteristically in moral discourse, whose meaning is to be explained (at least in part) in terms of the performance of a particular "speech-act," namely, prescribing. That is to say: in any discourse in which those words occur in their standard meanings, it must be the case that the speaker of that discourse is therein prescribing. He is, at any rate in part or implicitly, "telling someone what to do."

One might think that, as a general thesis about the occurrence in discourse of moral words, this is too obviously false ever to have been seriously believed. How could it possibly have been supposed that moral discourse, in all its almost endless diversity of forms and contexts, must consist essentially and always in the performance of any *single* speech-act? No one would think of saying this about discourse in general: but moral discourse, discourse in which moral words occur, is not much, if at all, less versatile in this respect than discourse in general; there are at any rate dozens of things which those who employ moral words may therein be doing. They may be prescribing, certainly; but also they may be advising, exhorting, imploring; commanding, condemning, deploring; resolving, confessing, undertaking; and so on, and so on. But here we may note as a possible explanatory factor the fairly obvious fact that, when Hare thinks of "moral discourse," he thinks first of such discourse as occurring in one particular context—that, namely, in which one speaker addresses to another a moral judgment upon some course of action currently open to, and possibly to be undertaken by, that other person; in which *A* asks "What shall I do?", and *B* answers his question. This half-conscious restriction of context was in fact already present, we may note further, in emotivism; for the context in which one typically "creates an influence" is that in which one talks to another party with an eye to his present or future behaviour. That Hare is apt to carry over this tacit restriction is evident from his recurrent concern with imperatives, which, of course, are also typically issued by one speaker to another with an eye to what that other is currently to do. Now it is certainly not grossly false to say of imperatives (though it is not quite true either) that they are tied, so to speak, to the performance of a particular speech-act. It is not very badly wrong to say, that is, that one who engages in "imperative discourse" is therein, in virtue of what imperatives are, performing the speech-act of telling someone what to do. But if, as Hare seems to, one half-consciously restricts one's attention to the kinds of contexts in which imperatives would naturally occur, then it may seem fairly plausible to say that "moral judgment" too consists in the performance of, is tied to, one particular speech-act, that of prescribing. This is not, indeed, a truth about moral judgment, still less about moral *words*; it might be a truth, at best, about the particular class of moral utterances which might naturally be issued in that particular kind of situation. But if the very narrow restriction of context is not noticed, the gross absurdity of the generalised thesis may not be noticed either.

The prescriptive thesis, however, cannot yet be dismissed; for it is not merely the gross absurdity that we have just considered. Though that plainly false doctrine has certainly been propounded in its name—and even, at the price of desperate paradox, explicitly defended—the thesis is susceptible of a much less absurd interpretation. The false doctrine, in fact, has probably managed to hold the field not only because the above-mentioned half-conscious restrictions have masked its full absurdity, but also because it has not been properly distinguished from the more plausible doctrine that we have now to consider.

The more plausible doctrine, and the one that is really central in Hare's account, is that moral discourse is prescriptive in the sense that, in discourse of this kind, there obtains a quite special connection between words and deeds. Here we may glance once again at the comparison with imperatives. Suppose that I issue to you the imperative utterance "Spare that tree"; in what would acceptance by you of my utterance consist? It seems that we must say: it would consist in your *doing* what I say, namely, sparing that tree. Generalising, we may say that imperative discourse is such that acceptance of what is said in that mode consists in appropriate *action* on the part of those to whom it is addressed: you have not accepted what I said if you do not do as I say. Now it is in this respect, Hare believes, that moral discourse is analogous, that it too is prescriptive. We need not embrace (though he sometimes does) the rather obvious falsehood that to issue a moral utterance is always to tell someone what to do; but we can and must say that any proposition in morals, whatever the speaker may be doing in issuing that proposition, is such that acceptance of it consists in acting in a certain way, either here and now, or if the appropriate circumstances should arise. Moreover (since moral judgments, unlike imperatives, are universalisable and "apply" to the speaker himself no less than to other persons), any proposition in morals also commits the speaker to acting in a certain way; if he does not so act, then he does not mean what he says. If I remark to you that it was very wrong of Jenkins to get so horribly drunk at his daughter's wedding, I surely am not telling you—still less myself—not to get horribly drunk at weddings of daughters: perhaps we have no daughters, or our daughters are already firmly settled in the married state, and in any case I am talking about Jenkins, not you or me. Nevertheless, my remark is such that anyone who really accepts it stays sober at his daughter's wedding and on occasions of that *kind*, or at least, like you and me, would do so if so placed. If you would not, then you do not really accept what I say: and if I would not, then I do not sincerely mean what I say. It is not only that, as we are told, actions speak louder than words; it is that, in the case of prescriptive discourse, actions confirm or refute words, in acting we "accept" or "reject" them. And it is, of course, by no means obviously false that moral discourse is prescriptive in this sense; for we should all be inclined to agree that, as Hare puts it, "If we were to ask of a person 'What are his moral principles?' the way in which we could be most sure of a true answer would be by studying what he *did*".

Now that there is, in moral discourse, this kind of close connection, of interdependence, between words and deeds is, at the very least, a very plausible view. It needs, I think, to be hedged and qualified in certain respects, some of great importance; but let us for the moment postpone those operations. We must first consider whether, assuming this view to be correct, it follows that in *this* sense the prescriptivist thesis is true.

This may seem at first sight to be a very extraordinary question; for it may seem that Hare's prescriptivist doctrine—not indeed in its absurd, but in its other, more persuasive sense—just *is* the doctrine that in moral discourse this interdependence of words and deeds obtains. But this is not so. Prescriptivism has, I think, looked persuasive to many because it has been thought simply to be this doctrine. But it is not; for it not only asserts this interdependence, it seeks to explain it; and the explanation is far indeed from being obviously correct.

We come up here, once again, against the seductive influence of the imperative model. It is indeed true (or true enough) to say that to accept the imperative "Spare that tree" just is to spare that tree, and that accordingly we have a case here of a very intimate relation between words and deeds. The relation in this case, furthermore, is susceptible of relatively simple explanation. The deed—or non-deed perhaps—of sparing that tree is thus intimately related to the words in question in that the words *prescribe* that course of action; and it is for that reason that the course of action constitutes acceptance of what was said, and any other course of action would constitute its rejection. Now the prescriptivist thesis says (as its name implies) not only plausibly, that in moral discourse there obtains a comparably intimate relation between words and deeds, but also, much less plausibly, that that relation holds here for the *same reason:* the words prescribe, and the deeds are consonant or dissonant with the words in so far as, and because, they do or do not follow the prescription given. It is not exactly that (as on the absurd view) to issue a moral judgment is itself always actually to prescribe; it is rather that any moral judgment either is, or presupposes, or implies, or both, a prescription. As we put it at an earlier stage, it "entails an imperative;" and it is in virtue of *that* that our relation obtains here between words and deeds, and that moral discourse can be said in general to be "action-guiding".

But why, we may now ask, should the relation be explained in this way? Some may have thought—some have certainly written as if they thought— that it must be explained in this way because there is no other way; the *only* way in which deeds can be consonant, or dissonant, with words is for their doing to be, or not be, what the words *prescribe*. But it is really quite obvious that this is not the only possibility; there are dozens of others. I may express a liking for the modern dance, and my behaviour may show that I do not really like it at all. I may say that I want a classless society, and my actions may betray that I really want no such thing. I may express a resolution always to be kind to children, and so act as to show that I was wholly insincere in doing so. I may say that my ideal is perfect self-mortification, and live in a way that makes clear that this is idle verbiage. I may say that I value social justice above all things, and show in practice, when it comes to the crunch, that I value many things much more. And so on and so on. Thus, from the fact, if it be a fact, that a man's moral principles are revealed most decisively in his behaviour, it does not follow in the least that those principles have to be conceived as, or as implying *prescriptions*. They might, so far as that point goes, equally well be conceived as expressions of taste or of approval, as avowals of wants or aims, as views about values or ideals, as resolutions, as beliefs about interests, and in many other ways too. On this score at any rate, "Eating people is wrong" is no more closely akin to "Don't eat people" than it is to "I don't want people to be eaten:" for in each of these cases the eating of people, or looking on complacently while people are eaten, would be in some sort of conflict with, even in a sense would contradict, what is said. Why then should we, having conceded, as we must, that moral judgments in general *are* not imperatives, still maintain that they are all in this respect *like* imperatives, that their relation to conduct is to be explained in the same way?

MORAL DISCOURSE AND CONDUCT

The fact is, as I think we are now in a position to see, that the thesis of "prescriptivism" errs, at bottom, in attempting to answer an impossible question—a question, that is, to which *any* answer would be bound to be wrong. Imperative discourse, as we may say reasonably enough, is in some way intimately related to conduct; and here we may go on to ask: in what way, exactly? Now this is a question, as it happens, that has quite a good answer; for in virtue of what imperatives are, it is broadly true to say that one who issues an imperative, employs an imperative expression, is therein telling someone to do something, whose behaviour may accordingly conform with, or go against, what is said. Now Hare, it appears, goes on from this point to ask the same question of *moral* discourse—this is intimately related to conduct: in what way, exactly? But here we have a question without an answer; for, whereas imperative expressions form a particular grammatical class whose members (roughly) are standardly employed for one particular purpose in one particular type of situation, "moral expressions" are of the utmost grammatical diversity, may occur in very widely varied types of situations, and may be employed in doing very many quite different things. Thus, while it is reasonable to suppose that the relation of imperatives to conduct can be characterised, broadly at any rate, in *one* way, it is entirely unreasonable to suppose that the same can be done for "moral discourse". Sometimes, certainly—namely, in that type of situation which seems always to be at the front of Hare's mind—moral discourse will be prescriptive: the speaker will be, roughly speaking, telling another person what to do, instructing, advising, or "guiding" him. But at other times not. As Nowell-Smith very properly remarks: "The words with which moral philosophers have especially to do . . . play many different parts. They are used to express tastes and preferences, to express decisions and choices, to criticise, grade, and evaluate, to advise, admonish, warn, persuade and dissuade, to praise, encourage and reprove, to promulgate and draw attention to rules; and doubtless for other purposes also." It is probably true that in all these cases *someone's* conduct will be *somehow* related to, consonant or dissonant with, what the speaker says— sometimes his own conduct, sometimes that of the person he addresses, sometimes that of specific other persons, or of people in general But the actual relations, quite clearly, will be widely diverse, and not to be summed up in any *single* formula whatever.

At the end of the last section we took note of a number of different ways in which deeds, as we put it, may be "consonant or dissonant" with words, otherwise than by being or not being what the words prescribe. We can now see that it would be a complete mistake to raise the question which of these ways is exemplified, or even most nearly exemplified, in moral discourse. For the fact is that they all are; and so are a great many more. Resolutions on my own part, advice offered to another; the profession of aspirations or ideals; the expression of distaste, criticism, or commendation; reference to wants of my own, or to the needs or aims or interests of others—*all* of these commonly occur in "moral discourse," just as they occur also, of course, in discourse that is not moral. In each case there is, no doubt, some relation to conduct, but by no means the same kind of relation in every case. We thus find in the end that our two versions of prescriptivism err, not indeed in quite the same way, but still in very similar ways. In its absurd form the doctrine seeks to incorporate into "moral discourse," and even into the meanings of moral words, the performance of just one particular speech-act, that of *prescribing*—as if, whatever the moral discourser is saying and in whatever situation, this is the *only* thing that he can ever be doing. The other version is not so blatantly misguided as this, for it does not construe the term "prescriptive" so narrowly as to imply that one who uses a prescriptive expression must always be, literally and strictly, prescribing; the suggestion is only that what is thus said is always related very intimately to what is done. But at this point there creeps in the very similar error of supposing that this relation is always to be explained in the same way, and explained, furthermore, on the model of actual prescription. But that moral discourse in general is related to conduct in *one* way is no more true than that one who engages in moral discourse is always doing *one* thing.

A legislator, a judge, an advocate, and a juryman may all engage in "legal discourse". But on the one hand they will not, of course, all therein be doing the same one thing; nor, obviously, will the things they are severally saying be related in any one way, though probably all are in some way, to human conduct. A possible "prescriptive theory of legal discourse"—which would consist, perhaps, in taking the language of *legislation* as that in terms of which all legal talk would be sought to be explained—would share most of the merits and demerits of its analogue in ethics. It would throw practically no light on the law. I am not suggesting, of course, that there is no truth whatever in "prescriptivism" as an ethical theory; but I do suggest that there is less truth than falsehood. The grain of truth is to be located in the very general claim that "moral discourse" is not purely, theoretically, informative—it bears on conduct, what is done may be in conflict or in harmony with what is said. But in so far as the theory does not merely state this unexceptionable platitude, but purports to offer an explanation of it, it appears to me to be completely mistaken—and mistaken, not only in that it wrongly proposes "prescribing" as the link between moral words and deeds, but, more seriously, in that it tacitly embodies the grossly false idea that there is some *one* way in which this linkage can usefully be described. The question how "moral discourse" bears on conduct really needs to be separately considered for many quite different kinds of moral utterance, and for many quite different situations or contexts in which moral utterances may occur. It seems a considerable disservice to obscure this diversity beneath the appearance of a single, rather simple, monolithic doctrine.

We are left, then, with a number of questions still disconcertingly open. The intuitionist's characterisation of moral discourse we have seen to be distressingly taciturn. That moral discourse is "emotive" is, we have further observed, not universally true nor in any case distinctive. But we now have to say, it appears, much the same about prescriptivism. For if moral discourse is in some contexts prescriptive, that is not because it is moral discourse, but because it is, in those particular contexts, discourse in which prescribing happens to be going on. How then *is* moral discourse to be, in general, distinguished? What makes it moral? What, in fact, does "moral" mean? This is a question, far too seldom considered with the care and attention it deserves, to which we shall revert, somewhat sketchily, in later sections.

ARGUMENT IN MORALS

We took note, in introducing the prescriptivist amendment to emotivism, that it had at least *prima facie* the considerable advantage of not representing moral discourse and debate as fundamentally non-rational. To guide, we observed, unlike to influence, is essentially to engage in a rational activity; advice, whether accepted or not, may be good or bad, I may have good or bad reasons for offering you the guidance I do. But now we must observe that this advantage turns out to be illusory: prescriptivism too cannot find much place for argument.

In Hare's own account of moral reasoning, very great importance is attached to the feature of moral judgment, already mentioned, which he calls "universalisability". It is, Hare seems to say—and, as we shall see, not without reason—solely in virtue of this feature that argument, properly so called, is possible in morals; and he is naturally disposed to make quite substantial claims as to what such argument can achieve. Now to say that any proposition in morals is "universalisable" is, as we briefly noted earlier, to say that one who affirms or accepts that proposition is thereby committed—as a matter of logic—to a certain view of any cases of a certain kind. For me to assert that you ought not to do X in situation Y commits me, as a matter of logic, to the general "principle" that no one should do things *like X* in situations *like Y*—"like" meaning here "not relatively distinguishable from". Generality of this sort is implicit in all moral judgment.

Now one might think at first sight that, while argument on the basis of this feature is certainly possible, yet such argument could not really achieve very much. For what, on the basis of this feature, can be argued about? What is put in issue? It is plain, I think, that what is put in issue is simply consistency. To appeal, in discussion of some moral judgment that I make, to the feature of universalisability is not to raise the question whether my judgment of the case before me is *right*, but only the question whether it is the same as, or compatible with the judgments that I make or would make of other cases of the same kind. It is not, indeed, that this matter is unimportant. For people are indeed very commonly prone, from prejudice or bigotry or thoughtlessness, to judge differently cases which are not relevantly different—to make, for example, unjustifiable exceptions in favour of themselves or their friends, and to the detriment of foreigners, or political opponents, persons they dislike, or persons whose existence is inconvenient to them. And in such cases they may indeed be logically obliged—though not necessarily induced—to change or amend their judgments, when the requirement of consistent universalisability is forced upon their attention. Nevertheless, if it appears to you that my judgment of some particular case is morally quite wrong, you may well achieve nothing by appealing to universalisability; for all that may emerge may be that I am perfectly prepared to make the same (in your view) wrong judgment of any case of this kind. All my standards and principles may seem to you highly objectionable; but, provided that I apply them consistently in every case, they will be quite invulnerable to any argument of this pattern.

But is this point, one may wonder, too abstractly stated? Is the case we envisage really, and not merely theoretically, a possible one? It is easy to say that, in theory, practically any moral judgment, however objectionable, might be consistently "universalised", and so might stand unscathed against argument founded upon this consideration. But may it not be the case in fact that not many highly objectionable judgments actually would emerge from such scrutiny unscathed? One might think that this would probably be so for the following reason. What is really objectionable, one might think, about many objectionable moral judgments is that one who makes them does so in disregard of, or without giving proper weight to, the wants, or the needs, or the interests, of those concerned (other than himself); he ignores, let us say, or does not properly consider, the fact that the interests of other persons will be gravely damaged by the course of action which he professes morally to approve. But if so—if he is prepared seriously to hold, as a general principle, that such action to the detriment of others' interests is to be morally approved—we can point out that, in virtue of the condition of universalisability, he is committed to approving of the neglect or damage of *his own* interests if and when, as may occur, he is himself in the position of those whose interests will be damaged by the action in this case. If their interests may properly be neglected now, so, when he finds himself in their shoes, may his. But surely only the most irrational of men could want the neglect or frustration of his own interests; and if so, the requirement of universalisability may seem to impose upon any rational man the condition that, in his practical judgments, he *must* pay that regard to the interests of others which, in general, he would want to be paid to his own interests. And it is plain that this would constitute, in practice, a condition of very substantial moral significance and effect.

I think, however, that there is an important equivocation here. It is true—perhaps even necessarily true—that no rational man *wants* the frustration of what he sees as his own interests, or *likes* it when his interests are frustrated. But then what a man wants, or would like, is scarcely the point at issue here: the question is what he would morally approve or find morally objectionable; and that, of course, may not be at all the same thing. If I commend, or adopt as right, some course of action which grossly damages the interests of another, you may point out to me, correctly no doubt, that I would not like it if my own interests were damaged in that way; there is, however, no reason why I should not admit this, and yet still maintain that, if our positions were reversed, that other person would be *right* to damage my interests exactly as I now propose to damage his. The ruthless landlord, for instance, on the point of ejecting his aged, ailing, and needy tenants into the snow, may concede not only that they will greatly dislike this treatment, but that he himself would dislike it no less if he were in their place; nevertheless, he may hold, it is right that they should be ejected, and that he himself should be ejected too, if he were in similar case. That he would not like it, he says, is neither here nor there; the point is that business is business, the economic show must go on. In order, that is, consistently to defend as unobjectionable my neglect of another's interests, I do not have to go to the somewhat unbalanced length of positively wanting my own interests to be neglected, or of somehow not disliking it when they are: all that I am required to do is to concede that neglect of my own interests by others would be unobjectionable. And there is nothing particularly strained or unbalanced about this; it is, for instance, the very essence of the gospel of self-help, of untrammelled competition in the old capitalist style—a gospel which, however morally disagreeable one may find it, has been consistently adopted by very many entirely sane men, and not only by those who have been winners in the jungle war. A man cannot, in effect, by the argument from universalisability be constrained to attach *much* weight, if any, to the interests of others; for he may be entirely ready to concede that others are not morally required to attach much weight, if any, to his own, however intensely he may dislike it when, in the competitive free-for-all, it happens that he comes out on the losing side. But if this is true, the requirement of universalisability appears, whether in theory or in practice, to set almost no limit to the practical judgments which *can* be consistently made and maintained by sane men; and if so, it does not, as a weapon of moral argument, carry much fire-power.

Why then is Hare inclined to make such large claims for this real, but limited dialectical weapon? Because (it is not, I think, unfair to say) his doctrine does not allow for genuine argument of any other kind. If asked to give reasons for some moral view I have expressed—that is, on this view, for some "prescription" that I have issued—I may do one or both of two things: I may adduce certain facts about the case under consideration, or some principle, or principles, of which my presently-expressed view is an instance or application. But my principles, of course, are on this view themselves "prescriptions" of mine; and such facts as I may adduce about the present case constitute *reasons* for my expressed view of it in so far as I have adopted, i.e. "prescribed", some principle in accordance with which that view is derivable from those facts. Thus my giving of "reasons" for my expressed prescription consists, on this view, essentially of my referring to and relying on *further* prescriptions of my own: what are reasons for me, are, for you, not only not necessarily good reasons, but possibly not reasons at all. And thus, what we speak of as argument between two parties emerges essentially as nothing more than the articulation by each of his own position. For you to say that my view is *wrong* is to say only that your position excludes that view; for me to "argue" that my view is *right* is to show only that my position includes it. And there is nothing else, on this view, that argument can do; for there are no "reasons" that either party can appeal to independently of, and so genuinely in support of, his own prescriptions. In this way it must inevitably appear to Hare that *real* argument can address itself only to the question of consistency; for so long as a man prescribes consistently, then on this view he has (since he has provided himself with) all the "reasons" that any of his particular pronouncements may require; and if I have "reasons" for views that differ from his, he need claim only that my reasons are not reasons for him.

It is, I believe, often not really noticed how surprising (at least) Hare's view of this question is. Most of us, no doubt, would agree readily enough that in moral matters we have to make up our own minds; we ourselves must decide on, embrace, commit ourselves to our moral standpoint. Further, we are probably ready enough to agree that moral discourse seems little susceptible of demonstrative argument; we have seldom much hope, in moral controversy, of confronting an opponent with a cogent proof of our views. Now it may seem that Hare is saying no more than this; but he is saying much more. For he is saying, not only that it is for us to decide what our moral opinions are, but also that it is for us to decide what to take as grounds for or against any moral opinion. We are not only, as it were, free to decide on the evidence, but also free to decide what evidence is. I do not, it seems, decide that flogging is wrong because I *am* against cruelty; rather, I decide that flogging is wrong because I *decide to be* against cruelty. And what, if I did make that decision, would be my ground for making it? That I am opposed to the deliberate infliction of pain? No—rather that I *decide to be* opposed to it. And so on. Now there are people, I think, whose moral views do seem to be formed and defended in this way—who, as one might say, not only make up their own minds, but also make up their own evidence; who pick and choose not only on the question what is right or wrong, but also on the question what are even to be admitted as relevant considerations. But such a person, surely, is not so much a model as a menace; not an exemplar of moral reasoning, but a total abstainer from any serious concern with reason. And if this really were a general feature of the human predicament, then to find cogent arguments in morals would not merely be difficult; it would be as hopeless as trying to play a competitive game in which each competitor was making up his own rules as he went along.

Quasi-Cognitivism and Quasi-Naturalism—Further Readings

Braithwaite, R. B., "Critical Notice. *The Language of Morals*, By R. M. Hare," *Mind*, LXIII (1954), pp. 249–262. Exposition; criticism; but expresses some basic agreement.
Ewing, A. C., *Second Thoughts in Moral Philosophy* (New York: Macmillan, 1959), Chap. 1. Critic.
Hancock, Roger, N., *Twentieth Century Ethics* (New York: Columbia U.P., 1974), Chap. 5. Exposition and criticism.
Hare, R. M., "Critical Notice. *Contemporary Moral Philosophy*, By G. J. Warnock," *Mind*, LXXVII (1968), pp. 436–440. Hare answers Warnock's criticisms of his views.
——, *Essays on the Moral Concepts* (Berkeley, Calif.: U. of California Press, 1972).
——, *Freedom and Reason* (New York: Oxford U.P., 1963).
——, *The Language of Morals* (Oxford: Clarendon, 1952).
Hudson, W. D., *Modern Moral Philosophy* (Garden City, N.Y.: Doubleday, 1970), Chap. 5. Exposition; criticism; but also a generally sympathetic defense.
Kerner, George C., *The Revolution in Ethical Theory* (New York: Oxford U.P., 1966), Chap. 4. Exposition and criticism.
MacIntyre, Alasdair, "What Morality is Not," *Philosophy*, XXXII (1957), pp. 325–335. Critic.

D THE REVIVAL OF COGNITIVISM AND NATURALISM: *DESCRIPTIVISM*

Contemporary philosophic controversy has witnessed a strong revival of naturalism and cognitivism. "Descriptivism" has become a standard name for the contention that normative conclusions can be inferred from descriptive, or factual, premises. Since these premises contain terms which sometimes designate natural properties of men and things, the word "naturalist" applies. One of the most controversial arguments directed against the prescriptivist and emotivist tradition, and against non-naturalism, was produced by J. R. Searle, in an article entitled "How to Derive 'Ought' from 'Is'." It was later revised in his book *Speech Acts*.* He attacks the hoary principle that one cannot derive

*J. R. Searle, *Speech Acts* (Cambridge: Cambridge University Press, 1969).

normative conclusions from factual or descriptive premises, a principle
he credits specifically to Hume, and to Moore, Hare, and the emotivists
by inheritance and persuasion. He claims that from the factual premise
"Jones uttered the words 'I hereby promise to pay you, Smith, five
dollars',," along with some tautologous principles and empirical reports
(which make up three more premises), the normative conclusions "Jones
ought to pay Smith five dollars" can be deduced. The additional premises
are, "Jones promised to pay Smith five dollars"; "Jones placed himself
under (undertook) an obligation to pay Smith five dollars"; "Jones is
under an obligation to pay Smith five dollars." He says that each premise
is connected to the one preceding it by a logical relation that is not so
strong an entailment, but is not a contingent relationship. This relation
is usually called implication or presupposition. By the addition of further
statements as premises, the relationship becomes one of entailment.
These further statements will be empirical assumptions, tautologies,
and descriptions of word usage.

The argument rests on a distinction between two kinds of fact:
"brute fact," i.e., "Jones utters the words 'I hereby promise to pay
you, Smith, five dollars',," and "institutional fact." The second premise
involves appeals to what Searle calls the "constitutive rule" of promising, and the third is tautologous. There is also a distinction between
two kinds of rules which is important to his argument. First, there are
constitutive rules, which govern *invented* systems, as in the game of
chess; and, second, there are regulative rules, which govern antecedent
activities, for example, the rules of table manners as related to the antecedent activity of eating. Searle identifies institutional facts as systems of
constitutive rules and characterizes promising as an institutionalized
activity. Intuitionists, prescriptivists, and emotivists have, in his opinion,
confused these related but different conceptions. The conclusion that
Jones ought to pay Smith five dollars follows from him uttering the
words "I hereby promise . . ." in a way similar to the way "Jones
scored six points for his team" follows from "Jones crossed the goal
line."

Other thinkers whose work is not included in this book have contributed significantly to the dialogue and should be mentioned. Peter
Geach, in "Good and Evil,"* submits a powerful argument in support of
the naturalistic position, claiming that the intuitionists, emotivists, and
prescriptivists are led to their mistaken conclusions by confusing two
different ways in which adjectives are used and justified. He distinguishes
them under the names "attributive" and "predicative." The criteria

---

*Peter Geach, "Good and Evil," *Analysis*, XVII, 1956.

for the correct use of adjectives like "good" are drawn from the nouns to which normative or evaluative adjectives are attached, and are not subject to choice. "Good" and "evil" are always attributive, and never predicative, adjectives. Failure to recognize this has led other thinkers, in Geach's opinion, to the mistaken search for common properties named by normative and evaluative terms. Not finding them, theorists were forced into prescriptivism and emotivism. Normative adjectives are, in Aristotle's words, "syncategorematic." Paul Ziff, in *Semantic Analysis*,* provides a detailed analysis of the conditions for the uses of the word "good." These theories have in common the conviction that normative and evaluative terms are parasitic upon the nouns and noun constructions they modify, and that the nouns relate to empirical conditions—states of affairs.

It was to be expected that Searle's work would be the target of much negative criticism, and the expectations have been fulfilled. His view has invited attacks from such divergent strongholds of ethical theory as intuitionism and prescriptivism. Antony Flew thinks that he can show that Searle has begged the all-important evaluative question in his first premise. He argues that the evaluative "ought" is incapsulated in an unstated but assumed commitment which is an ingredient in the first premise. Searle's first premise looks like the neutral and actual report of verbal usage which his argument necessitates; but it is not. There must be an engaged, committed participant. This commitment, of course, is not a part of the fact, yet its presence makes the premise normative or evaluative. Further, it is this commitment that provides whatever it is that bridges the gap between "ought" and "is."†

In several extremely influential articles, Phillipa Foot is perhaps mainly responsible for the counter-attack against the antinaturalistic tradition which had dominated the British and American philosophical scene. She argues that such theories lead to strange conclusions. For one thing, their commitment to the existence of an unbridgeable logical gap between facts and values implies that there are no limits to the kinds of

---

*Paul Ziff, *Semantic Analysis* (Ithica: Cornell University Press, 1960).

†Hare argues in "The Promising Game," (*Revue Internationale de Philosophie*, No. 70 (1964), pp. 398–412) that Searle's first premise is a synthetic moral principle. He claims in support of his contention that when one combines Searle's principle and its sub-principle he gets an evaluative statement; so, again, the normative conclusion follows, but not from wholly factual premises. It is difficult to see the resolution of this kind of conflict, and we see it continued in Foot's arguments, and in their criticism by Phillips and Mounce. For excellent coverage of this controversy, see Hudson, *Modern Moral Philosophy*, *op. cit.*, pp. 282–331; R. A. Hancock, *Twentieth Century Ethics*, *op. cit.*, pp. 197–275.

things to which a moral agent could meaningfully attribute moral predicates. Anything can be judged good or evil, right or wrong, subject to prescriptivity and the principle of universalizability. But this means, in her opinion, that a man could claim that it is good to clasp and unclasp his hands. Such a result occurs because values and norms are *externally* related to their objects, either by decisions and choice, as in the case of Hare's theory, or by pro-attitudes and emotions, as in the cases of Nowell-Smith and Stevenson. Thus, a person could refuse to count as his reasons whatever is offered by others in the way of justification for the value or obligation connected with an action.

She denies that the relations between the reasons which set out descriptions of factual conditions, and the norms or rules which set out values, are external; their relation is internal or logical. Therefore, if we carefully attend the factual descriptions of the objects we value and the human beings who value them, it will be seen that there is no logical gap or wedge between them and the presupposed or implied evaluations. Taken as reasons, such factual statements can logically imply evaluative conclusions.

Her examples, which have become famous, are concerned with pride, fear, a feeling that something is dangerous, bodily injury, courage, and justice. It is clear that feelings of pride are not externally related to their objects—one cannot meaningfully or logically justify feelings of pride for, say, the sky or sun, because one cannot, in fact, claim responsibility for them. The case of fear is similar. The feeling of danger, however, is different in an important respect. If the belief in the possibility of injury by the dangerous object turns out to be wrong, the attribution of danger must be withdrawn; this is not true in the cases of fear and pride. Foot's analysis of injury shows that evaluative terms are linked to factual conditions which give point to them. The harm involved in the loss of needed and wanted functions of eyes, ears, arms, etc., is internally related to the badness involved. We do not attribute injury or harm to a state or condition which people generally want, desire, or need. Justice, as well as other virtues, must likewise be related to function, purpose, need, desire. Notice, first, that Foot does not make moral terms name natural properties; rather, natural properties form criteria for the use of moral terms. Second, she does not claim that value terms are such that attribution of good is reducible to a particular individual wanting or desiring something—she distinguishes between want and need. Third, she need not, and does not, commit herself to the dubious proposition that men *per se*, like knives, have *a* purpose, point, or function: her analogies are to the determinate functions of arms, legs, or eyes, and other conditions that characterize men's actions, wants, or needs, in particular contexts. Men obviously have needs and wants, and it would be difficult to describe men in any detailed way without including these needs and wants and their relation to bodily organs. "Danger of physical injury," then, in standard cases, is ruled out as a criterion for deciding whether something is good. Foot concludes that facts, cited as reasons in justification of the good or bad character of actions and evaluations, function as criteria for moral judgments. What ought to be the case can be derived from what is the case. Virtues are non-contingently related to human good and harm.

D. Z. Phillips and H. O. Mounce believe that they can show that the claimed internal relation between, say, bodily injury, and the negative evaluation of it, follows only when a background of moral ideals and standards is assumed. This "way of life" will determine whether, say, the loss of an ear, or clapping one's hands, or rudeness, is "good" or "bad" in a normative sense. Therefore, the factual or descriptive proposition that a person lost an ear will not legitimize the evaluative conclusions that the event and condition are bad. Phillips and Mounce claim that, in fact, the reverse of Foot's thesis is often true; i.e., very often religious and other evaluative principles determine whether something is, in fact, valuable. They grant that related factual matters are not irrelevant to moral conclusions; they grant, therefore, that moral judgments are not reducible to persuasions, coercions, likes and dislikes. They also agree that it is false to claim that just anything can count as a reason for a moral belief. For them, the relations between facts and values are not contingent. Nevertheless, they maintain that the ultimate principles which make up the aforementioned "backgrounds" are not subject to proof or justification. They argue that one cannot set out clearly what men's functions are, by any analogy with knives and other things, such that their descriptions imply moral predicates. (We might recall Siegler's criticism of Aristotle on a similar point.) They conclude that although propositions such as "*x* is harmful," are descriptive, they are nevertheless not evaluatively neutral. Their use of examples is sometimes puzzling, although the technique is common among philosophers— the "counter-example" technique. It is as if we could deny the general function and value of a nose if we could locate a person who cut it off in order to spite his face. Or, that loss of a leg would not count as an injury in the evaluative sense if we could locate a case where a person avoided running into a stream and drowning for lack of a leg. Many of the examples used against Foot and Searle appear, in other words, to rest upon aberrant and borderline cases of the use of normative terms. Since normative terms are vague, family-type words, the supply of such counter-examples is virtually unlimited. In the future, we may expect the debate over the revival of cognitivism and naturalism to continue. For now, the reader must judge whether Searle and Foot, or their critics, have the better of the argument.

43

How to derive "Ought" from "Is"[1]

John R. Searle

I

It is often said that one cannot derive an "ought" from an "is." This thesis, which comes from a famous passage in Hume's *Treatise*, while not as clear as it might be, is at least clear in broad outline: there is a class of statements of fact which is logically distinct from a class of statements of value. No set of statements of fact by themselves entails any statement of value. Put in more contemporary terminology, no set of *descriptive* statements can entail an *evaluative* statement without the addition of at least one evaluative premise. To believe otherwise is to commit what has been called the naturalistic fallacy.

I shall attempt to demonstrate a counter-example to this thesis.[2] It is not of course to be supposed that a single counter-example can refute a philosophical thesis, but in the present instance if we can present a plausible counter-example and can in addition give some account or explanation of how and why it is a counter-example, and if we can further offer a theory to back up our counter-example—a theory which will generate an indefinite number of counter-examples—we may at the very least cast considerable light on the original thesis; and possibly, if we can do all these things, we may even incline ourselves to the view that the scope of that thesis was more restricted than we had originally supposed. A counter-example must proceed by taking a statement or statements which any proponent of the thesis would grant were purely factual or

FROM "How to Derive 'Ought' from 'Is' " by John R. Searle (*Philosophical Review*, Vol. 73, January 1964). Reprinted by permission of Philosophical Review and the author.

---

[1] Earlier versions of this paper were read before the Stanford Philosophy Colloquium and the Pacific Division of the American Philosophical Association. I am indebted to many people for helpful comments and criticisms, especially Hans Herzberger, Arnold Kaufmann, Benson Mates, A. I. Melden, and Dagmar Searle.

[2] In its modern version. I shall not be concerned with Hume's treatment of the problem.

"descriptive" (they need not actually contain the word "is") and show how they are logically related to a statement which a proponent of the thesis would regard as clearly "evaluative". (In the present instance it will contain an "ought.")[3]

Consider the following series of statements:

1. Jones uttered the words "I hereby promise to pay you, Smith, five dollars."
2. Jones promised to pay Smith five dollars.
3. Jones placed himself under (undertook) an obligation to pay Smith five dollars.
4. Jones is under an obligation to pay Smith five dollars.
5. Jones ought to pay Smith five dollars.

I shall argue concerning this list that the relation between any statement and its successor, while not in every case one of "entailment," is none the less not just a contingent relation; and the additional statements necessary to make the relationship one of entailment do not need to involve any evaluative statements, moral principles, or anything of the sort.

Let us begin. How is (1) related to (2)? In certain circumstances, uttering the words in quotation marks in (1) is the act of making a promise. And it is a part of or a consequence of the meaning of the words in (1) that in those circumstances uttering them is promising. "I hereby promise" is a paradigm device in English for performing the act described in (2), promising.

Let us state this fact about English usage in the form of an extra premise:

(1a) Under certain conditions C anyone who utters the words (sentence) "I hereby promise to pay you, Smith, five dollars" promises to pay Smith five dollars.

What sorts of things are involved under the rubric "conditions C?" What is involved will be all those conditions, those states of affairs, which are necessary and sufficient conditions for the utterance of the words (sentence) to constitute the successful performance of the act of promising. The conditions will include such things as that the speaker is in the presence of the hearer Smith, they are both conscious, both speakers of English, speaking seriously. The speaker knows what he is doing, is not under the influence of drugs, not hypnotised or acting in a play, not telling a joke or reporting an event, and so forth. This list will no doubt be somewhat indefinite because the boundaries of the concept of a promise, like the boundaries of most concepts in a natural language, are a bit loose.[4] But one thing is clear; however loose the boundaries may be, and how-

---

[3] If this enterprise succeeds, we shall have bridged the gap between "evaluative" and "descriptive" and consequently have demonstrated a weakness in this very terminology. At present, however, my strategy is to play along with the terminology, pretending that the notions of evaluative and descriptive are fairly clear. At the end of the paper I shall state in what respects I think they embody a muddle.

[4] In addition the concept of a promise is a member of a class of concepts which suffer from looseness of a peculiar kind, viz. defeasibility. Cf. H. L. A. Hart, "The Ascription of Responsibility and Rights," *Logic and Language*, first series, ed. A. Flew (Oxford 1951).

ever difficult it may be to decide marginal cases, the conditions under which a man who utters "I hereby promise" can correctly be said to have made a promise are straightforwardly empirical conditions.

So let us add as an extra premise the empirical assumption that these conditions obtain.

(1b) Conditions C obtain.

From (1), (1a), and (1b) we derive (2). The argument is of the form: If C then (if U then P): C for conditions, U for utterance, P for promise. Adding the premises U and C to this hypothetical we derive (2). And as far as I can see, no moral premises are lurking in the logical woodpile. More needs to be said about the relation of (1) to (2), but I reserve that for later.

What is the relation between (2) and (3)? I take it that promising is, by definition, an act of placing oneself under an obligation. No analysis of the concept of promising will be complete which does not include the feature of the promiser placing himself under or undertaking or accepting or recognising an obligation to the promisee, to perform some future course of action, normally for the benefit of the promisee. One may be tempted to think that promising can be analysed in terms of creating expectations in one's hearers, or some such, but a little reflection will show that the crucial distinction between statements of intention on the one hand and promises on the other lies in the nature and degree of commitment or obligation undertaken in promising.

I am therefore inclined to say that (2) entails (3) straight off, but I can have no objection if anyone wishes to add—for the purpose of formal neatness—the tautological premise:

(2a) All promises are acts of placing oneself under (undertaking) an obligation to do the thing promised.

How is (3) related to (4)? If one has placed oneself under an obligation, then, other things being equal, one is under an obligation. That I take it also is a tautology. Of course it is possible for all sorts of things to happen which will release one from obligations one has undertaken and hence the need for the *ceteris paribus* rider. To get an entailment between (3) and (4) we therefore need a qualifying statement to the effect that:

(3a) Other things are equal.

Formalists, as in the move from (2) to (3), may wish to add the tautological premise:

(3b) All those who place themselves under an obligation are, other things being equal, under an obligation.

The move from (3) to (4) is thus of the same form as the move from (1) to (2): If E then (if PUO then UO): E for other things are equal, PUO for place under obligation and UO for under obligation. Adding the two premises E and PUO we drive UO.

Is (3a), the *ceteris paribus* clause, a concealed evaluative premise? It certainly looks as if it might be, especially in the formulation I have given it, but I think we can show that, though questions about whether other things are equal frequently involve evaluative considerations, it is not logically necessary that they should in every case. I shall postpone discussion of this until after the next step.

What is the relation between (4) and (5)? Analogous to the tautology which explicates the relation of (3) and (4) there is here the tautology that, other things being equal, one ought to do what one is under an obligation to do. And here, just as in the previous case, we need some premise of the form:

(4a) Other things are equal.

We need the *ceteris paribus* clause to eliminate the possibility that something extraneous to the relation of "obligation" to "ought" might interfere.[5] Here, as in the previous two steps, we eliminate the appearance of enthymeme by pointing out that the apparently suppressed premise is tautological and hence, though formally neat, it is redundant. If, however, we wish to state it formally, this argument is of the same form as the move from (3) to (4): If E then (if UO then O); E for other things are equal, UO for under obligation, O for ought. Adding the premises E and UO we derive O.

Now a word about the phrase "other things being equal" and how it functions in my attempted derivation. This topic and the closely related topic of defeasibility are extremely difficult and I shall not try to do more than justify my claim that the satisfaction of the condition does not necessarily involve anything evaluative. The force of the expression "other things being equal" in the present instance is roughly this. Unless we have some reason (that is, unless we are actually prepared to give some reason) for supposing the obligation is void (step 4) or the agent ought not to keep the promise (step 5), then the obligation holds and he ought to keep the promise. It is not part of the force of the phrase "other things being equal" that in order to satisfy it we need to establish a universal negative proposition to the effect that no reason could ever be given by anyone for supposing the agent is not under an obligation or ought not to keep the promise. That would be impossible and would render the phrase useless. It is sufficient to satisfy the condition that no reason to the contrary can in fact be given.

If a reason is given for supposing the obligation is void or that the promiser ought not to keep a promise, then characteristically a situation calling for an evaluation arises. Suppose, for example, we consider a promised act wrong, but we grant that the promiser did undertake an obligation. Ought he to keep the promise? There is no established procedure for objectively deciding such

---

[5] The *ceteris paribus* clause in this step excludes somewhat different sorts of cases from those excluded in the previous step. In general we say, "He undertook an obligation, but none the less he is not (now) under an obligation" when the obligation has been *removed*, e.g. if the promisee says, "I release you from your obligation." But we say, "He is under an obligation, but none the less ought not to fulfil it" in cases where the obligation is *overridden* by some other consideration, e.g. a prior obligation.

cases in advance, and an evaluation (if that is really the right word) is in order. But unless we have some reason to the contrary, the *ceteris paribus* condition is satisfied, no evaluation is necessary, and the question whether he ought to do it is settled by saying "he promised." It is always an open possibility that we may have to make an evaluation in order to derive "he ought" from "he promised," for we may have to evaluate a counter-argument. But an evaluation is not logically necessary in every case, for there may as a matter of fact be no counter-arguments. I am therefore inclined to think that there is nothing necessarily evaluative about the *ceteris paribus* condition, even though deciding whether it is satisfied will frequently involve evaluations.

But suppose I am wrong about this: would that salvage the belief in an un-bridgeable logical gulf between "is" and "ought"? I think not, for we can always rewrite my steps (4) and (5) so that they include the *ceteris paribus* clause as part of the conclusion. Thus from our premises we would then have derived "Other things being equal Jones ought to pay Smith five dollars," and that would still be sufficient to refute the tradition, for we would still have shown a relation of entailment between descriptive and evaluative statements. It was not the fact that extenuating circumstances can void obligations that drove philosophers to the naturalistic fallacy fallacy; it was rather a theory of language, as we shall see later on.

We have thus derived (in as strict a sense of "derive" as natural languages will admit of) an "ought" from an "is." And the extra premises which were needed to make the derivation work were in no cause moral or evaluative in nature. They consisted of empirical assumptions, tautologies, and descriptions of word usage. It must be pointed out also that the "ought" is a "categorical" not a "hypothetical" ought. (5) does not say that Jones ought to pay up if he wants such and such. It says he ought to pay up, period. Note also that the steps of the derivation are carried on in the third person. We are not concluding "I ought" from "I said 'I promise'," but "he ought" from "he said 'I promise'."

The proof unfolds the connection between the utterance of certain words and the speech act of promising and then in turn unfolds promising into obligation and moves from obligation to "ought." The step from (1) to (2) is radically different from the others and requires special comment. In (1) we construe "I hereby promise . . ." as an English phrase having a certain meaning. It is a consequence of that meaning that the utterance of that phrase under certain conditions is the act of promising. Thus by presenting the quoted expressions in (1) and by describing their use in (1a) we have as it were already invoked the institution of promising. We might have started with an even more ground floor premise than (1) by saying:

(1b) Jones uttered the phonetic sequence/:ai$^+$hirbai$^+$pramis$^+$təpei$^+$yu$^+$smiθ$^+$faiv$^+$dalərz/

We would then have needed extra empirical premises stating that this phonetic sequence was associated in certain ways with certain meaningful units relative to certain dialects.

The moves from (2) to (5) are relatively easy. We rely on definitional connections between "promise," "obligate," and "ought," and the only problem which arises is that obligations can be overridden or removed in a variety of ways and we need to take account of that fact. We solve our difficulty by adding further premises to the effect that there are no contrary considerations, that other things are equal.

II

In this section I intend to discuss three possible objections to the derivation.

First Objection

Since the first premise is descriptive and the conclusion evaluative, there must be a concealed evaluative premise in the description of the conditions in (1b).

So far, this argument merely begs the question by assuming the logical gulf between descriptive and evaluative which the derivation is designed to challenge. To make the objection stick, the defender of the distinction would have to show how exactly (1b) must contain an evaluative premise and what sort of premise it might be. Uttering certain words in certain conditions just *is* promising and the description of these conditions needs no evaluative element. The essential thing is that in the transition from (1) to (2) we move from the specification of a certain utterance of words to the specification of a certain speech act. The move is achieved because the speech act is a conventional act; and the utterance of the words, according to the conventions, constitutes the performance of just that speech act.

A variant of this first objection is to say: all you have shown is that "promise" is an evaluative, not a descriptive, concept. But this objection again begs the question and in the end will prove disastrous to the original distinction between descriptive and evaluative. For that a man uttered certain words and that these words have the meaning they do are surely objective facts. And if the statement of these two objective facts plus a description of the conditions of the utterance is sufficient to entail the statement (2) which the objector alleges to be an evaluative statement (Jones promised to pay Smith five dollars), then an evaluative conclusion is derived from descriptive premises without even going through steps (3), (4), and (5).

Second Objection

Ultimately the derivation rests on the principle that one ought to keep one's promises and that is a moral principle, hence evaluative.

I don't know whether "one ought to keep one's promises" is a "moral" principle, but whether or not it is, it is also tautological; for it is nothing more than a derivation from the two tautologies:

All promises are (create, are undertakings of, are acceptances of) obligations,

and

One ought to keep (fulfill) one's obligations.

What needs to be explained is why so many philosophers have failed to see the tautological character of this principle. Three things I think have concealed its character from them.

The first is a failure to distinguish external questions about the institution of promising from internal questions asked within the framework of the institution. The questions "Why do we have such an institution as promising?" and "Ought we to have such institutionalised forms of obligation as promising?" are external questions asked about and not within the institution of promising. And the question "Ought one to keep one's promises?" can be confused with or can be taken as (and I think has often been taken as) an external question roughly expressible as "Ought one to accept the institution of promising?" But taken literally, as an internal question, as a question about promises and not about the institution of promising, the question "Ought one to keep one's promises?" is as empty as the question "Are triangles three-sided?" To recognise something as a promise is to grant that, other things being equal, it ought to be kept.

A second fact which has clouded the issue is this. There are many situations, both real and imaginable, where one ought not to keep a promise, where the obligation to keep a promise is overridden by some further considerations, and it was for this reason that we needed those clumsy *ceteris paribus* clauses in our derivation. But the fact that obligations can be overridden does not show that there were no obligations in the first place. On the contrary. And these original obligations are all that is needed to make the proof work.

Yet a third factor is the following. Many philosophers still fail to realise the full force of saying that "I hereby promise" is a performative expression. In uttering it one performs but does not describe the act of promising. Once promising is seen as a speech act of a kind different from describing, then it is easier to see that one of the features of the act is the undertaking of an obligation. But if one thinks the utterance of "I promise" or "I hereby promise" is a peculiar kind of description—for example, of one's mental state—then the relation between promising and obligation is going to seem very mysterious.

Third Objection

The derivation uses only a factual or inverted-commas sense of the evaluative terms employed. For example, an anthropologist observing the behaviour and attitudes of the Anglo-Saxons might well go through these derivations, but nothing evaluative would be included. Thus step (2) is equivalent to "He did what they call promising" and step (5) to "According to them he ought to pay Smith five dollars." But since all of the steps (2) to (5) are in *oratio obliqua* and hence disguised statements of fact, the fact-value distinction remains unaffected.

This objection fails to damage the derivation, for what it says is only that the steps *can* be reconstrued as in *oratio obliqua*, that we can construe them as a series of external statements, that we can construct a parallel (or at any rate related) proof about reported speech. But what I am arguing is that, taken quite literally, without any *oratio obliqua* additions or interpretations, the derivation is valid. That one can construct a similar argument which would fail to refute the fact-value distinction does not show that this proof fails to refute it. Indeed it is irrelevant.

III

So far I have presented a counter-example to the thesis that one cannot derive an "ought" from an "is" and considered three possible objections to it. Even supposing what I have said so far is true, still one feels a certain uneasiness. One feels there must be some trick involved somewhere. We might state our uneasiness thus: How can my granting a mere fact about a man, such as the fact that he uttered certain words or that he made a promise, commit *me* to the view that *he* ought to do something? I now want briefly to discuss what broader philosophic significance my attempted derivation may have, in such a way as to give us the outlines of an answer to this question.

I shall begin by discussing the grounds for supposing that it cannot be answered at all.

The inclination to accept a rigid distinction between "is" and "ought," between descriptive and evaluative, rests on a certain picture of the way words relate to the world. It is a very attractive picture, so attractive (to me at least) that it is not entirely clear to what extent the mere presentation of counter-examples can challenge it. What is needed is an explanation of how and why this classical empiricist picture fails to deal with such counter-examples. Briefly, the picture is constructed something like this: first we present examples of so-called descriptive statements ("my car goes eighty miles an hour," "Jones is six feet tall," "Smith has brown hair"), and we contrast them with so-called evaluative statements ("my car is a good car," "Jones ought to pay Smith five dollars," "Smith is a nasty man"). Anyone can see that they are different. We articulate the difference by pointing out that for the descriptive statements the question of truth or falsity is objectively decidable, because to know the meaning of the descriptive expressions is to know under what objectively ascertainable conditions the statements which contain them are true or false. But in the case of evaluative statements the situation is quite different. To know the meaning of the evaluative expressions is not by itself sufficient for knowing under what conditions the statements containing them are true or false, because the meaning of the expressions is such that the statements are not capable of objective or factual truth or falsity at all. Any justification a speaker can give of one of his evaluative statements essentially involves some appeal to attitudes he holds, to criteria of assessment he has adopted, or to moral principles by which he has chosen to live and judge other people. Descriptive statements are thus objective, evaluative statements subjective, and the difference is a consequence of the different sorts of terms employed.

The underlying reason for these differences is that evaluative statements perform a completely different job from descriptive statements. Their job is not to describe any features of the world but to express the speaker's emotions, to express his attitudes, to praise or condemn, to laud or insult, to commend, to recommend, to advise, and so forth. Once we see the different jobs the two perform, we see that there must be a logical gulf between them. Evaluative statements must be different from descriptive statements in order to do their job, for if they were objective they could no longer function to evaluate. Put metaphysically, values cannot lie in the world, for if they did they would cease to be values and would just be another part of the world. Put in the formal mode, one cannot define an evaluative word in terms of descriptive words, for if one did, one would no longer be able to use the evaluative word to commend, but only to describe. Put yet another way, any effort to derive an "ought" from an "is" must be a waste of time, for all it could show even if it succeeded would be that the "is" was not a real "is" but only a disguised "ought" or, alternatively, that the "ought" was not a real "ought" but only a disguised "is."

This summary of the traditional empirical view has been very brief, but I hope it conveys something of the power of this picture. In the hands of certain modern authors, especially Hare and Nowell-Smith, the picture attains considerable subtlety and sophistication.

What is wrong with this picture? No doubt many things are wrong with it. In the end I am going to say that one of the things wrong with it is that it fails to give us any coherent account of such notions as commitment, responsibility, and obligation.

In order to work towards this conclusion I can begin by saying that the picture fails to account for the *different types* of "descriptive" statements. Its paradigms of descriptive statements are such utterances as "my car goes eighty miles an hour," "Jones is six feet tall," "Smith has brown hair," and the like. But it is forced by its own rigidity to construe "Jones got married," "Smith made a promise," "Jackson has five dollars," and "Brown hit a home run" as descriptive statements as well. It is so forced, because whether or not someone got married, made a promise, has five dollars, or hit a home run is as much a matter of objective fact as whether he has red hair or brown eyes. Yet the former kind of statement (statements containing "married," "promise," and so forth) seem to be quite different from the simple empirical paradigms of descriptive statements. How are they different? Though both kinds of statements state matters of objective fact, the statements containing words such as "married," "promise," "home run," and "five dollars" state facts whose existence presupposes certain institutions: a man has five dollars, given the institution of money. Take away the institution and all he has is a rectangular bit of paper with green ink on it. A man hits a home run only given the institution of baseball; without the institution he only hits a sphere with a stick. Similarly, a man gets married or makes a promise only within the institutions of marriage and promising. Without them, all he does is utter words or make gestures. We might characterise such facts as institutional facts, and contrast them with non-institutional, or brute, facts: that a man has a bit of paper with green ink on it is a brute fact, that he has five dollars is an institutional fact.[6] The classical picture fails to account for the differences between statements of brute fact and statements of institutional fact.

The word "institution" sounds artificial here, so let us ask: what sorts of institutions are these? In order to answer that question I need to distinguish between two different kinds of rules or conventions. Some rules regulate antecedently existing forms of behaviour. For example, the rules of polite table behaviour regulate eating, but eating exists independently of these rules. Some rules, on the other hand, do not merely regulate but create or define new forms of behaviour: the rules of chess, for example, do not merely regulate an antecedently existing activity called playing chess; they, as it were, create the possibility of or define that activity. The activity of playing chess is constituted by action in accordance with these rules. Chess has no existence apart from these rules. The distinction I am trying to make was foreshadowed by Kant's distinction between regulative and constitutive principles, so let us adopt this terminology and describe our distinction as a distinction between regulative and constitutive rules. Regulative rules regulate activities whose existence is independent of the rules; constitutive rules constitute (and also regulate) forms of activity whose existence is logically dependent on the rules.[7]

Now the institutions that I have been talking about are systems of constitutive rules. The institutions of marriage, money, and promising are like the institutions of baseball or chess in that they are systems of such constitutive rules or conventions. What I have called institutional facts are facts which presuppose such institutions.

Once we recognise the existence of and begin to grasp the nature of such institutional facts, it is but a short step to see that many forms of obligations, commitments, rights, and responsibilities are similarly institutionalised. It is often a matter of fact that one has certain obligations, commitments, rights, and responsibilities, but it is a matter of institutional, not brute, fact. It is one such institutionalised form of obligation, promising which I invoked above to derive an "ought" from an "is." I started with a brute fact, that a man uttered certain words, and then invoked the institution in such a way as to generate institutional facts by which we arrived at the institutional fact that the man ought to pay another man five dollars. The whole proof rests on an appeal to the constitutive rule that to make a promise is to undertake an obligation.

We are now in a position to see how we can generate an indefinite number of such proofs. Consider the following vastly different example. We are in our half of the seventh inning and I have a big lead off second base. The pitcher whirls, fires to the shortstop covering, and I am tagged out a good ten feet

---

[6] For a discussion of this distinction see G. E. M. Anscombe, "On Brute Facts," *Analysis*, 18 (1958).

[7] For a discussion of a related distinction see J. Rawls, "Two Concepts of Rules," *Philosophical Review*, LXIV (1955).

down the line. The umpire shouts, "Out!" I, however, being a positivist, hold my ground. The umpire tells me to return to the dugout. I point out to him that you can't derive an "ought" from an "is." No set of descriptive statements describing matters of fact, I say, will entail any evaluative statements to the effect that I should or ought to leave the field. "You just can't get orders or recommendations from facts alone." What is needed is an evaluative major premise. I therefore return to and stay on second base (until I am carried off the field). I think everyone feels my claims here to be preposterous, and preposterous in the sense of logically absurd. Of course you can derive an "ought" from an "is," and though to actually set out the derivation in this case would be vastly more complicated than in the case of promising, it is in principle no different. By undertaking to play baseball I have committed myself to the observation of certain constitutive rules.

We are now also in a position to see that the tautology that one ought to keep one's promises is only one of a class of similar tautologies concerning institutionalised forms of obligation. For example, "one ought not to steal" can be taken as saying that to recognise something as someone else's property necessarily involves recognising his right to dispose of it. This is a constitutive rule of the institution of private property.[8] "One ought not to tell lies" can be taken as saying that to make an assertion necessarily involves undertaking an obligation to speak truthfully. Another constitutive rule. "One ought to pay one's debts" can be construed as saying that to recognise something as a debt is necessarily to recognise an obligation to pay it. It is easy to see how all these principles will generate counter-examples to the thesis that you cannot derive an "ought" from an "is."

My tentative conclusions, then, are as follows:

1. The classical picture fails to account for institutional facts.
2. Institutional facts exist within systems of constitutive rules.
3. Some systems of constitutive rules involve obligations, commitments, and responsibilities.
4. Within those systems we can derive "ought's" from "is's" on the model of the first derivation.

With these conclusions we now return to the question with which I began this section: How can my stating a fact about a man, such as the fact that he made a promise, commit me to a view about what he ought to do? One can

---

[8] Proudhon said: "Property is theft." If one tries to take this as an internal remark it makes no sense. It was intended as an external remark attacking and rejecting the institution of private property. It gets its air of paradox and its force by using terms which are internal to the institution in order to attack the institution.

Standing on the deck of some institutions one can tinker with constitutive rules and even throw some other institutions overboard. But could one throw all institutions overboard (in order perhaps to avoid ever having to derive an "ought" from an "is")? One could not and still engage in those forms of behaviour we consider characteristically human. Suppose Proudhon had added (and tried to live by): "Truth is a lie, marriage is infidelity, language is uncommumicative, law is a crime," and so on with every possible institution.

begin to answer this question by saying that for me to state such an institutional fact is already to invoke the constitutive rules of the institution. It is those rules that give the word "promise" its meaning. But those rules are such that to commit myself to the view that Jones made a promise involves committing myself to what he ought to do (other things being equal).

If you like, then, we have shown that "promise" is an evaluative word, but since it is also purely descriptive, we have really shown that the whole distinction needs to be re-examined. The alleged distinction between descriptive and evaluative statements is really a conflation of at least two distinctions. On the one hand there is a distinction between different kinds of speech acts, one family of speech acts including evaluations, another family including descriptions. This is a distinction between different kinds of illocutionary force.[9] On the other hand there is a distinction between utterances which involve claims objectively decidable as true or false and those which involve claims not objectively decidable, but which are "matters of personal decision" or "matters of opinion." It has been assumed that the former distinction is (must be) a special case of the latter, that if something has the illocutionary force of an evaluation, it cannot be entailed by factual premises. Part of the point of my argument is to show that this contention is false, that factual premises can entail evaluative conclusions. If I am right, then the alleged distinction between descriptive and evaluative utterances is useful only as a distinction between two kinds of illocutionary force, describing and evaluating, and it is not even very useful there, since if we are to use these terms strictly, they are only two among hundreds of kinds of illocutionary force; and utterances of sentences of the form (5) – "Jones ought to pay Smith five dollars" – would not characteristically fall in either class.

44

On Not Deriving "Ought" from "Is"

ANTONY FLEW

In *How to do Things with Words* (Oxford 1962) there is a promise which Austin, unfortunately, did not live to try to fulfil. In introducing his fivefold classification into verdictives, exercitives, commissives, behabitives, and expositives Austin suggests that this classification is "quite enough to play Old Harry with two fetishes which I admit to an inclination to play Old Harry with, viz.

FROM "On Not Deriving 'Ought' from 'Is' " by Antony Flew (*Analysis*, Vol. 25, no. 2, 1964).

[9] See J. L. Austin, *How to Do Things with Words* (Cambridge, Mass. 1962) for an explanation of this notion.

(1) the true/false fetish (2) the value/fact fetish" (p. 150). Perhaps it is; but Austin made there no attempt to show why the possibility of making his fivefold classification must qualify or undermine the possibility of distinguishing issues of fact from issues of value, or the need sometimes to insist on the difference. Indeed from what he actually says it is not clear precisely what he wished to play Old Harry with; and hence even less clear how the exercise was to be performed.

The word nevertheless seems to have gone round that the idea that there is a radical difference between *ought* and *is* is old hat, something which though still perhaps cherished by out-group backwoodsmen has long since been seen through and discarded by all with-it mainstream philosophers. For instance, in a penetrating article on "Do illocutionary forces exist?"[1] Mr. L. Jonathan Cohen offers some provocative asides: "the statement-evaluation dichotomy, whatever it may be, is as erroneous on my view as on Austin's"; and "Indeed there is a case for saying that Austin's recommendation about the word "good" is itself a hangover from the fact-value dichotomy" (pp. 136 and 137). Cohen gives no hint as to where and how this dichotomy was so decisively liquidated. But a recent paper by Mr. John R. Searle, on "How to derive 'ought' from 'is' " can perhaps be seen as an attempt to plug the gap. Searle's stated aim is to show that the Naturalistic Fallacy is not a fallacy, and he gives many signs of thinking of his aspirations in Austinian terms. My object is to show that Searle is entirely unsuccessful, and to suggest that anyone who hopes to succeed where he has failed will have to find other and more powerful arguments.

2. The first point to remark about Searle's article is that he chooses to start from his own characterisation of what the Naturalistic Fallacy is supposed to consist in; and that he neither quotes nor gives precise references to any statements by the philosophers with whom he wishes to disagree. His characterisation runs:

> It is often said that one cannot derive an "ought" from an "is." This thesis, which comes from a famous passage in Hume's *Treatise*, while not as clear as it might be, is at least clear in broad outline: there is a class of statements of fact which is logically distinct from a class of statements of value. No set of statements of fact by themselves entails any statement of value. Put in more contemporary terminology, no set of *descriptive* statements can entail an *evaluative* statement without the addition of at least one evaluative premise. To believe otherwise is to commit the naturalistic fallacy. (Italics here and always as in original.)

Let us consider alongside this paragraph from Searle some sentences written by a contemporary protagonist of the view which Searle is supposed to be challenging. These quotations come from K. R. Popper and – significantly – they come from *The Open Society* (1945):

> The breakdown of magic tribalism is closely connected with the realization that taboos are different in various tribes, that they are imposed and enforced by man,

---

[1] *Philosophical Quarterly*, 14 (1964).

and that they may be broken without unpleasant repercussions if one can only escape the sanctions imposed by one's fellow-men. . . . These experiences may lead to a conscious differentiation between the man-enforced normative laws or conventions, and the natural regularities which are beyond his power. . . . In spite of the fact that this position was reached a long time ago by the Sophist Protagoras . . . it is still so little understood that it seems necessary to explain it in some detail. . . . It is we who impose our standards upon nature, and who introduce in this way morals into the natural world, in spite of the fact that we are part of this world. . . . It is important for the understanding of this attitude to realize that decisions can never be derived from facts (or statements of facts), although they pertain to facts. The decision, for instance to oppose slavery does not depend upon the fact that all men are born free and equal, and no man is born in chains . . . even if they were born in chains, many of us might demand the removal of these chains. . . . The making of a decision, the adoption of a standard, is a fact. But the norm which has been adopted, is not. That most people agree with the norm "Thou shalt not steal" is a sociological fact. But the norm "Thou shalt not steal" is not a fact; and it can never be inferred from sentences describing facts. . . . *It is impossible to derive a sentence stating a norm or a decision from a sentence stating a fact;* this is only another way of saying that it is impossible to derive norms or decisions from facts. (Vol. 1, pp. 50–3)

Popper's account, even in this abbreviated form, is of course much fuller than that given by Searle; and, partly for that reason, it says or suggests many things which are not comprised in Searle's short paragraph. It presents the idea of the Naturalistic Fallacy as involved in the clash of world-outlooks and personal commitments; and it is governed throughout by the notion that "we are free to form our own moral opinions in a much stronger sense than we are free to form our own moral opinions as to what the facts are.[2] But the most relevant and important difference is that Popper at least suggests, what is true, that the fundamental discrimination in terms of which the Naturalistic Fallacy is being characterised is not, and does not have to be thought to be, a clearcut feature of all actual discourse. It is not something which you cannot fail to observe everywhere as already there and given, if once you have learnt what to look for. There is, rather, a differentiation which has to be made and insisted upon and the distinction is one the development of which may go against the grain of set habits and powerful inclinations. Our situation in this case is not at all like that represented in the second chapter of the book of *Genesis*, where God presents to Adam the beasts of the field and the fowl of the air, leaving it to him merely to supply names for each natural kind.

Searle's account of the opposing position seems to suggest, what his later criticism appears to be assuming, that its misguided spokesmen must be committed to the notion: that an *is/ought* dichotomy is something which the alert

---

[2] R. M. Hare, *Freedom and Reason* (Oxford 1963) p. 2. The same author's *The Language of Morals* (Oxford 1952) is another excellent source for the sophisticated and flexible handling of the idea of the Naturalistic Fallacy; and Hare is, of course, perfectly well aware that the same terms and expressions may combine both descriptive and normative meanings – and hence that normative standards are incapsulated in certain uses of such terms. See, for instance, especially *LM* pp. 119–21 and pp. 145–50 and *FR* pp. 188ff. and pp. 25ff.

natural historian of utterances could not fail to notice, as somehow already given; and that no utterances can either combine, or be ambiguous as between, these two sorts of claim. Yet when we turn to Popper, and allow him to speak for himself, we find in his account nothing at all to suggest any commitment to the erroneous ideas: that all the utterances which are actually made must already be clearly and unambiguously either statements of fact or expressions of value; or that every actual utterance is either purely a statement of fact or purely normative. What Popper emphasises is, rather, the epoch-marking importance of the development of this sort of distinction, the great need to insist upon it, and the difficulty of appreciating fully what it does and what it does not imply.

It is perhaps possible that Searle here, like so many others elsewhere, has been misled by Hume's irony; notwithstanding that Searle himself disclaims concern "with Hume's treatment of the problem." For Hume does indeed write as if he was quite modestly claiming only to have noticed, and to have become seized of the vast importance of, a distinction which, however unwittingly, everyone was always and systematically making already:[3]

> I cannot forbear adding to these reasonings an observation, which may, perhaps, be found of some importance. In every system of morality, which I have hitherto met with, I have always remarked, that the author proceeds for some time in the ordinary way of reasoning, and establishes the being of a God, or makes observations concerning human affairs; when of a sudden I am surprised to find, that instead of the usual copulations of propositions *is*, and *is not*, I meet with no proposition that is not connected with an *ought*, or an *ought not*.

3. After this somewhat protracted introduction, designed to refresh memories about what is and is not involved in the position which Searle is supposed to be attacking, we can now at last turn to his arguments. He works with the example of promising: "The proof unfolds the connection between the utterance of certain words and the speech act of promising and then in turn unfolds promising into obligation and moves from obligation to 'ought'." The idea is to start with a purely descriptive premise such as "Jones uttered the words 'I hereby promise to pay you, Smith, five dollars', " or that Jones uttered the corresponding phonetic sequence, and to proceed by a series of deductive moves to the purely normative conclusion "Jones ought to pay Smith five dollars." Considerable elaboration is necessary, and is provided, in the attempt to deal with the complications arising: because the utterance of such words or sounds will not always rate as a making of the promise; and because the prima facie obligation to keep a promise can be nullified or overriden.

It will, in the light of what has been said in section 2, be sufficiently obvious what sort of moves the critic must make if he hopes to drive a wedge into such a proposed proof. He has to distinguish normative and descriptive elements in the meaning of words like *promise*; and to insist that, however willing we may be to accept the package deal in this particular uncontentious case of promising, it is nevertheless still not possible to deduce the normative from the descriptive

[3] D. Hume, *Treatise*, III. i. 1.

part of the combination. The best place to insert the wedge in Searle's argument seems to be where he maintains: "one thing is clear; however loose the boundaries may be, and however difficult it may be to decide marginal cases, the conditions under which a man who utters 'I hereby promise' can correctly be said to have made a promise are straightforwardly empirical conditions." The weakness becomes glaring if we summon for comparison some obnoxious contentions of the same form. Terms such as *nigger* or *Jewboy, apostate* or *infidel, colonialist* or *kulak* no doubt carry, at least when employed in certain circles, both normative and descriptive meanings; and, presumably, the descriptive element of that meaning can correctly be said to apply whenever the appropriate "straightforwardly empirical conditions" are satisfied. But in these parallel cases most of us, I imagine, would be careful to use one of the several linguistic devices for indicating that we do not commit ourselves to the norms involved, or that we positively repudiate them. Thus, to revert to Searle's example, one could, without any logical impropriety, say of the man who had in suitable circumstances uttered the words "I hereby promise . . ." that he had done what is called (by those who accept the social institution of promising) promising. The oddity of this non-committal piece of pure description would lie simply in the perversity of suggesting a policy of non-involvement in an institution which is surely essential to any tolerable human social life.

4. It remains to ask either why these moves do not impinge on Searle as considerable objections or how he thinks to dispose of them. We have already in section 2 offered suggestions bearing on these questions. But more light is to be found by considering in the second part of his article his discussion of "three possible objections to the derivation."

(a) The first of these objections consists in simply asserting that "Since the first premise is descriptive and the conclusion evaluative, there must be a concealed evaluative premise in the description of the conditions . . ." To which Searle replies that as it stands this objection just begs the question: it requires to be supplemented with some account of the precise location and nature of the concealed evaluative premise. So far, so unexceptionable. The crunch comes when he continues: "Uttering certain words in certain conditions just *is* promising and the description of these conditions needs no evaluative element." For, as we have been urging in section 3, the normative element enters: not with the neutral description of the conditions in which those who accept the social institution of promise-making and promise-keeping would say that someone had made what they call a promise; but at the moment when, by using the word *promise* without reservation, we commit ourselves to that institution.

(b) The second objection considered runs: "Ultimately the derivation rests on the principle that one ought to keep one's promises and that is a moral principle, hence evaluative." To this Searle responds that, whether or not this is a moral principle, "it is also tautological." He then proceeds to offer three suggestions to explain "why so many philosophers have failed to see the tautological character of this principle." This is, perhaps, to go rather too fast. For the sentence "One ought to keep one's promises" is not in itself and unequivocally either tautological or not. It could without too much strain be given either tautological or substantial or even equivocal employments. If the user is prepared to accept that the absence of obligation is a sufficient reason for withdrawing the word *promise*, then the employment is clearly tautological. But if he is to be taken to be referring to certain specific descriptive conditions, and maintaining that, granted those, certain specific things ought to be done, then, surely, the employment is substantial. And if he is insisting that, granted these specific descriptive conditions, then necessarily those things ought to be done; then he would seem to be equivocating between a substantial and a tautological employment.

The first of Searle's suggestions is that some of his opponents have failed "to distinguish external questions about the institution of promising from internal questions asked within the framework of the institution." No doubt some have: though it would be slightly surprising and wholly deplorable to find that many philosophers in an Humean tradition had neglected a distinction of a kind for which one of the classical sources is to be found in the third appendix of the second *Inquiry*. Even so this particular charge rings very badly in the present context. For, as we were urging in section 3, the weakness of Searle's attempted derivation lies precisely in the refusal to allow that the acceptance of a social institution must come between any statement of the purely descriptive conditions for saying that a promise was made, and the drawing of the normative conclusion that something ought to be done.

A more subtle version of the same fault can be seen in Searle's reply to a variant of his first proposed objection, which would protest: "all you have shown is that 'promise' is an evaluative, not a descriptive, concept." This variant, he claims, "in the end will prove disastrous to the original distinction between descriptive and evaluative. For that a man uttered certain words and that these words have the meaning that they do are surely objective facts. And if the statement of these two objective facts plus a description of the conditions of the utterance is sufficient to entail the statement . . . which the objector alleges to be an evaluative statement . . . then an evaluative conclusion is derived from descriptive premises . . . ." But here again it is both necessary and decisive to insist on distinguishing: between a detached report on the meanings which some social group gives to certain value words; and the unreserved employment of those words by an engaged participant. For it is between the former and the latter that there comes exactly that commitment to the incapsulated values which alone warrants us to draw the normative conclusions.

Searle's other two suggestions both refer to peculiarities which make his chosen example especially tricky to handle: the second notices the difficulties which arise because the prima facie obligation to keep a promise made may sometimes properly be overridden by other claims: and the third takes cognisance of the fact that the first person present tense "I promise" is performative. It is not perhaps altogether clear why failure to take the measure of this insight – for which again a classical source can be found in Hume[4] – is supposed to

[4] *Treatise*, III. ii. 5, "Of the obligation of promises."

encourage the idea that "One ought to keep one's promises" is not tautological. What Searle says is: "If one thinks the utterance of 'I promise' or 'I hereby promise' is a peculiar kind of description . . . then the relation between promising and obligation is going to seem very mysterious." Certainly if one thinks that, then there will be a mystery as to why the utterance of these words is construed, by anyone who accepts the institution of promising, as involving the incurring of an obligation. But this is no reason at all for saying that the same misguided person must also by the same token find something mysterious about the notion that, supposing that someone has promised, it follows necessarily that he is obliged.

This is a good occasion to say that where we have spoken of a descriptive element in the meaning of *promise*, we were, of course, intending to include only uses other than the first person present performative. Fortunately the complications connected with that use can for present purposes be largely ignored. For in Searle's candidate proof "I promise" is mentioned, not used; and so our criticism insists that the normative premise is to be found at the point where the performance is characterised, unreservedly, as a promise.

(c) The third objection considered is that: "The derivation uses only a factual or inverted-commas sense of the evaluative terms employed." This discussion is the most interesting for us. It is here that Searle comes nearest to recognising, and to trying to deal with, the rather obvious sort of criticism which we have been deploying. In formulating this objection Searle recognises the distinction: between the employment of a term like *promise* in a detached anthropological description of a social practice; and the use of the same term, without reservation, by a committed participant. His reply is: "This objection fails to damage the derivation, for what it says is only that the steps *can* be reconstrued as in *oratio obliqua*. . . . That one can construct a similar argument which would fail to refute the fact-value distinction does not show that this proof fails to refute it. Indeed it is irrelevant."

This, of course, is true. And if all spokesmen for the opposition were such men of straw it would be a very easy matter to consign them to the garbage dump. What is so extraordinary is that, having apparently allowed the crucial distinction, Searle fails to notice the decisive objection: that his step from 1, "Jones uttered the words 'I hereby promise to pay you, Smith, five dollars' " to 2, "Jones promised to pay Smith five dollars" is fallacious; unless, that is, we are supposed, as we are not, to construe 2 as being purely descriptive, as being, as it were, in *oratio obliqua*.

To explain Searle's oversight the only philosophically relevant suggestions we can offer are those indicated in section 2. Yet it really is extremely hard to believe that he is attributing to his opponents the assumptions: that all our discourse is already divided into elements which are either purely normative or exclusively descriptive; and that no legitimate expression could combine in its meaning both normative and descriptive components. For, though such misconceptions could conceivably be derived from a wooden and unsophisticated reading of some of those sentences in the *Treatise*, such a construction must at once make a mystery of any claim that attention to this distinction "would subvert all the vulgar systems of morality." This sort of thing could scarcely even be thought – as quite clearly it has been thought by many of the most distinguished protagonists of the idea of the Naturalistic Fallacy – if what was at stake really was just a matter of noticing a division already clearly and universally obtaining; rather than, as of course it is, a matter of insisting on making discriminations where often there is every sort of combination and confusion.

45

Moral Beliefs

PHILIPPA FOOT

To many people it seems that the most notable advance in moral philosophy during the past fifty years or so has been the refutation of naturalism; and they are a little shocked that at this late date such an issue should be reopened. It is easy to understand their attitude: given certain apparently unquestionable assumptions, it would be about as sensible to try to reintroduce naturalism as to try to square the circle. Those who see it like this have satisfied themselves that they know in advance that any naturalistic theory must have a catch in it somewhere, and are put out at having to waste more time exposing an old fallacy. This paper is an attempt to persuade them to look critically at the premises on which their arguments are based.

It would not be an exaggeration to say that the whole of moral philosophy, as it is now widely taught, rests on a contrast between statements of fact and evaluations, which runs something like this: "The truth or falsity of statements of fact is shown by means of evidence; and what counts as evidence is laid down in the meaning of the expressions occurring in the statement of fact. (For instance, the meaning of 'round' and 'flat' made Magellan's voyages evidence for the roundness rather than the flatness of the Earth; someone who went on questioning whether the evidence was evidence could eventually be shown to have made some linguistic mistake.) It follows that no two people can make the same statement and count completely different things as evidence; in the end one at least of them could be convicted of linguistic ignorance. It also follows that if a man is given good evidence for a factual conclusion he cannot just refuse to accept the conclusion on the ground that in his scheme of things this evidence is not evidence at all. With evaluations, however, it is different. An

FROM "Moral Beliefs" by Philippa Foot. (*Proceedings of the Aristotelian Society*, Vol. 59, 1958–9). Reprinted by courtesy of the Editor of The Aristotelian Society. © 1959 by The Aristotelian Society.

evaluation is not connected logically with the factual statements on which it is based. One man may say that a thing is good because of some fact about it, and another may refuse to take that fact as any evidence at all, for nothing is laid down in the meaning of "good" which connects it with one piece of "evidence" rather than another. It follows that a moral eccentric could argue to moral conclusions from quite idiosyncratic premises; he could say, for instance, that a man was a good man because he clasped and unclasped his hands, and never turned NNE after turning SSW. He could also reject someone else's evaluation simply by denying that his evidence was evidence at all.

"The fact about 'good' which allows the eccentric still to use this term without falling into a morass of meaninglessness, is its 'action-guiding' or 'practical' function. This it retains; for like everyone else he considers himself bound to choose the things he calls 'good' rather than those he calls 'bad.' Like the rest of the world he uses 'good' in connection only with a 'pro-attitude'; it is only that he has pro-attitudes to quite different things, and therefore calls them good."

There are here two assumptions about "evaluations," which I will call assumption (1) and assumption (2).

Assumption (1) is that some individual may, without logical error, base his beliefs about matters of value entirely on premises which no one else would recognise as giving any evidence at all. Assumption (2) is that, given the kind of statement which other people regard as evidence for an evaluative conclusion, he may refuse to draw the conclusion because *this* does not count as evidence for *him*.

Let us consider assumption (1). We might say that this depends on the possibility of keeping the meaning of "good" steady through all changes in the facts about anything which are to count in favour of its goodness. (I do not mean, of course, that a man can make changes as fast as he chooses; only that, whatever he has chosen, it will not be possible to rule him out of order.) But there is a better formulation, which cuts out trivial disputes about the meaning which "good" happens to have in some section of the community. Let us say that the assumption is that the evaluative function of "good" can remain constant through changes in the evaluative principle; on this ground it could be said that even if no one can call a man *good* because he clasps and unclasps his hands, he can commend him or express his *pro-attitude* towards him, and if necessary can invent a new moral vocabulary to express his unusual moral code.

Those who hold such a theory will naturally add several qualifications. In the first place, most people now agree with Hare, against Stevenson, that such words as "good" only apply to individual cases through the application of general principles, so that even the extreme moral eccentric must accept principles of commendation. In the second place "commending," "having a pro-attitude," and so on, are supposed to be connected with doing and choosing, so that it would be impossible to say, e.g. that a man was a good man only if he lived for a thousand years. The range of evaluation is supposed to be restricted to the range of possible action and choice. I am not here concerned to question these supposed restrictions on the use of evaluative terms, but only to argue that they are not enough.

The crucial question is this. Is it possible to extract from the meaning of words such as "good" some element called "evaluative meaning" which we can think of as externally related to its objects? Such an element would be represented, for instance, in the rule that when any action was "commended" the speaker must hold himself bound to accept an imperative "let me do these things." This is externally related to its object because, within the limitation which we noticed earlier, to possible actions, it would make sense to think of anything as the subject of such "commendation." On this hypothesis a moral eccentric could be described as commending the clasping of hands as the action of a good man, and we should not have to look for some background to give the supposition sense. That is to say, on this hypothesis the clasping of hands could be commended without any explanation; it could be what those who hold such theories call "an ultimate moral principle."

I wish to say that this hypothesis is untenable, and that there is no describing the evaluative meaning of "good," evaluation, commending, or anything of the sort, without fixing the object to which they are supposed to be attached. Without first laying hands on the proper object of such things as evaluation, we shall catch in our net either something quite different, such as accepting an order or making a resolution, or else nothing at all.

Before I consider this question, I shall first discuss some other mental attitudes and beliefs which have this internal relation to their object. By this I hope to clarify the concept of internal relation to an object, and incidentally, if my examples arouse resistance, but are eventually accepted, to show how easy it is to overlook an internal relation where it exists.

Consider, for instance, pride.

People are often surprised at the suggestion that there are limits to the things a man can be proud of, about which indeed he can feel pride. I do not know quite what account they want to give of pride; perhaps something to do with smiling and walking with a jaunty air, and holding an object up where other people can see it; or perhaps they think that pride is a kind of internal sensation, so that one might naturally beat one's breast and say "pride is something I feel *here*." The difficulties of the second view are well known; the logically private object cannot be what a name in the public language is the name of.[1] The first view is the more plausible, and it may seem reasonable to say that given certain behaviour a man can be described as showing that he is proud of something, whatever that something may be. In one sense this is true, and in another sense not. Given any description of an object, action, personal characteristic, etc., it is not possible to rule it out as an object of pride. Before we can do so we need to know what would be said about it by the man who is to be proud of it, or feels proud of it; but if he does not hold the right beliefs about it then whatever his attitude is it is not pride. Consider, for instance, the suggestion

---

[1] See L. Wittgenstein, *Philosophical Investigations* (1953), especially sections 243–315.

that someone might be proud of the sky or the sea: he looks at them and what he feels is *pride*, or he puffs out his chest and gestures with *pride* in their direction. This makes sense only if a special assumption is made about his beliefs, for instance, that he is under some crazy delusion and believes that he has saved the sky from falling, or the sea from drying up. The characteristic object of pride is something seen (*a*) as in some way a man's own, and (*b*) as some sort of achievement or advantage; without this object pride cannot be described. To see that the second condition is necessary, one should try supposing that a man happens to feel proud because he has laid one of his hands on the other, three times in an hour. Here again the supposition that it is pride that he feels will make perfectly good sense if a special background is filled in. Perhaps he is ill, and it is an achievement even to do this; perhaps this gesture has some religious or political significance, and he is a brave man who will so defy the gods or the rulers. But with no special background there can be no pride, not because no one could psychologically speaking feel pride in such a case, but because whatever he did feel could not logically be pride. Of course, people can see strange things as achievements, though not just anything, and they can identify themselves with remote ancestors, and relations, and neighbours, and even on occasions with Mankind. I do not wish to deny there are many far-fetched and comic examples of pride.

We could have chosen many other examples of mental attitudes which are internally related to their object in a similar way. For instance, fear is not just trembling, and running, and turning pale; without the thought of some menacing evil no amount of this will add up to fear. Nor could anyone be said to feel dismay about something he did not see as bad; if his thoughts about it were that it was altogether a good thing, he could not say that (oddly enough) what he felt about it was dismay. "How odd, I feel dismayed when I ought to be pleased" is the prelude to a hunt for the adverse aspect of the thing, thought of as lurking behind the pleasant facade. But someone may object that pride and fear and dismay are feelings or emotions and therefore not a proper analogy for "commendation," and there will be an advantage in considering a different kind of example. We could discuss, for instance, the belief that a certain thing is dangerous, and ask whether this could logically be held about anything whatsoever. Like "this is good," "this is dangerous" is an assertion, which we should naturally accept or reject by speaking of its truth or falsity; we seem to support such statements with evidence, and moreover there may seem to be a "warning function" connected with the word "dangerous" as there is supposed to be a "commending function" connected with the word "good." For suppose that philosophers, puzzled about the property of dangerousness, decided that the word did not stand for a property at all, but was essentially a practical or action-guiding term, used for *warning*. Unless used in an "inverted comma sense" the word "dangerous" was used to warn, and this meant that anyone using it in such a sense committed himself to avoiding the things he called dangerous, to preventing other people from going near them, and perhaps to running in the opposite direction. If the conclusion were not obviously ridiculous, it would be easy to infer that a man whose application of the term was different from ours throughout might say that the oddest things were dangerous without fear of disproof; the idea would be that he could still be described as "thinking them dangerous," or at least as "warning," because by his attitude and actions he would have fulfilled the conditions for these things. This is nonsense because without its proper object *warning*, like *believing dangerous*, will not be there. It is logically impossible to warn about anything not thought of as threatening evil, and for danger we need a particular kind of serious evil such as injury or death.

There are, however, some differences between thinking a thing dangerous and feeling proud, frightened or dismayed. When a man says that something is dangerous he must support his statement with a special kind of evidence; but when he says that he feels proud or frightened or dismayed the description of the object of his pride or fright or dismay does not have quite this relation to his original statement. If he is shown that the thing he was proud of was not his after all, or was not after all anything very grand, he may have to say that his pride was not justified, but he will not have to take back the statement that he was proud. On the other hand, someone who says that a thing is dangerous, and later sees that he made a mistake in thinking that an injury might result from it, has to go back on his original statement and admit that he was wrong. In neither case, however, is the speaker able to go on as before. A man who discovered that it was not his pumpkin but someone else's which had won the prize could only say that he still felt proud, if he could produce some other ground for pride. It is in this way that even feelings are logically vulnerable to facts.

It will probably be objected against these examples that for part of the way at least they beg the question. It will be said that indeed a man can only be proud of something he thinks a good action, or an achievement, or a sign of noble birth; as he can only feel dismay about something which he sees as bad, frightened at some threatened evil; similarly he can only warn if he is also prepared to speak, for instance, of injury. But this will only limit the range of possible objects of those attitudes and beliefs if the range of these terms is limited in its turn. To meet this objection I shall discuss the meaning of "injury" because this is the simplest case. Anyone who feels inclined to say that anything could be counted as an achievement, or as the evil of which people were afraid, or about which they felt dismayed, should just try this out. I wish to consider the proposition that anything could be thought of as dangerous, because if it causes injury it is dangerous, and anything could be counted as an injury. I shall consider bodily injury because this is the injury connected with danger; it is not correct to put up a notice by the roadside reading "Danger!" on account of bushes which might scratch a car. Nor can a substance be labelled "dangerous" on the ground that it can injure delicate fabrics; although we can speak of the danger that it may do so, that is not the use of the word which I am considering here.

When a body is injured it is changed for the worse in a special way, and we want to know which changes count as injuries. First of all, it matters how an injury comes about; e.g. it cannot be caused by natural decay. Then it seems clear that not just any kind of thing will do, for instance, any unusual mark on the body, however much trouble a man might take to have it removed. By far the most important class of injuries are injuries to a part of the body, counting as injuries because there is interference with the function of that part; injury to a leg, an eye, an ear, a hand, a muscle, the heart, the brain, the spinal cord. An injury to an eye is one that affects, or is likely to affect, its sight; an injury to a hand one which makes it less well able to reach out and grasp, and perform other operations of this kind. A leg can be injured because its movements and supporting power can be affected; a lung because it can become too weak to draw in the proper amount of air. We are most ready to speak of an injury where the function of a part of the body is to perform a characteristic operation, as in these examples. We might hesitate to say that a skull can be injured, and might prefer to speak of damage to it, since although there is indeed a function (a protective function) there is no operation. But thinking of the protective function of the skull we may want to speak of injury here. In so far as the concept of *injury* depends on that of *function* it is narrowly limited, since not even every use to which a part of the body is put will count as its function. Why is it that, even if it is the means by which they earn their living, we would never consider the removal of the dwarf's hump or the bearded lady's beard as a bodily injury? It will be tempting to say that these things are disfigurements, but this is not the point; if we suppose that a man who had some invisible extra muscle made his living as a court jester by waggling his ears, the ear would not have been injured if this were made to disappear. If it were natural to men to communicate by movements of the ear, then ears would have the function of signalling (we have no word for this kind of "speaking") and an impairment of this function would be an injury; but things are not like this. This court jester would use his ears to make people laugh, but this is not the function of ears.

No doubt many people will feel impatient when such facts are mentioned, because they think that it is quite unimportant that this or that *happens* to be the case, and it seems to them arbitrary that the loss of the beard, the hump, or the ear muscle would not be called an injury. Isn't the loss of that by which one makes one's living a pretty catastrophic loss? Yet it seems quite natural that these are not counted as injuries if one thinks about the conditions of human life, and contrasts the loss of a special ability to make people gape or laugh with the ability to see, hear, walk, or pick things up. The first is only needed for one very special way of living, the other in any foreseeable future for any man. This restriction seems all the more natural when we observe what other threats besides that of injury can constitute danger: of death, for instance, or mental derangement. A shock which could cause mental instability or impairment of memory would be called dangerous, because a man needs such things as intelligence, memory, and concentration as he needs sight or hearing or the use of hands. Here we do not speak of injury unless it is possible to connect the impairment with some physical change, but we speak of danger because there is the same loss of a capacity which any man needs.

There can be injury outside the range we have been considering; for a man may sometimes be said to have received injuries where no part of his body has had its function interfered with. In general, I think that any blow which disarranged the body in such a way that there was lasting pain would inflict an injury, even if no other ill resulted, but I do not know of any other important extension of the concept.

It seems therefore that since the range of things which can be called injuries is quite narrowly restricted, the word "dangerous" is restricted in so far as it is connected with injury. We have the right to say that a man cannot decide to call just anything dangerous, however much he puts up fences and shakes his head.

So far I have been arguing that such things as pride, fear, dismay, and the thought that something is dangerous have an internal relation to their object, and hope that what I mean is becoming clear. Now we must consider whether those attitudes or beliefs which are the moral philosopher's study are similar, or whether such things as "evaluation" and "thinking something good" and "commendation" could logically be found in combination with any object whatsoever. All I can do here is to give an example which may make this suggestion seem implausible, and to knock away a few of its supports. The example will come from the range of trivial and pointless actions such as we were considering in speaking of the man who clasped his hands three times an hour, and we can point to the oddity of the suggestion that this can be called a good action. We are bound by the terms of our question to refrain from adding any special background, and it should be stated once more that the question is about what can count in favour of the goodness or badness of a man or an action, and not what could be, or be thought, good or bad with a special background. I believe that the view I am attacking often seems plausible only because the special background is surreptitiously introduced.

Someone who said that clasping the hands three times in an hour was a good action would first have to answer the question "How do you mean?" For the sentence "this is a good action" is not one which has a clear meaning. Presumably, since our subject is moral philosophy, it does not here mean "that was a good thing to do" as this might be said of a man who had done something sensible in the course of any enterprise whatever, we are to confine our attention to "the moral use of 'good.' " I am not clear that it makes sense to speak of a "moral use of 'good,' " but we can pick out a number of cases which raise moral issues. It is because these are so diverse and because "this is a good action" does not pick out any one of them, that we must ask "How do you mean?" For instance, some things that are done fulfil a duty, such as the duty of parents to children or children to parents. I suppose that when philosophers speak of good actions they would include these. Some come under the heading of a virtue such as charity, and they will be included too. Others again are actions which require the virtues of courage or temperance, and here the moral aspect is due to the fact that they are done in spite of fear or the temptation of pleasure; they must indeed be done for the sake of some real or fancied good, but not necessarily what philosophers would want to call a moral good. Courage is not *particularly* concerned with saving other people's lives, or temperance with leaving them their share of the food and drink, and the goodness of *what is done* may here be all kinds of usefulness. It is because there are these very diverse cases included (I suppose) under the expression "a good action" that we should refuse to consider applying it without asking what is meant, and we should now ask what is intended when someone is supposed to say that "clasping the hands three times in an hour is a good action." Is it supposed that this action fulfils a duty? Then in virtue of what does a man have this duty, and to whom does he owe it? We have promised not to slip in a special background, but he cannot possibly have a *duty* to clasp his hands unless such a background exists. Nor could it be an act of charity, for it is not thought to do anyone any good, nor again a gesture of humility unless a special assumption turns it into this. The action could be courageous, but only if it were done both in the face of fear and for the sake of a good; and we are not allowed to put in special circumstances which could make this the case.

I am sure that the following objection will now be raised. "Of course clasping one's hands three times in an hour cannot be brought under one of the virtues which we recognise, but that is only to say that it is not a good action by our current moral code. It is logically possible that in a quite different moral code quite different virtues should be recognised, for which we have not even got a name." I cannot answer this objection properly, for that would need a satisfactory account of the concept of a virtue. But anyone who thinks it would be easy to describe a new virtue connected with clasping the hands three times in an hour should just try. I think he will find that he has to cheat, and suppose that in the community concerned the clasping of hands has been given some special significance, or is thought to have some special effect. The difficulty is obviously connected with the fact that without a special background there is no possibility of answering the question "What's the point?" It is no good saying that here would be a point in doing the action because the action was a morally good action: the question is how it can be given any such description if we cannot first speak about the point. And it is just as crazy to suppose that we can call *anything* the point of doing something without having to say what the point of *that* is. In clasping one's hands one may make a slight sucking noise, but what is the point of that? It is surely clear that moral virtues must be connected with human good and harm, and that it is quite impossible to call anything you like good or harm. Consider, for instance, the suggestion that a man might say he had been harmed because a bucket of water had been taken out of the sea. As usual it would be possible to think up circumstances in which this remark would make sense; for instance, when coupled with a belief in magical influences; but then the harm would consist in what was done by the evil spirits, not in the taking of the water from the sea. It would be just as odd if someone were supposed to say that harm had been done to him because the hairs of his head had been reduced to an even number.[2]

---

[2] In face of this sort of example many philosophers take refuge in the thicket of aesthetics. It would be interesting to know if they are willing to let their whole case rest on the possibility that there might be aesthetic objections to what was done.

I conclude that assumption (1) is very dubious indeed, and that no one should be allowed to speak as if we can understand "evaluation," "commendation" or "pro-attitude," whatever the actions concerned.

II

I propose now to consider what was called assumption (2), which said that a man might always refuse to accept the conclusion of an argument about values, because what counted as evidence for other people did not count for him. Assumption (2) could be true even if assumption (1) were false, for it might be that once a particular question of values—say a moral question—had been accepted, any disputant was bound to accept particular pieces of evidence as relevant, the same pieces as everyone else, but that he could always refuse to draw any moral conclusions whatsoever or to discuss any questions which introduced moral terms. Nor do we mean "he might refuse to draw the conclusion" in the trivial sense in which anyone can perhaps refuse to draw *any* conclusion; the point is that any statement of value always seems to go beyond any statement of fact, so that he might have a reason for accepting the factual premises but refusing to accept the evaluative conclusion. That this is so seems to those who argue in this way to follow from the practical implications of evaluation. When a man uses a word such as "good" in an "evaluative" and not an "inverted comma" sense, he is supposed to commit his will. From this it has seemed to follow inevitably that there is a logical gap between fact and value; for is it not one thing to say that a thing is so, and another to have a particular attitude towards its being so; one thing to see that certain effects will follow from a given action, and another to care? Whatever account was offered of the essential feature of evaluation—whether in terms of feelings, attitudes, the acceptance of imperatives or what not—the fact remained that with an evaluation there was a committal in a new dimension, and that this was not guaranteed by any acceptance of facts.

I shall argue that this view is mistaken; that the practical implication of the use of moral terms has been put in the wrong place, and that if it is described correctly the logical gap between factual premises and moral conclusion disappears.

In this argument it will be useful to have as a pattern the practical or "action-guiding" force of the word "injury," which is in some, though not all, ways similar to that of moral terms. It is clear I think that an injury is necessarily something bad and therefore something which as such anyone always has a reason to avoid, and philosophers will therefore be tempted to say that anyone who uses "injury" in its full "action-guiding" sense commits himself to avoiding the things he calls injuries. They will then be in the usual difficulties about the man who says he knows he ought to do something but does not intend to do it; perhaps also about weakness of the will. Suppose that instead we look again at the kinds of things which count as injuries, to see if the connection with the will does not start here. As has been shown, a man is injured when-ever some part of his body, in being damaged, has become less well able to fulfil its ordinary function. It follows that he suffers a disability, or is liable to do so; with an injured hand he will be less well able to pick things up, hold on to them, tie them together or chop them up, and so on. With defective eyes there will be a thousand other things he is unable to do, and in both cases we should naturally say that he will often be unable to get what he wants to get or avoid what he wants to avoid.

Philosophers will no doubt seize on the word "want," and say that if we suppose that a man happens to want the things which an injury to his body pre-vents him from getting, we have slipped in a supposition about a "pro-attitude" already; and that anyone who does not happen to have these wants can still refuse to use "injury" in its prescriptive, or "acting-guiding" sense. And so it may seem that the only way to make a *necessary* connection between "injury" and the things that are to be avoided, is to say that it is only used in an "action-guiding sense" when applied to something the speaker intends to avoid. But we should look carefully at the crucial move in that argument, and query the suggestion that someone might happen not to want anything for which he would need the use of hands or eyes. Hands and eyes, like ears and legs, play a part in so many operations that a man could only be said not to need them if he had no wants at all. That such people exist, in asylums, is not to the present purpose at all; the proper use of his limbs is something a man has reason to want if he wants anything.

I do not know just what someone who denies this proposition could have in mind. Perhaps he is thinking of changing the facts of human existence, so that merely wishing, or the sound of the voice, will bring the world to heel? More likely he is proposing to rig the circumstances of some individual's existence within the framework of the ordinary world, by supposing for in-stance that he is a prince whose servants will sow and reap and fetch and carry for him, and so use their hands and eyes in his service that he will not need the use of his. Let us suppose that such a story could be told about a man's life; it is wildly implausible, but let us pretend that it is not. It is clear that in spite of this we could say that any man had a reason to shun injury; for even if at the end of his life it could be said that by a strange set of circumstances he had never needed the use of his eyes, or his hands, this could not possibly be foreseen. Only by once more changing the facts of human existence, and supposing every vicissitude foreseeable, could such a supposition be made.

This is not to say that an injury might not bring more incidental gain than necessary harm; one has only to think of times when the order has gone out that able-bodied men are to be put to the sword. Such a gain might even, in some peculiar circumstances, be reliably foreseen, so that a man would have even better reason for seeking than for avoiding injury. In this respect the word "injury" differs from terms such as "injustice"; the practical force of "injury" means only that anyone has *a* reason to avoid injuries, not that he has an overriding reason to do so.

It will be noticed that this account of the "action-guiding" force of "injury" links it with reasons for acting rather than with actually doing something. I do not think, however, that this makes it a less good pattern for the "action-guiding" force of moral terms. Philosophers who have supposed that actual action was required if "good" were to be used in a sincere evaluation have got into diffi-cuties over weakness of will, and they should surely agree that enough has been done if we can show that any man has reason to aim at virtue and avoid vice. But is this impossibly difficult if we consider the kinds of things that count as virtue and vice? Consider, for instance, the cardinal virtues, prudence, temper-ance, courage and justice. Obviously any man needs prudence, but does he not also need to resist the temptation of pleasure when there is harm involved? And how could it be argued that he would never need to face what was fearful for the sake of some good? It is not obvious what someone would mean if he said that temperance or courage were not good qualities, and this not because of the "praising" sense of these *words*, but because of the things that courage and temperance are.

I should like to use these examples to show the artificiality of the notions of "commendation" and of "pro-attitudes" as these are commonly employed. Philosophers who talk about these things will say that after the facts have been accepted—say that X is the kind of man who will climb a dangerous mountain, beard an irascible employer for a rise in pay, and in general face the fearful for the sake of something he thinks worth while—there remains the question of "commendation" or "evaluation." If the word "courage" is used they will ask whether or not the man who speaks of another as having courage is supposed to have commended him. If we say "yes" they will insist that the judgement about courage *goes beyond the facts*, and might therefore be rejected by someone who refused to do so; if we say "no" they will argue that "courage" is being used in a purely descriptive or "inverted commas sense," and that we have not got an example of the evaluative use of language which is the moral philosopher's special study. What sense can be made, however, of the question "does he commend?" What is this extra element which is supposed to be present or absent after the facts have been settled? It is not a matter of liking the man who has courage, or of thinking him altogether good, but of "commending him for his courage." How are we supposed to do that? The answer that will be given is that we only commend someone else in speaking of him as courageous if we accept the imperative "let me be courageous" for ourselves. But this is quite unnecessary. I can speak of someone else as having the virtue of courage, and of course recognise it as a virtue in the proper sense, while knowing that I am a complete coward, and making no resolution to reform. I know that I should be better off if I were courageous, and so have a reason to cultivate courage, but I may also know that I will do nothing of the kind.

If someone were to say that courage was not a virtue he would have to say that it was not a quality by which a man came to act well. Perhaps he would be thinking that someone might be worse off for his courage, which is true, but only because an incidental harm might arise. For instance, the courageous man might have underestimated a risk, and run into some disaster which a cowardly man would have avoided because he was not prepared to take any risk at all. And his courage, like any other virtue, could be the cause of harm to him because possessing it he fell into some disastrous state of pride.[3] Similarly, those who question the virtue of temperance are probably thinking not of the virtue itself but of men whose temperance has consisted in resisting pleasure for the sake of some illusory good, or those who have made this virtue their pride.

But what, it will be asked, of justice? For while prudence, courage and temperance are qualities which benefit the man who has them, justice seems rather to benefit others, and to work to the disadvantage of the just man himself. Justice as it is treated here, as one of the cardinal virtues, covers all those things owed to other people: it is under injustice that murder, theft and lying come, as well as the withholding of what is owed for instance by parents to children and by children to parents, as well as the dealings which would be called unjust in everyday speech. So the man who avoids injustice will find himself in need of things he has returned to their owner, unable to obtain an advantage by cheating and lying; involved in all those difficulties painted by Thrasymachus in the first book of the Republic, in order to show that injustice is more profitable than justice to a man of strength and wit. We will be asked how, on our theory, justice can be a virtue and injustice a vice, since it will surely be difficult to show that any man whatsoever must need to be just as he needs the use of his hands and eyes, or needs prudence, courage and temperance?

Before answering this question I shall argue that if it cannot be answered, then injustice can no longer be recommended as a virtue. The point of this is not to show that it must be answerable, since justice is a virtue, but rather to suggest that we should at least consider the possibility that justice is not a virtue. This suggestion was taken seriously by Socrates in the Republic, where it was assumed by everyone that if Thrasymachus could establish his premise—that injustice was more profitable than justice—his conclusion would follow: that a man who had the strength to get away with injustice had reason to follow this as the best way of life. It is a striking fact about modern moral philosophy that no one sees any difficulty in accepting Thrasymachus' premise and rejecting his conclusion, and it is because Nietzsche's position is at this point much closer to that of Plato that he is remote from academic moralists of the present day.

In the Republic it is assumed that if justice is not a good to the just man, moralists who recommend it as a virtue are perpetrating a fraud. Agreeing with this, I shall be asked where exactly the fraud comes in; where the untruth that justice is profitable to the individual is supposed to be told? As a preliminary answer we might ask how many people are prepared to say frankly that injustice is more profitable than justice? Leaving aside, as elsewhere in this paper, religious beliefs which might complicate the matter, we will suppose that some tough atheistical character has asked "Why should I be just?" (Those who believe that this question has something wrong with it can employ their favourite

[3] Cf. Aquinas, *Summa Theologica*, I–II, q. 55, Art. 4.

device for sieving out "evaluating meaning," and suppose that the question is "Why should I be 'just'?") Are we prepared to reply "As far as you are concerned you will be better off if you are unjust, but it matters to the rest of us that you should be just, so we are trying to get you to be just"? He would be likely to enquire into our methods, and then take care not to be found out, and I do not think that many of those who think that it is not necessary to show that justice is profitable to the just man would easily accept that there was nothing more they could say.

The crucial question is: "Can we give anyone, strong or weak, a reason why he should be just?"—and it is no help at all to say that since "just" and "unjust" are "action-guiding words" no one can even ask "Why should I be just?" Confronted with that argument the man who wants to do unjust things has only to be careful to avoid the *word*, and he has not been given a reason why he should not do the things which other people call "unjust." Probably it will be argued that he has been given a reason so far as anyone can ever be given a reason for doing or not doing anything, for the chain of reasons must always come to an end somewhere, and it may seem that one man may always reject the reason which another man accepts. But this is a mistake; some answers to the question "why should I?" bring the series to a close and some do not. Hume showed how *one* answer closed the series in the following passage:

"Ask a man *why he uses exercise;* he will answer, *because he desires to keep his health.* If you then enquire, *why he desires health,* he will readily reply, *because sickness is painful.* If you push your enquiries further, and desire a reason *why he hates pain,* it is impossible he can ever give any. This is an ultimate end, and is never referred to any other object." (*Enquiries*, appendix I, para. v.) Hume might just as well have ended this series with boredom: sickness often beings boredom, and no one is required to give a reason why he does not want to be bored, any more than he has to give a reason why he does want to pursue what interests him. In general, anyone is given a reason for acting when he is shown the way to something he wants; but for some wants the question "Why do you want that?" will make sense, and for others it will not.[4] It seems clear that in this division justice falls on the opposite side from pleasure and interest and such things. "Why shouldn't I do that?" is not answered by the words "because it is unjust" as it is answered by showing that the action will bring boredom, loneliness, pain, discomfort or certain kinds of incapacity, and this is why it is not true to say that "it's unjust" gives a reason in so far as any reasons can ever be given. "It's unjust" gives a reason only if the nature of justice can be shown to be such that it is necessarily connected with what a man wants.

This shows why a great deal hangs on the question of whether justice is or is not a good to the just man, and why those who accept Thrasymachus' premise and reject his conclusion are in a dubious position. They recommend justice to each man, as something he has a reason to follow, but when challenged to show

---

[4] For an excellent discussion of reasons for action, see G. E. M. Anscombe, *Intention* (Oxford 1957) sections 34–40.

why he should do so they will not always be able to reply. This last assertion does not depend on any "selfish theory of human nature" in the philosophical sense. It is often possible to give a man a reason for acting by showing him that someone else will suffer if he does not; someone else's good may really be more to him than his own. But the affection which mothers feel for children, and lovers for each other, and friends for friends, will not take us far when we are asked for reasons why a man should be just; partly because it will not extend far enough, and partly because the actions dictated by benevolence and justice are not always the same. Suppose that I owe someone money; ". . . what if he be my enemy, and has given me just cause to hate him? What if he be a vicious man, and deserves the hatred of all mankind? What if he be a miser, and can make no use of what I would derpive him of? What if he be a profligate debauchee, and would rather receive harm than benefit from large possessions?"[5] Even if the general practice of justice could be brought under the motive of universal benevolence—the desire for the greatest happiness of the greatest number—many people certainly do not have any such desire. So that if injustice is only to be recommended on these grounds a thousand tough characters will be able to say that they have been given no reason for practising justice, and many more would say the same if they were not too timid or too stupid to ask questions about the code of behaviour which they have been taught. Thus, given Thrasymachus' premise Thrasymachus' point of view is reasonable; we have no particular reason to admire those who practise justice through timidity or stupidity.

It seems to me, therefore, that if Thrasymachus' thesis is accepted things cannot go on as before; we shall have to admit that the belief on which the status of justice as a virtue was founded is mistaken, and if we still want to get people to be just we must recommend justice to them in a new way. We shall have to admit that injustice is more profitable than justice, at least for the strong, and then do our best to see that hardly anyone can get away with being unjust. We have, of course, the alternative of keeping quiet, hoping that for the most part people will follow convention into a kind of justice, and not ask awkward questions, but this policy might be overtaken by a vague scepticism even on the part of those who do not know just what is lacking; we should also be at the mercy of anyone who was able and willing to expose our fraud.

Is it true, however, to say that justice is not something a man needs in his dealings with his fellows, supposing only that he be strong? Those who think that he can get on perfectly well without being just should be asked to say exactly how such a man is supposed to live. We know that he is to practise injustice whenever the unjust act would bring him advantage; but what is he to say? Does he admit that he does not recognise the rights of other people, or does he pretend? In the first case even those who combine with him will know that on a change of fortune, or a shift of affection, he may turn to plunder them, and he must be as wary of their treachery as they are of his. Presumably the

---

[5] Hume, *Treatise*, III. ii. 1.

happy unjust man is supposed, as in Book II of the *Republic*, to be a very cunning liar and actor, combining complete injustice with the appearance of justice: he is prepared to treat others ruthlessly, but pretends that nothing is further from his mind. Philosophers often speak as if a man could thus hide himself even from those around him, but the supposition is doubtful, and in any case the price in vigilance would be collosal. If he lets even a few people see his true attitude he must guard himself against them; if he lets no one into the secret he must always be careful in case the least spontaneity betray him. Such facts are important because the need a man has for justice in dealings with other men depends on the fact that they are men and not inanimate objects or animals. If a man only needed other men as he needs household objects, and if men could be manipulated like household objects, or beaten into a reliable submission like donkeys, the case would be different. As things are, the supposition that injustice is more profitable than justice is very dubious, although like cowardice and intemperance it might turn out incidentally to be profitable.

The reason why it seems to some people so impossibly difficult to show that justice is more profitable than injustice is that they consider in isolation particular just acts. It is perfectly true that if a man is just it follows that he will be prepared, in the event of very evil circumstances, even to face death rather than to act unjustly—for instance, in getting an innocent man convicted of a crime of which he has been accused. For him it turns out that his justice brings disaster on him, and yet like anyone else he had good reason to be a just and not an unjust man. He could not have it both ways and while possessing the virtue of justice hold himself ready to be unjust should any great advantage accrue. The man who has the virtue of justice is not ready to do certain things, and if he is too easily tempted we shall say that he was ready after all.

46

On Morality's Having a Point

D. Z. PHILLIPS AND H. O. MOUNCE

I

It has come to be thought important once again in ethics to ask for the point of morality. Why does it matter whether one does one thing rather than another? Surely, it is argued, if one wants to show someone why it is his duty to do something, one must be prepared to point out the importance of the proposed action,

FROM "On Morality's Having a Point" by D. Z. Phillips and H. O. Mounce (*Philosophy*, Vol. XL, No. 154, 1965). Reprinted by permission of The Royal Institute of Philosophy and the authors.

the harm involved in failing to do it, and the advantage involved in performing it. Such considerations simply cannot be put aside. On the contrary, the point of moral conduct must be elucidated in terms of the reasons for performing it. Such reasons separate moral arguments from persuasion and coercion, and moral judgements from likes and dislikes; they indicate what constitutes human good and harm.

If we take note of the role of reasons in morality, we shall see that not anything can count as a moral belief. After all, why does one regard some rules as moral principles, and yet never regard others as such? Certainly, we *can* see the point of some rules as moral principles, but in the case of other rules we cannot. How is the point seen? There is much in the suggestion that it is to be appreciated in terms of the backgrounds which attend moral beliefs and principles. When rules which claim to be moral rules are devoid of these backgrounds we are puzzled. We do not know what is being said when someone claims that the given rule is a moral rule.

Normally, we do not speak of these backgrounds when we express and discuss moral opinions. It is only when we are asked to imagine their absence that we see how central they must be in any account we try to give of morality. Consider the rules, "Never walk on the lines of a pavement," and "Clap your hands every two hours." If we saw people letting such rules govern their lives in certain ways, taking great care to observe them, feeling upset whenever they or other people infringe the rules, and so on, we should be hard put to understand what they were doing. We fail to see any point in it. On the other hand, if backgrounds are supplied for such rules, if further descriptions of the context in which they operate are given, sometimes, they can begin to look like moral principles. Given the background of a religious community, one can begin to see how the rule, "Never walk on the lines of a pavement," could have moral significance. Think of, "Take off thy shoes for thou art on holy ground," and its connections with the notions of reverence and disrespect. It is more difficult, though we do not say it is impossible, to think of a context in which the rule, "Clap your hands every two hours," could have moral significance. Our first example shows how we can be brought to some understanding of a moral view when it is brought under a concept with which we are familiar. By linking disapproval of walking on the lines of a pavement with lack of reverence and disrespect, even those not familiar with the religious tradition in question may see that a *moral* view is being expressed. Such concepts as sincerity, honesty, courage, loyalty, respect, and, of course, a host of others, provide the kind of background necessary in order to make sense of rules as moral principles. It does not follow that all the possible features of such backgrounds need be present in every case. The important point to stress is that unless the given rule has *some* relation to such backgrounds, we would not know what is meant by calling it a moral principle.

The above conclusion follows from a more extensive one, namely, that commendation is internally related to its object. Mrs Foot, for example, suggests that there is an analogy between commendation on the one hand, and mental attitudes such as pride and beliefs such as "This is dangerous" on the other. One cannot feel proud of *anything*, any more than one can say that *anything* is dangerous. Similarly in the case of commendation: how can one say that clapping one's hands every two hours is a good action? The answer is that one cannot, unless the context in which the action is performed, for example, recovery from paralysis, makes its point apparent.

Certainly, those who have insisted on the necessity of a certain conceptual background in order to make sense of moral beliefs and moral judgements have done philosophy a service. They have revealed the artificiality of locating what is characteristically moral in a mental attitude such as a pro-attitude, or in a mental activity such as commending. They have shown the impossibility of making sense of something called "evaluative meaning" which is thought of as being externally or contingently related to its objects. One could have a pro-attitude towards clapping one's hands every two hours, and one could commend one's never walking on the lines of a pavement, but neither pro-attitude nor commendation would, in themselves, give a point to such activities.

If the point of virtues is not to be expressed in terms of pro-attitudes or commendations, how is it to be brought out? It has been suggested that this could be done by showing the connection between virtues and human good and harm. But this is where the trouble starts, for if we are not careful, we may, in our eagerness to exorcise the spirit of evaluative meaning, fall under the spell of the concept of human good and harm, which is an equally dangerous idea. Unfortunately, this has already happened, and much of the current talk about human good and harm is as artificial as the talk about "attitudes" in moral philosophy which it set out to criticise.

The point of calling an action (morally) good, it is suggested, is that it leads to human good and avoids harm. Further, what is to count as human good and harm is said to be a *factual* matter. Thus, one must try to show that there is a logical connection between statements of fact and statements of value, and that the logical gap supposed to exist between them can be closed. Men cannot pick and choose which facts are relevant to a moral conclusion, any more than they can pick and choose which facts are relevant in determining a physical ailment. Admittedly, the notion of a fact is a complex one, but this makes it all the more important to exercise care in the use of it. Let us try to appreciate this complexity in terms of an example.

Someone might think that pushing someone roughly is rude, and that anyone who denies this is simply refusing to face the facts. But this example, as it stands, is worthless, since it tells one nothing of the context in which the pushing took place. The reference to the context is all important in giving an account of the action, since not any kind of pushing can count as rudeness. Consider the following examples:

a. One man pushing another person violently in order to save his life.
b. A doctor pushing his way through a football-match crowd in response to an urgent appeal.
c. The general pushing which takes place in a game of rugby.
d. A violent push as a customary form of greeting between close friends.

In all these cases, pushing someone else is not rude. If someone took offence at being pushed, he might well see in the light of the situation that no offence had been caused. But what of situations where there is general agreement that an offence *has* been caused? Is the offence a fact from which a moral conclusion can be deduced? Clearly not, since what this suggestion ignores is the fact that *standards already prevail* in the context in which the offence is recognised. If one wants to call the offence a fact, one must recognise that it is a fact which already has moral import. The notion of "offence" is parasitic on the notion of a standard or norm, although these need not be formulated. The person who wishes to say that the offence is a "pure fact" from which a moral conclusion can be deduced is simply confused. What are the "pure facts" relating to the pushing and the injury it is supposed to cause? A physiological account of the pushing (which might be regarded as pure enough) would not enable one to say what was going on, any more than a physiological account of the injury would tell us anything about what moral action (if any) is called for as a result. It makes all the difference morally whether the grazed ankle is caused by barging in the line-out or by barging in the bus queue. Any attempt to characterise the fact that an offence has been caused as a non-evaluative fact from which a moral conclusion can be deduced begs the question, since in asserting that a *kind of offence* has been caused, a specific background and the standards inherent in it have already been invoked.

But our opponent is still not beaten. He might give way on the confusion involved in the talk about deducing moral conclusions from "pure facts," and agree that "pushing" does not constitute rudeness in all contexts. Nevertheless, he might argue, where the circumstances *are* appropriate, it is possible to determine the rudeness of an action in a way which will settle any disagreement. But, again, this is clearly not the case. Whenever anyone says, "That action is rude," there is no logical contradiction involved in denying the assertion, since although two people may share a moral concept such as rudeness, they may still differ strongly in its application. This is possible because views about rudeness do not exist *in vacuo*, but are often influenced by *other* moral beliefs. A good example of disagreement over the application of the concept of rudeness can be found in Malcolm's Memoir of Wittgenstein. Wittgenstein had lost his temper in a philosophical discussion with Moore, and would not allow Moore sufficient time to make his point. Moore thought that Wittgenstein's behaviour was rude, holding that good manners should always prevail, even in philosophical dicussion. Wittgenstein, on the other hand, thought Moore's view of the matter absurd: philosophy is a serious business, important enough to justify a loss of temper; to think this rudeness is simply to misapply the judgement. Here, one can see how standards of rudeness have been influenced by wider beliefs; in other words, how the judgement, "That is rude," is not entailed by the facts.

The position we have arrived at does not satisfy a great many contemporary moral philosophers. They are not prepared to recognise the possibility of permanent radical moral disagreement. They want to press on towards ultimate agreement, moral finality, call it what you will. They propose to do this by considering certain non-moral concepts of goodness in the belief that they will throw light on the notion of human good and harm. The non-moral example, "good knife," has been popular in this respect. The word "knife" names an object in respect of its function. Furthermore, the function is involved in the meaning of the word, so that if we came across a people who possessed objects which looked exactly like knives, but who never used these objects as we use them, we should refuse to say that they had the concept of a knife. Now when a thing has a function, the main criterion for its goodness will be that it serves that function well. Clearly, then, not anything can count as a good knife. But how does this help out understanding of moral goodness? Moral concepts are not functional. One can see what is to count as a good knife by asking what a knife is *for*, but can one see the point of generosity in the same way? To ask what generosity is *for* is simply to vulgarise the concept; it is like thinking that "It is more blessed to give than to receive" is some kind of policy!

Yet, although moral concepts are not functional words, they are supposed to resemble them in important respects. The interesting thing, apparently, about many non-functional words, is that when they are linked with "good" they yield criteria of goodness in much the same way as "good knife" and other functional words do. For example, it seems as if "good farmer" might yield criteria of goodness in this way. After all, farming is an activity which has a certain point. To call someone a good farmer will be to indicate that he has fulfilled the point of that activity. What "the point" amounts to can be spelled out in terms of healthy crops and herds, and a good yield from the soil. The philosophical importance of these examples is that they show that the range of words whose meaning provides criteria of goodness extends beyond that of functional words. But what if the range is even wider than these examples suggest? It is clear what the philosophers who ask this question have in mind: what if the meaning of moral concepts could yield criteria of goodness in the same way? If this were possible, one need not rest content with expounding "good knife" or "good farmer"; "good man" awaits elucidation. The goal is to find out what constitutes human flourishing. Furthermore, once these greater aims are achieved, all moral disputes would be, in principle at least, resolvable. Anyone claiming to have a good moral argument would have to justify it by showing its point in terms of human good and harm. And, once again, not anything could count as human good and harm.

The programme is nothing if not ambitious. Unfortunately, it will not work. The reason why is no minor defect: the whole enterprise is misconceived almost from the start. As far as land farming is concerned, the confusion could have been avoided had one asked why "farming" yields criteria when joined with "good." To say that this type of farming is an activity which has a point, that farming serves some end, and that to call someone a good farmer is to say that he achieves this end, is only to tell part of the story. The most important part is left out, namely, *that the end in question is not in dispute.* That is why it makes sense to talk of experts in farming, and why problems in farming can be solved by technical or scientific means. For example, farmers might disagree over which is the best method of growing good wheat, but there is no disagreement over what is to count as good wheat. On the other hand, the situation is different where animal farming is concerned. Suppose it were established that the milk yield was not affected by keeping the cattle indoors in confined quarters, and by cutting their food supply.[1] Many people would say that no good farmer would be prepared to do this, despite the economic factors involved. Others may disagree and see nothing wrong in treating animals in this way. The point to note is that here one has a *moral* dispute. We recognise it as such because of the issues of cruelty, care, and expediency involved in it. The dispute cannot be settled by reference to the point of farming in this instance, since it is agreed that whichever side one takes, the milk yield remains the same. One must recognise that there are different conceptions of what constitutes good farming. Similarly, we shall find that there is no common agreement on what constitutes human good and harm. We shall argue presently that human good is not independent of the moral beliefs people hold, but is determined by them. In short, what must be recognised is that there are different conceptions of human good and harm.

II

The above argument would not satisfy the philosophers we have in mind. For them, moral views are founded on facts, the facts concerning human good and harm. We shall argue, on the other hand, that moral viewpoints determine what is and what is not to count as a relevant fact in reaching a moral decision. This philosophical disagreement has important consequences, for if we believe that moral values can be justified by appeal to *the* facts, it is hard to see how one man can reject another man's reasons for his moral beliefs, since these reasons too, presumably, refer to the facts. If, on the other hand, we hold that the notion of factual relevance is parasitic on moral beliefs, it is clear that deadlock in ethics will be a common occurrence, simply because of what some philosophers have unwisely regarded as contingent reasons, namely, the different moral views people hold.

Many philosophers are not convinced that there need be a breakdown in moral argument. It is tempting to think that anyone who has heard *all* the arguments in favour of a moral opinion cannot still ask why he ought to endorse it, any more than anyone who has heard all there is to say about the earth's shape can still ask why he ought to believe that the earth is round. Anyone who has heard *all* the reasons for a moral opinion has, it seems, heard all the facts. Sometimes the facts are difficult to discern, but there is in principle no reason why moral disagreement should persist. Therefore, it is difficult to see how "*x* is good" can be a well-founded moral argument when "*x* is bad" is said to be equally well founded. So runs the argument.

[1] We owe this example to Dr. H. S. Price.

Certainly, it is difficult for philosophers who argue in this way to account for moral disagreement, since for them, moral judgements are founded on the facts of human good and harm, and the facts are incontrovertible. It is not surprising to find Bentham being praised in this context, since he too alleged that there is a common coinage into which "rival" moral views could be cashed. The rivalry is only apparent, since the felicific calculus soon discovers the faulty reasoning. On this view, moral opinions are hypotheses whose validity is tested by reference to some common factor which is the sole reason for holding them. Bentham said the common factor was pleasure; nowadays it is called human good and harm. Whether one's moral views are "valid" depends on whether they lead to human good and harm. But how does one arrive at these facts? One is said to do so by asking the question, "What is the point?" often enough.

Philosophers are led to argue in this way by misconstruing the implications of the truth that a certain conceptual background is necessary in order for beliefs to have moral significance. Instead of being content to locate the point of such beliefs in their moral goodness, they insist on asking further what the point of *that* is. If one does not give up questioning too soon, one will arrive at the incontrovertible facts of human good and harm which do not invite any further requests for justification. Injury seems to be thought of as one such final halting place. To ask what is the point of calling injury a bad thing is to show that one has not grasped the concept of injury. To say that an action leads to injury is to give *a* reason for avoiding it. Injury may not be an overriding reason for avoiding the action which leads to it, as injustice is, but its being *a* reason is justified because injury is necessarily a bad thing. Even if we grant the distinction between reasons and overriding reasons, which is difficult enough if one asks who is to say which are which, is it clear that injury is always a reason for avoiding the action which leads to it?

The badness of injury, it is argued, is made explicit if one considers what an injury to hands, eyes, or ears, prevents a man from doing and getting; the badness is founded on what all men want. Mrs Foot, for example, expounds the argument as follows,

... the proper use of his limbs is something a man has reason to want if he wants anything.
I do not know just what someone who denies this proposition could have in mind. Perhaps he is thinking of changing the facts of human existence, so that merely wishing, or the sound of the voice, will bring the world to heel? More likely he is proposing to rig the circumstances of some individual's existence within the framework of the ordinary world, by supposing for instance that he is a prince whose servants will sow and reap and fetch and carry for him, and so use their hands and eyes in his service that he will not need the use of his.

But, Mrs Foot argues, not even this supposition will do, since the prince cannot foresee that his circumstances will not change. He still has good reason to avoid injury to his hands and eyes, since he may need them some day. But there was no need to have thought up such an extravagant example to find objections to the view that injury is necessarily bad. There are more familiar ones close at hand which are far more difficult to deal with than the case of the fortunate prince. For example, consider the following advice,

And if thine eye offend thee, pluck it out, and cast it from thee: it is better to enter into life with one eye, rather than having two eyes to be cast into hell fire. (Matt. xviii. 9.)

Or again, consider how Saint Paul does not think "the thorn in the flesh" from which he suffered to be a bad thing. At first, he does so regard it, and prays that it be taken away. Later, however, he thanks God for his disability, since it was a constant reminder to him that he was not sufficient unto himself. Another example is worth quoting.[2] Brentano was blind at the end of his life. When friends commiserated with him over the harm that had befallen him, he denied that his loss of sight was a bad thing. He explained that one of his weaknesses had been a tendency to cultivate and concentrate on too many diverse interests. Now, in his blindness, he was able to concentrate on his philosophy in a way which had been impossible for him before. We may not want to argue like Saint Paul or Brentano, but is it true that we have no idea what they have in mind?

A readiness to admit that injury might result in incidental gain will not do as an answer to the above argument. True, there would be a gain in being injured if an order went out to put all able-bodied men to the sword, but are we to regard the examples of Saint Paul and Brentano as being in this category? In some peculiar circumstances where this gain could be foreseen, we might even imagine a person seeking injury rather than trying to avoid it. But is this the way we should account for saints who prayed to be partakers in the sufferings of Christ? Obviously not. It is clear that Paul himself does not regard his ailment as something which happens to be useful in certain circumstances. But in any case, why speak of *incidental* gain in any of these contexts, and why speak of the contexts themselves as *peculiar?* In doing so, is not the thesis that injury is necessarily bad being defended by calling any examples which count against it incidental or peculiar? In so far as moral philosophers argue in this way, they lay themselves open to the serious charge which Sorel has made against them:

The philosophers always have a certain amount of difficulty in seeing clearly these ethical problems, because they feel the impossibility of harmonising the ideas which are current at a given time in a class, and yet imagine it to be their duty to reduce everything to a unity. To conceal from themselves the fundamental heterogeneity of all this civilised morality, they have recourse to a great number of subterfuges, sometimes relegating to the rank of exceptions, importations, or survivals, everything which embarrasses them. . . .[3]

---

[2] We owe it to Mr. Rush Rhees.
[3] Georges Sorel, *Reflections on Violence*, trans. T. E. Hulme (Collier-Macmillan, 1961) pp. 229–30.

Is it not the case that we cannot understand Brentano's attitude to his blindness unless we understand the kind of dedication to intellectual enquiry of which he was an example, and the virtues which such dedication demands in the enquirer? Again, we cannot understand Saint Paul's attitude to his ailment unless we understand something of the Hebrew-Christian conception of man's relationship to God, and the notions of insufficiency, dependence, and divine succour, involved in it. These views of personal injury or physical harm cannot be cast in terms of what all men want. On the contrary, it is the specific contexts concerned, namely, dedication to enquiry and dedication to God, which determine what is to constitute goodness and badness. We can deny this only by elevating one concept of harm as being paradigmatic in much the same way as Bentham elevated one of the internal sentiments. We can say that injury is necessarily bad at the price of favouring one idea of badness.

In so far as philosophers construct a paradigm in their search for "the unity of the facts of human good and harm," they are not far removed from the so-called scientific rationalists and their talk of proper functions, primary purpose, etc. One of these, in an argument with a Roman Catholic housewife over birth control, stressed the harm which could result from having too many children. He obviously thought that the reference to physical harm clinched the matter. The housewife, on the other hand, stressed the honour a mother has in bringing children into the world. It seems more likely that the scientific rationalist was blind to what the housewife meant by honour, than that she was blind to what he meant by harm. Are we for that reason to call the honour incidental gain?

How would the scientific rationalist and the housewife reach the agreement which some philosophers seem to think inevitable if all the facts were known? It is hard to see how they could without renouncing what they believe in. Certainly, one cannot regard their respective moral opinions as hypotheses which the facts will either confirm or refute, for what would the evidence be? For the rationalist, the possibility of the mother's death or injury, the economic situation of the family, the provision of good facilities for the children, and so on, would be extremely important. The housewife too agrees about providing the good things of life for children, but believes that one ought to begin by allowing them to enter the world. For her, submission to the will of God, the honour of motherhood, the creation of a new life, and so on, are of the greatest importance. But there is no settling of the issue in terms of some supposed common evidence called human good and harm, since what they differ over is precisely the question of what constitutes human good and harm. The same is true of all fundamental moral disagreements, for example, the disagreement between a pacifist and a militarist. The argument is unlikely to proceed very far before deadlock is reached.

Deadlock in ethics, despite philosophical misgivings which have been voiced, does not entail liberty to argue as one chooses. The rationalist, the housewife, the pacifist, or the militarist, cannot say what they like. Their arguments are rooted in different moral traditions within which there are rules for what can and what cannot be said. Because philosophers believe that moral opinions rest on common evidence, they are forced to locate the cause of moral disagreement in the evidence's complexity: often, experience and imagination are necessary in assessing it. One can imagine someone versed in the views we have been attacking, and sympathetic with them, saying to an opponent in a moral argument, "If only you could see how wrong you are. If only you had the experience and the imagination to appreciate the evidence for the goodness of the view I am advocating, evidence, which, unfortunately, is too complex for you to master, you would see that what I want is good for you too, since really, all men want it." Such appeals to "the common good" or to "what all men want" are based on conscious or unconscious deception. It may be admitted that the majority of mothers nowadays want to plan the birth of their children, to fit in with the Budget if possible, and regard the rearing of their children as a pause in their careers. But this will not make the slightest difference to the housewife of our previous example. She believes that what the majority wants is a sign of moral decadence, and wants different things. But she does not believe because she wants; she wants because she believes.

The view that there are ways of demonstrating goodness by appeal to evidence which operate *independently* of the various moral opinions people hold is radically mistaken. Sometimes, philosophers seem to suggest that despite the moral differences which separate men, they are really pursuing the same end, namely, what all men want. The notion of what all men want is as artificial as the common evidence which is supposed to support it. There are no theories of goodness.

The Revival of Cognitivism and Naturalism—Further Readings

Anscombe, G. E. M., "Modern Moral Philosophy," *Philosophy*, XXXIII (1958), pp. 1–19. Proponent.

Bennett, Jonathan, "Whatever the Consequences," *Analysis*, XXVI (1966), pp. 83–102. Critic, concentrating on Anscombe's views.

Foot, Philippa, "Goodness and Choice," *Proceedings of the Aristotelian Society*, Suppl. XXXV (1961), pp. 45–60.

——, "Moral Argument," *Mind*, LXVII (1958), pp. 502–513.

Franklin, R. L., "Recent Work on Ethical Naturalism," in Nicholas Rescher, (ed.), *Studies in Ethics, American Philosophical Quarterly Monograph Series* No. 7 (Basil Blackwell: Oxford, 1973), pp. 55–95. Critical discussion of contemporary writing on ethical naturalism, with an excellent bibliography.

Geach, P. T., "Good and Evil," *Analysis*, XVII (1956), pp. 33–42. Proponent, especially concerned with criticizing "Oxford Moralists," including R. M. Hare.

Hare, R. M. "Geach: Good and Evil," *Analysis*, XVIII (1957), pp. 103–112. A critical response to Geach.

Hudson, W. D. (ed.), *The Is-Ought Question* (London: Macmillan, 1969), especially Parts III and IV. Collection of twenty-two papers by contemporary authors on issues related to the revival of cognitivism.

——, *Modern Moral Philosophy* (Garden City, N.Y.: Doubleday, 1970), Chap. 6. Exposition and qualified criticism.

Phillips, D. Z., "Does It Pay to Be Good?" *Proceedings of the Aristotelian Society*, n. s., LXV (1964–65), pp. 45–60. Critic of Foot's "Moral Beliefs."

Phillips, D. Z., and H. O. Mounce, *Moral Practices* (New York: Schocken Books, 1970), Chap. 5. Critics.

Warnock, G. J., *Contemporary Moral Philosophy* (London: Macmillan, 1967), Chaps. 5 and 6. Proponent.

——, *The Object of Morality* (London: Methuen, 1971), Proponent.

Biographical Notes

ST. THOMAS AQUINAS (c. 1225–1274) was an outstanding Catholic philosopher and theologian of the Medieval period whose writings continue to have wide influence. His major works include *Summa Contra Gentiles* (c. 1260) and *Summa Theologica* (1265–1272).

ARISTOTLE (384–322 B.C.) was a Greek philosopher whose works have been among the most influential in the history of Western civilization. Of special interest to the student of ethics are his *Nicomachean Ethics, Eudemian Ethics,* and *Politics.*

WILLIAM HARRY BAUMER (1932–   ) is Professor of Philosophy and Assistant Vice President of Academic Affairs at the State University of New York at Buffalo. He has written several articles in contemporary journals on Kant, egoism, and confirmation.

JEREMY BENTHAM (1748–1832) was a founder of utilitarianism. Among his major works are *An Introduction to the Principles of Morals and Legislation* (1789) and *Theory of Legislation* (1802).

FRANCIS HERBERT BRADLEY (1846–1924) was a leading English philosopher who served as Fellow of Merton College, Oxford, for many years. His major works include *Ethical Studies* (1876) and *Appearance and Reality* (1893).

HEINRICH EMIL BRUNNER (1889–1966) was Professor of Theology at the University of Zurich from 1924 to 1953. Among his many works on religion and ethics are *The Divine Imperative* (1932), *The Philosophy of Religion from the Standpoint of Protestant Theology* (1937), and *Christianity and Civilization* (1948–49).

JOSEPH BUTLER (1692–1752) was a leading Anglican theologian of the eighteenth century. His major works are *Fifteen Sermons Preached at the Rolls Chapel* (1726; 2d ed., 1729) and *The Analogy of Religion* (1736).

CHARLES ARTHUR CAMPBELL (1897–) is Professor Emeritus at the University of Glasgow. His major publications include *On Selfhood and Godhood* (1957) and *In Defence of Free Will with Other Philosophical Essays* (1967).

JOHN DEWEY (1859–1952) taught for many years both at the University of Chicago and Columbia University. One of America's leading philosophers, his major works include *Ethics* (with James H. Tufts, 1908; rev. ed., 1932), *Democracy and Education* (1916), *Reconstruction in Philosophy* (1920; 2d ed., 1948), *Human Nature and Conduct* (1922), *A Common Faith* (1934), and *The Theory of Valuation* (1939).

ALFRED CYRIL EWING (1899–) taught at the University of Cambridge. Among his major works are *The Definition of Good* (1947), *Ethics* (1953), and *Non-Linguistic Philosophy* (1968).

GUY CROMWELL FIELD (1887–1955) taught at the University of Bristol. His major works include *Moral Theory* (1921; 2d ed., 1932), *The Philosophy of Plato* (1949), and *Political Theory* (1955).

ANTONY GARRARD NEWTON FLEW (1923–) is Professor of Philosophy at the University of Reading. Among his major works are *God and Philosophy* (1966), *Evolutionary Ethics* (1967), *An Introduction to Western Philosophy* (1971), and *Crime or Disease?* (1973).

PHILIPPA RUTH FOOT (1920–) is Senior Research Fellow, Somerville College, Oxford, and Professor in Residence at the University of California, Los Angeles. She is the editor of *Theories of Ethics* (1967), the author of *Morality and Art* (1970), and has written several influential articles on the subject of ethics for contemporary journals.

RICHARD MERVYN HARE (1919–) is White's Professor of Moral Philosophy and Fellow of Corpus Christi College, Oxford. His major ethical works are *The Language of Morals* (1952), *Freedom and Reason* (1963), *Essays on the Moral Concepts* (1972), and *Applications of Moral Philosophy* (1972).

THOMAS HOBBES (1588–1679) was one of the major English philosophers of the seventeenth century. His principal works include *Leviathan* (1651) and *Philosophical Rudiments concerning Government and Society* (1651).

PAUL HENRI THIRY, BARON D'HOLBACH (1723–1789) was one of the most outspoken materialists and atheists during the Enlightenment. In addition to contributing to Diderot's *Encyclopedia*, he wrote *The System of Nature* (1770) and *Good Sense* (1772).

JOHN HOSPERS (1918–) is Professor and Director of the School of Philosophy at the University of Southern California. Among his works are *Introduction to Philosophical Analysis* (1953; 2d. ed., 1967), *Human Conduct* (1961), and *Libertarianism* (1971).

WILLIAM DONALD HUDSON (1920–   ) is Reader in Moral Philosophy and Sub-Dean of Arts at the University of Exeter. His major published works include *Ethical Intuitionism* (1967), *Reason and Right* (1970), and *Modern Moral Philosophy* (1970). In addition, he has contributed to, and edited, a well-known collection of papers, *The Is-Ought Question* (1969).

IMMANUEL KANT (1724–1804) taught at the University of Königsberg in East Prussia and became one of the most original and influential writers in the history of philosophy. Among his major works are *Critique of Pure Reason* (1781; 2d ed., 1787), *Fundamental Principles of the Metaphysic of Morals* (1785), *Critique of Practical Reason* (1788), *Critique of Judgment* (1790), *Religion Within the Limits of Bare Reason* (1793), and *Perpetual Peace* (1795).

ALASDAIR CHALMERS MAC INTYRE (1929–   ) is Professor of Philosophy and Political Science at Boston University. Among other works, he is the author of *Marxism and Christianity* (1953), *The Unconscious* (1957), *A Short History of Ethics* (1966), and *Against the Self-Images of the Age* (1971).

BRIAN H. MEDLIN (1927–   ) teaches at Flinders University of South Australia. He is the author of articles on a variety of philosophical topics in contemporary journals.

JOHN STUART MILL (1806–1873) was an outstanding English philosopher of his time. Included among his major works are *On Liberty* (1859), *Considerations on Representative Government* (1861), *Utilitarianism* (1863), and *The Subjection of Women* (1869).

GEORGE EDWARD MOORE (1873–1958) was Professor of Philosophy at the University of Cambridge and became one of the leading English philosophers of the twentieth century. His major ethical works are *Principia Ethica* (1903) and *Ethics* (1912).

HOWARD OWEN MOUNCE (1939–   ) is Lecturer in Philosophy, University College, Swansea. In addition to writing articles on ethics for contemporary journals, he is co-author (with D. Z. Phillips) of *Moral Practices* (1970).

FRIEDRICH NIETZSCHE (1844–1900) was one of the most influential German philosophers of the nineteenth century. Among his major works are *Beyond Good and Evil* (1886), *The Genealogy of Morals* (1887), *Thus Spake Zarathustra* (1883–85), and *The Will to Power* (1909–10).

DANIEL JOHN O'CONNOR (1914–   ) is Professor of Philosophy, University of Exeter. Among his works are *Introduction to the Philosophy of Education* (1957), *Aquinas and Natural Law* (1967), and *Free Will* (1971).

DEWI ZEPHANIAH PHILLIPS (1934–   ) is Professor of Philosophy, University College, Swansea. His works include *The Concept of Prayer* (1965), *Death and Immortality* (1970), *Faith and Philosophical Inquiry* (1970). He is also co-author (with H. O. Mounce) of *Moral Practices* (1970).

PLATO (427/8–347/8 B.C.) was a Greek philosopher whose writings provide the foundation of most subsequent developments in Western philosophy. Among his works related to ethics are *Euthyphro, Apology, Crito, Meno, Phaedo, The Republic, Protagoras, Gorgias,* and *Philebus.*

HASTINGS RASHDALL (1858–1924) taught at Oxford University. His works include *The Theory of Good and Evil* (1907; 2d ed., 1924), *Philosophy and Religion* (1910), *Is Conscience an Emotion?* (1914), and *Ideas and Ideals* (1928).

JOHN BORDLEY RAWLS (1921–   ) is Professor of Philosophy at Harvard University. He has written several well-known articles on ethics and social philosophy for contemporary journals and is the author of *A Theory of Justice* (1971).

SIR WILLIAM DAVID ROSS (1877–   ) was for many years Professor of Philosophy and Provost of Oriel College, Oxford. Among his major ethical works are *The Right and the Good* (1930), *Foundations of Ethics* (1939), and *Kant's Ethical Theory* (1954).

BERTRAND ARTHUR WILLIAM RUSSELL (1872–1970) was one of England's most influential philosophers. Of special interest for ethics, his works include *Marriage and Morals* (1929), *The Conquest of Happiness* (1930), *Religion and Science* (1935), *Human Society in Ethics and Politics* (1955), and *Why I Am Not a Christian* (1957).

JEAN-PAUL SARTRE (1905–   ) is a leading French existentialist who refused the Nobel Prize for Literature in 1964 on the ground that he rejected all official distinctions. Among his major works are *Being and Nothingness* (1943); *No Exit* (a play, 1945); *Existentialism and Humanism* (1946); *The Roads to Freedom:* (1) *The Age of Reason* (1945), (2) *The Reprieve* (1945), (3) *Troubled Sleep* (1949) (novels); and *The Words* (autobiography, 1963).

JOHN ROGERS SEARLE (1932–   ) is Professor and Chairman of the Department of Philosophy at the University of California at Berkeley. In addition to contributing numerous articles to contemporary journals, he is the author of *Speech Acts* (1969) and *The Campus War* (1971).

FREDERICK SIEGLER (1932–1975) taught at the University of Chicago and the University of Washington. He has written several papers on ethical topics for contemporary journals.

JOHN JAMISON CARSWELL SMART (1920–   ) is Emeritus Professor, University of Adelaide, and Reader in Philosophy, La Trobe University. In addition to various articles, his major works in ethics are *An Outline of a System of Utilitarian Ethics* (1961) and (with Bertrand Williams) *Utilitarianism: for and against* (1973).